JUVENILE LAW VIOLATORS, HUMAN RIGHTS, AND THE DEVELOPMENT OF NEW JUVENILE JUSTICE SYSTEMS

This volume brings together the work of scholars and practitioners specializing in juvenile justice from the USA and Europe alongside scholars from Africa and Asia who are working on human rights issues in developing countries or countries in transition. The book presents two types of papers: descriptive and analytical academic papers on entire systems of juvenile justice or aspects of those systems (eg aftercare, restorative justice, etc.), and papers which deal with efforts to promote reform through international activity (PRI, DCI, DIHR) and through efforts to utilize modern theory in national reforms in developing countries (Malawi and Nepal) or in countries experiencing current or recent political and systemic changes or developments (South Africa, Germany, Serbia and Poland). The volume is also intended to throw light on recent trends in juvenile crime in various countries, the relationship between actual developments and popular and political perceptions, and reactions to such developments (including efforts to find alternatives to the incarceration of young offenders). A streak of new moralism is clearly discernible as a counteracting force against more humane reform efforts. The volume discusses developments within the actual parameters of juvenile offending, public and political demands for security and public intervention, and measures to provide interventions which are at the same time compatible with international human rights instruments.

Titles in this Series

Juvenile Law Violators, Human Rights, and the Development of New Juvenile Justice Systems

Edited by

Eric L Jensen
and
Jørgen Jepsen

·HART·
PUBLISHING
OXFORD AND PORTLAND, OREGON
2006

Published in North America (US and Canada) by
Hart Publishing
c/o International Specialized Book Services
920 NE 58th Avenue, Suite 300
Portland, OR 97213-3786
USA
Tel: +1 503 287 3093 or toll-free: (1) 800 944 6190
Fax: +1 503 280 8832
E-mail: orders@isbs.com
Website: www.isbs.com

Hart Publishing, 16C Worcester Place, Oxford, OX1 2JW
Telephone: +44 (0)1865 517530 Fax: +44 (0)1865 510710
E-mail: mail@hartpub.co.uk
Website: http://www.hartpub.co.uk

British Library Cataloguing in Publication Data
Data Available

ISBN-13: 978-1-84113-637-0 (hardback)
ISBN-10: 1-84113-637-9 (hardback)

ISBN-13: 978-1-84113-636-3 (paperback)
ISBN-10: 1-84113-636-0 (paperback)

Typeset Compuscript, Shannon
Printed and bound in Great Britain by
Biddles Ltd, King's Lynn, Norfolk

Foreword

on behalf of
The Danish Institute for Human Rights

The present report on the international workshop entitled Juvenile Law Violators, Human Rights, and the Development of New Juvenile Justice Systems represents a joint effort in the field of comparative law and sociology between the International Institute for the Sociology of Law (IISL), Oñati, Spain, the Danish Institute for Human Rights (DIHR) and a number of legal and sociological scholars within the field of juvenile justice.

The DIHR is involved in a programme of support to a number of developing countries in this field and renders this support in the light of international conventions, of which the Convention on the Rights of the Child (CRC) is a major instrument for reform. The CRC is relevant not only for developing countries, but certainly also for most countries in the West, not least in Europe.

Support and advocacy for reform requires a solid knowledge base. For this reason, the research basis which the workshop and the present volume represent is an indispensable means for development. The DIHR appreciates that its own experience and work in the provision of assistance to developing countries can benefit from the fruits of the work of scholars contributing to the combination of theory, policy and practical work. The ultimate test of theory is in its application. And the furthering of human rights can only be effective if it is based upon equal measures of knowledge, reform and compassion. This, in my opinion, is needed more in relation to juvenile justice than to most other fields. The future of our societies is dependent upon the way we treat our young generations. This can only be acceptable if it is based upon a solid foundation of human rights.

I therefore take the opportunity to express my sincere thanks to the IISL and the other contributors to the conference and to this book.

Morten Kjaerum, Director, DIHR
Copenhagen, June 2004

Acknowledgements

A project of the scope of the international conference held at the International Institute for the Sociology of Law and this resulting book requires the energies and ideas of many people. First and foremost we would like to thank all the conference participants for a lively, congenial and stimulating experience in Oñati.

We thank the International Institute for the Sociology of Law for providing excellent facilities for the conference and for generous financial support, and the wonderful staff with whom we worked. It was a pleasure working with Professor Dr. Manuel Calvo Garcia, former Scientific Director, on-site in Oñati. We would like especially to thank Malen Gordoa Mendizabal for her superb assistance in all phases of planning the conference, for the execution of the conference, and for her unflagging attention to detail.

The Danish Institute for Human Rights (previously known as the Danish Centre for Human Rights) was an important supporter of this conference. We thank Charlotte Flindt Pedersen for her efforts in this regard. In addition, DIHR hosted the editors during March 2004 and provided an excellent environment for editing many of the chapter drafts. We also thank Johnny Juhl Sørensen for his support of this project and for his enthusiasm for linking the present book to the Durban volume.

The School of Law at Aarhus University, where Dr. Jensen was on a Fulbright Lecturer/Research Scholar appointment during the spring of 2002, provided important support services during the application process. Dr. Jensen would like to thank the University of Idaho for providing financial support for the conference and for a sabbatical leave during the spring of 2004 to work on the book.

Thanks also to Dr. Troy Armstrong for financial support of the conference from the Center for Delinquency and Crime Policy Studies, California State University, Sacramento.

We would like to thank Ian Jensen, Sarah Eilers and Paul Dalton for their assistance in proof reading sections of the manuscript.

Finally, thanks go to the staff of the International Juvenile Justice Observatory for sharing their website information service with us at the conference in Oñati (http://www.oijj.org).

The editors

Preface

The present publication emerges as the product of a conference held in Oñati, Spain, at the International Institute for the Sociology of Law in June 2003. The editors of this volume organised the conference based on their experiences and interests in the juvenile justice field. Dr. Eric L. Jensen is Professor of Sociology at the University of Idaho. Jørgen Jepsen is Associate Professor Emeritus of Criminology at the University of Aarhus, Denmark, and has worked for several years as a consultant to the Danish Institute of Human Rights (DIHR) on juvenile justice reform in Africa, Nepal and other non-Western countries. The idea behind the conference was to bring together scholars and practitioners specialising in juvenile justice from the U.S.A., Western Europe and Poland with colleagues from African countries, Serbia and Nepal working on human rights issues in developing countries or countries in transition.

The Danish Institute for Human Rights was one of the contributing organisations to the conference at Oñati. The DIHR provides human rights support to a number of developing countries in Africa and Asia, as well as to countries in the former Eastern Bloc. In addition to three staff members from DIHR, Penal Reform International (PRI) was represented by its African section manager, and Defence for Children International (DCI) was represented by a consultant on juvenile justice. Two of the developing nations, Malawi and Nepal, were involved in the Juvenile Justice Program of DIHR. Thus, organisations working with human rights were represented at the conference.

The idea behind the conference was to bring together the two groups—academics and practitioners in the human rights field—for the mutual exchange of knowledge and ideas and to discuss how such knowledge could be applied in promoting developments in juvenile justice. Discussions about the application of international human rights instruments, most notably the Convention on the Rights of the Child (CRC), formed an important part of this exchange and this topic was dealt with in several of the papers presented. It might be said that the conference was a workshop for the applied sociology of law.

It should also be noted that participation in this process was part of an effort by the DIHR to further developments in juvenile justice in a number of its partner countries in Africa and Nepal. Later in the year (November 2003) a workshop on juvenile justice and diversion was held in Durban, South Africa, arranged in co-operation between DIHR, colleagues in the field of juvenile justice reform in South Africa (again a mix of academics and practitioners) and participants from partner countries, including Malawi, Tanzania, Uganda and Nepal (see J.J. Sørensen and J. Jepsen (2005) *Juvenile Justice in Transition: Bringing the Convention on the Rights of the Child to Work in Africa and Nepal* (Copenhagen, Danish Institute for Human Rights)). The idea was to utilize some of the materials from the Oñati conference on a more practical level in connection with efforts to promote the use of diversion of juveniles from the adult criminal justice system. DIHR therefore saw the two conferences as mutually complementary, pushing further to put academic knowledge, international instruments and collected experience to work in this process of reform of laws and practices. The ideas of an increased use of diversion and the development of restorative justice as important parts of this process comprised an agenda that tied the representatives of diverse legal systems together.

The content of the present volume reflects this combination of ideas and goals. The book is a combination of two types of papers. Some are traditional academic papers which present whole systems of juvenile justice in a combination of description and analysis or certain parts thereof (e.g. aftercare, restorative justice, etc.). These topics were seen as important background material for the development of new juvenile justice systems. The other papers deal with efforts to promote reform through international activity (PRI, DCI, DIHR), and through efforts to utilize modern theory in national reforms in developing countries (Malawi and Nepal) or in countries experiencing current or recent political and systemic changes or developments (South Africa, Germany, Serbia and Poland).

The present volume is also intended to throw light on recent trends in juvenile crime in various countries, the relationship between actual developments and popular and political perceptions, and reactions to such developments, including efforts to locate effective alternatives to the incarceration of young offenders. At the same time as the search for such alternatives is being intensified through international exchange and experimentation, the amelioration of harsh measures against juvenile law violators is often countered by political and public cries for security and demonstrative public intervention against misbehavior. A streak of new moralism is clearly discernible as a counteracting force against more humane reform efforts. The volume (like the conference) is intended to throw light on the developments, in the countries represented at the conference, relating to three elements: the actual parameters of juvenile offending, public and political demands for security and public intervention, and measures to provide such interventions as best concord with the humanistic concerns expressed by the CRC and other international Human Rights instruments.

This volume is therefore a mixture of papers with different content and styles, but with the common aims outlined above. The discussions at the seminar were fruitful in furthering mutual gains of knowledge and insights, and some of this is reflected in the revision of some of the papers after the conference. It was not intended that the papers should use a common template. Rather the general ideas behind the conference were outlined for the presenters and different reactions to these came to the fore. It is therefore diversity that characterizes the present volume. This diversity demonstrates that the aims described require such a combination of contributions. Ultimately, it is hoped that the volume will be useful to both academics and practitioners and that the latter group will recognize that the sociology of law is more than an academic discipline: it can be an active force in promoting human rights and juvenile justice reform.

Jørgen Jepsen and Eric L. Jensen
July 2005

Contents

Contributors

Bruce Abramson, Consultant, Defence for Children International, Geneva, Switzerland.

Troy L Armstrong, Professor Emeritus, California State University, Sacramento, California, U.S.A.

José Luis de la Cuesta, Professor of Criminal Law and Director of the Basque Institute of Criminology, University of the Basque Country, San Sebastian, Spain.

James Dumesnil, California State Director, National Association of Forensics Counselors, Mather, California, U.S.A.

Frieder Dünkel, Professor of Criminal Law and Criminology, University of Greifswald, Germany.

Barry C Feld, Centennial Professor of Law, University of Minnesota, Minneapolis, Minnesota, U.S.A.

Eric L Jensen, Professor of Sociology, University of Idaho, Moscow, Idaho, U.S.A.

Jørgen Jepsen, Senior Consultant, The Danish Institute for Human Rights, Associate Professor Emeritus (Criminology), University of Aarhus, Denmark.

Desmond Kaunda, Capacity Development Manager, Malawi Human Rights Resource Centre, Lilongwe, Malawi.

Krzysztof Krajewski, Professor of Criminology, Department of Criminology, Jagiellonian Univeristy, Krakow, Poland.

Barbara Mendenhall, Research Analyst, Mincucci Associates, Sacramento, California, U.S.A.

Charlotte Flindt Pedersen, Project Manager, Danish Institute for Human Rights, Copenhagen, Denmark.

Jerzy Sarnecki, Professor of Criminology and Chair, Department of Criminology, Stockholm University, Stockholm, Sweden.

Kishor Silwal, Director, Center for Legal Research and Resource Developments, Kathmandu School of Law, Kathmandu, Nepal.

Ann Skelton, Director, Litigation Project, Centre for Child Law, University of Pretoria, Pretoria, South Africa.

Adam Stapleton, Regional Director, Penal Reform International, Lilongwe, Malawi.

Ivana Stevanovic, Researcher, Yugoslavia Child Rights Centre, Belgrade, The Republic of Serbia and Montenegro.

Lola Vallés, Researcher, The Police Academy of Catalonia, Barcelona, Spain.

1

Introduction

ERIC L JENSEN AND JØRGEN JEPSEN

T HE CHAPTERS IN this book are organised around the themes of the Oñati conference. One of the major objectives of the conference was to bring together experts in juvenile justice from nations at various stages of development or transition, thus allowing for comparison of rather diverse legal and social systems. We were seeking an exchange of research findings and cross-cultural comparisons of the societal and political contexts from which juvenile justice systems emerge and evolve. In pursuit of this objective, the authors described the juvenile justice systems in their nations and several authors discussed the extent and parameters of juvenile law violation in their countries. These descriptions then opened up discussion of a critical issue: are current reactions and proposals within these nations' juvenile justice systems in line with the empirical reality of changes in youth law violation? This discussion emerged as a frequent theme in the conference contributions. We will return to this theme in the concluding chapter.

Another important objective of the conference was to consider the mutual application of system models and research findings across the juvenile justice systems or emerging juvenile justice systems in the nations represented. That is, what can we learn from each other? In addition, we encouraged the participants to explore the practical application of the various juvenile justice models under different social and cultural conditions. For example, a developing nation which to date has primarily used the adult criminal justice system to respond to juvenile delinquency may consider the ideas and philosophies of the Anglo-American juvenile court system, the Scandinavian welfare board system, or the proposals for a combined juvenile justice and family court system in Serbia for potential adoption. Conversely, traditional modes of conflict resolution in developing nations (e.g. mediation and restorative justice) are currently being implemented in several Western societies, in part inspired by examples from New Zealand, South Africa and other African countries (see Braithwaite 2002). This exchange of ideas and experiences with examples of attempts at practical implementation of various models of juvenile justice broadened the horizons of all the participants in the conference.

MODELS OF JUVENILE JUSTICE

The juvenile justice system was created in Western nations—the U.S.A., Britain, and Australia—around the turn of the twentieth century (see Platt 1977, Cunneen and White 1995). These new separate systems of justice for children and youth were based on the legal doctrine of *parens patriae*. That is, the state is the ultimate guardian of children. The state was empowered to exert its authority over that of the parents when the best interests of the child demand state intervention (see the chapters by Jensen and Dünkel). Similar developments took place at this time in the Scandinavian countries, with the elimination of adult criminal court jurisdiction for juvenile offenders and the creation of municipal welfare boards instead of juvenile courts.

The original juvenile courts were based on a social welfare model (also referred to as a child welfare model). That is, the court was intended to guide and assist children, not punish them. The juvenile court was seen as a quasi-social welfare institution which dispensed assistance to children in trouble. Since the juvenile court was perceived as helping youth and not punishing them, no due process requirements were included in the early American legislation (see Jensen's chapter in this volume).

Over time the pendulum has gradually swung in many Western nations toward a social control model (also referred to as the correction/repression model and the 'get tough' movement) (see Bernard 1992, Feld 1999). This shift to a social control model is documented in the chapters on the American experience, Spain (with the possible exclusion of Catalonia), South Africa, and Denmark.

The age of criminal responsibility varies considerably by nation (see Table 1.1). In most Western nations the maximum age under the jurisdiction of the juvenile court is 16–18 years. In the Scandinavian countries the minimum age of criminal responsibility is 15 years, with provisions for compulsory measures by the social welfare authorities below that age, and overlapping jurisdiction of criminal courts and social welfare boards for persons aged 15–17 years.

A unique feature of the original American juvenile court model was the creation of 'status offenses'. These are behaviors which are defined as a violation of law only for children or youth. Common examples of status offenses in the U.S.A. are: running away from home, being beyond the control of one's parents or guardians, violation of curfew, and unexcused absences from school. These behaviors were included in the early American juvenile court legislation because it was believed that they were signs of future criminality. Thus, this version of the social welfare model suggested that offending youth should be assisted by the juvenile court early in their lives before they proceed on a projected path of more serious adult offenses. The Scandinavian welfare board model was based on the same tenets, but without status offenses.

Table 1.1: The Age of Criminal Responsibility in Europe

Country	Diminished criminal responsibility (juvenile criminal law)	Criminal responsibility (adult criminal law can/ must be applied)	Legal majority
Austria	14	18/21	18
Belgium	16**/18	16/18	18
Belarus	14***/16	14/16	18
Bulgaria	14	18	18
Croatia	14/16*	18/21	18
Czech Republic	15	18	18
Denmark	15	15/18	18
England/Wales	10/12/15*	18	18
Estonia	14	18	18
Finland****	15	15/18	18
France	13	18	18
Germany	14	18/21	18
Greece	13	18/21	18
Hungary	14	18	18
Ireland	7/15*	18	18
Italy	14	18/21	18
Latvia	14	18	18
Lithuania	14***/16	14/16	18
Macedonia	14***/16	14/16	18
Moldova	14***/16	14/16	18
Netherlands	12	18/21	18
Norway****	15	18	18
Poland	13*****	15/17/18	18
Portugal	16	16/21	18
Romania	16/18	16/18/21	18
Russia	14***/16	14/16	18
Scotland	8/16	16/21	18
Slovakia	15	18	18
Slovenia	14***/16	18	18
Spain	14	18/21	18
Sweden****	15	15/18	18
Switzerland	7/15*	15/18	18
Turkey	11	15	18
Ukraine	14***/16	14/16	18
Former Yugoslavia	14/16*	18/21	18

* criminal majority concerning juvenile detention (youth imprisonment etc.)
** only for road offences
*** only for serious offences
**** only mitigation of sentencing without a separate juvenile justice act
***** no criminal responsibility *strictu sensu*, but application of the Juvenile (Welfare) Law

Source: Dünkel 2003, 135.

As illustrated by the examples cited above, nations working to revise a juvenile justice system or to create one anew have several models to either adopt or use as templates. Increasingly Western nations have moved toward a social control model. As the chapters by Jensen, Feld, Jepsen and Skelton note, this move is fraught with problems. On the other hand, more traditional social welfare-based models continue in Poland, Germany and Sweden despite recent demands for more repressive policies, particularly against violent young offenders.

THE CONVENTION ON THE RIGHTS OF THE CHILD AND RELATED INTERNATIONAL INSTRUMENTS

The Convention on the Rights of the Child (CRC) was enacted by the United Nations in 1989 and has been signed by all but two nations in the world (the U.S.A. and Somalia). The CRC is used as the major framework by the Danish Institute for Human Rights and other organizations, including UNICEF and Penal Reform International, in assisting nations to develop humane, human rights-based juvenile justice systems.

The conditions in prisons and remand facilities in many developing nations are so poor and inhumane that they violate basic human rights standards when seen from any point of view. Because of this, many developing nations are currently trying to keep juveniles from being detained in jail while awaiting trial and from being sent to institutions for adult offenders. These facilities often subject young offenders to much hardship and humiliation, such as physical, sexual and psychological abuse.

In recent years a number of nations and international organizations have supported developing nations in designing juvenile justice systems that exempt young offenders from these hardships and divert them into non-institutional forms of intervention (see also the 'Tokyo Rules' on non-institutional measures and the other instruments mentioned below). Even in cases where such systems of diversion are badly needed, recommended by international instruments and supported by foreign donors and national progressives, they are often met with opposition from the public, repressive legal systems, and system representatives such as judges, prosecutors and the police.

The basic principles of the CRC (and the related international instruments) as they apply to juvenile justice systems are as follows (United Nations 2000, 275–300):

- the best interests of the child should be the primary consideration;
- states parties shall take all appropriate measures to protect the child from all forms of physical or mental violence, injury or abuse, neglect

or negligent treatment, maltreatment, or exploitation, including sexual abuse;

- no child should be subjected to torture or other cruel, inhuman or degrading treatment or punishment;
- neither capital punishment nor life imprisonment without possibility of release shall be imposed for offenses committed by persons below eighteen years of age;
- the arrest, detention, or imprisonment of a child shall be in conformity with the law and shall be used only as a measure of last resort and for the shortest appropriate period of time;
- every child deprived of liberty shall be separated from adults unless it is considered in the child's best interests not to do so;
- every child deprived of his or her liberty shall have the right to prompt access to legal and other appropriate assistance, as well as the right to challenge the legality of the deprivation of his or her liberty;
- the right to be presumed innocent until proven guilty according to law;
- the right to be informed promptly and directly of the charges against him or her;
- the right to have legal or other appropriate assistance in the preparation and presentation of his or her defense;
- the right not to be compelled to give testimony or to confess guilt;
- the right to have examined adverse witnesses and to obtain the participation and examination of witnesses on his or her behalf;
- if considered to have infringed the penal law, to have this decision and any measures imposed in consequence thereof reviewed by a higher competent, independent and impartial authority or judicial body;
- the right to have his or her privacy fully respected at all stages of the proceedings;
- the establishment of a minimum age below which children shall be presumed not to have the capacity to infringe on the penal law; and
- a variety of dispositions shall be available to ensure that children are dealt with in a manner appropriate to their well-being and proportionate both to their circumstances and their offense.

Several other international instruments set out and reinforce these human rights guidelines for establishing and maintaining juvenile justice systems. These instruments are: the U.N. Standard Minimum Rules for the Administration of Juvenile Justice 1985 (the Beijing Rules), U.N. Guidelines for the Prevention of Juvenile Delinquency 1990 (the Riyadh Guidelines), U.N. Rules for the Protection of Juveniles Deprived of their Liberty 1990 (Havana Rules), U.N. Standard Minimum Rules for Alternative Penal Measures 1990 (the Tokyo Rules), and the European Rules on Social Sanctions and Measures 1992.

PLAN OF THE BOOK

Our basic goal in organizing the Oñati conference was to provide information for the participants to review and subsequently to allow us to consider which models or portions of other nations' juvenile justice systems may be the most effective and applicable to our societies. We were thus offering a variety of options from which the convened experts could choose. Our intention was to facilitate productive policy choices, but not dictate to any nation's representatives what path they should follow.

The book is divided into three sections, based on our objectives for the conference. Section One contains papers dealing with the practicality of human rights-based juvenile justice models for diverse social and cultural conditions. Section Two of the book contains chapters that provide information for the comparison of the juvenile justice systems of various nations. Section Three contains chapters that focus on what can be learned about both productive and negative elements of juvenile justice systems from the nations represented.

The papers in Section One are authored by Abramson, Flindt Pedersen, Stapleton, and Skelton. These authors represent international or national organizations directly involved in providing consultation, support and inspiration to developing countries.

The first paper, by Bruce Abramson, deals with the framework for juvenile justice issues set out by the CRC. Mr. Abramson has worked as a consultant to Defense for Children International (DCI) on projects which attempt to implement the CRC via the Committee on Child Rights. In this chapter he describes the system of reporting under the CRC, and the advantages and problems of this procedure as a means of promoting children's rights.

The chapter by Charlotte Flindt Pedersen, formerly the Project Manager of the Juvenile Justice project at DIHR, analyzes the experience of the Institute in providing assistance to developing countries. She has worked on juvenile justice projects in Africa and Serbia. She has also been on fact-finding missions for UNICEF to study juvenile justice in Kazakhstan and Uzbekistan.

Ms. Flindt Pedersen discusses the needs to utilize research and monitoring to provide a knowledge base for reform and development, and to locate partners and stakeholders in the co-operating nations in order to achieve changes in policies and programs. Her experience attests to the need for a respect for cultural differences in the nations involved. In addition, she notes that developed nations can learn from the co-operating developing nations, particularly in the case of the current trend toward diversion and restorative justice in developing countries.

In his chapter, Adam Stapleton discusses regional co-operation. Mr. Stapleton is director of the African Office of Penal Reform International (PRI) in Lilongwe, Malawi. PRI has a program of assistance for nations around the world to improve conditions in prisons and juvenile justice systems (recall that in many developing nations children are detained in adult prisons). In connection with its work on juvenile justice in Uganda, PRI has developed and promoted ten 'principles of juvenile justice' which form the backbone of PRI's support of regional development efforts in several developing nations. International assistance for Africa has expanded considerably in recent years. A number of donor countries and organizations have created, developed, or supported programs in juvenile justice. To some extent this assistance has taken the form of sending selected local officials to Europe to learn about developments in the field. But it has been the experience of PRI—and DIHR—that bringing relevant stakeholders together within the same region may be as effective as importing advice and models from Europe. This chapter discusses the conditions necessary for such regional co-operation to become effective and sustainable, and provides insights into overcoming obstacles to these goals.

Ann Skelton writes on the situation in South Africa. For several years the South African Law (Reform) Commission has worked on a juvenile justice bill which many considered to be a potential model for developed nations, particularly given its emphasis on restorative justice. The bill has been through a number of revisions and has not been passed by the South African Parliament. The revisions have mostly been in a conservative direction, influenced by a moral panic surrounding juvenile crime. The progressive proposals regarding diversion and restorative justice have been attenuated due to pressures from politicians and public opinion for increased formal social controls. In the period of transition in South Africa—which Skelton sees as presenting opportunity for reform—the process which the bill on juvenile justice has been through exemplifies the difficulties presented by moral panics, and the media and political reification of these.

The chapters in Section Two of the book are authored by Jensen (U.S.A.), de la Cuesta (Spain), Dünkel (Germany), Krajewski (Poland), Sarnecki (Sweden), Jepsen (Denmark), and Silwal (Nepal).

Eric L. Jensen describes the history of the juvenile court in the U.S.A., tracing its roots to the late 1800s and what has been called the child savers movement. The view of juveniles as immature individuals in need of time and support to mature, and to pass through difficult periods of life adjustment without being marginalized were the basis of the first juvenile courts in the U.S.A. These ideals are similar to those underlying the CRC and the current movement to create diversion programs in developing nations. The chapter then discusses the contemporary movement toward a crime control model in the U.S.A. Recent positive contributions to juvenile justice research and practice are also reviewed.

Spain has revised its juvenile justice system in recent years. The chapter by José Luis de la Cuesta provides an historical account of these developments, which in some ways are reminiscent of the developments in Scandinavia. Spain had experienced, to a limited extent, changes in its legislation after the Franco years, but it was not until 2000 that a major act on juvenile justice was passed. This act increased the procedural safeguards for juveniles, and provided new options for reactions—some with the goal of social control and some more welfare-oriented. A number of these changes have been slow to come to fruition, however, due to a lack of funding from the autonomous regions.

The chapter by Frieder Dünkel charts the developments in juvenile offenses and justice reactions to them in Germany. With the advent of reunification, Germany presents a case study of two systems of juvenile justice coming together—at least in theory. The former East German system—which was characterized by a relatively low level of juvenile crime—has gradually approached the West German system but has so far avoided its more repressive characteristics. In general, the contemporary system in the German Federal Republic is characterized by a social welfare approach. It has developed a traditional system of probation and parole, and a number of other non-punitive reactions to juveniles including mediation and diversion.

The chapter on Poland by Krzysztof Krajewski describes the difficult process of changing legislation and systems of reaction away from some hard and fast traditions into a more welfare-oriented system. Polish juvenile court judges seem receptive to welfare approaches, at least for less serious offenders. To some extent, this process of development resembles that of East Germany, but the very process of changing legislation seems more resistant than in the former East Germany. On the other hand, the treatment-oriented social welfare view of juvenile delinquency seems rather well entrenched. In spite of a modest rise in violent crime and a related moral panic, the social welfare approach has preserved its place in Poland.

Scandinavian nations have a long-established social welfare tradition. Both the chapter on Sweden by Jerzy Sarnecki and the chapter on Denmark by Jørgen Jepsen deal with systems based on the Scandinavian welfare boards. While in juvenile court systems the decision-maker is a judge, under a welfare board model decisions are made by a board of social administrators and local politicians. In cases where involuntary removal from the home is sought, the board is assisted by a judge, and a psychologist or other child specialist. The judge deals with procedural issues and the psychologist assists in fitting the reaction to the personality and circumstances of the juvenile. A number of issues arise under both systems regarding the protection of procedural safeguards for the alleged young law violator and the issue of appropriate reaction(s). Although the variety of reactions utilized in both systems is similar, the American juvenile court is characterized primarily by a judicial element supplemented by a number of social and other services, and the Scandinavian systems consist primarily of a social welfare organization supplemented by a judicial element on relevant occasions.

Both the American system and the Scandinavian systems have been exposed to demands for increased social control reactions to young offenders. In Scandinavia, Sweden has to a large extent resisted the pressure for more repressive policies. In Denmark, on the other hand, the system has become more social control-oriented as a result of a moral panic and conservative politicians rising to power, particularly in connection with reactions to violent offenses committed by youngsters of non-Danish origin.

As Kishor Silwal reports in the last chapter of Section Two, Nepal is a country in which the conditions for young offenders caught by the police are worse than, or at least as bad as, those in Africa. However, in recent years, the Centre for Legal Research and Resource Development (CeLRRD) in conjunction with the Kathmandu School of Law (KSL) has developed a program of assistance for young offenders in remand holds. A number of cases have successfully been brought to the attention of the Supreme Court. These cases have been used as an instrument for change and to put pressure on the government to live up to its obligations under the CRC and other international instruments. With support from the DIHR and other donors, the two organizations have begun a process of reform of juvenile justice involving all relevant stakeholders, including high-ranking police officials, the judiciary, prosecutors, and NGOs. A steering committee has been created to promote reform and provide a research basis for these efforts. A number of relevant research projects have been conducted and coordinated by Kishor Silwal. Nepal has actively participated in the DIHR juvenile justice project and the KSL has created a website which collects information on juvenile justice. Nepal's efforts are an example of successful progress towards a more humane juvenile justice system inspired by co-operation with other developing countries and international organizations. The Nepalese movement toward positive change comes in spite of very limited resources.

The third section of the book contains chapters that focus on examples of what practitioners and scholars involved in the varying juvenile justice systems can learn from each other. These chapters address the role of the police in juvenile cases in Catalonia (Vallés), an innovative and established model of aftercare (Armstrong), indigenous Native American restorative justice practices (Mendenhall and Dumesnil), processes for creating human rights-based juvenile justice systems in developing nations (Kaunda), the development of a mixed model of juvenile justice and family law reform in Serbia (Stevanovic), and the pitfalls of the American version of the social control model (Feld).

One of the innovations to emanate from the revisions in Spanish law on juvenile justice is the creation of special police units which deal with juveniles in Catalonia. In her chapter, Lola Vallés describes this development.

The system she describes both allows more effective police work with juveniles and stimulates more youth-friendly behavior on the part of the police.

The chapter by Troy Armstrong discusses the issues surrounding an effective aftercare system for juveniles coming out of institutional settings. The Intensive Aftercare Project is a theory- and research-based program designed to aid in the transition of youth from correctional placements back into the community. Just as the U.S.A. was at the forefront of developing a juvenile court system in the late 1800s, it has also been a leader in developing improved services for troubled youth based on the extant research (see also the chapter by Jensen). The level of resources invested in this aftercare model is of course far beyond those available in the developing nations, but it can be hoped that some of the lessons learned from the Intensive Aftercare Project are generalisable to all societies.

The numerous Native American nations that exist within the borders of the U.S.A. each have their own traditionally-based forms of justice. These resemble the systems of (other) developing nations more than those in the non-Native communities in the U.S.A. Mendenhall and Dumesnil have studied Native American reactions to youth law breaking. They find these reactions to be based on restorative ideals and practices. Restoration and apology are preferred to more repressive formal sanctions. A number of similarities between these practices and those of indigenous peoples in Africa, New Zealand and Canada are evident in this chapter. Developed nations are now learning from these restorative practices.

Desmond Kaunda has written the chapter on the juvenile justice system in Malawi. The original system of justice in Malawi was characterized by repressive attitudes and disorganization, combined with a notable lack of resources. Initiatives from foreign donors, including PRI, have led to co-ordinated work between various parts of the system. This effort began with the Juvenile Justice Forum at Zomba in the southern part of the country. A magistrate in co-operation with a local NGO began by looking at the situation wherein a large number of juvenile offenders were detained in dismal conditions in a section of an adult prison. A closer look at their records indicated that their detention was not legal. In conjunction with a legal aid organization, several of the juveniles had their cases reviewed and were released.

This model inspired the creation of a National Juvenile Justice Forum and juvenile justice forums in other parts of the country (e.g. Lilongwe). The DIHR has supported these developments and has given support to a process of monitoring juvenile delinquents and their treatment in the system.

Kaunda's chapter describes these developments and points to a need for further assistance, in relation to the legal system, the judiciary and law enforcement. Here the CRC and other international instruments have functioned as important guidelines for humanizing the system and counter-acting repressive reactions. Similar projects in Tanzania and Uganda formed part of the DIHR program of assistance in juvenile justice (see Sørensen and Jepsen 2005).

Serbia, as part of the former Yugoslavian Federation until 2004, is in a complicated political and legal situation. These complications extend to issues of human and child rights. The transition from the former commu-nist regime has been slower than was the case for Poland or East Germany, and it is not yet complete. Repeated shifts in the political status of the nation and constantly changing governments in the former Yugoslavia and in the remaining republic of Serbia-Montenegro have protracted the process of reform. In Chapter 17 Ivana Stevanovic discusses a proposal which has recently been presented and advocated in Serbia by a group of child special-ists working for new legislative initiatives. It combines proposed changes in the law regarding juvenile delinquency, juvenile justice, and child and fam-ily law. Thus, the situation of children is dealt with in terms of their roles as both perpetrators of offenses and as victims abuse and neglect. This holistic view of the child is in concordance with emerging international trends. Whether this proposal will succeed in surmounting the numerous obstacles currently presented by the political situation in Serbia is at pres-ent uncertain.

Barry Feld's chapter criticizes the social control direction that the American juvenile court has taken. Underlying these demands for 'getting tough on crime' is the role of the media in creating public perceptions of youth as dangerous. As Feld points out, juveniles are subject to rather severe sanctions yet continue to be deprived of many of the due process protections available to adults in the U.S.A. Feld also points to the role of racial tensions in the creation of these more repressive juve-nile justice policies. He issues a warning to other societies to beware of the pitfalls of the current approach in the U.S.A. Other paths should be pursued in an effort to satisfy the guidelines for juvenile justice systems as set out in the CRC.

In the concluding chapter Jensen and Jepsen review the themes that have evolved in these chapters. Some of the themes were anticipated and others were unexpected. On the one hand, the editors were aware of the moral panic over youth crime in the U.S.A., the emergence of one in Denmark, and the failed attempt to incite panic in Sweden (see Estrada 2001). On the other hand, we were unaware of the moral panic in South Africa and the movement toward one in Poland. In this chapter we also discuss the inte-gral role of the social construction of childhood and youth in shaping juve-nile justice policy, the restorative justice movement that has influenced several of the nations represented in this book, and the importance of implementing juvenile justice practices in line with human rights guidelines and the available evaluative research.

REFERENCES

Bernard, T.J. (1992) *The Cycle of Juvenile Justice*. (New York, Oxford University Press).

Braithwaite, J. (2002) *Restorative Justice and Response Regulation*. (New York, Oxford University Press).

Cunneen, C. and White, R. (1995) *Juvenile Justice: An Australian Perspective*. (Oxford, Oxford University Press).

Dünkel, F. (2003) 'Youth Violence and Juvenile Justice in Germany'. In F. Dünkel and K. Drenkhahn (eds.), *Youth Violence: New Patterns and Local Responses—Experiences in East and West*. (Mönchengladbach, Forum Verlag Godesberg).

Estrada, F. (2001) 'Juvenile Violence as a Social Problem: Trends, Media Attention and Societal Response'. *British Journal of Criminology* 41: 639–55.

Feld, B.C. (1999) *Bad Kids: Race and the Transformation of the Juvenile Court*. (New York, Oxford University Press).

Platt, A. (1977) *The Child Savers: The Invention of Delinquency*. 2nd edn (Chicago, University of Chicago Press).

Sørensen, J.J. and Jepsen, J. (2005) *Juvenile Justice in Transition: Bringing the Convention on the Rights of the Child to Work in Africa and Nepal*. (Copenhagen, Danish Institute for Human Rights).

United Nations (2000) *Bringing International Human Rights Law Home: Judicial Colloquium on the Domestic Application of the Convention on the Elimination of All Forms of Discrimination against Women and the Convention on the Rights of the Child*. (New York, United Nations).

Section One

The Practicality of Human Rights-Based Juvenile Justice Systems for Diverse Nations

2

Juvenile Justice:
The 'Unwanted Child'

Why the potential of the Convention on the Rights of the Child is not being realized, and what we can do about it

BRUCE ABRAMSON

INTRODUCTION

THE CONVENTION ON the Rights of the Child is the centerpiece of an international movement that is aimed at promoting the human dignity of all children and adolescents. Unfortunately, juvenile justice issues are being marginalized. Moreover, specialists in the field of juvenile justice have not climbed on board the CRC bandwagon. Sadly, juvenile justice is the 'unwanted child' of the 'children's rights movement'. Why is this so? And more importantly to those of us who work in the area of juvenile justice, What can we do about the 'unwantedness' problem? How can we juvenile justice professionals—lawyers, judges, sociologists, criminologists, law professors, and public servants in the field of juvenile justice—harvest the rich potential of the Convention on the Rights of the Child?

Marginalization is a comparative notion. Part I therefore begins with an overview of the Convention on the Rights of the Child, discussing the seven main ways in which the CRC is making an important difference in the lives of boys and girls throughout the world. Major steps are being taken in all of the other main areas of concern, such as child labor, sexual exploitation, and universal education. It is relative to all of the action that is taking place in these other areas that we can say that juvenile justice is being marginalized, both within the children's rights movement, and within the broader human rights movement. Part II then discusses the six principal reasons for this relative neglect and lack of progress. Part III suggests a way forward. While this last part is addressed primarily to juvenile justice professionals, the discussion is also relevant to CRC activists.

PART I

THE SEVEN WAYS IN WHICH THE CRC MOVEMENT IS
TRANSFORMING THE WORLD OF CHILDREN AND ADOLESCENTS

Overview

The CRC movement is the social and political campaign that aims to realize all the promises contained in the Convention on the Rights of the Child.
The Convention is the 'clockwork' of the CRC movement, which, despite
the misleading term 'Child', encompasses everyone up to the age of 18
years. The CRC therefore covers adolescents, the age group that makes up
the vast majority of the juvenile justice 'client' population.[1]

The CRC movement is a part of the broader international human rights
movement, but, interestingly, there are things about the Convention that
have given it an edge over the other main human rights treaties—the
International Covenant on Civil and Political Rights (ICCPR), and the
International Covenant on Economic, Social and Cultural Rights (ICESCR).

For one, the CRC has been far more popular with governments than
other UN treaties. Since 1989 when the Convention was opened for ratification, all but two states have joined it, a record that no other human rights
treaty comes close to matching. (The United States and Somalia are the two
hold-outs.) For another, unlike the other treaties, the Convention on the
Rights of the Child is holistic: it combines the so-called 'civil and political
rights' with the 'economic, social and cultural rights'. Moreover, while the
CRC recognizes that the right-holder is the individual boy or girl, it also
recognizes more clearly than the Covenants that each person is also a member of a family, a community, and a society.

Not only have nearly all states ratified the Convention on the Rights of
the Child, many have done comprehensive reviews of their laws, institutions,
and social practices, and most of them have taken meaningful steps to bring
themselves into compliance with the treaty's obligations. Another indication
of the positive response to the CRC is that states are actually turning in compliance reports to the Committee on the Rights of the Child, the body that
monitors the implementation of the treaty. And these reports are usually not
just token gestures; they often provide candid assessments of the problems
that children and adolescents are facing, and concrete information about the
measures that the state is taking to realize their rights.[2]

[1] The Convention on the Rights of the Child, along with all the other UN treaties mentioned
in this paper, is available at www.unhchr.ch.
[2] The key documents are the state's implementation report; the Committee's List of Issues;
the state's supplementary report addressing the List of Issues; the Summary Records of the
Committee's dialogues with the state; and the Committee's Concluding Observations (or recommendations). These are available at www.unhchr.ch/tbs/doc.nsf, under Treaty Body
Database: Documents—by type.

The seven ways in which the CRC is having an impact

The situation is far from perfect, needless to say. States are frequently accused of hypocrisy, of making fancy speeches about respecting the rights of kids, and then going on with business as usual. But this contradiction between words and actions is a problem that runs throughout all of life. While there is indeed a great deal of superficiality in 'rights-talk', there have also been many tangible accomplishments.

The power of the CRC is its catalytic effect in stimulating activism at all levels of society. In this section, I will outline the seven ways that the Convention is being put to work to improve the lives of children and adolescents.

1. Coalition building

Perhaps the most dramatic catalytic effect is the *networking and coalition building* that is going on, particularly among NGOs, but also with intergovernmental organizations and states. The CRC movement is a social-political movement, and the 'bandwagon' is precisely the extensive collaboration that is required to effect change.

Local and national NGOs form coalitions to push their governments to implement the CRC. For instance, many nation-wide coalitions meet with government officials who are preparing the state's implementation report to the Committee on the Rights of the Child; they write their own 'alternative reports'; and they come to Geneva to meet with Committee members to help ensure that the Committee's dialogue with the government will address the priorities. There is an international NGO liaison office that facilitates this process, even paying the expenses of national NGOs from developing countries to come to Geneva! And the liaison office follows up by assisting national NGOs to maintain their coalitions as on-going forces within their countries (Allen 1999).[3]

NGOs are teaming up to create a 'multiplier effect'. They pool resources; they form partnerships to carry out research and assessments in support of reform proposals; they conduct training; they share information; they run projects; and they influence public policy. There are many different types of coalition. Some are made up of NGOs that specialize in particular areas, like street children, while others are composed of a wide diversity of human rights and humanitarian organizations, as in the campaign against underaged (or 'child') soldiers.

---

[3] The one-stop-shop for information on the Convention is CRIN (Children's Rights Information Network), at www.crin.org. For information on coalitions, check the menu under Organizations: NGO Group For CRC: National coalitions.

NGOs that specialize in kids' rights and welfare also join forces with human rights organizations and humanitarian organizations in many forums, such as the General Assembly, the UN Commission on Human Rights, and the Sub-Commission. They have been active in the creation of the International Criminal Court, and in the negotiations of other human rights and humanitarian treaties, for instance.

2. Changing attitudes

Advocates on the CRC bandwagon are using the Convention to achieve a variety of goals. At the most basic level, advocates aim at *changing attitudes*.

Overcoming the invisibility of children and adolescents in government decision-making, changing social norms that permit cruelty, abuse and exploitation, and getting adults to value the opinions of kids and to pay more attention to their feelings, are some of the measures being taken to raise the status of youngsters in society. Anywhere from a third to half of a country's population is made up of people under the age of 18 years—citizens without the power to vote, and who lack, whether by reason of immaturity or their lower social status, the ability to shape the laws and policies that are critical to their survival and development. Simply acknowledging that kids are bearers of rights is a big step for a society to take.

The CRC, and the other UN human rights treaties, like the two Covenants and the Convention Against Torture, are springboards for mobilizing public outrage against injustices. The human rights movement is very much a battle for the hearts and minds of society, which means that it is a struggle over values, attitudes and beliefs (Laurent 1998).

3. New governmental structures

The CRC movement has also helped to create *new governmental structures* to better serve the needs of kids. For instance, some states have created omnibus offices for children and adolescents, as well as intra-departmental co-ordinating mechanisms; they have instituted better data collection and information sharing procedures on indicators of well-being (such as disaggregated statistics on school drop-out rates); they analyze their annual budgets to ensure more equity for children and their families; and they conduct impact assessments on kids' welfare before passing legislation. These are mega-structures in that they are not specific to any particular category of concern, like education or sexual abuse; they are institutional changes that affect the overall process of government in order to better realize all of the rights in the CRC (Hodgkin and Newell 1996; Newell and Holmberg 2000).

At the international level, I think we can include under this heading some of the new United Nations treaties, as well as treaties created under other law-making systems. For instance, we now have two additions to the CRC—the Optional Protocols On the Sale of Children, Child Prostitution and Child Pornography, and On the Involvement of Children in Armed Conflict; the new ILO Convention on the Worst Forms of Child Labor[4]; the European Convention on the Exercise of Children's Rights[5]; and the African Charter on the Rights and Welfare of the Child.[6]

International forums devoted to the rights of children and adolescents should also be mentioned here. Some notable examples include: The General Assembly's Special Session on Children in 2002, with the resulting Declaration and Plan of Action; the two World Congresses Against Commercial Sexual Exploitation of Children; the 'Machel Study' on children and war; and the study on Children and Violence that is just now getting underway, and which should be of real interest to specialists in juvenile justice. These are structural innovations in the sense that they are frameworks for generating international, national and local actions.[7]

4. Participation of young people

One of the most exciting developments is the pioneering work in promoting the *participation* of kids at all levels of society.

Participation is a broad concept. It includes the effective involvement of individual youngsters in decisions that directly affect them, as in the case of disciplinary actions at school. It also refers to the involvement of young people as a social group. This occurs when adults consult with kids when they conduct needs-assessments, or when they design and monitor programs. It also happens when young people are included in the running of these programs. Training and employing young people as peer councilors is just one such example (Hart 1992; Petrén and Hammarberg 2000).

5. Developmental needs

The CRC movement promotes *understanding of the developmental needs* of adolescents and children. What distinguishes youngsters from adults is that they are in a process of rapid development, physically, mentally, morally, and socially. This is what entitles them to 'special care and assistance', in the

---

[4] ILO Convention No. 182, available at www.ilo.int, buried under Child Labour (IPEC): Ratification Campaign.

[5] ETS No. 160; available at www1.umn.edu/humanrts, under Treaties: Regional Conventions: All Council of Europe Conventions.

[6] Available at www1.umn.edu/humanrts, under Treaties: Regional Conventions: African Human Rights Instruments.

[7] Information on these initiatives is available at www.crin.org, under Themes.

words of the preamble to the CRC. Kids 'grow in developmental sequences, like a tower of bricks, each layer depending on the one below it' (UNHCR 1994, 1). Our job as adults is to make sure that each brick is in the right place at the right time.

Unfortunately, promoting the understanding of developmental needs is perhaps the least advanced part of the movement. For instance, advocates place great emphasis on training government officials about human rights, but their programs tend to concentrate on the various UN treaties as sets of rules. What is usually missing is training about the psychological, social and physical needs of the kids. As Elizabeth Scott has argued in *A Century of Juvenile Justice*, 'good policy cannot ignore the empirical reality of adolescence as a developmental stage' (Scott 2002, 140). Many juvenile justice specialists have expertise in the developmental needs of young people, and the CRC movement could profit from collaborating with them.

6. *Law reform*

One of the chief aims of human rights activists is to get states to change their laws. This is primarily a political process, which is why all the other NGO activities—changing attitudes and coalition building, in particular—are so important. While there is a slight trend in courts directly using the various UN treaties in their decisions (Conforti and Francioni 1997; Cotran and Sherif 1997; Jayawickrama 2002), for the most part the process of 'implementing' the human rights treaties is political, rather than legal (Heyns and Viljoen 2001; Heyns and Viljoen 2002).

Legislative reform is always a major topic of concern to juvenile justice specialists. The state implementation reports, together with the CRC Committee's recommendations, give a good snapshot of the successes, and the gaps, in this area.

7. *Budgets: getting bigger pieces of the pie*

Governmental budgets are a type of law, to be sure, but they are so different from other legislation that they need special mention.

Nearly all human rights are resource-intensive. Just because a piece of legislation says that such-and-such is to happen does not mean that it will. The state must spend money to put its programs and policies into effect, so the actual enjoyment of human rights will largely depend on successful competition for government spending.

Here, too, is where the other activities that I have mentioned have their pay-off. Like a rising tide lifting all the boats, elevating the status of children and adolescents in society, mobilizing societal sentiment against specific outrages, and ensuring transparency and accountability through better governmental structures, all help to ensure fairer allocations to young people.

While I have separated out these seven types of impacts, what is important to emphasize is that all of these activities are going on simultaneously, and it is the combined effect, the synergistic interaction, that produces the results (Woll 2000).

PART II

THE SIX PROBLEMS THAT MAKE JUVENILE JUSTICE THE
'UNWANTED CHILD'

While the Convention on the Rights of the Child is proving itself to be a highly successful human rights treaty, the potential of the CRC is not being realized with respect to the youngsters who are in trouble with the law. Of all the major areas covered by the Convention, juvenile justice is the most neglected.

Marginalization of juvenile justice reform

Several years ago, Defence for Children International (2000) made a study of 140 state implementation reports, and the corresponding recommendations of the Committee on the Rights of the Child. The study identified a number of indicators by which to gauge the seriousness of the neglect of juvenile justice issues.

The first indicator is the frequency with which the Committee has called for 'comprehensive reform' of the juvenile justice system. Of course, states need to do better in all areas, including education and health, but the need for 'comprehensive reform' of juvenile justice reflects the degree to which the fundamental obligations of the CRC have not been understood, accepted, or acted upon by governments. Another indicator is the number of times that the Committee has had to urge states to end inhumane practices that constitute *per se* violations of international law, like using the death penalty on minors, or flogging and torture. What distinguishes human rights abuses against minors in the juvenile justice system from other serious issues, such as sexual abuse and child labor, is that these youngsters are in the care and custody of the state, so what happens to them is often a result of conscious choices. For instance, the failure to separate minors from adults in detention, which is a bedrock requirement of international law, is the result of a policy decision to not make the investments necessary for a humane penal system. The picture that emerges is one of states failing to grasp the reasons for having a special system of justice for young people who are in trouble with the law. The depth of the problem is reflected in the difficulty that the Committee on the Rights of the Child has had in focussing on key juvenile justice issues, and in articulating the core messages of the Convention in this area.

This does not mean to say that there are no bright spots, that there are no improvements whatsoever. But when compared to other major areas covered by the Convention, the rights of youngsters in conflict with the law are being neglected. This is the justification for calling juvenile justice the 'unwanted child' of state human rights obligations.

How can we account for the relative neglect of juvenile justice, or, more accurately, the neglect of the youngsters who are caught up in the penal system? The next section will discuss the six major reasons for the relative neglect of juvenile justice reform.

Before I discuss the reasons for marginalization, I need to confront the problem that I face in addressing this issue. Of the six causes of the relative neglect of juvenile justice, four are internal problems, that is to say, they are barriers for which juvenile justice professionals or CRC activists themselves bear some responsibility. If I compare myself to a doctor trying to cure the 'unwantedness problem' of juvenile justice reform, then my diagnosis has to include attitudes and behaviors of my colleagues— fellow professionals in the field of juvenile justice, and fellow CRC activists.

I think of the story of Dr. Ignaz Semmelweiss when I use the metaphor of a doctor giving a diagnosis.

Dr. Semmelweiss noticed that the mothers in the hospital where he worked were dying from fever after childbirth at a much higher rate than in other maternity wards. This was in Europe in the 1840s. He finally concluded that the deaths were somehow connected to the fact that the medical students who were assisting the births had just come from dissecting cadavers, *and they were not washing their hands*. The very doctors who were 'helping' the mothers were the agents of their deaths, Semmelweiss concluded. But no one would listen. He was rebuffed, even vilified, and the strain broke him. He eventually went mad (Hellman 2001).

The medical world has changed greatly since then, thankfully, but human nature is still the same. Dr. Semmelweiss is a real-life case of 'shooting the messenger' who brings the bad news. This is the dilemma that I face. I want to encourage juvenile justice professionals to get on board the CRC bandwagon, and CRC activists to work more closely with them and with NGOs that specialize in juvenile justice reform. But, since four of the six sources of marginalization are internal problems, part of my message is 'Physicians heal yourselves'. I don't know of any way to avoid the proverbial shoot-the-messenger problem other than to candidly acknowledge it, and then move on to the discussion of the six sources of marginalization.

The six causes of 'unwantedness'

1. *Juvenile justice is about crime*

Perhaps the most serious problem is that minors in trouble with the law do not receive the same sympathetic understanding that is so freely given to other youngsters. Every penal offense has a victim, and fear of crime can erode the quality of life of everyone in society, and these are the roots of the unpopularity of penal reform.

When the public does become interested in juvenile justice it is often because politicians are exploiting law-and-order concerns. Too often politicians call for get-tough measures, and, typically, these 'solutions' turn out to be shortsighted, doing more harm than good. And the media just adds to the problem, since bad news sells better than good news.

The end result is that the public is usually either cold or outright hostile to the kids who are accused of breaking the law. It should not come as any surprise that juvenile justice remains unpopular, despite the popularity of the CRC as a whole. [8]

2. *Juvenile justice is not a system but an overlapping of systems*

It is standard practice to speak of 'the juvenile justice system', or to use short-cut expression like 'juvenile justice', rather than say more completely what we mean. The pressures of work, and the nature of bureaucracy, force us to simplify. But this simplification distorts reality because 'juvenile justice' is not a system but an overlapping of systems. The police, the lawyers, the judges, the prison staff, the probation officers, and the rehabilitation personnel are separate *occupational systems*. In addition to these occupational systems, 'juvenile justice' can be looked at from the perspective of *functional* systems, like prevention, apprehension (investigation and arrest), diversion, imprisonment, trial, and rehabilitation. Each of these systems has its own hierarchical structure and peer network, its own mission, and its own ethos. And each is in competition with the others for resources. In fact, sometimes there are even conflicts between the objectives or the working methods of the overlapping systems.

We are all familiar with the 'balloon effect' in juvenile justice reform: reformers grab hold of one part of the problem, and it bulges out somewhere else. One of the reasons for the balloon effect is that changes in one system put pressure on the other interlocking systems, and these other

---

[8] To fully appreciate this problem, we need to see the matter from the public's perspective. Ron Powers' article, 'The Apocalypse of Adolescents' (2002), is a good example of public perceptions in one developed country.

systems push back, defeating the reform, or creating new problems. This is why we must address 'juvenile justice' not as *a* system but as a set of *over-lapping systems*.

The two barriers to juvenile justice reform that we have just looked at are external problems in the sense that they are imposed upon juvenile justice professionals and CRC activists either by society or by the institutional structures of government. They are 'inherent' problems that will never go away completely; reformers will always need to take them into account. The other sources of marginalization, however, are to some extent internal problems. It is to these internal sources of marginalization that we now turn.

3. Rhetoric of 'the child'

There are several features of the CRC movement that have made it difficult for activists to take up juvenile justice reform. The dominant image in 'children's rights' advocacy is the innocence, vulnerability, helplessness, and victimization of 'the child'. There are two traps here, and perhaps you have already guessed what they are.

The first is that juvenile offenders are not innocent! And they certainly are not helpless! If they were, there would be no need for a juvenile justice system.

Of course, many juvenile offenders are themselves victims—of physical, sexual, or emotional abuse—and this victimization often plays an important causal role in the behavior that has got them into trouble with the law. But the fundamental premise of most CRC activists—the innocence and helplessness of the beneficiaries of their altruism—contradicts the very reason that the kids are in police custody and before the courts: they have intentionally caused serious harm to other people.

The second trap is that the overwhelming majority of juvenile offenders are not children: they are teenagers. CRC activists experience extreme difficulty with this fact.

We need to back up here and put the CRC into its historical context. The Convention on the Rights of the Child did not give birth to the 'children's rights movement'. Long before the United Nations was created there has been a 'child-savers' movement that has seen kids, children primarily, as objects of protection (Hawes 1991). After the UN system began creating human rights agreements, activists in the child-savers movement lobbied for a treaty specifically for children, and one that would be framed in terms of 'rights'. The early drafts of this treaty used the word 'child', meaning, basically, young people below the age of puberty. As the negotiations proceeded, it was suggested that the scope of the treaty should be enlarged to cover everyone under the age of 18 years; in other words, to add adolescents to the class of people who would be rights-holders under the new convention. The delegates agreed to this extension, but the 'child' language remained the same. The enlargement was handled by the technical device of a legal fiction: CRC article 1 says that '[f]or the purposes of the present Convention' the term *child* is to be read to mean everyone under 18 years.

CRC advocates love to say that the Convention 'defines' every human being under the age of 18 as a 'child'. Which is simply not true. The Convention does not say that all of these human beings *are* children, but only that the *word* 'child' in the treaty is *to be translated as* everyone under 18. Article 1 is an artificial definition: that's why it's a 'legal fiction'.

There is mental blocking going on here. While CRC advocates talk about the Convention applying to everyone under 18, they are nearly always thinking about children, not children *and* adolescents. Look at the photos in CRC promotional materials and you will find that they are exclusively, or overwhelmingly, of children—usually pictured as innocent, vulnerable, and often suffering. When you listen to a CRC advocate talk about 'children's rights', ask yourself: 'Is this speaker visualizing 16 and 17 year olds?' I believe you will nearly always say, 'Definitely not teenagers!' Unfortunately, rhetoric like 'child rights' and 'the child' is making adolescents invisible in the CRC movement (Abramson 1996).

Human rights are 'tools' for promoting respect for the human dignity of each and every person. All of us who work directly with young offenders know the importance of respect (Sennett 2003). There is no such thing as rehabilitation, or reinsertion, or prevention, or even a fair trial, without deep respect for the young person we are interacting with in the juvenile justice system. But I have never yet met a sixteen or seventeen year old who wants to be called a 'child'.

I cannot explain why CRC advocates find it so important to call older teenagers—young men and women, really—'the child'. It must be meeting the adults' emotional needs. As always, our greatest stumbling block to reform is human nature. Whether it's parents beating their children ('It's for their own good, dammit!'), or the medical profession fighting Semmelweiss ('We're *helping* these women!'), or countless other issues, we are always confronted with the gap between our words and our deeds. CRC advocates *say* that the Convention covers everyone under 18, but notwithstanding some exceptions, like the reproductive health of girls, teenagers are marginalized. And since the young offenders are overwhelmingly teenagers, juvenile justice gets sidelined, as compared with other areas covered by the CRC.

4. Over-reliance on the negative approach

The traditional NGO approach to human rights is to focus on abuses of civil and political rights, and the primary mode of action has been 'name-shame-and-blame', that is, to expose outrages, to shame governments into action through public denunciations, and to seek punishment of perpetrators. The traditional approach has succeeded in awakening the public's conscience on many issues, and it will always be a necessary part of human rights work. But by itself the 'negative approach' will not take us all the way to our destination—to achieving full realization of all human rights. We must also adopt 'positive approaches'.

The heart of the positive approach is a focus on *respecting the human dignity* of children and adolescents, which means, above all, *promoting their healthy development*: indeed, this is the essence of the Convention on the Rights of the Child. It's vital that we stop cruelty, of course, but our aim should be to *replace* cruelty with attitudes and practices that respect human dignity, which includes promoting the healthy development of young people. This objective is especially important in dealing with young offenders because only this perspective keeps the system focussed on prevention and rehabilitation. And only the positive approach can recapture the sympathetic understanding that all human beings who are in need are entitled to.

There are times when it is appropriate to argue for reform on the basis of social utility, such as when we show politicians the research studies proving that prevention is cost-effective, or when we argue for diversion programs on the grounds that detention is a scarce resource that is being over-used. Pragmatic arguments are always necessary, but they are not human rights arguments. Every kid has a *right* to an education, a *right* to family contact, a *right* to an adequate standard of living—all of which are 'social and economic rights', and all of which are critical to the well-being of the youngsters who are caught up in the juvenile justice system.

Human rights advocacy requires a combination of moral, legal and pragmatic arguments (Schulz 2002, 1–16). The more a state works towards realizing human right across the board, the more progress it will make in reducing juvenile offending, but this will require a more positive approach to human rights work than is currently the case.

5. The salami approach

As I've mentioned, one of the great strengths of the CRC is that it is holistic. 'Holistic' is actually a cluster of concepts, when it is used correctly.

In the human rights movement, 'holistic' usually means that 'civil and political rights' are not to be given priority over 'economic, social, and cultural rights'; all rights are said to be 'interdependent'.

In addition, holistic can refer to a particular way of looking at social problems, an approach which can best be illustrated by making a comparison. There is a tendency for people interested in juvenile justice to focus on two, so-called 'juvenile justice articles'—CRC article 37 (inhumane treatment) and article 40 (administration of justice). This is the 'salami approach', which chops up the holistic Convention into slices of rights; it's an approach that fails to see young people as having a full range of needs, and rights, at every moment they are within the justice system.

Under the salami approach, one divides life up into themes, such as education or juvenile justice, and then focusses an inquiry within the confines of the chosen heading. For example, one looks at schools and asks, 'What are the state's obligations with respect to education under the CRC?' or at prisons and inquires, 'What are the state's juvenile justice obligations?' By contrast, the holistic approach looks at *people as complete human beings* and asks, 'With respect to these boys and girls in detention, what are the obligations with respect to their education, to their health, to due process, etc., etc.' Under the holistic approach, virtually every CRC right can be seen as a juvenile justice right, from the point of view of the boys and girls who are in conflict with the law. The rights to education, to health, and to family contact, for instance, are vitally important to kids in the juvenile justice system. (Note my relapse into the singular 'system'.)

'Holistic' is all-encompassing. Generally speaking, a significant percentage of juvenile criminal activity is directed at income-generation. This includes certain kinds of property crimes (e.g. theft), crimes of violence (e.g. robbery, mugging), and illegal commerce (e.g. drug dealing, prostitution). If prevention and reintegration programs are to have a significant social impact, they must address the income-generation problems of teenage boys and girls, and their families. Unfortunately, the needs of minors who are at risk of offending, or who are already in trouble, are not taken into account in national economic development plans. 'Juvenile justice' is seen as the administration of justice to minors who have broken the law, unconnected to the larger problems of social justice, like poverty and other types of marginalization.

The truly holistic approach that I am talking about is, of course, simply another aspect of the positive approach: providing adolescents and children with the 'special care and assistance' that they are entitled to under the CRC. Society—both the state and civil society—must take measures that will promote healthy development, and this includes education, and the ability for them or their families to earn a living in a lawful manner.

The holistic approach, in its fullest sense, addresses all of the dimensions of life.[9]

6. Boys

Juvenile justice is overwhelmingly about boys. The kids who are being arrested and imprisoned are boys, ranging from about 85% to 99% of the total number of inmates in detention, depending on the country. The penal system, adult and juvenile, is the most heavily gendered institution in society, even more so than the military, given current trends. I think that this

---

[9] John Pitts' extraordinary book, *The New Politics of Youth Crime: Discipline or Solidarity?* (2001), compares the holistic strategy of the French government to the fragmented approach of the United Kingdom.

fact is one of the most important reasons for the marginalization of juvenile justice issues in the human rights movement.

The are a number of areas of life where the indicators of well-being show that boys are doing worse than girls, but the CRC movement routinely ignores this, with only modest exceptions. The expression 'particularly girls' appears throughout the CRC literature, but it is very unusual to see 'especially boys'. Unfortunately, the 'particularly' language is exclusionary: the word *particularly* focusses people's attention on girls, with the result that either the situation of boys is ignored, or boys are reduced to second class citizens as right-holders under the CRC.

For instance, when a state implementation report says that more boys than girls are hooked on cigarettes, the CRC movement expresses concern 'at the high and increasing' prevalence of tobacco use 'notably among girls' (Committee on the Rights of the Child 2002, para. 40). The situation is worse for the boys, but only the welfare of the girls is focussed on.

Apparently, the rationale for ignoring the boys is that the girls in this particular state have a higher rate of increase in tobacco usage, even though more boys smoke, and even though society is only closing the gender gap, as it makes females more like males in all areas of life not fixed by biology. The justification here is not only thin, it works in just one direction. When another state reports that boys are committing suicide two to three hundred per cent more often than girls, and that the rate of increase for the boys is greater (Australia 1996, Table F10), the situation still does *not* call for special attention to boys.[10] Instead, the CRC establishment merely expresses 'concern' at 'the incidence of suicide among *young people*', airbrushing out the gender issue altogether (Committee on the Rights of the Child 1997, para. 18) (emphasis added).

The indicators are staring us in the face. Everyone knows that girls are being severely discriminated against or excluded in education. Right? Well, the statistics tell us that *boys* are also being severely discriminated against and excluded in education.

For instance, boys are *under-represented* in secondary schools in *eighty-eight countries* (UNICEF 2002, 96–9). The pattern of female over-representation in education gets worse as the youngsters get older, the trend against boys is increasing with time, and the problem is global. In post-secondary education in Western states, for instance, males are under-represented in all

[10] Table F10 is not reproduced on the UN website. Australia's report has one short paragraph on suicide, and it makes no mention of the dramatic gender disparities that are reflected in Table F10 (Australia 1996, para. 884). In an interesting comparison, the report devotes eight paragraphs to what the Australian government is doing to combat female genital mutilation within its borders (Australia 1996, paras. 872–9). Eight paragraphs to one, with the one paragraph refusing to mention the greater problems that the boys are facing: that's a good summary of the position of boys in the human rights movement.

but a couple of countries. In Norway, females are over-represented by thirty percentage points (Doyle 1999, 22). And girls in Sweden are over-represented by an extraordinary thirty-seven percentage points (UNICEF 2002, 96–9). According to the experts, these trends are explained in part by the higher rates of learning disabilities in boys, and, even more importantly, by the absence of male role models, primarily as a result of the increase in female-headed households, and the over-representation of women in the teaching profession (Doyle 1999, 22). These two factors—learning disabilities and loss of male role models—are also significant in the over-representation of boys in the juvenile justice system.

Another indicator pertains to the most basic of all human rights: the right to life. In all but a couple countries of the world, females have disproportionately longer life expectancies than males. In some European countries, women are outliving men by as much as one hundred and twenty percent (UNICEF 2002, 110).[11] It is often said that the right to life is the most fundamental human right of all, since all of the other rights obviously require that the right-holder be alive to enjoy them. But even though males are not enjoying their right to live on a par with females, we do not see human rights activists identifying this gender disparity as a human rights issue, or as a gender issue, or, for that matter, even as a disparity. And one never hears CRC or human rights activists calling for 'affirmative action' to correct the imbalance in the enjoyment of the most fundamental of all human rights. Ensuring equal enjoyment of the right to life would require activists to think in terms of 'particularly men and boys', but this expression simply does not exist in human rights-talk.

I do not mean to imply that no government is making any effort to correct any of the various imbalances that are depriving boys of the equal enjoyment of CRC rights with girls, or that the human rights establishment invariably turns a blind eye to the fate of males. But overall, neither the human rights movement nor the CRC movement is treating imbalances in the well-being *of males* as a human rights issue, or even a 'gender issue'.

The relative neglect of juvenile justice is therefore a part of a wider phenomenon of the marginalization of boys and men wherein the problems that disproportionately harm males are routinely ignored or downplayed. And since juvenile justice is one of the most dramatic instances of boys as a social group faring worse than girls as a group, we need to give the gender dimension close attention.

---

[11] Compare the presentation of these disparities with other rhetoric in the human rights literature: 'Maternal mortality is a reflection of the devaluation of female life and a measure of the social neglect of women' (Center for Reproductive Rights 2003, 74). We never see a comparable statement about the lower life expectancies of boys and men.

Consider the remarks of Sir John Stevens, the Metropolitan Police Commissioner:

> In London, our research shows that there are about thirty to forty youths on each borough who have grown up in [state] care in an environment of physical and sexual abuse, each and every one . . . had been abused and when they had reported offences they had been ignored or enquires had not been successful. These youths have been excluded from school for four or five years and who have never experienced any form of parental control. Some of them wouldn't even recognize their parents if they met them in the street. Is it any wonder they become desensitised to society's norms and decencies. Maybe three hundred to four hundred of them are causing a huge upsurge in street crime and the pattern is repeating itself up and down the country. (Guardian 2002, 2)

What percentage of these 'thirty to forty youths' would you guess were males? Stevens does not give citations for the studies, but I would be willing to bet that 'youths' is 100% masculine. Sir John is obviously concerned about stopping the sexual and other abuses that he mentions; even though he is talking about hooligans, he has not lost his sympathetic understanding. But rather than say 'young males', he has chosen to use de-gendered language. Why do you think he made this choice?

Compare Sir John's speech with Amnesty International's report on juvenile justice in the United States. 'Many girls suffering sexual and physical abuse at home respond by fighting back or running away,' which, the report says, helps to explain why girls end up in the hands of the juvenile justice system (Amnesty International 1998, 52–3). And what about the history of sexual and physical abuse suffered by the boys who are in the system? Amnesty's report is totally silent about this. The report also decries the 'massive over-representation of black children' in the penal system (Amnesty International 1998, 53, 56–7). *Black children?* Not black *males?* Or just plain *teenage boys*, without the color coding? The Amnesty report does not recognize *any* over-representation of males in the jails of America. The report calls attention to the 'distinct link between the over-representation of black children in the justice system and the social and economic environment in which they live', but since males are not over-represented, nothing needs to be said about the sociological factors that propel boys into the arms of the law. Apparently, black *males* are in lock-up because that's where they're supposed to be. That's the implication, isn't it?

So much for the flagship of the human rights movement. Are the juvenile justice professionals doing any better in addressing the over-representation of boys in the penal system? Let's check with the International Centre for the Prevention of Crime. They say that we now have the knowledge and the tools to effectively prevent juvenile delinquency. They tell us that large-scale studies have identified the 'factors . . . associated with' delinquency, and this allows us to design effective programs (International Centre for the Prevention of

Crime 1999, 2–3). They name eight risk factors, such as poverty and dropping out of school, but the biggest statistical correlater—the sex of the youngster—is not on their list. Apparently, effective prevention of juvenile delinquency calls for androgynous measures; we are expected to believe that the young person's sex is irrelevant, despite the fact that males are grossly over-represented in the penal system.

Although the United Nations plays a major role in the promotion of human rights, we find this same exclusion of boys throughout its publications. For instance, the *World Youth Report 2003* has a chapter on 'Juvenile Delinquency' that is excellent in all respects—except when it comes to boys (United Nations 2004, 188–210). The title page has a large photo of two pre-teen girls looking out at the reader with beautiful, laughing smiles. The body of the chapter has three photos, all of smiling girls. Boys are overwhelming over-represented in jails and prisons of the world, but the chapter on juvenile delinquency does not contain a single photo of a male. The text of the chapter follows the same pattern of exclusion. For instance, a long section on 'Preventing Juvenile Delinquency' is framed in terms of 'adolescents', thereby ensuring that there is no gender analysis. The subject of gender comes up only a few times, and when it does the text is always slanted in favor of girls at the expense of boys.

The systematic exclusion of boys exists throughout the CRC movement. A UNICEF booklet, *Sport, Recreation, and Play*, illustrates the problem (UNICEF 2004). The booklet contains twice as many photos of girls than of boys, and for teenagers the imbalance jumps to a four-to-one ratio against the males. The exclusion of boys is also seen in the types of activities that the youngsters are engaged in. Girls are often shown in activities that require skill and dedication, like gymnastics and karate, but there is only one photo of a boy—a pre-teen—doing anything that takes comparable skill and that will win the youngster comparable social recognition. To appreciate the extent of the exclusion, we need to bear in mind that the booklet was produced in the United States, where, for a generation now, editors and publishers have been taking great care to ensure that photos reflect gender and racial or ethnic parity. Moreover, the booklet is a UN publication, and I know from my own experience in working on a number of publications that UN agencies are similarly vigilant. It is simply impossible for a booklet to contain such a gender imbalance by accident. And finally, let us not forget that the subject is sports, and that sports activities play an important role in juvenile delinquency prevention and reintegration programs for boys—the gender that makes up the vast majority of the inmates in penal detention facilities.

Whether we look at the CRC movement, or at the broader human rights movement, or at the specialized juvenile justice advocacy, we find the same pattern of avoiding the gender dimension of juvenile justice. Some adults are in deep denial of the gender issue when boys are on the losing end of the disparities. But most people recognize that there is a gender issue. The problem is that no one has found an effective, positive way to address it. I think that juvenile justice professionals and CRC activists are paying a dear price in credibility for their failure to address gender: the public knows—at some level of awareness—that the advocates for reform are not addressing the problem when they duck the gender dimension of delinquency.

This does not mean to say that no one is ever paying attention to the needs and rights of boys *as boys*, but the task here is to account for the difficulty of juvenile justice reform, and we can't ignore the fact that there is a gender dimension *within the advocacy itself*.

Social marginalization is not a problem of accidental forgetfulness, like not remembering to turn off the bathroom light. As in any type of social exclusion, the marginalization of boys is the result of active processes (Sommers 2002). Sad to say, there is outright sex discrimination against boys in the CRC movement.

PART III

WHAT TO DO?

I believe that there are two basic things that juvenile justice professionals can do to counteract the unwantedness problem, and to promote penal reform for children and adolescents. The first step is to climb on board the CRC bandwagon. The second is to get juvenile justice reform onto the international agenda.

Step one: become part of the CRC movement

I have argued in the foregoing sections that there is much to be gained by mainstreaming juvenile justice concerns within the CRC movement, and that there are some serious barriers that must be overcome before the full potential of the CRC can be realized. Almost all the obstacles are ones of attitude, which, I would suggest, make them ripe candidates for human rights advocacy.

Joining the CRC movement would require juvenile justice specialists to invest time and energy, which would mean an increase in their already over-stretched workloads. Whether they see this additional stress as worthwhile will depend upon their perceptions of both the immediate and the long-term payoffs. I think that the point that needs to be emphasized is that the investment will bear fruit only if the specialists form coalitions among themselves, and then, with a strategy in hand, branch out and enlist others, including NGOs, intergovernmental agencies, and states.

The juvenile justice situation is like a gigantic swimming pool where the water is near freezing, and where the kids are succumbing to hypothermia. We have a vast array of people bringing cups of hot water to the pool. But the 'tea cup brigade' will not raise the temperature of the water; it can provide relief to the individual swimmers in the immediate vicinity, but the pool is too vast for even an army of tea cups to effect a change.

I think that the only way to raise the temperature of the pool is for juvenile justice specialists to mainstream themselves in the CRC movement, and in the broader human rights movement of which it is a part. These movements are aiming at fundamental changes throughout society, and this is where the criminal-law and juvenile-justice experts need to be putting their efforts.

For instance, juvenile justice professionals have a lot to gain by teaming up with CRC advocates in the course of their present work. The techniques that are being developed to promote young people's participation has obvious value to juvenile justice workers, for example. But this is still the tea cup approach to reform. It will never overcome the attitude barriers that are keeping juvenile justice marginalized.

Juvenile justice experts can gain more by joining the national CRC coalitions. But 'joining' is not enough. A bandwagon is not a club that one becomes a part of by submitting an application. It is a social movement, which means that it's a series of alliances or partnerships that people form to advance their specific objectives. Juvenile justice advocates must be able to show the CRC advocates how the latter's aims will be advanced by enlarging their spheres of interests to include the young people who are in trouble with the law. Most NGOs have areas of specialization, like street kids, or education, or caste discrimination, to name a few concerns. Juvenile justice professionals must re-examine their work in light of these concerns, and then find ways to build upon the links between juvenile justice issues and the work of these other NGOs. Prevention, diversion, detention, and rehabilitation are in fact linked to the mandates of the traditional 'children's rights' organizations, but these links are not being made clear, and are not being capitalized on for their multiplier effects in the promotion of reform.

In other words, juvenile justice specialists must pull CRC specialists into their own corner of the bandwagon: they must be able to show how mainstreaming juvenile justice will have a pay-off in terms of implementing the CRC as a whole.

Raising the temperature of the pool will require a global strategy. Education is a good illustration of how thinking in global terms can change perceptions and behavior. Education activists have been waging a fierce campaign for a number of years to get political leaders to accept the notion that basic education is fundamental to the economic, social and political development of states. The idea has been planted, and the roots are now fairly deep. The World Bank, for instance, integrates education-for-all within its developmental plans and its lending packages. The major UN agencies are now actively supporting education. And governments are making real efforts to achieve educational results. As a consequence, we have seen tremendous progress, and the current rededication to education-for-all is even more promising. Juvenile justice professionals need to team up with CRC activists to take similar international action with respect to juvenile justice reform.

The education-for-all campaign is also a good example of the contributions that juvenile justice professions can make. Dropping-out and related problems at school are among the highest risk factors for teenager offending. So delinquency prevention programs and reintegration programs that will get offenders back into the educational system are extremely important. Moreover, school-based prevention and rehabilitation programs are cost-effective ways for the state to reduce crime levels. But despite the importance of these programs, the education-for-all campaign has not integrated the juvenile justice dimension into its activities. Juvenile justice professionals therefore have an important role to play in helping the campaign to overcome this blind spot. The education-for-all people, juvenile justice professionals, and CRC activists all share a common interest, and they need to work together to accomplish their reform objectives. My point is that the CRC movement is the best vehicle for this collaboration.

Step two: get juvenile justice reform onto the international agenda

A global juvenile justice strategy would likewise need to plant a powerful conceptual seed: *the development of society includes a progressively more humane penal system.* Economic developmental plans, and international lending and donor aid-packages, must include provisions for reforming the penal system.

To take one illustration, states are coming back to the Committee on the Rights of the Child on their second implementation reports without having complied with their obligations to separate minors from adults in detention. Even though separation has been a fundamental UN standard for fifty years, and even though it is specifically required by the CRC, and despite the fact that the Committee's first set of Concluding Observations urged the state to take action, the situation has not changed. The reason is always the same: no money. Which means, in translation, that the human rights of people in trouble with the law continue to lose out in the political competition for resources. And this will always be the case because developing countries are having a tough time providing even the popular services, like health and education; in fact, their education and health systems usually depend on large amounts of international aid. But note the salami approach here. Kids in detention have health and educational needs too! But their needs—their human rights—are not being integrated within the international aid assistance plans.

It's the same situation with diversion programs. Governmental officials can be persuaded that prevention and diversion are cost-effective measures for reducing delinquency, but they cannot get from where they are to where they would like to be without outside support. When there's not enough money to buy gas or radios for the police cars, and the police officers' salaries are insufficient to live on, and the state is three months behind in paying them, then we cannot expect the government to make the juvenile justice expenditures that are required today in order to reap important social gains in the future. Major reform will not occur without international support, and that support will not come in amounts sufficient to raise the temperature of the pool unless there is a new way of thinking among the leaders in the world of international aid.

It is not acceptable for inter-governmental bodies or states to promote multi-million dollar development projects without earmarking a portion for the progressive upgrading of the penal system, not when we consider the levels of inhumanity that we find in the juvenile and adult systems throughout the world. Economic development fuels social disruption, like migration and changes in family structures, and disruption of the social fabric will lead to additional crime; that's the human condition. A holistic, human rights approach will anticipate these problems, and will ensure that developmental packages have dedicated a certain portion to the rehabilitation of the penal system.

The international system has already laid a number of foundations that juvenile justice professionals, working together with CRC activists, can build upon. For instance, the Commission on Human Rights appeals to states to 'include in their national development plans the administration of justice as an integral part of the development process . . .' (Commission on Human Rights 2002).[12] The Commission on Human Rights is a subsidiary body of the UN General Assembly, and it is made up of states, so this recognition of the link between penal reform and development is an important step. But the abstract recognition of the link must be followed up by many concrete initiatives. Juvenile justice professionals have a vital role to play in showing national governments, donor states, UN agencies, and international financial institutions the concrete implications of the link. For example, the people who control the purse strings and the architects of development projects need to understand that juvenile delinquency prevention and rehabilitation programs do work, and that they are cost-effective ways for the state to reduce crime. But the only way that the gatekeepers of

---

[12] This part of the Commission's resolution is based on the Beijing Rules, rule 1.4 ('Juvenile justice shall be conceived as an integral part of the development process of each country within in a comprehensive framework of social justice for all juveniles').

development will know this is for juvenile justice professionals to present them with the research findings on prevention and rehabilitation.

Another foundation is the United Nations Millennium Declaration (General Assembly 2000). Adopted in the year 2000, this document is increasingly becoming the comprehensive framework for planning, co-ordination and monitoring of the work of states, UN agencies, and international organizations. While the Declaration contains a few concrete targets, such as the universal enjoyment of primary education by the year 2015, most of the goals are framed in highly abstract terms. The abstract goals are broad enough to embrace all aspects of juvenile justice reform, from ending inhuman prison conditions to the creation of prevention, diversion and rehabilitation programs, to ensuring due process in the handling of individual cases. But since the goals are abstract, it is up to juvenile justice professions to define the concrete links. A great deal of work is being done to turn the Millennium Declaration into a practical framework device in many spheres of life, but this work will just perpetuate the marginalization of juvenile justice reform. Unless, that is, juvenile justice professionals team up with CRC activists to ensure the technical and political integration of penal reform into the Millennium Declaration's follow-up activities.

CONCLUSIONS

The Convention on the Rights of the Child has proven itself to be a highly successful catalyst for promoting the human rights of children and adolescents, with the one principal exception of juvenile justice. Once the unwantedness problem is acknowledged, juvenile justice professionals and CRC activists can join together to create strategies that will counteract each of the six sources of marginalization. By climbing on board the CRC bandwagon, and by getting juvenile justice reform on to the international development agenda, juvenile justice professionals will help to fulfil the powerful potential of the Convention on the Rights of the Child.

REFERENCES

Abramson, Bruce (1996) 'The Invisibility of Children and Adolescents'. In E. Verhellen (ed.), *Monitoring Children's Rights*. (The Hague, Kluwer Law International).

Allen, D. (1999) 'Networking in the NGO Community'. In E. Verhellen (ed.), *Understanding Children's Rights*, vol. 5. (The Hague, Kluwer Law International).

Amnesty International (1998) *Betraying the Young: Human Rights Violations Against Children in the US Justice System*. (London, Amnesty International).

Australia (1996) *Australia's First Report*. UN Doc. CRC/C/8/Add.31.

Center for Reproductive Rights (2003) *Claiming Our Rights: Surviving Pregnancy and Childbirth in Mali*. (New York, Center for Reproductive Rights).

Commission on Human Rights (2002) Resolution 2002/47, para. 4, reproduced in UN Doc. E/2002/23, and UN Doc. E/CN.4/2002/2000, chap. XI.

Committee on the Rights of the Child (1997) *Concluding Observations of the Committee on the Rights of the Child*. Australia. UN Doc. CRC/C/15/Add.79.

Committee on the Rights of the Child (2002) *Concluding Observations of the Committee on the Rights of the Child*. Switzerland. UN Doc. CRC/C/15/Add.182.

Conforti, B. and Francioni, F. (1997) *Enforcing International Human Rights in Domestic Courts*. (The Hague, Kluwer Law International).

Cotran, E. and Sherif, A.O. (1997) *The Role of the Judiciary in the Protection of Human Rights*. (The Hague, Kluwer Law International).

Defence for Children International (2000) *Juvenile Justice: 'the unwanted child' of State Responsibilities*. (Geneva, Defence for Children International). The findings are available at www.defence-for-children.org, under International Network on Juvenile Justice: Juvenile Justice—the 'Unwanted Child': download the commentary.

Doyle, R. (1999) 'By The Numbers: Men, Women and College'. *Scientific American*, October.

The Guardian (2002) 'Sir John calls for criminal justice reform'. 6 March, available at www.guardian.co.uk/crime/article/0,2763,664344,00.html.

Hart, R. (1992) *Children's Participation*. (Florence, Italy, Spedale degli Innocenti).

Hawes, J. (1991) *The Children's Rights Movement*. (Boston, Twayne).

Hellman, Hal. (2001) *Great Feuds in Medicine*. (Hoboken, New Jersey, John Wiley & Sons).

Heyns, C. and Viljoen, F. (2001) 'The Impact of the United Nations Human Rights Treaties on the Domestic Level'. *Human Rights Quarterly* 23: 3: 483–535.

Heyns, C. and Viljoen, F. (2002) *The Impact of the United Nations Human Rights Treaties on the Domestic Level*. (The Hague, Kluwer Law International).

Hodgkin, R. and Newell, P. (1996) *Effective Government Structures for Children*. (London, Calouste Gulbenkian Foundation).

International Centre for the Prevention of Crime (1999) *Crime Prevention Digest II: Summary*. (Montreal, International Centre for the Prevention of Crime). Available at www.crime-prevention-intl.org, under Publications.

Jayawickrama, N. (2002) *The Judicial Application of Human Rights Law*. (Cambridge, Cambridge University Press).

Laurent, P.G. (1998) *The Evolution of International Human Rights: Visions Seen*. (Philadelphia, University of Pennsylvania Press).

Newell, P. and Holmberg, B. (2000) 'A "watchdog" for children's rights'. In A. Petrén and J. Himes (eds.), *Children's Rights: Turning Principles Into Practices*. (Stockholm, Save the Children Sweden).

Petrén, A. and Hammarberg, T. (2000) 'The Political Influence of Children'. In A. Petrén and J. Himes (eds.), *Children's Rights: Turning Principles Into Practices*. (Stockholm, Save the Children Sweden).

Pitts, J. (2001) *The New Politics of Youth Crime: Discipline or Solidarity?* (Dorset, United Kingdom, Russell House).

Powers, R. (2002) 'The Apocalypse of Adolescents'. *Atlantic Monthly*, March. Available at www.theatlantic.com/issues/2002/03/powers.htm.

Schulz, W. (2002) *In Our Best Interests*. (Boston; Beacon Press).

Scott, E. (2002) 'The Legal Construction of Childhood'. In M. Rosenheim, F. Zimring and D. Tanenhaus (eds.), *A Century of Juvenile Justice*. (Chicago, University of Chicago Press).

Sennett, R. (2003) *Respect in a World of Inequality*. (New York, W.W. Norton).

Sommers, C. (2002) *The War Against Boys*. (New York, Simon & Schuster).

UNICEF (2002) *The State of the World's Children 2003*. (New York, UNICEF).

UNICEF (2004) *Sport, Recreation, Play*. (New York, UNICEF).

United Nations (Dept. of Economic and Social Affairs) (2004) *World Youth Report 2003: The Global Situation of Young People*. (New York, United Nations).

Woll, Lisa (2000) *The Convention on the Rights of the Child Impact Study*. (Stockholm, Save the Children Sweden).

3

Support for the Implementation of Humane Responses to Children in Conflict with the Law in DIHR Partner Countries

CHARLOTTE FLINDT PEDERSEN

INTRODUCTION

C HILDREN AND ADOLESCENTS are the most important resource in a country's development. Providing good opportunities for children and adolescents to develop their potential remains vital in the light of future prosperity; however, it is not something that is necessarily easily done. Doing so implies that children have access to a safe environment, quality education, access to adequate health services, access to fair treatment in the justice system, as well as the right to participate in decision-making processes at various levels. This will give them the opportunity to become active partners in a democratic society. However, in most of the countries that the Danish Institute for Human Rights is working in, neither the economic foundations nor the professional ability of the government and its underlying structures are in place to provide these services to the children of their country.

In December 2001 the Danish Institute for Human Rights (DIHR) therefore initiated co-operation with NGO partners in four countries (Nepal, Uganda, Malawi and Tanzania) to establish a small juvenile justice platform with the purpose of exploring ways of addressing the challenges posed to the legal and social system in each of the partner countries, specifically targeting the issue of fair treatment of children in the justice system and support to government structures in improving their justice systems in relation to the treatment of children.

This article summarizes some of the experiences that can be drawn from this co-operation and describes the gradual formulation of a strategy on the implementation of humane responses to children in conflict with the law in this forum. Before going any further I would like to credit our partners, who through their commitment are the primary forces driving this process in each of their respective countries in formulating and designing strategies which fit their respective legal systems and social and economic conditions, and creating the possibilities for dialogue with the state parties needed for the promotion of the cause. I will be using examples and findings from our partners in my presentation; however, these should not be accredited to me, but to the Centre for Youth Children's Affairs (CEYCA) in Malawi, the Malawi Human Rights Resource Centre (MHRRC), the Centre for Legal Affairs (CELA), the Legal Human Rights Centre in Tanzania (LHRC), Ms. Lillian Tibatemwa-Ekirikubinza, Deputy Vice Chancellor Makarere University in Uganda, Centre for Legal Research and Development Research (CeLRD), Kathmandu School of Law (KSL) in Nepal, and the National Juvenile Justice Forum of Malawi. The role of DIHR is to facilitate co-operation between the five countries (including Denmark) and to support bilateral projects in terms of funding and coaching/advice on specific issues, providing inspiration for further development in terms of personnel and study tours, and providing the opportunity to meet and exchange information.

THE WORKING SEMINAR ON JUVENILE JUSTICE

Establishing a common frame of reference

In December 2001 the four countries took part in a working seminar in Copenhagen. The purpose of the seminar was to exchange ideas and perspectives with key stakeholders, resource personnel and partners with regard to improving the administration of juvenile justice in the four partner countries. Danida funded the seminar under our framework agreement.

The seminar's point of departure was the flow of criminal justice in relation to juveniles. General and specific features in the four countries were scrutinized:

- at the legislative level;
- at the judicial level;
- at the level of police and prosecution;
- at the level of sanctions and their implementation;
- regarding the role of the social welfare sector, NGOs and the local community;
- finally, to look into the data and analytical material that could support the direction of future interventions.

The seminar turned out to be a forum for positive exchange and, based on this, it was decided to set up a bilateral project of co-operation between each set of partners in each country on juvenile justice as well as to maintain regional co-operation in order to secure the exchange of experiences. One of the main conclusions of the seminar was that the participants had found more solutions to their endeavours to address their country's juvenile justice issues in the exchange with neighbouring countries than in the presentations providing the Danish perspective (see Pedersen and Jepsen 2001).

Compliance with CRC

It was also established at the seminar that the co-operation would take a rights-based approach, with the point of departure being the articles of the Convention of the Rights of the Child as well as trying to apply the minimum standards provided by the Beijing Rules and Riyadh Guidelines, which thereby provided purpose and direction in our work and gave us the methodological framework for all our activities.

In the course of the project of co-operation it has become clear that the challenges facing our partners in terms of achieving compliance with the international standards in relation to the administration of juvenile justice are huge. Below is an attempt to compile a list of some of the problems experienced in the juvenile justice systems of the four countries:

- The numbers of juveniles in detention and the way they are treated are difficult to monitor in the co-operating countries, as the reporting of such figures and information is poor. In none of the co-operating countries is there as yet any system in place that keeps proper track of the numbers of children involved in the criminal justice system. Therefore it is currently impossible to assess how well or how poorly the system is working. In Malawi the national juvenile justice forum is promoting the establishment of separate registries for juveniles at all levels of the justice system. And the regional forums are monitoring the number of children in the penal system and in remand facilities.
- There is no systematized collection of baseline data in the area of juvenile justice or criminal justice, which impedes the possibility of assessing the scope and types of juvenile delinquency, in creating meaningful preventive and reactive responses with regard to efforts in crime prevention, rehabilitation and improving the administration of juvenile justice in general. A systematized approach to understanding the system, scope, types and reasons for delinquency will provide the government and other stakeholders with the basis for developing strategies, social polices, and legislation.
- Some of the countries' legislation allows for sanctions such as corporal punishment and establishes a very low age of criminal responsibility.

The exception is Uganda. Here legislation has to a large degree been brought into compliance with the CRC, whilst at the same time trying to use existing resources and the local community court system outside the formal system instead of setting up new and costly structures. The Uganda children's statute was to the other participants a sort of model law for improving children's rights; however, the application of the statute is still far from perfect.

- There are insufficient legal guarantees with regard to due process and fair trial, and superficial or no legal representation in the different stages of the judicial process, with the effect that it is the most vulnerable and unprotected youth who end up in prison, such as street children and children from poor families.
- There are insufficient or no institutional structures providing for alternatives to the prison system, along with a lack of resources and professional capacity in these structures, in so far as they exist, with regard to possibilities for the reintegration and rehabilitation of child offenders. Often these institutions are placed far from public transportation and visits from relatives are therefore rare.
- There is a lack of awareness at the different stages of the judicial process (prosecutors, police investigators, judges, lawyers) of the special circumstances pertaining to child offenders and there are big gaps between legislation and practice. Even in places with knowledge of the procedures, the resources for applying special measures are often unavailable. Who should write the social report? How to get hold of the parents or guardians when telephone communication is only for the few? How to transport juveniles to a special place for remand or to a judge to assess the legality of the arrest, when transportation is not available? And so on.
- There is a lack of supporting mechanisms such as social and societal structures, resulting in a one-dimensional juvenile justice system which is compelled either to release juveniles without punishment or to give mainly custodial measures of punishment.
- There is a lack of resources in terms of human and material resources in the criminal justice system, such as means of transportation, which impedes the authorities in e.g. bringing children back into the community and to the family, and a lack of mattresses, food, medicine and other basic needs.
- There is a lack of child participation in the justice system as well as in society in general.

Seminar recommendations

A main recommendation of the seminar was not only to consider juvenile justice and juvenile delinquency as a problem pertaining to the legal system and as a legal problem, but to pay attention to the social dimension of the issue and seek solutions for children in conflict with the law in this sphere as well (Pedersen and Jepsen 2003).

This pointed towards the need for co-ordination, co-operation and the involvement of different sectors of society. Therefore a multi-sectored approach was recommended, promoting co-operation across social affairs, to the law enforcement agencies, to the courts, and to the youth penal institutions and prisons in order to successfully provide humane responses to children in conflict with the law.

Another recommendation stemming from the above was the need to explore ways of engaging in pre-trial activities so that this period is not spent in idleness. The pre-trial period can be spent trying to find a solution outside the justice system. Whilst stating that diversion is important, the question as to what type of diversions there should be remained unanswered. Nevertheless, those designing a juvenile justice system in each of the countries should take the issue of diversion into consideration.

Finally it was decided to proceed with the task of gathering more knowledge on the situation of children in the justice systems as well as looking into the provisions of the legislation with regard to children in conflict with the law and the institutional framework in each country. It seemed necessary to decide on the complexity of the situation in order to define the right strategy to address the issue properly as well as to promote the issue among decision makers and government justice agencies.

Aims and activities in the implementation process

It was clear from the outset that one of the aims of any intervention would be to support the establishment of a community-based infrastructure, utilising existing resources in the communities to support the justice system in providing alternatives to incarceration as well as through measures of crime prevention, diversion, rehabilitation and reintegration of children in conflict with the law, thus reducing the need for punitive interventions. A tentative model for such a network was the newly established Juvenile Justice Forum in Malawi and the Children's Statute of Uganda.

At the seminar in Copenhagen, specific steps in the implementation process were outlined:

- A systematic examination of national legislation, policies and practices to ensure that the letter and the spirit of the Convention and guidelines are reflected—that is, baseline studies conducted by each partner organisation based on bilateral partnership agreements.
- In connection with the above, development of monitoring and evaluation mechanisms and improving tools for the collection of credible information on the criminal justice system pertaining to children in conflict with the law.

- Dissemination of the collected baseline information to stakeholders from which to develop a strategy for implementation and improving practices, as well as providing information to a broader public about the rules and principles of juvenile justice instruments.
- Lobby for law reform based on the findings of the baseline study.

THE CONFERENCE ON JUVENILE JUSTICE AND HUMAN RIGHTS IN NEPAL

Consolidation and comparing findings, development of a toolbox

A year after the forum took place, the organisations and individuals in the four partner countries constituting the informal juvenile justice network met again in Nepal. This conference was entitled 'Juvenile Justice and Human Rights'. Its purpose was to share information and research findings among the participating countries which had been elaborated since the last meeting. Each country was asked to present a situation paper, especially reflecting the following:

- Problems of juvenile delinquency,
- Legal framework developed to address the problem,
- Mechanisms to deal with young people committing delinquency,
- Programs being implemented, with reference to diversion schemes,
- Institutions involved,
- Possibility of co-operation in future, and
- Presentation of Expert Inputs on Diversion Schemes, reflecting upon recent developments and the most efficient forms of diversion.

Network terminology

During the meeting of the juvenile justice network the term 'juvenile' came up for discussion. A working group was composed to try to create a common terminology for the network. Dissatisfaction was rooted in the fact that the term 'juvenile' is usually applied in relation to judicial proceedings and therefore has negative connotations associated with law breaking. However, in the common sense the words 'juvenile' and 'child' can be used interchangeably, referring to a human being who is not an adult. The working group appointed by the plenary to develop a working definition for words that do not carry negative connotations came up with the following to substitute 'juvenile':

A. Minors in conflict with the law/administration of justice (this should cover minors liable to a charge or in conflict with police administration procedures).

B. Minors in conflict with societal norms (this will cover minors who have not committed offences, runaways, children defined as beyond control).

C. Minors in need of care and protection (children who are abandoned, abused, victimized, exploited in e.g. child labour).

As was pointed out during the presentation to the plenary, these definitions are not unproblematic either: the term 'minor' as opposed to 'adult' reflects an element of discrimination as it implies that children are lesser or incomplete beings (and thereby maybe do not enjoy the same number of rights as adults). Another problem is that the term 'minor' is often used with respect to children who are not liable to a charge, and therefore it would seem that the targeted age group is not encompassed by this term.

Nevertheless, for the time being we settled for the term 'minor', because the age of the child differs from statute to statute in all the co-operating countries. The working committee decided to retain the term 'juvenile justice' in the statutes and names of the organisation/s but footnoted the working definitions in all the program documents. The retention of the term 'juvenile' is supported by the United Nations Standard Minimum Rules for the administration of juvenile justice (the Beijing Rules), which give us the following definition of juvenile: 'A Juvenile is a child or young person who under the respective legal system may be dealt with for an offence in a manner which is different from an adult.'

Legislation versus practice

Another issue discussed at the Nepal meeting was the role of legislation. Based on the experiences of Uganda and Malawi it was stated that laws are very important in strengthening the juvenile justice system; however, law reform is not a precondition for implementing more humane responses to children or initiating diversion programs. What are required are resources, political will and creative use of the existing legislation. But improving the law is necessary in order to sustain the results of improved practices as well as to develop the range of possibilities for diversion.

Diversion

Another dimension to the methodological toolbox was added and explored during this conference. Ricardo Mukonda from UNICEF in Mozambique talked about diversion and provided some principles and considerations for the application of diversion programs:

The need to divert children in conflict with the law stems from the fact that the criminal justice system in its present form subjects children to institutionalized human rights violations. With diversion the argument is that a humane way should be developed within the criminal justice system to deal with children in conflict with the law so as to minimize the dehumanising effect of the formal criminal adjudication process. (Ricardo Mukonda in Kathmandu School of Law 2003)

It was stressed that diversion programs should be designed to fit the community and its cultural and economic contexts, as well as the children in question. Therefore local partners are crucial to the successful implementation of such programs. In most of the countries we can find alternative measures to incarceration, but in only a few countries does '*diversion*' as a concept form part of the legal system when dealing with young offenders. Since the last meeting, Malawi has got so far as setting up a national system for facilitating a diversion process through the national and regional juvenile justice forums. A lesson can be learned from this process: in every justice system a certain opportunity for discretionary power always exists, which could be used in the direction of diversion: that is, the police, the prosecutor or the judge could take the initiative to divert the juvenile offender at any stage of the formal criminal process.

It was decided that each of the participating partners should start developing diversions schemes. The main elements in the initiation of these schemes would be as follows:

- Bringing stakeholders together to strengthen collaboration and the ability to produce alternative solutions to offences committed by children/minors, i.e. diversion, and the use of their discretionary power, and ensure that children are always granted a genuine spokesperson (NGOs, paralegals, teachers) as early as possible in the process. Ideally Malawi's model of juvenile justice forums should be applied, adapted to the local context.
- Empower/mobilize local resources (both financial and human).
- Initiate piloting diversion programs with educative effects (preventive diversion programs and life skills components).
- The next international network meeting would be solely devoted to this aspect and the dissemination of experiences and exposure to successful diversion programs should be high on the agenda.

Each national partner should formulate a second phase of individual project co-operation along these lines. At the international level DIHR should formulate terms of reference for the network's activities in consultation with the partners in the network. It was decided that DIHR should until further notice function as an informal secretariat for the international element of the network.

RESEARCH AND MONITORING

Research and monitoring was another important topic at the Nepal meeting. It was concluded that due to the urgency of the problems it is necessary to carry out continuous formative action research following already ongoing programs in order to adjust these to the complexity of issues and problems related to children and adolescents. The research should be carried out by domestic researchers—so that the ownership of the information obtained during the research is internalized and thereby maintained within the society in question and with people who have the legitimacy to act and take responsibility for acting upon the findings they make. This will also provide for a more exact interpretation of the findings in relation to the cultural context. A publication providing amongst other things a compilation and extracts of the baseline studies is in the making, which will, as was emphasized by the participants, provide an important comparative perspective to the situation of juvenile justice and thereby be useful for the purpose of promoting increased awareness of the problems involved in the administration of juvenile justice among decision-makers and justice sector stakeholders.

One of the aspects which is very important and where we see an important role for DIHR is supporting our partners in the collection of statistical information on children in the justice system. This is, however, extremely difficult due to a lack of centralized registration of crime and judicial activities. Ideally registers should contain information about the type of offence, where and when the offence was committed, former offences, the sanction, and so on. This is, however, very rarely the case, which makes it virtually impossible to follow developments in child-related crime or to compare whether children are more involved in criminal activities than previously and which type of activities they are involved in.

There is practically no tradition in our co-operating countries of using statistical information, and therefore this has been the most problematic part of the exercise. At the same time the partners are often confronted with problems of gaining access to the relevant authorities, which only partially are in possession of the required information. In the long run the gathering of this information should be a government responsibility, but the activities of the NGO can pilot this and show the way in relation to the usefulness of statistical information on children in conflict with the law. For example, answers to common questions could be found: Who commits the crime? Is it juveniles/adults, men/women, employed/unemployed? Where is the crime primarily committed? Is it in the city or in the countryside? What is the most common crime? Is it theft or violence? And what are the reactions of the formal/informal system to child-related crime? This information could be used in developing crime prevention strategies and in supporting the development of humane juvenile justice systems.

Upon presentation of the baseline studies to stakeholders (even though the studies gave a critical picture of the performance of the administration of justice in relation to children), the stakeholders were actually happy or grateful to be informed and have the information as a point of departure for discussion and for looking into improving the situation. The information thereby became a communication tool between the NGOs and the stakeholders in the juvenile justice system.

COMMON PROBLEMS AND SOLUTIONS

In both Denmark and the United States we have in recent years seen a trend towards demands for a more punitive approach when dealing with young offenders. Despite all our money and different psychological and pedagogical methods we have not been able to find sustainable solutions to the problems of the most marginalized and often most vulnerable youth/children and the problem of their reintegration into society.

I am convinced that some of the elements of a solution to the problems of Northern crime policies can be found with our partners in the South. What I see is that they have, forced by the inhumanity and imperfection of their own justice and penal systems, insufficient social welfare systems, and insufficient funds, been compelled to move towards finding solutions outside such areas, using existing resources in the communities and mobilising these to take responsibility for children. In Malawi, Uganda, Tanzania and Nepal there is among the most progressive justice stakeholders an increasing awareness and determination to keep children away from the criminal justice system.

In countries like Malawi and Tanzania the formal legal system interacts with informal structures, which must be taken into consideration when designing strategies for improving juvenile justice practices. Often there exist in these informal systems traditional, non-codified ways of taking care of children who lose their family or somehow fall outside societal norms. However, these informal systems and the values they are based upon are under influence from modernization and development and are therefore changing and cannot in the long run be relied upon to cater for the children of the local community. Sometimes the informal system will not take an approach that guarantees the best interests of the child, but neither, as can be seen above, does the formal system. In both instances a change of attitude and a possibility of finding other solutions and instituting other practices have to be provided: restorative justice, victim-offender mediation, compensation, community service, supervision and so on, involving a range of actors taking responsibility for children who fall outside societal norms.

In the North as well as the South we also share some common features. If we look at marginalized children's backgrounds in Denmark, Malawi or

Nepal the majority will come from single parent families, from severe poverty, be it in a material or spiritual sense, from unemployment, and/or have a minority background. They live on the brink of society and the challenge they pose to us is to bring them into the center of society again. The family has not been able to take care of the child's integration into society and therefore the task faced by the system is to support alternative resource personnel, communities or individuals who can take responsibility and replace the role of the family with respect to guiding the child into the womb of society.

One aspect which the network has to explore further is the development of ways of promoting children's participation not only in the juvenile justice system, but in general in decisions of relevance to their own lives. Juvenile offending often occurs as a reaction to a lack of influence. The ability to care, own and take responsibility for one's own life and reject a lifestyle connected with offending has to be based on the participation of the child and the sensation of being able to influence one's own life situation.

CONCLUSIONS

DIHR has from the outset of its engagement in juvenile justice aimed at a cross-sector and cross-regional approach (government, judiciary, civil society, social and criminal law enforcement which includes both preventive and reactive stages).

In order to promote sector-wide thinking on the part of domestic stakeholders and to ensure domestic ownership in the process, DIHR has applied a step-wise approach. The first step comprised the development of strong partnership relations to key actors in all of the co-operating countries. Together with these partners DIHR has initiated baseline studies on children and adolescents in the justice system, situational analysis and revision of the legislative provisions in the co-operating countries.

The contribution of diversionary methodologies and the development of diversion schemes suited to the context of each of the participating countries remains one of the most realistic avenues, and should be a crucial component in the achievement of a well-functioning juvenile justice system in poor countries as well as wealthy ones. These efforts should be seen together with parallel efforts that seek to achieve better national monitoring systems and to develop strong national Juvenile Justice Forums working for broad-based reform and sector co-ordination.

Up to this moment, the program of co-operation has achieved the initial part of its potential impact and has fertilized the growth and development of common understandings in relation to juvenile human rights standards, monitoring instruments, strategies and policies for diversion.

In the execution of juvenile justice there exists a situation in which many stakeholders and actors are involved. To become able to provide impetus to the development of the system, these different players must strike up a dialogue with each other. Co-ordination and sharing of information is an important basis for possible improvements. Therefore it is imperative that the sector develops its discussions around national forums for juvenile justice, such as that in Malawi. It is also necessary that the system becomes capable of producing reliable data and analyses that can describe developments within the sector, and thus produce and maintain the planning base for further deliberations and the drawing up of action plans, as in Nepal. Finally, in order for the results to be sustained, it is necessary that the work can inform the legislative process in the creation/design of viable and appropriate responses, as with the children's statute in Uganda.

To proceed in this direction *it is necessary*:

- to support national juvenile justice forums and to build up their capacity to conduct advocacy for reform, networking and their strength to secure co-ordination;
- to develop and institutionalize national monitoring systems that can produce reliable data and valid research for the benefit of stakeholders and key decision makers;
- to develop proper criteria for diversion programs and appropriate national diversion options.

The problems, challenges and objectives that compose our strategy have been formulated in co-operation with our partners as an ongoing process. I find this extremely important, as it means that the network belongs not only to the Danish Institute for Human Rights—it belongs to each and every member of the network.

REFERENCES

Kathmandu School of Law (2003) *Juvenile Justice System in Nepal.* (Kathmandu, Nepal).

Pedersen, C.F. and Jepsen, J. (eds.) (2003) *Report from Working Seminar on Juvenile Justice*, Copenhagen, 3–8 December 2001. (Copenhagen, Danish Centre for Human Rights).

4

Regional Co-operation and the Spread of New Ideas and Practices

ADAM STAPLETON

REGIONAL CO-OPERATION: AN OVERVIEW

REGIONAL CO-OPERATION IS problematic, particularly in Africa with its range of languages, religions, political and economic groupings, uncertain lines of communications, and prejudices. Francophones and Anglophones suspect each of making no attempt to understand the other. Angola is intimate with Brazil and distant from Namibia. The Sudan looks over to Saudi Arabia with barely a glance at Uganda. If you want to travel from west to east Africa, it is still quicker (and cheaper) to take a plane to Europe and reconnect there.

Co-operation between donor agencies on a regional basis is weak. Country missions report to desk officers in their capitals. They are neither required nor, it appears, encouraged to share information with other missions in the region. Donors still prefer to bring in consultants from their own countries rather than identify expertise and relevant experience within the region.

NGO 'networks' exist but appear to have little impact. Amnesty International assisted at the birth of the Southern Africa Human Rights NGO Network (SAHRINGON). After a promising beginning, it has been riven by internal squabbles and appears to continue in name only. The Southern Africa Legal Aid Network (SALAN) has active individual member organizations but lacks coherence of purpose to make it an effective body.

Yet the picture is not all negative. The groundbreaking work of the South Africa Human Rights Commission has made it a leader in its field. It has hosted Commissioners from other institutions around the continent and provided know-how and training. The Conference of Heads of Correctional Services in Central, Eastern and Southern Africa (CESCA) meets every two years and includes heads of prisons from 17 African countries. It provides a useful forum for senior prison officers to meet and discuss new trends in corrections and invite speakers from within and outside the continent to inform improvements in corrections.

PENAL REFORM IN AFRICA

In the area of penal reform, Penal Reform International (PRI) works around the world, *inter alia*, to promote and develop international standards with regard to law enforcement and prison conditions, to reduce the use of imprisonment and to increase the use of constructive non-custodial sanctions encouraging social reintegration while taking into account the interest of the victims.

In Africa, PRI has been working to develop an agenda of reform that is recognized and shared by African countries up, down and across the continent. This agenda is aimed at practitioners and informed by a plan of action that sets out good practices and 'models' from all over the globe.[1]

Conferences provide stepping stones in the process of reform. They provide a forum for interest groups to come together, exchange ideas, and chart a way forward. They can exert great moral influence and practical guidance.

The first Pan-African conference on prison conditions took place in Kampala, Uganda in September 1996. The conference convened 133 delegates from 47 countries, including 40 African countries. The delegates were heads of prison services, senior law officers, government ministers and representatives from NGOs working in the sector. From the outset, all delegates (from both governmental and non-governmental agencies) realized they shared common ground, namely that prison conditions were appalling and something had to be done. The conference issued the Declaration on Prison Conditions in Africa 1996 which drew particular attention to the plight of young prisoners, the need to separate them from adults, and the need for treatment 'appropriate to their age'.

Conference declarations need to be followed up if they are to enter the mainstream of current thinking on a given theme. In order to enhance the authority and visibility of the Kampala Declaration, it was translated and widely distributed throughout Africa, endorsed by the African Commission on Human and Peoples' Rights and, in 1997, adopted as a United Nations instrument.[2] The result today is that the Kampala Declaration 1996 is widely recognized as the starting point for penal reform on the African continent.

Concerned about the conditions of young people in conflict with the criminal law, PRI convened a regional seminar on juvenile justice in Lilongwe, Malawi in 1999. The conference (hosted by the Malawi Ministry of Justice and Constitutional Affairs) focussed considerable attention on a

---

[1] The first Index of Good Practices in a planned series focusses on reducing pre-trial detention and is available on the PRI website: www.penalreform.org.

[2] Sixth session of the UN Commission on Crime Prevention and Criminal Justice. International Co-operation for the Improvement of Prison Conditions. E/CN.15/1997/21.

model of juvenile justice drawn up by the National Institute for Care and Resettlement of Offenders (NICRO) in South Africa and developed in Namibia by the Legal Assistance Centre, a national NGO based in Windhoek. As a result of the recommendations of the meeting, PRI facilitated a pilot scheme in the following year in one magisterial area in Malawi and assisted in drawing up a two-year work program with national roll-out. The national juvenile justice forum continues to this day, chaired by a judge of the High Court of Malawi.

In 2002, a second Pan-African conference on prisons and penal reform in Africa took place in Ouagadougou, Burkina Faso.[3] The conference looked back over the past six years at what had been achieved as a result of the first conference held in Kampala. The record was encouraging, as the conference noted: the appointment of the Special Rapporteur on Prisons and Conditions of Detention by the African Commission on Human and Peoples' Rights (ACHPR); the extension of Community Service as an alternative to prison based on the Zimbabwe model to 13 new African countries; the increasing evidence of prison services entering into partnerships with NGOs to bring about reform; the development of a regional forum for heads of correctional services through the CESCA annual conference.

The Ouagadougou Declaration on Accelerating Prison and Penal Reform in Africa also recognized the 'considerable shortcomings' in the treatment of prisoners and issued a forward-looking Declaration set in a practicable seven-point framework, supported by a plan of action to address these shortcomings. The Declaration places emphasis on reducing the prison population, making prisons more self-sufficient, promoting greater reintegration of offenders into society, applying the rule of law to prison administration, and encouraging best practice 'at national, regional and international levels' drawing from the 'rich experience' from across the continent.

This is not mere rhetoric. The practice of the law in Africa is often highly creative and innovative—it has to be, given the constraints within which justice systems operate in many countries. Over the past ten years the sector has had to develop its own ways of making justice accessible to ordinary people. Good practices[4] have emerged: practices which adhere to international human rights standards, benefit the poor and vulnerable and are proven to be effective. A case in point is the Namibian juvenile justice forum.

[3] Pan-African Conference on Prisons and Penal Reform in Africa. Ouagadougou, Burkina Faso, 18–20 September 2002.

[4] The phrase 'good practices' is preferred to 'best practices' since the use of the superlative begs a number of questions that need not be addressed here (i.e.: who says so, in what context, when, and how much do they cost?).

These practices are being increasingly recognized and shared through such regional mechanisms as CESCA; through the associations formed by national co-ordinators of community service (with the mutual support and assistance they provide); and through a growing recognition of and reliance on regional expertise.

DEVELOPING NEW IDEAS

Developing and implementing new ideas in the justice sector is different from coming up with new and more efficient ways of laying down 200 kilometers of road or managing a forestry project. There is no 'kit' form like a new water well or communications system. In general, one size does not fit all. Nor do these new ideas and practices simply 'catch on'. They need to be introduced, planted, nurtured and supported—then, if the soil is receptive and the timing is right, they may 'take'.

Identify one problem in the justice sector and further analysis discloses a range of causes—all of which need to be treated to cure that one problem. One might take, for instance, the 'inhuman'[5] level of overcrowding in prisons in Africa. Overcrowding is not unique to African prisons, however in Africa it has reached epidemic proportions. The diagnosis is simple: too many people. The solution (also simple): reduce the numbers in prison.

So, in 1998 in Nigeria, a presidential taskforce on prison decongestion and reforms was constituted which approved criteria for release of prisoners and visited every prison in the country to verify data. Trials were speeded up and magistrates visited prisons. Between December 1998 and October 2000 over 8000 prisoners were released. Within three months the prisons were even more congested.

Again, in 1999 in Malawi, the juveniles in Zomba prison were suffering appalling conditions. Paralegals conducted a short study into the lawfulness of each boy's detention. The enquiry found that of the 179 young persons found in Zomba prison, not one was there in accordance with the laws of Malawi. The Chief Commissioner and Chief Resident Magistrate organized the closure of the section. Within two months it had re-opened and by the end of 12 months the population stood at 120 young persons and rising.

The work of the presidential taskforce in Nigeria and paralegals in Malawi are valuable in that they expose the extent of the problem; however they fail to achieve the cure sought because what is needed is an integrated course of treatment to tackle the multiple ills that cause a particular disease

---

[5] 'Considering that in many countries in Africa the level of overcrowding in prisons is inhuman', Preamble to the Kampala Declaration on Prison Conditions in Africa 1996.

within the system. A course that treats judicial and popular attitudes, sentencing principles and practice, access to legal advice and assistance, police investigation procedures, court administrative procedures and processes, prison conditions and so on and so forth. All this takes some money, considerable commitment and a great deal of time.

Some ideas ('access to justice') or 'products' (community service orders) may appear to work well in country A (i.e. they do what they set out to do; in a timely, inexpensive way; that can be demonstrated; and if you ask anyone involved they would be able to give you a clear explanation of what they are about and how they have assisted them), but on transplanting to country B, they do not appear to 'take'. The point of departure and approach, the institutions, the needs and problems will all differ to a varying degree such that the idea or product just does not work. The *context* is important. So too is *timing*. It is not much good starting something new in the middle of a war or 12 months before the next elections.

So, what are the features that should attach to this idea or product if it is to catch on and spread further afield? It would probably stand a better chance if it was *simple* and if the idea had been translated into practice and *tested* first. Then it would help gain ground if the idea was *unoriginal*—in the marketing sense of being NEW!—but had roots—if dormant—which people could identify and so claim as their own. Any idea is not much good if it does not address a widely shared *need*—and do so in ways which are *sustainable*, i.e. not merely affordable but providing '*sustainability of impact*'.[6]

This said, the real world is greatly influenced—some might say unreasonably so—by the opinions of economists. Notwithstanding the caveat of Einstein that 'not all that counts can be counted and not all that can be counted counts', where we can 'count' and measure the impact of these new ideas, we need to; where we cannot we need to illustrate in other ways how they build 'social capital', to use the phrase favored by the World Bank.

A case in point concerns the community service orders scheme developed in Zimbabwe. In 1992, research in Zimbabwe prisons showed that 60% of prisoners were serving terms of 3 months or less. Data also showed that the prison population was continuously rising. In 1994 a three-year pilot scheme on community service began. Almost 17,000 orders were made in this period and the prison population stabilized. 90% of orders were satisfactorily completed. The cost of supervising a person on community service is estimated to be one third of keeping the same person in prison. On schedule, the government took over the scheme from donors in 1997.

---

[6] 'Beyond Rule of Law Orthodoxy—the legal empowerment alternative', Golub (2003). The author goes on to explain: 'If a given legal services NGO serves enough people, or builds enough capacities for the poor to effectively assert their own rights, or affects enough laws—such impact is sufficient to justify past and future donor investment.'

SPREADING NEW IDEAS

The question becomes, having identified this 'new idea' or 'product', how to spread or export it?

In *starting up*, there is a need to develop clear and attractive literature and 'visual aids'. Film is particularly useful and provides greater outreach since not everyone can come and see for themselves. Criteria for the success of the product provides guidance to those interested in borrowing from it or adapting it to their own country contexts. Statistics should clearly demonstrate that the situation today is better than it was yesterday (from baseline data) because of the introduction of the new product. Key people from elsewhere may be invited to come and visit and see the product for themselves. Influential and respected individuals with close links with the establishment should be approached to sponsor the product's introduction in their country.

Having started, there is a need to *develop momentum (for change)*. A preliminary visit to the target country would identify effective link persons in key positions who will promote the product, together with a clear lead agency. By convening a national conference to introduce the idea (including all stakeholders and excluding none) with practitioners (from the region) as resource persons and a tangible outcome in the form of a time-bound action plan, the way forward becomes clear.

Follow up (sensitization) meetings targeting key groups assist in meeting objections, fears or criticisms. Emphasis on close co-ordination both nationally and within the region develops trust and confidence. A budget for publicity is important to get people talking about the idea or at least to recognize that others are talking about it. Then there is the task of securing funding for the period in question.

The next step is *national roll-out*. Teams will need to be recruited and trained. Materials will need to be 'packaged'. Pilot schemes will need to start and be closely nurtured in the earlier stages. This will require close support and encouragement from those charged with supervising its implementation (the High Court judge in Zimbabwe in charge of introducing community service encouraged every magistrate and volunteer to contact him directly as and when they felt the need for advice or guidance). Early wins/gains should be publicized as widely as possible. Once three countries are applying the product, a regional network could be established so that those charged with implementation are able to share information, discuss problems and develop materials jointly and set and agree common standards—whether through e-mail forums or annual meetings.

The need for *flexibility* in marketing the product is also key to its successful implementation, particularly in dealing with national rivalries or jealousy, thus it should be capable of adaptation so that it becomes 'ours' and not something borrowed from 'them' with space for 'local' creativity and ingenuity (so long as people do not lose sight of the criteria identified for its success in the originating country). In this way and by maintaining an open attitude to new ideas, investment in research and development based on practices elsewhere in the world, the product is in a state of constant evolution and change.

Any new idea or product is only as good as the results it can demonstrate and its overall impact on the sector in particular or society in general. The development of *objectively verifiable indicators* is required from the outset. These targets should be conservative in the first instance. Surpassing expectations builds confidence, failing to meet them does not and fuels the fears of its detractors. The data gathered needs to be scientifically provable and not anecdotal. In turn, this approach demonstrates a professional outlook and reassures those providing the funding that they are getting value for money. Regular evaluations that provide constructive criticism enable continuing improvements to be made to the product. Ways need to be identified how best to illustrate the impact of the non-countable benefits (film and interviews with beneficiaries greatly assist here).

'Between the idea and the reality falls the shadow'—converting the idea into practice: two case studies

Juvenile justice in Malawi based on the Namibian model

The Juvenile Justice Forum (JJF) in Namibia was established in 1994 and was made up of nine ministries, criminal justice agents, NGOs and individuals. It ran a successful pre-trial diversion program for children in conflict with the law.

Members of the JJF visited police cells each week and completed a cell visit form. They identified young people who were being held unlawfully and referred the case to a sub-committee of the JJF. Where parents had not been traced, volunteer tracing agents were employed.

JJF workers screened the children to identify the child's circumstances, to determine the nature of the crime, to ensure that children were placed in the custody of their parents/guardian, to monitor the treatment of arrested children, and to make recommendations to the prosecution regarding diversion.

The recommendations were either for prosecution or for diversion to one of the following: life skills program, prosecutor's warning, supervision, counselling, victim-offender mediation, pre-trial community service.

In conducting the screening, the guiding principle was the best interests of the child. Between 1997 and 2002, only 3% of those diverted to life skills programs were reported to have re-offended.[7]

---

[7] The JJF program in Namibia has undergone significant changes since and further information can be obtained from the program manager, Celeste Zaahl (czaahl@lac.org.na).

Following the paralegal study of juveniles in Zomba prison above (and other prisons), a national seminar was convened in Malawi (as mentioned above) with the Ministry of Justice, Malawi Human Rights Commission (MHRC), African Commission on Human and Peoples' Rights and Penal Reform International sharing the platform with UNICEF.

The participants at the seminar included judges, magistrates, lawyers, police and prison officers as well as human rights NGOs and constitutional bodies (such as the office of the Ombudsman, Inspectorate of Prisons and MHRC) with invited speakers from the region (Uganda, Namibia and South Africa). A library of contemporary papers and commentaries was put together thanks to the good will of organizations such as Defence for Children International, UNICEF (Florence) and Save the Children (UK) and circulated to all participants.

The seminar looked at initiatives that were underway in Uganda, Namibia and South Africa and international trends and thinking on the subject. Particular interest was shown in the Namibian Juvenile Justice Forum and it was decided by the seminar to test the scheme in Malawi by selecting one magisterial district to start a forum. The costs were minimal. The selected site also housed the prison where the worst conditions obtained (namely Zomba). A timely urgent action by Amnesty International on the plight of juveniles in custody added urgency to the process.

Over a period of 10 months (January–October 2000) the forum met locally, facilitated by PRI. The meetings were minuted and action for the next month agreed between all parties. The regional courts administrator took charge of follow up. At each meeting the parties reported on what they had done in the intervening four weeks. Those who were dragging their feet or failing to honor their commitments were soon shamed into activity by the activities of the others.

In the course of this period, the LAC provided technical assistance from Namibia in the shape of someone who had been chiefly responsible for the implementation of the scheme over five years in Namibia. He made several visits to Zomba over the period, in which time he assisted in adapting the Namibian model to suit the Malawi context, drew up a training syllabus, trained people, and drafted a training manual for future use. In consultation with members of the forum and judiciary, he then produced (with PRI support) a short term plan of action and two-year medium term work program.

In October 2000, a meeting was convened with members of the forum, the judiciary, NGOs and other interested parties (such as UNICEF) to discuss the work programs. They were unanimously adopted.

The National Juvenile Justice Forum was then established and the Chief Justice nominated a judge of the High Court to chair the Forum, assisted by a senior magistrate as national co-ordinator. PRI facilitated funding from UNICEF and DFID and then withdrew. The program has a dynamic national co-ordinator and in 2006 is running along the lines of the Namibian Forum.

The Malawi Paralegal Advisory Service—work in progress

The PAS began in December 1999 with a meeting of four NGOs and PRI to identify an intervention in prisons to facilitate legal advice, assistance and education to indigent offenders. Following discussions with the prison service, a 12-month pilot scheme began in May 2000 with eight paralegals from four national NGOs working in the four main prisons. No one outside the prisons expected the pilot to last six months, as NGO access to prisons was an entirely novel enterprise. The PAS is now in its fifth year, with 37 paralegals working in 13 prisons, four central police stations and court centers, and has attracted attention from a number of other countries in Africa and South Asia.

The type of assistance to be provided was developed over time according to the needs expressed by prisoners and observed by the paralegals. By the end of the 12 months a clear work program had been established based on legal advice and assistance and education. Each team submits a monthly report which is discussed at monthly meetings by representatives from each team with the co-ordinators.

In April 2002, after two years of activity, the program was independently evaluated (Kerrigan 2002). The highly positive report encouraged the donor agency to extend funding for three years (2003–2006), aimed at establishing a legal aid delivery service with national outreach on the frontline of the criminal justice system (in the police stations at interview, in the courts at first appearance and in the majority of prisons).

Entry into the police stations was initially resisted. This was a key objective of the program since most abuse takes place in police stations where 'confession-based' evidence remains the order of the day, and paralegals sought admission to police interviews.

Once the team decided to focus their support exclusively on young persons in conflict with the law, the police objections fell away. They readily agreed to paralegals assisting with parent tracing so that interviews could go ahead. After further discussion and collaboration with the judiciary, paralegals developed 'screening forms' so that in appropriate cases, young persons could be interviewed at the police station and promptly be diverted from the criminal justice process where the individual was a first offender, the offense charged was not serious and the person admitted his/her guilt. The paralegals drew heavily on the Namibian model in designing this approach.

After 12 months, the juvenile program in the police stations was evaluated in the four regions where it was operating. A national meeting was convened with senior police officers which agreed that paralegals should extend their activities to include adult accused and attendance at police interview—the initial goal of the intervention.

In 2004, the program was again positively evaluated.[8] The program was replicated in Benin (2002). The Kenyan Prison Service with members of the judiciary and NGOs sent a delegation to study the program in 2003 and a pilot started in four prisons around Nairobi in January 2004. In 2005, the Kenya Prisons Paralegal Project expanded to nine new prisons and three children remand homes in four provinces. In Uganda, again following a study visit, a similar pilot started in January 2005 under the aegis of the Law Society of Uganda. In December 2005, the Paralegal Advisory Service (Uganda) recruited 24 paralegals to work in prisons in the north, south, east and west of the country.

Elsewhere in the region, the Principal Commissioner of the Tanzanian Prison Service has invited PRI to facilitate the introduction of a pilot scheme in prisons around Dar es Salaam. An NGO in Niger[9] has proposed starting a similar scheme. Interest has been expressed by prisons in Ghana and Zambia. Beyond Africa, funding has been set aside in Bangladesh (UNDP and the European Union) for a pilot to begin.

The criteria identified for the success of the scheme to date are:

— a practical and effective work plan responding to the immediate needs of those in conflict with the law;
— a 'highly co-operative and trusting spirit' developed with the criminal justice agencies based on a low key approach;
— maximum participation of the stakeholders creating ownership of the scheme;
— a service provider that complements rather than competes with the legal profession by offering appropriate legal advice and assistance.

AFTERTHOUGHT

'Where shall I begin, please your Majesty?' he asked
'Begin at the beginning' the King said gravely, 'and go on till you come
to the end: then stop.' (Alice's Adventures in Wonderland)

Entry points: choosing where to start—is it really such a problem?

Public opinion is generally highly judgmental and intolerant of those who offend against society's laws. Former Malawi President Banda's much publicized comment about prisoners in his prisons—'let them rot'—strikes a chord with many people.

---

[8] By Thomas Trier Hansen, Deputy Judge, Denmark.
[9] Niger, with a population of 11 million, has 77 lawyers.

Yet there are persuasive arguments for moving penal reform up the political agenda even if there are no votes in improving prison conditions.

The prison population at any one time hides the real number of people passing through prisons in the course of a year, which is five or six times higher than the static population recorded on any given day. The overwhelming majority of people entering prison will one day leave and return to society.

Prisons are incubators of disease. The rise of tuberculosis in Russia in the late 1990s has been traced to the appalling state of the country's congested prisons. In most countries in Africa, HIV rates are proportionately higher in prison populations. The rates of tuberculosis are also on the increase in the congested closed environment that characterizes most prisons in Africa.

Most people in prison are there because they do not have the means to retain the services of a lawyer or because of the absence of effective alternatives to prison, not because they are dangerous or otherwise a threat to the community at large. This is especially the case with juveniles who are picked up for begging in the street (being a rogue or vagabond) or handed over by a parent (who lack the time, know-how or patience to deal with a rebellious teenager).

Where conditions are overcrowded, there is little prospect that the juvenile offender will receive an education or preferential treatment in accordance with international laws and guidelines on the treatment of young persons. The likelihood is abuse, criminalization and ultimately social marginalization.

There is greater sympathy for a young person detained in a police station or prison: few people would agree that it is in the best interests of the child to keep him/her in such institutions. However a disproportionate amount of energy is spent 'structuring' a correct response rather than agreeing a strategy with key players and implementing it. The ad hoc remedies applied in Nigeria and Malawi (above) were useful in allowing the system to let off steam. What was lacking was the follow up that would ensure that the head of steam did not build up again. In Malawi, a start has been made.

Ownership: maximizing participation and changing minds

It has become almost axiomatic to state that the more people are involved the greater the chance an activity has of succeeding. Time spent in small meetings—in Africa at least—rather than in large-scale workshops is useful to explain the purpose and clarify activities. It is easy to 'commit' to activities in a populous assembly, less so when you are 'face to face'.

A process approach (proceeding one step at a time) is also useful in 'building coalitions' of partners (both within and without government). The participation of all actors is important if the idea is to be able to gain the 'space' needed to develop and grow and establish the credibility of the program.

The head of the Female section at Zomba Central Prison was totally opposed to the Paralegal Advisory Service when it first started in 2000. Her advice to the prisoners was to have nothing to do with 'these NGO people' who were 'well paid' and 'do nothing'. Six months later her attitude had completely changed and she has become one of the strongest advocates within the Prison Service of the PAS. In 2004, she started her own nursery for the children of female prisoners in the prison, which the paralegals are assisting her to support.

Sustainability: making maximum use of scarce resources

A little money goes a long way in the justice sector. The Juvenile Justice Forum and PAS in Malawi arose from an initial investment of $1000.

While many of the 'institutional' problems identified by stakeholders are real—police officers *do* lack transport, communications equipment, adequate terms and conditions of service and training; prison structures *are* dilapidated; the judiciary *do* need properly equipped courts and registers and administrative support—the perceived solution, 'more funds and resources', is not going to fix the matter.

A wider ('sectoral') approach that involves the participation of all the actors in the sector may achieve more by simply enhancing communication, co-operation and co-ordination between them at the local level (a good example of this is the 'Chain Link' project in Uganda and the introduction of Caseflow Management Committees at the local and regional levels).

These can involve simple measures such as: issuing *cost orders* against lawyers who seek unnecessary adjournments; taking account of the *remand period* spent in custody when passing sentence; giving *credit* for an early plea of guilty; lowering the threshold for *bail* in appropriate cases, and stating a general presumption in favour of bail; *discharging* those cases that have taken too long to investigate or to come to trial; taking proactive measures to ensure that the *'equality of arms'* principle is maintained and that unrepresented accused persons are not unduly prejudiced; amending the law to include *custody time limits*; and so on (PRI 2003).

The reality of many governments is that, even with the best will in the world, insufficient capital is available to address so many competing priority needs—not only in the justice sector, but also in health, education, agriculture and infrastructure. This is why the Ouagadougou Declaration emphasizes the need for greater 'self-sufficiency' within prison services; and why PRI looks for relevant, low/no cost practices/models from elsewhere.

Visibility

If there is no 'quick fix' to the multitude of problems confronting the justice sector in many countries, some well crafted *'quick wins'* (i.e. discreet, high impact, (usually) low cost interventions that address a priority need in a short time-frame) help to show what can be done with little when the actors concerned work together. Publicizing these early gains raises morale, reassures policy makers, changes (often entrenched) attitudes and encourages confidence in those providing funding that the money is being well spent.

Public opinion is often ill-informed. In Zimbabwe, the community service scheme was initially criticized by the general population as being 'soft on crime'. By the end of the pilot scheme, public opinion had moved 180 degrees and demand for 'placements' from the courts was exceeding the number they could supply. Public opinion needs to be engaged through the dissemination of accurate information, publicizing success stories and encouragement of public debate (on the radio/television more than in the print media).

Change is disquieting for many people. In a time of political flux and financial and personal insecurity the very idea of more change engenders alarm and a measure of resentment sets in. Change should not be too sudden therefore nor too drastic. People need time to adapt gradually to the ideas tabled and see the practice so that they can observe the benefits for themselves. In this way the noble aspirations of so many UN instruments and texts are seen to transform into a living, practical reality.

REFERENCES

Golub, S. (2003) *Beyond Rule of Law Orthodoxy—the Legal Empowerment Alternative*. Rule of Law Series No. 41, Democracy and Rule of Law Project. (Washington, D.C., Carnegie Endowment for International Peace).

Kerrigan, F. (2002) *Energising the Criminal Justice System in Malawi—the Paralegal Advisory Service*. (Copenhagen, Danish Centre for Human Rights).

Penal Reform International (2005) *Index of Good Practices in Reducing Pre-Trial Detention*. (7th version, Lilongwe, Penal Reform International).

5

The South African Child Justice Bill: Transition as Opportunity

ANN SKELTON

INTRODUCTION

A N IMAGE THAT has echoed again and again in the minds of people working in the child justice sector in South Africa is that of Nelson Mandela, as he made his first address to Parliament as the newly elected President of South Africa in 1994. He promised that 'the basic principle from which we will proceed from now onwards is that we must rescue the children of the nation and ensure that the system of criminal justice must be the very last resort in the case of juvenile offenders' (Mandela 1994).

The impetus for this important commitment by the ANC led government was the history of the suffering of children in South Africa's police cells and prisons. In the 1970s and 1980s many of these children had been political detainees, subject to arbitrary arrests, detention without trial, sometimes to torture (Wilson and Ramphele 1987). By the late 1980s the political detentions had stopped, but many children continued to be swept up into the criminal justice system because of 'ordinary' crimes, the majority of which were non-violent crimes, mostly theft. Non-governmental organisations and human rights lawyers did what they could during the apartheid years; there were detainee's parents committees and free legal representation during the years of intense political activity. Later, there was a concerted campaign by a group of non-governmental organisations to have children released from prisons and police cells and to call for reform of the way in which the criminal justice system dealt with children. In the early 1990s a strong child rights movement began to develop in South Africa, and thus children's rights became an important theoretical framework underpinning the efforts at law reform (Sloth-Nielsen 2001). All this history must have been ringing in Nelson Mandela's ears as he made his first promises of action.

With a President as a champion for the rights and protection of children in the criminal justice system, anything and everything seemed possible, and indeed—at least for a while—sweeping changes to the way that things had been done in the past were more than possible, they were expected. In this chapter I will show that the transition to democracy in South Africa flung open the door to change, but that the door has been inching back to position over the years that have ensued. It is not yet closed, but the gap is narrower, and there is concern that some of the reform initiatives may not come to fruition.

This chapter examines the efforts of law reformers in South Africa in relation to children accused of crimes. The efforts have culminated in the Child Justice Bill, which at the time of writing has been through two rounds of deliberations of the Parliamentary Portfolio Committee on Justice and Constitutional Development. The chapter details the background to the law reform efforts and describes some of the issues relating to concern about public safety that have influenced the process. Some aspects of the parliamentary debates about the Bill are then explored and analysed.

TRANSFORMATION

The coming to power of the first democratically elected government in South Africa provided an opportunity to transform organs of society and government policy. There was an obligation to leave the apartheid past behind and embrace a new era of justice and equality. After the elections and the installation of the government of national unity in 1994, government began to lead a consultative process aimed at the development of criminal justice policy. The early period of the new democracy was a highly consultative phase of government, and many members of civil society such as academics and experts from the non-governmental sector were invited to participate in this phase of policy-making. The period of transition was a window of opportunity for legal transformation. The word 'transformation' is in itself significant: the early stage of the new democracy was a period in which South Africans spoke about 'transforming' rather than 'reforming' laws, 'creating' rather than 'redrafting' policy. Every sector produced white papers, green papers or policy frameworks in the years following the first elections in 1994.

Van Zyl Smit (1999) records that during the early years of the new government there was a conscious effort by criminologists and human rights activists to build a coalition of progressive forces that united around new ideas for dealing with juveniles. Van Zyl Smit is of the view that in the transitional period juvenile justice attracted more debate and development resources than any other criminal justice issue and therefore the ideas of how society should ideally be organized in the future were articulated most fully in this context. Van der Spuy *et al* (2004) note, however, that the proposed new juvenile justice dispensation was only one of many dramatic and far-reaching schemes for the transformation of the criminal justice system competing for resources and for the favourable attention of the legislature, and consequently progress from research to policy formulation to draft statute was slow.

Van Zyl Smit then moves on to sketch the reality that, within only a few years of the new government being established, the pressure of keeping the electorate happy began to show in some very mixed messages that government was sending out with regard to its approach to criminal justice policy. Quick on the heels of producing a National Crime Prevention Strategy (1996) which was rooted in ideas of social crime prevention, and whilst still running a Truth and Reconciliation Commission based on ideas of restitution and healing, the government began what Van Zyl Smit calls an 'erratic flirtation' with law and order responses to crime. The responses ranged from 'an almost farcical police undertaking to arrest thousands of known criminals in a short period ..., through the introduction of mandatory minimum sentences, to the bizarre (and only half-heartedly denied) suggestion that disused mine shafts be used to house dangerous prisoners' (Van Zyl Smit 1999, 201). He traces the genesis of this swing towards a law and order response to a sense of 'popular punitiveness'. The fears of the white minority about the myriad of societal changes they were experiencing tended to be most effectively articulated in terms of fear about crime. Thus government was faced with the reality that keeping the business sector happy and promoting investor confidence was becoming threatened by what appeared to be a lack of commitment or ability on their part to deal effectively with crime.

Camerer (1997) defines the tension in a slightly different way. Her view is that within a few years of coming to power the South African government found itself doing a balancing act; on the one hand protecting the hard-won commitment to human rights (including those of suspects and perpetrators), and on the other hand addressing the angry calls for vengeance and retribution by many South Africans who have been victimised by crime. Camerer maintains, however, that the only way that the government can hope to restore faith in the criminal justice system is by focussing on the needs and rights of crime victims and providing an adequate response to them.

It is evident from what has happened in criminal justice policy making in South Africa during the first ten years of democracy that popular sentiment does not always remain supportive of vision-based policy. South African policy analysts Simpson *et al* (2001) observe that South Africa has experienced a backlash to the ultimate vision-based policy, namely the Bill of Rights contained within the Constitution. The authors contend that the experiences of crime and violence, as well as government's apparent non-delivery of solutions to deal with the problem, has increasingly stimulated a popular backlash which is about a resistance to those mechanisms in the Bill of Rights which are seen as servicing criminals rather than victims. Children who commit crimes have not been immune to this backlash, and the influence that it has had on the process of drafting legislation is palpable.

Crime and its control became a pivotal theme in South Africa within two years of the first democratic government coming to power. South African policy and law makers have in recent years begun to embrace a number of 'law and order' ideas relating to crime control, primarily borrowed from the United States. The 'broken window approach to policing' championed by the former Commissioner for New York City, William Bratton, was discussed enthusiastically in the South African press when Bratton visited South Africa in 1996. In the United States Bratton had achieved much success by encouraging police to 'crack-down on the squeegee boys'—a reference to young (mainly black) males who washed car windscreens in New York streets (Simpson 1997). This approach is somewhat at odds with the idea of diversion of children away from the criminal justice system, which is based on an attitude of tolerance for the reality that young people often commit minor crimes. If such children can be diverted away from the criminal justice system rather than exposed to its brutalising effects, they are more likely to grow up to be law-abiding citizens than those who are swept into the penal system. This is the idea that underpins rule 11 of the United Nations Standard Minimum Rules for the Administration of Justice (1985) which encourages dealing with juvenile offenders, where appropriate, without resorting to a formal trial.

Swart (2000), a member of the South Africa Parliament, observes that 'In South Africa—with the unacceptably high crime rate—what may seem a desire for retribution is actually a concern for public safety'. Swart believes that a restorative justice approach can still provide a solution because it can potentially deliver at least as much public safety as the present system. 'Therein lies the appeal to policy makers grappling with the demands of society for safer streets' (Swart 2000, 2).

The development of the proposed child justice system was strongly influenced by the movements of restorative justice and children's rights but concerns have been raised about whether these two movements remain strongly influential, or whether public concern about crime has caused the mood in South Africa to shift to a point where the crime control imperatives are overriding some of the previous policy commitments, and a more punitive approach is emerging (Skelton, 1999). The government's approach to children in the criminal justice system is ambivalent. 'Criminal justice responses to young offenders continue to oscillate between the iron fist and the velvet glove' is the vivid description offered by Van der Spuy *et al* (2004, 177). To illustrate this, the authors note that according to Muntingh (2001, 6) the number of children under 18 years in prison rose by 158.7% from January 1995 to July 2000, compared to only a 33.2% increase in the 18–20 year-old bracket. Sentences of children are also getting longer. Yet at the same time, diversion has also rapidly increased during the same period.

THE LAW REFORM PROCESS

The extent to which the law and order approach has dislodged the original intention of those involved in the development of new policy and legislation for child offenders needs to be examined by going back to the end of 1996 when the official process of law-making began. In December 1996 the Minister of Justice, Dullah Omar, requested the South African Law Commission (now called the South African Law Reform Commission) to include an investigation into juvenile justice in its programme. He appointed individuals from civil society to be members of the juvenile justice project committee, whom he knew had been part of the non-government lobby group calling for substantial reform to the juvenile justice system. The juvenile justice project committee of the South African Law Commission commenced its work in January 1997. The Law Commission process of law reform is a very consultative one, and there was a high level of participation by people working in the system, and even by children themselves who were directly consulted on the Bill in order to obtain their views and reflect on them in the final report.

The first step taken by the juvenile justice project committee was to publish an issue paper setting out the general direction that was to be taken. A quote from the issue paper indicates the broad approach:

The South African Constitution and international instruments give an outline of what should be included in a future South African juvenile justice system. In line with these principles the project committee is of the view that the overall approach should aim to promote the well-being of the child, and to deal with each child in a individualised way. A key aspect should be diversion of cases in defined circumstances away from the criminal justice system as early as possible ... The involvement of family and community is of vital importance, as is sensitivity to culture, tradition and empowerment of victims. There should be an emphasis on young people being held accountable for their actions. This should be done in a manner which gives them an opportunity to turn away from criminal activity. (South African Law Commission 1997, 5)

In the final report, which was published almost three years later in 2000, the Commission enumerates various factors that influenced the law reform process, namely the recognition of children's rights, the theory of restorative justice, fiscal constraints, and public concern about crime. In relation to the last-mentioned factor, the Commission had the following to say:

Increasingly, however, during the three year investigation into Juvenile Justice by the Commission, a further influence has been brought to bear, and that is the deep concern in South African society about the high levels of crime. The public have expressed the need for a system of justice which deals effectively with serious violent criminals. This factor, too has shaped the process of law reform, and this is evidenced by provisions in the draft Bill which allow for children charged with serious, violent offences to be tried in a criminal court at a higher jurisdictional level, to be imprisoned both during the awaiting trial period and as a sentence option. It is also recommended that criminal records for serious and violent offences should not be expunged. These features were not originally envisaged by the Commission in the early stages of the investigation. Indeed, the Issue Paper made the assumption that there would be no children in prison awaiting trial in the proposed new system. The realisation has grown, as the investigation has unfolded against a backdrop of rising public concern about crime, that in order to give the majority of children (those charged with petty or non-violent offences) a chance to make up for their mistakes without being labelled and treated as criminals, this Bill would need to be very clear about the fact that society will be protected from the relatively small number of children who commit serious, violent crimes. (South African Law Commission 2000, 9)

The Commission went on to say that although the draft Bill was pragmatic and cognisant of the realities of the crime problem in the country, the initial commitment to children's rights had not been sacrificed. This demonstrated that law reformers had committed themselves to what they believed could realistically be achieved in South Africa, with an eye on the need for proper implementation.

The 'pragmatism' referred to by the Commission also became a recurring theme in the developing process of child justice law reform as the Bill moved into Parliamentary discussions. The juvenile justice project committee had, with a great deal of foresight, predicted that the Bill would not succeed if questions about implementation could not effectively be answered. Consequently, the project committee made history at the South African Law Reform Commission by being the first project committee to undertake a costing of their proposals (Barberton and Stuart 1999). Following the handover of the South African Law Commission Report on Juvenile Justice to the Minister of Justice in August 2000, work on implementation planning began. The Child Justice Project, a United Nations technical assistance project of the government of South Africa, followed up on the costing work already done by assisting government to produce a comprehensive budget and implementation strategy for the Child Justice Bill. This is an inter-sectoral budget developed with the involvement of Treasury, and linked to the government's medium term expenditure framework. The Deputy Minister of Justice and Constitutional Development has described it as a model according to which all future Bills should be costed and planned for.

Sloth-Nielsen (2003), in her innovative article entitled 'The Business of Child Justice', undertakes an in-depth analysis of the pragmatic approach which was followed by the project committee and by government. She concedes that children's rights and restorative justice were important influencing factors in the development of the Child Justice Bill, but she makes the following observation:

The article has described and explained how, in the child justice sphere, a growing realism about the transition South Africa is facing resulted in a measurable shift in emphasis from human rights values (as philosophical constructs), and from a stance based on the righteousness derived from the worthiness of the cause. The increasing reliance for both law reformers and government's technical advisors on arguments and practices related to economic modelling and cost efficiency have been illustrated here in support of the contention that, while providing a useful backdrop, children's rights and restorative justice ideology have been eclipsed by business-speak. This could give the impression that an efficiency model, along corporatist lines, has supplanted the idealism of the endeavour. (Sloth-Nielsen 2003, 192)

Sloth-Nielsen, a well-known South African children's rights advocate and academic, is no doubt being a little provocative in this statement. In the closing remarks of her article she concludes that a children's rights ideology and pragmatic management philosophy are not competing discourses if we want to ensure that we provide a system that can actually deliver rights to children.

THE ROLE OF THE POLITICIANS

The Child Justice Bill was introduced into Parliament in November 2002 as Bill 49 of 2002. South Africa has a participative style of law making, with every Bill being deliberated on by Portfolio Committees made up of elected representatives from various political parties. Public hearings were held on the Bill in February 2003 and the deliberations on the Bill by the Portfolio Committee on Justice and Constitutional Development (hereafter the portfolio committee) followed in March 2003[1].

Although the process of finalising the Bill is not yet complete, there are a number of observations that can be drawn from the deliberations that have taken place thus far. A number of themes have emerged from the nature and content of the debates.

The portfolio committee has continued with the emphasis on the pragmatic that began earlier in the law-making process. The policy makers' earlier decisions to focus on practical issues such as budgeting and implementation were based at least in part on the knowledge that the Parliament has previously passed laws for which there was no clear implementation plan or budget, and they have subsequently seen that government has struggled to implement such legislation[2]. In order to demonstrate

---

[1] The minutes of these portfolio committee deliberations can be found at www.pmg.org.za.
[2] The Maintenance Act 1998 and the Domestic Violence Act 1999 are examples of legislation that had laudable aims but have proved difficult to put into practice. Government had to undertake costings and develop infrastructures after the Acts came into operation.

that they had learned from these previous experiences and that they were well prepared for the Child Justice Bill, government handed to the portfolio committee a comprehensive budget and implementation strategy to support the Bill. The preparatory work that had been supported by the UN technical assistance project on Child Justice as described above proved invaluable, as the chairperson of the portfolio committee noted that, had government been unable to demonstrate their readiness to implement the Bill, the Bill may not have been debated at all[3]. The chairperson of the portfolio committee has also mentioned the possibility of a 'phased in' approach to implementation, and it may be that the final version of the Bill will indicate a 'staggered' implementation date, with the Bill perhaps being put into operation on different dates in the various provinces according to their state of readiness to implement certain provisions.

The focus on practicalities is further evidenced by the portfolio committee's current position on the imprisonment of children below of the age of 14 years during the pre-trial and trial stage. The intention of the Bill as presented to Parliament was to place a complete ban on the imprisonment of children below the age of 14 years. The portfolio committee has shown reluctance to accept this complete ban, at least in part because they fear that there will not be sufficient appropriate alternative secure facilities to accommodate such children. They therefore propose, in the case of pre-trial detention of children below the age of 14 years, that such children may be imprisoned only if there are no alternative facilities within a reasonable distance from the court, and the portfolio committee further proposes that this should be a temporary measure, to be reviewed by parliament within two years of the Bill being passed 'with a view to establishing whether the factual situation in respect of the availability of suitable placement facilities warrants the continued application of those provisions and, if necessary, every two years thereafter' (redrafted Child Justice Bill, clause 24 (5)). The idea behind this appears to be that parliament is using its oversight powers to force government to deliver on the policy commitment that has been made.

A second identifiable trend is the portfolio committee's tendency to emphasise regulation rather than discretion. The original drafters relied on translating their vision through principles, objectives and substantive clauses which left the details regarding the decisions to be made in each case to the discretion of various role players in the system, within a broad framework of norms and standards. This was considered to be the best way of ensuring that each child would be dealt with in an individualised way, and it was also in line with the United Nations Standard Minimum Rules for the Administration of Juvenile Justice (1985) which state at rule 6 that in view of the varying special needs of juveniles as well as the variety of measures

---

[3] PMG minutes (see n 1), 28 February 2003.

available, appropriate scope for discretion should be allowed at all stages of the proceedings. A trend that can be identified in the portfolio committee deliberations thus far is that the politicians do not want to leave such decisions solely in the discretion of prosecutors or magistrates. They have tended to seek more regulation and a limitation of the choices that can be made. An example of this is the question of which cases may be diverted. The Bill as it was placed before parliament did not set any limits on the discretion of the criminal justice role players. The decision whether or not to divert a particular matter was to be taken in the context of a broad set of principles and minimum standards, and based on the particular circumstances of the child and the facts of the case. The approach of the politicians has been to the contrary. In an apparent need to obtain legal certainty and to ensure that the public feels that their interests have been protected, the portfolio committee has chosen to link diversion to schedules of offences. The Bill as placed before parliament did contain schedules of offences, but the main intention of the schedules as devised by the original drafters had been to place limits on the use of imprisonment. Instead, the portfolio committee has built a tight regulatory framework based on the use of these schedules. With regard to diversion, for example, the portfolio committee has directed that the system should allow for petty offences as listed in schedule 1 to be diverted informally by a prosecutor, whilst certain serious offences listed in schedule 3 are to be rendered 'not divertable'. The rationale for this highly regulatory approach appears to be, at least in part, a tendency towards a more 'determinate' approach to sentencing, and therefore to diversion. This approach has already been shown by the Justice portfolio committee in relation to both bail and minimum sentencing (Skelton 1999). Both of these areas of criminal procedure have now been stringently linked to schedules of offences, and there is also evidence of a 'grading' of offences. For example, rape is no longer just rape, it has been broken down to indicate the level of violence used, whether the offender acted alone or as part of a group, or the degree of vulnerability of the victim. Politicians appear to think that this will make the public safer, or at least feel safer. Leggett observes that 'the Mbeki administration has made sure that those given responsibility for criminal justice talk the tough line. Harsh legislation on sentencing and bail has been passed, prompted in no small part by perceived public opinion ... Surprisingly, public surveys have indicated that the South African public might not be so unreasonable as the politicians believe' (2003, 1).

The Child Justice Bill as introduced into Parliament did not allow for minimum sentences for children. The second round of deliberations at the portfolio committee resulted in the committee deciding to graft the current law in relation to minimum sentences (which applies to 16 and 17 year olds) onto the Bill. This despite the fact that such provisions are clearly at odds with the overall policy approach of the Bill. Since the last round of

Parliamentary deliberations, however, the Supreme Court of Appeal has handed down a judgment in the case of *Brandt v the State* [2005] 2 All SA I(SCA), which may shape the legislature's final decision on the whether or not to include minimum sentences in the Child Justice Bill. The case involved a 17 year old boy who had been convicted of murder. The court *a quo* had applied the minimum sentence of life imprisonment on the boy. His appeal against this sentence was upheld on the basis that, in the opinion of the Court, minimum sentences do not apply and should not automatically apply to persons below the age of 18 years. A constitutional argument was invoked, namely that the Constitution provides that children should not be detained except as a last resort, and that a minimum sentence implies a first resort of imprisonment. The Court held that the traditional aims of punishment for child offenders have to be re-appraised in the light of the Constitution and the United Nations Convention on the Rights of the Child, the Riyadh Guidelines, the Beijing Rules and the African Charter on the Rights and Welfare of the Child. Any sentencing court must have discretion when sentencing a child, in order to give effect to the requirements of international law for individualisation and the need for proportionality to be applied to the young offender, as well as the crime and circumstances surrounding it.

The Bill as it was introduced into parliament had followed the *doli incapax* approach, but provided that the minimum age of criminal capacity be increased from 7 to 10, with this age group being presumed to lack criminal capacity until such capacity is proven beyond a reasonable doubt by the State. Children of 14 years and older, but below the age of 18 years are presumed to have criminal capacity, but are still considered to be children. This is in line with section 28 (3) of the South African Constitution. Generally, the portfolio committee has accepted this approach. There is, however, a worrying tendency shown by the committee to exclude 16 and 17 year olds from some protections. The committee has excluded diversion on a charge of rape for 16 and 17 year olds, and has decided that there shall be no automatic right of appeal for 16 and 17 year olds, and—if the portfolio committee insists on pushing through minimum sentences, they will apply only to 16 and 17 year olds. This is disappointing to the Child Rights sector, and the original draft of the Bill published by the Law Commission did not treat this category of children differently from 14 and 15 year olds. Part of the reason for the approach of the portfolio committee on this issue seems to be that the members of the committee, basing their views on what they believe to be public opinion, are more comfortable to accept special protection for young children if they can show that they are protecting the public from older children who commit serious offences. This approach is not altogether a surprise, and although it is not the ideal, the committee has not gone so far as to say that 16 and 17 year olds should be treated as adults, as is the case in many foreign jurisdictions such as a number of states in the

USA which try children as young as 13 years of age as adults on certain serious charges (Stafford and Kyckelhahn 2002).

A further factor leading to the highly regulatory approach mentioned above may be a lack of faith in functionaries in the criminal justice system, such as the police, the prosecution and the judiciary. All of these sectors are undergoing transformation, with efforts being made to increase the number of black and women candidates at all levels of the criminal justice system. There is a fear that inexperienced personnel will not use their discretion wisely, thus the tendency to centralise decision making through the more peremptory style of law making.

A third identifiable trend has been the portfolio committee's tendency to focus on the exceptional cases, and shape the law to cater for the extraordinary. This is again contrary to the approach of the original drafters. The South African Law Commission noted that the majority of children do not commit serious, violent crimes for example, and thus several sections of the Bill focus on the first 48 hours following the arrest of the child and the attempts to divert such a child from trial in the courts.

Although the portfolio committee has not proposed changing the basic structure of the Bill, there is a tendency for them to reframe certain sections to deal with the exceptional case. Numerous hypothetical examples have been raised by politicians who are members of the portfolio committee along the lines of 'what if an eleven year old child who has committed a heinous crime is arrested in an area where there are no secure alternatives to prison and the police station has only one vehicle which cannot be tied up all day to transport the child to another town that has a secure care facility ...'. The approach inherent in the Bill that was published by the Law Commission was that there should be a generally applicable scheme with limited powers available to deal with the exceptional case. In order to help this approach in practice the drafters built in rules, such as 'every child must be assessed by a probation officer within 48 hours of arrest' and then have a proviso to that rule allowing for departure if there are substantial reasons for such departure, which reasons should be recorded by the presiding officer. Instead, the politicians appear to be haunted by the idea of passing the legislation and a few years down the line being confronted with a case which presents an enormous challenge, such as the case involving the killing of James Bulger in the UK, a case which has been referred to by the politicians during the deliberations on the Child Justice Bill on numerous occasions.

The portfolio committee's approach in this regard is not unique. Brunk (2001) makes the fascinating observation that people tend to form their thinking about punishment when pondering the most horrendous cases. Thus pressures are created for a criminal justice system that is designed to deal with the 'worst case'. Brunk cautions that 'legal responses appropriate for the worst cases are not necessarily the best way to handle the vast majority of the routine offences that come to the attention of the criminal justice system. There is always a danger in making "worst case" scenarios the standard for policy' (Brunk 2001, 32).

Oddly enough, opposition politics have not played a very distinctive role in the deliberations. By and large the parties represented on the portfolio committee all appear to agree with the general approach of diverting as many children as possible away from the system. All of them, regardless of political affiliation, appear to be afraid of political embarrassment, hence their 'worst case' scenario discussions. They want to pass a Bill that can be said to take a long term approach of leading children away from crime, but they do not want any difficult come-backs that might lead to fingers being pointed at them for not being tough enough on crime. It is a difficult balance for them to strike.

CONCLUSION

Transition creates opportunities. These must be seized with both hands, but there is a need to be thorough as well. New democracies require a high level of consultation. Doing all these things properly takes time, and as time passes, politics normalise—it is soon back to 'business as usual'. It is therefore necessary to have a pragmatic approach that goes beyond policy articulation. It is necessary to try to foresee how patterns of thinking may change once the euphoria of the new-found freedom has waned.

Simpson *et al* (2001) point out that the word 'transition' does not adequately describe the changes that South Africa was going through in the early years of the new democracy. 'Transition is not the same as regime change,' the authors remark, and in the early years of a new democracy it is not certain whether the basic liberal-democratic features will be permanent.

A lesson that can be learned from the unfinished journey of juvenile justice reform in South Africa is that there needs to be an awareness that societies do not remain static and that as a new democracy emerges so popular expectations change. The initial impetus that is brought about by a regime change is characterised by the desire to create legitimate structures and systems that reflect the new order. Thus, when the new ANC-led Government of National Unity came to power, bolstered by a rights-based constitution and a children's rights lobby, it demonstrated the political will to bring about dramatic changes to the way that children were dealt with by the criminal justice system. But it did not take long before the public were asking new and different questions about crime and justice.

One of the difficulties that needs to be faced in countries that undergo regime change is that *everything* is in transition. There are probably not enough personnel to run current or future systems properly and new people are being appointed who have to be trained. Procedures, institutions and infrastructure have to be built or strengthened as the process unfolds. The proof of the policy pudding is in the implementation thereof. Van der Spuy *et al* (2004) observe that the juvenile justice reform initiatives are very ambitious and far-reaching innovations. The authors speculate that 'transformation fatigue' may be setting in as the complexities of social reform become apparent to government officials trying to implement them, and they have doubts about whether the criminal justice system can cope with yet another restructuring and the new infrastructure and staffing re-organisation that will be necessary to make things work.

Looking back with the benefit of hindsight, it was probably inevitable that the pendulum would swing back around 'rights' debates in relation to criminal justice matters, as concerns about high levels of crime and the need to prioritise community safety came to the fore. In South Africa the sense of new-found freedom amongst the public was soon eclipsed by a sense of fear—a fear of crime, a fear that young people were out of control. And thus politicians began to feel some pressure from the electorate to articulate the fears of voters and to show that they are tough on crime. As an antidote, it has been necessary to keep the history of South Africa's children to the fore, to stress that those who will benefit most from the new provisions are the poorest and most marginalized children, such as street children. This has helped to keep many of the provisions intact. Advocates for child justice have had to develop arguments about balancing the need for managing children in a fair and just system that takes account of their age, with the need to ensure the safety and protection of the community.

The sector has demonstrated resilience and the Child Justice Bill drafting and implementation planning process was certainly characterised by a forward-looking, pragmatic approach. Van Zyl Smit and Van der Spuy sum up their view of the situation as follows:

> Pragmatism among the moral entrepreneurs may not, however, be enough to keep the communitarian ideas afloat. As elsewhere in the criminal justice system, the gap between theory and practice, between social policy and bureaucratic implementation may loom large. This may be the case despite the fact that the bill was placed before Parliament together with an implementation strategy and detailed costing. Notwithstanding such initiatives, the political will to sustain this model of child justice may prove to be fickle in the face of contradictory pressures to 'tough justice' elsewhere in the criminal justice system. (Van Zyl Smit and Van der Spuy 2004, 201)

Only time will tell whether, and to what extent, the final Child Justice legislation will reflect the aspirations of the post-apartheid child rights and restorative justice reform movements. However, the approach of the judiciary as evidenced in the *Brandt* decision is encouraging, and perhaps the judgment will nudge the legislature away from minimum sentencing for 16 and 17 year olds. It may well have broader positive effects on the sentencing provisions in the Bill. The judgment illustrates the importance that the courts place on the international instruments relevant to juvenile justice as well as on South Africa's constitution—one of the few constitutions in the world that contains rights protections specifically applicable to children. Members of the legislature will have to keep in mind that the child justice legislation they enact needs to pass muster with the courts, within a framework of international and constitutional law.

REFERENCES

Barberton, C. and Stuart, J. (1999) *Costing the Implementation of the Child Justice Bill*, Research Monograph 14. (Cape Town, Applied Fiscal Research Centre, University of Cape Town).

Brunk, C. (2001) 'Restorative Justice and the Philosophical Theories of Criminal Punishment'. In M Hadley (ed.), *The Spiritual Roots of Restorative Justice*. (Albany, New York, State University Press).

Camerer, L. (1997) 'Crime, Violence and Punishment—Putting Victims on the Agenda'. *African Security Review* 6, 46 at 47.

Leggett, T. (2003) 'Are South African Victims Interested? Insight from an Inner City Victim Poll'. (Pretoria, Institute for Security Studies).

Mandela, N. (1994) Inaugural Speech to Parliament, available at www.polity. org.za/govdocs.

Muntingh, L. (2001) 'Sentencing and Diversion Statistics, 1999–2000'. *Article 40*, 3(3), 8.

Simpson, G. (1997) 'Youth Crime in South Africa'. Conference paper presented at a conference entitled *Appropriate Justice for Young People: Exploring Alternatives to Retribution*, hosted in Cape Town by the Institute of Criminology (UCT) and NICRO, 5 and 6 February 1997.

Simpson, G., Hamber, B. and Stott, N. (2001) 'Future Challenges to Policy-Making in Countries in Transition'. Paper delivered at a conference entitled *Comparative Experiences of Policy Making and Implementation in Countries in Transition*, 6–7 February 2001, Derry/Londonderry, Northern Ireland. Available at www.csvr.org.za/ papers.

Skelton, A. (1999) 'Juvenile Justice Reform: children's rights and responsibilities versus crime control'. In C.J. Davel (ed.), *Children's Rights in a Transitional Society*. (Pretoria, Protea Book House).

Skelton, A. (2002) 'The Child Justice Bill: Implementing the United Nations Convention through the process of law-making'. Unpublished paper presented at the ISPCAN Conference in Implementing the UN Convention on the Rights of the Child: *Myth or Reality*, Durban, September 2000.

Sloth-Nielsen, J. (2001) *The Role of International Law in Juvenile Justice in South Africa*, LLD thesis. (Cape Town, University of the Western Cape).

Sloth-Nielsen, J. (2003) 'The Business of Child Justice'. *Acta Juridica* 175–93.

South African Law Commission (1997) *Issue Paper on Juvenile Justice*, Project 106, Pretoria.

South African Law Commission (2000) *Report on Juvenile Justice*, Project 106, Pretoria, available at www.law.wits.ac.za/salc/salc.html.

Stafford, M.C. and Kyckelhahn, T.L. (2002) 'Delinquency and Juvenile Justice in the United States'. In J.A. Winterdyk (ed.), *Juvenile Justice Systems: International Perspectives*. 2nd edn (Toronto, Canadian Scholars Press).

Swart, S. 'The Appeal of Restorative Justice to Policy Makers'. Paper presented at the United Nations Crime Congress: Ancilliary Meeting, Vienna, Austria, 2000.

United Nations Standard Minimum Rules for the Adminstration of Juvenile Justice (1985).

Van der Spuy, E., Scharf, W. and Lever, J. (2004) 'The Politics of Youth Crime and Justice in South Africa'. In C. Sumner (ed.), *The Blackwell Companion to Criminology* (Oxford, Blackwell).

Van Zyl Smit, D. and Van der Spuy, E. (2004) 'Importing Criminological Ideas in a New Democracy: Recent South African Experiences'. In T. Newburn and R. Sparks (eds.), *Criminal Justice and Political Cultures: National and International Dimensions of Crime Control*. (Collumpton, Willan Publishing).

Van Zyl Smit, D. (1999) 'Criminological Ideas and South African Transition'. *BJC* 39(2), 198–215.

Wilson, F. and Ramphele, M. (1987) 'Children in South Africa'. In *Children on the Frontline: the impact of apartheid, destablization and warfare on children in southern and South Africa*. (New York, UNICEF).

Section Two

Juvenile Justice Systems

6

An Historical Overview of the American Juvenile Justice System

ERIC L. JENSEN

T HE OBJECTIVE OF this chapter is to provide a broad overview of the origins of the juvenile justice system in the United States and subsequent major changes in the system. This historical overview provides the groundwork for the chapters by Armstrong and Feld on contemporary issues in American juvenile justice. In addition, since the American juvenile court has been a major influence on the systems in a number of Western and Eastern European nations, this chapter provides an historical background for those systems which are described in this book.[1]

THE HISTORICAL ORIGINS: THE SOCIAL CONSTRUCTION OF CHILDHOOD AND THE SOCIAL WELFARE MODEL

The American model for the juvenile court, and more broadly the juvenile justice system, was created in Chicago in 1899. Just as the discipline of sociology emerged out of a period of massive economic and related social changes in Europe, the juvenile justice system was created during the transition from an agricultural economy to an industrial economy, and from a rural to an increasingly urban society in the U.S.A. (see Platt 1977). In a sense, these events may parallel the economic and social transitions taking place in the developing nations today. Of course, additional influences on the legal institutions in developing nations today are the forces of economic and cultural globalization.

A number of societal forces influenced this change in the American legal institution. These underlying societal forces cannot be discussed thoroughly in this chapter but they are detailed in Platt's *The Child Savers* (1977) and Feld's *Bad Kids* (1999).

---

[1] Cunneen and White (1995) show that separate juvenile courts were also appearing in Australia and England in the late 1800s and early 1900s (see also Farrington 1984). In fact, the similarities underlying the development of separate courts for juveniles in the U.K. and the U.S.A. are striking.

Two cultural changes in the U.S.A. that were central to the creation of the juvenile justice system were the social construction of childhood as a distinct stage of life, and the later social construction of adolescence. The social construction of childhood began hundreds of years earlier in Europe (Aries 1962). By the late 1800s it had become part of American culture. Children were no longer seen as simply little adults, but as immature and in need of 'proper' socialization and nurturing to develop into responsible adults.

The social construction of adolescence was beginning in the late 1800s. As the economy changed from agricultural to industrial, the traditional pattern of becoming independent through employment and marriage in one's teenage years was no longer the norm. Persons in their teenage years were now expected to continue to be economically dependent on their parents, to attend school, and in essence prolong their childhood.

The Progressive Movement of the late 1800s and early 1900s was a crucial force in creating policies directed at young people. The Progressives were attempting to improve the life circumstances of the working class and poor in this increasingly urban, industrial America, and at the same time impose their rural, Protestant values on the lives of the waves of immigrants coming into the United States at the time. One element of the Progressive Movement has been termed the 'child savers'.

Three of the youth-centered policies advocated by the Progressive Movement were: (1) child labor laws, (2) compulsory school attendance, and (3) the juvenile court (see Feld 1999). These were major changes in social policy toward youth in the U.S.A.

Child labor laws

Laws were passed that limited the number of hours children could work and set minimum ages at which children could work, among other things. These laws were, on the surface, intended to protect children from the harsh conditions of the industrial workplace of the time, but at the same time to open up more jobs for adults.

Compulsory school attendance

Youth were required to attend school until they reached a specified age; for example, 16 years. These laws were intended to require that youth learn the basic skills necessary to become a productive part of the adult workforce and 'good' citizens. Of course, these laws also took youth out of the workforce and opened up industrial jobs for adults.

The origins of the juvenile court

One small, localized part of the Progressive Movement that became a major force in the creation of the juvenile justice system was the Chicago Women's Club. Out of the industrial economy emerged a new upper-middle class in the U.S.A. The cultural ethos of this newly affluent stratum of urban society expected women to stay in the home and to be responsible for the 'proper' upbringing of their children. Given their affluence and their related ability to hire others to perform the household labors for their families, these women had the free time, the motivation, and the resources to be an active part of the Progressive Movement in Chicago.

One of their priorities was to improve conditions in local jails. To familiarize themselves with the conditions in jails, they visited the Cook County jail in Chicago. Upon visiting the jail, they were appalled not only at the physical conditions there, but also that children were being held with adults. In conjunction with several other progressive-minded groups, they worked to create the first juvenile court in Chicago in 1899.

The juvenile court model was based on the ideology of protecting and guiding children to mature into responsible, law-abiding adults. The espoused purposes of the juvenile court were to 'help' or rehabilitate, not punish. Since its formal child welfare function was not to be punitive, the originators of the juvenile court did not believe that it was necessary to provide due process protections to youth in the court. These rights of due process are provided to adults in the American criminal courts, at least in theory if not always in practice. In line with this lack of due process protections, the procedures of the court were informal, not formal as in the adult criminal court system.

The juvenile court in the U.S.A. was based on the legal doctrine of *parens patriae*. This doctrine was originally used in 1500s in English chancery courts to protect the Crown's interests in the property of children whose parents had died and left an estate, that is, the state would take over managing the property of the child until they were of majority age. The state was 'parent of the country', and thus acted as parent for the estate of the child (see Bernard 1992, Feld 1999).

The *parens patriae* doctrine emerged in the U.S.A. in the case of Mary Ann Crouse in 1838. In that case, the Pennsylvania Supreme Court ruled that the child Mary Ann could be removed from the custody of her father and placed in the Philadelphia House of Refuge because she was a poor child and in danger of growing up to be a pauper; she had committed no crime. The court asserted the *parens patriae* doctrine when affirming the decision of a lower court to remove custody from the father and place her in an institution (see Bernard 1992, Feld 1999).

Another change in the treatment of juveniles under the law that came with the juvenile court was the creation of 'status offenses'. These are behaviors that are illegal for youth only. Examples of these are truancy from school, running away from home, and being beyond the control of parents. The child savers believed that these behaviors were early signs, or predictors, that a youth would become involved in crime. So the rationale was that the juvenile court should intervene early in the lives of 'wayward' children to prevent the development of criminal behavior. This belief led to an entire new category of behaviors becoming illegal for youth.

The American juvenile court eventually evolved into an entire juvenile justice system. This new juvenile justice system included age-specific courts, probation and parole (or aftercare) services, short-term detention facilities, and long-term correctional facilities. The states were free to set the age limits for the juvenile court. Today 39 of the 50 states have a maximum age of 17 years (i.e., under 18 years of age). Eight states have upper age juvenile court jurisdiction limits of 16 years and three states have upper age limits of 15 years.

REFORMS IN THE SYSTEM: DUE PROCESS, DIVERSION, DEINSTITUTIONALIZATION AND DECRIMINALIZATION (THE FOUR Ds)

Following these beginnings, the juvenile justice system carried out its duties relatively unchanged until the 1960s. At this time, societal and legal changes in the U.S.A. led to changes in the juvenile justice system. Specifically, during the 1960s it was discovered by civil liberties attorneys and criminologists that many youth were being treated punitively in the juvenile court but they did not have the due process protections provided to adults in the criminal justice system. This realization and subsequent U.S. Supreme Court decisions led to major changes in the juvenile justice system. The initial phase of these legal changes has been called the due process revolution.

The most influential and far-reaching of these decisions was the *Gault* case in 1967. In this decision, the U.S. Supreme Court held 8 to 1 that individuals in juvenile court hearings had the constitutional right to certain due process protections when the youth was in jeopardy of being incarcerated. These were: the right to counsel, the right to a notice of the charges, the right to confront and cross-examine witnesses against them, and the privilege against self-incrimination.

The next major juvenile court decision by the U.S. Supreme Court came in the *Winship* case (1970). In this decision, the Supreme Court ruled that juveniles are entitled to the highest standard of proof 'beyond a reasonable doubt' during the adjudication proceedings (known as the trial in the adult criminal court). The Court ruled that the 'preponderance of evidence' is not a sufficient basis for a decision of delinquency when youths are charged with acts that would be criminal if committed by adults.

These two Supreme Court decisions began a due process revolution in the American juvenile court and, at the same time, served as the beginnings of a more adversarial system. The social welfare model of justice for juveniles was ending and a more legalistic orientation began to emerge.

In addition to these important Supreme Court decisions, the national political agenda in the U.S.A. changed in the late 1960s. President Lyndon Johnson appointed a series of task forces to examine the rise in 'street' crime at the time. The juvenile delinquency and juvenile justice task force called for four major policy directions: due process for juveniles in the juvenile court, diversion from handling in the juvenile justice system for minor offenses, 'decriminalization' of status offenses, and deinstitutionalization (i.e. a reduction in the use of incarceration for juveniles, particularly for status offenses and less serious violations of criminal law) (President's Commission on Law Enforcement and Administration of Justice 1967). These policy directions have been referred to as the four Ds. These changes moved across the nation, although not always with the results that were anticipated by their advocates (i.e. an unanticipated consequence of diversion programs was often an increase in youth being touched by state controls or 'net widening') (Polk 1984, see also Feld 1999, 173–85).

In 1974 the federal Juvenile Justice and Delinquency Prevention Act codified many of the changes recommended in the President's Commission report into law. This Act required states to remove status offenders from secure detention and correctional facilities, to remove juveniles from jails where they were held with adults, and to encourage the development of community-based alternatives to detention and correctional facilities, among a number of other progressive changes. This Act allowed the federal government to withhold juvenile justice funds from states if they did not comply with the required policies.

Research on the deinstitutionalization of status offenders found that this new policy was effective. The number of status offenders held in secure short-term detention and in long-term correctional institutions decreased substantially between 1974 and 1982 (Schneider 1984, Krisberg *et al* 1986, see also Feld 1999, 175–9). An unanticipated consequence of this change was that many more status offenders were subsequently held in private mental health and substance abuse treatment facilities, in some instances with levels of security comparable to those in public correctional institutions (Feld 1999, 179–85). This change in the handling of status offenders is not in line with the objectives of the federal deinstitutionalization legislation. Feld (1999) has referred to this new development as the 'hidden system' of social control for youths.

This reform movement of the 1970s appears to have laid the framework for portions of the juvenile justice sections of the Convention on the Rights of the Child (1989). For example, Article 37.b states in part, 'The arrest, detention, or imprisonment of a child shall be in conformity with the law and *shall be used only as a measure of last resort and for the shortest appropriate period of time*' (emphasis added). The latter part of this section is referred to as the 'least restrictive alternative' among professionals in the U.S. This notion is grounded in the diversion and deinstitutionalization portions of the four Ds. The least restrictive alternative method of handling a youth is also covered in Article 40.3.d and 4. In Article 37.c it is stated that '... every child deprived of liberty shall be separated from adults unless it is considered in the child's best interest not to do so ...'. While this notion was one of the founding tenets of the origins of the juvenile court, as noted above it was only realized more fully in the U.S. with the passage and enforcement of the Juvenile Justice and Delinquency Prevention Act of 1974. The removal of children from adult remand facilities and prisons is currently a major issue being pursued by various non-governmental organizations and legal practitioners in the developing nations included in this book (see chapters in the present volume by Kaunda and Silwal).

In addition, several of the due process rights delineated in Article 40.2.b.i–iv derive from the U.S. Supreme Court decisions reviewed in this chapter. For example, Article 40.2.ii: 'To be informed promptly and directly of the charges against him or her, and if appropriate, through his or her parents or legal guardians, and to have legal or other appropriate assistance in the preparation and presentation of his or her defense'; the portion of Article 40.2.iii referring to the right to legal counsel; and Article 40.2.iv 'not to be compelled to give testimony or to confess guilt; to examine or have examined adverse witnesses' were first required in the U.S.A. by the *Gault* decision (1967).[2]

In the next U.S. Supreme Court decision on due process rights for juveniles, *McKeiver v Pennsylvania* (1971), the Court began to retract its support for additional due process rights in the juvenile court. The Court ruled in this case that there was not a constitutional requirement for juveniles to have the right to a jury trial. The Court noted in this decision that the juvenile court had become somewhat similar to the adult criminal court with the rights guaranteed in *Gault* and *Winship*. The Justices did not want this trend to expand.

Breed v Jones (1975) was the last of the major cases in the due process revolution. In this case the Supreme Court held that a juvenile could not be tried in an adult court after being adjudicated in the juvenile court for the same offense since this was forbidden by the double jeopardy protection.

CHANGE CONTINUES: THE CRIME CONTROL MODEL

Another crucial political change that influenced juvenile justice policy in the United States was the presidency of Ronald Reagan. Almost immediately

[2] The United States of America has not ratified the Convention on the Rights of the Child. The primary reasons behind this failure to ratify the CRC are that some states allow capital punishment for juveniles, and that some rights accorded to children under the CRC are not recognized as rights in the United States, such as the fundamental right to an education (see Walker *et al* 1999, 36–8). The U.S. Supreme Court recently ruled in *Roper v Simmons* (2005) that a person cannot be executed for a crime they committed when under the age of 18 years.

upon entering office in 1980, Reagan began to alter the direction of federal initiatives for juvenile justice policy from prevention programs and related research to an emphasis on serious, violent youth offenders and incarceration. Specifically, the Reagan administration emphasized the following policies: (1) preventive detention—holding juveniles believed to be a risk to public safety in secure holds before appearing in court; (2) transfer of juveniles charged with specified crimes to an adult criminal court; (3) mandatory and determinate sentencing for violent juveniles; (4) increased confinement of juveniles; and (5) enforcement of the death penalty for juveniles convicted of committing aggravated murder. This direction in juvenile justice policy has been termed the 'crime control model'. The crime control model continues to be the dominant presence in U.S. juvenile justice policy today.

Alfred S. Regnery, director of the federal agency responsible for juvenile justice policy and funding under President Reagan, explained their objectives as follows:

In essence, we have changed the outlook of the office from emphasizing the lesser offenses and the non-offender to one emphasizing the serious juvenile offender. We have placed less emphasis on juvenile crime as a social problem and more emphasis on crime as a justice problem. In essence, the office now reflects the general philosophy of President Reagan and his administration rather than that of Jimmy Carter and his administration. (Regnery 1986, 40)

Interestingly, there was not a major increase in youth violent crime at the time. Although there was a small increase in the homicide rate for 14–17 year olds in 1980 (www.ojp.usdoj.gov/bjs/homicide/teens.htm), the rate of serious violent crime for juveniles—homicide, aggravated assault, forcible rape and robbery combined—declined between 1975 and 1985 (see Empey *et al* 1999, 63). Furthermore, the proportion of persons under 18 years of age who were arrested for serious violent crime steadily decreased from 1975 through 1982, reaching its low point in 1987. Juveniles accounted for an average of 11.5% of arrests for serious violent crimes in the years 1978 to 1982 and this declined to an average of 9.3% in the years 1981 to 1989 (Maguire and Pastore 2001, 389).

The anti-youth sentiment underlying this Reagan administration policy shift has been interpreted by many social scientists and others as a sociopolitical construction to capture public attention and galvanize a voting block for the Republican party that began under the Nixon administration (see Baum 1996, Jensen and Gerber 1998, Beckett and Sasson 2004). Although this 'get tough' trend began with conservative Republicans, it has subsequently spread throughout the American political spectrum (see the chapter by Jepsen in this volume for a similar experience in Denmark and Ann Skelton on South Africa).[3]

---

[3] See White (1990) regarding a moral panic about youth as a dangerous class in Australia.

Later, homicide rates of youth exploded. Between 1987 and 1993 the juvenile arrest rate for murder increased substantially, as did the murder arrest rate for 18 to 25 year olds. This escalation in lethal violence was widely covered by the media and served to support both in public opinion and politically the 'get tough' policies that the Reagan administration had been advocating for several years.

One of the crime control model changes that swept across the nation was the increase in statutory or legislative transfer (or waiver) of juveniles to the adult criminal court. Under this policy juveniles are automatically sent to the adult criminal court for trial in certain instances. These statutes usually specify an age range (e.g. 15–17 years) and specific offenses (e.g. first-degree murder, forcible rape, robbery) for which a juvenile is automatically transferred to an adult court for trial and sentencing. These statutes were created because conservative legislators believed that juvenile court judges were 'too soft' on juveniles accused of serious offenses. Of course, legislative transfer to the criminal court allows for or requires more severe punishments since juveniles are subject to sanctions in the adult criminal justice system.

The research shows that legislative transfer of juveniles to the adult criminal court has been ineffective in deterring serious violent crime among youth. The first two studies of legislative transfer of juveniles to the adult criminal court in the urban high crime rate state of New York (Singer and McDowell 1988) and the rural low crime state of Idaho (Jensen and Metsger 1994) both concluded that this policy was ineffective. Jensen and Metsger (1994, 102) stated, 'the movement away from the traditional juvenile court model to the more punitive criminal justice system did not deter youth from committing violent crimes'.

The most recent research on this topic follows two matched groups of youth prosecuted for serious crimes for seven years after their appearances in the adult criminal court or juvenile court. This research not only confirms the findings of the earlier studies, but also concludes that serious adolescent offenders prosecuted in the adult criminal court are more likely to be rearrested for violent, property and weapons offenses than are those prosecuted in the juvenile court. In addition, 'they are rearrested for these crimes more quickly and more often, and they are more likely to be returned to incarceration' (Fagan *et al* 2003, i). The authors go on to state:

Law and policy facilitating 'wholesale waiver' or categorical exclusion of certain groups of adolescents based solely on offense and age, are ineffective at ... specific deterrence of serious crime, despite political rhetoric insisting the opposite. Non-individualized transfer to criminal court may increase the risk of serious crimes by adolescents and young adults, by heavily mortgaging their possibilities to deflect their behavioral trajectory and resume a path of pro-social human development (Fagan *et al* 2003, ii; see also Sampson and Laub 1993).

The crime control era was solidified further with the decision in *Schall v Martin* (1984). In *Schall* the U.S. Supreme Court ruled that the preventive detention of juveniles is legal under the U.S. Constitution. That is, if the judge believes the youth to be at risk of committing a serious crime, he/she can be incarcerated until the adjudicatory hearing. There is no provision for bail for juveniles in the U.S.A. Procedures in the adult criminal system are very different. Bail is allowed for nearly all adult criminal cases. As Feld (1999, 138) has noted, 'juvenile pretrial detention practices contrast sharply with the limited circumstances under which criminal courts preventively detain adult defendants'.

As we have seen with the legislative waiver policy, the research reveals a major flaw in this preventive detention policy. In a remarkable 'natural experiment' study of the effects of preventive detention, Fagan and Guggenheim found that judges predicted future violent crime incorrectly in four out of five cases. 'The high rate of false positives demonstrates that the ability to predict future crimes—and especially violent crimes—is so poor that such predictions will be wrong in the majority of cases' (Fagan and Guggenheim 1996, 447).

In summary, with the U.S. Supreme Court decisions of the due process revolution, the American juvenile court has experienced the addition of several due process protections for juveniles in juvenile court, but these continue to be fewer than for adults accused of a crime. In the *McKeiver* and *Schall* decisions the scope of the due process revolution was initially stalled and later reversed. In a landmark study of the juvenile justice system in the U.S., Feld (1999, 162) concluded:

The United States Supreme Court's jurisprudence of youth possesses two competing cultural constructions and legal conceptions of young people. On the one hand, it views them as innocent, vulnerable, fragile and dependent *children*. When the Court characterizes youths as *children*, it invokes 'paternalistic' rationales to enable their parents and the state to protect and nurture them and subordinates their autonomy to the longer-term interests of the adults they will become. On the other hand, the Court's jurisprudence sometimes characterizes young people as autonomous and responsible *adult-like* people.

The Court adopts this 'liberationist' posture when young people engage in adult-like activities, such as frightening criminal behavior, and treats them as the formal and legal equals of their elders. ... [A]s a result ... *young offenders* continue to receive the 'worst of both worlds'.

THE OFFICE OF JUVENILE JUSTICE AND DELINQUENCY PREVENTION

The Office of Juvenile Justice and Delinquency Prevention (OJJDP) is the federal agency with the responsibility for recommending juvenile justice policy, providing funding for juvenile justice programming, and compiling and reporting statistical data on the juvenile justice system in the U.S. Although OJJDP's primary missions have changed to meet the philosophical positions of each federal administration since its inception, it continues to furnish valuable information and services to practitioners and researchers today, despite cut-backs by the George W. Bush administration.

One example is the OJJDP Model Programs Guide (http://www.dsgonline.com/Model_Programs_Guide/Web.mpg_index_flash .htm). This easily accessible website contains descriptions of model programs throughout the continuum of care, from prevention through re-entry into society following residential care (see the Intensive Aftercare Model chapter by Armstrong in this volume).[4]

OJJDP also sponsors numerous training sessions and workshops on juvenile justice practices. A major event of this type was the Justice for Children national conference held in December 2000 in Washington, D.C. Justice for Children was attended by hundreds of practitioners and researchers from across the country. Numerous workshops were held on cutting-edge juvenile justice practices (e.g. the Intensive Aftercare Model and the Social Development Model).

As part of its mission, OJJDP produces a number of statistical reports on juvenile crime, juvenile victimization, and juveniles in the justice system (http://ojjdp.ncjrs.org/; then go to 'statistics'). The information contained in these reports is widely used by practitioners and researchers alike.

THE ROLES OF EXPERTS AND FOUNDATIONS

Although the formal role of neo-conservative governmental agendas has been deleterious to juvenile justice policy in the U.S.A. in the opinions of many scholars specializing in this field (see Fagan *et al* 2003, Howell 2003, Krisberg 2003, Fagan and Guggenheim 1996, Laub *et al* 1995), experts based at universities or research institutes, and child welfare foundations have been at the forefront of progress in programs to aid troubled youth, especially since the late 1970s (see Tables 6.1 and 6.2). These efforts are a continuation of the policies and programs that emerged during the four Ds movement. Three examples of theses are Multisystemic Therapy (www.mstservices.com), the Social Development Research Group (http://depts.washington.edu/sdrg/index.html), and the Annie E. Casey Foundation (www.aecf.org).[5]

---

[4] Unfortunately, thorough explanations of the research support necessary to identify a program as a model for other jurisdictions is lacking in many cases.

[5] Other programs and organizations of note are Functional Family Therapy (www.fftinc.com), the Oregon Social Learning Center (www.oslc.org), and the Center for Restorative Justice and Peacemaking, School of Social Work, University of Minnesota, St. Paul, Minnesota, U.S.A. (http://ssw.che.unm.edu/rip).

Table 6.1: Positive Outcomes of the American Juvenile Justice Experience

Increased due process rights for juveniles

Least restrictive alternatives

Deinstitutionalization

Removal of juveniles from adult jails

Independent research and programming efforts by experts and foundations

The 'decriminalization' of status offenses

Table 6.2: Negative Outcomes of the American Juvenile Justice Experience

The creation of status offenses

The increased use of incarceration

The expanded use of preventive detention

The increased use of legislative transfer of juveniles to the adult criminal court

The failure to ratify the Convention on the Rights of the Child

Widening the net of the juvenile justice system in response to efforts at diversion

Less than full rights of due process for juveniles

The multisystemic therapy program and the Social Development Research Group have developed theory-based methods of treating youth and empirically evaluated their effectiveness. Multisystemic therapy (MST) is an intensive, short-term, in-community family treatment that addresses the known determinants of serious antisocial behavior in adolescents and their families. These determinants may include individual psychological problems of the youth, family problems, peer relations, and school problems. The treatment approaches include cognitive behavior therapy and family therapies. MST has been thoroughly researched and found to be very effective in reducing delinquent behavior (see Aos *et al* 2001, Henggeler *et al* 1992).

The Seattle Social Development Project (SSDP) was created as a delinquency prevention program by the Social Development Research Group. SSDP is a three-part intervention for teachers, parents and students in the first six years of schooling (i.e. beginning at about 6 years of age). The primary intervention tool is training teachers to manage classrooms to promote bonding to school (see Catalano and Hawkins 1996; see also Hirschi 1969). Training to promote bonding to school and family is also offered to parents. This program has been thoroughly researched and found to be effective in reducing several law violating behaviors among the youth after they grow into the teenage years (see Aos *et al* 2001, Hawkins *et al* 1999).

The Annie E. Casey Foundation is supporting a program to reduce racial disparities in juvenile detention (i.e. short-term incarceration). Minority youth represent two-thirds of detained juveniles in the U.S.A., but comprise only about one-third of the total youth population. As part of its Juvenile Detention Alternatives Initiative, the Casey Foundation has disseminated information on effective strategies to curb the disproportionate numbers of minority youth who are incarcerated (www.aecf.org/initiatives/jdai/).

These successful programs to help youth in trouble with the law have been adopted in various jurisdictions throughout the nation. Indeed, the Social Development Research Group currently has programs operating in several nations including the U.K. The foresight, dedication and devotion to methodological rigor in testing the effectiveness of these programs has led to advances in treatment of both youth at-risk of involvement in delinquency and those who are experiencing serious problems in their lives.[6]

CONCLUSION

Juvenile justice policy in the U.S.A. has experienced a number of major shifts in emphasis and practice since its creation. To understand these changes one must examine the underlying cultural traditions of the society, changing values which are rooted in the shifting social and economic dynamics of the society, and more recently the social constructions of youth and youth crime created by political claims-makers and solidified in public perceptions by the media.

Based on the American experience, it is prudent to advise nations in the midst of developing and implementing juvenile justice systems to take a path based on empirically supported models of human development, research on the causes of delinquency and the associated theories, best practices as established by research, and human rights principles (see Sampson and Laub 1993, Catalano and Hawkins 1996, Laub *et al* 1995, Aos *et al* 2001, Welch *et al* 2001; see also Abramson's chapter in this volume). Such efforts have been exemplified by experts and foundations such as those noted in this chapter.

However, based on the material contained in this book, we see that research-based best practices give way to ideologically driven policies in many instances. A path comprised of ideology, political self-interest, and swings in public opinion—which are often stimulated by political and moral claims-makers—is not only ineffective in solving problems of the social development of youth and their related law violating behaviors, but has also proven to be subject to problems of inequality under law, or the 'worst of both worlds' (see Feld's chapter in this volume and Feld 1999).

---

[6] See also relevant advances in developmental psychology discussed by Feld in his chapter in this volume.

REFERENCES

Aos, S., Phipps, P., Barnoski, R. and Lieb, R. (2001) *The Comparative Costs and Benefits of Programs to Reduce Crime.* Version 4.0. (Olympia, Washington: Washington State Institute for Public Policy).

Aries, P. (1962) *Centuries of Childhood: A Social History of Family Life.* (New York, Knopf).

Baum, D. (1996) *Smoke and Mirrors: The War on Drugs and the Politics of Failure.* (Boston, Little, Brown).

Beckett, K. and Sasson, T. (2004) *The Politics of Injustice: Crime and Punishment in America.* 2nd edn. (Thousand Oaks, California, Sage Publications).

Bernard, T.J. (1992) *The Cycle of Juvenile Justice.* (New York, Oxford University Press).

Catalano, R.F. and Hawkins, J.D. (1996) 'The Social Development Model'. In J.D. Hawkins (ed.), *Delinquency and Crime: Current Theories.* (New York, Cambridge University Press).

Cunneen, C. and White, R. (1995) *Juvenile Justice: An Australian Perspective.* (Oxford, Oxford University Press).

Empey. L.T., Stafford, M.C., and Hay, C.H. (1999) *American Delinquency: Its Meaning and Construction.* 4th edn (Belmont, California, Wadsworth Publishing).

Fagan, J.A. and Guggenheim, M. (1996) 'Preventive Detention and Judicial Prediction of Dangerousness for Juveniles: A Natural Experiment'. *Journal of Criminal Law and Criminology* 86, 415–48.

Fagan, J.A., Kupchik, A. and Liberman, A. (2003) *The Comparative Impacts of Juvenile versus Criminal Court Sanctions on Recidivism among Adolescent Felony Offenders: A Replication and Extension.* Final Technical Report submitted to Office of Justice Programs, U.S. Department of Justice, Washington, D.C.

Farrington, D.P. (1984) 'England and Wales'. In M.W. Klein (ed.), *Western Systems of Juvenile Justice.* (Beverly Hills, California, Sage Publications).

Feld, B.C. (1999) *Bad Kids: Race and the Transformation of the Juvenile Court.* (New York, Oxford University Press).

Hawkins, J.D., Catalano, R.F., Kosterman, R., Abbott, R. and Hill, K.G. (1999) 'Preventing Adolescent Health-risk Behaviors by Strengthening Protection during Childhood'. *Archives of Pediatrics and Adolescent Medicine* 153, 226–34.

Henggeler, S.W., Melton, G.B. and Smith, L.A. (1992) 'Family Preservation Using Multisystemic Therapy: An Effective Alternative to Incarcerating Serious Juvenile Offenders'. *Journal of Consulting and Clinical Psychology* 60, 953–61.

Hirschi, T. (1969) *Causes of Delinquency.* (Berkeley, California, University of California Press).

Howell, J.C. (2003) *Preventing and Reducing Juvenile Delinquency: A Comprehensive Framework*. (Thousand Oaks, California, Sage Publications).

Jensen, E.L. and Gerber, J. (1998) 'The Social Construction of Drug Policies: An Historical Overview'. In E.L. Jensen and J. Gerber (eds.), *The New War on Drugs: Symbolic Politics and Criminal Justice Policy*. (Cincinnati, Ohio, Anderson Publishing Co. and the Academy of Criminal Justice Sciences).

Jensen, E.L. and Metsger, L. (1994) 'A Test of the Deterrent Effect of Legislative Waiver on Violent Juvenile Crime'. *Crime and Delinquency* 40, 96–104.

Krisberg, B. (2003) 'The End of the Juvenile Court: Prospects for our Children. In J.D. Hawkins, S. Meyers, and R. Stone (eds.), *Crime Control and Social Justice: The Delicate Balance*. (Westport, Connecticut, Greenwood Press).

Krisberg, B., Schwartz, I., Lisky, P. and Austin, J. (1986) 'The Watershed of Juvenile Justice Reform'. *Crime and Delinquency* 32, 5–38.

Laub, J.H., Sampson, R.J., Corbett, R.P. Jr. and Smith, J.S. (1995) 'The Public Policy Implications of a Life-Course Perspective on Crime'. In H. Barlow (ed.), *Crime and Public Policy: Putting Theory to Work*. (Boulder, Colorado, Westview Press).

Maguire, K. and Pastore, A.L. (eds.) (2001) *Sourcebook of Criminal Justice Statistics 2000*. (Washington, D.C., United States Government Printing Office).

Platt, A. (1977) *The Child Savers: The Invention of Delinquency*. 2nd edn (Chicago, University of Chicago Press).

Polk, K. (1984) 'Juvenile Diversion: A Look at the Record'. *Crime and Delinquency* 30, 648–59.

President's Commission on Law Enforcement and Administration of Justice (1967) *Task Force Report: Juvenile Delinquency and Youth Crime*. (Washington, D.C., U.S. General Printing Office).

Regnery, A.S. (1986) 'A Federal Perspective on Juvenile Justice Reform'. *Crime and Delinquency* 32, 39–51.

Sampson, R.J. and Laub, J.H. (1993) *Crime in the Making: Pathways and Turning Points Through Life*. (Cambridge, Massachusetts, Harvard University Press).

Schneider, A. (1984) 'Deinstitutionalization of Status Offenders: The Impact on Recidivism and Secure Confinement'. *Criminal Justice Abstracts* 16, 410–32.

Singer, S. and McDowell, D. (1988) 'Criminalizing Delinquency: The Deterrent Effects of the New York Juvenile Offender Law'. *Law and Society Review* 22, 521–35.

Walker, N.E., Brooks, C.M. and Wrightsman, L.S. (1999) *Children's Rights in The United States: In Search of a National Policy.* (Thousand Oaks, California, Sage Publications).

Welch, B.C., Farrington, D.P. and Sherman, L.W. (2001) *Costs and Benefits of Preventing Crime.* (Boulder, Colorado, Westview Press).

White, R. (1990) *No Space of their Own: Young People and Social Control in* Australia. (Cambridge, Cambridge University Press).

Cases Cited

Breed v Jones 421 U.S. 519 (1975)
Ex parte Crouse (4 Whart. 9 [Pa. 1838])
In re Gault 387 U.S. 1 (1967)
In re Winship 397 U.S. 358 (1970)
McKeiver v Pennsylvania 403 U.S. 528 (1971)
Roper v Simmons 125 S. Ct. 1111 (2005)
Schall v Martin 467 U.S. 283 (1984)

7

The New Spanish Penal System on Delinquency

JOSÉ LUIS DE LA CUESTA

GENERAL BACKGROUND

URING MOST OF the twentieth century, the Spanish system with regard to minors and juvenile delinquency was based on a welfare model (*modelo tutelar*). This model experienced a deep crisis in the 1970s, particularly after the approval of the Spanish democratic Constitution in 1978. This led to a progressive abandonment of the traditional system (de la Cuesta 2001a, 7). The protection of abandoned minors, which since 1987 has been the responsibility of the regions (*Comunidades Autónomas*)[1] and the civil judges, was specially regulated by the 1996 Minors' Legal Protection Act. The reform on delinquency came later.

In 1985 the new Act on Judicial Power created Judges for Minors and required the Government to present to the Parliament a new Draft on Minors. This legal mandate was not immediately acted upon, however. Only after the Constitutional Tribunal Decision on the unconstitutionality of the 1948 system in 1991 did the process to reform the old model begin. The first reform—legally classified as 'urgent'—became effective in 1992.

The true transformation of the system arrived with the new century. Act 5/2000 of 12 January was approved in the application of Article 19 of the new 1995 Penal Code, with the aim of regulating the penal responsibility of minors. After several reforms—the most important of which was created by Act 7/2000 regarding very serious crimes and terrorism (Etxebarria Zarrabeitia 2001a, 77)—the Act entered into force in January 2001.

Act 5/2000 regulates all of the material, procedural and executive aspects of intervention against minors and juvenile delinquents (14–18 years old), establishing a system integrated within the criminal justice system. The new system is co-ordinated with the social services working to protect minors as established in the Autonomous Communities; these are competent to give

[1] Spain is a unitary state, but constitutionally divided into 17 regions that have political autonomy and are called *Comunidades Autónomas*.

their support to the judicial system and to the application of judicially adopted measures. Delinquency and penal responsibility of minors is declared according to the general basis established by the Penal Code. A special regime, currently suspended, is foreseen for juveniles 18–21 years old.

PENAL RESPONSIBILITY OF MINORS

The new model is a mixed one; it follows the trend begun in 1992 and is fully respectful of the Convention on the Rights of the Child. This model admits the 'penal responsibility' (or criminal responsibility) of minors under 18, and intends to reduce the importance of the ideas of protection and paternalism. According to the new model, minority of age (under 18) is no longer a circumstance that relieves the person of responsibility for a criminal offense (against, Feijóo Sánchez 2001, 24); culpability is also required to declare the penal responsibility of minors (Cuello Contreras 2001, 49). Minority of age is thus a personal limit to the application of the adult Penal Code that opens the way to the application of the Act on the Penal Responsibility of Minors. The new absolute limit of criminal responsibility is therefore established at 14 years of age (Article 3), and those who are between 14 and 18 years can be criminally responsible.

Formally, the penal responsibility of minors is exclusively based on the commission of a penal infraction with certain exemptions (Article 5.1). This responsibility differs from that of adults because it opens the door to treatment intervention. Allowing non-punitive intervention justifies important differences and avoids (but not in an absolute way) essential principles of adult penal law: proportionality, general deterrence, victim's participation in the penal process (de la Cuesta 2001b, 59), etc.

The application of treatment intervention for those minors who are deemed to be without sufficient maturity is also possible, but this question has not been yet adequately approached by Act 5/2000 and requires reconsideration. If criminal responsibility must be declared, proof of sufficient maturity (in particular, of those under 16) should be required, and not only the absence of the general circumstances of exemption from penal responsibility provided by the adult Penal Code. On the other hand, in cases of absence of capacity for forming criminal intent, the imposition of therapeutic measures should always require a documented risk of criminal dangerousness.

Penal responsibility and re-education

According to the Act, the declaration of penal responsibility is the first step in the process of re-education and resocialization of minors. Via a declaration of penal responsibility, minors should realize the importance of their conduct and of the social intervention; this is possible only if they are capable of understanding the process and the aim of the intervention. Although the new Act insists on this point and explicitly recognizes it, procedural norms are not clear and it will be very difficult for many minors to participate adequately in the penal process.

The special educative nature of the intervention also determines the prominent position of the technical team, and the need for the specialization of all professionals who take part in the penal process (4th Final Disposition).

The best interests of the child

According to the legal regulation, the entire legal intervention should be based on the 'minor's superior interest' (Palacio Sánchez Izquierdo 2000, Juan and López Martín 2001) or 'the best interests of the child' (CRC)—a principle repeatedly mentioned by the Act; additionally, the prosecutor's intervention and the intervention of the minor's lawyer should follow this principle. In fact, every decision and, in particular, choosing and determining the measure to be applied (Article 7.3) should be adopted in the light of this principle. Thus, judges must sentence based not solely on the seriousness of the penal infraction, but also based on the relevant psycho-social and family conditions (Article 7.3). Furthermore, the prosecutor is not obliged (as in adult penal law) to prosecute whenever a penal infraction has been committed; he can decide whether to prosecute or not (Articles 18 and 19).

However, the Act is not clear enough on the content of this concept. This is an important limitation that should have been avoided by adequate references to the minor's personal development, their educational needs, etc. The 'minor's interests' should indeed be connected to a minor's re-education and resocialization (Palacio Sánchez Izquierdo 2000, 58), especially as defined by the technical team and according to non-legal criteria in close co-ordination with the prosecutor and the judge (Funes Arteaga 1997, 65).

Field of application

The new Spanish Penal Law on Minors is applied to those between 14 and 18 years of age[2] who commit a penal infraction defined by the Penal Code or by a Penal Special Act (Article 1). Those under 14 who commit a penal infraction are sent by the Prosecutor to social services experienced in the protection of minors (Article 3) (Lorca Martínez 2001, 79).

---

[2] In 1992, the age limits were from 12 to 16 years.

An important legal distinction is made between those minors between 14 and 16 years old and juveniles (16–18 years old) (Article 9.4–5). The latter can be subjected to penal intervention of a greater intensity in serious cases.

Attainment of the age of majority does not put an end to the execution of the measure imposed. The measure goes on until its goals are achieved (Article 15), but internment of persons 23 years old, if necessary, will continue in a penitentiary institution.

According to Article 69 of the Penal Code, the system of penal responsibility of minors may apply in certain circumstances to those between 18 and 21 who have committed a less serious penal infraction,[3] committed without violence, coercion or serious danger to the life or personal integrity of others (Article 4). However, Act 9/2002 suspended this possibility until 2007.

Special features of procedure

The penal process for minors as regulated by the Act is a judicial process— possibly too similar to the one for adults—conducted by a specialized magistrate, the Judge of Minors, and fully respectful of the basic penal guarantees: presumption of innocence, right of defense, and the right of appeal (before the '*Audiencia Provincial*'). Even a final appeal to the Supreme Tribunal is possible in the interest of the law in the most serious cases.

The Prosecutor's participation in the process is an intensive one. The prosecutor conducts the investigation and prepares the instruction (Article 23). At the same time, the Prosecutor must guarantee the minor's rights and protect their interests (Article 6). A Prosecutor cannot make decisions that restrict a minor's fundamental rights; only the Judge of Minors is competent to adopt decisions restricting minors' fundamental rights based on a request by the Prosecutor (Article 23.3).

Diversion

A characteristic feature of the legal processing of juveniles is the recognized flexibility in the prosecution.

Article 18 authorizes the Prosecutor not to begin proceedings in cases of first offenses of less serious infractions committed without coercion or violence. Discretion is very broad in this instance and not sufficiently controlled. The decision should be based upon the possibilities for correction in a familial or educational milieu, under the control of the regional institutions competent in the protection of minors (critically: Landrove Díaz 2001, 287).

---

[3] Less serious offences are nowadays those punished by a prison term of up to five years (Article 33.3.a PC).

An investigation that has already opened can be closed (Article 19) if conciliation or reparation occurs. The Prosecutor must in this case take into account the seriousness of the infraction (in particular, the absence of coercion or violence) and the minor's circumstances. Mediation is conducted by the technical team.

Conciliation is deemed to have been achieved 'if the minor acknowledges the harm and apologizes to the victim and the latter accepts it' (Article 19.3). Reparation—operating here in the framework of 'penal responsibility' (Richard González 2000, 4) and not as a civil liability—is legally identified with the agreement of the minor to do something in the victim's favor or in favor of the community. Goodwill on the part of the minor is not enough: the victim must accept conciliation (critically: Gómez Rivero 2001, 168) or the reparation compromise. The literature considers, however, that the victim's acceptance need not necessarily be an explicit one; the absence of rejection is adequate (Martí Sánchez 2001, 77). Success in the application of the educative measure proposed by the technical team could also, in certain cases, be valid as reparation.

If conciliation and reparation are effective, only then (except if reparation was not possible due to reasons other than the minor's consent) can the Prosecutor close the investigation and propose that the Judge dismiss the case. If reparation (or the educative activity) is not fulfilled, the process goes on (Article 19.5).

Once the process has begun and even once the measure of intervention has been pronounced, there are possibilities for the suspension, modification and/or substitution of the measures imposed (Articles 14 and 51) that can put an end to the penal intervention (Mena Álvarez 2001, 221).

Provisional measures

Article 28 allows the Prosecutor—if they consider that there is sufficient reason to suppose or a risk that the minor may elude justice—to demand of the Judge of Minors the adoption of provisional measures in order to guarantee the custody and defense of the minor.

These provisional measures (Gisbert Jordá 2001, 103) can consist of internment, controlled freedom, or custody by a family member or an educational group. The Judge must order the measures in the interests of the minor after having heard the minor's defense and having taken into consideration, amongst other opinions, the input of the technical team.

The time a youth spends in a provisional measure is counted as time served as part of a sanction, if a measure is finally imposed. This can also be applied to minors who are not capable of culpability but who are suspected of the commission of a criminal behavior. In these cases, the prosecutor (Article 29) should demand the adoption of civil measures for the protection and custody of the minor. However, the process is not interrupted because it is the responsibility of the Judge of Minors to impose, according to the minor's interests, either a therapeutic internment or an ambulatory treatment—the two therapeutic measures contained in the Act.

Detention and provisional internment

1. In case of detention by the police, minors should be kept in adequate facilities, different from the ones used for people over 18 years of age (Article 17.2). Detained minors have the right to speak formally in the presence of their counsel and their parents or legal guardian and the Prosecutor. The Prosecutor must be informed of the detention within 24 hours. After 48 hours the minor must be either released or appear before the Judge of Minors (Article 17).

A detained minor has all the rights of an adult detainee and, in particular, the right to counsel (Article 520 Criminal Process Act) and *habeas corpus* (Article 17.6). They also have the right to protection and to social, psychological, medical and physical assistance according to their age, sex and individual characteristics (Article 17.3).

The detention of minors requires detailed regulation, with an explicit determination of the applicable means of control and coercion. Some 'Provisional norms on the police treatment of minors' have created specialized teams or police groups for the treatment of minors.

2. Before the end of detention, the Judge for Minors—in accordance with the gravity of the conduct, the 'social concern' and always taking into account the minor's personal and social circumstances—can order provisional internment. This internment can extend to three months and may be extended by an additional three months (Article 28).

3. In case of terrorism, the reform operated by Act 7/2000 foresees the establishment of specific facilities, eventually created with the collaboration of the Autonomous Communities, and kept under the control of the specialized staff of the *Audiencia Nacional*[4] (4th Additional Disposition).

Other special features

1. The penal process for minors did not allow the intervention, as actors, of victims (Article 25). Victims could denounce, but it was the Prosecutor's task to accuse. This exclusion of the victim from the legal processing of the minor has been criticized (Landrove Díaz 1998, 293; Ventura Faci and Peláez Pérez 2000, 124), although in exceptional circumstances the victim was allowed to participate during the instruction as well as in the hearing regarding certain cases, but only in a limited way.

---

[4] The National Audience is a central judicial body competent to deal with certain crimes, particularly terrorism and organized crime.

Act 15/2003 has put an end to this exclusion of the victim and has modified Article 25. It allows the victim's intervention as an actor in the penal process for minors.

Victims' exclusion from the penal process has never affected their involvement in the process of establishing civil liability. The civil process is examined in a 'separate file' (Articles 61–64) (de la Cuesta Arzamendi 2001c, 175; Navarro Mendizábal 2001, 121). Act 5/2000 has indeed established a new procedure (Ventura Faci and Peláez Pérez 2000, 212), before the Judge of Minors but independent of the penal action. In this 'separate file' victims can intervene and they are allowed to present their civil claim to the Judge (Article 109.2 Penal Code).

Act 5/2000 also regulates the liability of parents and legal guardians to pay victims compensation for damage caused by the minor's behavior.

2. An important feature of the new penal process for minors is the special position of the technical team (Dolz Lago 2001, 129). It is usually composed of a psychologist, a teacher and a social worker (although the Autonomous Communities are allowed to establish their exact composition). The technical team has important responsibilities: to investigate and report on the minor's situation; to explore the possibilities of conciliation or reparation; to advise on the appropriateness of application of the provisional measures; and to advise on the final measures and their order of application, modification, substitution or suspension. They can also present proposals for the non-prosecution of the case, in the minor's interests, if the 'social concern' has already been shown sufficiently or it is deemed inadequate due to the time that has elapsed since the commission of the facts (Article 27.4).

The hearing

Flexibility is also assured in the hearing, where the Judge of Minors again has broader discretion than in the adult criminal process.

A minor's agreement with the Prosecutor's petition leads directly to a 'conformity sentence' (Article 32). The hearing takes place in the presence of the prosecutor, the lawyer, a representative of the technical team and the minor, who can be accompanied by their legal representative unless barred from doing so by a judicial decision. Participation of a representative of the public entity responsible for the protection or reform of minors is also allowed (Article 35).

According to Article 35.2, and although as a general rule (Tomé García 2001, 176) hearings are public, the Judge can decide to keep the hearing private if it is in the best interests of the minor or the victim. The Judge can also order the minor to leave the hearing temporarily if, officially or at the parties' request, they consider that it is in the minor's best interests to do so (Article 37.4).

After the hearing, the Judge makes public the sentence within five days. The sentence establishes the measures and their content, duration and objectives in a clear manner and with explanations appropriate to the minor's age (Article 39).

Special protection against mass-media publicity

Article 35.2 explicitly establishes that the mass media cannot obtain or disseminate the minor's photograph or any data that will identify them. The judge and the prosecutor must strictly enforce this mandatory rule.

The system of sanctions

In general

The primary task of the technical team (Article 27.3) is to detect the possibilities of conciliation and reparation and, eventually, to propose the content and aims of the reparatory activity that can lead either to the abandonment of the process as foreseen in Article 19 or to the decision to put an end to the execution of the measure already applied (Article 51.2). Often, the elaboration of this proposal will require mediation by the technical team.

By virtue of the accusatory principle, the Judge of Minors cannot impose a more severe measure than the one demanded by the Prosecutor. Internment measures cannot exceed the length of deprivation of liberty penalties foreseen by the Penal Code for the commission of the same offence by an adult (Article 8). The general rules for the selection of measures are contained in Article 7.3: the judge must take into account with flexibility not only the evidence and the legal importance of the conduct, but in particular the minor's age, social and family conditions, and personality. The technical team must provide this information to the Judge in their reports; in addition the public institutions competent for the protection and reform of minors can advise the judge in this way.

In case of the minor's non-culpability, only therapeutic internment or ambulatory treatment can be imposed, and always taking into account the risk of dangerousness by the minor.

Measures

1. Act 5/2000 establishes a list of 'measures'. An important part of the academic literature considers them to be 'punitive sanctions' (Sánchez García de Paz 2000, 719) and prefers to call them 'juvenile punishments'

(Cerezo Mir 2000, 106, García Pérez 2000, 686, Etxebarria Zarrabeitia 2001b, 32. Measures consist of the following (Muñoz Oya 2001, 185):

Measures consisting of the deprivation of liberty: internment in a closed regime, in a semi-open regime or in an open regime; and therapeutic internment (Ortiz González 2001, 185).

Other measures: ambulatory treatment, visiting a day-center; weekend arrest; supervised freedom (eventually with intensive supervision); custody by a family or educative group; community service; warning; socio-educative tasks; deprivation of driving license for motorcycles; revocation of other administrative licenses (to hunt, to fish, or allowing the use of arms); absolute disqualification from taking part in political elections or becoming a public servant.

The list is broad, but more imaginative measures are lacking; maybe they could be applied through the socio-educative programs. It is also very doubtful whether this kind of measure will really help to achieve rehabilitation.

2. Measures, in general, may not exceed two years (community service 100 hours, and weekend arrest 8 weekends) (Article 9.3). However, for those over 16 years of age who have committed an offence with violence or coercion or presenting a great risk to life or one's physical well-being, measures can extend up to five years (200 hours community service, and up to 16 weekend arrests) (Article 9.4). In extremely serious cases (and recidivism is always considered so) internment in a closed regime for 1–5 years is allowable, followed by supervised freedom with educative assistance for up to 5 additional years. This measure cannot be suspended or substituted before one year of effective execution (Article 9.5).

In the case of very serious offences (murder, homicide, rape, violent sexual aggressions and those punished by the Penal Code with 15 years' imprisonment or more), minors of 16 years can receive a measure of internment in a closed regime (1–4 years) followed by supervised freedom (up to three years further); those over the age of 16 will receive a measure of internment in a closed regime (1–8 years) followed by supervised freedom (up to five years further) and the measure will not be modified, suspended or substituted until half of the internment has been executed (4th Additional Disposition).

If the offence is terrorism and the minor is held responsible for more than one offence—and one of them is punishable by 15 or more years' imprisonment for an adult—internment in a closed regime can extend up to 5 years for those under 16, and up to 10 years for those aged 16 and over. Furthermore, taking into account the seriousness of the offence, the number of acts committed and the perpetrator's circumstances, an absolute disqualification from taking part in political elections or becoming a public servant (4 to 15 years) can follow internment (4th Additional Disposition).

3. Act 5/2000 foresees the possibility of conditional suspension of the execution of measures after two years (Article 40). Conditional suspension requires both the absence of new convictions during the probation period

and the minor's promise not to commit further offences. The Judge can submit the minor to a regime of supervised freedom during the conditional suspension or to a socio-therapeutic activity (eventually with the participation of parents or tutors), if the technical team or the public entity competent to protect or reform minors proposes it.

The judicial capacity to modify, suspend, reduce, substitute or put an end to the measure is an important feature of the system. These decisions can take place 'at any moment', in accordance with the minor's best interests and if the social concern of the minor's behavior has been sufficiently expressed (Article 14).

Relations among different measures

The judge can impose one or more measures, if he/she considers this to be most suitable and in the best interests of the minor. Nevertheless, if different measures are pronounced and they cannot simultaneously be applied, the Judge can substitute all (or some) of them or indicate the order of application. The total amount of time cannot exceed twice the most serious one (Article 13).

As a general criterion, the order of application should begin with internment measures (particularly therapeutic internment). In cases of measures of the same nature, the preferred order according to the law is the chronological one (Article 47). However, judges are free to establish a different order.

If, during the measure's execution, an 18 year old is punished by application of the Penal Code and the simultaneous execution of this punishment and the juvenile measure is not possible, priority is given to the juvenile measure, unless, taking in account the defendant's circumstances, the judge considers the immediate execution of imprisonment more suitable (Article 47.5).

Special sentencing rules

For misdemeanors only, warnings, weekend arrest (up to 4 weekends), community service (up to 50 hours) and deprivation of licenses can be applied (Article 9.1).

Internment in a closed regime is foreseen only for intentional offences committed with violence or coercion or causing a great risk to the life or personal integrity of others (Article 9.2 and 9.6).

Regulation of concurrence of infractions is 'very much inspired' in the Penal Code (Articles 11 and 12). In addition, special statutory limitations are foreseen (Article 10), although offences committed by persons aged 18 to 21 years or very serious crimes and terrorist offences (4th Additional Disposition) will be submitted at this point to the general rules of the Penal Code.

Special features of the execution of measures

The execution of measures (San Martín Larrinoa 2001, 141; also López Martín and Dólera Carrillo 2001, 141) is founded upon the principle of legality (Article 43) and is placed under the control of the Judge for Minors (Article 44).

The Autonomous Communities are competent to execute the measures directly or by means of contracts with other public or private, not-for-profit entities. However, responsibility for the execution of measures remains in the hands of civil servants (Article 45). Proximity is an important principle: minors must be kept in institutions close to their residence, but the Judge can decide to the contrary if there are indications that this will be in the best interests of the minor (Article 46.3).

To execute a measure, the competent public entity designates a professional who assumes responsibility for oversight of the youth's sentence. He must report periodically to the Judge, the Prosecutor and counsel for the minor on the execution of the measure and the minor's progress (Article 49).

If a minor escapes, as soon as they are apprehended they are returned to the same institution where they were interned or to another institution better adapted to their situation. If the measure was weekend arrest, they will be obliged to remain at home for the rest of the time. If the measure did not consist of deprivation of liberty, the prosecutor can propose to the judge that it be substituted by another measure or, in exceptional cases, that the minor be interned in a semi-open regime (Article 50).

The execution of the measure of internment (López Cabello 2001, 155) is divided in two periods: effective internment and supervised freedom (Article 7.2). The Act contains particular rules for the execution of measures of deprivation of liberty in specific centers outside the penitentiary administration: these can be centers for the protection of minors or psychiatric facilities (Article 54).

Measures imposed as sanctions against terrorism are executed under the control of specialized staff and in the centers of the *Audiencia Nacional*, eventually established by means of a contract with the Autonomous Communities (4th Additional Disposition).

A fundamental principle of treatment in the centers must be resocialization of the youth (Article 55). By virtue of this principle, those rights of the inmate that are not affected by the conviction (and regulated by Article 56)[5] must be guaranteed, and the internal life of the institution should be guaranteed; in addition, life inside must be organized in a manner that is similar to the outside world (Article 55.2). Administrative regulations establish the system of ordinary and extraordinary leaves and releases (Article 55.3), and all the other aspects of the establishment's functioning. Minors have the

---

[5] Duties are defined by Article 57.

right to be informed in writing and in comprehensible language of all these points and of their rights to present petitions and claims and to appeal (Article 58).

Particularly important rules are the disciplinary rules (Article 60) and the rules related to surveillance and security measures (Article 59). Disciplinary sanctions must respect the constitutional principles and norms in their content, form and procedure. Disciplinary sanctions can always be appealed—either in writing or orally—before the Judge for Minors (Article 60.7). Personal dignity, the right to nourishment, the right to mandatory education, the right to be visited, and the right to communicate are guaranteed (Article 60.1).

Act 5/2000 does not establish the different disciplinary infractions; it is the task of the Regulation to define them. Disciplinary sanctions are, however, contained in Article 60: separation from the group (in cases of aggression, violence or serious breach of the rules of communal life), separation during the weekend, deprivation of weekend leave; deprivation of other leave; deprivation of participation in leisure activities; and warning. These sanctions are also legally classified according to their applicability to very serious, serious or light infractions, respectively.

FINAL REMARKS

Five years ago, a new minors' and juveniles' penal justice system entered into force in Spain, established by Act 5/2000 on the Penal Responsibility of Minors. The new model is fully respectful of the CRC. Far from the ancient social welfare approach, it does not follow a purely correctional and repressive approach, but a mixed one. It is a responsibility model: minors can be held responsible, but the declaration of their penal responsibility is not answered by (minors' or juveniles') punishments, but by 'measures' that should be oriented to serve the best interests of the child.

In order to be effectively applied, any new system needs not only sufficient investment in structures, facilities and means, but also, usually, normative development by the government of the general legal provisions.

Both aspects are essential. Without new and improved means and facilities, the new system has no real opportunity to succeed in such a difficult field. Without sufficient normative development, individual rights will suffer and many of the new provisions will never be applied. Several years have elapsed and these two essential preconditions for guaranteeing the adequate application of the new system have needed a lot of time to be fulfilled or are even still lacking.

At the regional level, only Catalunya urgently approved a new Regional Act (Act 27/2001) on Juvenile Justice, in order to regulate the principles of the interventions of the Autonomous Community. At the national state level, only in summer 2004 was the administrative regulation necessary to ensure the adequate application of the Act approved (see Royal Decree 1774/2004 of 30 July; published by the Official Journal—*Boletín Oficial del Estado*, 209—on 20 August 2004). The time that has elapsed since it entry in force is too short to give an accurate evaluation of its provisions.

Regarding facilities and resources, after the approval of Act 5/2000 by the parliament, the Autonomous Communities estimated that more than seven million euros (Ríos Martín 2001, 241) of public investment were needed to implement the new system. Five years after Act 5/2000 entered into force, a large proportion of these funds are still awaited.

REFERENCES

Cerezo Mir, J. (2000) *Derecho Penal. Parte General: Lecciones*. 2nd edn (Madrid).

Cuello Contreras, J. (2001) *El nuevo derecho penal de menores*. (Madrid).

de la Cuesta, J.L. (2001a) 'La abolición del sistema tutelar: evolución del Derecho español en materia de jóvenes y menores delincuentes'. *Harlax* 37.

—— (2001b) 'The Position of Victims and Victim Support in the New Spanish Juvenile Criminal Law'. In E. Fattah and Parmentier (eds.), *Victim Policies and Criminal Justice on the Road to Restorative Justice. Essays in Honour of Tony Peters*. (Leuven).

de la Cuesta Arzamendi, J.L. (2001c) 'Responsabilidad civil'. In Consejo Vasco de la Abogacía, *La Ley Orgánica 5/2000 de Responsabilidad Penal de los Menores*. (Bilbao).

Dolz Lago, M.J. (2001) 'Labor y funciones del equipo técnico'. *Estudios Jurídicos. Ministerio Fiscal*, I.

Etxebarria Zarrabeitia, X. (2001a) 'Algunos aspectos de Derecho sustantivo de la Ley Orgánica 5/2000, reguladora de la Responsabilidad Penal de los Menores y de su Reforma en materia de terrorismo'. *Icade* 53.

—— (2001b) 'Aspectos sustantivos'. In Consejo Vasco de la Abogacía, *La Ley Orgánica 5/2000 de Responsabilidad Penal de los Menores*. (Bilbao).

Feijóo Sánchez, B. (2001) 'Sobre el contenido y la evolución del Derecho Penal español tras la LO 5/2000 y la LO 7/2000'. *Revista Jurídica*, UAM, 4.

Funes Arteaga, J. (1997) 'Menores y jóvenes en situación de conflicto social: posibles respuestas'. *Justicia juvenil en la C.A.P.V. Situación y perspectivas*. (Vitoria-Gasteiz).

García Pérez, O. (2000) 'La evolución del sistema de justicia penal juvenil'. *Actualidad Penal* 32.

Gisbert Jordá, T. (2001) 'Las medidas cautelares'. *Estudios Jurídicos. Ministerio Fiscal*, I.

Gómez Rivero, M.C. (2001) 'Algunos aspectos de la Ley Orgánica 5/2000, de 12 de enero, reguladora de la responsabilidad penal del menor'. *Actualidad Penal* 10.

Juan, A. and López Martín, E. (2001) 'El interés del menor como columna vertebral de la Ley 5/2000 de 12 de enero'. In *Justicia de menores e intervención socioeducativa*. (Murcia).

Landrove Díaz, G. (1998) *La Moderna Victimología*. (Valencia).

Landrove Díaz, G. (2001) *Derecho Penal de Menores*. (Valencia).

López Cabello, P. (2001) 'Ejecución de las medidas privativas de libertad'. In Consejo Vasco de la Abogacía, *La Ley Orgánica 5/2000 de Responsabilidad Penal de los Menores*. (Bilbao).

López Martín, E. and Dólera Carrillo, M.A. (2001) 'Ejecución de las medidas no privativas de libertad'. In *Justicia de menores e intervención socioeducativa*. (Murcia).

Lorca Martínez, J. (2001) 'Las medidas de protección de menores y la intervención de la entidad pública en la LORPM 5/2000 de Responsabilidad Penal de los Menores'. *Estudios Jurídicos. Ministerio Fiscal*, I.

Martí Sánchez, J.N. (2001) 'Protección de la víctima y responsabilidad civil en la ley penal de los menores'. *Actualidad Penal* 4.

Mena Álvarez, F. (2001) 'Reglas para la determinación de las medidas aplicables: modificación y sustitución de medidas'. *Estudios Jurídicos. Ministerio Fiscal*, I.

Muñoz Oya, J.R. (2001) 'Estudio sobre las medidas en la Ley Orgánica Reguladora de la Responsabilidad Penal de los Menores'. *Estudios Jurídicos. Ministerio Fiscal*, I.

Navarro Medizábal, I. (2001) 'La responsabilidad civil en la Ley Orgánica de Responsibilidad Penal del Menor', 53 *Icade* 121–162.

Ortiz González, A.L, (2001) 'La medida de internamiento en la Ley Reguladora de la Responsabilidad de los Menores' 53 *Icade* 185–202

Palacio Sánchez Izquierdo, J.R. (2000) 'El principio del superior interés del menor'. *Surgam*, 466–7.

Richard González, M. (2000) 'El nuevo proceso de menores'. *La Ley*, 28 June.

Ríos Martín, J.C. (2001) 'La ley de Responsabilidad Penal de los Menores, cambio de paradigma: del niño en peligro al niño peligroso'. *Icade* 53.

San Martín Larrinoa, B. (2001) 'Ejecución'. In Consejo Vasco de la Abogacía, *La Ley Orgánica 5/2000 de Responsabilidad Penal de los Menores*. (Bilbao).

Sánchez García de Paz, I. (2000) 'La nueva ley reguladora de la responsabilidad penal del menor'. *Actualidad Penal* 33.

Tomé García, J.A. (2001) 'Aspectos procesales en la nueva ley del menor'. *Icade* 53.

Ventura Faci, R. and Peláez Pérez, V. (2000) *Ley Orgánica 5/2000 de 12 de enero reguladora de la responsabilidad penal de los menores. Comentarios y jurisprudencia.* (Madrid).

8

Juvenile Justice in Germany

FRIEDER DÜNKEL

HISTORICAL ASPECTS OF JUVENILE JUSTICE IN GERMANY: THE COMPROMISE BETWEEN WELFARE AND JUSTICE

PRELIMINARY REMARKS

GERMANY IS SITUATED at the centre of Europe, bordering Denmark, Poland, the Czech Republic, Austria, Switzerland, France, Luxemburg, Belgium and the Netherlands. The country has a geographical area of 357,026.55 square km. With about 82 million inhabitants, the population density per square kilometre is 231.

Germany, with its capital city Berlin, is a parliamentary democracy. Article 20 of the Constitution (Grundgesetz) defines the political system as 'a democratic and social welfare state under the rule of law'. Germany is a federal republic consisting of 16 federal states which exhibit a certain degree of autonomy, particularly concerning questions of education and culture, but not in criminal and prison law or juvenile justice. Therefore, in these matters the same federal law applies for all federal states.

In 2004 the gross domestic product was 108 € per capita (2004) and the unemployment rate stood at 12% (about 10% in West-Germany, 20% in East-Germany, i.e. the 5 states which formed the former German Democratic Republic prior to the re-unification of Germany in 1990).

The age structure is as follows (at 1 January 2004):

children under 8 years: 7.4%;
children 8–14 years: 6.1%;
juveniles 14–18 years: 4.7%;
young adults 18–21 years: 3.4%;
young adults 21–25 years: 4.8%;
adults 25–30 years: 5.7%;
adults 30–40 years: 15.5%;
adults 40–50 years: 15.7%;

adults 50–60 years: 12.0%;
adults 60 years and older: 24.6%.

Roughly 9% (7.3 million) of the population have a foreign passport, one quarter of which are Turkish passports. A further 25% come from other EU member states, particularly Italy, Greece and Spain. Population growth in Germany has been declining for years and this despite increases in the number of immigrants, which played a significant role in the 1980s and early 1990s. Immigrants from the former Soviet empire with German roots have been issued German passports and are not classed as foreigners.

HISTORICAL ASPECTS OF JUVENILE JUSTICE IN GERMANY: THE COMPROMISE BETWEEN WELFARE AND JUSTICE

The history of a system of specific social control for minors in Germany goes back to the beginning of the previous century. Since 1908, some courts, such as in Berlin, Frankfurt/Main and Cologne, began to develop special court chambers that specialised in issues concerning young delinquents. Only after World War I could the idea of specific legislation successfully be pursued by opting for the 'dualistic' approach of welfare *and* justice. Thus, in 1922, the Juvenile Welfare Act (JWA—*Jugendwohlfahrtsgesetz* of 1922) dealing with young persons in need of care was passed and in 1923 the Juvenile Justice Act (JJA—*Jugendgerichtsgesetz*, literally translated as the Juvenile Courts Act)[1] dealing with juvenile offenders who had committed a delinquent act proscribed by the general penal law (*Strafgesetzbuch*, StGB). A totally welfare oriented model of juvenile justice did not fit with the German 'mentality', which remained intent upon keeping the penal option to deal with young offenders. The compromise was a somehow 'mixed' system of juvenile justice, combining elements of educational measures with legal guarantees and a procedural approach in general which is characteristic of the justice model. The JJA did not create a new 'juvenile penal law'. Punishable crimes are the same as for adults, i.e. so-called status offences do not form an element of the JJA. The JJA consists of a specific system of reactions/sanctions applicable to young offenders and of some specific procedural rules for the juvenile court and its proceedings (e.g. the principle of non-public trials).

In comparison with the general penal law for adults, the legislator of 1923 for the first time 'opened the floor' for *educational measures instead*

---

[1] The literal translation of '*Jugendgerichtsgesetz*' reflects the historical roots of the JJA. It goes back to the adjudication of specialised judges of youth chambers at some courts in bigger cities like Berlin, Cologne and Frankfurt. The '*Jugendgerichtsbewegung*' ('movement for establishing juvenile courts') had a major influence on the first JJA in 1923; see Schaffstein and Beulke 2002, 34 ff.

of punishment (the corresponding slogan was '*Erziehung statt Strafe*'), particularly instead of imprisonment. Also opened was the possibility of abandoning the otherwise strictly applied principle of obligatory prosecution (principle of legality, *Legalitätsprinzip*). The JJA was thus a forerunner to the notion of giving the prosecutor discretion as to whether, and how, to prosecute or dismiss a case because of the petty nature of the offence or educational measures taken by other institutions or persons (see §§ 45, 47 JJA and below). The third pillar of innovation contained in the 1923 legislation was to increase the age of criminal responsibility from 12 to 14 years.

In this context one can mention that only in the period of the Nazi regime between 1933 and 1945 was the 12- to 14-year age group 're-criminalised' for certain offences and behaviour. Today, the lowering of the age of criminal responsibility is only an issue (of a more rhetorical or symbolic nature, particularly at election time) for a few conservative politicians of the Christian Democratic Parties (CDU/CSU), but without any chance of being accepted by the majority of the political parties.

The law of 1923 and the amendments that followed did not define the principle of 'education'. History has demonstrated that this lack of precise definition of 'education'—under certain ideologies—can lead to a totally different meaning and use of the educational principle. Thus the Nazis defined 'education' as *education by* (not instead of!) *punishment*. In other words, a rather repressive meaning of education prevailed. The introduction of so-called disciplinary measures, particularly the short-term detention centre (up to four weeks of detention as a short sharp shock), by an administrative decree of 1940 and an amendment to the JJA in 1943 can be seen as a demonstration of the repressive '*Zeitgeist*' of the Nazi era.

After World War II the legislator decided to keep these measures, as they also existed in other European legislation (see e.g. the British detention centre). The reforms of the Nazi system are ambivalent insofar as they also included educational innovations that had been discussed in the previous era of the Weimar democracy of the 1920s. On the other hand it can be seen that a totalitarian ideology of education was linked to the general totalitarian ideology of the Nazis (see Wolff 1986; 1989).

The Juvenile Welfare Act of 1922 was a classic law providing intervention in the sense of the *parens patriae* doctrine. The state replaces parents who are not able or willing to fulfil their educational duties. The educational measures were similar to or even the same as the educational measures stipulated in the Juvenile Justice Act, such as supervisory directives, care orders, orders to improve the educational abilities of parents, placement in a foster family or in residential care, etc. In the years that followed, the interventions of the JWA were neither changed nor criticised very much. However, in the late 1960s, following social and political movements and changes, the reform debate emerged. The main criticism concerned closed institutions ('homes') as stipulated by the JWA; in the field of the JJA the concern was the disciplinary measures, particularly youth detention of up to four weeks (a kind of shock incarceration for repressive purposes). The reform movement in the early 1970s was strongly in favour of a unified welfare model (excluding classic sanctions of the justice model as far as possible). However, this idea had been abandoned by 1974 (see in detail Schaffstein and Beulke 2002, 41 ff). Thereafter reform proposals were made under the dualistic approach of separate welfare and justice legislation. Finally, in 1990, the JWA was replaced by a modern law of social welfare (under the concept of the *Sozialstaat*). The juvenile welfare boards should function as a help and offer help, not as agents of 'intervention'. At least in theory, the repressive measures of education, such as detention in secure (closed) residential care ('homes'), have been abolished. In the late 1980s and early 1990s a few closed welfare institutions were re-opened (about 150 places in total in some federal states—which is about 0.2% of all measures of placement in the welfare system; see Sonnen 2002, 330).

The juvenile justice system has experienced major changes since the 1970s. This has happened without any legislative amendment and has been called 'reform through practice' (*'Jugendstrafrechtsreform durch die Praxis'*), meaning that innovative projects have been developed by social workers, juvenile court prosecutors and judges. As a consequence the numbers of juvenile prison sentences lessened considerably in the 1980s after the introduction of 'new' community sanctions (see below and Heinz 2003).

THE SANCTIONS SYSTEM OF THE GERMAN JUVENILE JUSTICE ACT (JJA—*Jugendgerichtsgesetz*, JGG)

In cases of crimes the interventions of the JJA are characterised by the principle of 'subsidiarity' or 'minimum intervention' (see the diagram at the end of this chapter).[2] This means that penal action should only be taken if it is absolutely necessary. Furthermore, sanctions must be limited by the principle of proportionality. The legislative reform of the JJA in 1990, passed in the same year as that of the JWA, underlines the principle of juvenile court sanctions as a last resort (*'ultima ratio'*). Therefore the primary sanctions of the juvenile court are educational or disciplinary measures.

---

[2] The application of the JJA is restricted to crimes defined by the general penal law (StGB). The Juvenile Welfare Act (JWA) is applied when a child or juvenile in his personal development seems to be 'in danger' and needs help or measures provided by the JWA. The measures are chosen according to the estimated educational needs. They are not imposed in an 'interventionist' style, but are offered and taken upon the request of the parents. In part, the measures are the same as those provided by the JJA (e.g. social training courses, special care, etc.). The residential care order exists in both laws, too. If the authorities of the youth welfare department want to bring a child or juvenile to such a home (against the parents' will), they must ask the family court judge for a specific order (according to § 1631b Civil Code, *Bürgerliches Gesetzbuch*). Such homes are usually open facilities.

The most important response to petty offences is dismissal of the case without any sanction. In this context one should emphasise that police diversion, like the British form of cautioning, is not allowed in Germany. The underlying reasoning is the abuse of police power that occurred under the Nazi regime. Therefore all forms of diversion are provided for only at the level of the juvenile court prosecutor or the juvenile court judge. The police are strictly bound by the principle of legality. All criminal offences have to be referred to the public prosecutor. The situation is different from the one in England where police cautioning plays a considerable role.

The 1990 reform of the Juvenile Justice Act in Germany extended the legal possibilities for diversion considerably. The legislature has thus reacted to the reforms that have been developed in practice since the end of the 1970s (see Bundesministerium der Justiz 1989; Heinz in Dünkel, van Kalmthout and Schüler-Springorum 1997). The law now emphasises the discharge of juvenile and young adult offenders because of the petty nature of the crime committed or because of other social and/or educational interventions that have taken place (see § 45 (1) and (2) JJA). Efforts to make reparation to the victim or to participate in victim-offender reconciliation (mediation) are explicitly put on a par with such educational measures. There is no restriction concerning the nature of offences; additionally, felony offences (*'Verbrechen'*) can be 'diverted' under certain circumstances, e.g. a robbery, if the offender has repaired the damage or made another form of apology (restitution/reparation) to the victim.[3]

Four levels of diversion can be differentiated. Diversion without any sanction (*'non-intervention'*) is given priority in cases of petty offences. Diversion with measures taken by other agencies (parents, the school) or in combination with mediation is the second level (*'diversion with education'*). The third level is *'diversion with intervention'*. In these cases the prosecutor proposes that the juvenile court judge impose a minor sanction, such as a warning, community service (usually between 10 and 40 hours), mediation (*'Täter-Opfer-Ausgleich'*), participation in a training course for traffic offenders (*'Verkehrsunterricht'*) or certain obligations such as reparation/restitution, an apology to the victim, community service or a fine (§ 45 (3) JJA). Once the young offender has fulfilled these obligations, the juvenile court prosecutor will dismiss the case in co-operation with the judge. The fourth level is the introduction of levels one to three at the juvenile court proceedings after the charge has been filed. Fairly often in practice the juvenile court judge will face a situation where the young offender has, in the meantime (after the prosecutor has filed the charge), undergone some educational measure such as

---

[3] The situation is different in the general penal law for adults (>18 or 21 years old) where diversion according to §§ 153 ff of the Criminal Procedure Act is restricted to misdemeanours. Felony offences (i.e. crimes with a minimum prison sentence provided by law of one year) are excluded.

mediation, and therefore a formal court seems unnecessary. Section 47 of the JJA enables the judge to dismiss the case in these instances.

In addition, *formal sanctions of the juvenile court* are structured according to the *principle of minimum intervention* (*'Subsidiaritätsgrundsatz'*; see the diagram at the end of the chapter). Juvenile imprisonment has been restricted to a sanction of last resort, if educational or disciplinary measures seem to be inappropriate (see §§ 5 and 17 (2) JJA). The reform of the Juvenile Justice Act of 1990 extended the catalogue of juvenile sanctions by introducing new community sanctions such as community service, the special care order (*'Betreuungsweisung'*), the social training course (see Dünkel, Geng and Kirstein 1998) and mediation (see Dünkel 1996, 1999; Bannenberg 1993). The educational measures of the juvenile court, furthermore, comprise different forms of directives concerning the everyday lives of juvenile offenders in order to educate and to prevent dangerous situations. Thus the judge can forbid contact with certain persons and prohibit going to certain places ('whereabouts', see § 10 JJA). Disciplinary measures comprise the formal warning, community service, a fine and detention for one or two weekends or up to four weeks in a special juvenile detention centre (*'Jugendarrest'*).

Youth imprisonment is executed in separate juvenile prisons (see § 92 JJA). Youth prison sentences are a sanction of last resort (*'ultima ratio'*, see §§ 5 (2), 17 (2) JJA), in line with the view espoused by international rules such as the so-called Beijing Rules of 1985.[4] For 14–17 year-old juveniles the minimum length of youth imprisonment is six months, the maximum five years. In cases of very serious crimes for which adults could be punished with more than ten years of imprisonment, the maximum length of youth imprisonment is ten years. In the case of 18–20 year-old young adults sentenced according to the JJA (see below), the maximum penalty is also ten years (see §§ 18, 109 JJA). The preconditions for youth imprisonment are either the 'dangerous tendencies' of the offender that are likely to exclude community sanctions as inappropriate, or the 'gravity of guilt' concerning particular, serious crimes (like murder, aggravated robbery, etc.; see § 17 (2) JJA).[5]

Youth imprisonment sentences of up to two years can be suspended in case of a favourable prognosis; in all cases the probation service gets involved. The period of probationary supervision is one to two years; the period of probation two to three years.

---

[4] See United Nations 1991, Dünkel 1994, 43; Rule No. 17.1 of the Beijing Rules restricts youth imprisonment to cases of serious violent crimes or repeated violent or other crimes if there seems to be no other appropriate solution.

[5] The precondition of 'dangerous tendencies' for imposing a prison sentence is very often heavily criticised as it causes stigmatisation and possibly contributes to an 'inflation' of prison sentences where the juvenile court judge cannot find appropriate alternatives, see Dünkel 1990, 466 f; law reform proposals urge for the abolition of the term 'dangerous tendencies' and for keeping only the precondition of the 'gravity of guilt', see Albrecht 2002; Deutsche Vereinigung für Jugendgerichte und Jugendgerichtshilfen 2002; Dünkel 2002 with further references.

HUMAN RIGHTS ASPECTS OF CRIMINAL PROCEDURE IN THE JUVENILE JUSTICE SYSTEM

Juvenile justice systems, particularly those following the welfare model, are often criticised for failing to guarantee human rights. Compared to the general criminal procedure for adults, the right of access to a legal defence counsel and other basic human rights issues seem to be underdeveloped and some critical scholars denounce the juvenile justice system as 'second class justice'.

The German juvenile justice system shares these criticisms only to a very minor extent, as in general the legal procedural rules are very similar for juvenile and adult criminal justice. The JJA states that the procedural rules, for example the rules of evidence, are the same as for general criminal procedure. Deviations from this general rule are based on educational aims. So, for example, court hearings are not open to the public (see § 48 JJA) in order to protect the juvenile's privacy and to avoid stigmatisation. In juvenile trials the participation of the so-called social court assistant (*'Jugendgerichtshilfe'*), i.e. a social worker from the community youth welfare department, is required (see § 38 (2) JJA). They have to prepare a social report and are required to participate in the court trial in order to give evidence about the personal background of the juvenile and to assist the judge in finding the appropriate sanction. The right to a defence counsel, in principle, is more extensive in the juvenile justice system, as every juvenile who is put in pre-trial detention must have an advocate appointed immediately (see § 68 No. 4 JJA), whereas in criminal cases for adults this right is realised only after having suffered three months of pre-trial detention. Furthermore, there are restrictions for imposing pre-trial detention on juveniles, particularly for 14 and 15 year-old offenders (see § 72 (2) JJA). Residential care in a juvenile home should always be given priority to pretrial detention. The reality, however, sometimes indicates that the legal preconditions are not always complied with. Therefore the criticism of inappropriate forms of pre-trial detention cannot be refuted.

Another problematic issue is the appeal against juvenile court decisions. A court decision cannot be appealed solely in order to receive another educational measure (see § 55 (1) JJA). This seems to be problematic in cases where the judge imposes a rather 'severe' educational measure, such as several hundreds of hours of community service. Unlike in other countries, in Germany the community service order is not limited by a maximum period (in Austria for example it is limited to 80 hours, in other countries 120–240 hours). Thus, in individual cases, a violation of the principle of proportionality has been observed.

Another critical issue concerning the system of judicial review in juvenile justice is that the juvenile can only appeal once, either to the district court (*'Landgericht'*) in order to get a second hearing, or to the high court of a federal state (*'Oberlandesgericht'*) for a review of legal questions (see § 55 (2) JJA). This shortening of review procedures has been introduced in order to speed up trials and to enforce the educational approach of juvenile justice. However, from a legal and human rights perspective this puts juveniles at a disadvantage compared to their adult counterparts. On the other hand, juveniles profit from the exclusion of a joint procedure by the victim or their representative counsel ('*Nebenklage*') and of the so-called private criminal procedure ('*Privatklage*', i.e. the private charge if the public prosecutor refuses prosecution in the public interest), both of which are disallowed in the juvenile justice system (see § 80 (1), (3) JJA).

A few (practically unimportant) rules disadvantage juveniles for the sake of educational concepts. For example, the period of pre-trial detention— according to the discretion of the judge—will not be taken into account if the remaining period of a juvenile prison sentence is less than six months and therefore estimated as being insufficient for the educational process of reintegration (see § 52a JJA).

In general one can say that the orientation of the German juvenile criminal procedure towards preserving fundamental rights is quite well developed and that disadvantages as compared to adults are restricted to more exceptional cases. Thus the German juvenile justice system does not share the shortcomings of welfare systems that rely more on informal procedures (e.g. round tables, family conferences etc.) than on formal legal rights.

TRENDS IN JUVENILE DELINQUENCY, PARTICULARLY OF VIOLENT OFFENCES

In Germany no longitudinal studies of victimisation and delinquency on the basis of representative surveys exist, unlike in the USA or some European countries. Police and court-based data are, besides the well-known shortcomings, problematic as the counting methods were changed in the 1970s and 1980s. Thus, more or less comparable data is at our disposal only from 1984 onwards. These indicate that juvenile delinquency was stable or even slightly decreased in the 1980s up until 1989, and then increased until the mid-1990s. From then on, a rather stable rate of young offenders, and of violent offenders in particular, can be seen when looking at the rates of convicted offenders (see Figures 8.1–8.3).[6] Police data indicate, however, a stabilisation only for robbery offenders, whereas serious and bodily injury after 1993 was still increasing for juveniles and young adults. A particular increase can be observed in the five new federal states of the former East Germany (Brandenburg, Mecklenburg-Western Pomerania, Thuringia, Saxony, and Saxony-Anhalt). The rates for certain offences, particularly

---

[6] For a comprehensive overview of the development of juvenile crime in Germany see Bundesministerium des Inneren and Bundesministerium der Justiz 2001; for a similar development in other European countries see Estrada 1999; 2001.

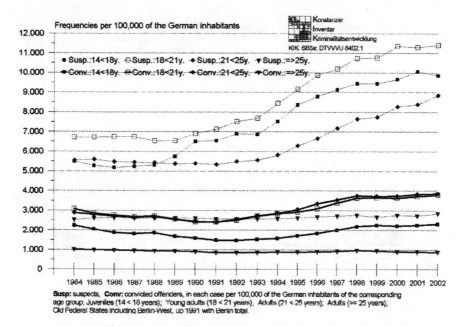

Figure 8.1: Male German suspects and convicted offenders by age group, 1984–2002. All offences (without traffic offences)).

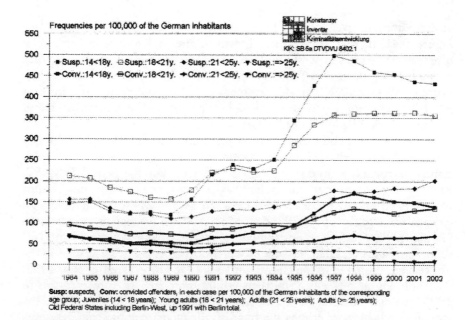

Figure 8.2: Male German suspects and convicted offenders by age group, 1984–2002. Robbery (§§ 249–56, 316a PC).

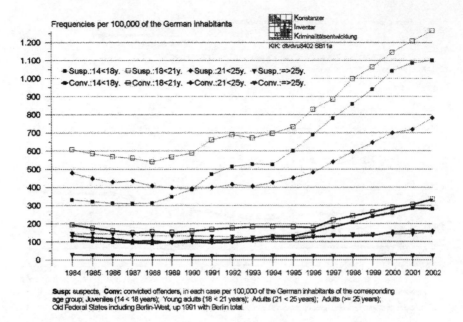

Figure 8.3: Male German suspects and convicted offenders by age group, 1984–2002. Serious and dangerous bodily injury.

violent offences, even exceeded the ratio of the western federal states (see Figure 8.4). In the last 8 years, however, the violent and other young offender crime rates in West and East Germany have grown closer together because of an increase in West Germany and a stabilisation or even reduction in East Germany. This development could be interpreted as a kind of normalisation after a period of particular problems of social transition and anomie or 'normlessness' in East Germany.

Young migrants and members of ethnic minorities have become a major problem for the criminal justice system in Germany. They are overrepresented, particularly concerning violent offences. For the period 1984–97, 83% of the increase in the police registered juvenile and young adult offenders crime rate (persons aged between 14 and 21) was due to foreign citizens (see Pfeiffer *et al* 1998, 48). Most of these foreigners were born in Germany. The Turkish minority plays a specific role in this problem. Self-report studies reveal that the rate of violent offenders is twice as high in the Turkish as compared to the German juvenile age group (Pfeiffer *et al* 1998, 81). Looking at different groups of ethnic minorities or foreigners up to 1993, asylum seekers played a predominant role, which explains the increase in the general crime rate, but also the increase in pre-trial detainees and sentenced prisoners. This problem disappeared after a change of immigration legislation in 1993 reduced the influx of immigrants considerably.

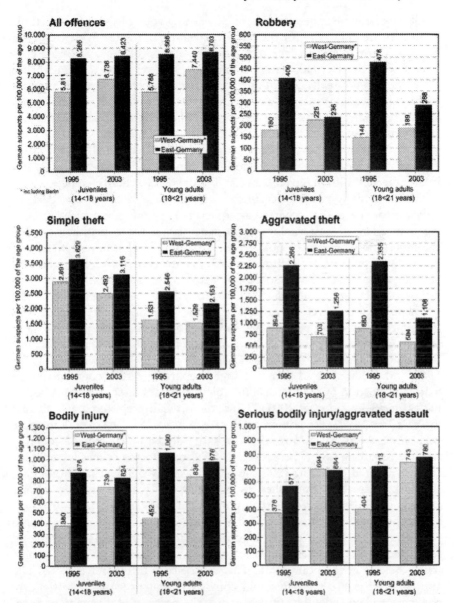

Figure 8.4: Suspected juveniles and young adults per 100,000 of the age group in East and West Germany, 1995 and 2003.

A specific problem has emerged with the so-called '*Aussiedler*', usually people from the former Soviet Union with a German passport, who have severe problems integrating because of language deficiencies and other problems. Often they are sentenced for serious violent crimes and build a rather explosive prison subculture (see Dünkel 2005, Dünkel/Walter 2005).

All the phenomena described here concerning young migrants and ethnic minorities are only valid for the old federal states of former West Germany. The East German *Länder* face very different crime problems. These are connected with the German native population. As very few foreigners live there, they do not really contribute to the crime problem. However, they are worthy of particular interest as they are overrepresented as victims of violent crimes, particularly committed by xenophobic or right wing extremists (see Dünkel/Geng/Kunkat 2001; Dünkel/Geng 2003). However, right wing extremist and xenophobic attitudes as well as self reported violent crime since 1998 in East Germany have declined, too (see Wilmers *et al* 2002, 101 ff; Sturzbecher 2001; Dünkel/Geng 2003; all with further references).

There are many possible reasons for the increase in crime, and particularly violent crime, that occurred after German re-unification and the opening of borders in Eastern Europe in general and the concomitant social changes. One of the most popular explanations is Heitmeyer's theory of social disintegration (see Heitmeyer 1992; Heitmeyer *et al* 1996). The East German development can also be connected with the increase in opportunity structures and a lack of social control at the beginning of the 1990s, when police forces were re-established. One general argument to explain the violent crime increase in the 1990s is a changed sensibility to and reporting rate of violent crimes. One of the very few longitudinal victimisation studies, conducted by Schwind *et al* in the city of Bochum in 1975, 1986 and 1998, showed that a changed reporting rate accounted for the major proportion of the increase in violent offences (assault/serious bodily injury; see Schwind *et al* 2001). Thus, the officially registered assault rate increased by 128%; the non-reported rate only by 9%. The overall increase was only 24% from 1975 to 1998. What really had changed considerably was the reporting rate: whereas in 1975 7.2 unreported crimes were added to one reported crime, in 1998 the ratio was only 3.4:1. That means that the dark figure had diminished by half and the 'real' increase in violent crime is much less impressive than police data would suggest.

Another important statement is that the development of police registered crime rates is not on a par with court-based crime rates. The increase in sentenced young offenders is much less important than one would presume when looking at the police data. This can be seen in Figures 8.1–8.3. The gap between police registered and convicted (sentenced) young offenders has increased considerably. One reason is the practice of diversion by juvenile court prosecutors and judges (see below), which is partly the result of an increase particularly in petty property offences. There are, however, indications that reported violent offences are too often not very serious crimes and are therefore available for mediation and diversion as well (see Pfeiffer *et al* 1998). For instance, in Hannover during the 1990s, apparently, robberies causing very minor damage (of less than 15 Euros) have increased.

Table 8.1: Changes in police registered and non-registered violent crimes (assault) in Bochum 1975–98

	1975	1998	Changes: 1998 compared to 1975
Police registered offences	865	1,976	<u>+ 128%</u>
Non-reported offences	6,214	6,772	+ 9%
Police registered *and* non-reported offences	7,079	8,748	<u>+ 24%</u>
Ratio of reported to non-reported offences	1 : 7.2	1 : 3.4	

Source: Schwind *et al* 2001, 140.

Although violent crime rates, particularly robbery and (serious) bodily injury, increased in the early 1990s, it is still true that the vast majority of juveniles and young adults are not violent offenders. Non-violent property offences constitute about 70% of all crimes reported for young offenders (see Bundesministerium des Inneren/Bundesministerium der Justiz 2001; Walter 2001: 201 ff; H-J. Albrecht 2002, D 32). The victims of such crimes are often the peers of young offenders. Victims of violent adult offenders are also very often children or young persons (see for example the crimes of sexual child abuse or child maltreatment). Considering domestic violence, the First Periodic Security Report ('*Erster Periodischer Sicherheitsbericht*') of the German government states: 'Young persons deserve attention and the protection of society not so much as perpetrators than as victims of violent crimes' (Bundesministerium des Inneren/Bundesministerium der Justiz 2001, 2).

Violent and other crime is not equally distributed over the different regions. It is more widespread in cities than in rural areas and the official crime rates indicate an elevated prevalence rate in the northern compared to the southern federal states of Germany (on the differences between East and West Germany see Figure 8.4 above). Whether these differences are 'real' or the product of different reporting and selection strategies is not clear. Looking at the different federal states, an interesting observation is that the relatively high police registered general crime rates for juveniles and young adults in the northern and north-eastern states such as Bremen, Berlin, Hamburg, Schleswig-Holstein, Mecklenburg-Western Pomerania and Brandenburg, as compared with those of southern states like Bavaria and Baden-Württemberg, diminish if we take the ratio of court-sentenced young persons (always calculated per 100,000 of the age group). The ratio of sentenced young offenders in the southern states is even higher than in the abovementioned northern states (see Figures 8.5 and 8.6). This is a result not only of different reporting rates, but of very distinct and different styles of diversion, as will be amplified below.

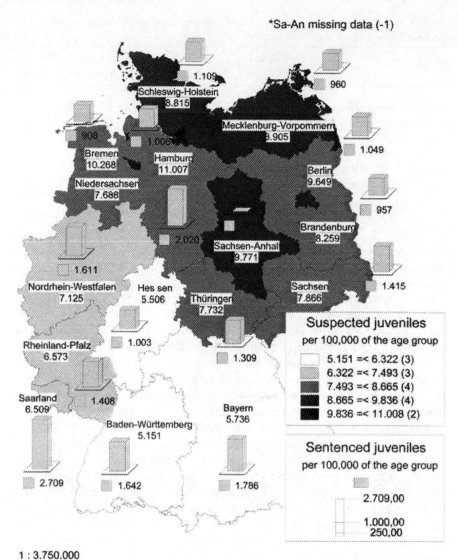

Figure 8.5: Suspected and sentenced German juveniles in a comparison of the federal states in 2003.

SENTENCING PRACTICE IN THE GERMAN JUVENILE JUSTICE SYSTEM (DIVERSION AND JUVENILE COURT DISPOSITIONS IN PRACTICE)

Diversion became the principal reaction utilised in the 1980s in juvenile justice in West Germany. In this context it has to be stressed that police registered juvenile crimes during the 1980s had been quite stable; even violent crimes

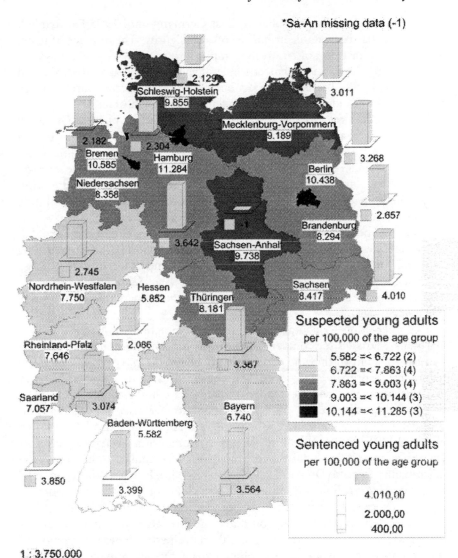

Figure 8.6: Suspected and sentenced 18–21 year old German young adults in a comparison of the federal states in 2003.

had diminished (see Heinz 2001a). The extension of diversion continued in the 1990s when official crime rates, particularly for violent offences, increased (see above). There was a real increase in crime after the opening of the borders in Eastern Europe and the occurrence of the phenomena of anomie and social disintegration in the youth subcultures in West Germany, but particularly in the East German federal states. The rate of young violent offenders registered by the police in East Germany until 1995 had tripled; since then it has been stable or has decreased slightly.[7] The practice of using diversion as a measure of controlling input into the juvenile justice system can clearly be shown in the Eastern federal states as well as in the so-called 'city-states': Berlin, Bremen and Hamburg. The elevated crime rates in these states have been reduced by a more extensive diversion practice.

Before the law reform, the discharge rates (diversion) in West Germany had already increased from 43% in 1980 to 56% in 1989. This increased steadily to 69% in 2003 (see Heinz 1994; 2003; Heinz in Dünkel/van Kalmthout/Schüler-Springorum 1997, and Figure 8.7). It should be stressed that in particular the increase concerned diversion without intervention (according to § 45 (1) JJA), whereas the proportion of diversion combined with educational measures remained stable (see Figure 8.7).

However, the large regional disparities had not been eliminated. The discharge rates varied in 2003 between 61% in Bavaria, 85% in Bremen and 84% in Hamburg. Apparently in all the federal states of Germany discharge rates in cities are higher than in the rural areas (see Heinz 1994; 1998/99). This contributes to the rather stable conviction rates and case-loads of juvenile court judges.

It is interesting to compare the diversion practices of East and West Germany. Statistics for comparison have only recently become available. It had been presumed that the penal culture in East Germany would be more severe and repressive. However, first calculations of diversion rates gave evidence of an even wider extended diversion rate in the new federal states, with an overall rate of 77% (Mecklenburg-Western Pomerania and Brandenburg as much as 82% and 81%; see Figures 8.8 and 8.9; see also Heinz 2003). In Mecklenburg-Western Pomerania statistical data is available from 2001. Its diversion rate of 82% is similar to the other new federal states (see also Dünkel/Scheel/Schäpler 2003). Here too, the 'economic' strategy of controlling the input and workload of the juvenile courts is evident. There is, however, another explanation that seems to be plausible. The expanded diversion rates could also be a reaction to different reporting behaviour. In East Germany possibly more petty offences are reported to the police, which are later excluded from further prosecution by the juvenile court prosecutors.

The strategy of expanding informal sanctions has proved to be an effective means, not only to limit the juvenile court's workload, but also with respect to special prevention. The reconviction rates of those first-time offenders who were 'diverted' instead of formally sanctioned were significantly lower. The re-offending rates were 27% : 36% (see Figure 8.10 and Heinz

---

[7] From 1995 onward one can observe a (slightly) diminishing juvenile crime rate in East Germany and an increasing rate in West Germany (also concerning violent offences), which results in a 'convergent' situation in both parts of Germany; see Heinz 2003 and Figure 8.4 above.

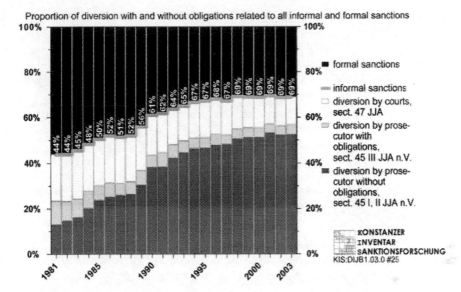

Figure 8.7: Diversion rates (dismissals by prosecutors or courts) in the juvenile justice system of Germany, old federal states, 1981–2003.

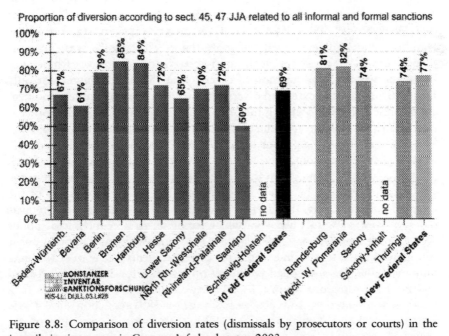

Figure 8.8: Comparison of diversion rates (dismissals by prosecutors or courts) in the juvenile justice system in Germany's federal states, 2003.

132   *Frieder Dünkel*

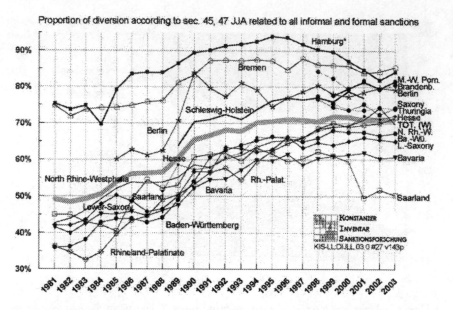

Figure 8.9: Comparison of diversion rates (dismissals by prosecutors or courts) in the juvenile justice system in Germany's federal states, 1981–2003.

1994; 2003; Dünkel 2003, 94). Even for repeat offenders the re-offending rates after informal sanctions were not higher than after formal sanctions (see Heinz/Storz 1992). The overall recidivism rates in states such as Hamburg with a diversion rate of more than 80% or 90% was the same (about 25%) as in states such as Baden-Württemberg or Rhineland-Palatinate where the proportion of diversion at that time counted for only about 40%. Thus the extended diversionary practice has had at least no negative consequences concerning the crime rate and general or special prevention. It also reflects the episodic and petty nature of juvenile delinquency.

At the same time, the proportion of 'formal' sanctions diminished to only 31% of all cases that could have entered the system at the juvenile court level. Interestingly, major changes in the juvenile court's sentencing practice in the 1980s and 1990s can be observed (see Figure 8.11). The proportion of the sanction of sentencing to short-term custody in a detention centre was reduced from 11% to only 6% (which amounts to a reduction of about 45%!) in the West German federal states. Unconditional youth imprisonment (six months up to five or, in exceptional cases, ten years; see above) accounts only for 1.5%; the suspended youth prison sentence for 3.5% of all formal and informal sanctions against 14–21 year-old offenders. The reduction in youth prison sentences from 8% to 5% means a 38% reduction since 1981. This is remarkable insofar as in the 1990s the proportion of youth prison sentences remained stable, although the number of violent offenders

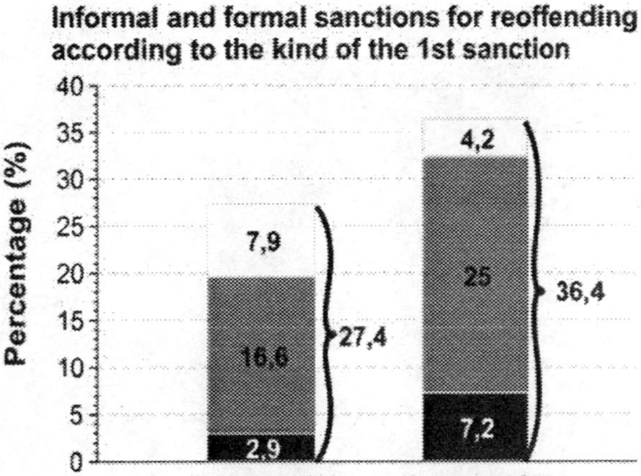

Informal and formal sanctions for reoffending according to the kind of the 1st sanction

Decisions after reoffending:	1st sanction informal	1st sanction formal
informal only (diversion)	7,9%	4,2%
reconviction without imprisonment	16,6%	25,0%
imprisonment	2,9%	7,2%
total reconviction rate	19,5%	32,2%
total	27,4%	36,4%

Figure 8.10: Rates of formal and informal sanctions after a first sanction for larceny and a risk period of 3 years (juveniles, cohort 1961).

increased considerably. The reduction in community sanctions by the court from 36% to 20% is attributable to the extended diversion practice.

About 70% of youth prison sentences are suspended (combined with the supervision of a probation officer). Since the mid-1970s, prison sentences of up to one year are suspended in about 80% of cases. Even the longer prison sentences of up to two years are now suspended in about 60% of cases, whereas in the mid-1970s this occurred only in exceptional cases (fewer than 20%). The extended practice of probation and suspended sentences (even for repeat offenders) has been a great success, as the revocation rates dropped to only about 30%. The probation service has apparently improved its efficiency, but on the other hand, the courts also have changed their practice by trying to avoid a revocation of the suspended sentence for as long as possible (see Dünkel 2003, 96 ff). Again it becomes clear that German juvenile court judges follow the internationally recognised principle of youth imprisonment as a last resort (*ultima ratio*) and for periods as short as possible (the minimum intervention approach).

The average length of youth prison sentences has slightly increased insofar as the proportion of sentences up to one year has decreased, the proportion of sentences of one to two years has increased. However, this has been 'compensated' by an extended rate of suspended sentences (see below). The proportion of youth prison sentences of more than two or more than three

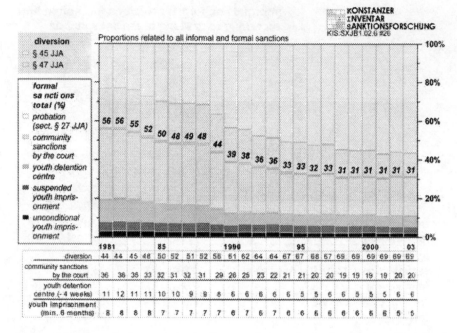

Figure 8.11: Sanctioning practice in Germany's juvenile justice system, old federal states, 1981–2003.

years remained stable (see Figure 8.12).

The practice of repeatedly suspending youth prison sentences of between one and two years had already preceded the reform of 1990 to a great extent by the suspension of not less than 54% of such sentences in 1990 (the ratio in 2003 went up to as much as 59%). The expansion of alternatives to youth imprisonment to young adults, who are more involved in crime than juveniles, particularly in respect of crimes such as robbery, contributed to the considerable decline, by about 40%, in the rate of imprisonment of juveniles and young adults between 1983 and 1990. This decline can be attributed to only a limited extent (5%) to demographic changes. Since 1990, however, youth prisoner rates have increased considerably. But, as can be shown by Figures 8.13 and 8.14, for crimes of robbery and assault this is not a result of more severe punishment by way of longer prison sentences, it is due simply to an increase in the absolute figures of sentenced persons.

89% of 'youth' prisoners in Germany are young adults between 18 and 25 years of age, whereas only 11% of the total population of 7,455 youth prisoners (31 March 2002) are 14 to 18 years old (see Dünkel 2003a).

We do not know much about court sentencing practice in East German federal states, as statistical data was until recently unavailable. A doctoral dissertation at Greifswald concerning the three states Brandenburg, Saxony

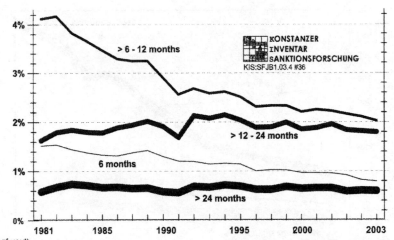

Rate of youth
prison sentences 7,8 8,2 7,9 7,5 7,2 7,2 7,2 7,4 6,7 6,0 6,7 6,5 6,6 6,4 5,8 5,9 6,0 5,7 5,8 5,8 5,5 5,4 5,2

= proportion of youth prison sentences related to all formally and informally sentenced juveniles and youn adults

Figure 8.12: Length of youth prison sentences under juvenile criminal law, 1981–2003.

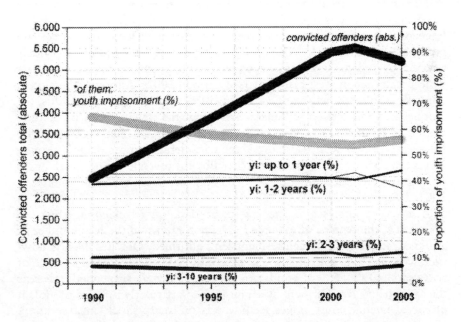

Figure 8.13: Length of youth prison sentences under juvenile criminal law, 1990–2003, Robbery.

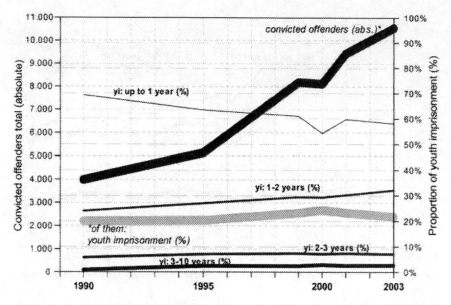

Figure 8.14: Length of youth prison sentences under juvenile criminal law, 1990–2003, Serious and dangerous bodily injury.

and Thuringia showed that (contrary to the presumption of some scholars) sentencing practice is not more repressive in the East. There are some differences in sentencing certain crimes, and particularly violent crimes are punished more severely. The youth detention centre option is widely rejected by judges, whereas suspended youth prison sentences are more widespread than in West Germany (see Kröplin 2002). Although the violent crime rates differed between East and West Germany in the mid-1990s, the number of youth prison sentences was about the same, as can be demonstrated by Figure 8.15 which itemises robbery offences. The main disparity between East and West Germany is the considerably lower risk of a young suspect in East Germany being sentenced by the juvenile court, which again reflects the extended practice of diversion (see Dünkel/Drenkhahn/Geng 2001; Kröplin 2002).

In a recent analysis of the statistical data on Mecklenburg-Western Pomerania, the pattern of extended diversion rates and the low number of sentences to a detention centre has been confirmed. One peculiarity, however, was the lower rate of suspending youth prison sentences (up to one or two years). Only 55% of youth prison sentences were suspended, whereas the average in West Germany is about 80%. Particularly in cases of violent offences, juvenile court judges seem to rely on 'sharp shock' incarceration. On the other hand, the study showed that 'new' community sanctions, such as social training courses, were given to 15% of all formally sanctioned

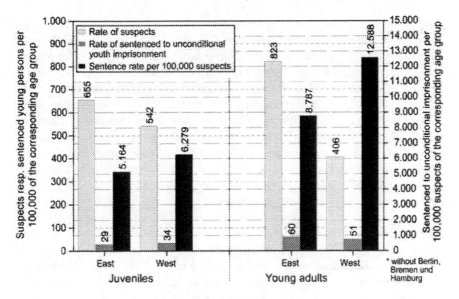

Figure 8.15: Comparison of juveniles and young adults suspected and sentenced to unconditional youth imprisonment for robbery offences in East- and West- Germany*, 1997.

young offenders (10% of young adults, 20% of juveniles; see Dünkel/Scheel/Schäpler 2003). One-third (36%) of all formally and informally sanctioned offenders received a community service order (16% of young adults and almost 80% of juveniles!). Mediation, making up about 8% (the same ratio for juveniles as for young adults), ranged far behind. However, like the care order (11%, 8% for young adults, 18% for juveniles), it is apparently not only an alibi for a 'repressive' sentencing practice, but an integrated part of a juvenile justice system that greatly relies on the educational ideal.

YOUNG ADULTS (18–21 YEARS OLD) UNDER THE JURISDICTION OF THE JUVENILE COURTS (§ 105 JJA)

In Germany, since the reform law of 1953, all young adults are transferred to the jurisdiction of juvenile courts. Comparing practices internationally, this decision is remarkable, because it points the way to extending the scope of juvenile courts for young adults between the ages of 18 and 21. So, for example, in 2000 Spain introduced regulations for young adults that are very similar to those of Germany. In 2001 Austria and Lithuania also introduced a flexible system for dealing with young adult offenders, and the option to choose an appropriate sanction from either the juvenile or the adult criminal law, when dealing with the aspect of the personality and maturity of the offender. Other countries, such the Netherlands and the former Yugoslavia, have long provided for the possibility of avoiding sentences according to the general penal law and instead impose sanctions according to juvenile law (see Dünkel 2002a). But, if in these latter cases the application of educational measures remained the absolute exception, the developments in Germany have gone in the opposite direction. Undoubtedly a major reason is that the reform of 1953 created the jurisdiction of the juvenile court for all young adult offenders independently of whether sanctions under the JJA or under the general Penal Law (StGB) were to be applied (see § 108 (2) JJA).

Section 105 (1) No. 1 of that law provides for the application of juvenile law if '*a global examination of the offender's personality and of his social environment indicates that at the time of committing the crime the young adult in his moral and psychological development was like a juvenile*'. In other words, he should be punished according to the JJA ('*Reifeentwicklung*').

Furthermore, juvenile law must be applied if it appears that the motives and the circumstances of the offence are those of a typical juvenile crime ('*Jugendverfehlung*', see § 105 (1) No. 2 JJA). In 1965 only 38% of young adults were sentenced under the terms of the Juvenile Justice Act, but by 1990 this proportion had nearly doubled to 64%. In 1995 the ratio decreased slightly to 60%, but then increased again to 64.5% in 2003 (see also Dünkel 2002a; these data refer to the 'old' West German federal states). This makes it clear that the full integration of young adults into the juvenile justice system has been accepted in practice. The regulations mentioned above have also been interpreted very widely by the courts to provide for the application of juvenile law in all cases where there were doubts about the maturity of the young offender (see BGHSt 12, 116; BGH *Strafverteidiger* 1989, 311; Eisenberg 2004, notes 7 ff to § 105). The Supreme Federal Court ('*Bundesgerichtshof*', BGH) held that a young adult has the maturity of a juvenile if '*elements demonstrate that a considerable development of the personality is still to be seen*' ('*Entwicklungskräfte noch in größerem Umfang wirksam sind*', BGHSt 12, 116; 36, 38. This is the case with the majority of young adult offenders. Thus the court does not rely on an imagined (prototype of) juvenile, but on aspects of each individual's personal development. There is no doubt that these arguments also hold for a further extension of the juvenile court's jurisdiction, for example for 21–24 year-old adults (see below). The interpretation of a 'typical juvenile crime', which is extensively used, follows a similar logic.[8]

---

[8] The examples mentioned in the cases are crimes committed in groups or under the influence of a group, as well as hooliganism, and sometimes very violent crimes that have derived from a specific situation (possibly in combination with alcohol abuse) etc.; see Eisenberg 2004, notes 34 ff to § 105.

However, in practice there are considerable regional differences with respect to specific crimes and different regions. For most serious crimes such as murder, rape and robbery, nearly all (more than 90%) young adult offenders are sentenced in terms of the (in these cases, milder) juvenile law (see Figure 8.16). The reason for this is that the higher minimum and maximum sentences provided by the 'ordinary' criminal law138 do not apply in the juvenile law (see § 18 (1) JGG). Juvenile court judges, therefore, are not bound by the otherwise obligatory life sentence for murder or the minimum of five years' imprisonment in the case of armed robbery. The German practice seems to be contrary to the so-called waiver decisions of the U.S.A., where the most serious young offenders are transferred to the 'ordinary' criminal justice system (see Stump 2003).

Only in the case of traffic offences are the majority of young adult offenders (in 2003: 57%) in Germany sentenced in terms of the criminal law for adults, because in these cases there is the procedural possibility of imposing fines without an oral hearing ('*Strafbefehl*', which is excluded from the juvenile penal law).

There are constitutional reservations about the regional inequalities that have emerged in practice. In North Rhine-Westphalia, for example, convictions in terms of the juvenile law according to research conducted in the 1980s ranged between 27% and 91% of all convicted juveniles (see Pfeiffer 1988, 96). When the (old) federal states are compared, the range in 2003

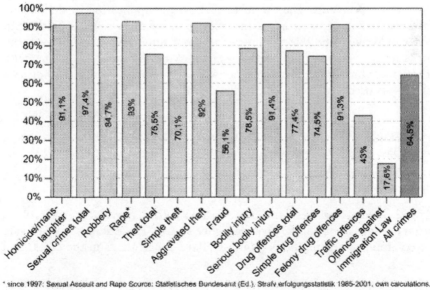

* since 1997: Sexual Assault and Rape Source: Statistisches Bundesamt (Ed.). Strafverfolgungsstatistik 1985-2001, own calculations.

Figure 8.16: Proportion of young adult offenders sentenced under juvenile criminal law (§ 105 JJA) according to different crimes, 2003, old federal states.

was from 48% in Baden-Württemberg, 49% in Rhineland-Palatinate to 86% in Hamburg and 91% in Schleswig-Holstein. Apparently juvenile court judges have different conceptions of the 'typical' personality of juvenile offenders and of the 'typical' nature of juvenile delinquency. Overall, there is a north-south divide, with the federal states in the north increasingly applying juvenile criminal law, whereas in the south juvenile court judges rely to a greater extent on the criminal law for adults. As to the new federal states, again a shortage of available data must be admitted. From individual studies we know that in 1998 the proportion of young adults sentenced according to the JJA was only 30% in Brandenburg and 34% in Saxony, but 60% in Thuringia (East-German average: 38%; West-German average: 59%, see Heinz 2001, 79 ff). In Mecklenburg-Western Pomerania the proportion in 2001 was 55%, in 2003 56% (see Dünkel/Scheel/Schäpler 2003 and Table 8.2). The low rates in Brandenburg and Saxony are not due to the 'distrust' of juvenile court judges towards the JJA, but are the result of a specific bureaucratic routine in the application of the '*Strafbefehlsverfahren*', a summary procedure with only a written file in cases of less severe offences.

In this context two discourses can be differentiated. On the one hand there is the 'rhetoric' debate in the field of criminal policy and the critique of conservative parties of too-lenient sanctioning by applying the sanctions of the JJA instead of the general criminal law.[9] Conservative politicians argue for young adults to be given increased 'responsibility', thereby allowing for the imposition of more severe punishment. On the other hand, practitioners have other problems. They want to eschew the application of the general criminal law in order to avoid the imposition of more severe punishment, but would like to be able to impose fines in a summary procedure (without an oral hearing), which up to now is not provided by the JJA ('*Strafbefehl*'). This procedure is very economical and time-efficient and—as indicated above—is used particularly for traffic offenders (drunk driving etc.).

REFORMS SINCE THE 1970S IN WEST GERMANY: INNOVATION FROM THE GRASSROOTS OF THE JUVENILE JUSTICE SYSTEM— THE NEW COMMUNITY SANCTIONS (MEDIATION, COMMUNITY SERVICE, SOCIAL TRAINING COURSES, CARE ORDER)

As indicated earlier, Germany experienced a reform movement that evolved from the 'grassroots' of the juvenile justice system. Practitioners from private or community organisations (youth welfare departments in the cities) and

---

[9] These arguments do not consider that in fact sometimes the application of sanctions of the JJA may be a disadvantage rather than a benefit, as can be shown by the fact that in the juvenile justice system the minimum prison sentence is six months, in the general criminal law only one month; for some empirical evidence of disadvantages in sentencing see Dünkel 1990; Pfeiffer 1991.

Table 8.2: Proportion of young adults (18–21 years old) sentenced according to the JJA (§ 105 JJA)

Federal states	Proportion of young sentenced according to adults the JJA (*all crimes*)			Proportion of young adults sentenced according to the JJA (*traffic offences*)		
	1998*	2001	2003	1997**	2001	2003
Baden-Württemberg	43%	47.9%	47.9%	20%	17.3%	19.2%
Bavaria	55%	60.5%	64.8%	35%	36.7%	39.3%
Berlin	57%	52.8%	54.4%	30%	45.5%	36.3%
Bremen	62%	70.8%	78.2%	61%	71.8%	77.8%
Hamburg	92%	83.2%	86.4%	95%	80.6%	82.3%
Hessen	71%	74.4%	77.2%	67%	64.8%	69.7%
Lower Saxony	71%	69.6%	71.9%	61%	56.9%	60.0%
Northrhine-Westfalia	63%	65.7%	69.4%	45%	47.9%	52.5%
Rhenania-Palatinate	47%	51.4%	49.2%	19%	20.2%	19.5%
Saarland	84%	87.4%	84.1%	77%	81.7%	68.9%
Schleswig-Holstein	89%	90.0%	91.2%	93%	87.8%	89.6%
Old federal states total	59%	62.3%	64.5%	38.8%	40.5%	43.0%
Brandenburg	30%	no inf.	no inf.	23%	no inf.	no inf.
Mecklenburg-Western Pomerania (2003)	no inf.	55%	56%	No inf.	41%	37%
Saxony	34%	no inf.	no inf.	12%	no inf.	no inf.
Thuringia	60%	no inf.	no inf.	44%	no inf.	no inf.
New federal states (1998 resp. 1997 without Saxony-Anhalt and Mecklenburg-Western Pomerania)	38%	no inf.	no inf.	21%	no inf.	no inf.

Sources: * Heinz 2001; ** Kröplin 2002; Strafverfolgungsstatistik 2001, 2003; Strafverfolgungsstatistik Mecklenburg-Western Pommerania 2001, 2003, own calculations.

juvenile court prosecutors and judges developed so-called new community sanctions (see for one of the first so-called 'Brücke'-initiatives Pfeiffer 1983) from 1974 when it became evident that legislative reforms would not be achieved in the near future. These projects were established close to the juvenile courts at the community level, very often by the communal welfare boards, but were then transferred to private organisations. This is a peculiarity of the juvenile welfare system that gives priority to privately run projects (principle of subsidiarity of state versus privately run organisations, see § 4 (2) JWA). The idea in the 1970s and 1980s was to establish appropriate and educational alternatives to the traditional, more repressive sanctions, such as short-term incarceration in a detention centre ('*Jugendarrest*', see above). The first 'new' community sanction to be implemented was the community service order. It was followed or accompanied by the special educational care order. This care order means that a social worker is attached to a juvenile offender, rather like a mentor, for a period of usually 6 to 12 months. It is seen as an alternative to the classic probation sanction where a probation officer sometimes has 70 or more cases. The care order amounts to more intensive oversight, as a social worker will have no more than 10 to 15 cases. It is evident that the care order can be much more efficient in providing help and social integrative services than a suspended prison sentence with supervision by a probation officer.

Since the beginning of the 1980s another 'new' community sanction has been developed: the social training course. This is a group-centred educational measure that targets both leisure-time problems and day-to-day living problems. Its aim is to improve social competence and the skills required in private and professional life. Social training courses are organised as regular meetings once or twice a week, often in combination with intensive weekend arrangements (sometimes sporting activities and 'adventure' experiences such as sailing, mountain climbing, etc.), usually for a period of up to six months (see Dünkel/Geng/Kirstein 1998).

The first mediation projects began in the mid-1980s (see Dünkel 1999, 108). At the beginning of the 1990s, 60% of the youth welfare departments reported that a mediation project had already been established. In 1995 a national poll revealed a total of 368 mediation projects, which is a 68% increase since 1992 (see Wandrey/Weitekmap in Dölling *et al* 1998). However, the authors reported that the majority of mediation schemes run on an 'ad hoc basis' to cater for individual cases and not as a priority measure within the ambit of educational measures provided by the JJA (see Wandrey/Weitekmap in Dölling *et al* 1998, 130 ff).

With the reform law of 1990 the legislator recognised the development of 'new community sanctions' by creating legal provision for their further and wider application. Mediation, in particular, in the draft bill was mentioned as 'the most promising alternative to the more repressive traditional sanctions'.[10]

The current JJA in Germany offers many opportunities for arranging mediation or damage restitution. Juvenile court prosecutors may waive prosecution if reformatory measures have already been implemented or introduced (§ 45 (2) JJA). The 1990 reform Act explicitly equates mediation with such a reformatory measure. Significantly, the legislator already recognises sincere efforts by juveniles to resolve conflicts or to provide restitution. This arrangement protects juvenile and young adult offenders if the victim of the crime refuses to co-operate. Successful damage restitution more frequently

10 The legal justification referred to the favourable experiences with assorted pilot projects launched since 1985, which increase consideration for the victim's special circumstances and 'settle the conflict between the offender and the victim that results from the criminal act more appropriately and more successfully ... than traditional sanctions have done in the past'; see *Bundesratsdrucksache*, No. 464/89, 44.

leads to a dismissal because of 'reduced culpability' (pursuant to § 45 (1) JJA; similar to § 153 of the Criminal Procedure Act in adult criminal law). Under the same conditions that apply to juvenile court prosecutors, juvenile court judges may waive prosecution to enable subsequent consideration of mediation efforts by the young offenders. Material loss restitution, as well as mediation as an independent sanction of the juvenile court, is a peculiarity associated with German juvenile law (see §§ 15, 10 JJA). The juvenile justice system, furthermore, provides for damage restitution in conjunction with a suspended term of detention in a remand home or imprisonment (the same applies for release on probation; for a summary see Dünkel 1999).

Providing mediation as a court sanction in juvenile justice (see § 10 (1) No. 7 JJA) was rightly criticised for violating the voluntary principle of mediation efforts. In practice, mediation as a juvenile court educational directive is almost never used (see Rössner/Klaus in Dölling *et al* 1998, 115), because suitable cases are dealt with in informal proceedings (diversion in the sense of § 45 (2) JJA, see above) prior to a court trial and therefore do not enter the level of formal court proceedings.

All of the above demonstrates that elements of restorative justice at different levels have been implemented in the German juvenile justice system.[11]

The juvenile law reform of 1990 somehow acted like a 'booster detonation' for the further extension of new community sanctions. In a nationwide poll conducted by the Department of Criminology at Greifswald we looked at the periods two years before and two years after the law came into force (1 December 1990). There was a 23% increase in the number of projects before and even a 60% increase after the statutory amendment in the case of mediation, which amounts to a relation of 1:2.6 (see Table 8.3). Considerable further increases can also be observed for the care order and for social training courses, but in absolute terms not for the community

Table 8.3: Increase in projects of 'new community sanctions' (offered by private or public organisations) in the old federal states before and after the amendment of the JJA in 1990

Educative measure	Increase *before* the law amendment (1 December 1990)	Increase *after* the law amendment (1 December 1990)	Relation
Mediation	23%	60%	1 : 2.6
Care order	17%	37%	1 : 2.2
Social training course	16%	30%	1 : 1.9
Community service	2%	5%	1 : 2.5

[11] After the juvenile justice legislation of 1990, the legislator also passed reforms of the general penal law and the Criminal Procedure Act (StPO) which included some innovation with emphasising mediation (see § 46a Criminal Law (StGB) of 1994 and §§ 155a, 155b Criminal Procedure Act; see also Dünkel 1999, 110).

service order. This is, however, due to the fact that before 1990 almost all youth welfare departments already ran community service schemes and therefore scope for a further increase was rather limited.

THE IMPLEMENTATION OF NEW COMMUNITY SANCTIONS IN EAST GERMANY AFTER RE-UNIFICATION IN 1990

The main aim of the nationwide Greifswald study on new community sanctions was to obtain empirical data about the establishment of these sanctions in the federal states, particularly in East Germany in the general context of implementing the JJA in the former GDR. The process of social transition proceeded very quickly in terms of legal reforms. The JJA came into force simultaneously with re-unification in October 1990, shortly before the amendment of the law in all of Germany. The poll was conducted in 1994 and 1995 and included a questionnaire sent to all community welfare departments, private organisations running mediation and other community sanction schemes and to juvenile court judges (see Dünkel/Geng/Kirstein 1998). The question was to what extent the new federal states had been able to implement the structure of juvenile welfare as compared to the established infrastructure in West Germany.

The results were astonishing as, a mere four years after re-unification, East German *Länder* had not only reached equivalent structures and quality of juvenile welfare, but had even overtaken the 'old' federal states (see Table 8.4).

This development continued in the five years that followed, as can be demonstrated by several further studies, particularly in the field of mediation (see Steffens 1999; Schwerin-Witkowski 2003). The German federal government sponsored and promoted many projects that focused on specific violent offender groups, such as right-wing extremist skin-heads. At present the police authorities estimate that there are about 10,000 right-wing, vio-

Table 8.4: 'New' educational community sanctions (offered by private or state organisations) in the old and new federal states of Germany in 1994

	Youth welfare departments	Social training course		Mediation		Care order		Community service	
	n	n	%	n	%	n	%	N	%
Old federal states (FRG)	479	350	73.1	336	70.1	408	85.2	461	96.2
New federal states (former GDR)	127	96	75.6	112	88.2	119	93.7	127	100
Total Germany	606	446	73.6	448	73.9	527	87.0	588	97.0

lence-prone skin-heads etc. in the whole of Germany. About half of them live in East Germany, although the East German population accounts only for 20% of the total German population (for an overview of right-wing extremism in Germany and particularly the East-German federal states see Dünkel/Geng 1999, 2003; Dünkel/Geng/Kunkat 2001). The overrepresentation of right-wing extremists in East Germany is a very striking phenomenon and can no doubt partly be explained by the specific problems generated by the economic situation (the unemployment rate is double that of West Germany), the lack of professional and personal perspectives, particularly in young people, and also the authoritarian style of rearing families in East Germany.

In consequence of the specific East German problems the youth welfare authorities face a tough workload. Nevertheless, the infrastructure and the number of social workers today is comparable to that of West Germany. In the old federal states youth welfare authorities and the juvenile justice system in general face different problems, particularly with young migrants and young drug addicts, which are not (yet) prevailing problems in the eastern part of Germany. The 'classic' drug in the Eastern *Länder* is alcohol. The illegal drug market has only recently increased there, too, although there is no real hard drugs scene yet (heroine, cocaine).

Community sanctions have made progress in the East, too. However, it is mainly the community service order that has gained major importance in the practice of juvenile justice. Table 8.3 shows that the other community sanctions, which are more educational and 'constructive' than community service or other traditional sanctions, have made little progress. Consequently, half of the community youth departments stated that they had no more than eight young offenders participating in mediation per year. In 50% of the cases in youth departments no more than eight young persons in West Germany and seven young persons in East Germany were under special educational care, and the number of participants at social training courses was 18 and 11, respectively. On the other hand, 80 and 78 community service orders were counted in 50% of the youth departments (see Table 8.5). The total number of young offenders sentenced to community service was six to eight times as much as that for the other educational sanctions mentioned in Table 8.5.

ACTUAL TENDENCIES IN JUVENILE CRIMINAL POLICY—BETWEEN TOLERANCE AND REPRESSION

The actual tendencies in juvenile criminal policy are ambivalent. Conservative parties demand a lowering of the age of criminal responsibility from 14 to 12, since the registered crime rate of children has increased (an argument that is not convincing as most of the increase is attributable

Table 8.5: Number of participants at educational measures of youth welfare departments, 1993

	Mediation			Care order			Social training course			Community service		
	25%* n =	50%** n =	75%*** n =	25% n =	50% n =	75% n =	25% n =	50% n =	75% n =	25% n =	50% n =	75% n =
Old federal states												
Participants at the measure	4*	8**	20**	4	8	16	9	18	32	41	80	152
Departments of youth welfare, n =		210			263			200			233	
Total participants, n =		3.346			3.758			4.926			28.130	
New federal states												
Participants at the measure	3	8	20	3	7	20	7	11	19	43	78	124
Departments of youth welfare, n =		107			99			47			106	
Total participants, n =		1.836			1.933			815			9.985	

* This means: 25% of the departments had X clients in the specific measure
** This means: 50% of the departments had X clients in the specific measure (= Median)
*** This means: 75% of the departments had X clients in the specific measure

to petty non-violent offences). Furthermore, they urge that the widely extended practice of sentencing young adults according to the JJA should be removed in order to impose harsher punishments on this age group and that the application of the JJA should be the exception and not the rule. The simple but enticing argument is that young adults have many responsibilities in civil law and therefore should be responsible like adults in penal matters, too. These arguments totally neglect the psychological and pedagogic foundation of the JJA. Today the development of personality and integration into the lives of adults takes even longer. Therefore, German juvenile criminologists and most of the practitioners in juvenile justice urge for the retention of the current age limits for young adults and even for going further in extending the application of the JJA to young adults, without any exception (for arguments of comparative law see Dünkel 2002a), and to include even 21–24 year-old adults in certain cases where the sanctions of the JJA seem to be more appropriate (see Deutsche Vereinigung für Jugendgerichte und Jugendgerichtshilfen 2002). Indeed, in Europe the age limits are not yet harmonised. On the one hand, in some countries the tendency to lower the age of criminal responsibility has been actualised, to as low as ten years, as in England and Wales (similar tendencies can be observed in the Netherlands); on the other hand the Scandinavian countries have retained their moderate approach with 15 as the age of criminal responsibility. It will be difficult to harmonise the different approaches in Europe, and perhaps it is not even desirable if one looks at the influence of the English 'get tough' policy. However, the majority of countries, particularly the Baltic and Central and Eastern European countries, have more or less developed a consensus about age limits of 14, 18 and 21 years (see the introductory chapter in this volume). So, in conclusion, it seems to be desirable that Germany maintains its juvenile crime policy and even extends the application of the JJA to young adults without exception.

A major reform debate took place in September 2002 when the German *Juristentag* (a biannual meeting of German lawyers) discussed the issue 'Is the German juvenile justice system up to date?'. The principal expert opinion was presented by Hans-Jörg Albrecht, director of the Max Planck Institute for Foreign and International Penal Law at Freiburg. His main proposal was to abolish the idea of education, but nevertheless to keep a separate juvenile justice system with proportionate (and with respect to adult offenders milder) sanctions (see Albrecht 2002). Concerning the abolition of the '*leitmotiv*' of education his ideas have been rejected by almost everyone in the German lawyers' assembly, as well as by juvenile criminologists and penal lawyers (see e.g. Dünkel 2002, Streng 2002, Walter 2002). Some of Albrecht's concrete proposals, however, corresponded with proposals of the Deutsche Vereinigung für Jugendgerichte und Jugendgerichtshilfen, an organisation of juvenile court judges, prosecutors, social workers active in juvenile justice and welfare, and criminologists. This organisation has influenced the reform debate of the last 30 years quite considerably. The DVJJ wants to keep the idea of education in the sense of special prevention and also to extend the scope of constructive solutions, like mediation and other community sanctions. In this context a 'reconstruction' of the system of community sanctions is being advocated as well as the restriction (limitation) of youth prison sentences (abolishing the possibility of imposing a prison sentence because of 'dangerous tendencies') and of pre-trial detention. They urge for young adults generally to be included in the JJA, for an extension of the maximum penalty from 10 to 15 years (in cases where a life sentence would be imposed for adults), and for a form of a summary written procedure to be introduced for this age group in order to deal with minor traffic or property offences (see Deutsche Vereinigung für Jugendgerichte und Jugendgerichtshilfen 2002 and the recommendations of the Deutsche Juristentag 2002: see www.djt.de).

Although the government of the social-democratic and the Green parties in Germany should not be tempted to follow a 'populist' and 'hysterical' criminal policy, it remains uncertain whether reform bills, including a reduction in penal severity, will pass through parliament successfully. Feelings of insecurity are exploited by most political parties (except the Green party) and right-wing populist parties in some state parliaments, as in Hamburg, have campaigned successfully during elections with law and order paroles. The role of the mass media is very important in this context. The German social-democratic party is sometimes badly influenced by the more repressive ideas of criminal policy of the British Labour Party. On the other hand, the 'culture of education' of those working in juvenile justice is strongly engendered in Germany by permanent further education of practitioners organised by the Deutsche Vereinigung für Jugendgerichte und Jugendgerichtshilfen and other organisations.

It was the honourable Franz von Liszt who, shortly after 1900, stated that a good social policy would be the best criminal policy. The idea of crime prevention has been developed more and more in the past 20 years in Germany. Successful projects have been established, e.g. to prevent violent or xenophobic crimes, in quite a few cities and communities (see e.g. Dünkel/Geng 2003). This development does not detract from the need for reforms of the juvenile justice system, but it points the way to dealing with the causes of crime. Juvenile justice can play only a marginal role in this regard and cannot solve general societal problems (such as poverty, unemployment and discrimination).

REFERENCES

Albrecht, H-J. (2002) *Ist das deutsche Jugendstrafrecht noch verfassungs-gemäß? Gutachten für den 64. Deutschen Juristentag.* (Munich, C.H. Beck).

Bannenberg, B. (1993) *Wiedergutmachung in der Strafrechtspraxis.* (Bonn, Forum-Verlag).

Bundesministerium des Inneren, Bundesministerium der Justiz (2001) *Erster Periodischer Sicherheitsbericht.* (Berlin, BMI/BMJ) (published also under **www.BMI.de/Berichte**)

Bundesministerium der Justiz (1989) (ed.) *Jugendstrafrechtsreform durch die Praxis.* (Bonn, Ministry of Justice).

Deutsche Vereinigung für Jugendgerichte und Jugendgerichtshilfen, 2. Jugendstrafrechtsreformkommission (2002) Vorschläge für eine Reform des Jugendstrafrechts. Abschlussbericht. *DVJJ-Journal Extra* No. 5 (see also *DVJJ-Journal*, vol. 13: 228–276).

Dölling, D. *et al* (1998) *Täter-Opfer-Ausgleich in Deutschland. Bestandsaufnahme und Perspektiven.* (Bonn, Forum Verlag).

Dünkel, F. (1990) *Freiheitsentzug für junge Rechtsbrecher. Situation und Reform von Jugendstrafe, Jugendstrafvollzug, Jugendarrest und Untersuchungshaft in der Bundesrepublik Deutschland und im interna-tionalen Vergleich.* (Bonn, Forum Verlag).

—— (1994) Les orientations actuelles de politique criminelle. In F. Dünkel *et al, Jeunes délinquants et jeunes en danger en milieu ouvert: utopie ou réalité? Cadres légaux et nouvelles pratiques – approche comparative.* (Toulouse, Erès, 41–78).

—— (1996) Täter-Opfer-Ausgleich. German experiences with mediation in a European perspective. *European Journal on Criminal Policy and Research*, vol. 4, 44–66.

—— (1999) La justice réparatrice en Allemagne. *Criminologie* vol. 32, 107–32.

—— (2002) Jugendstrafrecht—Streit um die Reform. Anmerkungen zum Gutachten von H-J. Albrecht zum 64. Deutschen Juristentag 2002. *Neue Kriminalpolitik*, vol. 14, 90–3.

—— (2002a) Heranwachsende im Jugendstrafrecht—Erfahrungen in Deutschland und aktuelle Entwicklungen im internationalen Vergleich. In R. Moos *et al* (eds.), *Festschrift für Udo Jesionek.* (Wien, Graz, Neuer Wissenschaftlicher Verlag, 51–66).

—— (2003) Entwicklungen der Jugendkriminalität und des Jugendstrafrechts in Europa—ein Vergleich. In F. Riklin (ed.), *Jugendliche, die uns Angst machen. Was bringt das Jugendstrafrecht?* (Luzern, Caritas-Verlag, 50–124).

150   *Frieder Dünkel*

—— (2003a) Situation und Reform des Jugendstrafvollzugs in Deutschland. *Recht der Jugend und des Bildungswesens* 51, 318–34.

—— (2005) Migration and ethnic minorities: impacts on the phenomenon of youth crime. The situation in Germany. In N. Queloz *et al* (eds.), *Youth Crime and Juvenile Justice. The challenge of migration and ethnic diversity.* (Bern, Staempfli, 45–71).

Dünkel, F., Drenkhahn, K., Geng, B. (2001) Aktuelle Entwicklungen der Sanktionspraxis und des Strafvollzugs in Ost- und Westdeutschland. In V. Bieschke and R. Egg (eds.), *Strafvollzug im Wandel: Neue Wege in Ost- und Westdeutschland.* (Wiesbaden, Kriminologische Zentralstelle, 39–81).

Dünkel, F., Geng, B. (1999) *Rechtsextremismus und Fremdenfeindlichkeit. Bestandsaufnahme und Interventionsstrategien.* (Mönchengladbach, Forum Verlag Godesberg).

—— (2003) (eds.) *Jugendgewalt und Kriminalprävention. Empirische Befunde zu Gewalterfahrungen von Jugendlichen in Greifswald und Usedom/Vorpommern und ihre Auswirkungen für die kommunale Kriminalprävention.* (Mönchengladbach, Forum Verlag Godesberg).

Dünkel, F., Geng, B., Kirstein, W. (1998) Soziale Trainingskurse und andere neue ambulante Maßnahmen nach dem JGG in Deutschland. (Mönchengladbach, Forum Verlag).

Dünkel, F., Geng, B., Kunkat, A. (2001) Einstellungen und Orientierungen zu Rechtsextremismus, Fremdenfeindlichkeit und Gewalt in Mecklenburg-Vorpommern. Internet-Publication www.uni-greifswald.de/~ls3/Veröffentlichungen, 1–71.

Dünkel, F., Lang, S. (2002) Jugendstrafvollzug in den neuen und alten Bundesländern: Vergleich einiger statistischer Strukturdaten und aktuelle Entwicklungen in den neuen Bundesländern. In M. Bereswill, T. Höynck (eds.), *Jugendstrafvollzug in Deutschland. Grundlagen, Konzepte, Handlungsfelder.* (Mönchengladbach, Forum-Verlag, 20–56).

Dünkel, F., Scheel, J., Schäpler, P. (2003) Jugendkriminalität und die Sanktionspraxis im Jugendstrafrecht in Mecklenburg-Vorpommern. *Zeitschrift für Jugendkriminalrecht und Jugendhilfe,* vol. 14, 119–32.

Dünkel, F., van Kalmthout, A., Schüler-Springorum, H. (1997) (eds.) *Entwicklungstendenzen und Reformstrategien im Jugendstrafrecht im europäischen Vergleich.* (Mönchengladbach, Forum Verlag Godesberg).

Dünkel, F., Walter, J. (2005) Young foreigners and members of ethnic minorities in German youth prisons. In N. Queloz *et al* (eds.), *Youth Crime and Juvenile Justice. The challenge of migration and ethnic diversity.* (Bern, Staempfli, 517–40).

Eisenberg, U. (2004) *Jugendgerichtsgesetz.* 10th edn (Munich, Beck).

Estrada, F. (1999) Juvenile Crime Trends in Post-War Europe. *European Journal on Criminal Policy and Research,* vol. 7, 23–42.

—— (2001) Juvenile Violence as Social Problem. *British Journal of Criminology* 41, 639–55.

Heinz, W. (1994) Flucht ins Prozeßrecht? Verfahrensrechtliche Entkriminalisierung (Diversion) im Jugendstrafrecht: Zielsetzungen, Implementation und Evaluation. *Neue Kriminalpolitik*, vol. 6, No. 1, 29–36.

—— (1998/99) Diversion im Jugendstrafrecht und im allgemeinen Strafrecht. Teil 1, *DVJJ-Journal*, vol. 9, 245–57; Teil 2, *DVJJ-Journal*, vol. 10, 11–19; Teil 3, *DVJJ-Journal*, vol. 10, 131–48; Teil 4, *DVJJ-Journal*, vol. 10: 261–7.

—— (2001) Die jugendstrafrechtliche Sanktionierungspraxis im Ländervergleich. In D. Dölling (ed.), *Das Jugendstrafrecht an der Wende zum 21. Jahrhundert*. (Berlin, New York, Walter de Gruyter, 63–97).

—— (2001a) Jugendkriminalität in Deutschland. Internet publication: www.uni-konstanz.de/rtf/kik

—— (2003) Das strafrechtliche Sanktionensystem und die Sanktionierungspraxis in Deutschland 1882–1999. Internet publication: www.uni-konstanz.de/rtf/kis Version 6/2003

Heinz, W., Storz, R. (1992) *Diversion im Jugendstrafverfahren der Bundesrepublik Deutschland*. (Bonn, Bundesministerium der Justiz).

Heitmeyer, W. (1992) Soziale Desintegration und Gewalt—Lebenswelten und Perspektiven von Jugendlichen. *DVJJ-Journal*, vol. 3: 76–84.

Heitmeyer, W. *et al* (1996) *Gewalt: Schattenseiten der Individualisierung bei Jugendlichen aus unterschiedlichen sozialen Milieus*. 2nd edn (Munich, Juventa).

Kröplin, M. (2002) *Die Sanktionspraxis im Jugendstrafrecht in Deutschland im Jahr 1997—ein Bundesländervergleich*. (Mönchengladbach, Forum Verlag).

Pfeiffer, C. (1983) *Kriminalprävention im Jugendgerichtsverfahren*. (Cologne, Heymanns).

—— (1988) *Jugendkriminalität und jugendstrafrechtliche Praxis—eine vergleichende Analyse zu Entwicklungstendenzen und regionalen Unterschieden*. Expertise zum 8. Jugendbericht.(Hannover, Kriminologisches Forschungsinstitut Niedersachsenz).

—— (1991) Wird nach Jugendstrafrecht härter gestraft? *Strafverteidiger*, vol. 11, 363–70.

Pfeiffer, C. *et al* (1998):*Ausgrenzung, Gewalt und Kriminalität im Leben junger Menschen: Kinder und Jugendliche als Täter und Opfer*. Sonderdruck der DVJJ zum 24. deutschen Jugendgerichtstag (Special print of Deutsche Vereinigung für Jugendgerichte und Jugendgerichtshilfen e. V., DVJJ). (Hannover, DVJJ).

Schaffstein, F., Beulke, W. (2002) *Jugendstrafrecht*. 14th edn (Stuttgart, Berlin, Cologne, Kohlhammer).

Schwerin-Witkowski, K. (2003) *Entwicklung der ambulanten Maßnahmen nach dem JGG in Mecklenburg-Vorpommern*. (Mönchengladbach, Forum Verlag Godesberg).

Schwind, H-D. *et al* (2001) *Kriminalitätsphänomene im Langzeitvergleich am Beispiel einer deutschen Großstadt. Bochum 1975–1986–1998.* (Neuwied, Kriftel, Luchterhand).

Sonnen, B-R. (2002) Juristische Voraussetzungen des Umgangs mit Kinderdelinquenz. *DVJJ-Journal*, vol. 13, 326–31.

Steffens, R. (1999) *Wiedergutmachung und Täter-Opfer-Ausgleich im Jugend- und Erwachsenenstrafrecht in den neuen Bundesländern.* (Mönchengladbach, Forum-Verlag).

Streng, F. (2002) Referat zum 64. Deutschen Juristentag. In Ständige Deputation des Deutschen Juristentages (ed.), *Verhandlungen des vierundsechzigsten Deutschen Juristentages.* Vol. II/1 (Munich, C.H. Beck, N 69–N 108).

Stump, B. (2003) ,Adult time for adult crime'—Jugendliche zwischen Jugend- und Erwachsenenstrafrecht. Eine rechtshistorische und rechtsvergleichende Untersuchung zur Sanktionierung junger Straftäter. (Mönchengladbach, Forum Verlag Godesberg).

Sturzbecher, D. (2001) *Jugendtrends in Ostdeutschland: Lebenssituationen und Delinquenz.* (Opladen, Leske und Buderich).

United Nations (1991) *The United Nations and Crime Prevention.* (New York, United Nations).

Walter, M. (2001) *Jugendkriminalität.* 2nd edn (Stuttgart, Richard Boorberg Verlag).

—— (2002) Das Jugendkriminalrecht in der öffentlichen Diskussion: Fortentwicklung oder Kursänderung zum Erwachsenenstrafrecht? *Goltdammer's Archiv für Strafrecht*, vol. 149, 431–54.

Wilmers, N. et al (2002) Jugendliche in Deutschland zur Jahrtausendwende: Gefährlich oder gefährdet? (Baden-Baden, Nomos Verlag).

Wolff, J. (1986) Die Geschichte der Gesetzgebung im Jugendstrafrecht. *Zeitschrift für Rechtssoziologie*, vol. 7, 123–42.

—— (1989) Spurensuche. *Neue Kriminalpolitik*, vol. 1, No. 1, 26–30.

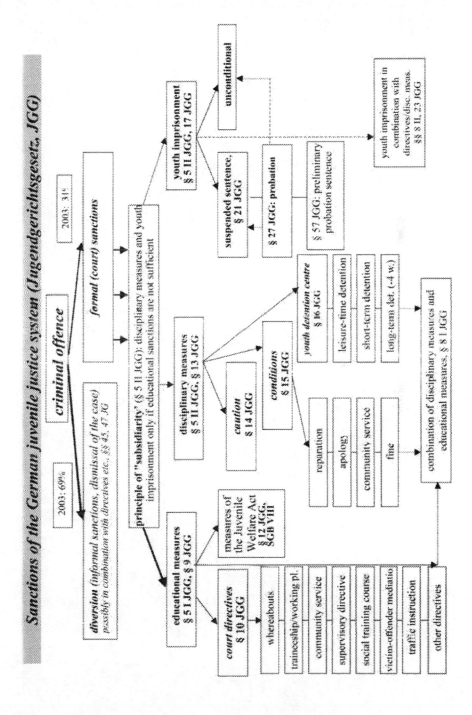

Sanctions of the German juvenile justice system (Jugendgerichtsgesetz, JGG)

criminal offence

2003: 69%

diversion (informal sanctions, dismissal of the case)
possibly in combination with directives etc., §§ 45, 47 JG

2003: 31%

formal (court) sanctions

principle of "subsidiarity' (§ 5 II JGG): disciplinary measures and youth imprisonment only if educational sanctions are not sufficient

youth imprisonment
§ 5 II JGG, 17 JGG

unconditional

suspended sentence,
§ 21 JGG

§ 27 JGG: probation

§ 57 JGG: preliminary probation sentence

youth imprisonment in combination with directives/disc. meas. §§ 8 II, 23 JGG

disciplinary measures
§ 5 II JGG, § 13 JGG

caution
§ 14 JGG

conditions
§ 15 JGG

youth detention centre
§ 16 JGG

leisure-time detention

short-term detention

long-term det. (-4 w.)

reparation

apology

community service

fine

combination of disciplinary measures and educational measures, § 8 I JGG

educational measures
§ 5 I JGG, § 9 JGG

measures of the Juvenile Welfare Act § 12 JGG, SGB VIII

court directives
§ 10 JGG

whereabouts

traineeship/working pl.

community service

supervisory directive

social training course

victim-offender mediatio

traffic instruction

other directives

9

The Juvenile Justice System in Poland

KRZYSZTOF KRAJEWSKI

INTRODUCTION

I
N POLAND, RESPONSIBILITY for juvenile offenders, as well as the measures that may be imposed upon juveniles showing other signs of social
maladjustment, are regulated independently of the adult criminal law.
Provisions regarding these issues are contained in the Proceedings in Cases
of Juveniles Act of 26 October 1982 ('Juveniles Act'). Despite its title, this
act regulates not only procedural aspects of juvenile justice but also most
issues of substantive law. After 1989 (i.e. the fall of the communist regime)
it was amended twice, namely in 1995 and in 2000, but these amendments
were not of a substantive nature. They both introduced certain important
modifications but the model of the juvenile justice system and basic regulations remained unchanged. This means that in Poland the area of juvenile
justice, as opposed to the 'adult' criminal justice system, is still regulated by
legislation dating back to the communist period.[1] Moreover, it may be
worth noting that this particular piece of legislation was adopted in the
autumn of 1982 (i.e. less than one year after martial law introduced by the
communist authorities crushed independent trade unions, and hopes for
reform and liberalization of the system had to be abandoned). As a matter
of fact, in the autumn of 1982 martial law was still in force, many activists
of the opposition were still held in internment camps, and communist
authorities were busy introducing various extraordinary measures contained in martial law decrees into 'regular' criminal law. In other words, in
general this period cannot be evaluated positively from the point of view of
its contribution to the development of criminal law in Poland (Wasek and
Frankowski 1995).

---

[1] Old criminal codes from 1969 (i.e. adopted under the communist regime), although substantially amended, remained in force until 1998. On 1 September of that year they were substituted by the completely new Criminal Code, the Code of Criminal Procedure and the Code
on Execution of Penalties adopted by Sejm (the Diet) in April 1997.

Interestingly enough, this does not necessarily apply to the Juveniles Act. Despite some controversial solutions and provisions which will be discussed later, it constituted quite a modern piece of legislation and did not differ substantially from models existing in many countries of Western Europe. The main proof that this act may be evaluated quite positively is that after only minor amendments, it has served over the last 15 years in democratic Poland. There was, of course, always some talk of the necessity of preparing a new juvenile regulation, but this was not considered to be an immediate task. Moreover, postulates and proposals voiced in this area indicate that the eventual new law may not necessarily bring real improvements and progress into the area of juvenile justice.[2]

Prior to the passing of the 1982 Juveniles Act, most issues of the juvenile law and juvenile responsibility were regulated by the provisions of Arts. 474–95 of the 1928 Code of Criminal Procedure, and Arts. 69–78 of the 1932 Criminal Code. The 1932 Polish Criminal Code, considered at that time to be one of the most modern pieces of penal legislation in Europe, remained under significant influence of the sociological school in penal law and positivist thinking in criminology. Because of this it adopted an approach based predominantly on the welfare model of juvenile law, and not a justice model of it (Beaulieu and Cesaroni 1999). As a consequence, juveniles under 17 were not assumed to be capable of forming criminal intent and thus of bearing criminal responsibility. Thus, priority has been given to special rehabilitative measures, not punishment, and to a separate system of procedure in cases of juveniles, as well as to the establishment of juvenile courts. From this point of view Poland was only following certain patterns established earlier in many countries of North America (Bernard 1992; Trépanier 1999b) and Europe (Christiaens 1999; Oberwittler 1999; Weijers 1999b), and all this despite the fact that traditions of welfare state and welfare based criminal policy were never very strong there.

In the period after World War II, communist authorities in principle followed this pattern. Moreover, a welfare approach to juvenile delinquency was even reinforced during the 1980s. During the drafting of the new Criminal Codes in the 1960s it was decided to take cases of juveniles completely out of the Criminal Code and the Code of Criminal Procedure, and to prepare a separate piece of legislation regarding these issues. Although it took years to prepare this legislation,[3] the Juveniles Act of 1982 continues

---

[2] At the end of 2003 the Ministry of Justice finally decided to call a committee of experts and entrust it with the task of preparing a draft of the new juvenile law. The work of this committee is currently at a very preliminary stage, and it is difficult to predict whether Poland will follow its own tradition and the example of the recent very liberal Czech juvenile legislation (Válková 2001), or make a switch towards a more punitive approach. Nevertheless, it is certain that the draft of a new law will not be ready soon.

with the 'child welfare' approach of the previous legislation.[4] It is based on the assumption that persons below a certain age, because of their mental development, shall not and cannot be held responsible for their wrongful acts in the same way as adults. This excludes first of all retributive purposes of punishment which may be acceptable in the case of adults. Moreover, it is assumed that possibilities of changing youthful law violators, or rehabilitating them, are, because of their young age, much better than is the case with older persons. This is due to the fact that their personalities are usually not fully developed and are more malleable. Because of this they may be more susceptible to measures of treatment and rehabilitation.

As a consequence, Polish legal language uses different terminology with respect to adult and juvenile lawbreakers. An offence may be only committed by an adult, and only adults may be held criminally responsible and punished in the strict meaning of the word. If a juvenile commits an act defined in the Criminal Code as an offence, it is referred to merely as a punishable act (*czyn karalny*), and not as an offence (*przestepstwo*). It is assumed that juveniles' culpability is different from that of adults, as juvenile acts lack *mens rea* in principle. It does not mean that juveniles are not held responsible for their wrongdoings in any way. They are, but according to different rules from adults.

Moreover, in juvenile cases courts do not impose punishments, as juvenile law contains a separate system of various measures aimed primarily at the treatment and rehabilitation of juvenile lawbreakers. This is stated clearly in Art. 3 § 1 of the Juveniles Act, which says that 'in cases of juveniles the guiding principle shall be the juvenile's welfare, and considerations aimed at achieving positive changes in his/her personality and behaviour, as well as encouraging and supporting proper fulfilment of their duties by the juvenile's parents or custodians'. This is completely different, exclusively rehabilitation oriented language compared with Art. 53 § 1 of the Criminal Code of 1997, which contains the main sentencing guidelines in cases of adults. This provision explicitly mentions both retributive purposes (punishment shall not exceed perpetrator's guilt, and be related to the harm done by the offence), as well as preventive and rehabilitative purposes of punishment. It refers also to the necessary influence of punishment on the law-abiding attitudes of the public, or what is commonly referred to as 'positive general prevention' (as opposed to general deterrence).

---

[3] The pre-war criminal codes went out of force in 'socialist' Poland not earlier than 1 January 1970. However, it took 12 more years to prepare and pass the new, separate juvenile legislation. Because of this, earlier mentioned provisions of the old codes regarding matters of juveniles remained in force until 12 May 1983 (i.e. until the entry into force of the Juveniles Act).

[4] For a general overview of the contemporary juvenile justice system in Poland see: Habzda (1992), Marek (1992), Stando-Kawecka (1995), Czarnecka-Dzialuk (2000), as well as Gaberle (2002).

This provision makes it clear that Polish criminal law, like the legal systems of most other European countries, does not treat retribution as an exclusive purpose of punishment, and still pays much attention to the treatment and rehabilitation of offenders. However, in case of juveniles it stresses practically exclusively diagnosis and treatment, and disregards guilt and punishment. Because of this the term 'juvenile penal law', which is used in some other countries (such as Germany), although used colloquially, does not constitute an official term in Polish. The term 'juvenile law' appears in legal terminology, in this way stressing the non-punitive and non-penal character of juvenile responsibility.

GROUNDS FOR APPLICATION OF JUVENILE MEASURES

General remarks

Provisions of the Juveniles Act of 1982 state that intervention in cases of juveniles (Art. 1 § 1), may be based on two different types of grounds. Under this act court intervention is possible first of all in cases of juveniles who show what the law refers to as *signs of demoralization* (*przejawy demoralizacji*), which means social maladjustment in a very broad sense of the term. Second, the law also allows for intervention in cases of *punishable acts* (*czyny karalne*), or what in the case of an adult would constitute an offence. What is interesting, and somewhat complicated, regarding these two grounds for intervention is that they are connected to two separate meanings of the term 'juvenile', or age limits for such court intervention (Górecki and Stachowiak 2002; Gaberle and Korcyl-Wolska 2002).

Signs of demoralization as a ground for intervention

Persons older than 18 years may not be subject to the proceedings instituted on the basis of demoralization. In that case, then, the term 'juvenile' is identical with the concept of a minor under Polish civil law. As a consequence there is no lowest limit whatsoever to judicial intervention in such cases, and even the youngest children may, at least theoretically, be subject to it.

One of the most controversial issues of this type of intervention under current Polish law is that the Juveniles Act of 1982 does not provide for a precise definition of the very term *signs of demoralization* (Korcyl-Wolska 2001). Article 4 of the Juveniles Act contains only some examples of behaviour types or circumstances which typically have to be treated as signs of demoralization. To those belong violation of the principles of community life, commission of a prohibited act, truancy, abuse of alcohol or illegal drugs, prostitution, vagrancy, as well as participation in criminal groups.[5] However, this list is by no means complete, and there may be various grounds for instituting proceedings in cases of demoralization which are not explicitly provided for on this list. In practice, about 30% of interventions due to this ground are based on grounds 'other' than those listed explicitly in Art. 4 (Habzda 1992). The above regulation was intended to provide flexibility and broad discretion in initiating state intervention in families' and youngsters' affairs, according to the classical formula of the 'child savers' ideology (Platt 1977) and the child welfare model of juvenile law. This flexibility and discretion may be considered to constitute an advantage from the point of view of social work. From the point of view of due process guarantees they may give grounds for serious doubts. Article 4 of the Juveniles Act is in certain parts extremely vague, and as such it may even be considered nowadays to be unconstitutional. This regards primarily the first category of Art. 4, or a violation of *the principles of community life*. This category is so broad and vague that it includes practically any-thing.[6] It constitutes no doubt the remnant of the communist rule, when communist authorities wanted to have as broad a 'safety valve' as possible, which could justify intervention in family affairs, also because of political reasons. Because of this it is rather surprising that since 1990 the lawmak-ers have undertaken some other changes in the Juveniles Act, but have not attempted to improve this particular provision of the most controversial section. Of course it must be remembered that this provision is currently construed and applied by the independent judiciary. The situation before 1989 was certainly different as there were various limitations on judicial independence, and various instruments of political influence on judicial decisions existed. Nowadays, with full guarantees of judicial independence the situation has changed substantially. Nevertheless the problem remains as to whether or not too much discretion has been granted here.

Punishable acts as grounds for intervention

The second possible ground for intervention in the case of juveniles is com-mission of what the law refers to as a punishable act. The Juveniles Act provides for various forms of responsibility and reactions which may be

[5] None of the forms of behaviour mentioned in this provision-with the exception of com-mission of a prohibited act-constitutes an offence per se under current Polish law. Because of this demoralization is something much broader than behaviour considered to be criminal. This means that the concept of demoralization under the Juveniles Act constitutes, as a matter of fact, an equivalent of status offences under the American legal tradition.

[6] The principles of community life clause is often used in various provisions of Polish civil law, and in this area it has a relatively clear meaning established by the jurisprudence and judi-cature of the Supreme Court and appellate courts. However, in the area of juvenile law its meaning is much less clear, and because of this its use may be questionable.

considered to constitute an equivalent of the 'adult' criminal law and procedure. Article 1 § 2.2 of the Juveniles Act provides this time a clear-cut definition of what is meant by this term. It means an offence (i.e. under Polish criminal law either a felony or misdemeanor) defined in any piece of legislation (i.e. not only in the Criminal Code), including the so-called fiscal offences (which under Polish law constitute a separate category), plus some selected contraventions[7] listed precisely in that provision. Intervention based on this ground applies to a narrower age group than in cases of demoralization, namely persons between 13 and 17 years. The lower limit of 13 years for juvenile responsibility for punishable acts is set by the Juveniles Act, and means that children under 13 who commit prohibited acts are dealt with exclusively as exhibiting signs of demoralization and treated accordingly. This also means that under current Polish law children under 13 cannot be held responsible for their 'offences' (i.e. actions which formally violate criminal law provisions), even in a quasi-penal sense.

The upper limit of special juvenile responsibility is set both in the Juveniles Act and in the Penal Code, the latter providing several further important regulations here. According to Art. 10 § 1 of the Criminal Code of 1997, criminal responsibility is possible if the perpetrator at the moment of the offence is at least 17 years old. Only such persons are considered under Polish law to be adults for the purposes of penal responsibility. Persons under that age are in general considered to be juveniles. However, the age limit of 17 years is not of an absolute character, as the law provides for some flexibility. Article 10 of the Criminal Code contains two exceptions to the above general rule: in some cases persons younger than 17 may be held responsible according to the rules of the Criminal Code (i.e. as adults). In other cases persons older than 17 may be treated as juveniles. The first exception applies to persons who are younger than 17 but older than 15 at the moment of their lawbreaking. According to Art. 10 § 2 of the Criminal Code, if such a person commits one of the prohibited acts (offences) listed in this provision,[8] waiver of juvenile jurisdiction and transfer of the case to the adult criminal court is possible. In other words, such persons may be tried and punished as adults. However, such waiver is by no means automatic. It must be based on an evaluation of all the relevant circumstances of a given case, including the personal circumstances of the

---

[7] Under the Polish criminal law system all adult prohibited acts are divided into offences and contraventions. Contraventions are defined as minor types of rule violations. They are generally dealt with by fines only, and are decided in a very simplified procedure. Nowadays contravention cases are handled in courts. Under communism special administrative boards had this jurisdiction.

[8] This list includes assassination of the President of the Republic, homicide and manslaughter, causing serious bodily harm with deadly consequences, causing a catastrophe of a serious character, hi-jacking, road accident with fatal consequences, aggravated rape, taking hostages, and robbery.

juvenile in question. The Code also states that the main grounds for such waiver of juvenile court jurisdiction is that juvenile measures were applied earlier without a positive effect (i.e. that the juvenile in question is in fact a 'recidivist'). But, if such a juvenile is tried as an adult, the Criminal Code provides a special sentencing rule, namely that the maximum penalty imposed in such cases shall not exceed two-thirds of the statutory maximum for a given offence. The court may also apply provisions on the extraordinary mitigation of punishment (Art. 60 of the Criminal Code) independently of all other requirements. This may result in imposing a sentence below the statutory minimum.

It may be worth noting that a similar provision was contained in the Criminal Code of 1969. However, the new Code introduced one significant modification that was important from the point of view of due process guarantees. The old Code was less specific about the types of offence which give grounds for the possibility of a juvenile being tried as an adult. It referred only in general terms to certain types of most serious offences; this gave—at least theoretically—prosecutors and juvenile judges more discretion in deciding on that issue. The new Code enumerates specific offences, thus making the use of discretion practically impossible. It must be underlined that in practice this provision is seldom used—no more than in a few cases each year.

The above regulation means that currently for persons under 15 (and above 12) waiver of juvenile jurisdiction is impossible. Such juveniles may never be held responsible for their wrongdoings according to the rules of the adult criminal law. For them responsibility under the Juveniles Act and specific juvenile measures remain the only possibility. It is only 15 to 16 years olds that may be subject to such responsibility, although the rule— applied in most cases—also constitutes special juvenile responsibility here. Since the beginning of the 1990s this regulation has been subject to some public discussion in Poland. Public perceptions of the serious growth of juvenile delinquency, as well as some very brutal and ruthless violent offences committed by juveniles publicized broadly by the media, resulted in demands for the age limit of 15 to be lowered and the possibilities for applying adult criminal law to juveniles to be broadened. As a matter of fact the new Criminal Code had lowered it already—in the Code of 1969 this limit was set at 16 years. For many the lowering of the age limit in 1997 was not enough and demands that it be lowered further to 13 or even 10 years are voiced from time to time, although the chances of such proposals being implemented remain rather small.

It may also be worth noting that there are certain possibilities for juvenile courts to impose penalties, and not only specific juvenile measures. This situation is regulated by Article 13 of the Juveniles Act. According to this article, in cases involving juveniles, who at the moment of adjudication of the case and sentencing are older than 18 years (although they are still treated as juveniles, if they committed their act before reaching 17), the juvenile court may waive juvenile measures if it considers them inappropriate and impose 'regular' punishment. However, in such cases extraordinary mitigation of punishment (i.e. its reduction below the lowest statutory limit) is mandatory.

A possibility of modifying the general age limit of 17 for juveniles in the opposite direction is regulated in Art. 10 § 3 of the Criminal Code. According to this article, persons who are older than 17 (i.e. who are in principle already adults) may be treated as juveniles under certain circumstances, if at the moment of their offence they were not older than 18. This rule applies in cases of misdemeanors, but not felonies. Courts adjudicating such cases may impose measures provided under the Juveniles Act instead of penalties, if the circumstances of the act and personal characteristics of its perpetrator warrant it.

Special Treatment of Adolescents

All of the above means that under Polish law persons 17 years and over—with the above-mentioned minor exceptions—are treated by penal law as adults and are subject to normal criminal responsibility. However, it must be noted that the Criminal Code designates a special category of adult offenders who receive special treatment because of their young age: the group labelled *adolescents* (*mlodociani*). Under Art. 115 § 10 of the Criminal Code, an adolescent is a person who at the moment of an offence was younger than 21 years and at the moment of sentencing younger than 24 years. Adolescents constitute only a subgroup within the category of adult offenders. This means that they are held criminally responsible for their law violations according to the general rules of penal responsibility. However, Art. 54 § 1 of the Criminal Code provides a special sentencing rule or directive which applies exclusively to this category of offenders. Namely, when sentencing such offenders courts shall consider primarily the need to rehabilitate them. Moreover, under Art. 60 § 1 of the Code, courts may always apply with respect to them an extraordinary mitigation of punishment. Additionally, an adolescent who at the moment of the offence was not yet 18 years old may not be sentenced to life imprisonment.[9] This means that while punishing adolescents, courts will always consider first of

---

[9] Life imprisonment constitutes the severest possible sanction under Polish criminal law. The death penalty was abolished in Poland in 1997 by the new Criminal Code, although since 1995 there has been a formal moratorium on executions, which was preceded by an informal one since 1989. The last execution took place under the communist regime in 1988. Even when capital punishment was still in use it was prohibited by the law to sentence persons under 18 to death.

all circumstances relevant from the point of view of individual prevention and rehabilitation, with retribution and general prevention practically set aside as purposes of punishment.

MEASURES IMPOSED IN JUVENILE CASES

As was mentioned earlier, with few exceptions juveniles under 17 years of age are assumed to be incapable of forming criminal intent in Poland. Thus they are not punished for their wrongdoings. For juveniles who show signs of demoralization or commit punishable acts, the law provides a special catalogue of measures intended exclusively for child care and rehabilitation of the lawbreaker. This catalogue is set out in Art. 6 of the 1982 Juveniles Act and contains the following measures:

— caution;
— obligation to behave in a certain way, especially to repair the damage, to offer an apology to the victim, to continue education at school or employment, to refrain from presence in certain milieus or places, to refrain from use of alcohol or drugs;
— responsible supervision by parents or by a custodian;
— supervision by a youth organization or other association, an employer or trusted person, who is obliged to guarantee the juvenile's proper conduct;
— supervision by a probation officer;
— directing the juvenile to a probation centre, a social organization or institution providing care, therapy or training for juveniles, applied with the consent of these institutions or organizations;
— ordering the juvenile to be put in a foster family, in an appropriate child or educational institution or in a training and educational centre;
— ordering the juvenile to undergo appropriate treatment for his/her mental handicap, mental illness, alcohol or drug abuse;
— withdrawal of driving licence;
— forfeiture of the proceeds of a punishable act;
— correctional centre (suspended or not);
— other measures under the Juveniles Act or Family Code.

Although this list of measures provided by Polish juvenile law is not necessarily extremely broad or innovative, it provides for flexible reactions in cases of misbehaving and lawbreaking children, that is, reactions aimed primarily at approaching the root causes of such misbehaviour and lawbreaking located either in the juvenile him/herself or in his/her environment (primarily the family). It must also be mentioned that the law and practice stress up to a certain point imposition of measures aimed at improving the child's performance in its 'natural' family environment. Measures having as a consequence change of this environment should be applied only if there is no other way to react. Because of this, measures provided by the Juveniles Act are usually connected in a more or less obvious way to elements of social work. Even if they impose certain limitations, deprive the juvenile of something etc., this is not intended primarily as a punitive reaction.

Flexibility and the possibility of adapting measures imposed earlier to changing conditions and circumstances constitute the main guiding principle in the execution of juvenile measures. This means first of all broad possibilities of changing earlier imposed child care and educational measures if this is justified by the welfare of a juvenile, as well as the possibility of imposing additional appropriate treatment measures during the execution of care, educational and reformatory measures (Art. 79). This is in accordance with the general rule regarding execution of juvenile measures. As a rule, all these measures have an indeterminate character (i.e. they are imposed in principle for an indefinite period of time). However, care and educational measures consisting of the duty to behave in a certain way, of establishing responsible supervision by parents or custodians, as well as the withdrawal of driving licence, automatically cease when a juvenile comes of age (i.e. when he/she becomes 18 years old) unless the court revokes them earlier. Execution of all other measures, including placement in a correctional centre, ceases automatically when a person is no longer a juvenile for the purpose of the execution of measures (i.e. when he/she becomes 21 years old).[10]

All measures listed in Art. 6 may be imposed both in cases of juveniles showing signs of demoralization, and in cases of juveniles who commit punishable acts. The most severe measure at the disposal of family courts does not fall into this category, namely placing a juvenile in a correctional centre of the borstal type. This measure may be imposed exclusively as a consequence of committing a punishable act. Moreover, it may be imposed only if a juvenile committed an offence or a fiscal offence. It may not be imposed as a consequence of a contravention (see footnote 6). An additional prerequisite for imposing this measure is a serious demoralization of the juvenile, the circumstances and character of his/her act, as well as the fact that earlier juvenile measures proved to be ineffective. These taken together become the grounds for a negative criminological prognosis (Art. 10). Execution of an order to place a juvenile in a correctional centre may be suspended for a probation period of 1 to 3 years. In such a case it is mandatory for the court

---

[10] This means that, apart from two earlier mentioned meanings of the term 'juvenile' (i.e. persons under 18 for the purposes of intervention in cases of demoralization, and persons between 13 and 17 years for the purposes of intervention in cases of punishable acts), the Juveniles Act recognizes a third meaning of this term. For the purpose of the execution of juvenile measures, juveniles are persons under 21 years.

to impose parallel care and educational measures. A decision to suspend such an order must be based on a positive prognosis with respect to the future behaviour of a juvenile (Art. 11).

Placement in a correctional centre is—like other measures under the Juveniles Act—of indeterminate character. It may be executed until a juvenile becomes 21 years old. The family court may also conditionally release (parole) a juvenile from a correctional centre, if the progress of his/her rehabilitation warrants the conclusion that he/she will not break law in the future. Conditional release is possible no earlier than after 6 months spent in a correctional centre. If the court decides to release a juvenile it has to ascertain a probation period of no less than 1 and no more than 3 years, and impose mandatory care and educational measures (Arts. 86, 87). Parole automatically ceases when a person becomes 21 years old.

It should also be mentioned that the Juveniles Act in its Art. 7 provides for some measures which are imposed not against juvenile him/herself, but against other persons, first of all his/her parents or custodians. These measures are:

— obligation of parents or custodians to improve educational, living and health conditions of the juvenile and to co-operate closely with the juvenile's school, educational centre, or employer, as well as his/her doctor or medical centre;
— obligation of parents or custodians to repair in part or in whole the damage done by a juvenile.

If the juvenile's parents do not comply with the above court orders, Art. 8 of the Juveniles Act provides for sanctions for such misbehaviour, beyond those which may eventually be imposed on the basis of the Family Code. The family court may impose a financial sanction in the amount of 50 to 1.500 PLN (currently about €10–350).

THE JUVENILE (FAMILY) COURT SYSTEM

Under the 1982 Juveniles Act, jurisdiction over all types of juvenile cases is placed with special family courts. It is a tradition under the Polish system that despite the child welfare orientation of juvenile law and juvenile interventions, measures provided for under juvenile law are imposed by the judiciary, and not by agencies of some other type. During the 1970s, as several drafts of the Juveniles Act were discussed in various commissions, there was an idea to introduce special juvenile boards of non-judicial character, consisting of specialists of various types involved in child welfare issues. This idea, based on Scandinavian examples, received relatively strong support among some specialists. It was expected that such boards may diminish even further any remaining punitive character of interventions in cases of juveniles and reinforce the welfarist orientation of the entire juvenile law system. However, these ideas were finally rejected, and the existing system of juvenile or family courts having jurisdiction over juvenile cases was retained. Interestingly enough, the main argument against the introduction of such boards of non-judicial character had something to do with the political situation in Poland at that time. There was fear that such boards may be much more susceptible to external influences, including political ones. Courts, although at that time hardly fully independent according to the standards of democratic states, were still better equipped to resist such eventual influences.

Family courts are created on the basis of Art. 18 of the Courts Act by an ordinance of the Minister of Justice. In practice they form special divisions within the county courts (i.e. the lowest courts within the court structure in Poland). In 2001 there were 314 family courts in Poland, with about 900 judges. The idea of such courts came about many years ago, during the 1970s (i.e., again under communism). According to the Courts Act, such courts shall have jurisdiction over all legal issues, both civil and criminal, related to the functioning of the family. This idea is quite similar to the stance once popular in the U.S. that understood 'the clientele of the juvenile court as "families with service needs"' (Weijers 1999a, 32). Because of this Polish family courts had jurisdiction not only over cases of juvenile delinquency, but also over cases resulting from family law matters (including divorce), and criminal cases against adults involving family issues (e.g. non-payment of alimony or subsistence, family violence, etc.). Judges of these courts should have better knowledge about all the problems of a given family. Second, they should have training broader than an exclusively legal one, including some additional knowledge of psychology, sociology, social work, etc. Family courts should also have on their staff specialists in these disciplines. During the 1990s the jurisdiction of family courts was limited, as divorce cases were transferred to provincial (district) courts, and family related adult criminal cases to penal divisions of county courts. Nevertheless, they retained jurisdiction over all juvenile cases under the 1982 Juveniles Act and all family cases under the Family Code, except divorce.

It may be worth noting that despite the very important role of juvenile courts within the Polish system of administration of justice, the position of family judge or juvenile judge is not necessarily very highly regarded. In the opinion of many judges this constitutes a sort of 'dead end' for a judicial career and for further promotion to district courts or appellate courts. The reason for this is that juvenile judges are considered to have very narrow specialisation, as a matter of fact neither in civil nor in penal law, and have experience which is useless from the point of view of the requirements for becoming an appellate judge.

PROCEDURE UNDER THE JUVENILES ACT

General rules of procedure in cases of juveniles

As was mentioned above, according to Art. 2 of the Juveniles Act, actions and interventions possible under this act may be undertaken either if a juvenile shows signs of demoralization, or if he/she commits a punishable act. In both cases imposing juvenile measures may be justified. However, circumstances justifying the imposition of such measures have to be established formally, in a special type of proceeding. Like 'adult' criminal procedure in any continental system, Polish procedure in cases of juveniles also consists of two basic phases. It starts with what Art. 33 of the Juveniles Act refers to as explanatory or investigative proceedings (*postepowanie wyjaśniajace*),[11] which constitutes roughly speaking the equivalent of a formal investigation in 'adult' criminal procedure. Depending on facts and circumstances revealed and established during the investigative phase, a case may be either dismissed or followed by the court phase, constituting an equivalent of the 'adult' trial. This phase may take two different forms, namely care and educational proceedings (*postepowanie opiekuńczo-wychowawcze*), or reformatory proceedings (*postepowanie poprawcze*).

Procedures under the Juveniles Act have several particular features. First, they constitute an unusual mix of rules and provisions of both civil and criminal procedure. The Act itself contains only some of the most basic procedural provisions and regulates only a few issues directly. Otherwise it provides in Art. 20 that in principle provisions of the Code of Civil Procedure on so-called non-litigious matters are applicable in cases of juveniles. Additionally the collecting and recording of evidence, participation of the defence counsel, and reformatory proceedings are subject to the provisions of the Code of Criminal Procedure. Thus, the basic idea underlying proceedings in cases of juveniles is that it should be procedure of a civil type, with criminal procedure applicable only on a supplementary basis. This decision of the Polish legislature not to create specific procedural regulations for juvenile cases, but to apply procedural provisions of other codes, is subject to some criticism in the Polish literature (Korcyl-Wolska 2001, 54–55). It is argued that the provisions of civil procedure are not able to regulate this type of proceeding properly. Moreover, civil procedure in non-litigious cases was created to regulate a completely different type of legal issue, thus it does not suit juvenile cases. Because of this, many practical

---

[11] The exact English equivalent of the Polish term *postepowanie wyjaśniajace* would be 'explanatory proceedings'. As this sounds rather artificial in English the term 'investigative proceeding' will be used here to designate this phrase.

problems were created, including several loopholes which had to be filled—also by the judicature of the Supreme Court—using some complicated legal arguments and interpretation rules. This led again to various doubts from the point of view of due process and other constitutional guarantees.

The investigative phase in cases of juveniles

A second feature of juvenile proceedings in Poland is the crucial role that is played by a family or juvenile judge. This includes the investigative phase which remains primarily in the hands of this judicial agency, having a position similar to the investigating magistrate in some continental criminal procedure systems, otherwise unknown in 'adult' criminal procedure in Poland. As a consequence public prosecutors have a very limited influence on juvenile cases in Poland. There is no special prosecutorial agency for juvenile matters (as there is in Germany). In addition, the role of the police during the investigative phase is—at least theoretically—of a very limited character.

Juvenile judges enjoy broad powers. One of the most important of these is regulated in Art. 21 § 1 of the Juveniles Act: it is the juvenile judge, and not the police or public prosecutor, who has the sole competence to institute formal investigative proceedings. The judge may do this if there is a good reason to suspect that a juvenile shows signs of demoralization or that he/she committed a punishable act. From the point of view of civil rights guarantees for both a juvenile and his/her family, it is important that if a juvenile is merely at risk of demoralization it is not enough to institute juvenile proceedings. According to the prevailing jurisprudence, he/she has to show actual signs of demoralization (Korcyl-Wolska 2001, Gaberle and Korcyl-Wolska 2002). If he/she is endangered only by demoralization, it is a matter for intervention by social welfare agencies and other measures, including judicial measures but under the Family Code regarding child care and custody.

Most importantly, as opposed to the 'adult' criminal procedure, which in Poland is governed strictly by the principle of mandatory prosecution, according to Art. 21 § 2 of the Juveniles Act proceedings in cases of juveniles are governed by the expediency principle, and juvenile judges enjoy broad discretionary powers. The judge may always refuse to institute proceedings or choose to discontinue them, if he/she considers imposing any care and educational or reformatory measures to be improper or unnecessary in a given case. In the latter situation it may also mean diversion of the case to be dealt with appropriately by a juvenile's school, or an organization or association he/she belongs to. In such cases the school or the organization or association to which the case has been transferred has the duty to inform the judge about actions undertaken and their results.

It is also worth mentioning that since the amendment to the Juveniles Act adopted in 2000, additional possibilities of diversion have been introduced. The new Art. 3a of the Juveniles Act provides that at any stage of the proceedings the juvenile judge, while acting on the initiative or with acceptance of both juvenile and victim, may transfer the case to mediation by an institution or a trustworthy person. Results of such mediation efforts shall be presented to the judge by this institution or person and taken into consideration while deciding the case. This provision constitutes a first attempt to introduce elements of restorative justice in a formal way into the Polish legal system. So far, practical experience with this form of deciding juvenile cases is rather limited. Nevertheless, Art. 3a was introduced as a result of the encouraging results of a pilot experimental program of mediating juvenile cases which has been running in eight family courts since 1995. This experiment has laid the groundwork for the development of certain institutional elements of a mediation system in Poland (Czarnecka-Dzialuk and Wójcik 2001).

It is important to note that the discretionary powers of the judge are not unlimited, as they are subject to appellate review. Decisions of the family judge to institute proceedings, as well as refusing to institute or to discontinue them, may always be appealed, also by the victim (Art. 21 § 3). This situation is the subject of intense discussion in the Polish literature. In principle the rights of the victim, and possibilities of influencing the course of proceedings with various motions—normally rather broad under 'adult' criminal procedure—are severely limited in juvenile proceedings. This is considered to be justified by the special purpose of this type of proceeding, namely that the welfare of a juvenile and his/her rehabilitation are the most important aims of intervention. Because of this right to appeal, the juvenile judge's decision to refuse to institute proceedings or to discontinue them constitutes one of the very few instruments which remain in the hands of the victim. For some time, especially due to some cases of serious violent offences committed by juveniles and publicized by the media, this regulation is hotly contested. Various victim organizations and associations are struggling for more victim rights in juvenile courts. However, so far and in accordance with the 'child welfare' ideology, the legal position of the victim in juvenile proceedings remains significantly weaker than in 'adult' criminal procedure.

The main purposes of the investigative phase of the proceedings in cases of juveniles are to reveal all relevant circumstances of the case, and to collect and record all relevant evidence for the purpose of future use during the trial. Due to the character of this proceeding devoted primarily to the welfare of the child, the juvenile judge also has the duty to collect all relevant personal data on the juvenile, as well as on his/her family. In this respect juvenile courts have to rely on specialized institutions, so-called family diagnostic and consultative centres. They are entrusted with the task of conducting complex examinations of juveniles and their families and preparing expert opinions in these matters for family courts. In 2001 there were 67 such centres in the country, and they employed 582 specialists of various types, including educational specialists, social workers, psychologists, psychiatrists and doctors of other specialization. As such they constitute an example of a bureaucracy based on the ideology of social work. People working within it consider themselves to be members of helping professions, rather than members of criminal justice agencies. This has an important influence on the way in which juvenile courts function, and on the non-punitive character of their dispositions.

The role of the police and public prosecutor during investigative proceedings is limited. All activities, including interviewing a juvenile, witnesses, expert witnesses, or taking any other evidence during the investigative proceedings are performed by the juvenile judge personally. According to the law the police may only perform certain activities which are necessary at the crime scene, or in case of a delay. Otherwise, they must act exclusively on the orders of the juvenile judge (Art. 37). Of course, the realities of modern investigation, especially in cases of serious and complicated offences, requiring various types of specialized police activities and forensic expertise, result in a situation in which juvenile judges must rely heavily on the police. Otherwise they would be unable to investigate many cases properly. Nevertheless, for a juvenile judge it would be a violation of the law to turn over the entire investigation of the case, or its substantial parts, to the police. The special role played by the juvenile judge during the investigation of juvenile cases of both types (cases of demoralization and cases of punishable acts) may mean that the role of the investigative phase in juvenile procedure increases, and it starts to dominate the court proceedings, with the role of the trial being marginalized. This may certainly be true, and corresponds with the general tendency towards the growing influence of the investigative phase in criminal proceedings (Schüler-Springorum 1999). This tendency, especially problematic in continental criminal processes, may be balanced in cases of juveniles in Poland, at least to a certain extent, by the fact that the investigation is conducted by an independent judicial agency.

A juvenile enjoys several civil rights guarantees during the investigative proceedings, independent of whether a ground for instituting proceedings constituted signs of demoralization or a prohibited act. First of all, he/she has the right to counsel. If there is a conflict of interests between the juvenile and his/her parents, participation of counsel is mandatory. Participation of counsel is also always mandatory during reformatory proceedings in court. Counsel has access to all files of the proceedings, and the right to participate in certain activities during the investigation. The most important of such activities is taking the testimony of the juvenile under investigation. Interestingly enough, he/she is not referred to as a 'suspect', a term used by 'adult' procedure, but as a juvenile. Such a hearing takes place in principle in front of the juvenile judge. Only in exceptional situations, namely in the case of delay, may it be performed by the police. But during the juvenile's testimony certain additional persons, apart from the judge or a policeman on the one side, and the juvenile on the other, must be present. Usually it has to be either the juvenile's counsel or his/her parents or both. If their participation is impossible it may be the juvenile's teacher, or a representative of an appropriate family welfare institution or of an NGO involved in helping families, who must be present during the testimony. Empirical research on this issue shows that, unfortunately, provisions on mandatory presence of these persons during the juvenile's testimony are often disobeyed (Korcyl-Wolska 2001, 174–83).

The Juveniles Act of 1982 also regulates issues of arrest and preliminary detention of juveniles. Special rules, which are different from those in adult criminal procedure, apply here. First, the police have the right to arrest juveniles suspected of prohibited acts (Art. 40 § 1). This means that arrest is not possible in cases of demoralization. Arrest may take place in cases of prohibited acts only if there is a possibility that a juvenile may escape, distort evidence or where it is impossible to establish his/her identity. The police have to inform the juvenile's parents and the family court about the youth's arrest within 24 hours. Arrested juveniles cannot be placed in 'regular' police jails or detention centres where adults are held. They must be placed in special institutions called police children shelters, intended exclusively for juveniles. Although they are run by the police, their staff usually have additional training and specialize in dealing with juveniles. The decision to arrest may be appealed to the juvenile judge, and the juvenile suspect shall be informed of this right. Under Art. 40 § 6.4 of the Juveniles Act and Art. 41.3 of the Constitution, a juvenile—like any other citizen—may be held under arrest for up to 72 hours. If the grounds for arrest are not confirmed, he/she must be released immediately. He/she must also be released if during the said 72 hours a family court does not impose an equivalent of preliminary detention in 'adult' criminal procedure (i.e. places the juvenile for a longer time in a special juvenile detention institution or remand house), or send him/her temporarily to a child care or educational institution.

Analogous to the regulations of 'adult' criminal procedure, the Polish Juveniles Act does not provide for the Anglo-American institution of bail. This means that after arrest the court must decide whether to apply any special measures intended to secure the suspect's presence during trial or not. In cases of juveniles these issues are regulated by Arts. 26 and 27 of the Juveniles Act of 1982. The first of these provisions states that it is possible to apply various preliminary measures such as supervision by an association, a youth organization or an employer, as well as preliminary supervision by a probation officer or a trusted person. A juvenile may also be temporarily placed in educational institutions of various types. Only in cases of prohibited acts which later may provide grounds for instituting reformatory proceedings and imposing a special measure of placement in a correctional centre is it possible (Art. 27) to apply during the investigative proceedings an equivalent of preliminary detention (i.e. place a juvenile in a remand house for a longer period of time). Such a decision may be justified either by the fact that there is a danger that the juvenile will escape or distort evidence, or by the fact that it is impossible to establish his/her identity, or he/she is suspected of having committed certain very serious prohibited acts (offences), listed in Art. 27 § 2 of the Juveniles Act—for example murder, rape or robbery. Decisions on placing juveniles in a remand house are made by the juvenile judge. Initially a juvenile may be placed in such remand house for no longer than three months. This may be extended by an additional three months by a panel consisting of one juvenile judge and two lay assessors. This means that detention in a remand house during the investigation cannot exceed six months. According to Art. 27 § 6 of the Juveniles Act, joint duration of detention until conviction by the court of original jurisdiction cannot exceed one year. This means that if the juvenile has to stay in a remand house during the entire proceedings, the investigative proceedings in a juvenile's case must be completed within 6 months, and the trial within the next six months. There are some possibilities of extending the stay in a remand house beyond this one-year term, but they are extremely limited.

Trial in juvenile cases

Depending on the results of the investigative proceedings, the juvenile judge has several options for completing it. He/she may resort to discretionary powers and discontinue proceedings, with or without diverting a case to other institutions. If he/she considers that discontinuation is not proper and further action is necessary, a decision to transfer the case for trial in the juvenile court, or to transfer it to the public prosecutor with a motion to waive juvenile jurisdiction and bring charges under Art. 10 of the Criminal Code according to the adult procedure, is required. Decisions of this latter type are extremely rare. This means that the most typical decisions ending investigative proceedings are decisions to open trial in the juvenile court (Habzda 1992).

Trial in the juvenile court, depending on the decision of the judge who investigated the case, may take one of two forms: care and educational proceedings or reformatory proceedings. The decision of the judge as to which type of procedure should be applied depends on what kind of measures he/she considers to be appropriate in a given case (i.e. either care and educational measures or reformatory measures). Care and educational measures may be applied in cases of both demoralization and prohibited acts, and constitute the vast majority of measures imposed by Polish family courts in juvenile cases of all types (see below). Reformatory measures may be applied only in cases of prohibited acts.

The two types of proceedings differ greatly. As was mentioned earlier, care and educational proceedings, with a few exceptions, are governed exclusively by provisions of the Code of Civil Procedure. Therefore this type of procedure is flexible. The punitive purpose is nearly totally absent, and thinking in categories of child welfare clearly dominates. Decisions are taken in a clearly non-adversarial environment,[12] and certain civil rights guarantees typical of criminal procedure are weakened or even totally absent. From this point of view it is necessary to stress that in practice the vast majority of juvenile cases are tried according to this form of procedure. Even in cases of punishable acts, more than 90% of cases are tried in this form, which means that in total this form on average constitutes more than 96% of juvenile cases. This practical domination of care and educational proceedings means also that an exclusively child welfare oriented type of procedure dominates the Polish juvenile justice system.

As opposed to care and educational proceedings, reformatory proceedings in juvenile courts are regulated by the provisions of the Code of Criminal Procedure (Górecki 1997). Thus, this type of procedure stresses to a greater extent civil rights and issues of procedural guarantees. It also has a quasi-penal character. However, there are some differences between reformatory trial proceedings in cases of juveniles on the one hand and 'adult' criminal procedure on the other. For example, during reformatory proceedings participation of counsel is mandatory. This is not always the case in 'adult' criminal procedure, and during investigative proceedings in juvenile cases it is only a possibility. This gives reformatory proceedings a more adversarial character that is reinforced by the fact that in some, although not all, cases participation of the public prosecutor is also mandatory.[13] In reformatory proceedings the court panel consists of a juvenile judge and two lay assessors (which is the rule in 'adult' proceedings), while in care and educational proceedings a single judge presides over the proceedings (Art. 50 of the Juveniles Act). Finally, as opposed to adult criminal procedure, juvenile trials are closed to the public, unless special educational interest warrants waiver of that rule.[14]

---

[12] Of course from an Anglo-American perspective any continental procedure is considered to be of an inquisitorial character. Nevertheless, the adversarial character of procedure may be subject to gradation, and continental procedures may contain various elements of an adversarial system. Because of this it may be rightly claimed that Polish juvenile court proceedings in cases of punishable acts have a much more adversarial character than such proceedings in cases of demoralization.

[13] This may be considered to be unusual, since the public prosecutor does not play any role in investigating juvenile cases, and does not prepare a charge sheet in such cases. Activities of an equivalent type are undertaken by the juvenile judge in such cases.

[14] In addition, court hearings in care and educational proceedings are closed to the public, but this is a rule in civil non-litigious proceedings, as opposed to criminal proceedings, where hearings are as a rule public.

Despite the fact that reformatory proceedings are regulated by the provisions of the Code of Criminal Procedure and bear a close similarity to the 'adult' criminal trial, it cannot and should not be considered to be of a primarily penal or punitive character. As was mentioned earlier, the only reformatory measure known to Polish juvenile law (i.e. correctional centre suspended or not) is not considered to constitute a punishment. And this is true despite the fact that it bears a certain similarity to deprivation of liberty or to a suspended sentence under 'adult' criminal law. Nevertheless a correctional centre is not a prison. It constitutes a juvenile measure, and its application and execution are governed by the general rule of Art. 3 § 1 of the Juveniles Act (i.e. child's welfare and rehabilitation). Moreover, if the court after trial comes to the conclusion that reformatory measures are not justified in a given case of a punishable act, it may always impose care and educational measures.

THE STATISTICAL PICTURE OF JUVENILE DELINQUENCY AND JUVENILE JUSTICE IN POLAND

The above description of the Polish juvenile justice system may be supplemented by some statistical data on the juvenile delinquency problem in Poland, as well as the functioning of the juvenile justice system. First of all it is necessary to stress that Poland, like all other countries of Central and Eastern Europe after the political, economic and social change which began in 1989, saw a serious growth in registered offences (Jasinski 1995; 1999, Widacki 2001, Krajewski 2004). A detailed presentation of this phenomenon and its causes goes beyond the scope of the present analysis—only a few general remarks are possible here. After a sharp jump in the registered offence rate in 1990 (from 1,440 per 100,000 inhabitants in 1989 to 2,317) during the first half of the 1990s this rate actually stabilized. It was only during the second half of the decade that it began to grow again in a significant way (Figure 1).

As a consequence, the rate of registered offences in 2001 was approximately 55% higher than it was in 1990. If one considers additionally the fact that especially rapid growth could be observed in the area of violent offences, such as assault, bodily injury, robbery and homicide, which were growing much quicker than property offences, it may be argued that the evolution of the crime problem in Poland took a very problematic direction. In the literature this picture is often countered with the argument that available results of victimization surveys do not necessarily confirm this dramatic growth trend. They show rather that the prevalence rate of victimization has stabilized or even decreased slightly during recent years, although readiness to report offences remains extremely low, which results in a large dark figure. However, this readiness to report seems also to be

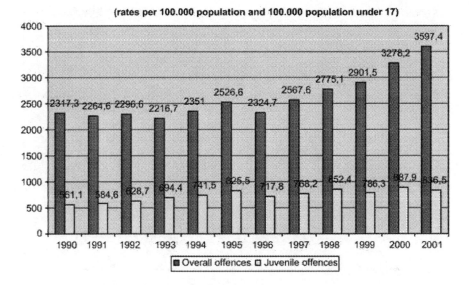

(rates per 100.000 population and 100.000 population under 17)

Figure 1: Overall offense rates and juvenile offences rates.

growing steadily. This means that the growth of registered offences may result primarily from increased readiness to report them to the police.

Nevertheless, if one compares the development of the adult offence rate and the juvenile offence rate during the 1990s, it becomes obvious, first of all, that the latter remained much lower than the former. Its growth was also somewhat less spectacular than in the case of adults, and at the beginning of the present decade even some slight decrease could be observed. Because of these different developments the juvenile offence rate in 2001 was 49% higher than in 1990, as compared to 55% growth in the overall offence rate. This picture certainly becomes more pessimistic if one considers developments in the area of some violent offences committed by juveniles (Krajewski 2003) (Figure 2).

Here growth rates were significant, sometimes even spectacular, such as in the case of robbery. They increased more than tenfold during the 1990s! But also in cases of assault or causing bodily harm these increases were very significant. This necessarily brought about changes in the structure of registered juvenile offences (Figure 3).

Prior to 1990, juvenile delinquency in Poland was dominated by property offences, such as simple theft and burglary, which even in 1990 still constituted almost 80% of all juvenile offences registered by the police. Certainly, this changed during the 1990s, as in the year 2001 the proportion of property offences among all juvenile offences decreased to about 40%, while the proportion of violent offences grew to more than 20%. Interestingly enough

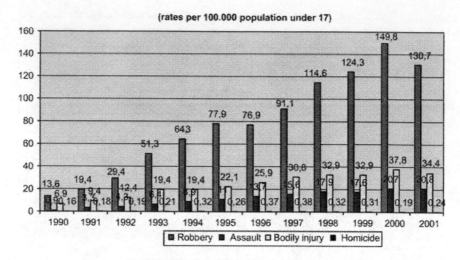

Figure 2: Development of selected violent juvenile offences.

it is the category 'other' which has also grown significantly, to slightly less than 20%. This was mainly due to a substantial growth in the drug offence rate. However, it may be interesting to note that despite all this, the proportion of juvenile offences among all registered offences (Figure 4) still remains fairly low (under 10%). Moreover, after growth during the first half of the 1990s it started to fall, and in 2001 it reached a historical low of 4.9%.

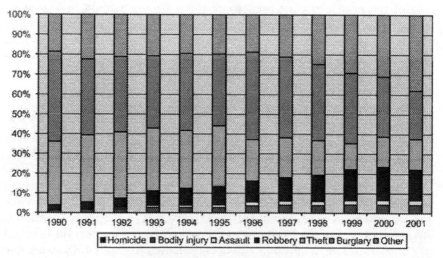

Figure 3: Structure of juvenile offences.

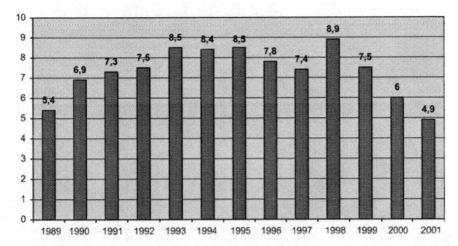

Figure 4: Proportion of offences commited by juveniles among all offences.

All this may indicate that juvenile delinquency in Poland does not necessarily pose a serious problem in quantitative terms, but undergoes certain
qualitative changes which may give reason for some concern: it becomes
more violent and generally more serious. This may be true, although some
reservations are necessary. A comparison of registration and processing patterns of juvenile delinquents in some central and western European cities
(Neubacher *et al* 1999) shows that these patterns are quite different. It
seems for example that in Hamburg a very high number of registered acts
is followed by an extremely intensive selection processes and very high
'drop-out' ratio. In Central European cities (Budapest, Prague, Krakow) the
number of registered offences is much lower, but at the same time selection
processes seem to be much less intensive. This may give grounds for the suspicion that a substantial proportion of less serious delinquent acts in
Central Europe either go unnoticed by the police or are selected-out in a
quite informal way and are never officially registered. This would mean of
course that the dark number of juvenile offences in Central Europe may
remain extremely high.

Similar patterns indicate data regarding juvenile suspects, although here
general rates of suspects and rates of juvenile suspects developed according
to a much more similar pattern than offence rates (Figure 5).

But the juvenile suspect rate was usually also 30–40% lower than the
respective adult rate. Interestingly enough, if one examines the age distribution of offenders (Figure 6), it becomes clear that although substantial
changes took place during the 1990s in the incidence of criminal behaviour
in all age brackets, it was not necessarily the bracket of 13–16 years that
was most problematic.

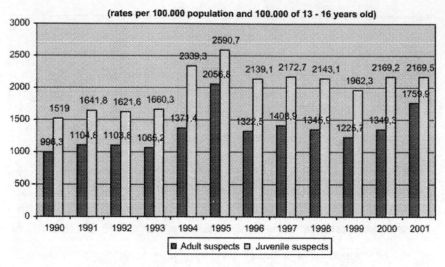

Figure 5: Adult suspect rates and juvenile suspect rates.

This distribution in 1989 was still relatively flat, and differences in the incidence of criminal behaviour between younger and older offenders were not very high. During the 1990s this changed, and younger age brackets experienced a sharper growth in offending than the other age categories. However, this growth was most substantial among 17–21 year olds (i.e. among adolescents), which have the highest offence rates, and not among juveniles. At the same time the proportion of juvenile suspects among all suspects remained fairly stable and low during the 1990s. In recent years this proportion decreased even further, following the same pattern as the number of registered offences (Figure 7).

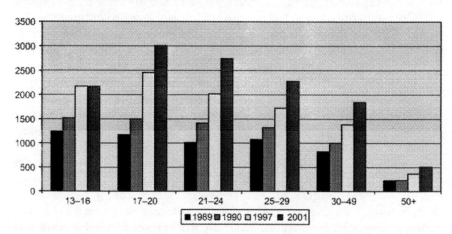

Figure 6: Age distribution of persons suspected of offences.

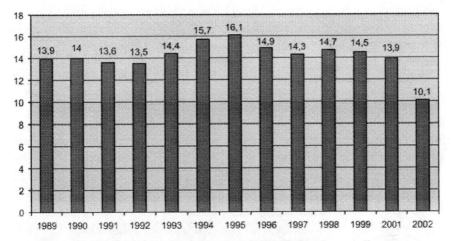

Figure 7: Proportion of juveniles suspected of offences among all suspects.

The remaining data illustrate the reality of the Polish juvenile justice system, and the way it adapted to the changing patterns of juvenile delinquency. First of all it is worth noting that the number of juvenile cases in family courts grew substantially during the 1990s (Figure 8).

The number of cases related to signs of demoralization doubled during that time, while the number of cases related to punishable acts more than doubled. The fact that the number of cases of the second type has been growing a little bit faster is confirmed by the fact that in 1990 their ratio was 1:2.5. In 2001 it became more than 1:3. This means that the majority (about three-quarters) of all juvenile interventions under Polish juvenile law

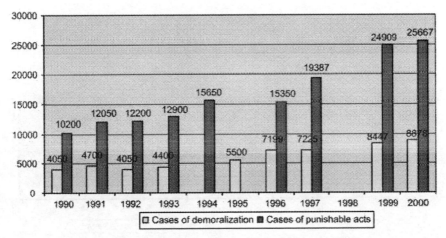

Figure 8: Juveniles dealt with by family courts because of demoralization and because of punishable acts.

are related to punishable acts. Despite these changes in the rate and structure of juvenile offending, the structure of sanctions imposed by juvenile courts remained almost unchanged (Figures 9 and 10).

There are even some indications that a more lenient and liberal approach actually established itself in the practice of family courts. In both types of juvenile cases, namely cases of demoralization and cases of punishable acts, the type of measure most often used, applied in about a third of cases of both types, is supervision by a probation officer. Although the use of probation decreased during the 1990s, it was followed by more intensive use of such measures as cautions and obligations of various types. This may

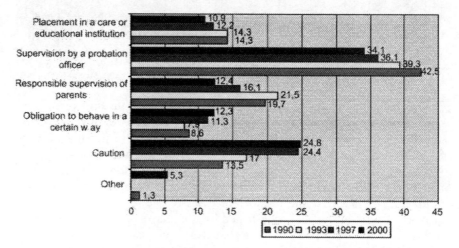

Figure 9: Structure of measures imposed in cases of demoralization.

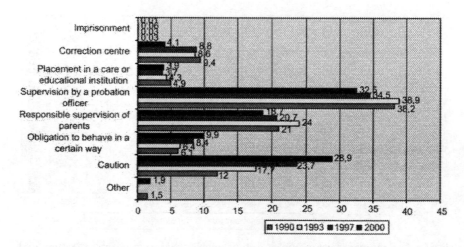

Figure 10: Structure of measures imposed in cases of punishable acts.

have two bases. First, during the 1990s Polish criminal policy in cases of adults underwent a significant process of liberalization, as compared with the communist period (Krajewski 2004). For example, a significant drop in the use of imprisonment and an increase in the use of fines took place. Additionally, the average duration of imprisonment went down. Something similar may occur also in cases of juveniles, as courts opt for less restrictive sanctions. But it may also be that the less intensive use of supervision by probation officers resulted from probation agencies being overloaded with work, which in turn forced courts to seek alternative measures.

Finally it is worth noting that the use of the most restrictive juvenile measure, namely the correctional centre, remained quite limited. This measure was and still is applied on average in less than 10% of all cases of punishable acts and showed decreasing use, which ended in a spectacular fall to 4.1% in 2000! And all of this despite the growing number of more serious juvenile offences. It seems that in the opinion of the judges, who have daily contact with the realities of juvenile delinquency, there is no need to react to these tendencies in a harsher way. This may be confirmed by the fact that a vast majority of measures imposed in cases of punishable acts are care and educational measures, and not the reformatory option (Figure 11).

At the same time, despite some growth in 2000, the majority of reformatory measures or correctional centre orders imposed by Polish juvenile courts (about three-fifths) remain suspended (Figure 12).

This indicates again that in face of the above mentioned qualitative changes in juvenile delinquency, Polish juvenile judges either moved in favour of a more lenient treatment of juvenile offenders, or do not perceive the problem of juvenile delinquency in such a dramatic way as the media and politicians.

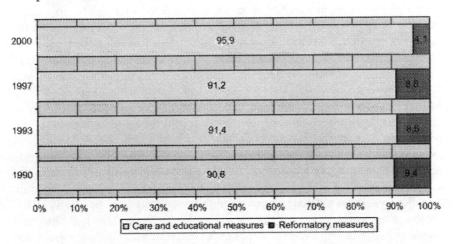

Figure 11: The proportions of care and educational, and reformatory measures imposed in cases of punishable acts

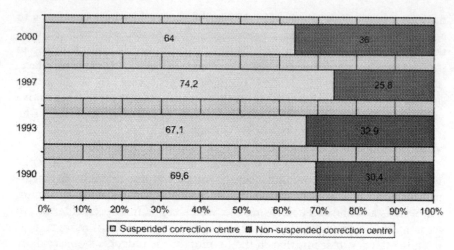

Figure 12: The proportions of suspended and non-suspended correction centre orders

CONCLUSIONS

Current laws regulating the juvenile justice system in Poland are clearly oriented towards a 'child welfare' model, with the rehabilitation of young
offenders constituting the main task of all actions undertaken in cases of
juvenile law violators. It means that the basic idea behind the creation of
the juvenile courts in the U.S. at the end of the nineteenth century, namely
that children in trouble ought to be 'saved' and not 'punished' (Weijers
1999a, 330), also underlies the Polish juvenile justice system. As a consequence, procedures in juvenile cases are constructed in a much more flexible way than in adult cases. Much more discretion is permissible, and the
law gives broader possibilities for intervention in a juvenile's life than is the
case with adults. Finally, juvenile measures are not aimed at punishment of
the lawbreaker, but almost exclusively at his/her treatment and rehabilitation. However, this does not necessarily mean that what Weijers (1999a,
341) refers to as efficiency and consequentialism have absolute priority over
civil rights. It is true that an emphasis on child needs often results in the
conviction that there is no need to safeguard all his/her procedural rights
(Trépanier 1999a, 314). It seems, however, that the Polish legislation was in
principle able to strike a common sense balance between these elements of
any juvenile justice system. As a recent major empirical study on this subject (Korcyl-Wolska 2001) shows, this balance may not be perfect, and
there are sometimes serious practical problems. Nevertheless, it does not
result in widespread excesses or abuses. Interestingly, such a model has
existed in Poland since before World War Two and its principles were not
changed under the communist rule. Because of this, the 1982 Juveniles Act

still remains in force as basic assumptions underlying its regulations were acceptable also from the point of view of the new democratic state. Notwithstanding this, since 1989 certain amendments were introduced which made some civil rights guarantees more explicit. This change was in accordance with the general tendency in penal and other types of legislation in Poland during the 1990s when issues of human rights and protection against abuses of power constituted the main point of attention. Such a tendency was absolutely natural in a country which has shaken off communist authoritarian rule.

Due to growing problems with juvenile delinquency and particularly juvenile violence, or rather a public perception of this, the public, media and politicians increasingly support a more punitive approach to the problem of juvenile delinquency. Demands to lower the age limit of criminal responsibility, or even to end the treatment ideology in the juvenile justice system altogether are often heard. This seems to be in accordance with certain tendencies that may be observed primarily in the U.S. and Canada (Trépanier 1999a; 1999b), but also to a much lesser extent in Europe (Weijers 1999a, Kilchling 2002). This return to classical thinking about the responsibility of juveniles, and stress on retribution and 'doing justice' can be observed especially clearly in the U.S. The prior ideology of child welfare is being substituted there by the tendency to make a 'sharp distinction between young offenders and children in need of protection' (Trépanier 1999a, 321). It is only the last group which is approached with the traditional welfare model. Young offenders are treated increasingly, in accordance with the general tendency of the American criminal justice system, in a punitive, retributive manner, like any other offenders.

So far, such tendencies have not prevailed in Poland, where the phenomenon of the 'cycle of juvenile justice' (Bernard 1992) seems to be absent (so far). This may be a general European pattern. In the opinion of Weijers (1999a, 339) this is mainly due to the fact that most European systems of juvenile justice never implemented the child welfare ideology in such a far reaching manner as was the case in the U.S. and never constituted agencies acting in such an informal and discretionary way. As a consequence, in Europe status offenders and children in need of care were always treated in a different manner from juvenile offenders (which does not necessarily mean that the latter were treated in a punitive way). Because of this, the position of juvenile courts in Europe and their special jurisdiction seems to be much more solid and stable than in the country of their birth. This seems to be the case also in Poland, where differentiation between children who show signs of demoralization and children who commit punishable acts results in a differentiated treatment of both categories. To the first group an exclusively welfare oriented approach applies, to the second—especially to perpetrators of the most serious offences—an approach in which more elements of penal reactions are included.

Interestingly enough, the child welfare approach to the problem of juvenile delinquency was—and still is—criticized from various points of view. It is not only the classical, retributive, justice oriented argument which is used. It is also an argument based on the principles of human rights and due process, which points out that the welfare and treatment ideology (not only in cases of juveniles) leads simply to unjust and unequal decisions and outcomes (Beaulieu and Cessaroni 1999, 374). From this point of view it may be asked what influence eventual changes in the direction of the *guilt and punishment* instead of the *diagnosis and treatment* model could have on issues of protecting the civil rights of juveniles. Paradoxically, a move towards more punitive, neo-classical elements in the juvenile justice system does not necessarily include increased protection of these rights. Experience teaches us that nowadays any reforms in the direction of an increasingly punitive character of criminal law usually involve a parallel dismantling of various guarantees of civil rights. Because of this, despite all its shortcomings and inadequacies, the current child welfare oriented model of juvenile justice in Poland seems to better serve not only the cause of controlling juvenile delinquency, but also the cause of protecting the civil rights of juveniles.

REFERENCES

Beaulieu, Lucien A. and Carla Cesaroni (1999) The Changing Role of the Youth Court Judge. *European Journal on Criminal Policy and Research*, vol. 7, No. 3, pp. 363–93.

Bernard, Thomas J. (1992) *The Cycle of Juvenile Justice*. (New York and Oxford, Oxford University Press).

Christiaens, Jenneke (1999) A History of Belgium's Child Protection Act of 1912. The Redefinition of the Juvenile Offender and His Punishment. *European Journal of Crime, Criminal Law and Criminal Justice*, vol. 7, No. 1, pp. 5–21.

Czarnecka-Dzialuk, Beata (2000) Juvenile Delinquency. In A. Siemaszko (ed.), *Crime and Law Enforcement in Poland on the Threshold of the 21st Century*. (Warszawa, Oficyna Naukowa), pp. 137–43.

Czarnecka-Dzialuk, Beata and Dobrochna Wójcik (2001) *Mediation in Cases of Juveniles in Theory and Practice* (Polish). (Warszawa, Typografika).

Gaberle, Andrzej (2002) Polen. In H–J. Albrecht and M. Kilchling (eds.), *Jugendstrafrecht in Europa*. (Freiburg, Max-Planck-Institut für ausländisches und internationales Strafrecht), pp. 303–16.

Gaberle, Andrzej and Marianna Korcyl-Wolska (2002) *A Commentary to the Proceedings in Cases of Juveniles Act* (Polish). (Gdansk, Arche).

Górecki, Piotr (1997) *Reformatory Proceedings in Cases of Juveniles* (Polish). (Sopot, Wydawnictwo Prawnicze Lex).

Górecki, Piotr and Stanislaw Stachowiak (2002) *Proceedings in Cases of Juveniles Act. A Commentary* (Polish). (Krakow, Kantor Wydawniczy Zakamycze).

Habzda, Ewa (1992) Sanktionsmöglichkeiten gegenüber Jugendlichen nach dem Gesetz über das Verfahren in Jugendsachen vom 26. Oktober 1982. In *Grundfragen des Jugendkriminalrechts und seiner Neuregelung, Symposium an der Kriminologischen Forschungsstelle der Universität zu Köln.* (Bonn, Forum Verlag Godesberg), pp. 303–10.

Jasinski, Jerzy (1996) Crime in Central and East European Countries. *European Journal on Criminal Policy and Research,* vol. 5, No. 1, pp. 40–50.

Jasinski, Jerzy (1999) Crime: Manifestations, Patterns and Trends of Crime 'traditional' versus 'new' crime; juvenile crime; fear of crime. *European Journal of Crime, Criminal Law and Criminal Justice,* vol. 7, No. 4, pp. 374–86.

Kilchling, Michael (2002) Vergleichende Perspektiven. Grundzüge des Jugendstrafrechts in europäischen Ausland und der Türkei. In H-J. Albrecht and M. Kilchling (eds.), *Jugendstrafrecht in Europa.* (Freiburg, Max-Planck-Institut für ausländisches und internationales Strafrecht), pp. 475–532.

Korcyl-Wolska, Marianna (2001) *Proceedings in Cases of Juveniles in Poland* (Polish). (Krakow, Kantor Wydawniczy Zakamycze).

Krajewski, Krzysztof (2003) Patterns of Juvenile Delinquency and Juvenile Violence in Poland. In F. Dünkel and K. Drenkhahn (eds.), *Youth violence: new patterns and local responses—Experiences in East and West.* (Mönchengladbach, Forum Verlag Godesberg), pp. 10–35.

Krajewski, Krzysztof (2004) Crime and Criminal Justice in Poland. *European Journal of Criminology,* vol. 1, No. 3 pp. 377–407.

Marek, Andrzej (1992) Das polnische Jugendrechtssystem in Theorie und Praxis. In *Grundfragen des Jugendkriminalrechts und seiner Neuregelung, Symposium an der Kriminologischen Forschungsstelle der Universität zu Köln.* (Bonn, Forum Verlag Godesberg), pp. 290–302.

Neubacher, Frank, Michael Walter, Helena Válková, and Krzysztof Krajewski (1999) Juvenile Delinquency in Central European Cities: A Comparison of Registration and Processing Structures in the 1990s. *European Journal on Criminal Policy and Research,* vol. 7, No. 4, pp. 533–8.

Oberwittler, Dietrich (1999) The Decline of Correctional Education, ca. 1900–1920. England and Germany Compared. *European Journal of Crime, Criminal Law and Criminal Justice,* vol. 7, No. 1, pp. 22–40.

Platt, Anthony M. (1977) *The Child Savers. The Invention of Delinquency.* 2nd edn, enlarged. (Chicago and London, The University of Chicago Press).

Schüler-Springorum, Horst (1999) Juvenile Justice and the 'Shift to the Left'. *European Journal on Criminal Policy and Research*, vol. 7, No. 3, pp. 353–62.

Stando-Kawecka, Barbara (1995) Polen. In F. Dünkel, A. van Kalmthout and H. Schüler–Springorum (eds.), *Entwicklungstendenzen und Reformstrategien im Jugendstrafrecht im europäischen Vergleich.* (Mönchengladbach, Forum Verlag Godesberg), pp. 419–35.

Trépanier, Jean (1999a) Juvenile Courts after 100 Years: Past and Present Orientations. *European Journal on Criminal Policy and Research*, vol. 7, No. 3, pp. 303–27.

Trépanier, Jean (1999b) Juvenile Delinquency and Youth Protection: The Historical Foundations of the Canadian Juvenile Delinquents Act of 1908. *European Journal of Crime, Criminal Law and Criminal Justice*, vol. 7, No. 1, pp. 41–62.

Válková, Helena (2001) Jugendstrafrechtsreform in Tschechien in Sicht? *Monatsschrift für Strafrechtsreform und Kriminologi*, vol. 84, No. 5, pp. 396–409.

Wasek, Andrzej and Stanislaw Frankowski (1995) Polish Criminal Law and Procedure. In S. Frankowski and P.B. Stephan (eds.), *Legal Reform in Post-Communist Europe. The View from Within.* (Boston, London, Kluwer International), pp. 275–308.

Weijers, Ido (1999a) The Double Paradox of Juvenile Justice. *European Journal on Criminal Policy and Research*, vol. 7, No. 3, pp. 329–51.

Weijers, Ido (1999b) The Debate on Juvenile Justice in the Netherlands, 1891–1901. *European Journal of Crime, Criminal Law and Criminal Justice*, vol. 7, No. 1, pp. 63–80.

Widacki, Jan (2001) Criminality in the Central and Eastern European Countries in the Period of Transformation 1989–1999. In J. Widacki, M. Maczynski, and J. Czapska (eds.), *Local Community, Public Security. Central and Eastern European Countries under Transformation.* (Warsaw, Instytut Spraw Publicznych), pp. 13–24.

10

Responses to Juvenile Crime: The Swedish System

JERZY SARNECKI

INTRODUCTION

T HE ENGLISH CONCEPT 'juvenile delinquency' has no direct equivalent in the Swedish language or in the Swedish legal system. Instead, in Sweden we usually speak of juvenile criminality, a concept which differs from juvenile delinquency in that it does not include so-called status offences, i.e. acts committed by juveniles which constitute a crime but are legal if they are committed by adults. Of course this does not mean that the Swedish authorities do not react if young people drink alcohol, run away from home or commit other acts which jeopardise their development. However, the authorities' reactions in such cases have the character of social measures and are regulated by social legislation, not penal legislation. In this paper the term 'juvenile delinquency' is used synonymously with the Swedish concept of juvenile criminality and thus covers all acts which are subject to penal sanctions according to Swedish law.

The objective of this paper is to describe the ways in which Swedish authorities respond to juvenile delinquency/criminality and also how this response has changed over the past two decades. These changes will then be related to existing knowledge of the extent and character of crimes committed by young people over the course of the period in question.

TRENDS IN JUVENILE DELINQUENCY OVER TIME

On the whole, criminality in Sweden has increased greatly since the mid-1920s. This is most frequently explained by the increase in the level of opportunities for crime. People today own a lot of attractive goods which are also relatively easily accessible. Cars constitute a good example of this. Considering their value, they are relatively easy to steal. The enormous expansion in private car ownership in Sweden (435 per 1,000 inhabitants in 2002) has affected the structure of Swedish criminality considerably, not only in terms of thefts, but also as a result of traffic offences and other kinds of offences. The introduction of self-service in shops constitutes another example of a social trend that has had a major effect on criminality.

However, changes in the level of criminal opportunities are by themselves insufficient to explain the changes that occurred in crime rates over the course of the last century. We can see this if we examine the number of individuals convicted[1] of offences in Sweden. This number has increased dramatically during the last century. The extent of the increase is very different across different age groups, however. According to statistics relating to persons convicted of serious offences[2] (von Hofer 2004 tab. 5.6) the proportion of 15 to 17 year olds convicted of such offences increased from approximately 0.35 per 100,000 individuals in this age group in the mid-19th century to 27.60 in the mid-1970s.[3] Thus we are looking at an increase of almost 80 times. The increase was considerably less marked within the older age groups (26 times for those aged 18 to 20, 16.5 times for those between 21 and 29 years of age, 6.0 for those aged between 30 and 39) and was low among the oldest group presented, i.e. individuals aged 40 years and over, where the proportion increased only 2.8 times (from 0.58 per 100,000 in the mid-19th century to 1.56 in the mid-1970s). Since the mid-1970s, the number of persons being registered has decreased.

The major differences in crime trends across different age groups suggest that changes in the opportunity structure are not sufficient to explain the increase in crime. Opportunities for crime have changed to the same extent irrespective of one's age. The fact that it is specifically juvenile crime that has increased suggests instead that changes have taken place in the social control of young people over this period. This is in fact not surprising, given the major changes that have taken place in relation to the position occupied by young people in the production process. Young people have been excluded from this process, which has led to a decrease in levels of control and has at the same time given them significantly more freedom, which in certain cases has led to an increase in their levels of criminality (Sarnecki 2003).

---

[1] The English term 'conviction' is used throughout this text as a translation of the Swedish 'lagföring'. This means that besides referring to persons adjudicated to have committed a given offence by a court, the term 'conviction' also covers two other responses to crime, these being 1) the issuance of a fine by the prosecutor (without proceeding through the court system) and 2) a so-called 'waiver of prosecution', which in effect amounts to a caution issued by the prosecutor (again in combination with a decision not to prosecute the offender through the courts). Both these responses require an admission of guilt on the part of the offender, and are thus treated as 'findings of guilt' in official statistics in the same way as court adjudications.

[2] Crimes where a prison term is included in the sanctioning scale.

[3] The final year for which von Hofer presents data is 1994. Unfortunately statistics relating specifically to serious offences were discontinued at the beginning of the 1990s.

Trends since the mid-1970s

The proportion of young persons (aged 15 to 17) convicted of offences peaked in the mid-1970s. As can be seen from Figure 10.1, there was then a substantial drop at the beginning of the 1980s. Following this point, the number of convictions then stabilised at a somewhat lower level, before undergoing a new decrease during the second half of the 1990s. The number of convictions relating to persons aged 18 to 20 has also declined. This decrease has been both considerably more substantial and more continuous than that witnessed among the juveniles. The total level of police reported crime in Sweden increased up until the beginning of the 1990s, at which point it stabilised.

Alternative sources of information on trends in juvenile crime also indicate that the offending of young people has been relatively stable and may possibly even have decreased over recent years. National self-report studies were first started in Sweden in the mid-1990s (Ring 1999; 2003). Since this point, four self-report surveys have been conducted on representative samples of pupils in school-year nine (aged approximately 15 years). The findings from these surveys show that levels of self-reported drug offences and violent crime were relatively stable between 1995 and 2001 whilst levels of theft offences and vandalism appeared to have fallen off somewhat. The proportion of young people who report not having committed offences of any kind over the course of the previous year increased somewhat from 19% in 1995 to 24% in 2001. At the same time, it is worth noting that a large majority of the 15-year-olds surveyed (approximately 75%)[4] still reported

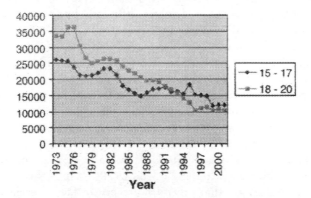

Figure 10.1: Absolute numbers of young people aged 15–17 and 18–20 years convicted of criminal offences in Sweden 1993–2000 (BRÅ, 2002).

---

[4] If certain minor offences such as thefts from school or the respondent's home, and fare dodging on public transport, are ignored, the proportion of youths reporting having committed one or more (non-minor) offences during the last year stood at 61% in 1995 and 52% in 2001 (Ring 2003).

that they had committed one or a few offences during the past year. Relatively few youths reported having committed large numbers of offences, however.

Since property crimes dominate among the reported offences, the total level of self-reported crime has decreased. This decrease is greatest among the most socially well-adjusted respondents and those reporting the lowest levels of participation in crime, but it is also discernable among youths presenting much higher levels of delinquent participation and among those from socially disadvantaged backgrounds. It should also be pointed out, however, that the study includes a number of questions relating to the young people's experience of criminal victimisation. In contrast with the levels of self-reported crime, levels of reported victimisation as regards certain types of theft, threatening behaviour and violence remain fairly constant over the period examined.

The first large self-report study of juvenile crime in Sweden was conducted in the town of Örebro in 1971. Twenty-five years later, in 1996, this study was repeated using the same survey instrument (Ward 1998). This study also indicated that variations in levels of self-reported crime were relatively small. Ward shows, however, a certain polarisation among the groups studied, with the group presenting the highest levels of criminal participation becoming both larger and more heavily involved in crime between the two surveys, whilst at the same time the size of the group reporting no involvement in crime whatsoever also became larger.

The majority of researchers in Sweden are more or less in agreement that the total level of juvenile crime has not increased over the last decades (Sarnecki 2003). The question of trends in juvenile *violence* is rather more controversial. According to official statistics (see Figure 10.2), the number of young people convicted of violent offences underwent a dramatic increase between the mid-1980s and the mid-1990s, after which point a certain decrease may be observed.

Certain academics (e.g. Kühlhorn 2003) have contended that this increase in recorded violent crime reflects a real increase, not least in relation to levels of serious violence. This contention has been called into question, however. Estrada and Sarnecki (2002), for example, have pointed out that the most serious form of violence—i.e. that resulting in death—has not increased among young people. The number of youths who die as a result of acts of violence has remained constant at approximately 16 individuals per year since the beginning of the 1970s. Whilst this does not constitute a direct indication that juveniles are not in fact committing crimes of this type, it does indirectly belie the perception that serious violence is on the increase among this group, since the perpetrators and victims of violence are most often drawn from approximately the same age group (Sarnecki 2001).

Nor does the apparent increase in the number of 15 to 17 year olds convicted of homicide (murder and manslaughter) during the second half of the

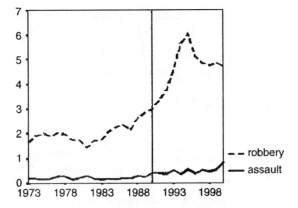

Figure 10.2: 15–17 year olds convicted of assault and robbery respectively, per 100,000 of population, 1973–2000 (Estrada and Sarnecki 2002, source: BRÅ, 2002).

1990s provide support for the contention that serious violence among juveniles is on the increase. On the contrary, a study from the Swedish National Council for Crime Prevention (BRÅ 2002) shows that the total number of convictions relating to violence resulting in death in fact decreased during this period. This decrease is a result of the fact that whilst convictions within the two most serious categories (murder and manslaughter) increased, the number of convictions relating to *aggravated assault resulting in death* fell. According to Lindström and Rying's calculations, *24 individuals* between the ages of 15 and 17 were convicted of murder, manslaughter or negligent homicide between 1990 and 1994, whilst the corresponding figure for 1995 to 1999 was *14 individuals*. This involves a reduction of slightly over 40%. One hypothesis that might be suggested in this context is that the courts today view cases of violence resulting in death more severely than they used to. It is not unreasonable to assume that this more severe view might relate not only to violence resulting in death, but rather to violence in general. Support for this hypothesis that Swedish society views violent crime more seriously than it did previously may be found, *inter alia*, in the findings from research into changes in the way violent crime is reported in the mass media (Estrada 1999, Pollack 2001).

As was mentioned earlier, the increase in levels of juvenile violence recorded by the police over recent years is not corroborated by either the self-report or victim surveys conducted among Swedish 15-year-olds since 1995. Victim surveys have been conducted among the general population in Sweden since the end of the 1970s. These surveys do not indicate any major increase in the level of youths' (16–24 years) exposure to violent crime either (Figure 10.3).

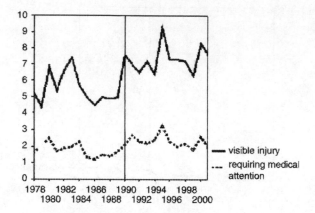

Figure 10.3: Proportion of youths aged 16–24 who report having been subjected to violence resulting in visible injury, or requiring medical attention, during the past year, 1978–2000 (Estrada and Sarnecki, 2002).

In particular, the figure provides no support for the thesis that more serious violence is on the increase, at least not since the beginning of the 1990s. Once again, this statement is based on the assumption that crimes against young people are for the most part committed by other young people.

RESPONSES TO CRIMES COMMITTED BY YOUNG PEOPLE

In Sweden social legislation is used to a great extent to regulate the authorities' responses to crimes committed by juveniles. The social services play a considerably greater role in society's response to criminal acts committed by young people, in comparison with most other countries. This also means that the goal of treatment characterises Swedish responses to deviant behaviour among young people to a greater extent than in many other parts of the world. Generally speaking, the social services and the public sector in Sweden have undergone a much more rapid expansion than in most other western countries. (The number of social services employees, for example, increased by about 500% during the 1960s and 1970s. Source: Näringslivets ekonomifakta 1983.) Since this time, the expansion has not been quite so pronounced and during the economic crisis of the first half of the 1990s, a number of cutbacks in the social sector were witnessed, as was also the case in the majority of areas of public sector activity in Sweden. One could nonetheless still argue that Swedish public sector social services remain relatively strongly resourced and influential (OECD 2003).

The responsibility for responding to crimes committed by young people is shared by the social services and the judicial system. The extent to which the judicial authorities and the social services share responsibility for the response to crimes committed by young people is mainly dependent on the age of the offender.

- For those below the age of 15, the main responsibility for the response to crime lies with the social services.
- For those aged between 15 and 17 (and in certain cases up to the age of 20), the responsibility is divided between the social services and the judicial authorities.
- From the ages of 18 to 20, the responsibility lies mainly with the judicial authorities.

The judicial system: the police

The Swedish justice system functions on the basis of the legality principle, which means that the police and other agencies within the justice system are obliged to intervene where the legal criteria that serve to define a criminal act are fulfilled. At the same time, however, the system allows for a large number of exceptions to this rule. In practice, therefore, as is the case in many other countries, the Swedish police have a large amount of discretionary power. When the police discover that a minor offence is being committed, their efforts are often limited to an order to cease and desist. If this is sufficient to stop the improper behaviour, the police do not report the matter. According to the legislation, the police have the right in certain cases to direct young offenders to repair the damage caused by their criminal acts. If the offender complies, the offence is not reported. In 1990, however, certain restrictions were introduced in relation to the police's right to exercise discretion in relation to the reporting of offences (RPS 1999).

According to Swedish law the police shall prevent, discover and investigate crimes. If a crime has been reported, the official task of the police is to investigate who committed the crime. As in most western countries, the police in Sweden have a low success rate (approximately 15%) when it comes to clearing up traditional crimes. This is true both for crimes committed by juveniles and for those committed by adults. Nevertheless the police, and in particular those police who work with juvenile crimes, are familiar with most of the highly criminally active juveniles within a police district. The criminal activities of these young people are so extensive that even given the low risk of discovery, they will become the subject of a police investigation at some time or other. Furthermore, the police obtain substantial knowledge about the more active juvenile offenders through contacts with and interrogations of other juveniles, neighbourhood police work and other police activities.

Up until 1985, the authority of the police in relation to the investigation of crimes committed by children less than 15 years of age was extremely limited. The police could not, for example, interrogate persons under the age of 15 unless they were investigating crimes involving adult suspects, looking for stolen goods or had other important reasons. (Establishing the guilt of a juvenile suspect was not, in normal cases, considered to be one of these 'important reasons'.) Beyond this, it was expected that the social services would be responsible for investigating the crimes committed by these young people. After a change in the law in 1985 the police were given broader powers regarding the investigation of juvenile crimes. Today, in normal cases, the police are expected to investigate crimes committed by young people over the age of 12, but such investigations are supposed to be carried out in collaboration with the social services. The principal objective with an investigation of this kind is to investigate the need for social measures. By law the police have the right to investigate crimes committed by younger children only in special cases. In addition, the last decade has witnessed a certain shift in praxis, such that schools, for example, have become more inclined to report offences committed by relatively young pupils to the police (Estrada 1999). The social services, however, still have the right to request that specific criminal investigations be suspended when they relate to persons under the age of 15.

Most investigations of juvenile crimes are relatively simple since the crimes committed by young people are usually not of a particularly serious nature. By law, the police are required to show great regard and care in their interrogations of juveniles. Parents and/or representatives of the social authorities should in most cases be present during an interrogation.

In different parts of Sweden the juvenile crime investigation issue has been resolved organisationally in variety of ways. In some areas, special units have been established which specialise in crimes committed by juveniles, or in some instances even certain types of juvenile crime, such as mugging, for example. In other areas, the less serious offences committed by juveniles are investigated by local community police officers whilst investigations into more serious offences are transferred to the central criminal investigation departments at the police district level. Irrespective of the way in which the police organise investigations of juvenile crime internally, this work always takes place in collaboration with the local social services.

If a suspect is under the age of 15, the police turn over the results of their investigation to the local social services. If the suspect is older then 15 the results of the investigation are turned over to the prosecutor. However, if the suspect is under 18, the social services are usually informed.

The judicial system: the prosecutor

According to current legislation, the police are to have a prosecutor assigned to an investigation if the offence is not of a 'straightforward nature' and where there is a suspected offender aged 15 or older involved. In certain cases the prosecutor is the head of the formal investigation. The prosecutor is also responsible for deciding whether the suspect should be arrested and whether an application should be made to a court for a detention order. However neither arrests nor detention orders are utilised very often in relation to offences committed by juveniles. For an individual aged 15 to 17 to be detained during an ongoing investigation, the law requires 'exceptional cause'.

One of the prosecutor's important tasks is that of deciding which measures should be taken regarding the suspect once the police investigation is finished:

- Should the preliminary investigation be discontinued?
- Should the prosecutor issue a prosecution waiver?
- Should he issue a summary sanction order?
- Should he prosecute the suspect in court?

A preliminary investigation may be discontinued, for example, if it turns out that the act committed by the individual did not constitute a crime. The prosecutor may also find that the evidence is insufficient to warrant prosecution.[5]

A waiver of prosecution still constitutes a relatively common form of decision taken by prosecutors in Sweden (see Figures 10.7, 10.8 and 10.9) although its use has decreased substantially since the mid-1980s (see Figure 10.4). This waiver means that the guilty party will not be subjected to any further measures by the legal apparatus (on the condition that they do not commit any further offences) as a result of the act. However, the act will be considered a crime and will be recorded as such in the register of convicted persons. The prosecutor may issue a prosecution waiver with regard to less serious crimes but only if the suspect has admitted to the offence. In the absence of an admission of guilt, the matter must be tried by a court.

---

[5] The prosecutor may also discontinue a criminal investigation if the crime in question may be deemed to be insignificant in relation to another offence and if the costs of the investigation would assume unreasonable proportions, providing the sanction would not exceed a fine or a waiver of prosecution. In such cases, however, the interests of other parties (e.g. those of the victim) may not be disregarded.

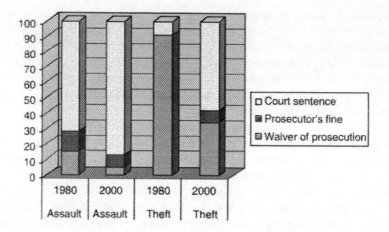

Figure 10.4: Youths aged 15–17 years who have been convicted by means of a court sentence, a prosecution waiver or a prosecutor's fine in 1980 and 2000, for assault and theft offences respectively.

The Swedish Young Offenders Act (LUL) gives prosecutors broad powers regarding the issuance of prosecution waivers when a suspect is below the age of 18, and in certain cases up to the age of 20. The rules are much more generous in relation to young people than older people. But the prosecutor may revoke a prosecution waiver if the young person returns to crime. In the legislation from 1988 on young offenders, the prosecutor's power to revoke such decisions was extended. The provisions regarding prosecution waivers were also made more formal and were to some extent given the form of a formal caution issued by the prosecutor to the juvenile and his parents. A further legislative change in 1994 (SFS 1994: 1760) produced a situation whereby waivers of prosecution may in principle no longer be used for youths who have previously been registered in connection with offences.

Over the course of 2001, approximately 111,000 court sentences, prosecutor's fines and waivers of prosecution were issued in Sweden. Approximately 16% of these convictions took the form of waivers of prosecution. Approximately 12,000 of the convictions related to young people aged between 15 and 17. Of these, approximately 24% were comprised of waivers of prosecution. Of the 10,000 or so convictions relating to youths aged between 18 and 20, approximately 11% took the form of waivers of prosecution. In the mid-1980s, these proportions were significantly higher among the youngest group (45%) whilst they lay at approximately the same level (9%) among the older youths.

Before a prosecutor issues a waiver of prosecution to a person under the age of 18, he often obtains an opinion from the social services if the offence is of a serious nature. When such a decision is issued it is often combined with the condition that suitable measures are to be undertaken by the social services. Prosecution waivers are issued only in extremely rare cases in relation to violent crimes or vandalism.

Another option available to a prosecutor is to determine the sanction for a crime himself. The conditions for the prosecutor to be able to issue a summary sanction order are similar to those for a prosecution waiver: the crime must be relatively minor and the suspect must have confessed. In addition, the suspect must have accepted the size of the sanction. Summary sanction orders may be issued only in the form of day-fines, where the number of days is determined by the seriousness of the crime while the size of each day-fine is determined by the guilty party's economic circumstances. Approximately 33% of all the entries into the register involve summary sanction orders. Among the youngest youths (i.e. those aged 15 to 17), the proportion is somewhat higher at 37%.

Finally, as was mentioned above, the prosecutor may decide to prosecute. Of the 15 to 17 year olds who were convicted of offences in 2001, 61% received these convictions in the form of a prosecutor's decision whilst 39% were convicted by a public court, having been indicted by the prosecutor. The corresponding proportions for 18 to 20 year olds were 51% and 49% respectively. Thus the majority of the younger youths and approximately half of the older ones are convicted by means of a prosecutor's decision. By contrast, 15 years ago a significantly larger proportion (83%) of 15 to 17 year olds were convicted by means of a prosecutor's decision as were 61% of the older group. Thus a considerably larger proportion and number of youths are today indicted for their crimes in a public court, whilst at the same time, the proportion and number of young people being convicted by means of a prosecutor's decision has fallen substantially.

The judicial system: the courts

When a prosecutor decides to prosecute an individual, his guilt and any possible sanction will be determined by the court. Of the approximately 4,600 juveniles aged 15 to 17 convicted annually by the courts in Sweden, 47% are sentenced to day-fines (the same type as can be decided upon by a prosecutor). A similarly common court-imposed sanction regarding juveniles involves being delivered into care in accordance with the Social Services Act. The proportion of sentences of this kind has doubled since the mid-1980s (see Figure 10.5); the number of juveniles given a sentence of this kind has increased almost fourfold. This sentence means that the court transfers the responsibility of finding a suitable measure for the guilty party to the local social services board.

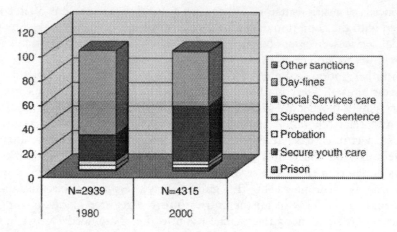

Figure 10.5: Comparison of distribution of court sentences for youths aged 15 to 17, 1980 and 2000.

Approximately 11% of all registered offenders in Sweden are sentenced to prison. Prison sentences are employed very rarely in Sweden for persons who have not yet reached the age of 18.[6] Up until 1999, approximately 60 individuals per year aged under 18 at the time of their offences were sentenced to a prison term, whilst a further 25 or so were sentenced to a special form of probation that begins with a short stay in prison. Since the introduction of the new youth sanction *Secure youth care* in 1999, only very few persons under the age of 18 (to date no more than four per year) have been sentenced to prison. Individuals in this age group are today in principle only sentenced to a prison term if they are of an age such that the length of a sentence to secure youth care would extend beyond the date on which they turned 21 years of age (see figure 10.6).

The fact that so few young persons are sentenced to prison shows that the intention of the new Act—to minimise the number of youths sitting in prison—has been achieved. The new sanction does in fact involve young people being sentenced to a fixed term sanction (which according to the intentions of the Act should be of approximately the same length as the prison term for which one would be sentenced as a young offender, usually approximately half the length of the sanction that an adult would have received for the same offence) but is served in an institution established for

---

[6] According to Swedish law, exceptional cause is required before an individual aged between 15 and 17 may be sentenced to prison. The opportunities to sentence 18 to 20 year olds to prison are also limited, although the legislation is somewhat less restrictive in this case and only reasonable cause is required.

the care of young people (here referred to as a youth care facility). These are the same institutions where youths are placed in compulsory care by the social services (see below). These institutions are focused on the treatment of young people and have a staff to 'inmate' ratio approximately three times that of prisons (approximately three staff members per youth in care). Over the course of 2000 and 2001, approximately 100 annually youths have been sentenced to the new sanction (of which approximately 85% were aged between 15 and 17 at the time of the offence, whilst the remainder were over the age of 18). This constitutes a slightly higher number than those who were sentenced to prison (including probation with a prison term) prior to the new Act coming into force. In addition, the introduction of the secure youth care sanction has led to longer custodial sentences. Youths sentenced to prison prior to 1999 served an average sentence of approximately 5.4 months. Youths sentenced to the new sanction, on the other hand, spend an average of 9.5 months in custodial care (BRÅ, SOS, SiS 2002).

The other sanctions that a court can use in sentencing minors are:

- Suspended sentences (approximately 1% of convicted persons aged 15 to 17 and 13% of those aged 18 to 20 were given this sanction in 2001); and
- Probation (without prison) (approximately 1% of convicted persons aged 15 to 17 and 11% of those aged 18 to 20 were sanctioned in this way in 2001).

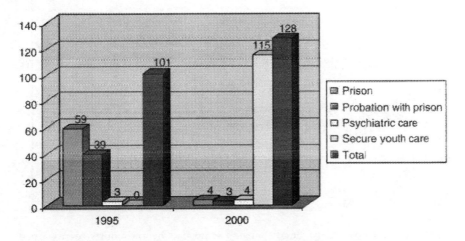

Figure 10.6: Number of youths sentenced to custodial sanctions 1995 and 2000.

Certain of the sanctions presented above may be combined with each other or with other forms of sanction. Thus probation may for example be combined with contractual care or community service. Combinations of this type are rare, however, for young persons under the age of 18. On the other hand, surrender into the care of the social services may be combined with the sanction youth service, which comprises community service specifically adapted to younger people. For approximately 20% of the 15 to 17 year olds sentenced to care within the social services, the sanction is combined with youth service in this way. In rare instances, youth service is also applied in combination with probation for young people over the age of 18. Fines may also be awarded in combination with other sanctions. Finally, young people are in rare cases sentenced to psychiatric care. This sanction is however extremely rarely used in relation to the youngest age group.

The distribution of sanctions in 2001 for all those convicted, and for young people aged 15 to 17 and 18 to 20 respectively, is presented in Figures 10.7, 10.8 and 10.9.

The social services

The social services do not have the task of punishing young people for their crimes. Therefore, when the social services make a decision regarding a measure suitable as a response to a criminal act, the decision should be

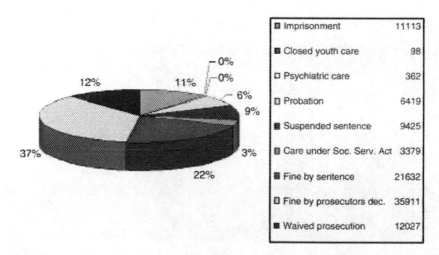

Imprisonment	11113
Closed youth care	98
Psychiatric care	362
Probation	6419
Suspended sentence	9425
Care under Soc. Serv. Act	3379
Fine by sentence	21632
Fine by prosecutors dec.	35911
Waived prosecution	12027

Figure 10.7. Convictions for all persons sentenced by the courts, or awarded prosecution waivers or summary sanctions by the prosecutor, 2001. 110,711 convictions in total.

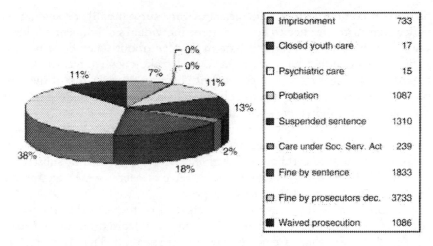

Imprisonment	733
Closed youth care	17
Psychiatric care	15
Probation	1087
Suspended sentence	1310
Care under Soc. Serv. Act	239
Fine by sentence	1833
Fine by prosecutors dec.	3733
Waived prosecution	1086

Figure 10.8: Convictions for all 18 to 20 year olds sentenced by the courts, or awarded prosecution waivers or summary sanctions by the prosecutor, 2001. 10,333 convictions in total.

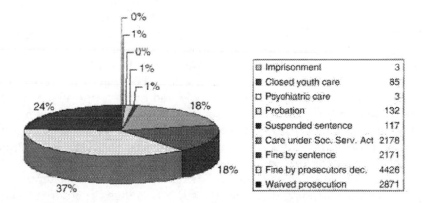

Imprisonment	3
Closed youth care	85
Psychiatric care	3
Probation	132
Suspended sentence	117
Care under Soc. Serv. Act	2178
Fine by sentence	2171
Fine by prosecutors dec.	4426
Waived prosecution	2871

Figure 10.9: Convictions for all 15 to 17 year olds sentenced by the courts, or awarded prosecution waivers or summary sanctions by the prosecutor, 2001. 12,029 convictions in total.

based solely on the young person's social situation. (If an individual has a serious history of criminality, that is naturally included in the overall picture of his social situation.) Swedish law places the entire responsibility for responding to crimes committed by individuals under the age of 15 on the social services. Thus the criminality of this group is regarded as a social welfare problem.

Accordingly the measures of the social services are to have the aim of helping the young offender out of the social situation that is causing him/her to commit crimes. The measures vary substantially, depending on which factors are deemed to be causing the individual's delinquency. Several years ago there was a heated debate in Sweden about whether or not the social services should have the right to undertake coercive measures with regard to their clients. The opponents of coercion thought that if the purpose of the social services was to help an individual, then it could hardly be done against the individual's will. It was also feared that the social services' right to use coercion would make the development of confidential contacts between social workers and clients impossible. The supporters of coercive measures felt that in certain cases, e.g. extensive drug abuse or substantial antisocial behaviour by young people, coercive measures were necessary, at least at the beginning of the treatment process.

The compromise that was finally reached came to mean that the use of coercive measures was limited greatly in the social legislation. In the Social Services Act (SoL) there are no coercive measures at all. This Act, which in most cases is also applicable to young offenders, states that those measures which have the aim of removing the causes of an individual's criminality are to be undertaken in terms of co-operation between the individual himself, his parents and the social services. Regarding individuals with minor criminal histories, these measures are usually limited to one or a series of talks with the young offender and his parents. If it becomes apparent through these talks that there are serious problems in the home (economic problems, internal conflicts, etc.), an attempt will be made to resolve these problems. The family is then given certain opportunities to receive economic support, therapy, a contact person and other forms of support. In certain cases the family may get a social worker who can meet with them at home over a longer period in order to help the family members resolve various problems (e.g. the family's economic planning, their leisure time problems, and conflicts in relations).

In cases of extensive antisocial behaviour that constitutes a threat to a young person's ongoing development, a law containing coercive measures known as the Act with Special Provisions on the Care of Young People (LVU) may be utilised. Another law containing coercive measures which can be used by the social services is the Act on the Care of Drug Abusers in Certain Cases (LVM). The rules governing when an individual may be forcibly taken into custody for the purposes of social services care are very restrictive. According to the Social Services Act (1982) the local social welfare boards have the right to decide about taking a child or young person into custody for social care. These boards, which are made up of local politicians and reflect the political party breakdown at the local government level, have been established by law in every Swedish municipality. In the larger municipalities, additional local boards have been set up. All decisions on custody for social services care made by these boards must be approved by a county administrative court. These courts have an organisation which is completely separate from that of the criminal courts. Decisions arrived at in the county administrative courts may be appealed to higher courts.

In approximately 2,000 cases per year, the social services arrive at a decision to place a young person outside of the family home. In the majority of these cases (approximately 80%, see Figure 10.10), the decision relates to voluntary care in accordance with SoL. The young person is usually placed in a family home or a so-called home for residence and care (HVB). HVB placements are also used relatively often in relation to compulsory (LVU) placements. (In 33% of compulsory care orders, the young person is placed in an HVB home).

The most common form of placement used in connection with compulsory care orders is placement in a youth care facility. Unlike the other institutions, these facilities have the right to use compulsion to keep the youth in place, and they often have secure units. In addition to placements in accordance with LVU, and in rare cases SoL, youths sentenced to secure youth care are also placed in these institutions (see above). Thus both youths placed in care in accordance with LVU and those sentenced to secure youth care are given compulsory care at these institutions. The difference is that youths in the LVU group are placed in these institutions by the social services (once the care order has been confirmed by the county administrative court) and are discharged in accordance with a decision reached by the social services which must however be re-examined every six months, and

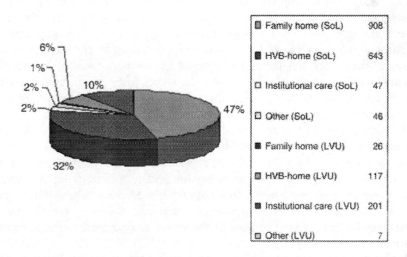

Figure 10.10: Youths aged 15 to 17 placed outside of their own home by the social services in accordance with SoL and LVU in 2001. 1,995 persons in total. (Source: BRÅ, SoS, SiS).

which may in this context be appealed in the county administrative court, whilst those sentenced to secure youth care are placed in these institutions by means of a court sentence and stay throughout the term of this sentence.

It is common that young people who have been placed in youth care facilities by the social services or by the courts are there for the same reason— i.e. involvement in crime. The social services may however also take a decision to issue care orders and place youths in institutions (although not usually youth care facilities of this kind) as a result of other problems experienced by the young person, such as the parents' inability to look after the young person, and different forms of behaviour which are self-destructive but not criminalised.

Other institutions

Thus, according to Swedish law, the social services and the judicial system are the institutions which are responsible for society's response to juvenile delinquency. The social services are also responsible for the response to other forms of antisocial behaviour among young people. On the other hand, young people with social problems also come into contact with other societal institutions and they are often the subject of measures taken by these institutions.

The largest and most important of these institutions is the school system. Sweden has a system involving nine years of compulsory education, but most young people (approximately 97%) go on to some form of further education. The 3% or so who do not continue their education are to a large extent young people with serious adjustment problems (Sarnecki 1983). According to Swedish law, they are to be followed up by the local authorities until they reach the age of 18. In those cases where these young people do not obtain jobs on the open labour market, they are offered various types of assistance by the local authority such as short training programs, job counselling, educational guidance, etc.

The school system has no formal responsibility for the control of deviant behaviour among young people. However, its de facto role is of course very large. Schools have to a great extent replaced the social control previously placed upon young people by working life and to a certain extent by the family and the neighbourhood. In a country like Sweden, where the majority of women work outside the home, the school constitutes the most important agent for social control of the young during most of the hours of a normal working day.

In Sweden, just as in other countries, there is a strong correlation between behaviour in school and criminality as well as other forms of deviant behaviour, both in the teenage years and in adulthood (SOU 1972, 76; Sarnecki 1986; Torstensson 1987; Ring 1999). Swedish teachers recognise very well the symptoms related to a heightened risk of persistent criminality, alcohol and drug abuse, etc., even if not all teachers are conscious of how important these observations may be.

Schools usually have their own organisation for dealing with student problems. Many schools have a school psychologist, a social worker (school curator) and medical personnel (doctor, nurse) attached to them. These personnel, along with those heading the administration of the school and certain teachers, constitute a student care team which, among other things, has the task of deciding how to react when students show symptoms of deviant behaviour. Most schools also have teachers who are specially trained to take care of students with school problems, behavioural difficulties, etc. Initially schools try to resolve problems that arise by means of talking with the student and his parents. Another possibility open to schools is that of taking students out of normal classes and placing them in special education groups, where they may receive more support and be subject to more control. In certain difficult cases the students can be placed in special separate schools run by local school boards. The goal, however, is to separate students with adjustment problems as little as possible from other students and to make sure that they are kept in their ordinary classes to as great an extent as possible. In addition, according to current law, schools within the compulsory school system cannot completely exclude students from the educational system. Instead, students with serious problems among the older age groups are given the option of taking a part-time class schedule and working the rest of the time (without pay) at some workplace nearby. In such cases, the school is responsible for providing the student with suitable guidance.

In general, the school staff will initially try to resolve a student's behavioural problems themselves. The social services are usually not contacted until the measures put in place by school staff have been seen not to produce the desired results. Even though school personnel see their students' behavioural problems at an early stage, schools make relatively few reports to the social services. In Sweden, the level of co-operation between the social services and schools varies from municipality to municipality.

The social services and the schools are also supposed to co-operate with the mental health care authorities responsible for children and juveniles, which have an independent status in Sweden. Parents, especially parents of younger students with behavioural problems, are often given a recommendation to make contact with this institution which offers various forms of individual, family and group therapy. However, contacts with the mental health care authorities are in principle voluntary and in most places they do not accept clients who are not clearly motivated regarding treatment. Sometimes the social services also utilise psychiatric experts to analyse young people with more serious behavioural disturbances. Certain young people with substantial criminality in their backgrounds can also be taken in for observation and in rare cases even for treatment in the county's psychiatric clinics for children and juveniles.

In the context of the debate on juvenile delinquency, the issue of leisure time is usually ascribed major importance. Sometimes juvenile criminality is simply defined as a leisure time phenomenon. A significant portion of the leisure time activities available to young people in Sweden are either financed or directly organised by public sector agencies. The financing of leisure activities for young people is provided through payments to an extensive number of organisations. It is estimated that at least half of the young people in Sweden are members of one or more organisations, most often sporting associations. In many places, especially in some of the country's smaller cities, the degree of association membership is significantly higher. However, associational activity seems to a large extent to be characteristic for young people from socially well-functioning families and, accordingly, for young people among whom the risk of developing serious antisocial behaviour is relatively low. The number of organisations that successfully recruit young people in the risk zone for criminality, and that may serve as an effective alternative to their antisocial network is relatively small (Sarnecki 1983, 1986).

As was mentioned earlier, the economic problems affecting Sweden at the beginning of the 1990s resulted in certain cutbacks within the public sector. The local authorities, which are responsible for schools, the social services and the leisure sector, were forced to make savings and did so primarily in areas of activity that are less well regulated in law than the social services. Amongst other things, substantial savings were made in the area of leisure provision for young people and student care within schools. During the second half of the 1990s, as the economy improved, more resources were once again devoted to these sectors, but one has to work on the assumption that preventive efforts, not least within schools, are less comprehensive than they were previously. At the same time as the resources available to schools for social measures have been reduced, schools have turned to an increasing extent to the police for support in connection with criminality among pupils (Estrada 1999). Several local authorities have made policy decisions that all crime in schools is to be reported to the police.

CONCLUSIONS

Sweden is a pluralistic welfare society with a highly developed public sector. Until the middle of the 1970s Sweden experienced a substantial increase in levels of criminality and other social problems among juveniles. From that point onwards the trends seem to have stabilized, and there are even signs that levels of juvenile crime may have diminished.

The ideas of welfare and pluralism also contribute to the relatively large amount of tolerance and humanity shown in Sweden towards persons who deviate from the norm. These ideas are considered to be important in the formulation of the measures to be used in relation to young offenders. Relatively substantial and long-term criminality is required before the authorities are allowed to undertake more far-reaching measures. The emphasis on treatment instead of punishment is also considered to be more humane, even though the ideas behind it have been questioned (BRÅ Rapport 1977, 7; SOU 1993, 35). The criticisms directed at the strong treatment focus within the Swedish justice system, and primarily within that part of the justice system focused on young people, comprised two elements. One related to the lack of scientific evidence that treatment was an effective method, the other to the perception that the system was unfair. In the light of more recent research, the first of these arguments against employing treatment as a means of responding to crime has shown itself to overstate the case (e.g. Lipsey 1992, 1995; Loeber and Farrington 1998 and BRÅ 2001b). The treatment of young offenders has shown itself capable of producing positive effects, even if these effects are rarely all that strong (CUS, SiS, Andersson 2003). The criticism of the system's unfairness, on the other hand, is still relevant. In this context, a hypothetical case is usually referred to whereby two youths who have committed the same offence are responded to in quite different ways. One comes from a well-functioning social background and is merely given a caution, whilst the other comes from much more difficult conditions and is therefore taken into care and placed in an institution.

In general, one can argue that in Sweden, the 1980s and 1990s were characterised by increasing levels of concern for juvenile violence which has been perceived both within the media and among the public as undergoing a substantial increase. Discussions of the trends in violent crime of the kind presented above seldom reach the public and tend to be contrasted in the press with descriptions of tragic and particularly bloody cases of violence. The general perception among the public at large may be assumed to be that the country has suffered a dramatic increase in the levels of violent crime committed by young people and other forms of serious youth crime. In the context of this climate of opinion, there is a general questioning of methods used to treat young offenders that are perceived to be too lenient. Certain treatment measures, such as taking youths with a long criminal record on sailing trips, have been presented in the media as both ineffective and at odds with the public's general sense of justice. This atmosphere has led politicians to perceive a need to show that they take juvenile crime seriously, and in particular violent crime (cf. Garland 1990, Estrada 2001, von Hofer 2004). Many of the reforms of legislation and praxis relating to young offenders appear to have the objective of accentuating the idea that this is a problem that cannot be taken lightly.

The substantial reduction in the number of young persons convicted of crime has therefore been followed by a substantial tightening of both the law and its application in relation to young offenders. This has led, for example, to a dramatic reduction in the number of young people being awarded waivers of prosecution and to a larger number of youths being sentenced by the courts. This and a long list of other measures suggest that there are efforts afoot to limit the measures of the social services, which are perceived as rather diffuse by many, and instead to emphasise the more transparent means of dealing with young offenders that is manifested by the justice system. These efforts, however, have not been allowed to go so far as to sentence young people to prison. On the contrary, Swedish legislators have made it clear that they do not regard prison as a suitable sanction for youths. Placing juveniles in prison is regarded as inhumane and as running contrary to the UN's Convention on the Rights of the Child. Parallel with the general increase in the severity of the response to juvenile crime, then, the prison sanction has in effect been abolished for the youngest individuals who have reached the age of criminal responsibility. Instead of a prison term, the sanction of secure youth care has been introduced, which takes the form of a treatment measure but which is imposed by a public court and in accordance with the proportionality principle. In this way, the 'lenient' influence of the social services is removed from this sanction. Given the current social climate, however, the introduction of secure youth care has in fact had a 'net-widening' effect, if not with regard to the number of youths being given custodial sentences then at least with regard to the length of the custodial sentences being imposed. Despite the fact that it was not the intention of the legislators, the courts appear to feel that they may sentence youths to a longer stay in a youth care institution than they could when the youths in question were instead being sent to prisons.

It is nonetheless highly doubtful that the influence of the social services over measures relating to young offenders has declined in any general way as a result of the neo-classicist trend witnessed within the Swedish justice system. It is true that the social services do not exert an influence over the length of stay in youth care institutions, but the treatment provided is nonetheless of a social nature and is provided in a collaboration between the National Board of Institutional Care, which falls under the Ministry of Health and Social Affairs and the local social welfare authorities. Further, the fact that a larger number of young people are being indicted and sentenced in public courts has resulted in more youths being delivered into the care of the social services. In connection with this sanction, the measures are formulated by the local social services even if the court has a certain influence over the way they are formulated.

The general conclusion of the above presentation is thus somewhat surprisingly that the combination of a general critique of the treatment ideology, a neo-classicist focus within the judicial system and a stiffening of sanctions against young offenders, has led to a situation where the influence of the treatment ideology and the social services has in fact become more powerful in relation to the way society responds to the crimes of young offenders. The fundamentally humanist view of youth crime and of measures for young offenders that has been dominant in Sweden over recent decades appears at least for the moment to remain intact, although the authorities have become more inclined to intervene against young offenders. The pressure from various quarters to change this system and to make it 'more effective', or even simply 'tougher', remains, however. The Swedish Government recently appointed a new inquiry with the task of reviewing the way Swedish society responds to crimes committed by young persons. The Government's directive to the inquiry states amongst other things that:

> The measures taken are to be dedicated to preventing the youth from reoffending. The commission's objective, whilst maintaining the penal law principles of proportionality, predictability and consistency, is to make progress with the work to develop a sanctioning system for young persons whose content is both clear and instructional, and to create improved conditions, on the basis of the young person's needs, for a return to a life characterised by good social function, thus producing positive change. (Ju 2002, 14)

By means of these formulations, the Government appears to be opening the way for both a more powerful element of neo-classicist thinking but also a continued treatment focus within the new legislation. The future will tell which of these directions the inquiry and the future legislation will take and what the consequences of coming reforms will be for the system's humanist focus.

REFERENCES

Andersson, T. (2003) *Institutionsbehandling av ungdomar. vad säger forskningen?* [Institutional treatment of young people. What does the research have to say?] (Stockholm, Förlagshuset Guthia).

BRÅ Report (1977) National Council for Crime Prevention, *Nytt straffsystem*. [The New Penal System], 7.

BRÅ PM (1982) National Council for Crime Prevention, *De unga lagöverträdarna. Åtgärder vid brott av ungdomar under 15 år*. [Young offenders. Measures in response to crimes committed by youths under fifteen years of age], 3.

BRÅ Report (2001a) National Council for Crime Prevention Sweden, *Kriminalstatistik*. [Crime statistics], 16.

BRÅ Report (2001b) National Council for Crime Prevention Sweden, *Kriminell utveckling: tidiga riskfaktorer och förebyggande insatser*. [Criminal development: early risk factors and preventive measures], 15).

BRÅ Report (2002) National Council for Crime Prevention Sweden, *Crime Trends in Sweden 1998 - 2000*

BRÅ, SOS and SiS (2002) National Council for Crime Prevention, National Board of Health and, National Board for Institutional Care, *Sluten ungdomsvård—en uppföljning*. [Institutional care of youths—follow-up].

Estrada, F. (1999) *Ungdomsbrottlighet som samhällsproblem: utveckling, uppmärksamhet och reaktion.* [Youth crime as a social problem] (Stockholm, University of Stockholm, Department of Criminology).

Estrada, F. (2001) 'Juvenile violence as a social problem: trends media attention and social response'. *British Journal of Criminology,* Vol. 41.

Estrada, F. and J. Sarnecki (2002) *Har ungdomsvåldet ökat?* [Has youth violence increased?] (Stockholm, University of Stockholm, Department of Criminology).

Garland, D. (1990) *Punishment and Modern Society: A Study in Social Theory.* (Oxford, Clarendon).

von Hofer, H. (2004) Criminal violence and youth in Sweden: a long-term perspective. *Journal of Scandinavian Studies of Crime and Crime Prevention,* 1.

—— (2000) Crime and reactions to crime in Scandinavia *Journal of Scandinavian Studies in Criminology and Crime Prevention.* Vol. 5, 2004, pp. 148–166

Ju (2002) *Utredningen om översyn av det allmännas ingripanden vid ungdomsbrott* [Commission of inquiry on revision of intervention in case of youth crime] http://www.riksdagen.se/debatt/dir/index.asp

Kühlhorn, E. (1979) 'Barnavårdslagen—en klasslag?' [The Child Care Act—Class Law?] *Socionomen.*

—— (2003) *Sluten ungdomsvård. Rättliga reaktioner på de ungas brott förre och efter införandet 1999.* [Institutional Care of Youths. Juridical reaction on youth crime before and after introduction 1999] (Stockholm, Statens institutionsstyrelse).

Lipsey, M.W. (1992) 'Juvenile Delinquency Treatment: A Meta-analytic Inquiry into the Variability of Effects'. In T.D. Cook, D.S. Cooper, D.S. Cordray, H. Hartmann, L.V. Hedges, R.J. Light, T.A. Louis and F. Mosteller (eds.), *Meta-analysis for Explanation: A Casebook.* (New York, Russell Sage Foundation).

—— (1995) 'What do we Learn from 400 Research Studies on the Effectiveness of Treatment with Juvenile Delinquents?'. In J. McGuire (ed.), *What Works? Reducing Reoffending: Guidelines from Research and Practice.* (Chichester, Wiley).

Loeber, R. and Farrington, D.P. (1998) *Serious & Violent Juvenile Offenders: Risk Factors and Successful Interventions.* (London, Sage Publications).

Näringslivets ekonomifakta (1983) *1983: Offentliga sektorn—Ekonomi, sysselsättning och trender.* [1983: The public sector—economy, employment and trends]. (Stockholm: Economic facts of Industry).

OECD (2003) *Basic Structural Statistics,* http://www.oecd.org/dataoecd/8/4/1874420.pdf

Pollack, E. (2001) *En studie i medier och brott.* [A study of the media and crime] (Stockholm, University of Stockholm, Department of Journalism, Media and Communication Studies).

Ring, J. (1999) *Hem och skola, kamrater och brott.* [Home and school, peers and crime] (Stockholm, University of Stockholm, Department of Criminology).

—— (2003) *Stöld, droger och våld bland Sveriges elever.* [Theft, drugs and violence among Swedish pupils] (Stockholm, National Council for Crime Prevention).

RPS (1999) *Polislagen* [The Police Law] National Police Board Sweden. http://www.polisen.se/inter/mediacache//4347/4734/2671/polislagen_pdf.pdf

Sarnecki, J. (1983) *Fritid och brottslighet* [Leisure and criminality] (Stockholm, National Council for Crime Prevention, Report No. 17).

—— (1986) *Delinquent Networks.* (Stockholm, National Council for Crime Prevention Report No. 1986: 1).

—— (1987) *Skolan och brottsligheten.* [School and crime] (Stockholm, Carlssons).

—— (2001) *Delinquent Networks: Youth Co-offending in Stockholm.* (Cambridge, Cambridge University Press).

—— (2003) *Introduktion till kriminologi.* [Introduction to criminology] (Lund Studentlitteratur).

SCB (1989) *Ungdomar och Brott.* [Youth and crime] (Stockholm, Statistic Sweden).

SCB (2002) *Undersökning av levnadsförhållanden (ULF)* [Survey of living conditions] http://www.scb.se/statistik/le0101/le0101.asp

SFS (1994:1760) Svensk Författningssampling, författningarna 1994:1604 till 1994:1800 http://www.notisum.se/rnp/reg/SF9941.HTM–226K

SOU (1972) Carlsson, G., *Unga lagöverträdare II. Familj, skola och samhälle i belysning av officiella data. 1956 års klientelundersökning rörande ungdomsbrottslingar.* [Young Offenders 11. Family, school and society in the light of official data. The 1956 Clientele Investigation Relating to Juvenile Delinquents] (Stockholm).

SOU (1993) *Reaktion mot ungdomsbrott.* [Reaction to juvenile delinquency] (Stockholm, Ungdomsbrottskommitten. B Statens offentliga utredningar).

Torstensson, M. (1987) *Drug Abusers in a Metropolitan Cohort.* (Stockholm, Department of Sociology, University of Stockholm, Report No. 25).

Ward, M. (1998) *Barn & brott av vår tid?: självdeklarerad ungdoms-brottslighet 1971 och 1996: en jämförelse utifrån Örebroprojektets data.* [Children and crimes of our time? Self reported juvenile crime in 1971 and 1996: a comparison employing data from the Örebro project] (Stockholm, University of Stockholm, Department of Criminology).

11

Juvenile Justice in Denmark: From Social Welfare to Repression

JØRGEN JEPSEN

INTRODUCTION

THE FOLLOWING ACCOUNT of developments in juvenile justice in Denmark in recent years was originally intended to demonstrate how a so-called welfare state has handled the problems of youth crime with non-repressive measures based upon social and personal support to young law violators, rather than through harsh repression with an emphasis on crime control. The somewhat unique use in Denmark—as in Scandinavia—of communal welfare boards instead of juvenile courts or adult courts was at the time of the presentation at Oñati seen as a model that might serve as an inspiration for developing nations or nations wanting to reform more repressive juvenile justice systems in a welfare direction, all in pursuance of the goals of the Oñati conference.

In the process of re-writing the original contribution after the Oñati conference it became increasingly clear, however, with the passage of time and the emergence of new information, that this would have amounted to presenting much too rosy and optimistic a picture of the actual developments. Tendencies that were discernible in the first years of the new millennium have become more prominent and the optimism originally expressed has been replaced by serious concern over the increasing repression characterizing juvenile justice—like criminal justice in general—in Denmark up until July 2005.

The following account will take up some of the characteristics of the original Danish welfare model of juvenile justice and look at the transformation it is undergoing which is bringing it closer to the crime control model of other Western countries such as the U.S.A. Both the welfare board model and the use of social support instead of institutionalization have come under pressure. The system of sanctions against youth in trouble with the law in recent years has been superseded by symbolic legislation aimed primarily at signalling official disapproval of juvenile deviance and instituting new forms of punishment emphasizing protection of the public. We shall return to this later, but first some words about the history of the Danish welfare state and its model of juvenile justice.

DENMARK AS PART OF SCANDINAVIA AND AS PART OF THE MODERN WORLD

Denmark is a small country (some 5.4 million inhabitants, with 6–7% in the age group 15–20) and forms part of Scandinavia, which until recently was characterized by great homogeneity in population and in politics and social structure. Abroad, Scandinavia has been seen as an important stronghold for social welfare traditions and for social and economic equality. Until Denmark and later Sweden joined the European Union, there was close co-operation between the Scandinavian countries on legislation and social conditions for many years. There is a joint Nordic passport union and there are rules for mutual assistance in legal and social matters. These similarities also characterize the fields of youth policy and juvenile justice (Nordisk Ministerråd 2000). Developments in crime patterns and in reactions to crime and deviance also display considerable similarities—as evidenced e.g. by Sarnecki's contribution to the present volume—with Finland earlier presenting a somewhat different case. Norway has lower offending rates than Sweden and Denmark.

Denmark long had a reputation for being the most permissive Nordic country in relation to deviance, both as to criminal sanctions and as to its drug policies. Denmark has also been seen as more pragmatic and less ideological than Norway and Sweden, working out policies on a more ad hoc basis and with relatively little inclination to base policy upon research and knowledge as opposed to public sentiment. Denmark was regarded—and regarded itself—as very tolerant and broad-minded with good foreign relations.

This picture has changed in recent years. Danish politics have evidenced a swing to the right, the Social Democratic hegemony has been replaced by neo-liberalistic governments based upon the more well-to-do segments of the population, but with a parliamentarian basis in a populist party—the Danish People's Party—reminiscent of other right-wing parties in Europe. Both this party and the conservative and liberal parties seek constituencies in the middle and so profess to be strong adherents to the welfare state. In later years, however, the influence of the Danish People's Party in particular has led to a tightening up of the legislation on immigration and refugees, accompanied by a clearly xenophobic rhetoric. This has also been a response to increasing public concern about the influx of foreigners who have not been well integrated, have tended to cluster in urban ghettoes, are not well versed in the Danish language and are beginning to exhibit the characteristics of a marginalized underclass (Socialforskningsinstituttet 2005).

Second generation immigrants in particular have displayed problems of adjustment in a spiralling interaction with discrimination in housing, in the labour market and on the streets. Signs of such maladjustment have been increasing crime levels, particularly among the young, and conflicts with the police, often of a quite dramatic nature.

In addition, Denmark has experienced a rise in gang phenomena, both in the form of motorcycle clubs (*Hells Angels, Bandidos*) with a high level of violent crime and drug dealing and in the form of street gangs, some of them consisting of immigrant youth. The Danish gangs have engaged in fights with immigrant gangs, thus a picture is formed which bears considerable similarity to American juvenile and racial gang wars over turfs and drug markets.

These developments have in recent years had the consequence that ordinary citizens have become afraid of foreigners and have demanded tough public action against perceived risks of violence, in particular from immigrant youth. The fears were nourished by dramatic media coverage of a few incidents involving 'ethnic' (i.e. coloured) youth—including a group rape in 2001 in the centre of Copenhagen.

Politicians were quick to grasp these sentiments and turn them into political capital in the struggle for power. The result has been harsher reactions to deviance, starting out with several 'violence packages' of legislative and law enforcement measures carried by the Social Democratic government in the 1980s and the early and mid-1990s. This trend was taken up much more forcefully by the later right-wing government, which took power in late 2001 and went on to win the elections in January 2005.

In the early spring of 2005, street gangs of very young immigrant youth in Copenhagen ghettoes who committed repeated acts of street robberies and violence, primarily against young Danish children, aroused worries among local inhabitants. The Copenhagen police and local politicians have called for stricter reactions towards these under-age groups, and again the issue of lowering the age of criminal responsibility has come up.

The following sections will deal with the original social welfare model as it was seen in operation until the late 1990s, and will then go on to chart changes towards the control model, which accelerated from around 2000 up until spring 2005. It will highlight some of the perceived assets of the welfare model, look at the ways in which this model has been challenged and is undergoing change, and finally try to chart the background to the changes and the prospects for further development. Finally we will look at the lessons that might be learned from this course of events.

These developments will be related to some of the key elements in juvenile justice raised by the Convention on the Rights of the Child (CRC) and to issues found relevant in work on juvenile justice reform in developing countries.

THE AGE OF CRIMINAL RESPONSIBILITY

A caveat

In relation to the following consideration of criminal responsibility it should be noted that although children below the relevant age ('minors') are considered as objects of assistance and treatment rather than punishment, some of the measures applied within the system of social welfare—in particular in secure residential institutions—in actual practice may be quite as harsh as institutions within the prison sector (some of the Danish open prisons have very permissive regimes and almost pleasant infrastructures). It is therefore worth considering how the interests of minors are safeguarded under the welfare system. It must also be noted that some offenders of minor age actually commit serious acts, including violence and robberies, and represent such a danger to their surroundings that protection of the public (and staff!) is an inescapable consideration.

Historical development[1]

In the mid 19th century steps were taken to limit the use of penal sanctions for children and juveniles. Ten years as the minimum age of criminal responsibility was made statutory while sentencing of children between 10 and 15 years came to be dependent on individual evaluation. They were only to be punished if they were evaluated to have been sufficiently mature to understand the criminal nature of the behaviour (Greve 1996). Punishment was seen as both unsatisfactory and burdensome and in 1905 an absolute age limit of 14 was introduced. Simultaneously, a law on child welfare was introduced, which was based on the still valid principle that children and juvenile offenders under 18 years should be educated, not punished (Greve 1996). Child welfare committees were set up and reformatories established to take care of 'erring and wicked children' as well as young offenders as the new law gave the committees the authority to detain children on the basis of behavioural problems and neglect.

The inspiration to form *child welfare committees* came from Norway, where a similar arrangement was established in 1900 (Dahl 1985). Moreover, the new radical ideas about criminal policy and about possibilities for treating the offender, which emerged in Europe around the turn of the 19th century, also influenced the changes concerning children and child welfare. It was the idea developed from the positivist school that led to a paradigm shift in the view of the offender and later on to a change in the classical penal ideology based strictly on proportionality.

[1] The following historical account is based largely upon Kyvsgaard (2004b).

These trends had a pronounced influence on the new Danish Criminal Code of 1930, which is still in force. The minimum age of criminal responsibility was then raised to 15 years (Nielsen 1999). Despite many attacks, this legal age limit has remained unchanged since then. Fifteen is also the age of criminal responsibility in the other Nordic countries (Nordisk Ministerråd 2000, 11–14).

An important aspect of the administrative implementation of the age of criminal responsibility is the question of the actual placement of the youngest offenders. Up until 2004 the youngest offenders—below 15— could not be placed in secure wards under the social welfare system by the communes (municipalities) without special permission from the county, which was supposed to safeguard the interests of children. In 2004 an administrative change was promulgated, allowing the communes to place children between 12 and 15 in secure wards without such permission. This has been seen by some (Vestergaard 2004a, Boerneraadet 2005) as a covert way of reducing the age of criminal responsibility to 12. It coincided with a demand set forth by the Danish Peoples Party for lowering the age of criminal responsibility to 12—a demand which found some support within the government itself.

In other words, the Danish history of the age of criminal responsibility shows a move between a fixed age limit and the maturity criteria discussed also in developing countries. Internationally, there are great variations in setting the limit (Mehlbye and Walgrave 1998, see also Table 1.1 in the Introduction), and it is more interesting to look at the overlap between the two systems rather than seeing them as divided according to sharp criteria.

DEVELOPMENTS IN DANISH JUVENILE JUSTICE LEGISLATION 1933–73 AND BEYOND

The Criminal Code of 1930 (in force in 1933) introduced a number of special sanctions, all based on the idea of treatment and all partly or totally indeterminate. For youth justice it resulted in the establishment of the *youth prison sanction*, a sentence for juveniles between 15 and 21 years of age with the intention of educating and training juveniles with criminal proclivities. The youth prison sanction was partly indeterminate as it was to last for a minimum of one year and maximum of three years, in case of readmission up to four years.

Even though the youth prison sanction was meant only for juveniles in need of care and education, it gradually became the most important prison sentence for juveniles. Most youth prison sentences, however, concerned offenders between the ages of 18 and 20, as offenders under 18 years in most cases had their charges withdrawn and were instead subjected to child and youth welfare. During the last decades of the existence of the youth prison, however, there was an increasing tendency to use the sanction for juveniles under 18 years.

The youth prison sanction was abandoned in 1973 together with the other (indeterminate) special sanctions based on the idea of treatment. Since then, no legislation concerning only juveniles and young adults was passed until 2001 when a new Youth Sanction, indicating the partial re-emergence of treatment-related ideas, was introduced.

THE DANISH SYSTEM OF JUVENILE JUSTICE TODAY

Denmark has no juvenile justice system

Denmark, in essence, has no separate juvenile justice system. Put simply, *children* below the age of criminal responsibility (15) are dealt with exclusively by the social welfare authorities—the municipalities and the counties. Persons above 15—be they adolescents aged 15 to 17 or young adults aged 18 to 21—are in principle dealt with by the ordinary courts. There is no juvenile court system.

Nevertheless, there is an overlap between the social welfare system for juveniles aged 15–17 and the adult criminal justice system, as young offenders may be dealt with within the welfare system until the age of 18 (and in a few cases until 21). Social welfare measures—including involuntary placement in a residential institution—may be extended below the age of 15 and may also be prolonged for youth turning 18 while in care, or may be the result of a decision by the welfare boards for juveniles aged 15–17. This may happen either independently of criminal behaviour or as a reaction to law violations. In the latter case, an interplay between the criminal law system and the welfare system occurs.

The criminal law system as a gateway to juvenile justice

The initiative from the criminal law system may occur either through a waiver of prosecution—granted by the prosecutor, but subject to limited review by the local court—or via a court decision. The latter type of decision may take the form of a conditional sentence (probation) with conditions subjecting the juvenile to supervision or placement within the welfare system or to a specific type of treatment, e.g. for psychiatric disease, or an unconditional 'Youth Sanction' (see below). When the young offender turns 18, however, (s)he becomes the responsibility of the adult probation system, which normally takes over supervision for the remaining period.

Adolescents may, however, become the responsibility of the Department of Corrections (Kriminalforsorgen, translated as the Department of Prisons and Probation (DP&P)), from the age of 15 in more serious cases, e.g. serious violence and repeated grave offences. This decision is up to the sentencing court, which may also pass an ordinary prison sentence.

According to the provisions of the CRC (Art 37), juveniles below 18 are presumed not to serve an unconditional sentence together with adult offenders, i.e. in adult prisons, and they are not supposed to be held in custody with adults in adult jail. Due to lack of slots in secure wards under the social welfare system, several young offenders aged 15–17 are still placed in local jails or prison rather than in secure social service institutions (*Politiken*, 27 March 2005).

The DP&P, in a count as of 13 August 2002, found a total of 16 juveniles aged 15–17 in its institutions, consisting of 5 in local jails, 4 in the Copenhagen jails, 1 in the special psychiatric prison at Herstedvester, 1 in an open prison and 5 in the closed prison at Ringe (in a special section for juvenile prisoners). In 1999 the Danish Supreme Court decided (UfR 1999.1415) that the CRC does not expressly prohibit placing a juvenile in isolation (solitary confinement) in an adult prison in extraordinary situations.

Adolescents aged 15–17 who are sentenced to prison are supposed (since 1998) to serve their prison sentence in an alternative way under section 78, subs. 2 of the Act on Execution of Sentences. *Serving in alternative way* covers a number of different options, some of them involving specialized treatment (e g in a psychiatric or other hospital), some involving placement by the welfare authorities in a foster family or other group setting and some of them involving special institutions for juveniles, including so called 'secure wards'. See figure 11.1 for an overview of the Danish system.

Social welfare, secure wards and budgets

The fact that the latter category of placement is under the auspices of the welfare authorities (run by the counties) may cloud the fact that the secure wards are tough institutions not so different from prisons. They are supposed to maintain maximal security, i.e. protection against escape. They are also supposed to contain elements of treatment, particularly for those young offenders serving a Youth Sanction (see below), but in practice treatment is rather limited and lacks any clear theoretical or professional basis (Vestergaard 2004b). The treatment element is clearly subordinate to the element of security. Some of the secure wards are specifically authorized to hold the most violent and dangerous categories of young offender, and even within these there are special isolation units or cells used for the most recalcitrant and escape-prone young offenders.

The secure wards are also to some extent used as alternatives to remand in ordinary jails for young offenders aged 15–17, as they are supposedly

	12	15	18	21	Age group
Decision makers	(Police) Welfare Board (CYB)	Police-prosecution-court Welfare Board (CYB) Prison- Probation- & Parole	Police-Prosecution-Court (Welfare Board), Dept. of Prison- Probation & Parole	Police-Prosecution-Court Prison- Probation & Parole Dept.	
Appeal to:	Social Board	Nat.Board of Appeal (CYB) High Court :invol.placement	Criminal court/ High Court	Prosecution (waiver) Criminal court, High Court	
---- Reactions: Preliminary custody decision	Police: interrogation, custody up to 4 hours CYB: voluntary/involuntary placement. Preventive measures (supervision etc.)	Police: arrest up to 24 hours,Court: remand custody – in spec.inst.s, jails prosec.. no charges cautionoing, fines, waivers of prosec., Youth Contract referral to CYB Prosecution. court sentence	Remand (jail) (court) Fines, waivers.(prosecution) (Court:conditional sentence (probation, Comm.Service), Uncond. Sent. (prison)	Remand custody (isolation) Fine, waiver Conditional sentence (Probation), Uncond. Sent. (prison, preventive detention)	
Implementors	Welf.system, CYB, County institutions	Welfare system (CYBs, county institutions) Department of Prisons, Probation & Parole	Welfare institutions (extension of stay), support Department of Prisons, Probation & Parole	Department of Prisons. Probation & Parole	
Measures (other than fines 6 warnings)	Support, supervision, placement in: Foster care, institutions. residential institutions Secure institutions Special secure wards	Welfare measures – Youth contract, supervision. support, placement, resid. institutionss. secure institutions, special secure wards, Youth Sanction Serving in alternative ways (treatment institutions). Prison (spec. wards)	Extended welfare measures (support). resid. institutions Supervision by DP;P&P Probation with do. Extended Youth Sanction Prison Transfer to treatment inst.s Parole (Supervision by DPP&P)	Probation, supervision by DP&P, Prison (open or closed) Preventive detention Transfer to special treatment institution (eg. Psychiatric hosp.) Parole – with supervision by DPP&P	

Figure 11.1: Denmark's juvenile justice system: an overview. The measures for different age groups ('juveniles' primarily 15–17)

more geared to housing young offenders and fulfil the CRC principle that juveniles should not be institutionalized with adult offenders. Still, occasionally a juvenile awaiting trial may be transferred to (or housed in) an adult jail when no room is available in a secure ward or when even these are insufficient to prevent escape and repeated offending.

The decision to place a juvenile in a secure ward is usually taken by the ordinary courts in connection with a remand custody order or as part of a Youth Sanction, as is transfer to an ordinary institution for juveniles.

According to current provisions and agreements, the local social welfare authorities at the municipal level do not have to cover the specific costs for each individual placement in a secure ward. According to available accounts, from a purely budgetary point of view, local authorities may therefore prefer placement in more restrictive, secure wards or even in prison.

It is understandable that the communes are also reluctant to remove a child from its home if this is not deemed absolutely necessary. But this reluctance has given rise to criticism that the communes are unwilling to bear the costs necessary for safeguarding the welfare and best interests of children. A parliamentary proposal was put forward in 2004 to move responsibility for decision making from the municipalities to a different forum which is independent of economic considerations (Forslag til Folketings-beslutning B 77/2004, Socialministeriet 2004). It resulted in a limited reform on placements, but without any major change in the organizational setup.

In principle, the economic responsibility should be a factor persuading the communes to prefer preventive social measures to institutionalization, also for children at risk of entering into or extending a criminal career. In practice, however, the communes are less effective at providing such preventive measures, particularly when they involve economic support to a child/juvenile and his/her parents. In recent years the economic burdens upon the communes of institutional placement after a removal of a child from the family—be it voluntarily or against the will of the parents and the child—have grown considerably, at the same time as the state increasingly limits their budgets. Thus at the end of 2002 a total of 14,360 children and juveniles were placed outside their home (Mehlbye and Rohde 2004, 13). Ten per cent of these placements were made against the will of the parents and/or the juvenile. The number of children and youth placed in residential institutions has been fairly stable at around 3,000 since the mid-1990s. Therefore, the growth in placements is primarily due to increased placements in social-pedagogical institutions and in foster family care. The former category today amounts to some 25% of all placements, foster families amount to 45% and residential institutions 25%. Compared to the other Nordic countries, Denmark has a high level of placements, particularly in the form of social-pedagogical collectives, boarding schools and 'own residence' (with municipal payments) (Mehlbye and Rohde 2004, 13).

THE SOCIAL WELFARE SYSTEM AND YOUNG OFFENDERS

In principle, decisions in children's cases, with or without a penal sanction, but involving removal of the child from the home, are made by the municipality (the local commune) through its 'welfare board', named the *Child and Youth Board* (CYB). In cases of compulsory removal of a child from its home, the local communal administration presents the proposal and its basis to the CYB. This board normally consists of three municipal politicians, supposed to represent a political and lay element with local insight. In cases of compulsory removal of a child or juvenile the committee is joined by a local judge and a person with special insight into children's matters. This is supposed to safeguard the legal position of the child/juvenile. The parents and the juvenile above 15 are provided with a lawyer free of charge. This structure—and in particular the CYB—is the Danish parallel to the Juvenile Court.

The role of the welfare boards—delimitation and co-operation between the social and justice sectors

The rules on administration and structure in placement cases are found in the Act on Social Service, the Act on Due Process (Retssikkerhedsloven), and the Act on Administration (Forvaltningsloven).

According to section 40 of the Act on Social Service the commune (municipality) makes decisions on *voluntary* measures. A number of measures are enumerated, such as consultancy, day care, youth clubs, practical and pedagogical support to parents, economic support, and placement outside the home. Most of these measures require the parents' consent, although appointment of a personal consultant or contact person for the child can be decided without consent under certain circumstances. 'Voluntary' placement outside the home of adolescents above 15 also requires consent by the adolescent. The commune decides on the placement and carries out supervision. Such voluntary measures may be appealed to the *Social Board* ('det sociale nävn') as far as the legality of the measure is concerned. The local Social Boards consist of five members and the County Chairman. In 2002 the Social Boards decided 855 cases, particularly in relation to questions of social support. These decisions are final.

If the commune finds that the case cannot be solved by voluntary measures it sends a proposal to the CYB for compulsory measures, accompanied by a case analysis and a plan of action for the measure.

A decision to remove a child/juvenile from the home against the will of the parents must be made by at least four of the five members, i.e. either the judge or the child specialist must be in favour. The CYB's decisions may be appealed to the *National Board of Appeal* (Ankestyrelsen) within four weeks, and from there—also within four weeks—to the *High Court* (Landsretten). Appeal may be made both by the parent and by the juvenile, if over 15. The complaint may concern the placement as such and the type of placement (foster home, institution) but not in which specific institution or home of those available the placement should take place.

Participants in the meetings of the National Board of Appeal are four ordinary members (civil servants), a chairman and a medical consultant, most often a specialist in child psychiatry. In 2002 the National Board handled 489 complaints, mostly concerning involuntary placements (Socialministeriet 2004, 18).

Appeals to the High Court involve the parents as parties to the case, along with the youth, if above 15. A lawyer is appointed free of charge for the complainant(s). The case is decided by two judges, one whom must be a specialist in child/youth psychiatry or psychology, the other a specialist in child and youth welfare measures. The case is handled according to the rules of the Act on Administration of Justice (Retsplejeloven) dealing with appeals against administrative deprivation of liberty.[2]

---

[2] These statements are based upon the Analysis of Procedures in Children's cases (Socialministeriet 2004).

Involuntary placements. Placement in secure wards

Placement in a secure unit under the general rules of the Social Welfare Act is an available option in the following circumstances: (1) if such a measure is considered absolutely necessary to protect an individual from harming himself or others, (2) for initial observation, or (3) to implement a decision regarding a longer period of treatment (section 58 of the Social Service Act). For juveniles above 15 the total duration of placement in a secure unit may be up to 14 months and the decision is made for 2 months at a time with the possibility, however, of two lots of 6 months in connection with a treatment program. In addition, the court may make a decision concerning placement in a secure unit at a juvenile institution as a surrogate for pre-trial custody according to the provisions of the Administration of Justice Act.

In connection with recent criticism of CYBs, a parliamentary initiative (Forslag til Folketingsbeslutning, B 77/2004) gave rise to an analysis of procedure in these cases (Socialministeriet 2004). Four considerations were seen as essential: decision-making should be improved in relation to (1) professionalism, (2) legal safeguarding of the interests of parents (to a lesser extent the child), (3) uniformity in decisions, and (4) counteracting of irrelevant economic considerations (i.e. the interest of the communes in saving money). Various reform models were presented in the analysis, one of them involving the removal of the judge from the local CYB and letting the local court be the first instance for complaints about decisions of the communal administration, another introducing a new national board as decision-maker, and a third variation involving regional centres. It was alleged that having a judge present in the CYB creates confusion between the administrative and the judicial powers. This discussion, however, did not result in any change in the organization of children's and juvenile cases within the communal sector.

In a separate piece of legislation (Act No. 1442 of 22 December 22 2004) the duty of the communes to provide preventive and supportive measures before removing children from the home was stressed, and a specific obligation for the communes to provide a cohesive policy for children was introduced. Also a duty was introduced to provide a quick plan of action (within 7 days from the receipt of documentation from the police), for children below 18 having committed violent crimes. The act further specified the options for support etc. that should be available, the rules for complaints and the rules for distribution of expenses. The system of decision-making was not changed in any fundamental way, however.

Within the next few years a major communal reform will be implemented, which involves a significant reduction in the number of communes, and the counties will be abandoned in favour of a limited number of regions (five). How the professional qualifications for dealing with cases of children in trouble with the law will be provided and improved is at present unclear.

Summing up—the welfare board model

The Danish experience of welfare boards (CYBs) undertaking some of the functions handled by juvenile courts elsewhere is thus by no means unambiguous. The idea that the CYBs should provide both legal safeguards and professionalism has not been clearly demonstrated. Furthermore, it has been noted that in Denmark there is a scarcity of research on the effects and efficacy of different organizational structures. It has also been pointed out in relation to placement outside the home that very little research on this topic has been carried out in Denmark. Thus the scientific basis for choosing between different models of organization and securing professional treatment of serious young offenders—or for that matter children and juveniles at risk—is lagging behind (even if this problem was finally taken up in 2004) (Vestergaard 2004a). This has led to increasing pressure to establish methods and routines for evaluation and documentation. A start has been made with the publication *Unge i dögnanbringelse—indsats- og resultat-dokumentation* (Youth in 24-hour placements—documentation of efforts and results) (Mehlbye and Rohde 2004). A number of illustrative cases are quoted, and proposals for the development of methods and systems to be applied by communes and counties in the coming years are presented.

DEVELOPMENTS IN THE SYSTEM OF REACTIONS

Cautious experiments with *family conferencing* within the welfare sector and *victim-offender mediation* in the criminal justice sector have begun. The latter has been only half-hearted and the development of alternatives to imprisonment or institutionalization has been quenched by the demand for security, for being 'tough on crime'—and on juveniles. There has been little respect for the type of research that questions the effectiveness of incarceration in preventing or reducing (re-)offending. Instead the demand has been for 'signal-legislation' expressing moral condemnation of law violation and of law violators, almost regardless of their age.

The development from the extensive use of waivers of prosecution for juvenile offenders through the special category of Youth Contracts to secure wards and the Youth Sanction is illustrated in the following sections. The public and political demands for demonstrative condemnation of young offenders and for harder sanctions have been based upon the perception that juvenile offending—like crime in general—and in particular violent crime, has been on the rise due to former *laissez-faire* criminal policy and that there has been a growing need for harder sanctions and more incarceration with an emphasis on protecting the public.

Are these perceptions borne out by the actual developments in juvenile crime, and to what extent are the problems adequately represented in the media? We will look at these questions in conjunction with an analysis of the statistics on registered offences committed by children (under 15), juveniles (15–17) and young adults (18–20) and with developments in the system of reactions during the period 1992–2002.

It should be noted, however, that the statistics on offences are hard to interpret and are subject to perceptual distortions due to the way they are created. The statistical entity for counting *offences* in the tables is decisions or '*dispositions*' under the Penal Code and so-called 'special legislation', i.e. less serious offences carrying maximum penalties of no more than two years. The decisions—either by the prosecution (waivers) or by the courts (conditional or unconditional prison sentences)—are distributed according to the 'main type of offence', i.e. the offence carrying the highest penalty under the law, which means that other offences in the same case (decision) are not counted. Furthermore, most of the official statistics concern decisions, not people—and some individuals appear in the annual statistics more than once in a year. These are the conditions that inescapably colour the presentation of reality in statistics.

THE DEVELOPMENTS IN CHILD AND YOUTH CRIME AND REACTIONS

Studies on self-reported crime among 14–15 year olds

Research on self-reported crime among school children in grade nine (14–15 years old) indicates a decline from 1979 and 1989 to 1999 both in the number of juveniles engaging in crime and in the number of juveniles committing serious offences. The former is especially pronounced (see Figure 11.2). Furthermore, the studies show that while the number of youth who have committed repeated serious offences has decreased, offenders tend to exhibit an increasing crime frequency (serious offences include car theft, burglary and robbery, while minor offences include *inter alia* shoplifting, theft of bicycles and vandalism).

The studies thus reveal an increased polarization in crime prevalence and frequency among juveniles, and similarly patterns of increased polarization are found in the lifestyles of the juveniles and in school life (Balvig 2000, Kyvsgaard 1992).

The decrease in prevalence among juveniles has been explained by demographic changes as small cohorts face different and better life circumstances than bigger cohorts and children of large families. It has furthermore been explained by an increased tendency among the youth to focus more on future opportunities and to view crime as risk behaviour (Kyvsgaard 1992, Balvig 2000). Finally, it has been pointed out that intensified crime prevention measures might have diminished the number of minor thefts (Balvig 2000, Kyvsgaard 2004b, 364–5).

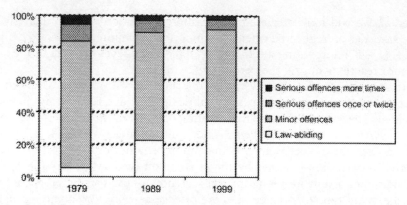

Figure 11.2: Self reported crimes among 14-15 year olds in 1979, 1989 and 1999
Source: *Flemming Balvig: RisikoUngdom, 2000.*

Children below 15—registered offence patterns

A set of preliminary statistics on offences registered for children aged 10–14 years during the period 1992–2002 has been published by the Danish Ministry of Justice, which stresses, however, the limited validity of the data (Justitsministeriet 2003, Kyvsgaard 2003a, 2003c).

Table 11.1 shows that the total number of reported crimes perpetrated by children under 15 years during the 1990s fluctuated somewhat and there was neither a clear upward nor a clear downward trend in crime prevalence among children. However, certain types of offences, especially violence and partly also robbery and shoplifting, showed a tendency to increase. The level of cases involving violence was rather stable until 1998 but in later years considerably more children were registered for violence. 'Joy-riding' (car theft) and in particular burglary decreased. Thus the number of children registered for burglary in 2002 was a third of the 1992 level. The table also indicates that the number of children registered for shoplifting heavily influences the total number of registered crimes for children below 15 (Justitsministeriet 2002).

Reactions, children, 12–14 years old

Since children below the age of criminal responsibility cannot in principle be punished, neither can they be formally 'charged' with violations they are suspected of having committed. But they can, in practice, be interrogated by the police.

In 2003 a set of rules on administrative coercive measures in criminal procedure against children below 15 were introduced in the Act on the

Table 11.1: Cases concerning children aged 10–14 'charged' with offences, distributed by type of offence and year (absolute numbers)

	1992	1993	1994	1995	1996	1997	1998	1999	2000	2001	2002
Violence (§ 244–6)	64	76	54	67	60	63	99	133	163	208	199
Burglary	526	336	385	256	240	211	182	108	173	165	185
Robbery	25	30	22	22	68	30	39	47	97	75	113
Shoplifting	1194	1374	1285	1261	1344	1271	1490	1550	1734	1310	1099
Joy-riding	325	252	261	261	203	254	230	217	290	246	317
Other	1074	1038	924	927	763	644	798	784	992	959	901
Total	3208	3106	2931	2794	2678	2473	2838	2839	3449	2963	2814
No. of 10–14 year olds	298752	290752	280521	273930	272987	276633	280579	289167	298751	308866	318443
Per 1,000 10–14 year olds	11	11	10	10	10	9	10	10	12	10	9

Source: *Danmarks Statistik, Kyvsgaard 2004b.*

Administration of Justice for the first time, limiting the time the police are allowed to keep under-age children in custody while investigating their suspected offences to 6 hours and regulating the way 'charges' might be presented. The Social welfare authorities are required to be represented during questioning of such underage suspected 'offenders'. These rules—which were drawn up pursuant to a report by the Criminal Procedural Committee of the Ministry of Justice (Justitsministeriets Strafferetsplejeudvalg 2003)—have been criticized for giving the police too wide powers in this respect (Boerneraadet 2005).

Only a small fraction of children below 15 are removed from their home by the social welfare authorities primarily because of acts which, if committed by an adult, would amount to a crime. Law violation should in principle be seen as a signal of trouble and interventions are seldom implemented due to crime exclusively, as other circumstances are indicators of a need for help.

Statistics on child welfare do not tell us the number of measures initiated on the basis of criminality. At the end of 2000 nearly 1,800 boys between 12 and 14 years of age were placed outside their home, which amounts to 19 per 1,000 population in that age group (Kyvsgaard 2004b, 368). Placement in foster families is the most common type, while placement in institutions constitutes around one-fourth of the placements (Socialministeriet 2003a).

A study on Fyn (='Fünen'—one of the major Danish islands) estimated that if the figures from Fyn were calculated up to the national level an estimated 2,300 cases involving law violations would be brought before the CYBs. Of these, some 800 would result in a juvenile being placed outside their home.

Adolescents 15–17 years old, patterns of offences—decisions

The registered offence pattern as measured by dispositions ('decisions'—which are based upon the unit of the decision for the most serious offence registered for the youth in question in the relevant year) is about the same for 15–17 year old offenders as for younger juveniles, as violence, robbery and shoplifting have increased while burglary has decreased. Dispositions (sanctions) for shoplifting increased especially from 1991–2, which was, however, primarily due to changes in sanctions policy and not to changes in offence rates.[3]

The number of juveniles aged 15–17 who during the period 1992–2002 received a penal reaction (waiver of prosecution, fine, or a court sentence) is quite stable and there are no clear tendencies towards increase or decrease. In absolute numbers there has been a decline, but this is negated when relative figures are applied (see Table 11.2).

---

[3] Until July 1991 around half of all charges for shoplifting were dropped and a warning was issued. By 1 July 1991 this practice had changed and instead a fine was imposed. Offences not leading to a charge are not included in the table.

Table 11.2: Number of sanctions (waivers of prosecution, fines, prison sentences (conditional and unconditional)) 1992–2002 for juveniles aged 15–17

	1992	1993	1994	1995	1996	1997	1998	1999	2000	2001	2002
Sex offences, total	21	22	19	34	19	28	19	28	39	23	21
Of which Rape	2	2	3	9	0	3	5	5	11	2	3
Violence, total	264	380	482	493	424	407	441	482	693	748	777
Of which Murder	1	0	0	0	1	1	0	0	0	0	0
Attempted murder	0	0	0	0	0	0	0	0	0	0	0
Penal Code § 244 (simple vi.)	207	292	364	372	309	308	311	334	522	548	572
PC § 245 (aggravated violence)	19	31	40	49	54	46	34	51	66	81	73
PC § 246 (v. with death or serious damage)	0	0	3	0	0	2	0	0	1	0	0
Property Crimes, total	4172	4065	4103	4246	3951	3744	3680	3345	3583	3527	3194
Of which Burglary	705	515	534	512	451	434	322	297	299	318	302
Shoplifting	1217	1294	1335	1320	1315	1282	1371	1210	1194	1024	911
'Joy-riding'	284	311	333	394	359	405	341	365	340	345	271
Robbery	61	58	70	86	87	112	110	113	142	152	134
Other Penal Code offences	48	79	90	102	51	73	75	76	84	111	103
Of which Drug offences	2	1	0	3	1	0	7	2	1	7	4
Penal Code offences, total	4505	4546	4699	4875	4445	4252	4215	3931	4399	4409	4095
Other law* violations, total	677	636	613	569	465	349	388	313	332	397	379
Of which Drug Act violations	59	77	81	61	66	57	99	70	91	109	119
Act on weapons	441	374	328	266	246	196	182	145	156	213	213
Total	5182	5182	5312	5444	4910	4601	4603	4244	4731	4806	4474
Per 1,000 15–17 year olds	25	26	27	29	27	26	27	26	29	29	26

Source: *Danmarks Statistik*, Kyvsgaard 2003c.

* 'Other laws' include traffic offences and violations of other 'special laws', including the Weapons Act and the Act on Euphoriant Drugs.

In relation to violence, there was a marked increase in the number of cases involving juveniles (15–17): the number has tripled since 1992. The great majority of cases concern simple violence (Penal Code section 244), but there has also been an increase in the number of cases of aggravated violence (section 245). Juveniles in Denmark, however, are very rarely involved in murder or attempted murder or particularly dangerous violence (section 246). Juveniles commit rather few sex crimes. In 2000, when several cases occurred in which juveniles had participated in group rapes, 11 juveniles were sentenced for rape, but this figure has diminished considerably since then.

The system of reactions, 15–17 year old offenders

For offenders in the age group 15–17 years the system is mixed: the great majority of these adolescent offenders are referred by the police, prosecution and/or the court for action to the welfare boards (CYBs), which are also exclusively responsible for dealing with child offenders below 15 years of age, and are often already in contact with the adolescent offenders and their families.

The board may decide to remove the adolescent offender from their home, but the majority of cases consist of measures not involving deprivation of liberty (Socialministeriet 2003b). Furthermore, 15–17 year olds are not normally placed in jail on remand awaiting a decision on their case. The most serious young offenders may be placed in substitute remand ('surrogatfängsling'), normally in an institution within the welfare system. For the most serious of these, such remand may take place in high security institutions but still within the social service system, normally in small institutions (Socialministeriet 2003a).

Types of disposition

The formal basis for special welfare measures against juvenile offenders aged 15–17 is a conditional waiver or suspension of prosecution[4], where referral to the welfare board and to the social services for youthful offenders is a condition for suspension of prosecution. After the lapse of a probation period of up to two years—or upon reaching 18—without further offending and without serious infractions of the condition(s) of submission to possible welfare measures the case is closed.

The 'traditional' waiver will only be kept on the juvenile's criminal record for two years after the initiation, if the conditions have not been violated. This may be seen as a partial expression of the wish not to stigmatise young offenders unnecessarily. It was further reduced in 1998 along with the introduction of the youth contract.

---

[4] Sections 722 and 733 of the Act on Administration of Justice (Retsplejeloven); see Rigsadvokaten (1998).

In addition to the condition of non-offending for a certain period, the waiver—which is formulated in co-operation between the prosecutors and the welfare authorities—may include a number of other conditions. Some of the conditions will be related to welfare measures, others may involve the payment of a fine or of restitution (damages) to the victim. Conditions which involve economic burdens upon the juvenile must be accepted by the court. Both in these cases and where other conditions are applied the case must be presented to the court, which has to be satisfied that the offender admits guilt and the judge is convinced of the truthfulness of this statement. If not, the case will have to go through an ordinary court process.

The conditions relating to social welfare measures may include placement outside the home according to the decision of the welfare board, or specific types of treatment, e.g. for the abuse of alcohol or other drugs.

Within the non-institutional measures the social authorities can use a wide array of measures, most of them parallel to those conditions that may be imposed under a conditional sentence under section 57 of the Penal Code. They may include various kinds of economic support for the juvenile or the family, the appointment of a personal advisor (mostly for administrative matters) and a contact person (for personal support and control), and special provisions for education. For families without means the welfare board may grant subsidies for such purposes.

As a measure of intermediate severity, the juvenile may receive a conditional sentence with probation (Kyvsgaard 1998). This may involve the setting or non-setting of the penalty in advance. In some cases the length of sentence will only be set in the case of violation of the conditions and a new appearance in court. A conditional sentence will normally be to a prison term, and the court may set a 'combination-sentence' which is in part suspended and in part unsuspended. The latter usually involves a short period (maximum three months) of deprivation of liberty or a fine.

For those young offenders who are given a conditional sentence, probationary supervision is normally carried out by the services of the Department of Prisons and Probation, but it may be delegated to the social services. When the juvenile reaches 18 years of age, further supervision is transferred from the social services to the Department of Prisons and Probation. This department is in charge of the supervision of all offenders above 18 years who receive a conditional sentence.

Remand placement and prison sentences for youth aged 15–17

Remand

As of January 15 1999 new rules came into force under which juvenile offenders aged 15–17 were to be placed as far as possible in surrogate remand custody in one of the secure institutions under the child and youth welfare authorities and could not normally be placed in ordinary jails. Still, a few of the most recalcitrant and escape-prone youths are occasionally placed in adult jails (see below).

Young prisoners

Until January 1999, young offenders aged 15–17 sentenced to prison under the Department of Prisons and Probation (DPP) were placed in special prison wards separate from adult offenders, one of them in a former youth prison, others in the Copenhagen Jail. These placements were, however, found to be problematic for geographical reasons and due to difficulties of providing suitable activities.

Thus, in the period 1999–2002 there was at any one time an average of 13–14 young inmates in prisons or jails, of whom 7–8 were serving a sentence and 6 were in remand custody. In 2003, however, the figures were notably higher: as of 25 February 2003 a total of 32 offenders below 18 were in prison or jail, of whom 12 were serving a sentence and 20 were on remand awaiting trial. This latter group would normally be put in a jail in Copenhagen or near their home.

Usually, young prisoners aged 15–17 serving a sentence in an open prison are also placed according to the principle of proximity to the home. At least every two weeks the prison staff are supposed to discuss the juvenile's situation and decide whether there might be grounds for placement elsewhere. Prisoners aged 15–17 sentenced to serve time in a closed institution should, as a rule, serve in the State Prison at Ringe—normally in a special section for the youngest group—or in a jail. The institutions are supposed to provide individual treatment programs according to the motivation of the youth. Cognitive skills programs, treatment of abuse, training in daily living (ADL), supplementary school education and other activities are offered.

At the state prison in Ringe, a special three-year project on separate wards in co-operation between the prison service and the social welfare system was introduced for young prisoners aged 15–18. These slots should aim specifically at the small group of young offenders repeatedly committing serious (or) violent crimes. It is maintained that these placements have a double objective:

—Taking care of the needs of the adolescent for relevant pedagogical and therapeutic measures, and
—fulfilling the demands of society for sanctioning the criminal activities of the juvenile (the public sense of justice), including keeping the offender in a closed environment as long as and to the extent that he violates the environment with his illegal behaviour.' (Socialministeriet 2003a)

The project includes the special section at Ringe and two open residential institutions with a mobile unit to assist in critical situations. The special ward at Ringe was fully occupied in 2002 and has a waiting list.

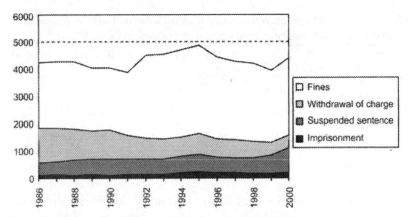

Figure 11.3: Sanctions for Criminal Code offences for 15-17 year old offenders by type of sanction, 1986-2000. Absolute numbers, cumulated

Source: Statistics Denmark, Kyvsgaard (2004b).

Within the social welfare sector 23% of the 3,000 slots for young persons were occupied by youthful offenders in 2000. In secure residential institutions (for placements based upon administrative deprivation of liberty) there was in 2003 a total of 85 slots in 7 institutions (Socialministeriet 2003a, 47); this number later increased to a total of 94. In one of the secure institutions a special secure ward was established in 1998 to provide for those young remand prisoners who represent the greatest danger to their surroundings and to themselves.

In critical situations, the most difficult and violent young offenders are moved around among the secure institutions and the jails. The pressure on the secure wards has also meant that an increasing number of young offenders on remand have to be held in ordinary jails instead of the secure welfare institutions (*Politiken*, 27 March 2005).

Regarding prison sentences imposed on young offenders, the length of the sentence will normally be shorter than is the case for adults irrespective of the fact that a prison sentence for young offenders typically embraces offences for which the juvenile has earlier been given a withdrawal of charge and/or a suspended sentence. For youth aged 15–17 a prison sentence may not be for more than 8 years.

In the year 2000, the average length of a prison sentence was 4.4 months for young offenders (aged 15–17) compared to 6.5 months for older offenders (aged 18–30), and none of the sentences for the juveniles exceeded 3 years (Kyvsgaard 2004b).

Until 2001, a provision in the Penal Code (section 49 subs. 2) was used to grant transfers from a prison to a treatment institution[5]. In connection with a change in the legislation which established the new Youth Sanction

---

[5] See Hagemann and Olsen (2001) for an evaluation of the effects of the application of section 49, subs. 2.

Table 11.3: Number of young offenders aged 15–17 sentenced to imprisonment and the number serving the sentence in an alternative way, respectively, 1991–99

	1991	1992	1993	1994	1995	1996	1997	1998	1999
Sentenced to imprisonment	51	69	70	91	113	105	111	111	89
Serving in an alternative way	10	23	27	44	55	53	58	75	60
Actually imprisoned	*41*	*46*	*53*	*47*	*58*	*52*	*53*	*36*	*29*

Source: *Ekspertgruppen om ungdomskriminalitet 2001* Kyvsgaard (2004b).

in 2001, a special provision was introduced in the Act on the Enforcement of Sentences (section 78) for such transfers. About half of them involve transfers to pensions or other (semi-open) institutions under the Department of Prisons and Probation; others involve transfer to a treatment institution within the social welfare system and a few to a psychiatric institutions; and yet others involve transfer to a special 'secure ward', also within the welfare organisation (these measures are referred to here as 'serving in alternative way').

The number of juveniles serving their prison sentences in an alternative way increased greatly after the ratification of the UN Convention on the Rights of the Child in 1991. During spring 2001 the practice of combining imprisonment with serving the sentence in an institution was established, enabling those who had not initially been allowed to serve a sentence in an alternative way to be transferred to an institution outside the prison system after some time (see table 11.3).

The numbers and types of sanctions (dispositions) imposed against Criminal Code offenders aged 15–17 in 2003 can be seen from Figure 11.3. (p. 233) (Kyvsgaard 2004b, 374).

Figure 11.3. shows the results of the Danish youth justice policy for the age group 15–17 years. In 2000, 5% of the sanctions for these young offenders were prison sentences, 20% suspended sentences, 11% were waivers of prosecution and the majority (nearly two thirds) of the sentences were fines.

For offenders over the age of 17 the corresponding figures were as follows: 22% prison sentences, 21% suspended sentences, 5% withdrawal of charge (waivers), and 53% fines. Fines and withdrawal of charge are thus

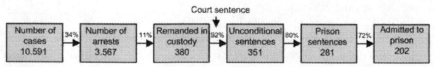

Figure 11.4: The flow of juvenile justice in Denmark 2003, age group 15–17

Table 11.4: Data on Reactions to ('sanctions') in Denmark, young offenders (aged 15–17 years) 2003

				% of total decisions	Overall total decisions
					10591
Acquittals (in court)		117			
Charges not sustained (no grounds for prosecution)		1720			
No guilt, total			1837	17%	
Guilt established			8754	83%	
Fines, total			6659	76%	8754
ticket fines		5972			
other fines		687			
Waivers, total			496	6%	8754
youth contacts		184			
ordinary waivers		114			
other wavers		198			
Court Sentence, total			1574	18%	8754
conditional			1223	78%	1574
cond. sent. alone		908			
cond. sent.+ comm. serv (80) + finc (16)		126			
cond. sent. + fine		189			
Measures (Greenland)			25		
Unconditional sentences			351	22%	1574
unconditional. sentences. alone		175			
youth sanction	70				
unconditional sentences		176			
combination sentences	14				

more frequently used for young offenders (Kyvsgaard 2004b, 374), and most fines are ticket fines[6].

The annual number of prison sentences for young offenders increased somewhat in the 1990s due to both an increase in robberies and violence

---

[6] Ticket fines are imposed by a police officer or a prosecutor without being taken to court— unless the offender denies guilt or is unwilling to pay the amount stipulated.

among juveniles and to harsher sentences for violence. Withdrawal of charge (waiver of prosecution) has been declining for many years: while 40% of all sanctions for offenders below 18 years were withdrawals of charge in 1980, this had decreased to 11% by 2000.

In 2003, the great majority—76% (6,659)—of all reactions to youth aged 15–17 (involving established 'guilt') were fines and 6% (496) were waivers of prosecution. Of these waivers, 184 (37%) involved Youth Contracts and 114 (23%) were 'traditional' waivers conditioned upon child and youth welfare measures. 1,574 decisions—or 18% of the total—involved a court sentence. Of this latter group, 1,223 were conditional and 351 unconditional (prison) sentences. 70 of the 351 were sentences to the 'Youth Sanction' (see table 11.4 (p.235)).

The most recent figures for reactions towards juvenile offenders aged 15–17 (from 2003) are summarized in Figure 11.4, which illustrates the flow of cases in the criminal justice system.

It should be noted that the number of admissions to prison does not quite correspond to the numbers in the table above as they stem from a different source from the ordinary crime statistics (namely information from the Department of Prisons and Probation) and thus overestimate the number of juveniles actually put in prison.

The overall system of reactions is illustrated in Figure 11.5, with available numbers for 2003 included (p.237).

Young adult offenders (18–20)—crime pattern (sanctions)

Regarding offenders aged 18 to 20 years, the crime pattern between 1992 and 2002 was much more stable than is the case for younger offenders, as shown in Table 11.5 (p.238).

It is difficult to point to a clear increase in violence and robbery among young adult offenders in this period, whereas the downward trend in burglary is pronounced. In general, the level of violence is somewhat higher for 18–20 year olds than for those aged 15–17, but during the period the two groups approached each other.

It should be noted, however, that to some extent the described development in types of offences is a statistical artefact, due to legislative changes—higher penalties—particularly in the field of violence. This has meant that violence will appear more often as the main offence in cases involving several counts of different offences. In general this means that the statistics overestimate the level of juvenile violence for 1992–2002 by some 20%.

For violation of the provisions on drugs in the Penal Code, as well as for violations of the Act on Euphoriant Drugs, there has been an increase in the number of cases since the end of the 1990s concerning youth aged 18–20.

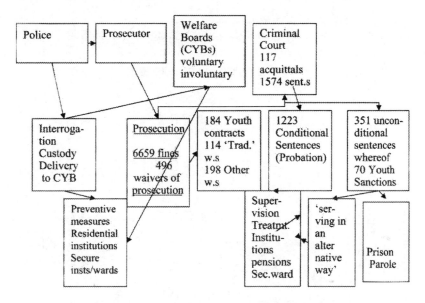

Figure 11.5: Flow of cases, juvenile offenders, aged 15–17 (2003)

Cases involving violation of the Act on Weapons declined during the period, which is also the case for 15–17 year olds. However, after 2002 the police launched systematic crackdowns on illegal weapons—knives, in particular. The knife-killing of a young Italian tourist in a street in Copenhagen by two young second generation immigrants in 2003 triggered a heated debate on the carrying of knives. The anger generated by this crime led to a (Supreme Court) sentence stating that the two young killers, after serving prison sentences of 10 and 8 years respectively, should be deported to Turkey, from where their families originated (one of them was born there, but came to Denmark with his parents at the age of three, the other was born in Denmark and both of them had lived most of their lives in Denmark).

As can be seen from the last row in Table 11.5, the number of dispositions per 1,000 population aged 18–20 years increased from 1992 to 1994 and has since then returned to the level we saw at the beginning of the 1990s. The figures reflect a decrease in the number of 18–20 year olds during the 1990s, down 23% from 1992 to 2002 (Kyvsgaard 2004b, 364).

The pattern of sanctioning for young offenders aged 18–20 in the year 2003 is shown in Table 11.6 (p. 239).

For youth aged 18–20, the proportion of waivers (2%) is just one third of those for 15–17 year olds (6%). Fines (the majority of which are for traffic offences) clearly dominate the picture (75% of all sanctions).

The development in relative offence rates, distributed by sex and age group (15–17 and 18–20), can be seen from Table 11.7 (see p. 241).

Table 11.5: Number of penal sanctions (waivers of prosecution, fines and prison sentences (conditional and unconditional)) 1992–2002 for the age group 18–20

	1992	1993	1994	1995	1996	1997	1998	1999	2000	2001	2002
Sex crimes, total	33	30	33	42	27	34	24	35	33	38	35
Of *which* Rape	4	5	3	4	6	7	3	7	4	6	7
Violence, total	680	829	1069	909	858	889	830	862	852	997	970
Of *which* Murder	2	2	2	6	2	2	1	4	2	1	1
Attempted murder	0	0	2	0	0	0	1	0	0	0	0
Simple violence (PC § 244)	524	601	793	616	596	608	562	559	592	652	610
Aggravated violence (PC § 245)	61	111	109	125	104	102	103	95	88	141	144
Very serious violence (PC § 246)	2	0	4	2	3	4	1	1	5	2	0
Property crimes, total	5470	5699	5606	5220	4821	4577	4332	4010	3817	3825	3525
Of *which* Burglary	1108	1087	958	829	804	662	601	504	474	486	450
Shoplifting	1139	1300	1318	1110	1056	1025	990	985	894	811	719
'Joy-riding'	360	434	521	500	540	551	514	452	362	403	363
Robbery	119	121	89	110	115	112	115	103	140	133	157
Other Penal Code Offences	191	199	228	288	232	214	246	224	282	285	362
Of *which* Drug crimes	11	20	17	17	20	16	28	36	35	49	79
Penal Code decisions, total	6374	6757	6936	6459	5938	5714	5432	5131	4984	5145	4892
'Special laws', total	1583	1598	1563	1390	1145	1073	1123	1074	1137	1232	1199
Of *which* Drug Act violations	465	463	468	388	353	401	402	476	511	565	559
Act on Weapons	487	496	461	329	305	264	288	219	208	268	243
Total	7957	8355	8499	7849	7083	6787	6555	6205	6121	6377	6091
Per 1,000 15–17 year olds	36	38	39	37	35	35	34	33	34	37	36

Source: *Danmarks Statistik, Kyvsgaard 2003c.*

Table 11.6: Reactions to youthful offenders (aged 18–20) in Denmark, 2003

(Penal Code and 'special laws')				*per cent* of
Decisions, total:		16.148		
Acquittals (in court)		241		
Charges 'dropped' (insuff.evidence etc.)		2532		
'Guilt' not sustained, total		2773	2.773	
'Guilt sustained', total		13.375		
Dispositions				
Fines: police fines:				
ticket fines (traffic laws etc.)		7.150		
fines + disqualif., prosecution		842		
court fines:				
fine sentences	1590			
fines accepted	361			
fines acc. + disqualif.	63			
court fines, total	2014	2.014		
Fines, total	10.006		10.006	75% 13.375
Waivers of Prosecution				
Youth contracts		6		
Conditions of youth measures		29		
'other waivers'		264		
waivers, total		299	299	2% 13.375
Court decisions (excl. acquittals)				
Sentences, suspended (probation)				
'suspended sentences alone'		1.098		
Suspended sent.s + fine		303		
suspended + Comm.Service		323		
suspended + CS + fine		113		
Suspended sentences, total		1.787		
Unsuspended sentences (prison)				
Unsusp. 'alone'	846			
partly suspended	204			
partly susp + CS	48			
unsusp. + fine	95			
served on remand	19			
Unsusp.sent.s, total	1.212	1.212		
Other court decisions				
'Measures' (Greenland)	43			
no penalty,	28			
Other court decisions total		71		
Court decisions, total		3.070	3.070	23% 13.375
(Acquittals)		241		
All decisions involving guilt		13.375		

It is notable that in 2001 and 2002 the proportion of sanctions for older boys was pretty much the same as in the period 1993–95. And for boys aged 15–17 the relative sanctioning level in 2002 returned to a fairly low level when looking at the period as a whole.

'NEW SANCTIONS'

Youth Contracts (1998)

In 1998 a new form of waiver of prosecution was instituted under the name Youth Contract (YC). The YC came into force on 1 July 1998 (Kyvsgaard 2000, Rigsadvokaten 1998, Stevens 2003). These contracts were to replace the traditional waivers of prosecution for most young offenders aged 15–17. At the same time, the use of fines and warnings were recommended by the Attorney General as the primary measures for young (first) offenders committing only less serious acts (Rigsadvokaten 1998).

On the basis of a pre-decision study, a contract is drawn up by the welfare services in conjunction with the prosecutor's office and the juvenile, and in some cases his or her parents. If the juvenile does not accept the contract at the end of the negotiations, prosecution resulting in a conditional sentence (i.e. a higher level of sanction) or an unconditional prison sentence is the presumed result.

The conditions of a youth contract might involve a promise to conscientiously attend school or another type of education, spend leisure time in a certain way, e.g. in a youth club, perform some type of work, etc. The types of promises are not necessarily different from the conditions that might be attached to the old style waivers or to a suspended sentence with probation. In addition, traditional welfare measures, including placement in an institution or foster family, may be used as a condition in a Youth Contract.

The Youth Contract was designed to gradually replace the old style waivers, particularly in cases of a somewhat serious nature. It was thus meant for a 'medium severity' type juvenile offender, who could not adequately be sanctioned by a warning or a fine. However, it was not meant for 'youth who seem to be involved in a fairly stable pattern of crime', i.e. repeated burglaries, theft etc. of a more serious nature. Robbery, drug crimes and drunken driving were also exempt from the Youth Contract system.

The ideology behind the Youth Contract was that young offenders should receive a more serious warning than implied by the traditional waivers. They should be warned that this was 'a last chance' and that more serious reactions would occur in the case of further offending or violation of conditions. On the reward side the law stated that if a youth contract was fulfilled,

Table 11.7: Number of sanctions (waivers of prosecution, fines, prison sentences (conditional and unconditional)) per 1,000 in the respective age groups, distributed by sex

		1992	1993	1994	1995	1996	1997	1998	1999	2000	2001	2002
Age 15–17 years	Girls	8	9	9	10	9	10	11	11	11	10	9
	Boys	40	42	45	47	44	41	42	40	46	47	42
Age 18–20 years	Girls	10	10	10	9	9	9	9	9	9	9	9
	Boys	60	64	67	63	59	59	59	56	59	64	63

Source: Danmarks statistik, Kyvsgaard 2003c.

the decision would only remain on the offender's criminal record for one year after the court's decision (as opposed to two years for ordinary waivers). The idea was to make youthful offenders accountable for their deeds (Kyvsgaard 2000).

There was at that time no willingness to use community service in the patterns of reactions towards juveniles. However, in connection with a tightening up in 2001of sanctions for car theft (classified as 'joy-riding') it was assumed that community service as condition of a suspended sentence would be a normal reaction towards young car thieves (15–17 years of age) and preliminary data show that the number of community service orders for young first offenders actually rose in the following year (Kyvsgaard 2004a).

In Denmark there has been no clear tendency towards more imaginative sanctions, e.g. restorative justice. Even the importation of conflict councils ('Konfliktraad') from Norway was carried out in a way that did not involve any real alternative. Participation in a conflict council meeting was not supposed to reduce the sanction to be imposed and the system was tried only on a pilot basis in a few circuits. In 2004 there was a proposal to expand its application on a national basis, but in April 2004 the government declared its intention to abandon the measure altogether. Its use has continued, however, on a limited experimental basis in a few circuits.

Youth contracts and the level of juvenile crime

The tightening up in relation to the traditional waiver was a reaction to the oft vented allegation that young offenders did not really get any serious reaction early enough, that they received several waivers, one after another—an impression which was not actually substantiated by statistics (Hansen 1996, Stevens 2003, 16), and that the supervisory roles were not very authoritative, but rather implied lenient reactions to breaches of conditions. Only very few violators were reported for breaches of conditions, and even fewer received any significant sanctions (Clausen 2002, Stevens 2003).

It was also a reflection of an increased fear of youth and angry reactions to publicity about a few, much discussed serious incidents (see further below). The public perception at that time was that juvenile crime—in particular violent crime—was on the rise and that society had failed to stem the tide of criminality.

In actual practice, however, juvenile crime had decreased over the years 1990–99 by almost 20%, except for its more serious forms. Thus the number of cases against 15–17 year olds for burglary declined from 867 in 1990 to 297 in 1999 (i.e. a reduction of almost two-thirds), theft of bicycles and mopeds from 505 to 277, and 'other theft' from 657 to 453. It should be noted, however, that part of the decline was due to the fact that the population of youth in the relevant age bracket—15–17 years—declined from 220,000 in 1990 to 165,000 in 1999, i.e. a decline of some 25%, so that the relative level of youth crime had not reduced so markedly as might first be assumed.

On the other hand, robbery cases rose from 72 to 113, serious violence from 27 to 51 and simple violence from 208 to 334. This is possibly worrying—percentage-wise—but not large in absolute numbers.

The application of Youth Contracts

In actual practice it turned out that YCs were used increasingly over the following years (1998–2001) against young offenders within the intended age brackets, but particularly for 15–16 year olds (Kyvsgaard 2000). Out of a total of 482 waivers in 1999, 162 involved YCs.

But in general the late 1990s and the early 2000s were characterized by a decline in the use of waivers altogether. Furthermore, in the sanctioning pattern we see a development resembling a polarization. Relatively more juveniles received fines (or warnings) rather than waivers and suspended sentences, and relatively more were sentenced to deprivation of liberty. The proportion of prison sentences thus rose from 17% of all dispositions in 1989 to 22% in 2003.

The explanation for this development may be an increasing level of crime among the more active juvenile offenders—more serious offenders, and serious offenders commit more crimes—or it may be that the prosecutors demand heavier penalties than previously.

This development in the sanctioning pattern parallels to some extent the developments in Sweden, where likewise 'a substantial reduction in the number of young persons convicted of crime has ... been followed by a substantial tightening of both the law and its application ... a dramatic reduction in the number of young offenders being awarded waivers of prosecution and to a large number of youth being sentenced by the court'— a paradox possibly explained by a perceived serious increase in juvenile violence (see Sarnecki's article in the present volume).

The demise of the Youth Contract

As indicated above, the idea of the Youth Contract was to provide a more constructive reaction to juveniles aged 15–17. In actual practice, however, this sanction did not take the place of the traditional waiver of prosecution, which still represents a large proportion of sanctions not involving deprivation of liberty. This may be due to a number of factors. One factor could be their increasingly limited use by local courts, which make decision based upon proposals from local prosecutors (Rigsadvokaten 2000). It also seems as though prosecutors have not been as enthusiastic about the YC measure. The concept of swift and harsh reactions to breaches of conditions relating to social welfare measures did not quite materialize either. The welfare services were late in reporting violations and most reported violations were met with quite mild sanctions—if any (Stevens 2003).

The use of waivers in general had been decreasing over the preceding years. Only 3% received more than one waiver with conditions and if those waivers without conditions are included, only 7% received more than one waiver. This was in contrast to the public perception of extreme leniency in granting repeated waivers.

The results in relation to recidivism were studied by Stevens (2003), who compared recidivism among those young offenders who received YCs with those who received only an 'old style' waiver, with or without conditions of social welfare measures. Among those young offenders who in the period 1996–99 received a waiver with conditions, 20% committed a new offence resulting in a penalty more serious than a fine within the first two years. The corresponding figure for youth receiving a conditional sentence was 33% and for those receiving an unconditional sentence, the rate of recidivism was 48%. For those receiving a prison term of more than 3 months, the rate was 65% (Stevens 2003, 5). It must be noted, of course, that these differences are to some extent a product of selection mechanisms placing the more recidivism-prone offenders in the prison category.

Stevens' study compared those young offenders who in the period 1 July 1998 to 31 December 2000 received a waiver of prosecution conditioned upon a youth contract with those who in a comparable prior period received a traditional waiver with (other) conditions. The result was that the two groups largely recidivated to the same extent and at the same frequency and speed. Even when controls were made for age, sex and prior criminal record as well as for the type of crime leading to the waiver with conditions, it was impossible to demonstrate significant differences in their inclination to commit new crimes. The conclusion that there were no significant differences is probably what might be expected as there are in reality only rather minor differences between the two types of sanction—namely the contractual element in the YC group (Stevens 2003, 40).

Thus one might say that neither youth contracts nor other waivers of prosecution have succeeded in holding or expanding their place in the total pattern of sanctions for offences committed by 15–17 year olds, even though their results must be considered to be fairly positive.

Although the use of fines had been rising for some years, it decreased again in the early 2000s. This development may be said to imply that 'the soft approach' has been seen as insufficient to handle the perceived problems of juvenile crime. But—more importantly—it did not seem to fulfil the alleged public demand for security and for notable and serious reactions to juvenile deviance, hence the ensuing upsurge of 'signal legislation'.

Waivers of prosecution have also been a major traditional reaction towards juvenile offenders in Sweden, where their use has reduced substantially since 1980, but it is still a relatively common form of decision taken by prosecutors (see Sarnecki's contribution in the present volume, Figures 10.4, 10.7, 10.8 and 10.9). Legislative changes in 1988 and 1994 involved further restrictions on the provisions for such waivers. Today a larger proportion and number of youths are indicted for crimes in public courts in Sweden (Sarnecki, this volume).

THE DEMAND FOR MORE SERIOUS SANCTIONS

During the early 1990s and the years 2000–02 an increasing concern was noted in relation to serious juvenile crime. It had three main components: (1) Fear of (serious) violence, (2) the 'Rocker War', and (3) the unruly behaviour of ethnic minorities.

(1) Increasing violence?

The early 1990s and the following years were characterized by increasing public alarm about violence. This concern was nurtured by the public, media and politicians alike. Even if the crime statistics did not reflect any great increase in violence in general, there was some increase in serious violence, also committed by 15–17 year olds (see Table 11.2 above). The result was the enactment of two consecutive 'violence packages', involving new legislation with higher penalties for violence—a dramatic inflation—and a 'violence secretariat' to launch a number of violence prevention activities. Between 2003 and 2005 a heavy investment in fighting the perceived increase in (youth) violence has by far overshadowed the beginnings in earlier years.

(2) The 'Great Danish Rocker War'[7]

This 'War' involved gunfights and other battles during the 1990s between the motorcycle clubs *Hells Angels* and *Bandidos* and their respective supporters and 'prospects'. It resulted in a number of killings and spectacular events which frightened the public and resulted in a special law prohibiting their residence in so-called 'Rocker fortresses' (*Rockerborge*).

---

[7] The term 'rockers' was imported to Denmark from England. It is erroneously applied to designate national chapters of international motorcycle clubs with provocative jacket decorations ('colors'). In Germany they have been outlawed as 'criminal organizations', but not in Denmark. See Jepsen (1998).

The fighting went on for several years, but seemed to end in 1999 when a truce between the two gangs was negotiated. The police played a large role in investigating and prosecuting members for a large number of crimes—not only the murders, but also drug trafficking and property crime. On only one occasion were innocent non-members exposed to serious risk and on another occasion a visitor to a rocker fortress party was killed when the opponent group fired an anti-tank missile into the fortress.

In 2003 a number of extraordinary legal and enforcement measures were processed through parliament to fight this problem. Part of the problem is that a large proportion of the offences are committed by supporters and recruits who try to obtain status and membership in the groups. The motor-cycle groups seem to be extremely attractive to young persons impressed by their macho image. Keeping youngsters away from them has become a major goal of crime preventive activities.

(3) Ethnic disturbances and crime

Xenophobic reactions to increased immigration, not least from (Northern) African countries and the Middle East, has triggered a very repressive atti-tude towards juvenile delinquency committed by immigrants, escalating almost infinitely to the time of writing (spring 2005). There were and are some real grounds for concern, however.

Young immigrants—and particularly second generation immigrants, born in Denmark and speaking Danish, but carrying foreign names and skin colours—contribute disproportionately to juvenile crime statistics, par-ticularly in the more serious offence categories, including violence and rob-beries. And a couple of spectacular cases, one of them involving the rape of a Danish woman in a public toilet in the very heart of Copenhagen by a small group of immigrant youth, triggered enormous public concern and demand for harsher penalties. In the spring of 2003 this resulted in legisla-tion significantly raising the penalties for violence and rape.

It is disputed, however, to what extent the higher offence rates among young—in particular second generation immigrants—are due to their eth-nic status as such. When account is taken of social factors such as the young offenders' social status and geographical location—which place them in the distinctly lower strata of society—their crime rates do not seem significantly higher than those of Danish youth in the same social category (see Kyvsgaard 2001a and 2005, and *Politiken*, 26 February 2003).

A study from the University of Copenhagen indicates that 75% of all charges against Danish youth end with a sentence, as compared to only 62% for second generation immigrants and 68% for first generation immigrant youth. This may indicate police discrimination at the point of charging (Kyvsgaard 2001b), a view confirmed to some extent by Holmberg's study

(2003) on the daily operations of police in a police circuit with a high representation of ethnic youth. Kyvsgaard (2005) notes social and cultural discrimination of young persons of non-Danish ethnic origin as the most important factors in explaining juvenile crime, but not necessarily as a reflection of culture conflict in the traditional sense (Sellin 1938).

Furthermore, new immigrants to Denmark have tended to be clustered in certain sections of major towns: Copenhagen, Aarhus and Odense. Here they have come into conflict with Danish citizens and the police. Battles have been fought within the immigrant ghettoes: Nörrebro in Copenhagen and Vollsmose in Odense. Police cars have been turned over and set on fire, and a local police station in the ghetto was set alight. These areas are not as run-down and slum-like as American racial ghettoes or the huge French congregations of immigrants from the former colonies. Most of them are areas of rather expensive public housing that ordinary Danes cannot afford, but where consequently the immigration and refugee authorities have tended to place refugees and immigrants with considerable public subsidies. On the other hand, the inhabitants have not been properly integrated into the labour market and particularly the younger generations have been left to fend for themselves. Ordinary Danish citizens have moved out, leaving the ethnic composition characterized by people of dark skin colour. In 2005 this led to an official move to find ways of reducing the number of coloured persons in the ghettoes, *inter alia* by prohibiting them from moving in.

The immigrants and their offspring maintain—and seem to be right in doing so—that they are being discriminated against in relation to employment and participation in Danish society. They are increasingly forming a distinct underclass with all the characteristics of deprived minority groups known from the U.S.A. and elsewhere. Minority youth express their frustrations in violent behaviour. Many of them are also isolated from society by language barriers and by living within foreign cultures resistant to integration into the general institutions of society.

The situation of dark-skinned immigrants and asylum-seekers from a number of African and Middle Eastern countries is parallel to the situation of black youth in the U.S.A. in many ways, as demonstrated in Feld's paper in the present volume. Although the 'blacks' in Denmark cluster in urban ghettoes, the minorities there are more of a mixture of different cultures. But their social situation and the way their 'alien-ness' is perceived and reacted to by the conservative politicians and the majority of the population, stimulated by sensation-seeking media, is strongly reminiscent of the 'race problem' in the United States.

By contrast, the minority problems in Sweden are less pronounced and the public and political attitudes are much more accepting and rational, although minority ghettoes are also becoming evident in Stockholm and a few other larger cities.

The coming into power of the right-wing government in late 2001 and the influence of the Danish People's Party has contributed to the alienation of immigrants and their offspring in Denmark. This alienation results in both expressive crimes due to frustration and instrumental crimes due to economic underprivilege. Altogether, these factors have generated and fortified public demands for toughness on crime and particularly for attention to crimes committed by 'ethnic youth'.

Nevertheless, perceptions of public sentiment may have been overstated by politicians in search of a cause. Repeated annual surveys (with four measurements each year) of public opinion and fears about violence and crime (Institut for Konjunktur-Analyse, figures elaborated by the Ministry of Justice, see Kyvsgaard 2003b and 2004c) indicate that the proportion of respondents worrying 'a lot' about violence and crime declined from some 60–70% in most years within the period 1985–1996 to 50–60% at the end of the 1990s. In 2001 and 2002 this proportion was only 43%. This tendency towards fewer 'worriers' continued into 2003 and 2004 when only 37% of respondents stated that they worry a lot about violence and crime, and this despite the dramatic events that took place in the summer of 2003.

A recent report (2005) by 'Visionsudvalget' (Report on 'The Future of Danish Police' (*Fremtidens Politi*) by a Ministry of Justice Committee on visions for the Danish Police states the following regarding the public's feelings of security and insecurity:

In December 2004 a report was published by TrygFonden and Huset Mandag Morgen named *Tryghedsrapport 2004—en analyse af danskernes tryghed og utryghed (Report on Subjective Security 2004—an Analysis of Feelings of Security and Insecurity among Danes)*. The study demonstrates that the Danish population generally does not feel particularly insecure in relation to crime. Thus only one out of fifteen Danes feels insecure in relation to the risk of being hit by violence. It further indicates that four out of five Danes find that the media overstate the risk of many things. Two out of three Danes find in addition that society often uses large resources by doing something against risks which are in reality insignificant. It is finally concluded that 'more remote sources of insecurity, such as crime, violence and terrorism play no measurable role for the subjective quality of life of the Danes'.

These surveys indicate that when you ask the citizens themselves a much more nuanced picture appears than those signals on rise in insecurity and worries which often seem to be dominant in the media and in the legal-political debate.

Visionsudvalget thus finds that the predominant focus in the media and politics on 'citizens' feelings of insecurity' and 'a visible police'— which is thus not demanded by the citizens themselves—is very problematic in relation to an adequate and reasonable use of the resources of the police.

According to the report (Tryghedsrapport 2004/JJ), '... the citizens are aware of the risk of being exposed to scare propaganda—and are quite irritated by it' (Visionsudvalget 2005, 34).

The politicians' interpretation of public opinion led, however, to the establishment of two new elements in juvenile delinquency policy: Secure Wards and the Youth Sanction.

THE SECURE WARDS

Only a few of the former state institutions for juveniles—including the most closed ones—survived the municipal reform of the mid-1970s which initiated a massive movement of de-institutionalisation. A couple of them were high security institutions which held juveniles on remand awaiting trial (surrogat-fängsling). The 1990s—after Denmark had signed the CRC—saw an increase in the use of such institutions as alternatives to remand in traditional jails. Today, however, only a few juveniles, representing very serious behavioural problems and high escape risk, are held on remand in jails—ideally, but rarely in reality, jails with special sections for juveniles. As a consequence of the CRC the number of slots in secure wards within the social welfare system increased during the 1990s, but the capacity of these institutions has on repeated occasions been lagging behind the need.

The quest for security has led to an increase in the use of these wards. Between 1996 and 2001 the number of secure slots rose from 45 to 85 and in 2004 there were 94. In addition it was estimated that before the end of 2003 there would be a need for 120 more slots in open institutions (Socialministeriet 2003a).

The total number of placements in secure wards rose from 321 in 1996 to 509 in 2001, and jumped to 750 in 2002.

The need for secure wards was aggravated by the creation of the new Youth Sanction (in force 1 July 2001), which requires as part of the sentence initial placement in a secure ward, normally for at least two months. The time to be spent in institutions should not exceed 18 months in total. But re-institutionalization may take place as a reaction to new crimes or violation of conditions for release. The number of placements in secure wards in 2002 stemming from Youth Sanctions amounted to 10% of all secure placements. The utilization ratio for secure places was 65% in 1996 versus 91% in 2002 and 101 in 2004 (*Politiken*, 27 March 2005).

In 2002 a total of 185 stays in secure wards were interrupted: in 31 of these transfer to ordinary prison took place, and in 63 cases the interruption was due to violence or threats (Socialministeriet 2003a, 51). The placement of children below 15 in secure wards on the basis of criminality decreased, however, from 29 in 2002 to 11 in 2003 (Amtsrådsforeningen, quoted from *Söndagsvisen*, 21 March 2004).

THE YOUTH SANCTION

Background and rationale

The Youth Sanction (YS) was instituted in connection with legislation on youth crime (Act No. 469/2001—new provisions in the Penal Code and in the Act on Social Service). The legislation was based on a report by an Expert Committee appointed by the Ministry of Justice with a rather repressive mandate (Ekspertgruppen om Ungdomskriminalitet 2001). It was spurred by the demand for more severe—and effective—sanctions and better protection of society. The YS should normally be seen as an alternative to an unconditional (or combined) prison sentence in the interval between 30 days and one year (approximately—it might extend up to one and a half years). The ideology was that it should both take care of the individual treatment needs of the offender and protect society. In the latter respect it was also stressed that it should give expression to 'the public sense of justice', including a need to keep offenders securely behind bars for a certain period and in this way impress on them the concern of society with their transgressions. The measure was supported by both the right wing and the social democrats, not least the then (SD) prime minister, apparently being scared about being seen as soft on crime.

It is notable that in practice both the YS and the secure wards are to a great extent used to contain youth of 'a different ethnic origin'. This reflects both the xenophobia mentioned above and the fact that ethnic youth are overrepresented among juveniles with a serious criminal record, with violence, with social and emotional problems and—for some—low intelligence. They have a higher record of absconding and of resistance to efforts to involve them in treatment or social-pedagogical efforts. Their record of violence against staff is also higher.

The initial period of a Youth Sanction is followed by a stay in a social-pedagogical (normally open) institution for up to 16 months. Upon release from the institution, a program of treatment at liberty follows until the end of the two year period. The idea is that this program seen as a whole is of a social-pedagogical and even psychotherapeutic nature and that the increase in freedom is conditional upon the progress of the offender during the earlier stages. The judge may, however, initially set the stay in the secure ward at as much as 16 months, primarily based upon the seriousness of the offence and the problems of the offender.

The application of the Youth Sanction

From 1 July 2001 until the end of 2002 a total of 77 sentences involved a YS. In 2003 a total of 70 were imposed. This caseload somewhat exceeded the expectations of the preparatory expert committee which had expected some 36 sentences per year. In 71 of the first 77 sentences a maximum of 12 months for placement in a residential (open) treatment-institution was established.

During the same period a total of 265 unconditional sentences to prison were pronounced to youth below 18 years of age. Of these, however, 127 were partly conditional—'combination sentences'.

In the last quarter of 2001 and in the fourth quarter of 2002 some 20–25% of all sentences to deprivation of liberty were Youth Sanctions. In some 80% of cases the juvenile had been in remand custody.

More than half (41) of the first 77 juveniles were sentenced to YS with robbery as their main offence. Fourteen of 77 sanctions concerned serious violence (as compared with 50 of the 265 prison sentences) and 9 (compared to 55) simple violence. One case involved serious vandalism and one case sale of narcotics. Of those sentenced to prison for violence or threats, a large proportion concerned threats or violence against witnesses—the kinds of crimes that were central in the police-influenced media reports. 47% of the YS group had no prior record (including waivers of prosecution) as compared to 22% for the prison group. Prior unconditional sentences to prison are unusual for the YS group but around one third of the prison group had such a sentence.

Less than half of the YS group was of Danish descent, 40% were themselves immigrants and 14% were descendants of immigrants. For the prison group the corresponding figures were 56%, 31% and 11%, i.e. there was some over-representation of non-Danish in the YS group.

Critique of the Youth Sanction

In his review of the results of the YS legislation Jorn Vestergaard concludes:

A review of the 55 sentences to YS pronounced during the first year of the YS shows that the courts demonstrate a significant level of insecurity in relation to the field of application and formulation of YS, and on a number of points the scepticism expressed from several sides on this innovation has been justified. In some of the cases the crime criterion has not been clearly fulfilled. Some sentences give the impression that the YS in a doubtful fashion is used to obtain juridical and political social aims. This article demonstrates that the YS involves considerable aggravation of the intensity of intervention as compared to prior practice. It is particularly unfortunate that some sentences do not allow for flexibility concerning the initial stay in a secure ward. [Vestergaard 2003, 1, my translation]

Part of this critique touches upon the real need to extend deprivation of liberty in a highly secure institution for as long as indicated. In reality a fairly large proportion of these youth have already been in such an institution under remand as a surrogate for jail placement. A hard and fast rule of a minimum of 2 months' initial stay for all may lead to overly long stays in closed conditions. Further, problems arise concerning transfer between open and closed institutions. But the major problem is the potential (and at times real) disproportionality between the time to be spent in institutions under the YS as compared to the shorter time normally spent under an ordinary prison sentence for a similar—or even the same—crime committed by another youth, possibly involved in the same case. In addition the shorter, ordinary prison sentences are normally served in open institutions within the welfare system. This contributes to a sense of injustice among the YS clients who compare their fate to that of their peers.

These objections are by and large the same as those made against the former sanction of Youth Prison, which was used in Denmark between 1933 and 1973. It was terminated on the basis of exactly the same arguments about injustice and about abuse of the considerations for treatment as an excuse for keeping young offenders imprisoned for longer terms than would normally be deserved in relation to the severity of the crime. This was one of the major objections against the (relatively) indeterminate sentencing practice of the 1960s, which led to the abandonment of almost all of these types of measures, where the length of time served depended on the asserted treatment needs of the offender rather than the severity of the offence. The 'just deserts' discourse was part of this development.

Vestergaard also is critical of the limited protection of the human and due process rights of young offenders in the institutions under the welfare authorities:

The coercive powers which a sentence to a youth sanction confers upon the welfare system are extremely extensive and vague, which puts basic considerations for due process to a hard test. ... The exercise of power is regulated in an administrative regulation, which is sharply in contrast with the legislative regulation, which in 2000 was promulgated in the execution of sentences in the criminal law system and with recent legislative regulation of coercive measures in criminal procedure against children below 15. The social system, furthermore, is not at all professionally geared to safeguard considerations for proportionality and due process, which are traditionally in focus in the correctional services and in the rest of the system of law enforcement. [Vestergaard 2004a, 149, author's translation]

This leads Vestergaard to suggest considering moving responsibility for implementing penal measures against young offenders from the social welfare system to the criminal justice system—as seen in other countries (*ibid.* n. 27). Vestergaard (*ibid.* 158) finds it thought-provoking that Sweden introduced the sanction of 'sluten ungdomsvaard' (closed youth care) in 1999, which has the same target group as the Danish youth sanction, but is much more in accordance with usual considerations for the setting of penalties. In Sweden, prison sentences for young offenders have largely been replaced by the new sanction. It is applied in some 100 cases per year, which has led to a rise in sanctions involving deprivation of liberty. Furthermore, the average period of institutionalisation has risen to some nine months (*ibid.* 158 n. 50).

In relation to the legitimacy of the YS, Vestergaard (2004b) states:

The real situation is that the Youth Sanction in its principles as well as on its own grounds lacks legitimacy. As penalty it is generally unjust. As treatment it is fundamentally inefficient. As social practice it represents an extreme violation of individual liberty and personal integrity. ... The youth sanction has been introduced in direct opposition to researched knowledge, the consideration for elementary due process and common sense.

He concludes (2004b, 80):

Public security has been given priority to child welfare, just like a hundred years ago (Stang Dahl, 1978). The emergence of the youth sanction is due to a mixture of a well-founded concern regarding a neglected and consequently menacing segment of juveniles and of a moral crusade based upon public mores and political sentiments. Thus, once again, the individual juvenile offender will have to pay the price for the failure to develop adequate methods of dealing with the wild ones.

DENMARK AND THE CONVENTION ON THE RIGHTS OF THE CHILD

Denmark ratified the CRC in 1991, but has not yet incorporated it into Danish Law—as has happened with the European Convention on Human Rights.

In general, Denmark is reluctant to undertake such incorporation, particularly of conventions of a more general nature (Espersen 2002) which are not 'self executable'. Under the 'dualist principle' Denmark is, however, obliged to take the CRC into consideration in legislation and policy as well as in administration. For several years the Danish state has maintained a somewhat self-sufficient attitude, indicating that Danish law and practice is generally of a high standard in relation to the topics covered by conventions, but this assumption is becoming increasingly doubtful. Thus there has been repeated criticism from NGOs—and from the relevant UN committees—that Denmark has not sufficiently implemented or incorporated the Convention Against Torture (CAT) or the CRC. Thus in 2001 the CRC committee criticized Denmark for forming insufficient bases for initiatives in legislation. Most recently Danish policy in the CRC field has been criticized by the Danish Council On Children (Børnerådet—here BR[8]) for this deficit and for its policies *inter alia* in relation to youth in trouble with the law.

---

[8] Børnerådet is a state consultative institution composed of members with particular insight into children's affairs, and thus is not an NGO in a strict sense.

Thus, in its latest 'shadow report' on CRC—a supplementary report to Denmark's 3rd periodic report to the UN Child Rights Committee—the BR states:

In an international perspective Danish children belong to the most privileged in the world—in particular in relation to material conveniences, social welfare, education and cultural rights. But as documented in the present report there are areas where the protection of children's rights have suffered setbacks in the past five years, and there are quite a lot of fields where—in spite of the recommendations from the CRC of June 2001—no strengthening of children's rights has occurred.

The BR (Boerneraadet 2005) summarizes the situation as follows:

It is still practice in Denmark to imprison juveniles, even together with adult offenders, in violation of the CRC. In later years sanctions against children, even down to the age of 12 have been aggravated and old-fashioned methods of incarceration and the use of force are used more and more often.

The BR recommends that juveniles should never be incarcerated together with adults and new thinking should be developed in the direction of 'sanctions without the use of bars'. It also recommends that children should be heard more and that the age limit for children to be considered as parties to their own cases should be lowered to 12. In general, children should be better informed about their own situation, about their rights under the CRC and about their right to complain.

But the BR is in general worried by the implacable tone, devoid of humanism, which dominates the debate on the youngest law violators. This is also true in relation to the law on immigrants (aliens) where many restrictions have been added, in particular in practice. This is true also in cases on family re-unification where children are involved, and in dealing with rejected asylum seeking families with children. Here, too, government policy seems steeped in the same implacable tone, failing to prioritize the best interests of the child.

Although the recommendations offered by the BR are of a rather simplistic kind, they and the paper reflect a perception which is rather widespread among critics of the more recent repressive and security-oriented trends in juvenile justice in Denmark. A number of more 'well-established' NGOs in the child welfare field have in their own 'Shadow Report' to the CRC in the spring of 2005 expressed similar views, although in less ardent wording.

The trend described here is also marked in relation to criminal policy in general. It forms part of the right wing government's program of penal law reform, which represents a considerable tightening of the repressive screw. It is also a reflection of public demands for security and more accountability in reactions to deviance in general and offending behaviour in particular.

The Social Democrats seem to have interpreted public sentiments in such a way that they have accepted the criminal and immigration policies of the right wing, apparently in the hope of keeping their (former predominantly) working class constituency. The elections in February 2005 showed, however, that this did not suffice. Other parties have opposed both aspects of this development from the standpoint of justice and openness to currents from abroad, so the policy issues have been tied to issues of nationalism and retaining national identity.

This also means that criminal policy and juvenile justice since the mid-1990s—at least—have been increasingly politicized and have become a vehicle for parties fighting against the intellectual elites that used to dominate the debates over social problems, deviance and culture in general. 'Cultural radicalism' has become a dirty term and has been linked with 'leftism' and covert adherence to communistic ideals. 'Being soft on crime' is seen as an indication of this allegedly naïve do-gooder posture, leaving the ordinary population at a loss for protection.

THE DEVELOPMENT OF JUVENILE JUSTICE IN DENMARK—TRENDS AND INFLUENCES

It should be evident from the above that legislation and practice in the field of juvenile justice in Denmark since the 1930s has followed a pendulum course, swinging back and forth between a belief in welfare and treatment on the one hand and the demand for public security and control on the other. While the 1973 reform did away with some of the old paternalism and belief in indeterminate treatment, it probably shortened sentences and resulted in some de-institutionalization in the long run. It also emphasized proportionality and justice, i.e. that persons who commit similar crimes should receive similar sentences, regardless of their personal circumstances. After 1973, the term 'inmate' was changed back to 'prisoner' and Nils Christie's view of imprisonment as the intentional infliction of pain and the belief that 'nothing works' gained a foothold.

Juvenile justice, however, managed to resist the swing of the pendulum away from welfare thinking for a long time. Juveniles have continued to be excused many of their norm violations due to their immaturity and the hope of socialization with the passage of time. The aura of innocence or lack of reproach has lingered for several years in this field. Resocialization was seen as the best way to further public security (Socialministeriet 2003a).

But this view has become increasingly unpopular in later years. Moral panics about increasing violence, unsafe streets and violent gangs have dominated the public discourse. Cautious criminologists have been swept aside as 'self-pronounced so-called experts' and 'judges of taste'.

Balvig (2003) sees this development as an indication of a more fundamental change in the existential view of society and of one's fellow beings. The latter are—if they commit offences—not seen as persons in need of support and resocialization, but as mature and responsible individuals. Their transgressions are connected with guilt and ill will and the response to their lack of self-control is public control and incapacitation. The changes needed in society have nothing to do with changing social conditions, improving welfare and decreasing social inequalities and discrimination. Rather they involve more control, supervision and internment of transgressors.

CONCLUSION: THE DANISH EXPERIENCE OF JUVENILE
JUSTICE—LESSONS TO BE LEARNED

For many years the Danish model of juvenile justice and its primary elements—the social welfare boards, the extensive use of waivers of prosecution and the other elements for diverting young offenders into social service instead of the criminal justice system—worked reasonably well in Denmark. There was a widespread feeling that it might also serve as a model for other systems with similar goals. It was assumed to be in accordance with the letter and spirit of the CRC and other international instruments for safeguarding the interests of society and of wayward youth at the same time.

As can be seen from the history sketched above, today it is not seen in the same favourable light. First, the age of criminal responsibility is—if not in the law books—in reality slowly creeping down from 15 towards 12 years for the 'heavy end' of delinquent children aged 12–15 through administrative provisions for the placement of such children in secure institutions or wards. Control has become a key word in this respect, and these secure institutions, although placed within the social welfare system, have many characteristics in common with the closed prisons, but lack the same legal safeguards.

Secondly, the municipal social welfare boards (CYBs), as decision-makers in cases of forced removal of children and juvenile offenders from their homes, are coming under increasing criticism for not safeguarding the legal and social interests of youth, by not investing sufficiently in support of the family at an early point, by not removing neglected children and juveniles soon enough from unhealthy surroundings, and by not reacting adequately to their delinquency. This is due in part to economic reasons, partly to a lack of professionalism and partly to a lack of an adequate knowledge base. The construction of the boards with the judge present in cases of involuntary removal of children from the home has been criticized for being ineffective as a guarantee of due process. The system has also been criticized as an obfuscation of the separation of powers, which today is seen as a problem rather than as an asset.

Thirdly, the primary administrative responsibility for safeguarding the fundamental legal rights of youth in the sanctioning system—including the institutions under the Youth Sanction—has been found to be lacking, and there has even been a proposal to extend the responsibility of the ordinary courts for juveniles down to the age of 12.

Fourthly, the system for complaints against coercive measures has been found to be unsatisfactory and cumbersome. Reform plans are under way, but the scientific basis for such reforms is scarce, the ideology is seen as irrational and the resources insufficient.

Fifthly, secure wards and the provisions for exercise of power in them are seen as expressions of an extreme focus on security and control, based upon fears of a small group of aggressive and treatment-resistant youthful offenders committing serious and violent offences, even while under age. A large part of the public discourse on juvenile delinquency and juvenile justice has focused on this group, particularly the growing part of the group of non-Danish origin, and even more particularly second generation immigrants with dark skin.

Finally, in general the system of reactions towards youthful offending has been polarized. The intermediate sanctions of waivers of prosecution, youth contracts and sentences conditional upon the application of welfare measures have been significantly reduced. Instead, fines are used increasingly for young offenders at the 'soft end' and closed institutions with secure wards as part of the Youth Sanction at the hard end. Serving 'alternatives to sentence', i.e. in treatment institutions, has reduced in favour of youth sanctions or ordinary serving of a sentence in closed prisons. New separate secure institutions are being created to house difficult young offenders of 'ethnic' origin. The Youth Sanction is being criticized for having an obfuscating mantel of treatment—with no or little rationale or reality—and for violating basic tenets of proportionality in the setting of sentences (Vestergaard 2004b).

How has all this come about—and must the 'soft' welfare approach give way once and for all to outright repression and control?

The repressive development of the system of reactions is to a limited extent founded upon a rise in violent and serious offences committed to a disproportionate extent by young 'ethnic' boys—in a situation when crime in general and juvenile crime in particular has been decreasing for some time.

The overrepresentation of ethnic youth in certain types of crime is considerably reduced when socio-economic background is controlled, but even so, the increase in the number of ethnic youth in secure institutions is alarming. Immigrants and refugees in Denmark are to an increasing extent forming a distinct underclass, clustering together in ethnic ghettoes (which most of them would like to leave, but are unable to do so), with problems of high unemployment, linguistic difficulties and outright discrimination. Young groups in the larger cities are experiencing this situation, exacerbated by xenophobic rhetoric at the political level as well as in day-to-day interaction. The result is despair and aggressive reactions towards mainstream Danish society. In this way the fear of strangers is becoming a self-fulfilling prophecy and a downward spiral is the result.

Criminal policy and juvenile justice have been taken out of the hands of academic experts in the name of democracy and invocations of 'the public sense of justice'. And if the population is not sufficiently fearful, politicians and the media have demonstrated considerable capacity to turn realistic concerns into moral panics. This has put juvenile justice on the political platform in a way that has never been known in Denmark. It used to be a non-controversial issue, left to the good intentions of the welfare system in co-operation with a usually sensible system of law enforcement and penology. Today juvenile justice has become a battleground where populistic policies overshadow and counteract the opportunities for traditional social welfare action.

The Social Democratic politicians' fear of their own constituencies has led them down the same road as the parties to the right. Consequently there is no reason to expect a change of direction in any foreseeable future, even in case of a change in political constellations, which is rather improbable within at least the next four years.

Reformers and juvenile justice activists might therefore prefer to look to other welfare states—such as Sweden—for models. Or they might look back in history to the rather good results of original Danish welfare policy in dealing with all but the heaviest end of juvenile offenders.

REFERENCES

Balvig, Flemming (2000) *Risiko Ungdom. Ungdomsundersøgelse 1999* (Youth at risk—Youth Study 1999). (Copenhagen, Det Kriminalpräventive Raad).
—— (2003) 'Med Straf Skal Land Bygges' (With Punishment the Land shall be built). In Jepsen, J. and Lyhne, J. (eds.), *Retspolitiske Udfordringer.* (Copenhagen, Gjellerup), pp. 249–70.
Boerneraadet (2005) Report to the UN Child Rights Committee. Supplementary report to Denmark's 3rd periodic report (Copenhagen) www.boerneraadet.dk
Bonke, Jens and Lene Kofoed (2001) *Längerevarende behandling af börn og unge i sikrede pladser* (Long-term treatment of children and youth in secure wards). (Copenhagen, Socialforskningsinstituttet). Rapport 01:8.
Christie, Nils and K. Bruun (1985) *Den gode fjende* (The ideal enemy). (Copenhagen, Ejlers Forlag).
Clausen, Susanne (2002) *Undersøgelse vedrørende unge lovovertrædere— vilkaarsovertrædelser og reaktioner herpå* (Study of juvenile Offenders— violations of conditions and reactions thereto). (Copenhagen, Justitsministeriet).
Cornils, Karin (2001) 'Jugendstrafrecht in Dänemark' (Juvenile Penal Law in Denmark). In *Jugendstrafrecht in Europa.* (Max Planck Institut für Ausländisches und Internationales Strafrecht, Freiburg im Br.).
Dahl, Tove Stang (1985) *Child Welfare and Social Defence.* (Oslo, Norwegian University Press).

Ekspertgruppen om ungdomskriminalitet (2001) *Rapport om Ungdomskriminalitet* (Expert Committee on juvenile criminality, Report on juvenile criminality). (Copenhagen, Justitsministeriet).

Espersen, Ole (2002) *Notat om fordele og ulempler ved en inkorporereing af De Forenede Nationers konvention om barnets rettigheder i dansk ret* (A note on advantages and disadvantages of an incorporation of the UN Convention on Children's Rights in Danish law). (University of Copenhagen).

Greve, Vagn (1996) *Straffene* (Copenhagen, Dansk Jurist- og Økonomforbunds Forlag).

Hagemann, Helle and Claus B. Olsen (2001) *Alternativ afsoning efter Straffelovens par. 49, stk. 2—en effektundersøgelse* (Alternative serving of sentence—a study of effects). (Copenhagen, CASA).

Hansen, Lisbeth (1996) *Integrationen af 15–17 årige lovovertrædere—til et normalt voksenliv?—eller til end ungdom og manddom i fängsler?* (The integration of 15–17 year old law violators—into normal adult life?—or into youth and manhood in prisons?). Specialeopgave. Den sociale kandidatuddannelse, Aalborg Universitet. (University of Aalborg—unpublished masters thesis).

Holmberg, Lars (1999) *Inden for Lovens Rammer* (Within the limits of the law). (Copenhagen, DJØF Forlag).

Holmberg, Lars and Kyvsgaard, B. (2003) Are immigrants and their descendants discriminated against in the Danish criminal justice system? *Journal of Scandinavian Studies in Criminology and Crime Prevention*, vol. 4, pp. 125–42.

Jepsen, Jørgen (1998) The Great Danish Rocker War and Societal Reactions—A Moral Panic? In H-J. Albrecht *et al* (eds.), *Internationale Perspektiven in Kriminologie und Strafrecht, Festschrift für Günther Kaiser zum 70. Geburtstag* (Berlin, Duncker & Humblot), pp. 573–608.

Justitsministeriet (1988) *Rapport om unge lovovertrædere* (Report on young offenders). (Copenhagen, November 1988).

Justitsministeriet (2002) *Redegørelse om ungdomsssanktioner og ubetingede fängselsstraffe til unge lovovertrædere 1. juli 2001–31. Dec. 2002* (A study of youth sanctions and unconditional prison sentences to young offenders).

Justitsministeriet (2003) *Børnekriminalitet 1992–2002* (Ministry of Justice, Child Crime, 1992–2002). (Copenhagen, www.justitsministeriet.dk).

Justitsministeriets Strafferetsplejeudvalg (2003) *Betänkning om straffeprocesuelle tvangsindgreb over for börn under den kriminelle lavalder.* (Committee Report on coercive measures in criminal justice towards children below the age of criminal responsibility). (Betänkning No. 1431, Copenhagen).

Kyvsgaard, Britta (1992) *Ny Ungdom?* (New Youth?) (Copenhagen, Jurist- og Økonomforbundets Forlag).

260   Jørgen Jepsen

—— (1998) *Kriminalforsorg i frihed—mellem omsorg, hjälp og kontrol* (Probation and other non-institutional sanctions—between care, assistance and control). (Copenhagen, Department of Prisons and Probation).

—— (2000) *Undersøgelse af ungdomskontrakter* (Study of youth contracts). Attachment to Rigsadvokaten informerer, No. 2.

—— (2001a) *Notat vedrørende kriminalitet og national oprindelse 2000* (A note on crime and national origin), www.jm.dk

—— (2001b) 'Kriminalitet, retshåndhävelse og etniske minoriteter' (Crime, law enforcement and ethnic minorities). *Juristen*, 363–73

—— (2003a) 'Kriminalitet og alder' (Crime and age) *Justitsministeriets Forskningsenhed*, www.jm.dk

—— (2003b) 'Bekymring for vold og kriminalitet 2003' (worries about violence and crime). *Justitsministeriets Forskningsenhed.*

—— (2003c) 'Udviklingen i børne- og ungdomskriminalitet' (1992–2002) ('Developments in child and youth crime') *Justitsministeriets Forskningsenhed.*

—— (2004a) 'Udviklingen i antal samfundstjenestedomme' (The development in the number of community service orders) *Justitsministeriets Forskningsenhed.*

—— (2004b) 'Youth Justice in Denmark'. In M. Tonry and A.N. Doob (eds.), *Youth Crime and Youth Justice—Comparative and Cross-National Perspectives.* (University of Chicago, Crime and Justice Series, Vol. 31).

—— (2004c) 'Bekymring for vold og kriminalitet' (Worries about violence and crime) *Justitsministeriets Forskningsenhed.*

—— (2005) 'Etniske minoriteters høje kriminalitetshyppighed: Kulturkonflikter eller sociale og ökonomiske aarsager?' (The high crime rate of ethnic minorities—Culture conflicts or social and economic causes?). In *SFI Temarapport: Etniske Minoriteter—et nyt proletariat?* (Ethnic minorities—a new proletariat?). Social Forskning. Socialforskningsinstituttet, Copenhagen.

Lund, Anker Brink (2003) Kriminalitet i de danske massemedier (Criminality in Danish mass media). *Nordisk Tidsskrift for Kriminalvidenskab* 90 (3), 160–77.

Løkke, Anne (1990) Vildfarende børn (Wayward children). (Copenhagen, SocPol).

Mehlbye, Jill and Sommer, B. (1998) 'Denmark'. In Mehlbye, J. and L. Walgrave (eds.), *Confronting Youth in Europe—Juvenile crime and Juvenile Justice* (Copenhagen, AKF Forlag).

Mehlbye, Jill and Rohde, Peter (2004) *Unge i dögnanbringelse—indsats og resultatdokumentation* (Youth in 24-hour placement—documentation of efforts and results). (AKF/Forum for Kvalitet og Udvikling i offentlig Service, Copenhagen).

Mehlbye, J. and L.Walgrave (eds) (1998), *Confronting Youth in Europe— Juvenile crime and Juvenile Justice* (Copenhagen, AKF Forlag).

Nielsen, Beth Grothe (1999) 'Historien om den kriminelle lavalder' (The story of the age of criminal responsibility). *Social Kritik*, 11, No. 62.

Nordisk Ministerråd (2000) *Ungdomskriminalitet in Norden* (Youth Crime in the Nordic countries). Nord 200–30, Copenhagen.

Politiken (daily newspaper) (26 February 2003) *Kriminalstatistik uden overvægt af indvandrere* (Crime statistics without overrepresentation of immigrants).

—— (1 March 2003) *Kritik af politital om kriminelle* (Critique of police figures on offenders) (relating to misleading figures on crime rates among ethnic youth).

Rigsadvokaten (1998) Meddelelse No. 7, *Behandlingen af sager mod unge lovovertrædere* (The Attorney General: Instruction on measures against young offenders).

—— (2000) *Evaluering af ordningen med ungdomskontrakter* (The Attorney General, Evaluation of the youth contract measure). (Copenhagen, Rigsadvokaten informerer) No. 2.

Sarnecki, J. (2003) *Introduktion til Kriminologi.* (Lund, Studentlitteratur).

Scllin, Torsten (1938) *Culture, Conflict and Crime.* (New York, Social Science Research Council).

Socialforskningsinstituttet (2005) *Etniske minoriteter – et nyt proletariat? (Ethnic minorities – a new proletariat?)* (Social Forskning, Temanummer, Copenhagen).

Socialministcrict (2000) *Børn og kriminalitet. Et inspirationskatalog til hurtig indsats over for børn, der begaar kriminelle handlinger* (Children and crime—an inspirational catalogue for quick efforts towards children who commit offenses). (Copenhagen, Ministry of Social Affairs).

—— (2003a) *Rapport fra arbejdsgruppen om gränsefladen mellem kriminalforsorgen og social og sundhedssektoren.* (Ministry of Social Affairs, Report from the working group on the delimitation between the Prison and Probation Service and the social and health sector) www.sm.dk/ net-publikationer/2003p4grflade2605/index.htm

—— (2003b) *Guide til effektiv indsats over for kriminelle unge* (Guide to effective measures towards young offenders) www.sm.dk/krimguide/

—— (2004) Analyse af procedurer i børnesager (pdf) www.sm.dk/publika-tioner/born

Stevens, Hanne (2003) *Evaluering af ungdomskontraktordningen* (Evaluation of the Youth Contract measure). (Copenhagen, Justitsministeriets Forskningsenhed).

Söndagsavisen (weekly news) (21 March 2004) *Färre unge på institution* (Fewer young offenders in secure institutions).

Vestergaard, Jørn (1991) 'Juvenile Contracting in Denmark: Paternalism Revisited'. In Snare, A. (ed.), *Youth Crime and Justice,* Scandinavian Studies in Criminology, vol. 12. (Oslo, Universitetsforlaget).

—— (2003) 'Den särlige ungdomssanktion' (The special youth sanction). *Tidsskrif for Kriminalret* 1/2003.

—— (2004a) 'Unge kriminelle i strafferetten og socialretten' (Young offenders in social legislation and criminal law). In *Festskrift til Ole Espersen,* Copenhagen, DJØF forlag, pp. 141–62.

—— (2004b) 'A Special Youth Sanction'. *Journal of Scandinavian Studies in Criminology and Crime Prevention,* vol. 5, 62–84.

Visionsudvalget (2005) *Fremtidens Politi* (Police of the Future). (Copenhagen, Justitsministeriet).

12

Juvenile Justice in Nepal:
An Overview

KISHOR SILWAL

INTRODUCTION

THE LEGAL STATUS of children and adolescents is different from that of adults in every democratic country. In addition, children and youth are not held accountable for violations of the criminal law in the same way as adults in these systems. The ultimate aim of such treatment of children and adolescents is to protect them from the negative effects of the adult justice system and also to provide a more appropriate way of dealing with them. These notions are guaranteed by international human rights law, which substantially considers children who violate the law to be victims of social hardship, neglect, violence, and deprivation. The juvenile justice concept is based on the assumption that a person below a certain age, because they are at en early stage of mental development, shall not and cannot be held responsible for their wrongful acts in the same way as adults. For this basic reason, it is now a widely accepted notion that juvenile justice systems should be established differently from traditional criminal justice systems.

The Nepalese judicial system has, at least nominally, given such attention to child offenders. With the ratification by Nepal of the UN Convention on the Rights of the Child (1989) (CRC) in 1990 and the Covenant on Civil and Political Rights (1966) (ICCPR) in 1991, it has theoretically accepted the fundamental notion of juvenile justice systems adopted in most parts of the world. Enactment of a separate Children's Act (1992) is another strong commitment Nepal has made. It is the first Act entirely dedicated to children's rights. It is designed to safeguard the interests and welfare of children. The Nepal Treaty Act (1990) is another important step that Nepal has taken towards fulfilling its international commitments. This Act was adopted by the Parliament to implement the treaty provisions mentioned in the Constitution of 1990 to which the country is a party, and it foresees in section 9 (1) the superiority of international law (either customary or treaty-based) over national legislation. Under this provision, inconsistent domestic law is rendered void, and provisions of the treaty are to prevail as the law of Nepal. Therefore, any provision in the domestic Act may be set aside if it is found to be inconsistent with the provisions of the CRC or the ICCPR. These are some of the efforts Nepal has made to distinguish the juvenile justice system from the criminal justice system.

THE DOMESTIC LEGAL FRAMEWORK OF THE NEPALESE JUVENILE JUSTICE SYSTEM

The Constitution

The Constitution of the Kingdom of Nepal (1990) is the fundamental law of the country. It is the highest norm at the domestic level and 'contains a framework for government, and provides a legitimate vehicle for granting and limiting the power of government officials'.[1] With regard to juvenile justice, the relevant provisions of the Constitution of the Kingdom of Nepal (1990) are encompassed in Part Three, entitled *Fundamental Rights*. It guarantees the right to freedom,[2] rights regarding criminal justice,[3] and rights against preventive detention.[4] Similarly, Article 26 (8) safeguards the rights and interests of children as part of state policy. The Supreme Court, as per Article 88 (1) and (2) of the Constitution, ensures the observance and compliance of Nepalese law to the Constitution. When the political powers fail to enforce the fundamental rights enshrined by the Constitution, it is

---

[1] See Dhungel, Adhikari, Bhandari and Murgatroyd (1998), 1.

[2] Article 12 (1) of the Constitution of the Kingdom of Nepal states that no person shall be deprived of his personal liberty save in accordance with law, and no law shall be made which provides for capital punishment.

[3] Article 14 of the Constitution of the Kingdom of Nepal has the following provisions:

 1. No person shall be punished for an act, which was not punishable by law when the act was committed, nor shall any person be subjected to a punishment greater than that prescribed by the law in force at the time of the commission of the offence.
 2. No person shall be prosecuted or punished for the same offence in a court of law more than once.
 3. No person accused of any offence shall be compelled to be a witness against himself.
 4. No person who is detained during investigation or for trial or for any other reason shall be subjected to physical or mental torture, nor shall be given any cruel, inhuman or degrading treatment. Any person so treated shall be compensated in a manner as determined by law.
 5. No person who is arrested shall be detained in custody without being informed, as soon as may be, of the grounds for such arrest, nor shall be denied the right to consult and be defended by a legal practitioner of his choice.
 6. Every person who is arrested and detained in custody shall be produced before a judicial authority within a period of twenty-four hours after such arrest, excluding the time necessary for the journey from the place of arrest to such authority, and no such person shall be detained in custody beyond the said period except on the order of such authority.
 7. [...] nothing in clause 6 shall apply to any person who is arrested or detained under any law providing for preventive detention.

[4] Article 15 of the Constitution of the Kingdom of Nepal.

then for the highest court to ensure that the constitutional provisions are properly observed.

The Muluki Ain, 1963

The Muluki Ain, also called 'Law of the Land', is categorised into five parts. The first and last parts of the instrument deal respectively with generalities and repeal provisions; they are not related to the present topic. The second part refers to court procedures, both civil and criminal. This part is particularly relevant to the issue of juvenile justice, as it deals with the functioning of regular courts. However, it does not provide for a separate juvenile court or for specific procedures applicable to juveniles. Therefore the common law is applied. However, as soon as a specific juvenile justice system is adopted, in accordance with the CRC and the Children's Act of 1992, the provisions of the Muluki Ain will be set aside: *speciala generalibus derogant*, the special law supersedes the general law. The third and fourth parts are dedicated to civil and criminal offences respectively, and as such determine the legality of any offence that may be perpetrated by young offenders. In the absence of a proper and independent system of juvenile justice, the general law applies to juvenile cases.

The Nepal Treaty Act 1990

This Act, adopted by Parliament in order to implement the treaty provisions mentioned in the Constitution of 1990, foresees in section 9 (1) the superiority of international law (either customary or treaty-based) over national legislation: the domestic law shall be void to the extent of the inconsistency, and the provision of the treaty shall prevail as the law of Nepal.[5] Therefore, any provision of the domestic acts mentioned below may be put aside when it is inconsistent with the provisions of the CRC or the ICCPR.

The Nepal Children's Act 1992

This legislation was enacted after the ratification of the CRC. In fact, it was crafted to fulfil the obligation created by CRC. The Children's Act was enacted for the overall protection of children. Basically, the following six provisions of the Children's Act relate directly to juvenile justice.

Section 2(a) of the act defines 'child' as every human being below the age of 16. The age of criminal liability set by the Act is slightly lower than that recommended by the CRC. There is no universally acceptable standard for the age of criminality; there is also no uniform international standard for the age of criminal responsibility for children.

---

[5] See also Sapkota (2003), 10.

The CRC, Article 40.3.a, only requires State Parties to establish 'a minimum age' below which children should not be presumed to have the capacity to violate the penal law. The Commentary on Rule 4.1 of the Beijing Rules declares the principle that 'the beginning of that age shall not be fixed at too low an age level, bearing in mind the facts of emotional, mental and intellectual maturity'. Section 11 of the Children's Act establishes the age of criminal responsibility. Nepalese legal provisions establish three distinctions: below 10—age of complete innocence; between 10 and 16—age of quasi responsibility (with sub-divisions 10–14 and 14–16); above 16—age of complete responsibility.

The minimum age of criminal liability in Nepal is far below that recommended by international instruments. The CRC recommends 18 years as the upper age for a 'child'. Although it has given latitude for a lower age by domestic legislation it does not mean that there should always be a lower age than 18 years for that purpose.

Section 15 of the act clearly prohibits using handcuffs and fetters, solitary confinement and keeping a child in prison with a prisoner who has attained maturity. It ensures basic minimum protection by prohibiting rigorous punishment. Section 42 provides for the establishment and operation of children's rehabilitation homes, guaranteeing that children will be put in these homes rather than prison. Section 50 gives leeway to the concerned authority who hears juvenile cases to use alternative measures instead of police custody or imprisonment. Section 55 is another provision relating to juvenile justice. It creates the obligation to establish a juvenile court. This section also authorises the government to establish a special bench for juvenile justice in each District Court.

ACTORS WITHIN THE JUVENILE JUSTICE SYSTEM

The actors within the field of juvenile justice may be divided into two groups: institutional and individual. The major functions and roles of the actors as well as deficiencies in their structure and operation are described below.

Institutional actors

The police

One of the basic functions of the police is to enforce laws. The police is the first official body with which juvenile offenders come into contact after the commission of an offence.[6] Nepal's police force is headed by the Inspector

---

[6] The information mentioned in the present paragraph is derived from CeLRRd (2002a), 28 and CeLRRd (2002b), 10.

General of Police (IGP) and is organised under the Police Act 1955 and Police Rules 1992. It is under the direct line of command of the Home Ministry. Dealing with the pre-trial phase, the crime investigation branch is in charge of investigating juvenile cases. The Criminal Investigation Department operates through 5 Regional, 14 Zonal and 75 District Police Offices (DPOs). The DPOs are the grassroots law enforcement units, entrusted with the responsibility to investigate crimes within their territorial jurisdiction. There is no specialised mechanism for dealing with issues of delinquency, although a Women's and Children's Cell exists within the Crime Investigation branch of Nepal.

In Nepal, there is no separate police system handling cases relating to juvenile delinquency. In the absence of specialised police to deal with juvenile matters, the police officers who investigate crimes committed by adults have the power to investigate juvenile offences. Principally, the State Offence Act (1993) and State Offence Rules (1998) prescribe the process of crime investigation as well as prosecution. However, in the case of juveniles, the Children's Act (1991) has established special provisions for conducting investigations. Handcuffing and solitary confinement are prohibited even at this stage of the investigation. The presence of a lawyer has been made compulsory at every stage of trial.[7] But hardly any of these protections provided by the legislation have been implemented.

In juvenile matters as in other cases, the State Cases Act authorises all persons to report the commission of any offence to the nearest police office. The police are required to examine the place of commission of the crime and preserve any necessary evidence. The police can arrest a person suspected of committing a crime for investigation. If a juvenile is suspected or arrested, special procedures should be initiated. It is during this period that protection of juveniles is most important. It has been argued that of all phases of the juvenile justice procedure, it is at the point of arrest and immediately thereafter, while in police custody, that an accused juvenile is most likely to become the victim of torture or other forms of cruel treatment. As stated in the Commentary to Rule 10 of the Beijing Rules, the period of initial contact with law enforcement agencies is of great importance. In this sensitive period, juveniles need a high standard of protection. Unfortunately, rights to this protection are often denied, as seen in frequent failures to ensure the involvement of a juvenile's legal representative and guardians during the proceedings. The involvement of the above mentioned people are valuable not only in their support for the child but also as observers of how the case is handled.

In Nepal, there is legislative protection against maltreatment of juveniles. The Constitution prohibits physical or mental torture of a person who is

---

[7] Section 19 of the Children's Act states that children's cases are not to be entertained in the absence of a legal practitioner.

detained during investigation, for trial or for any other reason. It forbids cruel, inhuman or degrading treatment, and moreover provides for compensation to the victims of such treatment.[8] The Children's Act applies this provision more specifically to cases of juveniles. It states that, 'notwithstanding anything mentioned in the other law in force, no child shall be subjected to handcuffs and fetters, solitary confinement or put together in prison with a adult prisoner in case a child is convicted of any offence'.[9] However, this legislative protection is not matched by practice. His Majesty's Government has stated that no cases have been reported of children who have been the victims of torture or other cruel, inhuman or degrading treatment (CRC para. 22). Yet, handcuffing juveniles as well as adults is a common practice in Nepal.

The Supreme Court has condemned the practice of handcuffing, observing (*obiter dicta*) that it is immoral, and issuing a writ of *mandamus* to compel the removal of handcuffs from juvenile offenders who are travelling from the police cell to the court.[10] Surprisingly, against the spirit of the law and the earlier rulings of the Supreme Court, in another case the judge of the Supreme Court refused to remove the handcuffs of a juvenile who was produced before the bench with handcuffs under a writ of *habeas corpus*. When the lawyer representing the case demanded the removal of the handcuffs, the bench dismissed it, asking: 'Who would be responsible if the juvenile escaped?'[11] This sort of attitude is typical of the adult criminal justice system.

Protection against abuse of authority can be found in measures relating to its supervision and the encouragement of participation by different interest groups. This may be observed in the following procedures: the police are required to conduct interrogation of the suspect in the presence of a public prosecutor/government attorney. Furthermore, number 24 of the Chapter on Court Procedure directs that in the case of an individual who has not attained the age of 16 years, the statement may only be made in the presence of a guardian. This is in accordance with the international emphasis on the involvement of parents and guardians in the justice process for juveniles.[12] However, this sort of legal provision is regularly ignored by interrogation officers.

In Nepal the police can generally place a suspect in police custody for investigation, without judicial authority, for only 24 hours. If it is required that the person be kept in custody for more than 24 hours, this can only be

---

[8] Article 14 (4) of the Constitution of the Kingdom of Nepal.

[9] Section 15 of the Children's Act 1992.

[10] *Balkrishna Mainali v Ministry of Home Affairs and Others*, writ No 3505 of 1999, dated 7 August 2001.

[11] See *The Kathmandu Post*, 7 March 2002.

[12] CRC Art 40.2 expressly states that juveniles should be informed promptly and directly of the charges against them, and, if appropriate, through their parents or legal guardians.

extended by order of the court. In such a circumstance, the maximum period before the court appearance and submission of the charge sheet is 25 days. It has been observed that in such situations, regardless of jurisdiction, there is no guarantee that the case will be resolved at this hearing. There may be statutory provision for unusually lengthy remand. Under Nepal's Narcotic Drugs (Control) Act 1976, suspects may be detained for up to 90 days prior to trial. The detention situation may possibly be more serious in the event of political and social upheavals. Those suspected of being involved in opposition or rebel groups may face severe restrictions on their liberty, by law and through pressures on the system. There are a number of children who have been detained on suspicion of their involvement with the Maoists, which has been declared a terrorist group by the Nepalese Government. Under the Terrorist and Destructive Activities Prevention Act 2002, anyone accused of terrorist activities may be kept in remand for up to six months.

The concern for speed within the pre-trial process derives from the widely held belief that deprivation of liberty should be used only as a last resort, and then only for the minimum possible period. Indeed, Rule 13.1 of the Beijing Rules stipulates that '(d)etention pending trial shall be used only as a measure of last resort and for the shortest possible period of time'. Furthermore, as provided by Rule 13.2, whenever possible, 'detention pending trial shall be replaced by alternative measures, such as close supervision, intensive care or placement with a family or in an educational setting or home'. In Nepal there are no specific statutory provisions for the practical application of Rule 13 of the Beijing Rules. Juveniles in pre-trial detention can face a danger of 'criminal contamination', and as such, alternative measures should be sought to best ensure their well-being.[13] However, it has been argued that, despite the application of the 'last resort' principle of detention in the context of juvenile justice, this standard has been violated on a huge scale.

One important condition of detention is the separation of children from adults. This is one of the most basic and long-standing principles of criminal justice. It has a dual purpose: to protect children from exploitation, abuse and negative influences by adults, and to ensure that the detention of children occurs in facilities that cater for their special needs. It is a principle articulated in numerous international instruments. Article 10 of the ICCPR states: 'Accused juvenile persons shall be separated from adults and brought as speedily as possible for adjudication',[14] and furthermore, '... be accorded treatment appropriate to their age and legal status'.[15] Rule 13.4 of the Beijing Rules states that '(j)uveniles under detention pending trial

---

[13] See also JDLs Rules for the Protection of Juveniles Deprived of their Liberty, (General Assembly Resolution 45/113 Rule 17).

[14] Article 10.2.b.

[15] Article 10.3.

shall be kept separate from adults and shall be detained in a separate institution or in a separate part of an institution also holding adults'.[16]

In Nepal, provision for these requirements can be found in section 42 (2) (a) of the Children's Act, 2048 (1992). It clearly states: 'A child to be imprisoned pursuant to the existing law for the investigation or proceedings of the case being accused of any crime shall be kept in the Juvenile Reform Home'. Further, Section 50 (1) of the Children's Act provides that where under other laws in force any person accused of committing any offence is to be kept in custody for investigation of the crime, the court hearing the case may order a suspected juvenile to be placed in the custody of their father, mother, relatives or other guardian. Furthermore, the court may order the suspected juvenile to be placed in the care of a social organisation working for the protection of children's rights or in a child reform centre. Such order will be made on the condition that the party with whom the juvenile is placed can ensure the appearance of the juvenile at the necessary time. The court is empowered to make such orders if, considering the age and physical condition of the juvenile, the details of the crime and the place of custody, it is found to be inappropriate to put him/her in custody. However, despite such provision, in most of the cases studied so far there has been no practice of placing a child in the custody of any other person or entity except that of the police.

Generally, the police and prosecutors are blamed for inflating the age of juveniles above 16 years on the charge sheet. During the investigation period, the prosecution must record the age of the suspect. If there is any inconsistency between the suspect's statement and other evidence collected by the prosecution, it will be necessary to verify which facts are genuine after collecting other necessary evidence. If there is any doubt remaining after such a process, the prosecutors consider the higher age to be the genuine age. The suspect has the right to rebut the statement of the prosecution in court. After completion of the investigation, the police will send their report to the public prosecutor's office, along with their opinion of the crime for which the suspect should be prosecuted and what punishment (s)he should receive.

Nepal's justice system is characterised by procedure and the norms of a 'formal' justice system. However, it is slowly becoming more flexible. In juvenile cases, there is increasing recognition of the need to ensure care and assistance for young people and encourage their personal development and reintegration. Nonetheless, the system is still far from full compliance with the fundamental principles of juvenile justice. These principles can be seen in the use of 'diversion'. Diversionary approaches are those that seek to avoid 'unnecessary' contact with the formal justice system and its potentially harmful aspects.

---

[16] See also the Standard Minimum Rules for the Treatment of Prisoners 85 (2).

Instead, alternative responses are sought that are sensitive to the personal circumstances of the offender and the nature of the crime as well as the interests of the victims, such as cautions, mediation and life skills training. Diversion can occur at all stages of a case, but is perhaps most significant when initiated in the early stages, prior to a hearing. International instruments encourage its use, namely Guideline 58 of the Riyadh Guidelines, and Article 40.3.(b) of the CRC. Rule 11 of the Beijing Rules further expands on its application. In Nepal, there is presently no provision for diversion in the treatment of juvenile offenders. However, the development of such approaches should be a priority, along with allocation of resources to establish them. Despite some necessary investment, alternative approaches could eventually take pressure off the formal justice system and, moreover, improve the justice available to juveniles, particularly those committing first-time or non-serious offences.

The Office of the Attorney General

With regard to the administration of justice, Article 110 of the Constitution provides the Attorney General with the right to initiate or not to initiate prosecution against offenders[17]. The same rule applies in the case of a juvenile offence. Its role is to protect society from all types of offenders, be they adult or juvenile. At present, within the prosecution service there is neither special training on nor any awareness of the specific rights of children, at either the central or the district level. Nevertheless, it seems that the Central Office of the Attorney General is the major source for cases of the Supreme Court on the subject circulating through the various District Government Attorney offices. Furthermore, a recent internal policy instruction from the Office of the Attorney General, dated July 2003, seems to have established a new recording system for juvenile cases. Each District Government Attorney should submit a monthly report stating the number of cases in which children were involved. Those reports will then be compiled into an annual report on the activities of the Office of the Attorney General and will ultimately be submitted to the Parliament and to the Prime Minister. However, this system of monthly reporting is yet to be put into effect.

In the case of a juvenile accused, there is no special provision for the process of prosecution. Prosecutors have been following the traditional system of just mentioning the age of the accused in the relevant column on the charge sheet. If the age is stated as below 16 years, that is *prima facie* evidence to the court that the case needs special consideration due to the immature age of the accused. Generally, in practice, it has been found that

---

[17] At the district level, section 17 of the State Cases Act also provides the District Government Attorney with the authority to decide whether or not to initiate judicial proceedings against suspects. There are 75 district level offices and 16 appellate offices to discharge the responsibility of the Attorney General.

if the age of the accused is below 16 years, prosecutors ask for remission of the sentence as per section 11 of the Children's Act.

The judiciary

The judicial system is threefold and is presented in Part 11 of the Constitution of the Kingdom of Nepal, 1990. The first level of hearing is the district level. District Courts, also called Courts of First Instance, have jurisdiction over both civil and criminal cases (whether adult or juvenile) and are located in all the 75 districts. The second level of hearing lies with the Courts of Appeal, of which there are 16 throughout the Kingdom of Nepal. The third and highest court in the judicial hierarchy is the Supreme Court. It is composed of a Chief Justice and a maximum of 14 Associate Judges, all of whom are appointed by His Majesty the King, on the recommendation of the Judicial Council. Article 88 of the Constitution provides the Supreme Court with vast jurisdiction. Decisions made by the Supreme Court strongly influence the development of law and act as precedents.

The Nepalese judicial system is uniform; it does not have a separate system of courts for the hearing of civil and criminal cases. However, there are provisions regarding the establishment of Special Courts to hear exceptional cases, such as State Treason. In violation of Article 40.3 of the CRC, there are no juvenile courts in Nepal. In the year 2000 the government decided to create Juvenile Benches, composed of one judge, one psychologist and one social worker (on the model of the Juvenile Courts mentioned in the Children's Act). Many regarded that decision as a first step toward the establishment of independent juvenile courts. However, three years after that decision, Juvenile Benches were yet to be established. Now, of the 75 districts, Juvenile Benches are only partially operating in two districts, *viz.* in Chitwan and Dolakha.[18] Juvenile cases are therefore heard in the ordinary judicial system, which obviously does not have the same focus on child welfare and rehabilitation as a separate system of courts would have.

There are no differences in trial procedures for adults and juveniles. A juvenile is arrested and detained in exactly the same manner as an adult. The public prosecutor files a charge sheet, along with the evidence collected during the investigation, and, if the accused person is in custody, s/he presents the accused before the relevant District Court; then the trial begins. As a general rule, trial in a court of law is open, according to the principle of public hearing[19]. However, the proceedings of a case involving a juvenile should be conducted *in camera*. Children's cases must be taken up by a juvenile court or by a child bench. The name and address of the child

---

[18] Juvenile cases in these two districts have been heard in the presence of a social worker; there was no psychologist though. See CeLRRd (2003), 101.

[19] Number 6 in the Chapter on Court Management, Muluki Ain.

cannot be disclosed to the public. The juvenile's legal representative, father, mother, relatives or guardian are allowed to be present in court for the hearing. Similarly, the officer hearing the case may allow any person or the representative of a social organisation involved in safeguarding the rights and interests of the child to observe the proceedings.[20]

Unfortunately, in practice, the court is often open during the hearing of juvenile cases. If properly implemented, the above provisions could help to put a child at ease and facilitate his/her full participation in the process. Such measures are also important for the protection of the child's privacy, something guaranteed by, *inter alia*, Article 40.2.(vii) of the CRC, Rule 8 of the Beijing Rules and Article 22 of the Constitution of the Kingdom of Nepal (1990). The interests of the juvenile as well as justice are important in determining how open proceedings may be, and how the judgment may be published.[21]

In the area of juvenile justice, the Supreme Court recently rendered a number of decisions with important implications for the juvenile justice system. The first decision by the Supreme Court regarding juvenile justice was taken in 2001. The Court issued a writ of *habeas corpus* with the aim of removing a juvenile offender from the central prison and placing him in a Juvenile Reform House, as prescribed by section 42 (1) of the Children's Act 1992, or, at the very least, to a juvenile welfare home, an orphanage or a privately established centre, as per section 42 (3) of the said Act.[22] More recently, in *Bablu Godia v His Majesty's Government* (writ no. 3390/2002), the Supreme Court '... directed the Government to establish and operate Child Reform Houses and other beneficiary organisations respecting the rights of children to physical and mental development'.[23]

The District Officer

The role of the Chief District Officer (CDO) is to take care of the entire administration of the district s/he has been assigned to. These prerogatives are not confined to the exercise of executive power; s/he also enjoys quasi-judicial power. The Public Offence Act gives competence to District Administration Officers (DAOs) to hear and decide cases brought before them on the ground of public offences. District Courts therefore appear incompetent to adjudicate such cases. Public offences represent a substantial part of all juvenile offences. CeLRRd's survey on juvenile justice shows that 63% of all offences committed by juveniles between the years 1997–98 and 2002–03 were public offences.[24] However, proceedings before this

---

[20] Children's Act 1992, s. 49.
[21] See ICCPR, Article 14.1.
[22] *Bablu Godia v Banke District Court et al,* writ no 3390 of 2000, decided on 2000 Chaitra 12.
[23] See CeLRRd (2003), 25.

quasi-judicial institution are known for recurrent violations of fair trial and other fundamental rights. This characteristic of the Nepalese system appears to be to the detriment of a dedicated and professional juvenile justice system.

The prison system

The Nepalese prison system is composed of 73 prisons in 71 districts.[25] Inmates in Nepal are divided in two groups: those convicted by a court of law are called 'prisoners' whereas those undergoing trial are called 'detainees'.

The penal system in Nepal is inefficient and by any measure inhumane. The existing prison system focuses on punishment without introducing a reformative or rehabilitative regime. While we talk about the links between prison and juvenile justice, although imprisonment is internationally recognised as inappropriate for dealing with juvenile offenders, it remains the most common instrument of juvenile justice in Nepal. As per the norms mentioned in the international instruments, Nepalese legislation clearly prohibits the keeping of juveniles together with adults in prison but it is common practice in Nepal to do so. [26]

Individual actors

Children (juvenile delinquents)

The main actors in the juvenile justice system in Nepal, and anywhere else, are undoubtedly the children themselves. Juvenile delinquents, for whatever reason, have caused a wrong to society, and as a consequence are channelled through the legal system. The CRC and all other international instruments dealing with the subject promote a specific juvenile justice system, focusing primarily on the welfare of the child and on its reintegration rather than on mere repression. Thirteen years after the ratification of the CRC, the Nepalese political power (government and parliament), the police and the legal profession (judges, prosecutors and lawyers) have not yet fully realised the negative impact that the absence of a proper juvenile system may have on society as a whole, for it is proven that dealing with juvenile delinquency through traditional punitive-oriented channels is inviting adult criminality.

---

[24] See CeLRRd (2003), 98. Information and data were gathered from 63 districts (information on the remaining 12 districts was unobtainable).

[25] Four districts do not have prisons: Bara, Dhanusa, Bhaktapur and Sunsari.

[26] See supra note 10, at 5.

Who, in the eyes of the law, is considered to be a child? Under Art. 1 of the Convention on the Rights of the Child (CRC), every human being below the age of 18 is considered to be a child. With regard to Nepalese law, the Children's Act of 1992 provides in section 2 (a) that a '(c)hild means every human being below the age of 16'.[27] Persons under the age of 16 years make up 43.92% of the population of Nepal.[28] Of course, the issue of juvenile justice does not concern most of the young population; all children below the age of 10 do not have criminal capacity;[29] and among those who are 10 and over, only a minority commit crimes. However, the fact that juvenile delinquency is less frequent than adult criminality should not make it a sort of 'secondary criminality', subject to less attention. Indeed it requires special measures and care. Besides, the number of crimes perpetrated by minors has dramatically increased in the urban areas in the last few years.

Of all children, 'street children' are the most at risk. There are an estimated 30,000 street children in Nepal, of whom approximately 4,000 are children 'of the street', that is children who reside and work on the street (as opposed to children 'on the street' who have homes but who spend most of their time working or playing on the street).[30] The environment of poverty and neglect in which they grow up, along with the negative interpersonal associations they are likely to make on the street, put them in the front line of the juvenile justice system.

Lawyers

It is a fundamental right of any person accused of having infringed the law to be represented in court by a defence counsel, hence young offenders are also supposed to be in contact with lawyers. Legal assistance at each stage of the judicial process is extremely important, as it is often the only way to be informed of one's rights and to have them observed. In the absence of a real social-worker profession, the role of the lawyer may require more skills than mere legal knowledge. In dealing with juvenile justice, lawyers must target the best interests of the child as the most important objective to achieve.

Social workers

The role of social workers is essential in the administration of a proper juvenile justice system. However, due to lack of resources and political

---

[27] The Treaty Act 1990 specifies the superiority of provisions provided by international agreements to which Nepal is a party over national provisions that would be inconsistent with international law. Therefore, the legality of section 2 (a) of the Children's Act is questionable insofar as it does not comply with the definition given by the CRC (to which Nepal is party).

[28] See HMG (2002), 24.

[29] There are 5,513,485 children below the age of 10 in Nepal, and 2,727,710 between 10 and 16. See Central Bureau of Statistics (2003), 1.

[30] See CWIN (August–October 2003), *Juvenile Delinquency in Nepal*, Kathmandu, at p8.

willingness, their role is almost nonexistent in Nepal. Social workers are usually the actors who are most aware of the conditions in which a child may evolve or probably evolve to be a criminal. The Children's Act of 1992 foresees that each juvenile court will be constituted of one judge, one psychologist and one social worker. But at the moment, this kind of court only exists in legislation. Similarly, the Beijing Rules foresee in Article 16 that a social inquiry should be made before sentencing. This inquiry should be done by qualified and experienced social workers. These inquiries are an indispensable tool for reaching a decision that will respect the juvenile's best interests. An understanding of their background, and of the causes that led to the commission of the offence, is essential in order to tailor-make the sentence to maximise the juvenile's chances of social re-integration. Furthermore, the role of social workers does not stop with the court sentence but should carry on after the juvenile exits the criminal system. Social workers should be there to facilitate the re-integration of the juvenile; they should be landmarks to which juveniles may come to seek help and counselling.

Parents

Parents have an important role to play in explaining the reasons for juvenile delinquency and youth criminality. In an ideal world, parents take care of their children and surround them with love, affection and education throughout their youth, which ultimately prevents them from exhibiting socially deviant behaviour, the most obvious being the breach of penal law. But we do not live in an ideal world. Parental responsibility implies duties (legal and moral) toward children and rights owed by the State to the parents. The limited scope of the present paper excludes a discussion of the duties of parents toward their children; however, some of the parental rights are specifically linked to juvenile justice and may be considered as providing psychological support for young offenders.

FUNDAMENTAL ISSUES

The Nepalese juvenile justice system has undergone major reforms, resulting in a distinct change in the structure and function of the adult justice system. Theoretically, legislation relating to the juvenile justice system in Nepal is clearly oriented towards the child welfare model, thus complying with international standards. But in the practical aspects it has been generally observed that the state of juvenile justice is pitiful, hence there are calls for immediate reform at the practical level. The fundamental issues mentioned below are the major concerns to be addressed in order to make our system just, reasonable and fair.

Criminal responsibility

An important concern relating to criminal responsibility is establishing the age of the child. However, in many remote places there is no system of birth registration. How can the age and subsequently the criminal capacity of children be obtained in those conditions? Though there are few options, one is to ask a doctor to identify their age. A second is to refer to the school-class level of the child. The first option requires money, the second requires that the child attends school, which is of course not always the case when dealing with alleged young offenders.

Surveys and reports reveal that investigating officers falsify the ages of accused, putting them into the higher age category, thus making conviction and sentencing easier.[31] The Government should make a special effort to improve the birth registration system in order to make it systematic. Indeed, section 3 (1) of the Children's Act of 1992 recognises the right of a child to a name and determination of birth date. The Committee on the Rights of the Child recommended in its last Concluding Observations (1996) that registration of children could be undertaken through 'the establishment of mobile registration' offices and registration units in school'.[32] In practice, when there is no official birth registration, judges often refer to a medical examination or to a school certificate. Section 3 (2) of the Children's Act states that 'in cases where the date of birth of any child is not traced, the person or organisation bringing up the Child shall, in consultation with a registered medical practitioner, determine the birth date of the child. Unless otherwise proved, the date so determined shall be considered to be the date of birth of the Child'. So the following are some suggestions: a proper system of birth certificates in remote areas should be established, either through schools or through local doctors; the establishment of mobile registration units should be encouraged, such as those suggested by the UN Committee on the Rights of the Child; judges and police personnel should be sensitive to the issue of age falsification. Its negative impact on justice and therefore on society should be emphasised. They must realise that by unquestioningly accepting false ages they irrevocably damage a life and cause a wrong to the society that they are meant to serve.

Quasi-judicial bodies

Authorities in quasi-judicial bodies are not always legally qualified and skilled; they are civil servants and as such they may come from very different academic backgrounds and have no knowledge of issues of delinquency. They have not been sensitised to the requirement of fair trial, nor have they

---

[31] See *op cit* note 17, pp. 94 and 99.
[32] See CRC/C/15/Add.57, para. 31.

followed special courses on the implementation of the CRC or of the Children's Act, but it is a bitter fact that they have been equipped, through various pieces legislation, to hear and decide the majority of juvenile cases. The only solution regarding this is to change the legislation through Parliament or to challenge it before the Supreme Court to make it void on the basis of inconsistency with principles of juvenile justice. Alternative measures for diverting juveniles as soon as the investigation starts will be a vital step towards avoiding trial by quasi-judicial bodies.

Lack of information and co-operation

In Nepal there exists no official data regarding the extent of juvenile delinquency. There is an obvious lack of knowledge and understanding of the child issue at all levels of administration and of the judiciary. Section 52 of the Children's Act creates the obligation for police organisations to keep accurate records of the manifestation of juvenile justice in Nepal. As per the Act those statistics must be made available for any study or research work without mentioning the name, surname or address of the child. Further, Rule 12 of the Beijing Rules reads as follows:

> In order to best fulfill their functions, police officers who frequently or exclusively deal with juveniles or are primarily engaged in the prevention of juvenile crime shall be specially instructed and trained.

An internal policy letter from the Office of the Attorney General, dated July 2003, seems to have established a new recording system of juvenile cases:

> Each District Government Attorney should submit a monthly report stating the number of cases where children were involved. Police organisations should also take the initiative to maintain the records of delinquency as per the provisions of Children's Act. In large cities, special police units should be established for that purpose.

Establishment of effective juvenile benches

The Nepalese Children's Act prescribes the establishment of juvenile courts. This obligation has not been made effective yet; and the juvenile benches that were considered as a temporary alternative do not work as well as they should: neither social workers nor psychologists are involved in the judicial process as envisaged by the Children's Act. However, the question of need for special courts to hear cases involving delinquents is not even a subject of controversy: it is common sense. So there remains a need for children's specialists in the judicial process and training of judicial personnel on juvenile justice, focusing on the international framework, the national provisions, and the ways and means to implement both of them. Similarly there is an urgent need to equip social workers and psychologists with the skills to handle juvenile cases properly.

Incarceration of children in prison

Section 42 of the Children's Act stipulates that a child be kept in a Child Rehabilitation Centre both during the investigation and in the execution of the sentence. This provision clearly indicates that the child should not be sent to prison to live alongside adult prisoners, even during the trial stage. The Children's Act is not specific on whether or not a child may be kept in police custody with adults during the pre-trial stage, however. Nevertheless, section 42 rejects this outright. Similarly, section 50(1) and (2) provides that if a judge presiding over a trial finds it inappropriate to send the child to prison, s/he should deliver the child to the parents or social organisations for custody. The Supreme Court in the *Bablu Godia case* (see note 25) ruled that it is mandatory to send a child to a child reform centre, thus the court completely ruled out the incarceration of children in prison. But in practice, however, children are kept in police custody or sent to jail indiscriminately.

Where a delinquent is sent to a Child Rehabilitation Centre in lieu of punishment, it is not clear how long s/he should stay there if s/he becomes a 'mature person' (as per the Children's Act) while serving the sentence. In practice, when the child becomes mature they are sent to prison. This goes against the reformative approach of juvenile justice. Once s/he is sent to a rehabilitation centre for reformation, how can sending him/her to prison only on the grounds of crossing the age barrier be a reasonable justification? It clearly negates the previous reform s/he received at the centre. In this regard, clear-cut provisions should be incorporated in our legislation to send them to vocational training centres instead of sending them to prisons.

CONCLUSION

Nepal does not have separate comprehensive legislation regarding the treatment of juvenile delinquents. The Children's Act of 1992 contains some provisions which deal with delinquent behaviour. But these provisions have not proven sufficient to establish a separate justice system for juveniles. Even now, the process of investigation, prosecution and trial is almost identical to that applied in the adult criminal justice system. Although the notion of a modern juvenile justice system accepted by the international community has been partly incorporated in Nepalese legislation, it is far from being applied. Despite the constitutional guarantee of legal assistance to delinquent suspects, this right has been frequently denied. The use of friendly, polite language in extracting information from young offenders while conducting interrogations is not the practice of the investigating authorities. Except as applied in some court rulings, probation has not been applied to young offenders. In this scenario, there is an urgent need to incorporate into practice separate juvenile justice legislation diverting juvenile delinquents from the ordinary criminal justice system.

REFERENCES

CeLRRd (2002a) *Baseline Survey on Criminal Justice System of Nepal,* CeLRRd (Bhaktapur).
CeLRRd (2002b) *Research Report of Trial Court System in Nepal,* CeLRRd (Bhaktapur).
CeLRRd (2003) *Juvenile Justice in Nepal,* CeLRRd (Bhaktapur).
Central Bureau of Statistics (2003) *Statistical Year Book Of Nepal 2003.*
CWIN (2003), *Juvenile Delinquency in Nepal* (Kathmandu).
Dhungel, Adhikari, Bhandari and Murgatroyd (1998) *Commentary on the Nepalese Constitution,* DeLF (Kathmandu).
HMG (2002) *Population Census 2001, National Report,* National Planning Commission Secretariat, Central Bureau of Statistics (Kathmandu).
Mukonda, R. (2003) 'A Paper on Diversion'. In *Juvenile Justice System,* pp. 227–9. (Kathmandu, Kathmandu School of Law, Nepal).
Sapkota, T. (2003) *Review of the Environmental Laws of Nepal.* Report submitted to HMG/UNDP: Strengthening the Rule of Law Programme.

Section Three

Learning from the Experiences of Diverse Models

13

The Role of the Police within the Spanish Juvenile Justice System: The Results of Legal Reform in Catalonia

LOLA VALLÉS

INTRODUCTION

IN THE LAST twenty years, major reforms in the political, economic and social fields have taken place in Spain. Among these changes, the criminal justice system and its agencies have been through a process of modernisation and democratisation. One of the more recent reforms affected the juvenile justice system and was introduced by a new law in 2000.

The police are a law enforcement agency within the criminal justice system. They hold a key position in this system as they can be considered the main entrance to it. In Spain a specific justice system for juveniles was created at the beginning of the 20th century. If we follow the historical evolution of the Spanish juvenile justice system we can observe changes in the model legislation and ages for application of juvenile law that go from the *guardianship model*—a paternalistic model similar to the American social welfare model—to *treatment ideology*—a mixed model based on individual responsibility, as in the crime control model—that have shaped police intervention with juveniles (see the chapter by de la Cuesta in this volume for additional information on the new Spanish model).

The guardianship model (*modelo tutelary*) was introduced in Spain by the Law of Bases in 1918, which opened the door to the progressive creation of Children's Courts following the model of the Cook County juvenile court (Chicago, 1899). Thirty years later, in 1948, the Law of 1918 was replaced by the Law of Juvenile Courts. The juvenile courts sought to protect those under 16, whether victims or offenders, from the improper exercise by their parents or guardians of the right to custody and education. It was a very 'paternalistic' and 'male based' conception. For instance, the main prerequisites for membership of this court were being male, over 25 years of age and with irreproachable morals and an unblemished lifestyle.

After a long dictatorship, democracy was re-established in 1976 and the lack of procedural guarantees in the Law of 1948 conflicted with key articles in the Spanish Constitution of 1978. During the 1980s there was in general minimum intervention by the juvenile justice system against juvenile delinquency as the law was in conflict with some of the principles of democracy. In addition to this, the need to introduce international treaties and agreements in law created a need to promulgate a new law regarding justice for juveniles; this took place in 1992 (Act 4/1992). This law constituted an urgent and provisional reform prompted by the declaration of unconstitutionality of the Law of 1948. The year 1995 saw the change of lawful age to 18 years, which was introduced by the new Penal Code, bringing it into line with the civil age of majority. Following this approval, a new law on justice for juveniles became all the more necessary.

The promulgation of Act 5/2000 on minors' penal responsibility was a swift movement towards *treatment ideology*[1] as it puts judicial intervention regarding juveniles somewhere between a formal sanction and a 'materially educational intervention'. It emphasises the recognition of the special vulnerability and educational demands of the offending juvenile and his/her legal responsibility for his/her acts. The law mandates that children under 14 years will not be criminally responsible for their actions and they cannot go through the criminal justice system. In exceptional instances, the law can be applied to young people of 18–20 years of age[2] (i.e. 'young adults'). Treating young adults as juveniles seems to take into account structural changes in western societies where the beginning of adulthood has been moved to run in parallel with the increasing practice of delaying entry to the employment market.

The way the police intervene with juveniles has gone through an important transformation in the last decades, especially since the democratisation of the State.

CHANGES IN LAW AND CHANGES IN PRACTICE

Act 5/2000 introduced a variation in the age of criminal responsibility for juveniles, from 12–16 to 14–17[3]. This means that children up to the age of

---

[1] The 2000 reform follows the juvenile justice model promulgated by international law such as the United Nations Rules, the Council of Europe Recommendations, the Convention on the Rights of the Child and the European Charter on Children's Rights.

[2] Provided young people fulfil the conditions presented in Art. 4 of the law: having committed a less serious crime or penal misdemeanour without violence or intimidation to the persons, or putting them in serious danger; not having been condemned by a final sentence for crimes committed after reaching 18 years of age; and that the special circumstances and the degree of maturity of the accused make it advisable, all those being considerations assessed by the Technical Advice Team.

[3] The 2000 reform fixes the minimum age for applying the juvenile justice system at 14 years; this has also been done in Italy, Sweden and Germany. The maximum age is 17.

13 are exempt from the juvenile justice system and criminal intervention is limited according to what biology and psychology define as childhood and adolescence. As a result, police intervention with juveniles under 14 years who commit a crime must be oriented towards child protection and must be done in connection with the juvenile welfare system and under the supervision and direction of the juvenile prosecutor's office.

Concerning the police, the new legislation on juveniles is a shift towards better protection of juvenile rights and legal safeguards in police performance. In this sense the reform introduces an exhaustive list of formal considerations relating to the detention of juveniles[4]. It must be emphasised that the 2000 Law limits the time of detention by the police to 24 hours[5] and also diminishes police discretion by establishing external bodies to lead police interventions: a judicial body—the prosecutor, and an administrative one—the juvenile welfare board. Furthermore, the law implies the official recognition and adoption in law of practices that were already in force, such as the existence of specialised police units for juveniles.

Act 5/2000 emphasises the protection of the basic legal safeguards and basic rights of juveniles; for instance, juveniles can request the *habeas corpus* procedure,[6] which will be initiated by the chief of police. The competent preliminary investigation judge in the place where detention has taken place will intervene. When the police detain a juvenile they are clearly instructed to avoid 'using tough language, physical violence and exhibiting

---

[4] Art. 17 of Law 5/2000: the detention of juveniles must be exceptional and must always be put into practice in such a way that it should cause the minimum detriment to the juvenile; juveniles must be informed of their constitutional and legal rights in words that they can understand and that should allow them to understand also the events they are being charged for, and the reasons for their detention; the police must immediately notify the prosecutor and the juveniles' representatives of the arrest, and also the appropriate legal personnel, as the case may be; a lawyer must assist the juveniles at all times; they must be questioned before their parents and a defence lawyer; and in their absence, before a prosecutor other than the one in charge of the proceedings; juveniles must be retained in adequate facilities and separate from those used for adults of penal age; they must also receive any physical, medical, psychological and social assistance and all the care and protection their age requires according to their sex and individual characteristics; and finally, within a maximum period of 24 hours juveniles must regain their freedom, and must be handed over to their parents, guardians or relatives or put under the Public Prosecutor, as the case may be.

Whenever the crime committed gives rise to liability to a prison sentence of over three years, juveniles must be put under the custody of the prosecution; if the presumed sentence is shorter, juveniles will be freed after giving evidence under the guardianship of those responsible for it. The prosecutor has 48 hours from the time of the arrest to decide on their freedom or request from a judge the precautionary measures they see fit to apply to the juvenile's situation.

[5] All juvenile detentions must be immediately communicated to the juvenile prosecutor by telephone and fax. During detention juveniles should be kept separate from adults and also be transported separately. Normally the police statement should also be sent within 24 hours to the juvenile prosecutor's office. In those cases where both adults and juveniles are considered perpetrators of a crime, a copy of the police statement must be sent to the juvenile prosecutor within 24 hours.

[6] The juvenile's parents or legal representative, the prosecutor, the juvenile's lawyer and the ombudsman can also request *habeas corpus*.

weapons'[7]. Furthermore, the police are only to use special protective security measures, such as handcuffs, on juveniles between 16 and 18 in serious crimes (i.e. violent crimes, sexual crimes or terrorism)[8].

Regulations on juvenile arrest and detention are provided by the new law, including the issue of place of detention. The law states that juveniles must be detained in adequate facilities and separate from those used for adults. The experience of the Catalan Police proves that improving and adapting facilities leads to less violence during the detention of juveniles. The juvenile prosecutor's office in Catalonia had made repeated requests to adapt detention facilities for juveniles since December 2001, when the 2000 reform came into force. However, the adaptions were not completed until July 2003.

When juveniles were kept in the old-style cells, violent episodes arose continuously such as self-inflicted injuries or furniture destruction. The new facilities consist of two big rooms with natural lighting and capacity for 30 juveniles each. The rooms have TV, video and special furniture designed to resist vandalism. Juveniles' attitudes towards the police have changed radically since the new facilities were put into use. For instance, taking interviews and testimonies is much easier and there is less self-injury.

JUVENILE POLICE UNITS

Law mandates that specialised police units for juveniles should be the main actors within the police segment of the juvenile justice system at the different levels of political power. It must be mentioned that in Spain there are three levels of government—state, regional and local—and as a consequence different police services with different tasks coexist, each service corresponding to one of the following levels: (1) At the state level there are two services: the National Police Force and the Civil Guard. (2) At the regional level there are three regional police services, in Catalonia (Mossos d'Esquadra), in the Basque Country (Ertzaintza) and in Navarra. In Catalonia and the Basque country these regional police services are intended to replace the state police forces. (3) At the local level in municipalities with more than 5,000 inhabitants there are local police services, better known as *municipal police* or *guardia urbana*.

Both state and regional police services in Spain have special units for dealing with juveniles; these units form part of the judicial police. The 2000

---

[7] Following the 2000 law reform the State General Prosecutor's Office dictated Recommendation 1/2000 for Police Services [*Circular 1/2000 de la Fiscalía General del Estado sobre criterios de aplicación de la Ley Orgánica Reguladora de la Responsabilidad Penal del Menor*] containing instructions for implementing the new law on juvenile justice. In section 9 instructions are given for police intervention during the detention of juveniles.

[8] Section 12 of General Prosecutor Recommendation 1/2000 for police services.

reform specifies for the first time in Spanish law that the juvenile police units will be the main police body to implement juveniles' law. However, it should be noted that these units had been set up long before the 2000 reform.

In Spain during the 1980s constitutional safeguards and European standards on criminal justice were gradually introduced, and the legal treatment for juveniles set apart a child protection system and a separate criminal justice system for children (those under 18 years of age). However, the police are the only criminal justice agency in which staff still deal with both juvenile justice and child protection tasks[9]. The 2000 reform maintains this situation.

Child protection tasks are aimed at all juveniles under 18 and the police develop them in collaboration with the juvenile welfare system. They target children and juveniles who are unprotected or at specific risk, and victims of 'a crime likely to affect their normal development as individuals'. Intervention of the police with juveniles under 14 who have committed a crime is protective only and only civil legislation on child protection can be used. In these cases police services may intervene only for the purposes of civil identification or determination of age, and they cannot use techniques and measures that are used to fight crime in relation to older juveniles or adults. They should apply child protection regulations, inform the prosecutor, follow his/her instructions and hand the juveniles over to their parents, guardians or relatives or to the juvenile welfare system.

Juvenile justice tasks are aimed at juveniles between 14 and 17. The police act as a part of the juvenile justice system which targets juveniles below the legal age of responsibility who have violated the law in such a way that, had they been of age, they would have been considered perpetrators of an offence or crime. Regarding juvenile justice procedures, police intervention according to Act 5/2000 must be fitting for juveniles who have committed acts considered misdemeanours in the Penal Code. It should be emphasised that juvenile criminal law is not applicable to children under 14 years of age regardless of the crime committed, nor to youngsters over 18 years who are processed in the adult criminal justice system.

Police enforcement of immigration law also applies to juveniles. When dealing with foreign juveniles, juvenile police units perform controls and administrative restrictions as part of their tasks.

At the state level the most important juvenile police unit is the group under the National Police Force. In the late 1970s and as a result of the emergence of juvenile delinquency within urban settings (crimes against property, vehicle theft, climate of insecurity, violence), *Juvenile Delinquency Groups* were created within the National Police Force (NPF), aimed at focusing on the offending juvenile. The emergence of juvenile delinquency

---

[9] For instance, the Catalan police force's juvenile unit self-reports that 30% of their work relates to protection while 70% relates to juvenile justice interventions.

coincided with the appearance of drugs, major demographic growth and unemployment among the second generation of immigrants who had settled on the outskirts of the larger cities during the industrialisation process of the 1970s. From the mid-1980s onwards, this more reactive orientation was complemented by the implementation of police departments specialising in juveniles and youth-related problems with a strong emphasis on preventive strategies. This demand for specialisation on the part of the police was specified in Royal Decree 769/87 for Regulation of the Judicial Police, constituting the *Groups for Minors of the NPF* (GRUME) in 1987, with headquarters in three big cities: Barcelona, Madrid and Seville.

GRUME forms a part of the Judicial Police Provincial Brigades, and their field of action focuses on three main objectives:

(1)   To protect children and juveniles who are victims, in collaboration with the juvenile welfare system. Their duties include: detection of children and juveniles in situations of abandonment or danger; the prevention and investigation of crimes involving children and juveniles as victims; assisting children and juveniles who have been victims of misdemeanours, and so on.

(2)   To combat criminality of youth in the juvenile justice system. Their duties include: informing parents regarding slight breaches of the law by juveniles; collaboration with juvenile courts and institutions providing attention to juveniles; the prevention and investigation of crimes involving children and juveniles as perpetrators, etc.

(3)   To help children and juveniles in risk situations. Their duties include: control of school absenteeism; participation in discussions, conferences and informative activities at schools; the search for and location of children and juveniles who have run away from home, etc.

At the regional level there is a juvenile unit in the Catalonia police force: the *Minors Brigade*. It was created in June 1986 together with a *Minors Police Headquarters*. It began to deal with questions relating to the victimisation of children and juveniles and also with criminal lawsuits brought against them. Since the beginning, a social educator has been part of its staff.

As a consequence of an organisational change after the 2000 reform, the *Minors Police Headquarters* was disbanded and instead a *Minors Service Office* (MSO) was created in December 2001. The MSO is a police unit solely for children and juveniles, on duty 24 hours a day, covering the entire region of Catalonia[10]. Three operational groups were established: two working from the public prosecutor's office for juveniles and one from the police headquarters building. Their duties are similar to those performed by

---

[10] The Minors Service Office covers the whole region of Catalonia, which has a population of 6.5 million. The average number of juveniles the Minors Service Office receives is close to 15 juveniles per day, with an average of four declarations being taken for each juvenile (perpetrators, victims and witnesses).

the Juveniles Unit of the NPF. They include, on the one hand, the investigation of complaints and reports which require subsequent inquiries. On the other hand, the MSO undertakes all other investigations ordered by the public prosecutor's office for juveniles and the courts as well as all steps in pursuance of court orders and administrative requests, detentions, appearances, summons, locations, confiscations, etc.

RELATIONS WITH THE PROSECUTOR AND OTHER AGENCIES

The rapport between the police and the prosecutor is very close and since the reform it has become even closer. Act 5/2000 recommends to the Ministry of the Interior, at both the national and regional level, that the staff of the juvenile units of the Judicial Police Brigades be assigned to the juvenile sections of the prosecutor's office. This has already been done, for instance, in the Catalan regional police where there are two groups assigned to the prosecutor's office dealing mainly with investigations following complaints or judicial orders. Under the 2000 reform, juvenile prosecutors lead the police investigations. However, after the detention and release of a juvenile offender investigations can be followed by the police with or without the request of the prosecutor or the judge[11].

Co-ordination between prosecutors and police services is better at the local level than at the regional level. The 2000 reform introduced the figure of the regional prosecutor who specialises in juveniles, but the police are still building bridges with regional prosecutors.

At the local level some positive initiatives have been taken in order to fight certain types of violence or crime in a more global and effective way through the creation of specific *protocols* among the different agencies dealing with the problem, including the prosecutor and the police. In fact, collaboration with other agencies through protocols is encouraged in section 30 of the National Police Service's '2001 Provisional Rules on police intervention with juveniles'. For example, in the case of the protocol for domestic violence: '... consensual performing of all the agencies: schools, health services, hospitals, prosecutors, police, judges and so on'. Evaluation of the protocol outcomes shows an increase in the number of complaints reported to the police and to the criminal justice system and more convictions resulting from co-ordination of the different agencies.

POLICE DISCRETION UNDER THIS SYSTEM

Police services in Spain have a large amount of discretionary power, just as in many other countries. This is because police activities are not always

---

[11] Section 28 of the 'Provisional Rules on police intervention with juveniles' [*Normas provisionales sobre tratamiento policial de menores*] of the National Police Service, January 2001.

qualitatively equal. Within the Spanish system police cannot use diversion formally—only the prosecutor is allowed to do so. Following the law strictly, police should always report improper behaviour and offences committed by juveniles. However, they do use diversion informally. It must be said, though, that the 2000 reform has reduced police discretion to some extent: it has introduced certain limits to the performance of the police by regulating in more detail the conditions for the detention of juveniles. In addition, police services must follow the prosecutor's orders when they perform criminal investigations and are under the juvenile welfare system when they perform child protection tasks.

In Spain, law regulates police proceedings, as they must be subject to the rule of law. However, there is a common thought that the police should be 'softer' with certain groups, especially those not able to defend themselves or to attack. This is the case with youngsters and children. This is based on the assumption that juvenile offenders are not responsible for their acts, thus they are not guilty. Their offences are seen as the result of the failure of those institutions in charge of socializing juveniles. Therefore police have a difficult role when dealing with juveniles. They must react to juveniles' offences, so they do have to intervene, but at the same time they should try not to stigmatise juveniles while performing their control function. For instance, two of the common characteristics of juvenile police units are that police officers do not wear uniforms and they receive specific training on skills that encourage juveniles to trust them.

When facing juvenile delinquency the police use even more discretion. They tend to react only when there is clear evidence of a crime and then they will apply the least degree of sanction permitted. In fact, when dealing with juveniles, police services tend to perform in a manner different from that which the law strictly stipulates. The reason for this adjustment is to try to avoid the stigmatisation that any criminal justice system intervention generates. This informal diversion by the police is mainly done in two ways:

(1)   Use of conciliation and mediation: a mediation process between the two parties to avoid a legal proceeding. The aim is to reach an agreement and avoid a lawsuit and police inquiry.

(2)   Diversion to other social control agencies: i.e. diverting police intervention to another social agency or institution. The aim again is to avoid the stigmatisation associated with a lawsuit or police inquiry. For instance, parents or legal guardians assume control and responsibility for the young offender's further actions. Another method of diversion is to refer the case to less stigmatising social agencies such as education, health or welfare agencies/institutions.

Out of this informal diversion arises the problem that police officers are not trained to undertake mediation, conciliation or referral to other agencies These are not strictly legal actions because Spanish law does not regulate them as police actions. In the event that it becomes regulated by law, training could then be included in police curricula. In fact, conflict resolution strategies are already part of the training curricula of some police services in Spain[12].

CONCLUSION

As a result of the promulgation of the new law on the juvenile justice system in 2000, Spanish police have changed the way they work with juveniles. The reform is a shift towards *treatment ideology* which considers that juveniles are not responsible for their acts and envisions juvenile crime as a result of problems in their process of socialisation—so it is in fact a shift towards a 'softer' approach to juvenile delinquency.

The law has introduced a very detailed regulation on police intervention with juveniles. It lowers the maximum time of detention, introduces the possibility of claiming *habeas corpus*, and lowers the age of criminal responsibility. All in all it limits police intervention and stresses the protection of the basic rights of juveniles.

In Spain there were already special juvenile police units, but they are now regulated by law. Members of these units receive special training. The functions of the police under the new system are quite wide as they range from protecting children at specific risk to detaining juveniles who have committed a crime. The law reinforces co-ordination between prosecutors and police services. It appears to be a more effective way of fighting criminality and reducing victimisation of juveniles.

When dealing with juveniles, police services tend to use more informal diversion. In Spain this diversion consists mainly of conciliation and mediation, and diversion to other agencies. This still happens even though these functions are not recognised by law and policemen are not trained to do so.

REFERENCES

Ajuntament de Barcelona (2002) *Menors: Protecció i Reforma*. (Barcelona; Guàrdia Urbana de Barcelona).

Antón Barberá, F. and Colás Turégano, A. (2002) Ley reguladora de la responsabilidad penal del menor (LO 5/2000 de 12 de enero) Aspectos policiales. In *Justicia Penal de Menores y Jóvenes (Análisis sustantivo y procesal de la nueva regulación)*. (Valencia, Tirant lo Blanch).

---

[12] For instance, during the Basic Training Course of the Catalan Regional Police-Mossos d'Esquadra there is a 17 hour course on 'mediation and communication'. The course aims at teaching cadets how to use mediation for the alternative resolution of conflicts, how to analyse conflicts and decide whether mediation is suitable, and techniques of mediation.

Bueno Arús, F. (1999) El anteproyecto de ley orgánica reguladora de la justicia de menores elaborado por el Ministerio de Justicia. *Harlax* 29, 49–61.

Clemente, Miguel (1999) El menor como objeto de las diferentes diligencias policiales. *Harlax* 29, 19–33.

Colectivo IOE, Martínez Reguera, E. *et al* (1989) *¿Tratamiento penal para menores?* (Madrid, Cáritas Española).

Dolz Lago, Manuel-Jesús (2000) *La nueva responsabilidad penal del menor (Comentarios a la Ley Orgánica 5/2000, de 12 de enero).* (Valencia, Ediciones Revista General de Derecho).

Generalitat de Catalunya (2000) *El Model de Justícia Juvenil a Catalunya.* (Barcelona, Centre d'Estudis Jurídics i Formació Especialitzada).

Polo Rodríguez, J.J. and Huélamo Buendía, A.J. (2000) *La nueva ley penal del menor.* (Madrid, Colex).

Sancha, V. (1999) Los menores infractores ante la ley orgánica reguladora de la justicia de menores. *Harlax* 29, 65–81.

Sánchez García de Paz, Isabel (1999) Minoría de edad y derecho penal juvenil. Aspectos político criminales. *Harlax* 29, 37–45.

14

Achieving Positive Results with Serious Juvenile Offenders in a Reintegrative Framework: Strategies Essential for Rehabilitative Effectiveness with the Intensive Aftercare Program (IAP) Model

TROY L. ARMSTRONG

INTRODUCTION

DURING THE 1960s, the more progressive wing of American juvenile justice assumed a stance that professional expectations for improved performance and behavior among youth released into the community following placement in secure confinement facilities (i.e. reformatories, training schools, secure treatment units) were simply not being met (Abadinsky 1991). In fact, the growing legitimacy of a nascent community corrections movement nationwide was being derived in part from the critical findings of research studies that noted the failure of accepted practices within youth correctional systems to resolve the legal, social and developmental problems exhibited by juvenile offenders experiencing extended periods of confinement. Regarding this failure, Dean-Myrda and Cullen (1985, 19) observed:

> ... research on recidivism rates revealed that prisons did little to diminish criminogenic predispositions. It was estimated that somewhere between fifty and eighty-five percent of all children committed to a reformatory eventually returned to crime after release. (Jensen and Rojek 1980, 50; Horwitz and Wasserman 1977)

Culminating a period of professional discontent and insight about the unacceptably high level of continuing failure of the system to reform delinquents, major alterations in the way juvenile offenders were defined and processed—spurred largely by the emergence of important new ideas about human development and the negative effects of social isolation—began to occur in the late 1960s across the country. Underlying these changes were persistent criticisms of numerous principles and practices that had previously been highly regarded and viewed as virtually unassailable.

A significant development in this call for reform was the increasingly active role taken by the federal government in stimulating planned change in the juvenile justice arena. Particularly critical in these governmental efforts was the issuance of a major report by the President's Commission on Law Enforcement and Administration of Justice (Armstrong and Altschuler 1982a). This policy initiative called for reform in four key areas of juvenile justice: decriminalization, due process, deinstitutionalization, and diversion (Blackmore 1980). Within this mandate for change, the primary thrust of deinstitutionalization/diversion strategies to reverse the excesses of many years of overreliance upon secure, institutional placement was to promote the development of coherent systems of community-based alternatives for juvenile offenders at the state and local levels.

Although emphasis in this movement was initially placed on less severely delinquent youths, the community-based strategies eventually came to embrace youthful offenders exhibiting the entire gamut of criminal misconduct. Hence arose the idea for designing and implementing specialized programs and supervision modalities in the community for high-risk, chronic, and even violent delinquents (Armstrong and Altschuler 1982b). These experiments extended to serious juvenile offenders who had required commitment to secure correctional facilities and then needed to be successfully reintegrated in their home communities. Noteworthy in these earlier efforts to normalize juvenile parolees in the community was a series of programs designed and implemented by the California Youth Authority during the 1960s and 1970s (Armstrong 1991a). In spite of some promising results with normalization and long-term behavioral change (Johnson 1962; Palmer 1971, 1973, 1974; Pond 1970; Roberts 1970), funding for such aftercare programs began to disappear as interest in specialized treatment as a high priority began to wane by the mid-1970s.

Interest in developing strategies for achieving more effective reintegration did continue to surface sporadically throughout the 1970s and in the early 1980s with the design and testing of various innovative models of juvenile aftercare and community re-entry. Perhaps most notable among these efforts was the Violent Juvenile Offender (VJO) initiative, funded by the Office of Juvenile Justice and Delinquency Prevention (OJJDP) in 1981 for a three-year demonstration period and tested at four sites nationally (Boston, Detroit, Memphis, Newark). Underlying the conceptual framework for this project was the assumption that key to effective intervention with serious, confined juvenile offenders was the utilization of theoretically-driven steps and procedures to reintegrate them back into their home communities (Fagan, Rudman and Hartstone 1984). Yet, in spite of progress made through such experiments attention was increasingly deflected from treatment-oriented reintegration approaches by a national acceptance of the precepts and slogans of a burgeoning 'get tough' movement that asserted that severely delinquent youth could only be brought under control through the adoption of harsher policies and practices (Conrad 1982; Doleschal 1982; Gross 1982; Greenberg 1977; Von Hirsch 1976).

The redirection of resources, restatement of philosophy, and restructuring of programs that marked the decline of community corrections in the late 1970s was a direct reflection of this emerging 'get tough' movement. In part predicated on the notion that juvenile crime had reached epidemic proportions, 'get tough' proponents championed the use of much more stringent, punitive sanctioning approaches to judicial and correctional intervention characterized by a new set of goals and objectives for the system. The agenda for change relied almost exclusively on the increased use of automatic waiver/transfer of youth to criminal court jurisdiction, a lowered age for criminal court jurisdiction, mandatory sentencing, and the return to a much wider utilization of long-term, secure confinement. Treatment and rehabilitative strategies were relegated to a very minor role (Armstrong and Altschuler 1982a).

Perhaps more than anything else, the 'get tough' movement riveted the attention of the juvenile justice community and the general public alike on the serious, chronic and violent delinquent. Issues of offender accountability and community protection came to the fore as strategies were devised and programs restructured to guarantee the imposition of high levels of social control over this population, especially when such youngsters were being maintained in the community.

As with all correctional fads and movements, the 'get tough' school began to show signs of weakening during the latter part of the 1990s and into the the 21st century. This re-emergence of the value and effectiveness of community correctional programming for juvenile offenders has been driven by a variety of factors. For one, costs of confinement in and construction of secure correctional facilities have caused both elected officials and juvenile professionals to return to the drawing board to explore more cost-effective ways of sanctioning and supervising juvenile offenders. Another growing realization is the recognition that incapacitation has done little to stem rising crime rates, especially serious crimes being perpetrated by juveniles (Byrne and Kelly 1989; Hagan 1991; National Research Council 1993, 2001; Shannon *et al* 1988). The late 1980s and early 1990s were clearly showing a pattern of greatly increased violence among juvenile offenders at the same time that juvenile correctional facilities were again beginning to bulge at the seams. Third has been an acknowledgement by many in the justice field, as well as by the public at large, that just maybe some things 'do work' in the attempt to rehabilitate juvenile offenders and adjust them to normal community life. A new rehabilitative literature is beginning to emerge and is revealing that certain treatment modalities are demonstrating long-term positive effects with delinquents (Andrews *et al* 1990; Borum 2003; Gendreau and Ross 1987; Lipsey 1992, 1995, 1999; Lipsey and Wilson 1998; Lipsey *et al* 2000; MacKenzie 2000; Palmer 1992, 1994; Sherman *et al* 1997). As Gies has noted, 'Despite early skepticism regarding intervention programs, recent literature reviews and meta-analyses demonstrate that intervention programs can effectively reduce delinquency' (2003, 3).

Interestingly, the renewed interest starting in the mid-1980s in community-based intervention strategies both as alternatives to incarceration and as reintegrative approaches has largely focused upon the problems posed by the most severely delinquent segment of this nation's larger juvenile offender population (Palmer 1991). These developmental efforts and the particular nature of the reforms can readily be shown to follow both from the impact of the 'get tough' school and from a number of research-based but widely disseminated insights about the relative role of serious juvenile offenders within the larger crime patterns of adolescent offenders in the United States. With regard to the influence of the get-tough school of the late 1970s and early 1980s, juvenile justice planners and practitioners were forced to take into consideration in designing and operating new programs the public demands that serious juvenile offenders be held much more accountable for their criminal behavior and that relatively high levels of social control be imposed upon them, especially while being managed in the community. In fact, much of the interest shown in juvenile restitution and community service programs throughout the 1980s and beyond can be readily tied to their ability to satisfy the widespread call for more accountability.

The clearest result of targeting severely delinquent youth for intervention has been the system's response of launching experimental program initiatives under the rubric of intensive supervision (Krisberg *et al* 1991, 1995; Wiebush 1993). Intensive juvenile aftercare as a coherent programming approach can be traced to experiences during the past several decades in adult intensive probation supervision and then subsequently to experiments with intensive supervision in juvenile probation (Armstrong 1991b). Clearly, the spread of the juvenile intensive probation supervision movement (JIPS) throughout the country has had important implications for the design and operation of juvenile intensive aftercare programs (Clear 1991; Steenson 1986; Wiebush and Hamparian 1991). Although largely grounded in notions of enhanced surveillance and heightened social control, JIPS has assumed a number of forms, the majority of which include various combinations of intensified surveillance/monitoring and highly specialized treatment modalities along with supportive service provision. Programs geared almost totally to strategies of increased control have met with little acceptance or success; rehabilitation and treatment persist as central considerations in interventions with delinquents. From a long-term perspective the feared decline and demise of the rehabilitative ideal have simply not occurred.

OVERVIEW OF TRANSITIONAL AND AFTERCARE PROGRAMMING FOR HIGH-RISK JUVENILE OFFENDERS

As indicated above, juvenile justice officials in charge of youth correctional systems throughout the United States have historically compiled a dismal record in efforts to reduce the recidivism rates of juvenile offenders re-entering the community from secure confinement, whether facilities were being operated at state, county or local levels (Altschuler and Armstrong 1994a). Within this overall pattern of failure the rate of recidivism appears to be most pronounced among a subpopulation of incarcerated youth who have established long records of criminal misconduct usually beginning at an early age and often being quite serious and violent in nature. Not only do they exhibit a persistent pattern of intense and severe delinquent activity, but also large numbers of youth in this extremely high-risk group are plagued by a multitude of other problems. Often they experience a variety of emotional and interpersonal problems, sometimes accompanied by physical health problems; most come out of family settings characterized by high levels of violence, chaos, and dysfunction; many are engaged in excessive alcohol and drug consumption and abuse; and a substantial proportion have become chronically truant and have dropped out of school altogether (Hamparian *et al* 1978; Hartstone and Hansen 1984; Elliot *et al* 1989; Tolan and Gorman-Smith 1998; McCord *et al* 2001). It is precisely this group of juvenile offenders who populate many juvenile facilities and pose the greatest challenge for the delivery of effective aftercare services and supervision.

One of the most common problems besetting the aftercare segment of youth corrections has been the difficulty of supervising the offender's transition from the closely monitored and highly regimented life in a secure correctional facility to the relatively unstructured and often tempting life in the community (Altschuler and Armstrong 1994b, 1994c, 1995). The inability of correctional personnel (i.e. institutional staff and field workers) to provide continuity of service and supervision from facility confinement to community living has long plagued efforts to achieve conditions of stability and normalization. Lack of co-ordination and partnership among correctional facilities, parole authorities, and community social institutions such as schools, community organizations, the family, mental health agencies, drug and alcohol treatment centers, employment and training programs, churches, business associations, employers and the like, have been a grave impediment to the development of effective aftercare programs.

The recognition of the multi-faceted needs and problems of youth in correctional programs should lead us to realize more than ever that aftercare field staff and community social institutions must be directly involved with correctional facility staff. The key challenge is how to create and bolster these partnerships and then to maintain and institutionalize them.

Recommendations for improved communication, shared decision making, co-ordinated planning and clear lines of authority are certainly not new; they have been made numerous times. Unfortunately, however, these recommendations have met with only a modicum of success (Nelson *et al* 1978). Much of the problem is that because of funding limitations, bureaucratic and professional intransigence, disputes over jurisdictional authority, understaffing, inefficient deployment of existing staff, community fears and resistance, and inadequate or nonexistent community resources, juvenile parole agencies, correctional facilitators and community-based social institutions have been unable to unwilling to enter into active, working partnerships.

In sum, the ability to reduce failure in the programming area of community re-entry necessitates addressing shortcomings in the structure and collective mission of correctional/parole/community-based resource and behavioral management systems. This need is particularly urgent in the case of multi-problem, serious juvenile offenders who are re-entering the community and display extremely high rates of reoffending. Intensive aftercare programs for this population must be designed, implemented and maintained with a full understanding of the potential pitfalls and a sense of how continuous case management, intensified levels of supervision and surveillance, and improved service provision, evidence-based treatment and youth advocacy can be effectively applied.

THE CONCEPT AND ROLE OF AFTERCARE IN JUVENILE JUSTICE

In commenting upon issues tied to defining the aftercare function suitably, Drs. David Altschuler and Troy Armstrong, Co-Principal Investigators on the OJJDP-funded 'Intensive Aftercare Program' (IAP), suggested a definitional frame of reference with regard to the concept of aftercare that was marked by a degree of specificity necessary for noting fundamental structural characteristics, underlying operational requirements, and essential programming dimensions. The intent of this conceptual formulation to broaden how we as professionals in the field of juvenile justice think about aftercare reflects more than a decade and a half of research and program development in this arena nationwide on their parts. They state:

> Aftercare ... refers specifically to those activities and tasks that 1) prepare out-of-home placed juveniles for reentry into the specific communities to which they will return, 2) established the necessary arrangements and linkages with the full range of public and private sector organizations and individuals in the community that

can address known risk and protective factors, and 3) ensure the delivery of pre-scribed services and supervision in the community. As this definition makes clear, both the correctional facility and the community have a critical role to play in aftercare. This definition stands in marked contrast to the customary conception and practice of aftercare historically in America where the focus is primarily—if not exclusively—on supervision *in* the community, with little or no focus on what takes place *before* release back into the community (Altschuler, Armstrong and MacKenzie 1999). Moreover, all too commonly, post-release aftercare falls far short on service delivery and treatment, leaving aftercare as little more than sur-veillance and monitoring in the community. (Altschuler and Armstrong 2001, 2–3)

The central concern explored in this definitional framework is that aftercare practice within the juvenile justice system has been largely confined to those activ-ities in working with youth in the community once they had been released from confinement. Usually, little was done to pave the way for a more carefully designed reintegrative process in terms of pre-release planning and collaborative decision making by institutional and field staff as the youth transitioned from confinement. There has been a growing recognition among practitioners working with issues of re-entry that this approach to reintegration, often described as 'falling off the table,' tends to be fraught with a variety of inherent problems, fre-quently resulting in high rates of failure and recidivism. Yet, for the most part innovative strategies to make the step-down phase of the institution/community continuum smoother and less disjointed had not been developed and tested. Obviously, changes are now beginning to occur both in the way aftercare is defined and in how programming efforts are being configured.

PROBLEMS AND IMPEDIMENTS PLAGUING THE DESIGN AND DELIVERY OF AFTERCARE SERVICES

It has repeatedly been stated over the past two decades that greater empha-sis should be placed upon transitional and aftercare services for confined juvenile offenders, but progress in this area has been slow for a number of reasons. A matter of particular irony is that although this population of serious and chronic delinquents, given their high-risk behaviors and propensity for repeated illegal acts, should supposedly be receiving the ben-eficial, cumulative effects of residential treatment and community-based follow-up, the reality is one where this programming arena has been given, at best, short shrift and, at worst, has simply been overlooked or ignored. Programs designed to respond to the needs and difficulties of youth re-entering the community have, historically, been assigned low priority on a regular basis in the competition for scarce resources.

Another major concern has been the ongoing inability of staff (located both in facilities and in the community) to provide continuity of service delivery and supervision from the point of confinement to reinsertion in the community. The issue of boundary has long hampered transition and result-ingly plagued efforts to achieve successful long-term adjustment for juvenile offenders. The lack of communication, co-ordination and collaboration among professionals representing the wide array of involved agencies ranging across residential facilities (both public and private) and community-based social institutions such as schools, neighborhood organizations, the family, mental health agencies, drug and alcohol treatment centers, employment and training programs, churches, business associations, and individual employers have been a persistent impediment to the development of appropriate policies and procedures for assigning and monitoring delivery services in a timely and efficient manner.

Any programming framework designed to achieve successful reintegration must devise strategies for overcoming such problems of linkage and connectedness that impede collaborative interaction across segmented systems. Two other ongoing problems identified as major obstacles to behavioral normalization and emerging from justice practice are as follows: 1) the experiences and interventions during residential confinement do not adequately prepare youth for the vicissitudes of daily life upon community re-entry, and 2) those valuable lessons learned and skills acquired while in confinement are not being sufficiently built upon and reinforced in the community following release. As Altschuler and Armstrong have noted, the key service areas around which both residential facilities and community-based providers need to organize their respective efforts in tandem are family, peers, school, work and substance abuse (1999, 6). It is these areas, when plagued with problems, that have been shown to be most predictive of reoffending among delinquent youth.

THE IAP INITIATIVE

Within the past fifteen years, as the field has experienced a resurgence of experimentation with innovative community corrections programs, one area of particular interest has been initiatives to develop more effective transitional and aftercare services for high risk youth. Notable among them have been several well documented projects including the Skillman Foundation's Intensive Aftercare Project, the State of Maryland's Juvenile Drug Treatment Program, the Michigan Nokomis Challenge Program, the Philadelphia Intensive Probation Aftercare Project, and the OJJDP-funded Intensive Aftercare Programs (see Altschuler *et al* 1999 for a description of these initiatives). It should be noted that much of this recent experimentation with innovative juvenile aftercare programming has focused on ways to develop more effective 'intensive' approaches that combine an appropriate mix of increased social control and intensified service delivery/treatment. This resurgence of interest in community corrections has dovetailed with a renewed confidence in the efficacy of treatment (Palmer 1992; Lipsey and Wilson 1998; MacKenzie 2000).

Current insights about designing and implementing intensive aftercare programs are grounded not only in previous experiments conducted on intensive supervision models in the adult system and juvenile probation but also draw inspiration from the earlier movement to expand and improve upon non-custodial correctional alternatives that were prevalent during the 1960s and 1970s (Armstrong and Altschuler 1982b). Several of the approaches and strategies that proved useful in diverting offenders from secure confinement are, in fact, prime candidates for transferability to highly structured and programmatically rich aftercare settings (Altschuler and Armstrong 1990). Key among these innovations were:

(1) Involvement of private agencies and citizens as well as public agencies in the community corrections process through the use of both volunteer and paraprofessionals and through purchase of service agreements,
(2) Adoption of a new stance by the community corrections agency that stresses resource brokerage and advocacy rather than direct delivery of all services to clients, and
(3) A case management approach that stresses continuity of service delivery and ongoing communication/collective decision making among all involved parties.

These practices, which undergirded much of professional activity during the height of an earlier community connections movement, have more recently been combined with newly formulated strategies and procedures for the supervision and treatment of high-risk offenders returning to the community.

The Office of Juvenile Justice and Delinquency Prevention, U.S. Department of Justice, announced in July 1987 a competitive bidding procedure to conduct a research and development project, Intensive Aftercare Programs (IAP). The IAP project was designed to assess current knowledge and programs in the field of juvenile aftercare, to develop a promising program model, to disseminate information about the proposed model, and to test this model in selected jurisdictions. The Johns Hopkins University's Institute for Policy Studies, in collaboration with California State University at Sacramento's Division of Criminal Justice, was funded in the spring of 1988 to conduct this multistage project. The demonstration phase of IAP was concluded in June 2000, and subsequently steps have been taken to advance further the dissemination of information about the findings and experiences of this project, as well as to provide varying levels of technical assistance. A key direction that has emerged for follow-up activities to promote the IAP approach has been the development of an aftercare center with a clearinghouse capacity for responding to requests nationwide (Altschuler and Armstrong 2001).

The IAP model that resulted from the research and development process and was tested in four pilot sites nationwide represents a carefully designed attempt to combine in a coherent fashion the most innovative policies and practices identified nationally to facilitate effective transitioning of high-risk adjudicated offenders back into the community and to offer a reasonable chance of long term normalization of behavior and reduced recidivism (Altschuler and Armstrong 1996). The model is grounded in a set of assumptions about the need to specify clearly the range of factors that generate and are highly correlated with serious delinquency. This identification process logically suggests promising strategies of intervention that are theoretically linked with these factors. Consequently, the model is theory driven and provides a framework of differential responses designed to meet the problems and needs of individual juvenile offenders. It is our impression that when the basic conceptual or theoretical principles of a program model either have not been stated or are ambiguously stated, it is difficult if not impossible for staff, program participants, or any other observers to understand with any degree of clarity what practices, services and procedures should be pursued and why, how they should be conducted and when, with which particular youth, and under what circumstances.

The design of the model was driven by a growing recognition arising largely from the assessment phase of the research and development process that a small set of goals must be incorporated if reintegration was to be successful. In the broadest sense, the implementation and management of effective aftercare services depends upon operationalizing programmatically four central goals. They are:

(1) Defining the overall aftercare function in a fashion that guarantees the inclusion of staff and interlocking programs across the entire continuum from the point of judicial commitment and residential placement to the termination of community supervision;

(2) Designing the network of community-based service provision in a way to respond comprehensively to the problems and needs of chronic, multi-problem delinquents;

(3) Devising a framework for case management thateinsures the continuity of supervision (surveillance and social control) and service delivery (treatment and competency development), which matches clients scientifically with appropriate interventions, and that brings the most objective procedures to inform decision making in the areas of risk and need;

(4) Focusing upon collaborative, inter-agency approaches and solutions to the challenge of supervision and service provision for a high-risk, high-need population.

In light of these requirements, a model (see Figure 14.1) was configured to span four distinct but linked conceptual levels extending from the most abstract and theoretical to program operations and service delivery.

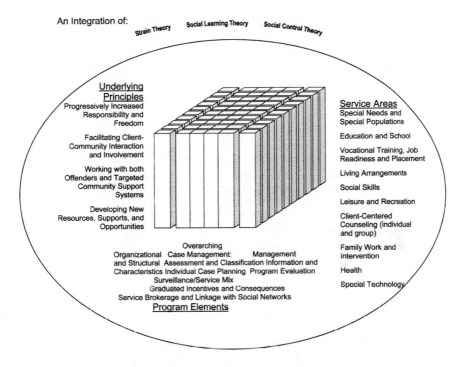

Figure 14.1: Intervention model for juvenile intensive aftercare.

In terms of descending levels of abstraction this framework (see Table 14.1) consisted of:

(1) An integration of social control, strain and social learning theories,
(2) Underlying principles of programmatic action,
(3) Program elements, and
(4) Service delivery areas.

At the level of integrating elements of various grand theories the design of co-relational pathways was consistent with a number of previously applied research initiatives to develop an intervention framework for serious juvenile offenders (Elliot *et al* 1985; Fagan and Jones 1984; Greenwood and Zimring 1985; Weiss and Hawkins 1981). The strength of these formulations has been that each of the three principal theories contributes a particular perspective and mode of reasoning, thereby deepening our understanding of the various causal and behavior-change processes involved. The proposed theoretically integrated framework for IAP postulates that serious delinquency, in general, and recidivism, in particular, are substantially related to: 1) weak controls produced by inadequate socialization, social disorganization and strain; 2) strain, which can have a direct effect on delinquency quite independent of

Table 14.1: The four conceptual levels that configure the IAP model

---

1. **Integrated Theory—A Synthesis of:**
   - Strain Theory
   - Social Learning Theory
   - Social Control Theory

2. **Underlying Principles of Programmatic Action**
   - Progressively Increasing Responsibility and Freedom
   - Facilitating Client-Community Interaction and Involvement
   - Working with both Offender and Targeted Community Support Systems
   - Developing New Resources, Supports, and Opportunities
   - Monitoring and Testing

3. **Program Elements**
   - Organization and Structural Characteristics
   - Overarching Case Management
     - Assessment and Classification for Client Selection
     - Individual Case Planning with a Family and Community Perspective
     - Surveillance/Service Mix
     - Incentives and Graduated Consequences
     - Service Brokerage and Linkage with Social Networks
   - Management Information and Program Evaluation

4. **Service Areas**
   - Special Needs and Special Populations
   - Education and Schooling
   - Vocational Training, Job Readiness, and Placement
   - Living Arrangements
   - Social Skills
   - Leisure and Recreation
   - Client-Centered Counseling (Individual and Group)
   - Family Work and Intervention
   - Health
   - Special Technology

---

weak controls and which is also produced by social disorganization; and 3) peer group influences, which serve as an intervening social force between youth with weak bonds and/or strain on the one hand and delinquent behavior on the other. The pathways by which these social forces and circumstances produce delinquency or recidivism are multiple, thereby requiring the availability of multi-modal interventions and treatment that can be tailored and targeted for individual problems and needs.

At the conceptual level of underlying principles of programmatic action, one sees a very distinctive domain within the IAP model, namely, the reintegrative demands for responding to circumstances of removal and isolation from community and the ensuing complexity of re-entry. Here, the model offers a very logical and structured guideline to overcome this condition of separation from the community. A focus is brought to bear upon the numerous issues and impediments arising out of the largely disconnected and fragmented movement of juvenile offenders from court dispositions to out-of-home custodial placement, to community step-down and aftercare supervision, and finally to discharge from the juvenile justice system. These principles are:

(1) Preparing youth for progressively increased responsibility and freedom in the community;
(2) Facilitating youth-community interaction and involvement;
(3) Working with both the offender and targeted community support systems (e.g. families, peers, schools, employers) on qualities needed for constructive interaction and the youth's successful community adjustment;
(4) Developing new resources and supports where needed; and
(5) Monitoring and testing the youth and community on their ability to deal with each other productively.

The five principles collectively establish a set of operational objectives and a reintegrative mission upon which the model rests (Altschuler and Armstrong 1991). In addition, these principles highlight the fact that intervening with confined youth for purposes of community re-entry requires not merely intensive supervision and service provision following release, but also planning and program activities that directly prepare these youth for what they will confront in the community. These pre-release activities, linked directly to street readiness, are followed by a carefully structured re-entry process keyed to a close monitoring of performance and progress by individual youth, and a close collaboration with other support and monitoring systems.

At the next conceptual level in the model, program elements, three critical areas have been identified as essential for developing an IAP implementation plan suitable for different jurisdictions, many of which face distinctly different challenges, barriers, and opportunities. They are: 1) organizational and structural characteristics, 2) case management, and 3) management information and program evaluation. Elements 1 and 3, organizational factors and the external environment, management information and evaluation, offer the means by which the overarching case management implementation and operations plan: 1) is developed to accommodate different settings, circumstances and contexts related to the targeted offenders, the structure of the juvenile justice system, nature of the juvenile code, and specific characteristics of the home community, and 2) can be monitored for the fidelity of implementation and program outcomes. However, at the heart of the program elements resides case management, truly the operational centerpiece of the IAP model. This is the operational centerpiece of any well-designed aftercare system since without its presence any attempt to identify, co-ordinate, monitor and deliver appropriate services would be futile. The exact configuration of required components specified as essential for aftercare case management emerged from a very extensive review of case management approaches being utilized nationwide in various jurisdictions to manage the behavior and deliver services to high-risk, multi-problem youth transitioning from out-of-home placements back into the community. The five discrete components we identified as essential are:

(1) Assessment, classification and client selection,
(2) Individualized case planning,
(3) Incentives and graduated consequences,
(4) Surveillance/service mix, and
(5) Brokerage and linkage to community resources.

Each of the five plays a role in determining how clients are targeted for particular levels and types of supervision, how clients are matched with appropriate resources and services, how clients can be tracked through the system without falling through the cracks, and how specific techniques can aid in the provision of supportive activities and sanctioning measures necessary for client supervision in the community.

At the most concrete and tangible level of the IAP model are the ten service areas identified as central to the comprehensive provision of supportive activities for juvenile aftercare. They are: 1) special needs and special populations, 2) education and school, 3) vocational training, job readiness and placement, 4) living arrangements, 5) social skills, 6) leisure and recreation, 7) client-centered counseling (individual and group), 8) family work and intervention, 9) health, and 10) surveillance and monitoring technology. While it is highly unlikely that any one program or participating provider would or even could provide this array of services, a strong argument can be made that a comprehensive system of aftercare offering an adequate continuum of interventions in a given jurisdiction must be equipped in some fashion to deliver this set of services to high-risk, multi-problem youth on aftercare status. These are the key service parameters that have been identified as relevant to juvenile populations transitioning from confinement. For a detailed discussion of each area, see Altschuler and Armstrong (1990).

A final but absolutely critical dimension of the IAP model's design and implementation concerns a conceptualization of the system domain for applying this framework. Here, the continuum for aftercare intervention is best viewed as consisting of three distinct, yet overlapping segments (See Figure 14.2). They are:

(1) Pre-release and preparatory planning during confinement,
(2) Structural transition requiring the participation of facility and community-based aftercare staff prior to and following community re-entry, and
(3) Long term, normalizing activities that ensure adequate service delivery and the necessary level of social control during the community phase.

This tripartite conceptualization represents a structural response to the systemic dilemma of being unable to smoothly transition youth with any major degree of success across the institution/community boundary. The review and analysis of promising juvenile aftercare approaches nationwide by the IAP staff, as well as the result of model building in the IAP project, have indicated the value of dividing the critical points of processing and movement across the continuum into three overlapping phases (Altschuler and Armstrong 1994a, 1994b). Within each of the three phases a set of aftercare-related activities should be initiated and then linked to activities to be conducted in subsequent phases (see Figure 14.3). Clearly, the first two of these three phases (i.e. pre-release planning and structural re-entry) are related programmatically to overcoming the difficulties posed by the facility/community boundary. It should be noted that these two phases are not mutually exclusive since their activities, procedures and goals are often intertwined.

Pre-release planning lends itself logically to the consideration of a series of activities that gradually lead to the full-time return of the confined youth to the community. This planning and treatment phase eventually merges into that part of the reintegrative process referred to as structured

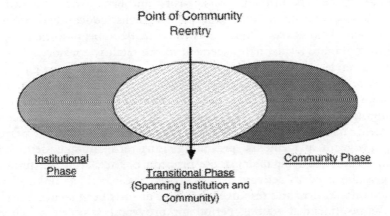

Figure 14.2: Reintegrative continuum.

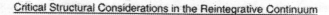

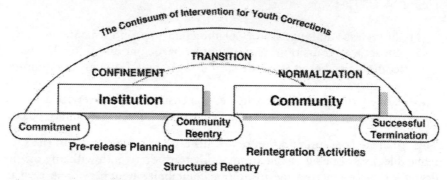

Figure 14.3: The structural configuration of and associated activities for juvenile aftercare across the institutional-community programming continuum.

transitioning. This phase, which includes both institutional and community segments (see Figure 14.4), involves providing well-planned and highly structured situations and opportunities through which gradual, progressively increased exploration and contact by the juvenile offender with the community can occur. A number of activities initiated in the facility during the institutional segment of transition can be used to launch the probing and testing of a youth's readiness and suitability for return to the community. These usually entail initial ventures into the community such as furloughs, home visits, and brief excursions to make contact with parents or other placement options, educational providers and potential employees. Once a decision is made to begin formal re-entry and to terminate residential placement in the facility, considerable attention is given to the use of various 'step-down' procedures during the community segment of transition prior to final community placement. These steps focus on relatively brief reintegrative procedures such as residential settings that include transitional cottages (often located close to the facility itself), halfway houses, short-term group homes, and other preparatory program placements preceding long-term independent living arrangements. Accompanying these procedures for step-down programming is the need to activate as quickly as possible those linkages with community services and resources that have already been identified. There can be no extended waiting period for provision of services following community re-entry.

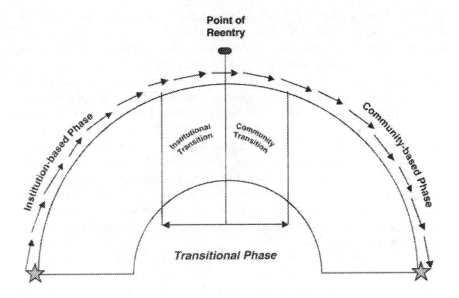

Figure 14.4: Segmentation of transitional phase.

From a supervision perspective, the period of structured transitioning usually should require a higher level of both face-to-face and telephone contact between the aftercare worker and the youth, as well as with other significant individuals, a more stringent use of curfew, the possible application of tracking services, the temporary use of electronic monitoring devices, and random use of drug and alcohol testing. All of these measures should, of course, be conditioned and influenced by the assessed circumstances of the youth at the point of release. In addition, this initial level of more intense social control and surveillance should hopefully be reduced as the youth moves through the aftercare experience, exhibiting improved performance and justifying increased freedom of action. Gradual decompression is a critical aspect of reintegration in the IAP model.

TESTING THE IAP MODEL AT MULTIPLE SITES

Challenges for implementation

During the research and development process four states were selected to test the model from a larger group of eight states that had initially participated in a series of three-day training conferences on IAP. These four states (Colorado,

Nevada, New Jersey, and Virginia) pursued a variety of preliminary tasks involving policy reformulation and fine-tuning essential features and components of their existing aftercare systems in preparation for moving forward to full operational status with the IAP Model. The major challenge faced across all four sites in the early stages of implementation was the complexity of adapting the generic IAP Model to the specific problems, needs and circumstances of the individual jurisdictions (Altschuler and Armstrong 1996). By design the model allows for a considerable degree of flexibility as long as implementation is consistent with basic underlying principles and program components. This strategy in designing the model anticipated the fact that program settings for juvenile aftercare are characterized by a diverse set of social, economic, political and organizational environments, often requiring considerable ingenuity in tailoring any conceptual model to the demands and constraints of specific concrete situations.

From an implementation perspective, pivotal to the success of this project at the individual demonstration sites has been the availability of content experts including the two co-principal investigators to provide extensive, ongoing technical assistance to guarantee that essential theoretical principles, program components, as well as required service provider agencies, were fully and precisely incorporated into the operational aspects of these pilot programs. Particular emphasis was placed on seeing that the five overarching case management components were applied and utilized in a way consistent with the intentions and stated requirements of the original model, generically defined. Also critical were key thematic features such as interagency collaboration, closer connections and open communication between institution and community-based aftercare, and strategies to facilitate backing representatives from community agencies and service providers, as well as significant others (family members and close friends), into the institution to interact with youth and staff to help achieve specified therapeutic outcomes.

Table 14.2 provides a brief summary of both positive and negative factors at the pilot sites which affected achieving a wide range of implementation goals. Only through a careful consideration of such factors can program planners and administrators hope to achieve full implementation of this complexly configured model. Perhaps the most objective comments and observations about implementation can be found in the process evaluation conducted by the national evaluation team from NCCD (Wiebush *et al* 2000). In discussing the degree of success achieved at the pilot sites in fully implementing the model, NCCD cited common programming factors that aided the implementation process. They were the following:

- high-risk, program-eligible youth are identified through the use of risk instruments that are site specific and empirically based,
- both institutional and aftercare case management are provided by staff who handle only IAP cases in small caseloads (i.e. 15 to 20 youth); in the community, parole officers work jointly with staff referred to as parole aides, field agents, or 'trackers',
- there is substantial co-ordination and continuity in case planning and case management across the institutional and aftercare phases; this co-ordination is facilitated by a team approach.
- team involvement and more frequent interaction between institutional and parole staff have helped overcome traditional turf and communications barriers,
- planning for aftercare begins shortly after the youth's institutional placement and is finalized at least 30 days prior to release into the community,
- there are formal structures to facilitate the transition from institution to aftercare, including the use of transitional facilities, furlough with intensive monitoring, or service delivery by community treatment providers that begins during the institutional phase and continues into the community,
- special services designed specifically for IAP youth have been developed and implemented in both the institutional and aftercare phases,
- aftercare services represent a mix of control measures and treatment interventions, and
- positive incentives and graduated sanction systems have been developed for the institutional and parole phases. (Wiebush *et al* 2000)

One should note that all of these factors are very consistent with essential requirements of the IAP model and represent 'doing business' in a way that is quite different from traditional, standard aftercare practice.

IAP demonstration sites

Within the IAP initiative, three states (Colorado, Nevada, Virginia) remained active in testing the model across the five years of pilot programming. Factors largely extraneous to implementing the model itself forced the state of New Jersey to discontinue the IAP test after two and a half years. While adhering closely to the fundamental design features and procedures that define the IAP framework, the three remaining states demonstrated considerable flexibility

Table 14.2: Factors affecting implementation

Positive Facilitators

• Previous well-established history of community, multi-agency collaborations for troubled youth where clear guidelines and procedures and guidelines have been identified and followed.

• The presence of scientifically valid assessment tools, both in the area of risk and need, to help match offenders with appropriate levels of supervision and relevant services.

• The availability of knowledgeable experts who can regularly provide technical assistance and training in the enhancement, fine-tuning and refinement of aftercare programs.

• Frequent interaction between institutional and parole staff to help overcome diverging interests and perceptions of relevant interventions.

• The presence or capacity to develop formal program structures and/or procedures to facilitate the transition from institution to aftercare.

• A jurisdictional history of contracting and brokerage for specialized services from various vendors in the community.

Impediments

• Difficulty of parole/aftercare line staff in adjusting to changing supervisory expectations and revisions in job description and responsibilities as aftercare evolves away from traditional casework practice.

• The fact of substantial physical distance between the home community of confined offenders and the institutions where they are being housed.

• The resistance of grassroots agencies and groups to embrace and provide opportunities for youth who have been identified as chronic, serious juvenile offenders and have been incarcerated due to the threat they pose to the community.

• The resistance of families—essential players in the intervention process—to agree to participate fully and openly in treatment and counseling along with their children.

• The inability to provide a condition of short-term 'lock-up' as the most stringent measure in a graduated sanctioning framework.

• An approach to intensive supervision that relies almost exclusively upon surveillance and social control techniques.

• A lack of creative approaches to work with older adolescent offenders on aftercare caseloads (generally tied to tendency to be inflexible in managing this population).

• Inability to find a common meeting ground, programmatically and philosophically, when working with other large and significant organizational entities in the community such as public schools and mental health.

---

and ingenuity in adapting the generic model to the specific circumstances and needs of their jurisdictions. The creativity revealed in these variations of the model served as a rich source of information and insight into the numerous ways the primary implementation goals of the IAP project could be achieved.

Colorado

The Colorado IAP project was operated by the State Division of Youth Services (DYS), Department of Institutions. The catchment area for eligible youth in confinement was comprised of parts of Jefferson, Arapahoe and Denver counties, including greater metropolitan Denver. The designated youth correctional facility for this project was Lookout Mountain Youth Services Center (LMYSC) and was located only 18 miles from downtown Denver, beneficial for close proximity to juvenile offenders' home communities. LMYSC was the state's most secure facility, housing the most severely delinquent youth in the DYS system. Project design required that all IAP participants be housed in a single cottage on the grounds of LMYSC.

Decision making about matching services with offenders and determining levels of supervision benefited from the availability of a battery of comprehensive assessment tools including the Youth Level of Service Inventory, the Adolescent Living Independently Via Education and Employment instrument, and a variety of privately provided tools focusing upon the assessment of family, vocation, and drug/alcohol problems and needs. These instruments supplemented the standard set of educational and psychological tools, completing other case file data already gathered to develop a youth's social, legal, medical, and personality profile. Within 60 days of confinement, a discrete case plan that established goals and procedures for successful community reintegration was developed. This master plan established guidelines for both institutionally based treatment and follow-up activities in the community.

To ensure adequate levels of supervision and service delivery, an IAP client manager (a DYS employee) provided oversight for each client from the point of institutional referral through transition and step-down into the community and throughout follow-up and eventual discharge. Specific standards for client management included monthly face-to-face contact with the youth during confinement and weekly contact that began 60 days prior to release and continued throughout community placement. A relatively intense level of contact was also maintained with ancillary individuals and agencies in the community including family members, school officials, employers and other involved parties. Caseload size was capped at 18 cases with a maximum of 6 institutional and 12 community clients.

Client managers assumed primary responsibility for all community contacts, but various service providers aided in the supervision process. Trackers employed by private providers were used extensively for daily face-to-face contacts. They were trained to make random spot checks, to monitor daily schedules and to employ electronic surveillance technology (following discussion with and approval by case managers). The majority of tracker contacts occurred outside normal working hours.

Each service provider developed an individualized treatment plan for referred youth, establishing goals and time frames for treatment consistent with the directives of the master case plan. Co-ordination and monitoring of these services were handled by the client managers through a brokerage model for contracted treatment and resource provision. The shaping of client behavior was greatly influenced through a graduated response framework in which both positive incentives and consequences/sanctions were utilized.

Nevada

The Nevada IAP project was operated by the State Division of Youth Corrections' Youth Parole Bureau. Clark County (Las Vegas), which had the greatest concentration of serious juvenile offenders in state confinement, was selected as the IAP pilot. The correctional facility identified for participation in the project was Caliente Youth Center, located approximately 150 miles from Las Vegas. This geographical factor of distances presented a substantial challenge in implementing the IAP Model.

Within the Caliente Youth Center, particular emphasis was placed on the special pre-release curriculum taught during the month prior to re-entry into the community. The curriculum focused major attention upon social skills training and issues related to street readiness. An aftercare worker (a parole agent) from Las Vegas resided and worked in the Caliente facility and in that role served as an ongoing liaison between the institution and community, ensuring regular, sustained contact and communication. All IAP youth returning to the Las Vegas area were required as part of transition to step-down into a highly structured and intensive day treatment program, the Center for Independent Living. Within this transitional setting existed the option of short-term residential placement for youth who were simply not prepared to return immediately to their homes for any one of a number of reasons. As a collaborative gesture, the Clark County School District employed an educational liaison specialist who spent considerable time at the institution and had primary responsibility for reintegrating IAP youth into public schools. Unfortunately, this strategy only achieved mixed results since retention proved to be a much greater obstacle than simply the act of enrolment.

The community supervision component relied on a team approach in which three parole officers assigned to the IAP project were collectively responsible for supervising 45 IAP parolees. This approach afforded 24-hour coverage in the community when required and facilitated a quick response when problems arose. Each officer managed a small caseload individually but contributed specialized expertise to the larger group of clients. Each officer had been encouraged to develop individualized expertise in areas such as substance abuse treatment, family therapy techniques, vocational education and training techniques, and job development and placement skills. These officers also traveled several times per month to Caliente to work with staff and IAP youth.

Additional personnel augmented the IAP supervision team. Two community outreach trackers provided expanded hours of supervision during evenings and weekends. Outreach workers blended surveillance with service provision that included life skills training and monitored recreation.

Virginia

The Virginia IAP project, commonly referred to as IPP (Intensive Parole Program), was designed to intervene and provide structured transition and community follow-up for serious, chronic juvenile offenders who had been committed to the Beaumont Juvenile Correctional Center by the Norfolk Juvenile and Domestic Relations Court. The Norfolk Court Service Unit appointed two senior parole counselors who supervised all IPP participants and co-ordinated the delivery of family services. These counselors visited confined youth at Beaumont at least once a month. Upon release participants were contacted on a face-to-face basis at least three times a week.

The parole counselors in this project managed caseloads with an average of 15 clients. They held weekly family meetings; conducted unannounced spot checks at school, home, and place of employment; continued the life skills curriculum that had been initiated in the institution; and co-ordinated other group activities involving participants and their families. These parole counselors also worked closely with the Norfolk School's Transition Specialist to address educational needs. A paraprofessional, serving as a parole aide, assisted with monitoring, transportation and other functions related to community supervision. Every 30 days IAP youth on parole status were required to appear in court for a judicial review, during which the counselor updated the court on the participant's progress.

As was the case with the Nevada pilot program where institution and community were at a considerable distance from each other, a similar situation existed in Virginia regarding the respective locations of the Beaumont facility and the city of Norfolk. A comparable strategy was adapted here to help overcome difficulties posed by the considerable distance separating the institution and the reentry community. A parole staff member was assigned to work exclusively in the institution with IAP youth and serve as liaison for them as they returned to the community.

Other examples of IAP implementation

The national attention that was given to the IAP Model during the formal demonstration period at the pilot sites resulted in a number of other jurisdictions across the U.S.A. beginning to experiment with variations of this basic framework in the mid-to-late 1990s. These sites have contributed substantially to the emerging knowledge base about issues in the design, implementation, and operation of intensive aftercare. Projects that were particularly valuable in providing insight were 1) the Network Aftercare System (NAS) in Mobile, Alabama; 2) the Intensive Parole Program (IPP) that was instituted throughout the state of Washington; 3) the Minority Youth Transition Program with the Oregon Youth Authority; 4) the Hennepin County Home School Intensive Aftercare Project in Minnesota; and 5) a number of statewide youth correctional system projects including the states of Alaska, Florida, Kentucky, New York, South Carolina, and South Dakota. Experimental or quasi-experimental design outcome evaluations have been conducted on a number of these projects.

At present, the most ambitious national juvenile re-entry/aftercare project grounded in the IAP design is the Targeted Re-entry Initiative. Managed by the Boys and Girls Clubs of America, the project has been funded by the Office of Justice Programs, U.S. Department of Justice, as a three-year demonstration at a number of pilot sites. Primary attention is being focused upon four intensive sites where a quasi-experimental design evaluation is being conducted by a research team from Indiana University, Indianapolis. A key element in this elaboration of the IAP Model is the introduction of a Boys and Girls Club providing recreational and other programming activities inside the participating juvenile correctional facility at each site (Barton *et al* 2004). In addition, major emphasis has been placed upon superimposing a strength-based, positive youth development component on more conventional correctional interventions that have traditionally targeted problems and deficits being exhibited by offenders in confinement (Armstrong 2004; Barton 2004).

Another widely discussed juvenile aftercare program that is currently in operation and builds upon IAP design features is the Minority Youth Transition Program (MYTP) housed within the state of Oregon Youth Authority. It represents an effort to adapt the IAP Model specifically to the needs and circumstances of African American youth in confinement as they transition into their home communities. This programming experiment has already been described in considerable detail in another publication (Armstrong and Jackson 2005).

The most serious manifestation of minority overrepresentation in the U.S. juvenile justice system can be found at the point of secure confinement, where the highest level of overrepresentation occurs. One strategic approach to reducing the problem that has received increasing attention over recent years involves programming steps being taken to reduce the number of minority youth returning to confinement as a result of new offenses or major technical violations being committed following release. Based upon the IAP framework for pre-release planning, structured transition, and intensified supervision/enhanced treatment during community follow-up, the MYTP utilized innovative policies and procedures that were especially sensitive to the needs of African-American youth in the youth correctional system. Between 1996 and 1999, the approach to aftercare began to show positive results in terms of reducing rates of recidivism, thereby reducing the extent of minority overrepresentation in Oregon's juvenile correctional facilities (Jackson 2002).

STRATEGIES ESSENTIAL FOR REHABILITATIVE EFFECTIVENESS

Other than insights gained and experiences noted during implementation of the IAP demonstration sites, five primary facets in design and application of the IAP Model were identified as being fundamentally important in achieving positive rehabilitative outcomes. Observations by the two co-principal investigators who probed issues relating to treatment impact across IAP demonstration and IAP-derived sites indicated that the following intervention strategies must be incorporated. Further, although the presence of appropriate evidence-based treatment modalities is mandatory, experiences in applying the IAP framework suggest that steps to success must be defined more broadly.

Appropriate mix of social control/surveillance and treatment/service

A major finding from prior research on intensive supervision programs has been that effective interventions aiming for long-term positive change with serious juvenile offenders need to provide programming modalities emphasizing treatment modalities and enriched service provision in addition to imposing the required level of social control (Armstrong, 1991). The important lesson of a fundamental need to mix social-control and treatment was not lost on the initial design of the IAP Model where the stated goal was to develop policies of intervention that assured the imposition of an appropriate mix of social control/surveillance and treatment/service provision. It was determined that the best way to guarantee this configuration was to incorporate into the screening/planning process a comprehensive assessment package for risk, need and resilience/strengths in order to guide decision making on an individualized basis, thereby resulting in a carefully calibrated deployment of resources to ensure appropriate levels of both

surveillance/social-control and treatment/service provision. Only by achieving the appropriate mix of these responses to high-risk, multi-problem youth
can program staff hope to maximize the overall impact of interventions; too
much or too little of either modality (social-control or treatment) can have
very negative implications in normalizing behavior and in seeking positive
change with this highly volatile, problematic group of adolescent offenders.
Fortunately, the assessment technology for guiding these complex decisions
is readily available to the juvenile system. These tools represent the major
innovation in the field over the past twenty years. At this point in the evolution of treatment and rehabilitation, the true challenge is to have available
those resources necessary to follow-up upon the indicated findings from
assessment for appropriate interventions.

Evidence-based treatment modalities and their inclusion across the reintegrative continuum

As emphasized early in this chapter, fundamentally important to current
efforts to design and deploy effective intervention approaches with high-
risk delinquents is the operational assumption that the assertion emerging
during the mid-1970s and stating 'nothing works' in youth offender treatment and rehabilitation has been shown through a number of research studies simply not to be true. The fact that correctional treatment can be
effective generally in reducing recidivism and renewed criminal activity
among adjudicated youth has a special relevance in programming intended
to remediate the antisocial behavior of severely delinquent juveniles. The
more severe the delinquent behavior, the more impact appropriately
matched treatment can have in terms of effect (Borum 2003; Gies 2003;
Lipsey *et al* 2000).

This narrower focus on issues of effectiveness with a particular offender
sub-population suggests an important set of considerations deriving from
the 'what works' debate and having a bearing upon the effectiveness of reintegrative programs. Carefully profiling confined youth who will be participating in transitional, re-entry and aftercare programs and being matched
with required levels of supervision/social control and linked with appropriate services and treatment modalities is a necessity for successful intervention. In large part this is a serious, chronic and often violent offender
population characterized by a pattern of early onset of delinquency, exhibiting frequent misconduct, and being plagued by a variety of social and personal problems. The axiom about what works best, with whom and under
which circumstances is especially relevant to situations where matching
treatment involves youth who have experienced multiple failures previously
in the juvenile justice system, are obviously resistant to interventions and
have reached the deep end of the system. Selection of appropriate modali-

ties must occur with a deep, comprehensive understanding of the nature and intensity of the problems, deficits and needs exhibited by this difficult group of youth.

At the heart of the procedures for selecting and matching treatment modalities is the need to understand the centrality of certain key factors referred to as criminogenic that ongoing research on recidivism has shown repeatedly to be the most predictive of reoffending (Andrews and Bonta 1994; Dembo *et al* 1991; Farrington 1989; Farrington and Hawkins 1991; Hawkins *et al* 1987, 1998; Lipsey and Derzon 1998; Loeber and Stouthamer-Loeber 1987; Osborn and West 1980; Patterson *et al* 1992; Thornberry and Krohn 1997; Thornberry *et al* 1993; Wiederanders 1983; Zarb 1978). These factors, often exhibited in combination by severely delinquent youth, are associated with problems such as dysfunctional and fragmented families, school disruption and conflict, negative peer influence, and substance abuse. Within the IAP Model special attention is given to identifying and measuring them early during the confinement experience and taking those steps through the individual case planning process to respond appropriately to their remediation.

In a recent article on effectiveness of aftercare programming, Altschuler and Armstrong (2002) noted that two bodies of research bear upon positive reintegrative outcomes. First, there is research that draws upon the nature of the confinement experience and its impact on subsequent success and failure in the community. Here, findings indicate the benefits of incorporating into the routine of confinement the delivery of those services and activities that maximize the choices of successful community reintegration. Second, another body of research examines the community side of transition and re-entry. Community intervention refers to what occurs: 1) in neighborhoods, 2) with families, friends, and acquaintances, and 3) with various socializing institutions (e.g. schools, faith-based organizations, neighborhood groups, recreational programs and clubs, employers). Correctional oversight and supervision must extend well beyond the formal role played by aftercare staff. These authors further note that among the several risk/need factors that must be included in this potent combination highly predictive of reoffending and must be targeted for intervention are those related to family dysfunction and conflict, negative peer group influence, school conflict and disruption, and drug/alcohol dependency.

Some of the specific programming/treatment principles and situational factors that have been shown to generalize well to effective interventions with more severely delinquent youth include the following:

A. *Role of the juvenile justice system*
   1. The site for service delivery not being a juvenile justice or law enforcement facility,

2. The juveniles in the program being referred or identified by a juvenile justice agency and their participation being mandated, and

3. The program being sponsored by a juvenile justice or law enforcement agency and having a tangible sense of requirements/performance standards and individualized accountability associated with operations.

B. *Amount/intensity/duration of service*
   1. The duration of the service period amounting to more than 18 weeks, and
   2. The average number of hours per week of service contact time being more than 5 hours.

C. *Targeted services*
   1. Designed to target the specific characteristics and problems of offenders that can be changed in treatment (dynamic characteristics), and
   2. Target the most intensive programs to those offenders who are at the highest risk of recidivism.

D. *Other promising strategies*
   1. Therapeutic integrity being high, i.e. the program's services are delivered as designed, having been fully implemented and staffed by trained personnel, and
   2. Research personnel playing a major role in designing and monitoring program activities.

E. *Promising treatment modalities*
   1. Intensive supervision with reduced caseloads (both probation and parole),
   2. Behavioral-based intervention (based on social learning or cognitive theories of change that emphasize positive reinforcement contingencies for pro-social behavior),
   3. Skill-oriented approaches that translate into improved interpersonal relations and readiness for more effective daily living,
   4. Multi-model approaches that allow simultaneous intervention into multiple problem areas of a single individual,
   5. Employment with the full complement of released activities including job training, job development, job placement, job shadowing, and associated activities, and
   6. Service brokerage with specialized providers in both public and private sectors and exhibiting state-of-the-art assessment and follow-up.

Essential structural characteristics of the reintegrative continuum

Another major development over the past decade in the evolution of experimentation with promising approaches and strategies for effective aftercare has been the growing recognition that emphasis must be placed upon critical structural features in the design of reintegrative systems. It has become evident on the basis of a small number of programming initiatives (Altschuler *et al* 1999) that any discussion of effectiveness and ensuing action-planning must go beyond simply a consideration of treatment modalities and move to incorporate certain essential structural characteristics. This aspect of program development and operations has only recently begun to be fully appreciated and incorporated with the newer wave of intensive aftercare initiatives beginning in the late 1980s and continuing into the 1990s. This lesson was not lost on the IAP project where a very concerted effort was made during the design phase to identify and implement those required structural characteristics of the reintegrative continuum (Wiebush *et al* 2000). The reader is referred to Table 14.3, which itemizes on the basis of IAP-related research what appear to be essential design features at each of the three interlocking phases of the continuum. It further provides a framework for conducting comparative analysis to determine the extent to which other recent aftercare initiatives have taken steps to incorporate such structural features (see Table 14.4).

A broad policy-driven challenge at the first, or institutionally-based phase of the continuum, is the need to inculcate a sense of reintegrative orientation among facility administrators and staff who are often heavily occupied with the demands and requirements of managing a confined offender population where issues of security and safety are critical and ongoing. An orientation toward reintegrative goals at this initial phase is essential for optimal results across the entire continuum.

Table 14.3: Baseline characteristics of IAP pilot programs for comparison with other intensive aftercare initiatives

---

I. **Program Design: Institutional Phase**
   A. Pre-release Planning
   B. Involvement of Outside Agencies and Individuals in Institution
   C. Targeted Community Activities during Confinement Period

II. **Program Design: Transitional Phase**
   A. Testing and Probing of Reentry Prior to Formal Placement in Community
   B. Structured Step-down Process Utilizing Residential Placement or Intensive Day Treatment.

III. **Program Design: Community Follow-up**
   A. Provision of Multimodal Treatment Services
   B. Discrete Case Management Services
   C. Use of Graduated Sanctions and Positive Incentives
   D. Provision of Supervision and Surveillance beyond Ordinary Working Hours
   E. Reduced Caseload Size/Increased Frequency of Client Contact
   F. Multi-stage Decompression Process

Table 14.4: Juvenile aftercare matrix

Program/Study Characteristics (IAP Model)	Philadelphia Intensive Probation Aftercare	Maryland Aftercare Program	Skillman Intensive Aftercare Project	Michigan Nokomis Challenge Program
PROGRAM DESIGN				
Institutional Phase				
Pre-release planning	Community sources offer input via probation officers. Preparation of post release plan.	Family therapist assesses, diagnoses, develops family contract, and begins weekly family group sessions. (Highly uneven implementation.)	Aftercare caseworker commences contacts with youth and family 3 months prior to release.	Planning for community re-entry is initiated 30 days after placement in residential phase.
Involvement of outside agencies and individuals in institution	Probation officers meet with institutional staff and juveniles.	Family visits facility at lease once; therapist involves youth in family assessment session. (Less than half of youth involved in family assessment session.)	Not indicated.	Parents meet with confined children, institutional staff and a community worker once every 2 weeks.
Targeted community activities during confinement period	Probation officers meet with parents on regular basis in the community.	Family attends weekly group sessions with therapist and support groups. (Low family involvement.)	Not indicated.	Community workers see parents once per week at their home.
Transitional Phase				
Testing and probing of re-entry prior to placement in community	Not indicated.	Not indicated.	Not indicated.	Not indicated.

Structured step-down process using residential placement or intensive day treatment	First 6 weeks with very high level of probation officer/client contact. No use of intensive day treatment or short-term residential treatment.	Initial period of intense contact, followed by lesser contact with case manager, additional counselor, and family therapist. No use of intensive day treatment.	First few weeks after facility release: carefully prescribed program. Average monthly contacts 10 over 67 months in Detroit; 60 over 6 months in Pittsburgh. Contacts taper off after first 2 months. Pittsburgh uses transition group home.	Initial month of virtual house arrest. Level of community worker/client contact also high during first 3 months. No use of intensive day treatment or short-term residential treatment.
Community Follow-up				
Provision of multimodal treatment services	Few prescribed activities but some emphasis on education and vocational activities.	Wide spectrum of services offered with links to community resources.	Efforts to improve family functioning through counseling and to link clients with education program. Jobs far short of expectations.	Variety of required programming activities. Some major questions about quality of delivery.
Discrete case management services	Required procedures neither highly developed nor clearly articulated.	Three articulated levels of intervention: pre-release, initial intensive aftercare, and transitional aftercare.	Not highly developed.	Not emphasized.
Use of graduated sanctions and positive incentives	Not indicated.	Not indicated.	Not indicated for incentives. Pittsburgh sanctions permitted return to group or wilderness program.	Not indicated.

Provision of supervision and surveillance beyond ordinary working hours	Thirty percent of contacts by probation officers required to occur outside normal office hours.	Not indicated.	Not indicated.	Supplemental surveillance activities provided by specialized community workers.
Reduced caseload size/increased frequency of client contact	Aftercare caseload of 12 youth under community supervision versus standard 70-120. Far higher level of contact than usual.	Caseload size unknown. Clients average 3.2 monthly contacts during aftercare or 32.4 contacts over approximately 10 months.	Caseload size of 6. Experimental group receives far more contacts than control group.	Aftercare caseload of 10 youth. Higher level of contact for supervision, treatment, and surveillance.
Multistage decompression process	Procedures for gradual, phased reduction in level of imposed control during 6 months of aftercare supervision.	Intensive aftercare 33 weeks long, not 8 weeks as planned; youth average less than 1 contact per week. During transitional aftercare phase, clients average meeting with case managers less than once every 3 weeks.	Contacts taper off over time in aftercare.	Framework and procedures for a diminishing level of supervision and control during aftercare.

From the perspective of more specific design features and associated activities at this structural phase is the deployment of a comprehensive assessment package to examine the nature and intensity of problems, needs and deficits being exhibited by the targeted youth. This procedure should be completed early during confinement and used to shape the treatment regimen in the facility, as well as to establish guidelines for interventions continuing after release into the community. Much of this activity needs to revolve around the identification of criminogenic factors exhibited by these youth and predictive of re-offending behavior if not directly addressed. Further, assessment at the point of institutional entry needs to incorporate variables for both measurement and clinical consideration along three primary dimensions: 1) risk, 2) need, and 3) resilience/protection. The next point in processing at which a thorough reassessment needs to be conducted is shortly prior to release into the community. This information is critical for determining the degree of positive change achieved during confinement, as well as identifying behavioral, attitudinal, and skill areas still in need of improvement. Such data are valuable for guiding decisions about timing of release and providing a baseline for subsequent reassessment of performance in the community. Additional reassessments should occur at designated points during the community phase of supervision.

The second, or transitional phase of the reintegrative continuum is undoubtedly that segment of aftercare planning and programming which has historically received the least attention. In a sense this phase has to be constructed since it does not have a tangible reality in the same way that both institutional and community-based phases of the system do. Without question the design and operationalization of the transitional phase received the greatest attention by administrators and staff at all of the IAP pilot sites. It is here that the potential exists for the highest level of communication, joint decision making, and collaborative activities by institutional and field staff. Since the baton of supervision and treatment is being passed during this phase, the opportunity and obligation for the greatest degree of interaction to facilitate a smooth and consistent step-down process is present. A number of possible design features to achieve transitional goals were recommended in the IAP initiative for testing at the pilot sites (see Table 14.5). Not surprisingly, the pilot sites took this set of generic recommendations and proceeded to greatly elaborate these features and configure them into highly innovative and somewhat distinctive constellations of transitional activities and programming components for transition at each of the sites (see Table 14.6).

Table 14.5: Operational procedures for structuring step-down at the point of transition: essential principles identified for effective transitioning in IAP

- Backing community-based agencies, individuals, and resources into the facility.
- Intensifying activities for a relatively short period in the facility prior to release and tied directly to re-entry requirements.
- Working with targeted community support systems prior to release to facilitate smoother transition into and linkage with the community.
- Testing and probing for youth adjustment and degree of street readiness in the community prior to final release.
- Providing a highly structured step-down (both short term residential and intensive day treatment) at the point of re-entry.
- Structuring caseload supervision on the basis of risk assessment procedures to ensure appropriate levels and forms of social control at the point of transition.

Table 14.6: Transition components of IAP programming*

Transition Component	Colorado	Nevada	Virginia
Early Parole Planning	Initial Plan complete 30 days after institutional placement; final plan complete 60 days prior to release.	Initial plan complete 30 days after institutional placement; final plan complete 30 days prior to furlough.	Initial plan complete 30 days after institutional placement; final plan complete 30 days prior to release.
Multiple perspectives incorporated in plan	Case manager, institutional staff, youth, parents, and community providers routinely involved.	Parole officer, institutional community liaison, institutional staff, and youth: parent participation limited.	Parole officer, institutional case manager, youth, interagency Community Assessment Team, parent.
Parole officer visits to institution	One to two times per week; routine.	Once per month; routine since spring 1997.	One to two times per month; routine.
Treatment begun in institution and continued in community	Via community providers. Includes multifamily counseling, life skills training, individual counseling, and vocational skills training; done routinely.	Via institutional-community liaison and parole officers. Includes life skills and drug/alcohol curriculums; done routinely until liaison vacancy.	Via one provider at Hanover only. Drug/alcohol treatment; sporadic use. State policy discourages contract services by community providers for institutionalized youth.
Youth pre-release visits to community	Supervised day trips to community programs, beginning 60 days prior to release.	Not allowed.	Not allowed.
Pre-parole furlough	Overnight/weekend home passes, beginning 30 days prior to release.	30 day conditional release to community, prior to official parole.	Not allowed.
Transitional residence	Not part of the design, but occurs for some youth.	Not part of the design.	Two group homes in Norfolk; 30- to 60-day length of stay; used for most youth.
Transitional day programming	Two day-treatment programs in Denver; used for almost all youth during the first few months after release.	One-day supervision/ treatment program; used for most youth.	Day treatment used for youth who do not go to group homes.

Phased supervision levels on parole	Informal system: contact once per week during the first few months, down to once per month later.	Four-phase system: contact 4 times per week during furlough; 3 times per week next 90 days; 2 times per week next 60–90 days; once per week next 30–60 days.	Four-phase system: group home; contact 5 to 7 times per week next 60 days; 3 to 5 times per week next 60 days; 3 times per week last 30 days.

* Source: Richard G.Wiebush, Betsie McNulty and Thao Le, 'Implementation of the Intensive Community-Based Aftercare Program', *OJJDP Juvenile Justice Bulletin*, U.S. Dep. of Justice (July 2000).

The third, or community follow-up phase of the reintegrative continuum, constitutes that segment of the system that was historically singled out as the focus of most aftercare or parole activities. Obviously, the IAP conceptualization of the overall continuum specifies this phase as only one of three critical segments involved in key decision making and programming activities for the delivery of effective aftercare services. Yet, it is within this part of the total system that the ultimate testing of the effectiveness of program design, policies and practices across the entire continuum occurs and is demonstrated through the successful stabilization and normalization of offenders or their failure to adjust. A number of key design features were identified for inclusion in the community follow-up during the development of the IAP Model (see Table 14.7). Although the importance of a number of these features has long been recognized as critical for successful community-based programming, the IAP project took a special initiative in fully conceptualizing the role and importance of the decompression process for designing the structure of community supervision. In addition, this formulation was closely linked to the increasing involvement of community organizations and agencies at the grassroots level as the youth under formal supervision moves ever closer to the completion of parole/aftercare status (see Figure 14.6).

Ideally following release, the youth experiences a relatively brief period (30–60 days) of intensive supervision and highly structured programming as he/she moves into the community on a full time basis (community transition phase). As adjustment and stabilization begin to occur, the youth progresses through a series of increasingly decompressed phases characterized by greater freedom of movement and a decreasing level of surveillance and supervision. This relaxation of control is triggered by evidence of positive performance and compliance with conditions of parole/aftercare. Progress is measured systematically on a periodic basis that is marked by the completion of a given stage of supervision, a thorough reassessment of performance and decreased level of risk, and specification of behavioral requirements for participation in the next stage of decompression. Key to

Table 14.7: Program design features for community follow-up phase

1. Multi-stage decompression process
2. Multi-agency collaboration including public organizations, private provider agencies, and key stakeholders
3. Increasing degree of community involvement at grassroots level
4. Provision of multi-modal treatment and service provision
5. Discrete case management framework
6. Provision of supervision and surveillance beyond ordinary working hours
7. Reduced caseload size/increased frequency of client contact

objective decision making for movement through this process is a procedure including formally administered instruments and a team review. IAP pilot sites defined the overall decompression experience in terms of three or four stages extending over a nine to twelve month period.

At the same time as decompression was occurring with respect to formal supervision of the offender in the community, efforts were being made repeatedly to link these youth to activities and organizations at the grassroots level. It was anticipated that this restorative strategy defined in terms of mobilizing community resources for the youth would provide ongoing support and stability when another critical transition occurred, namely, completion of

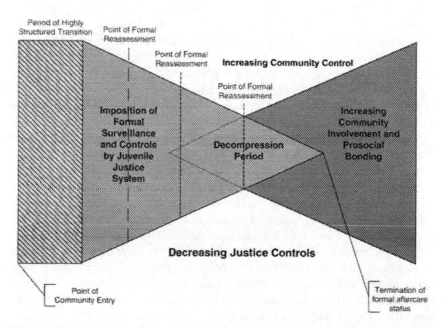

Figure 14.6: Multi-stage decompression in the community: reducing social control through formal reassessment and linkage to grassroots level.

parole/aftercare and termination of formal supervision. Advocacy for community involvement with and acceptance of high-risk juvenile offenders returning from confinement is essential if full normalization of this problematic population is to occur.

Overarching case management

At the heart of operational effectiveness for re-entry and aftercare programming there must reside a framework for overarching case management. As described earlier in the paper, this aspect of program design consists of five discrete components, sequential in nature and lending themselves to continuous, integrated case planning and management. The specifications for case management in the IAP Model reflect a number of imported factors that were taken into consideration in the model development process. For one, the targeting of a particular sub-population of juvenile offenders whose profile indicates the characteristics of high-risk and multi-need were key considerations for the inclusion of certain management components. For another, the research literature indicates limitations on effectiveness if there is sole reliance upon a casework approach to supervision; incorporation of multi-agency, collaborative arrangements through networking and service brokerage play a fundamental role in shaping management components. Perhaps above all is the recognition of the criticality of a state-of-the-art, comprehensive assessment package that drives much of the decision making for case management as the targeted offender is moved across the reintegrative continuum.

Coherence to ensure linkage and continuity across the entire set of case management components is best facilitated through the development of a unified or master case planning document. This tool must incorporate information derived from a number of sources and at various points in time, beginning with the judicial decision to commit a youth to confinement and continuing throughout the residential, transitional and community-based follow-up phases of the overall reintegrative experience. All IAP pilot sites were mandated with the requirement of developing such a tool to guide decision making and programming activities for each youth participating in the project.

A balanced approach to reintegrative intervention

Given their roots in the adult probation arena, intensive supervision programs within juvenile justice systems (the origins of IAP being traced to this approach) have a tendency to be or quickly become surveillance and social control approaches. However, research indicates that this tendency has negative implications for the long-term success of youth enrolled in such programs, namely, the relative lack of rehabilitative services precludes the option of promoting the development of skills and competencies in this population

(Armstrong 1988). High-risk, serious juvenile offenders require programming modalities that combine a set of intervention exhibiting both social control and treatment features. The prime mover for achieving this configuration is the presence of sophisticated assessment tools for both risk and need that guide decision making on an individualized basis and result in the deployment of surveillance/supervision and treatment/service provision techniques.

Having clearly designated procedures for achieving an objective, balanced approach to decision making in intensive supervision programs is essential. This challenge was addressed in the IAP initiative by identifying techniques (i.e. assessment technology and the resulting match with intervention modalities) that ensured an appropriate mix of program activities reflecting key juvenile justice principles (Altschuler and Armstrong 1994a). Direction for designing the relevant constellation of interventions was ultimately derived from an integrated theoretical framework where the predictive power of various risk and need factors for generating misconduct and reoffending behavior had been demonstrated through prior research. The key set of operant principles that were identified and used to guide this blending process were community protection, accountability, and competency development (see Figure 14.5). The operationalization of these principles was initiated through the individualized assessment of risk, need and resilience. This grouping has come to be known as the 'Balanced Approach' (Maloney *et al* 1988; Armstrong *et al* 1990), and the IAP Model is grounded in this conceptual framework, having been tailored for use in transitional and aftercare settings.

As a heuristic tool, the Balanced Approach is a convenient and highly objective point of reference for practitioners assigned the responsibility of matching high-risk juvenile offenders transitioning from confinement with the appropriate type and level of social control and rehabilitative services while at the same ensuring the imposition of a desired level of accountability. With regard to the significance of each of these principles, the single most important is the protection of the public from crime. The decision to move high-risk offenders back into the community in spite of their posing some level of risk requires that their supervision be sufficiently effective to reduce markedly the possibility of reoffending behavior. The array of techniques that have been developed for use with the IAP Model allow for the application of high levels of control, surveillance and intrusion. The second of the three principles, offender accountability, can be traced to the justice theme that the system must respond to illegal behavior in a swift and certain fashion so that the offender is expeditiously made aware of and responsible for the loss, damage or injury perpetrated upon the victim. The form and intensity with which the message is conveyed may vary considerably. Although the idea of punishment or revenge has never received substantial credibility in the juvenile justice system, a reasonable formulation of accountability is a critical component of system response for importing some sense of individual responsibility and psychological awareness on the part of the juvenile offender. A variety of techniques are available for achieving this goal and have been deployed widely in IAP programs. The third of the three principles, competency development, speaks to the value of rehabilitation as a critical factor in juvenile justice programming. Its pre-eminence derives from a body of research about youth being incompletely developed persons still in need of guidance and nurturing. Further, this concept in its most recent iteration points to a growing awareness in our field about the need for a basic redirection and redefinition of what juvenile justice treatment practices should be. At the center of this reformation process is an acknowledgement of the shortcomings of a pure 'medical model' based almost entirely upon the belief that delinquent behavior could most effectively be remediated through intense psychotherapeutic techniques. The central issue is not one of whether to treat, but rather how best to treat, given what is now known about the needs and developmental problems of delinquent youth. The primary challenge facing youth corrections for high-risk offenders in confinement is one of completing the basic habilitation process since these individuals exhibit multiple problems and deficits in the major areas of maturational development (Altschuler and Armstrong 1983).

CONCLUDING REMARKS

Juvenile justice systems throughout the United States have experienced a lengthy history of failure in managing populations of adjudicated youth transitioning from confinement back into the community. Unacceptably high rates of recidivism have been prevalent among those confined youth who are especially at high-risk of reoffending and tend to exhibit a wide range of problem behaviors and troubled personal histories. Beginning in the 1960s, a number of experimental program initiatives addressing issues of transition and aftercare were launched with the goal of achieving long-term normalization of offenders in the community (see Armstrong *et al* 2004, chapter 1). Although much has been learned collectively from these efforts, many of the inherent impediments and difficulties that plague the reintegrative process have persisted. In spite of valuable insights gained about more effective intervention strategies for juvenile offenders both within institutional settings and in community corrections, a sense of crisis over programmatic failure continued to mount in American youth corrections throughout the 1970s and 1980s.

Between the years 1988 to 2000 the Office of Juvenile Justice and Delinquency Prevention funded a long-term research and development project, Intensive Aftercare Programs, for the purpose of identifying promising approaches in juvenile aftercare, developing a model that was theoretically sound and incorporated state-of-the-art programming technology, and testing the efficiency of this model in order to reduce markedly the level of recidivism among the most severely delinquent youth transitioning from confinement. The development process in this initiative built upon a number of key ideas about effective policy and practice drawn partially from previous efforts and also incorporating new, untested strategies. Over the past several years, upon completion of the demonstration phase of the project, considerable effort has been devoted to generating findings and drawing conclusions about the initiative from a program development perspective. The resulting synthesis has allowed for considerable clarification about exactly what are the requisite dimensions for achieving successful treatment outcomes in reintegrative systems utilizing this approach.

Following a number of years of research and development activities tied to model design, implementation and operations, the broadly prescribed framework for systems utilizing the IAP approach appears to point to five basic programming dimensions that define procedural steps and practices essential in the effective delivery of treatment services and geared toward achieving positive outcomes. First, reflective of a number of earlier experiments aimed at providing highly structured interventions for serious juvenile offenders, the IAP Model clearly represents a version of reintegrative programming grounded in intensive supervision strategies and techniques. Yet, based upon extensive testing of the model, an essential aspect of intensification has been shown to be simultaneously placing a strong emphasis upon social control/supervision and service delivery/treatment. Decision making geared towards ensuring an appropriate mix of these two strategies must be guided by collaborative planning and assignment of responsibilities among agencies and sectors of the system managing various aspects of pre-release, transition and community follow-up.

Second, the IAP model is largely conceptualized as a rehabilitative framework operationalized by procedures through which participating youth are carefully profiled and then matched with proven, evidence-based treatment modalities. Deployment and co-ordination of these highly specialized interventions across the entire span of reintegrative process (i.e. from the point of placement in confinement to the completion of supervision in the community) is central to the model's design.

Third, application of the model within any juvenile justice system is highly dependent upon the recognition and incorporation of certain structural characteristics essential for mobilizing open communication, joint decision making, collaboration, and reinforcement in the community of gains made in the institution. These structural characteristics are directly tied to programming activities that characterize the three key phases of the reintegrative continuum: institutional pre-release, transition spanning institution and community, and long-term community follow-up.

Fourth, at the heart of operational effectiveness in the IAP Model resides a framework for overarching case management. This specification of case management components reflects a number of important factors that were taken into consideration in the model development process. For one, the targeting of a particular population of juvenile justice offenders whose profile indicates the challenge of managing a high-risk, multi-problem group was a critical consideration. For another, the research literature and practical experiences indicate limitations on effectiveness if there is sole reliance upon a casework approach to supervision; incorporation of multi-agency, collaborative arrangements through networking and brokerage play a fundamental role in shaping case management. Perhaps of most importance is the recognition of the criticality of a state-of-the-art, comprehensive assessment package driving much of the decision making for individual case planning as the targeted youth moves across the reintegrative continuum.

Fifth, a further guarantee that issues of both risk and need (i.e. social control and treatment) are being appropriately addressed in working with high-risk, multi-problem delinquents is readily facilitated through utilization of the Balanced Approach framework. This heuristic tool assures that consideration at key points in decision making is given in each case to the principles of community protection, competency development and offender accountability.

In conclusion, it is the perception of the two co-principal investigators of the IAP initiative, as well as of many juvenile justice professionals who have implemented the model in their jurisdictions, that reliance upon these five dimensions of program design as a collective point of reference is necessary if positive supervision and treatment outcomes are to be achieved.

REFERENCES

Abadinsky, H. (1991) *Probation and Parole: Theory and Practice.* (Englewood Cliffs, NJ, Prentice Hall).

Altschuler, D.M. and Armstrong, T.L. (1983) Four models of community-based interventions with serious juvenile offenders: Therapeutic orientations, educational strategies and reintegrative techniques. *Journal of Corrective and Social Psychiatry* 29 (4).

— (1990) Intensive community-based aftercare programs: Assessment report. Report submitted to Office of Juvenile Justice and Delinquency Prevention, U.S. Department of Justice.

—— (1991) Intensive Aftercare for the High-Risk Juvenile Parolee: Issues and Approaches in Reintegration and Community Supervision. In T. Armstrong (ed.), *Intensive Interventions with High-Risk Youths: Promising Approaches in Juvenile Probation and Parole* (pp. 45–84). (Monsey, NY, Criminal Justice Press).

—— (1994a) *Intensive aftercare for high-risk juveniles: An assessment.* Report. (Washington, DC, Office of Juvenile Justice and Delinquency Prevention, Office of Justice Programs, U.S. Department of Justice).

—— (1994b) *Intensive aftercare for high-risk juvenile offenders: A community care model.* (Washington, D.C., Office of Juvenile Justice and Delinquency Prevention, Office of Justice Programs, U.S. Department of Justice).

—— (1994c) *Intensive aftercare for high-risk juvenile offenders: Policies and procedures.* (Washington, DC, Office of Juvenile Justice and Delinquency Prevention, Office of Justice Programs, U.S. Department of Justice).

—— (1995) Managing aftercare services for delinquents. In B. Glick and A.P. Goldstein (eds.), *Managing delinquency programs that work* (pp. 137–70). (Laurel, MD, American Correctional Association).

—— (1996) Aftercare, not afterthought: Testing the IAP model. *Juvenile Justice* 3 (1).

—— (2001) Reintegrating High-Risk Juvenile Offenders into Communities: Experiences and Prospects. *Corrections Management Quarterly* 5 (3).

—— (2002) Juvenile Corrections and Continuity of Care in a Community Context—The Evidence and Promising Directions. *Federal Probation* 66 (2).

Altschuler, D.M., Armstrong, T.L. and MacKenzie, D.L. (1999) Reintegration, Supervised Release, and Intensive Aftercare. *Juvenile Justice Bulletin.* (Washington, D.C., Office of Juvenile Justice and Delinquency Prevention, Office of Justice Programs, U.S. Department of Justice).

Andrews, D.A. and Bonta, J. (1994) *The psychology of criminal conduct.* (Cincinnati, OH, Anderson).

Andrews, D., Zinger, I., Hoge, R.D., Bonta, J., Gendreau, P. and Cullen, F.T. (1990) Does correctional treatment work? A clinically-relevant and psychologically-informed meta-analysis. *Criminology* 28 (3), 369–404.

Armstrong, T.L. (1988) National Survey of Juvenile Intensive Probation Supervision, Parts I and II. *Criminal Justice Abstracts* 2 (2,3), 342–8, 497–523.

—— (1991a) Introduction. In T.L. Armstrong (ed.), *Intensive interventions with high-risk youth: Promising approaches in juvenile probation and parole.* (Monsey, NY, Criminal Justice Press).

—— (ed.) (1991b) *Intensive interventions with high-risk youths: Promising approaches in juvenile probation and parole.* (Monsey, NY, Criminal Justice Press).

—— (2004) Guidelines for Promising and Best Practices in the BGCA Targeted Reentry Project. Working paper prepared for Boys and Girls Clubs of America, Atlanta, Georgia.

Armstrong, T.L. and Altschuler, D.M. (1982a) Conflicting Trends in Juvenile Justice Sanctioning: Divergent Strategies in the Handling of the Serious Juvenile Offender. *Journal of Juvenile and Family Courts* 33 (4).

—— (1982b) Community-based program interventions for the serious juvenile offender: Targeting, strategies and issues. Report submitted to Office of Juvenile Justice and Delinquency Prevention, U.S. Department of Justice.

—— (2004) Intensive Juvenile Aftercare Reference Guide. Report submitted to Office of Juvenile Justice and Delinquency Prevention, U.S. Department of Justice. Available at www.csus.edu/ssis/cdcps

Armstrong, T.L. and Jackson, A. (in press) Overrepresentation of minorities in youth correctional confinement in the United States: A promising aftercare approach for ameliorating this problem. In N. Queloz, R. Brossand, F. Repand, Butikofer, B. Meyer-Birsch and D. Pittet (eds.), *Migrations in Ethnic Minorities: Impacts on Youth Crime and Challenges for the Juvenile Justice and Other Intervention Systems*, Proceedings from the 15th Conference of the International Association for Research into Justice Criminology.

Armstrong, T.L., Maloney, D. and Romig, D. (1990) The Balanced Approach in Juvenile Probation: Principles, Issues, and Application. *APPA Perspectives* 14 (1).

Barton, W.H. (2004) Incorporating the Strengths Perspective into Intensive Juvenile Aftercare. Paper presented at the 4th Annual Conference of the European Society of Criminology, Amsterdam, the Netherlands.

Barton, W.H., Jarjura, G.R. and Rosey, A.D. (2004) Evaluation of the Boys and Girls Clubs of America Targeted Re-entry Initiative: Phase I. Paper presented at the Annual Meeting of the American Society of Criminology, Nashville TN.

Blackmore, J. (1980) Community corrections. *Corrections Magazine* 6 (5) (October), 4–14.

Borum, R. (2003) Managing At-Risk Juvenile Offenders in the Community: Putting Evidence-Based Principles Into Practice. *Journal of Contemporary Criminal Justice* (19) 1.

Byrne, J.M. and Kelly, L. (1989) *Restructuring Probation As an Intermediate Sanction: An Evaluation of the Massachusetts Intensive Probation Supervision Program.* (Washington, D.C., United States Department of Justice).

Clear, T.R. (1991) Juvenile intensive probation supervision: Theory and rationale. In T.L. Armstrong (ed.), *Intensive interventions with high-risk youth: Promising approaches in juvenile probation and parole* (pp. 29–44). (Monsey, NY, Criminal Justice Press).

Conrad, J. (1982) Research and Developments in Corrections: A Thought Experiment. *Federal Probation* 46 (2).

Dean-Myrda, M.C. and Cullen, F.T. (1985) The panacea pendulum: An account of community as a response to crime. In L.F. Travis (ed.), *Probation, parole, and community corrections* (pp. 9–29). (Prospect Heights, IL, Waveland).

Dembo, R., Williams, L., Getreu, A., Genung, L. *et al* (1991) Recidivism among high-risk youths: Study of a cohort of juvenile detainees. *International Journal of the Addictions* 26, 121–77.

Doleschal, E. (1982) The Dangers of Criminal Justice Reform. *Criminal Justice Abstracts* 14.

Elliott, D.S., Huizinga, D. and Ageton, S.S. (1985) *Explaining Delinquency and Drug Use.* (Beverly Hills, CA, Sage).

Elliott, D.S., Huizinga, D. and Menard, S. (1989) *Multiple Problem Youth: Delinquency, Substance Use, and Mental Health Problems.* (London, Springer-Verlag).

Fagan, J.A. and Jones, S.J. (1984) Toward a Theoretical Model for Intervention with Violent Juvenile Offenders. In R.A. Mathias *et al* (eds.), *Violent Juvenile Offenders, An Anthology.* (San Francisco, CA, National Council on Crime and Delinquency).

Fagan, J.A., Rudman, C.J. and Hartstone, E. (1984) Interviewing with Violent Juvenile Offenders: A community reintegration model. In R.A. Mathias, P. DeMuro and R.S. Allinson (eds.), *Violent Juvenile Offenders: An Anthology.* (San Francisco, CA, National Council on Crime and Delinquency).

Farrington, D.P. (1989) Early predictors of adolescent aggression and adult violence. *Violence and Victims* 4, 79–100.

Farrington, D.P. and Hawkins, J.D. (1991) Predicting participation, early onset and later persistence in officially recorded offendings. *Criminal Behavior and Mental Health* 1, 1–33.

Gendreau, P. and Ross, R.R. (1987) Revivification of Rehabilitation: Evidence from the 1980s. *Justice Quarterly* 4, 3.

Gies, S.V. (2003) Aftercare Services. *Juvenile Justice Bulletin.* (Washington, D.C., Office of Juvenile Justice and Delinquency Prevention, Office of Justice Programs, U.S. Department of Justice).

Greenwood, P. and Zimring, F. (1985) *One More Chance: The Pursuit of Promising Intervention Strategies for Chronic Juvenile Offenders.* (Santa Monica, CA, The Rand Corporation).

Greenberg, D. (1977) The Correctional Effects of Corrections: A Survey of Evaluations. In D. Greenberg (ed.), *Corrections and Punishment.* (Beverly Hills, CA, Sage).

Gross, B. (1982) Some Anticrime Proposals for Progressives. *The Nation* (6 February).

Hagen, J. (1991) Destiny and drift: Subcultural preferences, status attainments and the risks and rewards of youth. *American Sociological Review* 56, 567–82.

Hamparian, D., Schuster, R., Dinitz, S. and Conrad, J. (1978) *The Violent Few: A Study of the Dangerous Juvenile Offender.* (Lexington, MA, Lexington Books).

Hartstone, E. and Hansen, K.V. (1984) The Violent Juvenile Offender. In P. DeMuro and R.S. Allison (eds.), *Violent Juvenile Offenders, An Anthology.* (San Francisco, CA, National Council on Crime and Delinquency).

Hawkins, J.D., Lishner, D.M., Jenson, J.M. and Catalano, R.F. (1987) Childhood Predictors and the Prevention of Adolescent Substance Abuse. Paper presented at the Research Conference on Juvenile Offenders with Serious Alcohol, Drug Abuse, and Mental Health Problems, Washington, D.C.

Hawkins, J.D., Herrenkohl, T., Farrington, D.P., Brewer, D., Catalano, R.F. and Harachi, T.W. (1998) A Review of Predictors of Youth Violence. In R. Loeber and D.P. Farrington (eds.), *Serious and Violent Juvenile Offenders: Risk Factors and Successful Interventions* (pp. 106–46) (Thousand Oaks, CA, Sage).

Horwitz, A. and Wasserman, M. (1977) *A cross-sectional and longitudinal study of the labeling perspective.* Paper presented at the Annual Meeting of the American Society of Criminology.

Jackdon, L. (2002) The Oregon Youth Authority's Gangbusters Program and the Office of Minority Youth Services. In *Juvenile Justice Today: Essays on Programs and Policies* (pp. 151–72). (Lanham, MD, American Correctional Association).

Jensen, G.F. and Rojek, D.G. (1980) *Delinquency: A sociological view.* (Lexington, D.C. Heath).

Johnson, B.M. (1962) Parole performance of the first year's releases—Parole Research Project: Evaluation of reduced caseloads. Research Report No. 27. (Sacramento, CA, California Youth Authority).

Krisberg, B., Currie, E., Onek, D. and Wiebush, R.G. (1995) Graduated sanctions for serious, violent, and chronic juvenile offenders. In J.C. Howell, B. Krisberg, J.D. Hawkins and J.J. Wilson (eds.), *Sourcebook on serious, violent, and chronic juvenile offenders* (pp. 142–70). (Thousand Oaks, CA, Sage).

Krisberg, B., Neuenfeldt, D., Wiebush, R. and Rodriguez, O. (1991) *Juvenile Intensive Supervision Program Model: Operations manual and planning guide.* (San Francisco, National Council on Crime and Delinquency).

Lipsey, M. (1992) Juvenile delinquency treatment: A meta-analytic inquiry into the variability of effects. In T.D. Cook, H. Cooper, D.S. Cordray, H. Hartment, L.V. Hedges, R.J. Light *et al* (eds.), *Meta-analysis for explanation: A casebook.* (New York, Russell Sage).

Lipsey, M. (1995) What do we learn from 400 research studies on the effectiveness of treatment with juvenile delinquents? In J. McGuire (ed.), *What works? Reducing reoffending* (pp. 63–78). (New York, John Wiley).

Lipsey, M. (1999) Can intervention rehabilitate serious delinquents? *Annals of the American Academy of Political and Social Science* 564, 142–66.

Lipsey, M.W. and Derzon, J.H. (1998) Predictors of Violent or Serious Delinquency in Adolescence and Early Adulthood. In R. Loeber and D.P. Farrington (eds.), *Serious and Violent Juvenile Offenders: Risk Factors and Successful Interventions* (pp. 86–105). (Thousand Oaks, CA, Sage).

Lipsey, M. and Wilson, D. (1998) Effective intervention for serious juvenile offenders: A synthesis of research. In R. Loeber and D.P. Farrington (eds.), *Serious and violent juvenile offenders: Risk factors and successful interventions* (pp. 313–45). (Thousand Oaks, CA, Sage).

Lipsey, M.W., Wilson, D.B. and Cothern, L. (2000) *Effective Intervention for Serious Juvenile Offenders*. Bulletin. (Washington, DC, U.S. Department of Justice, Office of Justice Programs, Office of Juvenile Justice and Delinquency Prevention).

Loeber, R. and Stouthamer-Loeber, M. (1987) Prediction. In H.C. Quay (ed.), *Handbook of juvenile delinquency* (pp. 325–82). (New York, John Wiley).

MacKenzie, D.L. (2000) Evidence-based corrections: Identifying what works. *Crime and Delinquency* 46, 457–71.

McCord, J., Widom, C.S. and Crowell, N.A. (eds.) (2001) *Juvenile Crime, Juvenile Justice*. (Washington, D.C., National Academy Press).

Maloney, D., Romig, D. and Armstrong, T.L. (1988) *Juvenile Probation: The Balanced Approach*. (Reno, NV, National Council of Juvenile and Family Court Judges).

National Research Council (1993) *Losing Generations: Adolescents in High Risk Settings*. Panel on High Risk Youth, Commission on Behavioral and Social Sciences and Education. (Washington, D.C., National Academy Press).

National Research Council (2001) *Juvenile Crime, Juvenile Justice-Panel on Juvenile Crime: Prevention, Treatment and Control*. J. McCord, C.S. Widom and N.A. Crowell (eds.), Commission on Behavioral and Social Sciences and Education. (Washington, D.C., National Academy Press).

Nelson, K., Ohmart, H. and Harlow, N. (1978) *Promising Strategies in Probation and Parole*, Office of Development, Testing, and Dissemination, National Institute of Justice, U.S. Department of Justice.

Osborn, S.G. and West, D.J. (1980) Do Delinquents Really Reform? *Journal of Adolescence* 3.

Palmer, T. (1971) California's Community Treatment Program for Delinquent Adolescents. *Journal of Research in Crime and Delinquency* 8(a), 74–92.

Palmer, T. (1973) The Community Treatment Project in perspective: 1961–73. *Youth Authority Quarterly* 26, 29–43.

—— (1974) The Youth Authority's Community Treatment Project. *Federal Probation* 38(a), 3–14.

—— (1991) Intervention with juvenile offenders: Recent and long-term changes. In T.L. Armstrong (ed.), *Intensive interventions with high-risk youths: Promising approaches in juvenile probation and parole.* (Monsey, NY, Criminal Justice Press).

—— (1992) *The Re-emergency of correctional intervention.* (Newbury Park, CA, Sage).

—— (1994) *A Profile of Correctional Effectiveness and New Directions for Research.* (Albany, NY, State University of New York Press).

Paterson, G.R. (1992) *Antisocial Boys: A Social Interactional Approach* (Vol. 4). (Eugene, OR, Castalic).

Pond, E.M. (1970) The Los Angeles Community Delinquency Control Project: An experiment in the rehabilitation of delinquents in an urban community. Research Report No. 60. (Sacramento, CA, California Youth Authority).

Roberts, C.F. (1970) A final evaluation of the Narcotic Control Program. Research Report No. 58. (Sacramento, CA, California Youth Authority).

Shannon, L., McKim, J., Curry J. and Haffner, L. (1988) *Criminal Career Continuity: Its Social Context.* (New York, Human Sciences Press, Inc).

Sherman, L.W., Gottfredson, D. MacKenzie, D., Eck, J., Reuter, P. and Bushway, S. (1997) *Preventing Crime: What Works, What Doesn't, What's Promising.* (Washington, D.C., U.S. Department of Justice).

Steenson, D. (1986) *A symposium on juvenile intensive probation supervision: The JIPS Proceedings.* (Minneapolis, MN, Hennepin County Bureau of Community Corrections, Juvenile Division).

Thornberry, T.P. and Krohn, M.D. (1997) Peers, drug use, and delinquency. In D. Stoff, J. Breiling and J.D. Maser (eds.) *Handbook of antisocial behavior* (pp. 218–23). (New York, John Wiley).

Thornberry, T.P., Krohn, M.D., Lizotte, A.J. and Chard-Wierschem, D. (1993) The role of juvenile gangs in facilitating delinquent behavior. *Journal of Research in Crime and Delinquency* 30, 55–87.

Tolan, P.H. and Gorman-Smith, D. (1998) Development of Serious and Violent Offending Careers. In R. Loeber and D.F. Farrington (eds.), *Serious and Violent Juvenile Offenders: Risk Factors and Successful Interventions.* (Thousand Oaks, CA, Sage).

Von Hirsch, A. (1976) *Doing Justice—The Choice of Punishments.* (New York, Hill and Wong).

Weiss, J.G. and Hawkins, J.D. (1981) *Reports of the National Juvenile Justice Assessment Centers: Preventing Delinquency.* (Washington, D.C., National Institute for Juvenile Justice and Delinquency Prevention).

Wiebush, R.G. (1993) Juvenile intensive supervision: Impact on felony offenders diverted from institutional placement. *Crime and Delinquency* 39, 68–88.

Wiebush, R.G. and Hamparian, D.M. (1991) Variations in 'doing' juvenile intensive supervision: Programmatic issues in four Ohio jurisdictions. In T.L. Armstrong (ed.), *Intensive interventions with high-risk youths: Promising approaches in Juvenile probation and parole.* (Monsey, NY, Criminal Justice Press).

Wiebush, R.G., McNulty, B. and Le, T. (2000) Implementation of the intensive community-based aftercare program. *Juvenile Justice Bulletin.* (Washington, D.C., Office of Juvenile Justice and Delinquency Prevention, Office of Justice Programs, U.S. Department of Justice).

Wiederanders, M. (1983) Success on Parole: The Influence of Self-Reported Attitudes, Experiences and Background Characteristics on the Parole Behavior of Youthful Offenders. Final Report.

Zarb, J. (1978) Correlates of Recidivism and Social Adjustment Among Training-School Delinquents. *Canadian Journal of Behavioral Science* 10.

15

Exploring Traditional Cultural Mechanisms of Conflict Resolution in American Indian Communities

BARBARA MENDENHALL AND JAMES DUMESNIL*

INTRODUCTION

A GROWING NUMBER OF Native American and Canadian First Nations communities, both reservation-based (Indian Country) and within urban areas, are going 'back to the future' (Jim Zion quoted in Rubin 2001) by using a variation of restorative justice conflict resolution based in their traditional culture. At the same time, mainstream communities are looking to restorative justice as a new way of resolving community problems, and American Indian communities are recognizing that their traditions are founded in conflict resolution through restorative justice. Reintroduction and revitalization of these traditions may provide a better system than the introduced Western criminal justice system for Native communities to respond to serious problems with juvenile delinquency.

In this chapter we will explore use of the traditional Native American variety of restorative justice conflict resolution with Native American juvenile offenders. This chapter relies on limited research on restorative justice, primarily Braithwaite (2002), and various sources on use and reintroduction of tradition in conflict resolution in Indian communities, including research conducted by one of the authors (Dumesnil), who interviewed friends and colleagues who manage prevention and intervention programs for Native American youths and adults about their use of tradition in their programs.

* The authors wish to thank Howard Bad Hand, Pat Bad Hand, John Beheler, Chuck Ross, Dorothy Brave Eagle, Dana Brave Eagle, Dawn Brave Eagle, and James W. Zion.

RESTORATIVE JUSTICE CONFLICT RESOLUTION AND AMERICAN
INDIAN COMMUNITIES

What is restorative justice and how does it work?

According to Braithwaite, 'restorative justice has been the dominant model
of criminal justice throughout most of human history for perhaps all the
world's peoples ... (and among indigenous peoples) restorative traditions
persisted into modern times' (2002, 5). Definitions of restorative justice
involve the notion of an egalitarian and respectful process in which all the
various parties with a stake in an offence collectively determine how to
resolve the situation so that all—victims(s), offender(s), and those affected
by the offence—are restored. It is up to those involved to determine what is
meant by restoration and when it is achieved.

It is this empowerment of the affected community to deal with consequences of injustice and to change private problems into public issues that
can be discussed and resolved through community action that gives restorative justice its effectiveness.[1] Note that in this sense, 'community' is defined
as those who have a stake in the particular offence. Depending on the situation, 'community' may have a narrow or wide inclusion of participants.
Collective decision making provides dignity and respect to all participants,
destigmatizes both offender and victim, and creates space for rehabilitation
of the offender. Note also, that in no community where restorative justice
has been implemented have government courts lost control over criminal
cases. It is usually the court that determines which cases will be 'allowed' to
be processed through restorative justice (Braithwaite 2002). Analysis of a
number of restorative justice programs in an international array of communities indicates that these programs can work in restoring victims, offenders, and communities (Braithwaite 2002). It usually becomes apparent
during restorative justice sessions that the offender has also been a victim
and needs restoration him/herself. As Ross (1996, 96) notes about restorative justice and conflict resolution, 'the real issue is how such states of
disharmony have come into existence and what can be done to turn them
around'.

The community that should be involved in a restorative justice process
consists of those individuals who have been affected by a specific problem,
and their roles should be as active participants in developing solutions and
as sources of informal social control and support (McCold and Wachtel
1997). David Moore (1997) called this a 'micro-community'. Below is an
example of a micro-community at work.

---

[1] In reviewing a draft of this paper James W. Zion commented: 'it [is also] changing public
issues into private problems in the sense of taking a dispute out of the "public", i.e. governmental, arena and returning it to where it belongs—the private scene' (personal communication).

In an upper middle class suburb a group of youths vandalized a number of ice fishing houses on a local lake. The public prosecutor, because of the difficulty of matching specific damage to specific offenders, decided not to pursue the case. The traditional justice system failed to deal with the crime. The police, however, had implemented a family group conference program for juvenile offenses and offered the victims an alternative response to the wrongdoing they had suffered. One particular victim, whose elaborate two-story ice fishing house had suffered considerable damage, was particularly irate, agreed only begrudgingly to attend the conference and threatened to display his rage at the conference.

The perpetrators, ice fishing house owners, and family and friends gathered for the family group conference. First, the offenders admitted their wrongdoing and described the damage that they had done. Then each of the victims expressed how they had been affected by the destruction of ice houses that they had built themselves, over many years, with their families and friends. The son of the owner of the two-story fishing house spoke for his father and expressed, in rather poignant terms, how he had spent much of his childhood working with his father and the rest of his family building their house for each winter fishing season. He suddenly realized, when faced with the destruction the youths had caused, how much that experience meant to him. His father, instead of expressing his rage as he had threatened, saved his comments for the close of the conference, after the whole group had worked out the terms of reparation.

Then he spoke with great emotion and thanked the youths for having vandalized his ice fishing house. He explained that until the conference he had never heard his son express how much all those years of shared experience meant to him. The father then invited all of the boys and their fathers, when the damage was repaired, to spend a weekend with his family fishing on the lake.

All of the people who participated in this conference lived in geographic proximity, but until they were grouped into a 'micro-community' through this powerful restorative justice process, they hardly knew each other. After the conference, bonds had been established that did not exist before the conference. Community can be defined identically to Goldstein's description of community that is used by good problem-oriented police officers: 'They use "community" rather deftly to describe those affected in any way by the specific problem they are attempting to address'. (McCold and Wachtel 1997, 10)

In this case, if the only truth that mattered was the conviction and sentencing of the offenders, healing for the individuals, the family and the community at large would not have occurred or even been possible. The opportunities for 'offender' and 'victim' restoration or rehabilitation would have been overlooked. Co-author Dumesnil is a forensic counselor who works with offenders and victims. The preponderance of forensic counseling suggests that offenders tend to be more open to therapeutic gains prior to adjudication. As the people of Hollow Water discovered (see below), the adversarial legal process positions an offender to deny, minimize or evade one's guilt. Accountability to family, victim, peers and community is required by the treatment process, and embracing responsibility and restoration routinely occurs. To satisfy legal obligations and accomplish full recovery, therapeutic clients turn themselves into law enforcement as a part of their healing. Dumesnil reports that when clients arrive for treatment post-adjudication, full recovery is very difficult to achieve or involves considerably more work.

What are the concerns and reservations about restorative justice?

Not all legal scholars agree that restorative justice is helpful or timely (Delgado 2000). Delgado concludes that restorative justice is typically no worse than conventional justice, but says that it can be an opportunity to promulgate middle class values upon minorities in society, and can allow and encourage the 'victim' to indulge in exacting revenge on the offender. What Delgado appears to be concerned with is the practice of mediation, where a court-appointed mediator referees differences between two parties with the primary goal being compensation paid to the victim by the offender. He is pessimistic about mediation allowing victims to indulge in revenge against offenders, with mediators perpetuating conservative middle-class values. His concerns may be valid since mediation is the one form of restorative justice that does not extend 'ownership of the crime problem beyond the victim and offender to concerned community members'. Presser and Gaarder (2000, 181) acknowledge that 'restorative justice has been inaccurately equated with mediation in the US'.

In addition, when this paper was initially presented at the 'Youthful Law Violators, Human Rights, and Development of New Juvenile Justice Systems Conference' at the International Institute for the Sociology of Law in Oñati, Spain, several participants raised concerns about the reintroduction of traditional methods of social control in restorative justice systems dealing with juvenile crime. Participants who worked in juvenile justice in Africa and with the United Nations cautioned that the use of severe corporal punishment is one traditional sanction that has been championed by indigenous groups wanting to re-establish traditional community-based restorative justice systems for juvenile offenders. The level of corporal punishment cited as traditional can be more severe than Western proponents of restorative justice can accept.

These participants also pointed to the United Nations Standard Minimum Rules for the Administration of Juvenile Justice ('the Beijing Rules') which expressly state in Part Three, section 17: 'Juveniles shall not be subject to corporal punishment.' In the commentary to the convention, it is explained that this statement is in line with Article 17 of the International Covenant on Civil and Political Rights, and the Convention Against Torture (i.e., corporal punishment is against international law). Although the Convention on the Rights of the Child does not forbid corporal punishment outright, it states that 'Every child deprived of his liberty shall be treated with humanity and the inherent dignity for human person and in a manner which takes into account the needs of the person and his or her age' (section 37a). Thus, the extent to which cultural traditions that advocate corporal punishment should be respected has been questioned by some within the framework of international instruments on the treatment of juveniles under the law.

Another possible limitation to the utility of community restorative justice programs is that to date evaluations of such programs are minimal and primarily anecdotal. Restorative justice system advocates have not produced evaluation reports demonstrating the benefits of such programs in a variety of Native communities. Finally, systems and individuals in positions of authority in some Native communities may be so damaged that restorative justice would only create another means of victimization. Such damaged communities will need to heal at a more fundamental level before introducing restorative justice programs using traditional healing methods with juvenile offenders. However, careful use of restorative justice may be part of healing Native communities to a point where traditional healing can be reintroduced.

In response to these criticisms, the research reported in this chapter indicates that restorative justice programs, including Peacemaker Courts, Sentencing Circles and Family Group Conferences are designed to address and manage Delgado's criticism of mediation. More systematic evaluations of restorative justice programs for juvenile law violators will be needed to answer the final criticism of the efficacy of restorative justice in Native (or other) communities.

The value of restorative justice

By constituting a micro-community made up of all in the relevant circle of the victim, the offender and the community, many perspectives are included. Equality of expression is an immediate goal of restorative justice (Haberfeld and Townsend 1993). If in the interest of efficiency, the process is truncated, time limits are set, and no effort is made to involve all stakeholders in the micro-community, then Delgado's concerns are salient. What this appears to mean is that the traditional variant of restorative justice cannot be employed in anything less than a comprehensive manner; a manner that honors the traditions and cultures where these methods originated. Native communities must have an ongoing level of cultural context of their tradition to reinstitute such programs. Otherwise the result would likely be another adversarial hierarchical process, only without judges or attorneys— simply more powerful and possibly abusive community members.

Braithwaite (2002) states that restorative justice may facilitate crime prevention and that the strongest outcome of restorative justice is that victims are more satisfied than with the criminal justice system. In addition, recidivism rates for those who participate in restorative justice conferences tend to be lower. This ties in with criminological research which shows that criminal rehabilitation most often occurs through the rehabilitation of the family of the offender—restorative justice strengthens family responsibility for dealing with crime in contrast to punitive court systems that weaken family responsibility for dealing with crime and deterring reoccurrence (Braithwaite 2002). There is also evidence of restorative justice efforts permeating the community at large and preventing potential offenders from offending (Braithwaite 2002; Ross 1996).

Finally, with regard to the integration of the modern restorative justice movement and indigenous communities, Braithwaite suggests the 'need ... to save and revive the restorative justice practices that remain in all societies' (2002, 142). He suggests '... helping indigenous community justice to learn from the virtues of liberal statism—procedural fairness, rights, protecting the vulnerable from domination (which did not get mandated along with Western legal systems or were corrupted by political and illiberal statism [authors' opinion]), ... and helping liberal state justice to learn from indigenous community justice—learning the restorative justice community alternatives to individualism' (2002, 142).

Attempts at eradication and foundations of restorative justice in American Indian communities

Although there have been recent efforts to reintroduce traditional restorative justice in Native communities, they come after a long period of public and private effort to eradicate Native American culture. American Indian tribes have been subjected to several hundred years of aggressive imposition of outside force that has seriously impacted every part of Native culture including systems of social control and conflict resolution. These forces have included invasion by Europeans and Americans; massive loss of population and social collapse due to inadvertent and deliberate spread of diseases (smallpox, tuberculosis, measles, malaria); complete eradication of tribes through war and disease; removal or restriction of tribes to reservations; total loss of tribal land base; decimation of subsistence resources; attempted forced assimilation that has included allocation of reservation lands to individuals (with much land subsequently lost through sale to non-Natives); imposition of American legal, political, medical, religious, educational, and other systems; forced removal of children to boarding schools; and criminalization of traditional social, ceremonial, and religious activities. Zion (2002b, 1) states: 'The Western world thought it was bestowing "civilization" on Indians, but instead, it created the foundations for anomie and institutionalized legal systems that do not work well.' The fundamental message to Native Americans until about 1960 was that 'nothing (Native) was of value to themselves: nothing of spiritual belief and practice, child-raising, pharmacology, psychology, dispute resolution, decision making, clan organization, or community governance' (Ross 1996, 46). This was conveyed despite mainstream adoption of much that came from Native American culture: domesticated crops, herbal medicine, governance structure, ideals of democracy.

Despite these enormous pressures to assimilate into American culture, Native American communities have maintained cultural values and traditional beliefs and practices. Fundamental to Native American values are: first, the importance of community and family; second, the responsibility of every individual to be part of community and family with a wide understanding of extended family; and third, the responsibility of the community and family to include each individual with social control and support operating through traditions of family responsibility (Ross 1996). This concept of interdependent society is expressed by the Lakota people as *Mitakuye Oyasin*, meaning 'we are all related'. Given these foundations of belief, restorative justice as a process of conflict resolution can work well in Native American communities presuming a certain level of social stability.

EXPLORING THE USE OF TRADITIONAL BELIEFS IN CRIME PREVENTION AND INTERVENTION IN NATIVE AMERICAN COMMUNITIES

There is little published documentation or description of the use of traditional restorative justice with crime prevention and intervention in Indian Country. Co-author Dumesnil interviewed people who run youth facilities and whose families have been in law enforcement and education in Native American communities for generations. While Native Americans have traditionally been suspicious of the written word, there is increasing concern that their ways are often unrecognized, undocumented, and even worse, misunderstood. As Native leaders have to compete for funding for programs to educate and rehabilitate their youth, many recognize that their ways need to be documented and reviewed. Their reluctance to write things down is a vestige of the oral tradition that defined their past. It is also partly about fear that something sacred will be taken from them or taken out of context. Another element is that Native societies have a strong ethic of non-interference (Ross 1992). Most learning traditionally occurred through modeling over a lifetime. It was a matter of observing repeatedly, and when the time came, being prepared to act. If not, then learning occurred through trial and error. Traditional leaders are very patient and trusting that people will learn from their own mistakes. Howard Bad Hand (2002) teaches that the most loving and spiritual stance towards another person is to accept them for who they are. Traditional elders try very hard to not tell anyone what to do but instead 'advise' through telling a traditional story (Zion, personal communication). Thus, if traditions are published, there is concern that the writer may be perceived as giving advice or direction. Please keep in mind that any pedantic quality in this chapter needs to be ascribed completely to the authors, as the original stories do not have this quality.

Those interviewed agreed that using traditional practices and ceremonies in character formation and dispute resolution with juveniles makes a great difference. They feel they are getting a little more support to institute these kinds of programs within their job duties and report that there is reason for cautious optimism. Recently, traditional methods have been used with good results in corrections by Chris Eagle Hawk of Pine Ridge Reservation Public Safety and in education by Florentine Blue Thunder of the Rosebud Reservation. Presently, they are being integrated into a new juvenile detention center, *Wanbli Wiconi Tipi*, which is opening on the Rosebud reservation. These leaders relate that providing services, especially ceremonies, as a way of confronting one's own history and issues has to be done with sincerity, honesty, humility, and integrity (described as 'a good way' by our Native American advisors); it has to be provided by someone who commands respect, and it works because the youth care about traditions and identify as 'Indian' even though they may not speak their indigenous language.

The critical importance of a living cultural context

In addition to concern about ceremonies being done in a good way, leaders have a concern that the cultural context of Native philosophy and way of life for applying traditional Native American beliefs in modern settings has been compromised or decimated. The problem as identified by Native leaders is whether the 'living cultural context' still exists to integrate traditional teachings into everyday life, especially as a method for dealing with juvenile crime. Although native teachers, treatment providers and corrections personnel report positive outcomes when traditional cultural mechanisms are used with children, they are concerned whether cultural context is adequate to meaningfully integrate traditional teachings into daily life, as well as into juvenile restorative justice systems.

For example, the Lakota (Sioux) way of life teaches a deep understanding of the interconnection and interdependency of all things and all nations. Reference to the term 'all our relations' establishes the foundations for the health and well-being of the individual and of the community.

For Lakota people, life is like a circle—continuous, harmonious, and cyclical, with no distinctions. Medicine and healing are a coming-together of all the elements in this circular pattern of life. The circle of healing is formed by the interconnections among the sick person, his or her extended family or relatives, the spirits, the singers who helped with the ceremonial songs, and the medicine practitioner. (Voss *et al* 1999, 235)

Much of the Native American cultural context was lost in the clash with European civilization. As noted previously, many, if not all, Native American traditional practices and ceremonies were made illegal in the late 1800s with recommendations and principles introduced by the Quaker Policy (Delano 1873) and establishment of codes for the Courts of Indian Offenses in 1883. The problem today is that traditional teaching without the living cultural context of tradition may result in the seed not taking root in young people. The teaching may be blamed for no longer having relevance to the modern world, as not being beautiful and powerful guideposts and landmarks in personal development and transformation.

As an example of this possibility, John Beheler, educator and principal of Marty's Indian School, relates a day where his school observed the 'Throwing of the Ball Ceremony'. This ceremony is a coming of age ceremony for a girl. As she comes into the age of motherhood, she is understood to have the 'world (or creation) in her hands'. Beheler involves parents and teachers and observes traditional forms to create the sacred space in an attempt to preserve or revive the living cultural context.

Beheler explains that the Sacred Ball, representing the universe and the Creator, is tossed over her back by a young girl dressed in traditional regalia representing purity, beauty and unspoiled humanity that are closely connected to the divine or creative. This ceremony teaches that challenges or opportunities may be dropped into a young person's life that will serve as a test. Will he/she reach out and bring the Creator into his/her life? How much conviction will he/she have in this effort? Will the young person be ready if it comes to him/her? Does he/she understand what it means to reach out for it? Does he/she understand what it means to accept it? If *the world* were dropped in his/her hands now, would the youth know what to do with it?

Bringing these questions to the students' consciousness following the ceremony is most important, according to John Beheler. This is the way the experience impacts education. It is how the child's development, the community and the ceremony take their role in sustaining one another. Beheler emphasizes that teachers and parents must have the capacity to provide a living cultural context to ensure this quality in education. If adults are not versed in traditions and song or are not allowed or encouraged to speak and to live them, then activities such as the Throwing of the Ball Ceremony become simply folklore. These concerns are echoed at schools within Indian Country. Bureau of Indian Affairs[2] (BIA) schools may have cultural directors,

---

[2] The Bureau of Indian Affairs is the agency of the U.S. Department of the Interior responsible for providing services to federally recognized Native American tribes and communities. Services include the array of government provided services that would ordinarily by funded and managed by special districts, cities, counties and states, including health, education, welfare, law enforcement and courts, community infrastructure (roads, water, etc.). In recent years there has been an effort to provide funds to the tribes and communities and to allow tribal authorities to manage many of these services directly.

but teachers who live and practice the tribe's sacred traditions cannot share personal experience with the children, or teach songs or crafts that honor their Native spirituality because BIA schools enforce the U.S. government standard of separation of church and state. Teachers who participate in tribal traditions are silenced.

Our advisors note that sharing information covertly helped to maintain knowledge and practice of traditional beliefs and ceremonies.[3] Children respect teachers who provide traditional knowledge; children also develop self-respect through knowledge of ancestral beliefs. At tribally administered schools, teachers and staff have more freedom to include rituals and ceremonies as part of the normal school routine. In these situations, teachers report that Native American practices have become powerful and helpful tools in early intervention and prevention work. Some traditions, such as Pow-Wows and costume and dance contests are preserved at BIA schools. Although these activities may maintain the social form of traditions, they were never intended to keep the spiritual context alive. There is also concern that the appointment of a school Cultural Director acknowledges that traditional culture no longer survives adequately in the community. Bad Hand states that ceremonies have always been a living and dynamic process. They are a product of time, place and tradition: handed down by history, and interpreted by elders and leaders to meet the demands of the time. He states that this element has been lost in much of contemporary ceremonial observances. Instead, Native Peoples have become concerned with 'getting it right', and the responsiveness, complexity and adaptability of living tradition has been lost. This dynamic is addressed further in our discussion of complex adaptive systems and complexity theory below.

In addition to schools, tribal juvenile justice systems are also incorporating traditional teachings and ceremonies into rehabilitation programming in their facilities. Pat Bad Hand is a director of the Rosebud Sioux Community's new (2005) Youth Wellness and Renewal Center, *Wiconi Wanbli Tipi*, serving a detained, court-ordered juvenile population. The project is committed to the use of traditional Lakota Sioux teachings in rehabilitating the youth who are in the facility. One of the major program goals of *Wiconi Wanbli Tipi* is to help youth to regain and reclaim an understanding of their *tios'paye*, which is a Sioux concept representing the story of one's relatives and ancestry, one's name, one's circle and one's life.[4]

---

[3] Howard Bad Hand (personal communication), A.C. Ross (personal communications) and Meyer (2002) share that such covert or secretive observance is a time-honored tradition for native peoples. Bad Hand states that for the century that the Sun Dance was outlawed, his people would sneak it in, early in the morning before July 4th celebrations. As Meyer indicates with the legal system, Native People often needed to disguise their teachings and practices in a European or American form in order to secretly pay honor to their knowledge and their ways.

[4] According to Black Elk; translated as '*ti* (where we live) *ospaye* (apart but not separated completely)' (DeMalle 1984, 320–1).

Witnessing generations come of age without an understanding of their place among their ancestors, their families and their community represents one of the most painful losses endured by Sioux elders.

Psychologists and anthropologists report that secure mother/infant attachment is the single greatest factor correlated with non-violent societies (Prescott 1980). Yet American Indian people have been subjected to Western hegemony telling them:

> ... from every direction and in every way, that (they) have no value to anyone, no purpose to (their) lives, no positive impact on the world around (them) ... At some point people brought to this position stand up and demand to be noticed, to be recognized as being alive, as having influence and *power* (author's emphasis). And the easiest way to assert power, to prove that you exist, is to demonstrate over people who are weaker still, primarily by making them do things they don't want to do. The more those things shame and diminish that weaker person, the more the abuser feels, within the twisted logic of victimizations, that they have been empowered and restored themselves. (Ross 1996, 48)

In many Native communities high levels of alcohol abuse, domestic violence, physical and sexual abuse, vandalism, and gang involvement illustrate the level of community social illness. Pat Bad Hand and colleagues at *Wiconi Wanbli Tipi* recognize the importance of these factors. They are committed and determined that their youth develop an intimate knowledge of *tios'paye*; their kinship circle, their relatives, their community, what it means for this individual to have his/her name and to be accountable to the legacy of his/her ancestors. It is the inclusion of the circles of family, community and ultimately the enveloping context of cultural/spiritual ceremony, values, beliefs and integrated system within the framework of restorative justice conflict resolution that provides a coherent context whereby delinquent youths and their families may choose to make whole their victims and their community. The same framework also provides the context whereby the community may choose to restore the offender and his/her family.

Attacks on the living cultural context

Zion (2002a, 9) reports that one contemporary theory of Indian crime and violence is that it is actually a form of 'mass post-traumatic stress disorder' (PTSD), resulting from centuries of failed European experiments to solve the 'Indian problem'. Europeans viewed the interrelated systems of education, religion, justice, science, medicine, agriculture, hunting, and governance as the 'Indian problem' that needed to be eradicated. Eradication attempts have been partially successful with severe damage to the integrated social systems of precontact Native America that has led to a prevalence of intergenerational learned violence among Indian families and communities (Zion 2002a). Likewise, many Native American teachers and elders observe that some of the greatest harm done to Indians today is by Indians themselves (Bad Hand 2002). This has caused great tension within communities (Bad Hand 2002, 35–6).

In trying to appreciate more fully the effects of European ways upon the living cultural context of Native Americans, Canadian Crown Prosecutor Ross has developed a story that was given to him by a Native teacher:

> Imagine that our two cultures are represented by a skin diver and a moon walker. Because they lived and worked in different environments, they developed different footwear to suit their needs. The moon walker created heavy boots, because there is less gravity on the moon. Without them, he would float off into space. The skin diver needed swimfins to propel him through the ocean. Without them, his ability to move about was diminished. As long as each stayed with his own footwear, in his own environment, he could move easily and well. If, however, the skin diver were forced to put on weighted moon boots, he would be at risk of drowning. Similarly, if the moon walker changed to swimfins, he would likely float off into space. In either case, each would be likely to come to grief if forced to wear the other's footgear.
>
> But imagine that Moon Boots came over to Swim Fins' land, and not appreciating why he needed flippers said 'You need to wear Moon Boots'. Believing in the 'rightness' of his ways, all measures were employed: from persuasion and ridicule right through to legal prohibition ... However, Swim Fins would not have changed environments, he would have only lost the ability to move around in his own world. Over time, his loss of mobility and power would take away his wish to move. No longer would he rejoice in his land and his relationships to it.
>
> Within that metaphor, the Western world has indeed done everything it could to force Aboriginal people to discard their traditional footwear. ... Instead of being encouraged to develop personal qualities and wide notions of responsibility, they found themselves trained into unthinking acceptance of codes of 'right' behavior established by others. Instead of a 'Natural Law' of interdependence requiring that they connect with each other as co-adventurers, they were trained to start thinking of themselves as 'better than' or 'worse than' their fellows ... .
>
> ... Traditional law makes no such assertion, and attempts no such imposition. Instead, it grants that each person, family, community and nation should be as free as possible to put their own wisdoms into practice within their own spheres of activity. Ironically, it is our very system of Canadian (American or English) law, especially its emphasis on absolute truths and one right answer, which seems to be the greatest felon where traditional law is concerned. (Ross 1996, 268–70)

Another example is that the Western/European way is intrinsically hierarchical in nature, and Native understanding is not. European invaders naturally saw their beliefs and their God as inhabiting the top spot, the right way and the truth. Native people did not propose that their God was better or that their spirits were stronger. They did not compete for the top spot in the hierarchy because they had no appreciation that a hierarchy existed (Neihardt 1932; Mails 1991; Ross 1989; Bad Hand 2002). For example, with regard to the Lakota:

> This spirit-centered worldview of the Lakotas is a worldview in which human beings are not superior to, but equal with other creatures of the earth. This view contrasts sharply with that of Judeo-Christian philosophy, which views human beings as superior to other creatures—'a little less than the angels ...' (Voss *et al* 1999, 230)

Or as Associate Chief Justice Murray Sinclair, Ojibway, of the Provincial Court of Manitoba stated:

> I am not a biblical scholar, but as I have come to understand it, in the Judeo-Christian tradition, man occupies a position just below God and the angels, but above all other earthly creation ... In sharp contrast, the aboriginal world-view holds that mankind is the least powerful and least important factor in creation ... Mankind's interests are not to be placed above those of any other part of creation ... In the matter of hierarchy, or relative importance of beings within creation, Aboriginal and Western intellectual tradition are almost diametrically opposed. (Ross 1996, 61)

Basil Johnston, an Ojibway scholar, relates that the Ojibway hierarchy of Creation is based on dependencies. 'It places the Mother Earth (and her lifeblood, the waters) in first place, for without them there would be no plant, animal or human life' (quoted in Ross 1996, 61). Next are the plant nations followed by the animal world. Last and clearly least important are humans, since 'Nothing whatever depends on our survival' (in Ross 1996, 61). By contrast, Western philosophy and religion place distance between human beings and the natural world, setting the hierarchical template institutionalized in Western civilization (Waldram 1994). It is reported that Native Americans had neither hierarchy nor permanence in their views on leadership, although there is recognition of the need for leadership.

Growing congruence between Native understanding and Western science

In the last century, breakthroughs in many scientific fields of research have led to transformations in how the world is viewed by Western science. These findings are locating Western philosophy and science closer to Native understanding than was previously thought possible. Recent developments in scientific study, including physics (Lipton 2001; Ross 1996), linguistics (Ross 1996), organic chemistry (Lipton 1998; 2001), the structure and action of DNA (Cairns *et al* 1988; Lipton 2001; Ridley 2003; Thaler 1994), cellular biology (Cairns, *et al* 1988; Lipton 1998, 2001; Thaler 1994), fetal development (Gibbons 1998a; Lipton 2001), early childhood development and psychology (Siegel 1999), chaos and complexity theories (Siegel and Hartzell 2003), study of complex adaptive systems (Peroff and Wildcat 2002; Siegel and Hartzell 2003), and Native American psychology (Bad Hand 2002) all point toward congruence between the previously dualistic nature of the Western worldview and the holistic nature of the Native American worldview. The predominant trend is toward the holistic viewpoint that healthy systems are interactive and naturally adaptive and self-organizing in the direction of increased complexity. Complexity lies between the extremes of sameness, rigidity and predictability, or randomness, unpredictability and disorder (Siegel and Hartzell 2003). Such systems are open, receive input from outside, have layers of components capable of chaotic behavior and are thus adaptable in changing circumstances.

Complexity is the path of harmony, the path of *wicozani or hozho'*, the path between the two extremes. It is the same as the 'Good Red Road' often referred to in Lakota life and prayer. It is similar to what Dr. A.C. Ross describes as the struggle of some Native people to live a sober life. On one side are the invitations of the comrades for drinking and excess. On the other are the tee-totalers and prohibitionists. For him and for other Native peoples their path to recovery consists of staying on the path between the chaos of excessive drinking and the rigidity of prohibitionists (Ross 1989). According to Zion (2002a), the Navajo spiritual path is similarly not the path of being 'all good'. It is a path of being in balance between the extremes of all good and all evil.

Howard Bad Hand, in responding to questions about Native American healing today, says: 'All dynamic systems require change. We are in the midst of change and transformation with our traditions, practices and beliefs. However, the truths I have learned about humanity and life from my people, especially from the old ones, have been solidly consistent and enduring' (Bad Hand 2002, 12). Further, Howard Bad Hand relates that, '... If you wish to know the independence of that which is idealized in life, the growth of that which is High cannot be based on the rigid and the unmoving ... All face the law of having to change with the times. Or, the times will come and shatter their rigidity' (Bad Hand 2002, 192). It appears that teachers (e.g. Bad Hand) are confirming that Native American spirituality and tradition endure because they honor the principles of complex adaptive systems.

There is a vibrant quality that emerges when systems are able to move in their natural, self-organizational flow toward complexity. The natural movement of the mind is also toward complexity and toward mental health. A stressed system, on the other hand, is one that tends to move away from complexity, toward extremes of rigidity or disorder (Siegel and Hartzell 2003). Psychological research with securely attached children and their parents reveals evidence of complex give-and-take in which each person contributes to the dialogue and can anticipate, but never fully predict, the response of the other. There is a vibrant matching, a pacing and aliveness present in the connection between parent and child. Through this process with an attuned and mindful adult, securely attached children learn to regulate behavior (Siegel and Hartzell 2003).

Most behavioral issues with onset in early childhood are caused by the child's inability to attach to or the unavailability of a primary parent figure. Such children will generally become the offenders of the next generation (Siegel 1999; Prescott 1979, 1980; Cline 2001). The Navajo would say about such an individual that 'he acts as if he has no relatives'. In this way, he betrays solidarity and kinship, and he becomes 'crazy' (Bluehouse and Zion 1993, 331). The Lakota would agree that this person has no relation with *tios'paye* and therefore is not open to the help his community and family can offer.

One reason why Western healing and corrections have not been effective with Native peoples is the overemphasis on the individual. Theories of relativity, complexity, and chaos; environmental influence; and the importance of a coherent narrative describe an evolution in Western science leading to a convergence with the values and traditions of Native philosophy. Patterns of the critical interplay of families, communities and the environment on genetic expression, individual development, health, healing, recovery and rehabilitation have become apparent. While these developments have occurred in science and health, a similar path can be traced in law and justice including the revitalization of restorative justice as a system for dealing with juvenile delinquency.

The Western legal system: when did victims of crime become victims of the criminal justice process?

An adversarial legal system is of necessity a hostile environment; it is organized as a battlefield in which strategies of aggressive argument and psychological attack replace those of physical force. (Herman 1992, 72)

Our children and the community can no longer afford the price the legal system is extracting in its attempts to provide justice in our community. (Community Holistic Circle Healing 1993, 5)

Traditional Native American and Aboriginal approaches to justice and corrections focus on harm done to victims and the community. Restitution is made to the victim and the victim's family, and optimally, the offender and victim will be *restored* to a mutually acceptable relationship. In so doing, the community is also wholly restored (LeResche 1993). Western justice shared this restorative focus until about the early 12th century.

However, with the passage of 'Leges Henrici' between 1112 and 1116, the English King, Henry I, declared that crimes were against the crown and that fines were payable to the crown prior to restitution made to victims.

Over time, restitution was viewed as interfering with the crown's right to exact a penalty for crime. Victims could sue for damages, but the state authority received what was originally direct restitution to the victim (Meyer 2002). The victim's role in providing evidence for the state's prosecution became more important than his/her need for healing, safety or compensation.

The justice system began to serve the needs of the abstract state, more than it served the needs of the victim and community (Umbreit and Bradshaw 1997).[5] This trend and pattern became so out of balance that by 1970 the 'Victim's Rights Movement' erupted in the United States, as well as movements for alternative and community policing, neighborhood watch, and other forms of more informal social control (Meyer 2002). In contemporary society most systems of adjudication and municipal law remain reactive adversarial processes, which are vertical and hierarchical in nature and use force to implement decisions or sanctions assuming one truth in any given situation. This reactive, adversarial, coercive and hierarchical system has essentially prevailed over traditional forms of justice, even in Tribal Courts. Most Native American scholars date the formal destruction of tribal justice systems at 10 April 1883, when the U.S. Commissioner of Indian Affairs created the Courts of Indian Offenses. With this ruling, followed by the Major Crimes Act of 1885, Native justice systems were completely transformed at the mandate of the federal government (Meyer 2002, 1380; Meyer and Zion 2000). Meyer notes:

> However, traditional justice was not completely annihilated; some tribal members were able to conceal their continued practice of traditional forms of justice from white view or found ways to embed some traditional thought in decisions issued from the Euro-American Courts of Indian Offenses. (Meyer 2002, 1380)

From a tribal perspective, the European model of justice imposed on Native Americans lacked the ability to deal with crime. How could ignoring the cause and origin of the problem reduce offensive behavior? In addition, victims could not expect justice from the federal courts. Not only were they left without reparations and compensation but they also lost the ability to tell their stories about how the offense had harmed them (Meyer 2002, 1386). Navajo healing understands that diagnosis and healing happen when a victim is able to give meaning to a problem through narrative; the person needs to 'talk about' and 'talk out' the problem in a social context (Zion 2002a, 28). When tribes lost their ability to use traditional techniques, they lost a powerful tool in their fight against crime

---

[5] Nowhere has this imbalance been as pronounced as the War on Drugs. Pre-1984, U.S. prison populations were largely made up of violent criminals. Today, 60% of those in prison are non-violent drug offenders (Jensen *et al* 2004).

and disorder. They lost the ability to develop a 'coherent narrative' to deal with what had occurred. The *tios'paye* of the tribe was no longer allowed to inform or be informed by the transgression and the corresponding opportunity for restoration. Recent efforts in Native communities are reinstituting forms of traditional justice by engaging in restorative justice conflict resolution.

LITERATURE REVIEW OF CONFLICT RESOLUTION/CRIME
PREVENTION AND INTERVENTION PROGRAMMING USING
TRADITION IN NATIVE COMMUNITIES

In addition to a brief review of the peculiarities of justice systems in Indian Country, this section will describe several restorative justice conflict resolution programs operating in Native communities as they have been presented in published material. In addition, other material will be synthesized in terms of various principles, theories, or other ideas germane to the topic. This is not the result of an exhaustive literature search.

One of the issues affecting the reintroduction of traditional restorative justice in Native communities is the matter of jurisdictional responsibility for managing justice. The central Canadian government is responsible for managing the justice system in Canadian First Nations communities. Within the United States there is a lack of coherence among the institutions of justice in Native communities. Responsibility for community social control is disjointed and spread between different governmental authorities that frequently do not work together, trust each other or communicate with each other. Many American Indian tribes and communities do not have authority over serious juvenile offenders in their own community. There is not even a consistent pattern to this lack of coherence across Indian Country. In some states the state court system and local law enforcement have responsibility for managing justice within Native American communities. In other states, some (but not necessarily all) Native American tribes manage their own tribal court systems and law enforcement agencies. However, in these communities the Federal courts have taken responsibility for investigating, prosecuting and adjudicating such major crimes as rape, murder, major drug dealing, and incest. Youths who are adjudicated for major crimes in Federal courts and enter the custody of the U.S. Bureau of Prisons are removed and incarcerated in contracted state or private facilities that may be distant from their home community. Where tribal courts do exist, they have limited ability to impose sentence (one year or less) or fine ($5,000 or less), which leaves these communities with many mid-range offenses which they have difficulty sentencing effectively. Given the low level of funding for intervention and prevention services, these peculiarities of adjudicating crime in Indian Country, and the ineffectiveness of punitive justice at reducing recidivism and preventing crime, it is particularly important that juvenile offenders be dealt with at the lowest level of offense or prevented from offending. Restorative justice conflict resolution can play a major role in this effort. The following briefly describes the attempts by some communities to use Native traditions to reinstitute restorative justice conflict resolution with juvenile offenders.

Emmonak Elders' Group

A recent restorative justice initiative in a Native community is the Emmonak Elders' Group in the Alaska Yukon Delta Yup'ik Eskimo community of Emmonak (total population of 800, with 200 youth enrolled in school) (Justice Center 2001). In agreement with the Alaska Division of Juvenile Justice, the Emmonak Elders' Group handles most non-felony juvenile cases within the community, which has allowed the youth to remain in the community while their case is being adjudicated through the elders. This process avoids the formal Alaska state justice system, which usually involves removal of the youth from the village and lengthy processing prior to consequences. Instead, youth are quickly held accountable within the context of community traditions.

The Elders' Group was started in 1997 in response to increasing social problems in the community. Their original goal was to pass down traditional knowledge and wisdom to younger generations. They have also addressed domestic violence by educating families and providing culturally based guidelines. The juvenile program started in 1999 with two goals: to reduce juvenile crime and recidivism, and to increase the skills, knowledge and control of local Native entities in solving village issues. These goals were to be achieved by increasing collaboration between state and local/tribal organizations and by restoring cultural relevance to community social controls and education by incorporating Yup'ik traditional values and beliefs into youth-serving systems.

One member of staff, funded by U.S. Department of Justice block-grant funding to the State of Alaska, is responsible for processing referrals from the state justice system and monitoring sentence completion. The person in this position is critical to the effectiveness of the restorative justice project but the Elders' Group is the essence of the project. The Alaska Division of Juvenile Justice (DJJ) regional office in Bethel, Alaska receives the case of every juvenile who is accused of violating the law (as determined by local police and magistrates or district court judges). Juveniles are assigned to a probation officer who determines whether the youth should have the choice of appearing before the Emmonak Elders' Group or stay in the state system for formal processing. The decision to offer the option is based on prior offense history, current charge, and offender's age. The juvenile and his/her parent(s) must agree to accept the authority of the Elders to administer the case. An increasing number of early interventions in the form of local referrals to the Elders' Group are also being made by families, community members and schools without DJJ involvement.

A hearing occurs in the community within 8–10 weeks following arrest or other referral. The Elders' Group, the youth and his/her family, and the staff member attend. Police are invited but infrequently participate. The agenda allows everyone to speak, there is then a break for the Elders to confer in private, and the process ends with sentencing the youth at which time all the Elders have a chance to speak to the youth and family. Sentencing is the core of the procedure and includes stories from the Elders about their own youth with discussion of values and guidance that were handed down to them, Yup'ik myths, and warnings about consequences for continued 'bad' behavior. Most sentences involve a period of community service. Finally, the youth is given a chance to speak.

The documented strengths of the program are the quick referral process, the community collaborations that have been built, expansion of referrals from local sources resulting in earlier intervention and resultant reduction of cases referred to the DJJ, and an expressed generalized positive feeling of community pride, as well as greater interest expressed in understanding the needs of community youth. Weaknesses are the lack of formal systems for providing case information to community referral agencies and poor record-keeping that makes it difficult to track recidivism. Comments about the program from families, elders and community members include the following:

> The elders opened her eyes. It doesn't make sense for the young people to sit in jail and not do anything. They should be here in the community at home doing something productive. In court the kids are just pieces of paper and with the elders' court the kids are people with families and histories ... She really changed, changed her attitude. They just sort of opened her eyes to what she was doing to herself. The whole community gets involved when the general elders' meetings occur.
>
> The elders provided very good advice. Within a week I noticed her face was glowing. We talk about things now that we never did before. By referring my daughter to the Elders' Group it made my daughter feel more cared about, both from me and also by people in the community.
>
> Our role is to pass on wisdom. It's knowledge, values, passed down. Knowledge is worthless unless it's passed on.
>
> We try to give advice without breaking their spirit. This is what I see when kids come back from Bethel. Their spirit is broken.
>
> Everyone can change their way of life. I've seen this for many years. The kids know we think this.
>
> The project is helping to bring back a new generation. Our dances are coming back and we are taping the elders' proceedings, saving the wisdom and the language.

To ensure ongoing success and continuity of operations, it will be important for this program to continue funding the administrative staff person position and to improve record keeping that can demonstrate the effectiveness of the program.

Navajo peacemaking

A similar program operated in one district of the Navajo Nation court system between 1996 and 1999 (Rubin 2001). The Navajo Nation operates its own tribal justice system with only those offenders who commit crimes falling under the Major Crimes Act being processed in the U.S. Federal justice system. Serious problems with juvenile delinquency exist in the Navajo Nation: over 2,000 charges were dealt with in the tribal court system in 1999. Gangs are well-established and cause serious violence (Rubin 2001). The Navajo Tribal Code directs the court to utilize Navajo common law and tribal statutes enacted by the Tribal Council as the laws of preference, followed by federal law, if applicable, and finally state law. Navajo common law is the traditional ways of the Navajo people, which are regularly argued in the Nation's courts and can be found in many publications and Navajo Supreme Court decisions, as well as by consulting elders, stories and oral history. Chief Justice Robert Yazzie states the vision of the tribal court system:

> It is not to punish, boss people around, have courts seen as powerful people who tell others how to live their lives, or courts being distant and alien from the people. It is a vision of courts as partners in the process of making it possible for Navajos to live freely as Navajos. (Rubin 2001, 2)

Within the Navajo courts, one method of increasing the use of tradition is to institutionalize historic Peacemaking practices by using community leaders and elders to resolve conflicts. Peacemaking is used primarily in family and civil disputes but it has also been used in juvenile delinquency cases as a diversion from court or as directed by a judge at judicial disposition. Navajo district courts employ liaisons who arrange for Peacemakers, who are elders with traditional Navajo wisdom, to meet with the concerned parties, keep records, and monitor implementation of an agreement. The Peacemaker Court heals relationships and achieves solidarity, balance and harmony. Lawyers and judges, as well as other professionals, are not involved. Restitution is only a small part of healing with a talking-out process being the major action that enables authentic healing.

Usually, three Peacemaking sessions are held for each case during a one year time period, with counseling occurring in between sessions. The first session gathers a wide range of information about the family and the youth with development of an individualized treatment plan that can include use of traditional ceremonial healing along with more standard counseling and other services. A second session several months later reviews progress and needs—service providers may participate and the treatment plan is reviewed. A final session assesses whether the treatment plan was completed and successful, and a follow-up plan is designed.

Rubin (2001) analyzed the Chinle District Juvenile Peacemaking Court for three years (1996–9) and states that the value of Peacemaking was demonstrated in the lives of juveniles and families. Records are scant, therefore it is difficult to know if juvenile delinquency has been reduced by Peacemaking. It is the author's impression that Peacemaking with juvenile offenders was only used within one district for a small number of cases. However, the potential exists for much more extensive involvement of Peacemaking throughout the Navajo Nation.

Healing Circles in Hollow Water, Canada

In the book *Returning to the Teachings*, Rupert Ross, Assistant Crown Attorney for the Canadian Justice Department, writes about his multi-year investigation of traditional healing among Canada's Aboriginal people (Ross 1996). Ross had worked in the system as the prosecutor in juvenile criminal cases in Aboriginal villages and was given the opportunity to work for several years finding and documenting those Native communities who were dealing with serious postmodern social ills. His description of the Healing Circles in Hollow Water, Manitoba, Canada are particularly engaging.

This effort came about when a group of Hollow Water residents—mostly Aboriginal women—met to discuss community problems, especially concerning youth. Many in the group were social service practitioners. In the process of working with the families of troubled youth it was discovered that the children's homes were plagued by high levels of substance abuse and family violence that was mostly not acknowledged or dealt with in the community. In looking at the cause of these problems among the adults the group of healing professionals discovered that in a community of 600 there was an extremely high level of historical and generational incest and sexual abuse. It was estimated that 80% of residents (male and female) had at one time or another sexually abused someone else.

The group determined that professional barriers had to come down—the former way of operating in separate agencies with confidentiality rules prevented them from achieving their shared goal of healing people to wholeness. A true team approach was created that incorporated outside professionals but required inclusion of lay team members as a means of sharing knowledge with the community. This partnership also created a way for the lay team members to train the outside professionals to work within the Native holistic framework. Extensive cross-training included information sharing across disciplines, Western models for intervention and healing, and exploring traditional ways and teachings being practised in other Aboriginal communities. As the level of sexual abuse in the community became clear to the team, members themselves had to confront the situation of their own histories of sexual abuse before they were ready to reach out to others. Since this work had occurred prior to Ross's exploration he could not describe it. The Healing Circles used with community members involve the practitioners sharing their own stories and sketching the pathways that lead victims and abusers away from self-hatred, alienation, anger and despair. Team members started on the healing path without traditional cleansings that were included later.

Ross (1996) reports that the strategy that the community team has developed involves a detailed protocol that leads all participants through a number of steps. These stages are truly restorative to all involved, and to the extent the participants choose, includes use of a number of traditional cleansing rituals. The process takes at least two years and some last much longer. The process occurs outside the criminal justice process, although links are maintained. When sexual abuse is alleged, the assessment team quickly evaluates the complaint and if it appears valid, swings into action with the organizational level described as 'a complex military action' (Ross 1996, 33).

The victimizer is confronted with the allegations (with police backup if needed), listened to, and offered support and accompaniment through the criminal justice process if sincere efforts are made to accept responsibility and go through the healing process. At the same time, team members contact others who will be affected by the disclosure to explain what has been alleged, the processes to be followed, and the help that might be made available. No one is left in the dark or alone in painful isolation. The victimizer is accompanied to the police station where formal charging occurs and he/she is asked to make a statement (not admissible in court but seen as a first step in accepting responsibility). The team then requires the victimizer to enter a guilty plea in court as quickly as possible. It asks the court to delay sentencing as long as possible so that the team can have the time it needs to work with the victim, offender, families, and community before presenting the court with a realistic assessment of the challenges and possibilities of the particular case. The team likes to see sentencing delayed until completion of the formal healing process, but frequently that is too long for the court system. Team members are involved in preparing sentencing reports and participating in court-based Healing Circles.

Ross (1996) reports that the Hollow Water Healing Circles' processes are evolving over time with greater participation of victimizers and victims and with greater interaction between community healing process and court process. A more recent step has been to require follow-up community Healing Circles at six month intervals following completion of the formal healing process but without the court's involvement to affirm the promises made, to honor further healing steps, and to maintain community expectations of victimizers. Of 48 offenders over a nine-year period, only five had gone to jail, primarily due to failure to participate in the healing program. Only 2 of the 43 completers had been charged with reoffending, one at an early stage in the process and the other during the infancy of the program. This latter person has since completed the formal healing program and gone on to become a valuable member of the Healing Circles team.

The strengths of the Hollow Water Healing Circles team and processes are its embeddedness in the community, its true team development, the commitment of the team members to work through the healing process with all parties concerned and at all stages of healing (including denial and joking about the offense from the victimizer—the shift from denial to joking is viewed as a positive step toward healing), the modeling of healing that team members (former victims and some of them former victimizers) provide to victims and offenders, and the openness of the process. Serious community ills such as sexual abuse can only exist at the level experienced in Hollow Water when they stay secret, private, and shameful.

Thoughts on the foundations, philosophy, and status of Native American law and restorative justice

This section will add to our discussion of Native American philosophy, psychology, point of view, and understanding of the role of humanity in the cosmos and the close fit between restorative justice and use of traditional healing for dispute resolution with delinquent juveniles in these Native conceptions. Carey Vicenti, Chief Judge of the Jicarilla Apache Tribe, writes that in stark contrast to American society:

> ... the Indian concept of the human being is one in which all aspects of the person and his or her society are integrated. Every action in daily life is read to have meaning and implication to the individual and guides how he or she interacts with tribal society or fulfills obligations imposed by society, law, and religion ... Therefore our institutions were not designed, as in American society, to discover the truth. Our institutions focused more upon determining the manner in which a transgression against social order would be remediated ... part of the remedy is in performing the exploration ... (It) is essential that the internal and external life of any perpetrator be examined to determine whether the individual is healthy or whole. And ultimately, we desire to reintegrate the individual back into tribal society. (Vicenti 1995, 3, 9–10)

Zion (2002b, 5) states that 'Traditional Indian Justice differs from Western models because it recognizes the healing component. Indian justice is not simply indigenous methods of resolving disputes, but a philosophy of life based upon respect and relationships'. Another contrast that Zion (undated) discusses is that Western justice does not try to reach into the mind or deal with psychological injuries, whereas traditional indigenous law does, which is why it heals and restores both victim and offender. Brill (1997) notes the emphasis of Indian justice on civil sanctions and diffusion of power rather than consolidation of political power. This writer also notes that 'civil refers to processes that attempt to restore relationships rather than permanently separate or stigmatize' (Brill 1997, 131). Chief Justice of the Navajo Nation, Robert Yazzie, recently called for a push by tribes, tribal courts, Indian Law organizations, Indian Country leadership and academics to promote and use Indian law as the law of preference (Yazzie 2003). Vicenti (1995) discusses the status of tribal courts across the U.S. and notes that lack of funding for sufficient competent staff to adequately justify the place and purpose of the court within the democratic structure of tribal government undermines the rest of tribal government. He also states that in 1995 'few tribes [had] reached a level of maturity where they can meaningfully make choices between traditional practice and American legal process' (Vicenti 1995, 15). However, it is our impression that progress is occurring rapidly in this area.

Others describe the benefits of indigenous or traditional justice in the forms in which it is being reintegrated into tribal court systems. Melton (1999, 24) notes that the indigenous process is 'non-adversarial and facilitates discussion between people in conflict in a safe environment that promotes resolution of underlying problems and keeping relationships intact. The communication process is fluid and allows for discussion of multiple viewpoints of the problem or conflict from those directly or indirectly affected'.

Native thought on adversarial courts is that opportunities are missed by offering healing to no one and only relying on deterrence and confinement, which works against the healing process and moves unbalanced persons further out of balance. One should not get the idea that traditional Indian law was without provision for dealing with dangerous individuals. Community welfare was paramount and those persons who resisted or were beyond community efforts aimed at healing could be killed (usually reserved for those considered truly evil, e.g. practitioners of witchcraft that harmed others) or banished to the wilderness (Ross 1996). In addition, traditional teaching could be quite painful to body and mind. The difference with Western justice is that it is not 'strictly ... punishment, unaccompanied by efforts to move people forward out of their problems ...' (Ross 1996, 14).

Vicenti (1995) points out that the American system of government with its adversarial system of justice is a large part of American culture. Imposition of this justice system with the purpose of correcting perceived rampant injustice creates greater injustice by forcing its culture on Indian peoples. Finally, Cruz says: 'an indigenous nation's sovereignty is strengthened if its law is based upon its own internalized values and norms ... traditional law is internal to a particular community, oral and for the most part, dynamic and not static in nature...(as) the fundamental principles of customary law do not change. They are simply extended to cover new situations' (Cruz undated, 2, 4).

Restorative justice and therapeutic jurisprudence and other original forms of dispute resolution (ODR) represent a horizontal legal system. Examples of such forms of justice are found in international law, in addition to the laws of many Native peoples. The core of the common law of most Native peoples is the 'segmentary lineage system', which is a method of tracing relationships and adjusting disputes among people who are related to each other in various ways (Barkun 1968). A horizontal legal system assumes and works for equality between participants (Haberfeld and Townsend 1993). It is a relationship-centered process, not agreement-centered. Its goal is to sustain community health (LeResche 1993). It is not a reactive adversarial process, and its preference is to avoid force or coercion.

According to Zion (2002b), 'therapeutic jurisprudence' is a new philosophy of using science and healthcare (including mental health services) to seize crime as an opportunity for healing rather than only for retribution and punishment. Zion (2002b) adds that we need therapeutic jurisprudence because people hurt each other. Violence is part of our human behavior; aggression is used as a form of intimidation and dominance, and aggression is redirected by people who have been hurt against weaker victims (e.g. women, children and animals). For many traditional peoples who hear of the possible healing nature of law, of 'appreciative inquiry', of 'Getting to Yes', of 'talking things out' in a circle and giving every person a voice and honoring mutuality, most would respond with 'What's new? Our ancestors were doing this for centuries' (Haberfeld and Townsend 1993; Whitney and Trosten-Bloom 2003; Zion 2002a, 2002b).

Original forms of dispute resolution revolve around the ability of offenders to completely restore themselves and their victims within their community, even in the case of very serious crimes. A prime example is the approach described above in Hollow Water, Manitoba, Canada. Instead of focusing on legal sanctions, prosecution and punishment, the community-based program focuses on full accountability, retribution to victims, and healing for all. The program involves a 13-step program over a period of several years. For some people, it would be easier to go to jail:

After completing the program, the former abuser goes through a cleansing ceremony to 'mark a new beginning for all involved'. During the ceremony, the former abuser washes his victim's feet (part of a traditional puberty rite), symbolically allowing her to re-enter womanhood, then throws a mask he has worn throughout the ceremony into a fire, symbolically destroying his identity as an abuser. Those who complete the program are welcomed back into society as though they had never offended in the first place. (Meyer 2002, 1382; see also Community Holistic Circle Healing 1993)

This program has a very low recidivism rate. In American society many accept the claim that adult sex offenders are incurable and need to be incapacitated, registered and monitored for life.[6] In the Hollow Water program recidivism for adult sex offenders is less than 5% (Aboriginal Peoples Collection 1997; Community Holistic Circle Healing 1993; Ross 1996).

As the restorative justice program for sexual abusers at Hollow Water indicates, there can be and needs to be a powerful healing component for all parties involved. Disharmony and crime are viewed as signs of problems with the health of the community, not only with an individual. By approaching the problem and intervention from a community standpoint, specific ceremonies aimed at eliminating the roots of disorder can be approached and accomplished as a community. In this way, Native Americans cope with emotional losses and other traumatic life altering occurrences at the same time as using crime as an opportunity for restoring offenders, victims and the community to greater strength, wholeness, integration and complexity (Meyer 2002).

While establishment of the Courts of Indian Offenses in 1883 and the Major Crimes Act of 1885 transferred prosecutorial power from Native American tribes to the federal government for certain serious offenses, the experience of Hollow Water indicates that for some very serious offenses, confinement may be inadequate (Ross 1996). In the words of the people of Hollow Water:

> What the threat of incarceration does do is keep people from coming forward and taking responsibility for the hurt they are causing. It reinforces the silence and therefore promotes, rather than breaks, the cycle of violence that exists. In reality, rather than making the community a safer place, the threat of jail places the community more at risk. (Aboriginal Peoples Collection 1997, 148)

As the women of Hollow Water have said, defense attorneys have destroyed their work with offenders on many occasions. 'We would do all this work, at our level here in the community, and in five minutes a defense lawyer can negate all your work. That offender is so weak and so vulnerable

---

[6] California's Megan's Law requires major and minor sex offenders to register for life. Minor offenses may include indecent exposure, pornography, or 'mooning' the basketball team as part of a drunken fraternity party. All registrants who attend college or work on a campus are required to have their identities made public. California's law distinguished between minor and major offenders, but due to a need to conform to federal law, the distinction has been lost in the renewed bill.

that he'll take what he doesn't have to face, what he doesn't have to acknowledge' (Aboriginal Peoples Collection 1997, 148). Hollow Water now has a few defense attorneys it can trust. These good attorneys do not encourage minimization or denial, and still protect rights and due process for clients.

Meyer and Zion (2000, 104) report that 'Navajos, as most Native American nations, have great contempt for the federal promise of incarceration as a solution to their crime problem'. Western jurisprudence does not deal with the causes of crime and recidivism.[7] Rather than dealing with the collapse of the living cultural context of Native communities, it has contributed to the demise of the indigenous cultural context.

Although its declared focus is on handing out punishment to fit the crime, *just desserts*, its punishments do not appear to help to restore the community, victims or offenders to wholeness and we find that increased incarceration has not reduced crime[8] (Koetting and Schiraldi 1997). Yet, our current policy increasingly requires mandatory minimum sentences resulting in lengthy sentences for minor drug offenses. In combination with disproportionately high rates of confinement for youth of color who are arrested, our policies have resulted in prison becoming a 'normal' socialization experience for poor minority youth (Anderson 2003) with little effect on creating safer communities. As expressed by Chairman Robert Horner, of the (Canadian) Parliament's Standing Committee on Justice: 'If locking up those who violate the law contributed to safer societies, then the United States would be the safest country in the world' (Ross 1996, 267).

CONCLUSION

If present science in a variety of areas demonstrates to us the importance of environmental interaction shaping behavior, then perhaps the Native therapeutic jurisprudence emphasis on restoring the community to wholeness and complexity, rather than simply punishing an individual, is where justice needs to focus. The reception that restorative justice has received indicates

---

[7] Francis Deisler (2002) has demonstrated that being incarcerated is frequently synonymous with receiving incompetent treatment. He argues that while prisoners are seen as 'second class citizens' they are still entitled to competent treatment. It is incorrect to conclude that people are incurable if they have not yet received treatment.
[8] Placing low-risk offenders in programs designed for high-risk offenders increases recidivism (Andrews *et al* 1990). After 3.5 years of incarceration, prisoners' coping skills become better suited to prison society than to mainstream life (Hammond and Chayen 1963). Thus longer prison sentences increase recidivism since recidivism is inversely related to evolving coping behaviors (Armentrout 2003).

that much of the American justice system is ready for reform (Zion 2002a, 2002b: Hora *et al* 1999; Winck and Wexler 1996; Boldt 1998; Schma 2000). However, adopting systems born from a culture that honored complexity, into a culture that currently tends toward rigid, reactive application of policy reforms can spell disaster. We need to embrace restorative justice while honoring the complexity of the living cultural context from which it sprang. Otherwise employing it may be no more meaningful or life changing than taking a souvenir home from a guided bus tour of the Black Hills. We must ask the question: are the victim, the offender and the community being restored through this process? If we cannot answer that question affirmatively, then the true purpose of restorative justice is not being fulfilled.

Native American peoples are in a dynamic process of revitalizing their traditions. One way in which this is occurring is by using restorative justice conflict resolution with delinquent juveniles outside of punitive court systems. This is being implemented in very different judicial structures such as tribal courts like the Navajo Nation or where state or federal courts have jurisdiction such as Alaska Native communities or Canadian Aboriginal villages. These communities are finding that by applying the principles of restorative justice toward conflict resolution with delinquent youth they are able to:

- save children from progressing deeper into the system and being lost to the community;
- restore families to better relations and restore relations between families;
- bring healing to victims;
- prevent other youths from becoming delinquent;
- restore and recognize the value and usefulness to the community of elders;
- further restore traditional values, beliefs, and practices throughout the community, which restores the locus of social control in families and community; and
- restore the whole community as a functioning integrated system based in traditional Native philosophy and spirit.

The Native perspective needs to be honored and salvaged fully intact and not in pieces, not only for Native communities but for the modern world. We need belief systems that understand how deeply interrelated we are to each other, to time, to place and to every thing in the environment, and how constantly responsive, flexible and adaptive we need to be. With new knowledge, Western science has shown us that helping professionals must value context, relationships, story telling, and family history to heal through restorative justice.

REFERENCES

Aboriginal Peoples Collection (1997) *The Four Circles of Hollow Water.* Public Works and Government Services, Canada APC 15 CA.

Anderson, C. (2003) '5.6 Million Have Prison Experience', The Associated Press. See Bureau of Justice Statistics: http://www.ojp.usdoj.gov/bjs

Andrews, D.A., Zinger, I., Hodge, R.D., Bonta, J., Gendrau, P. and Cullen, F.T. (1990) 'Does correctional treatment work?' *Criminology* 28, 369–40.

Armentrout, D.P. (2003) 'Objective Standards for Values in Therapy'. *The Forensic Psychologist* 2(3), 5–7.

Bad Hand, H. (2002) *Native American Healing.* (Chicago, Keats).

Barkun, M. (1968) *Law Without Sanctions: Order in Primitive Societies and the World Community.* (New Haven CT, Yale University Press).

Bluehouse, P. and Zion, J.W. (1993) 'Hozhooji naat'aanii: The Navajo Justice and Harmony Ceremony'. *Mediation Quarterly* 10(4), 327–37.

Braithwaite, J. (2002) *Restorative Justice & Responsive Regulation.* (New York, Oxford University Press).

Brill, E.J. (1997) 'Review of Indigenous North American jurisprudence'. *International Journal of Comparative Sociology* 38(1–2), 131–49.

Boldt, R.C. (1998) 'Rehabilitative Punishment and the Drug Treatment Court Movement' *Washington University Law Quarterly* 76, 1205.

Cairns, J., Overbaugh, J. and Miller, S. (1988) 'The Origin of Mutants'. *Nature* 335, 142–5.

Cline, F. (2001) *Uncontrollable Kids: From Heartbreak to Hope.* (Golden, CO, The Love and Logic Press).

Community Holistic Circle Healing (1993) *CHCH Position Paper on Incarceration,* CHCH files, Hollow Water, Manitoba, Canada.

Cruz, C.Z. (undated) 'Tribal Law as Indigenous Social Reality and Separate Consciousness—[Re]incorporating Customs and Traditions into Tribal Law' http://tlj.unm.edu/articles/czc/content.htm

Deisler, F.J. (2002) *Understanding and Treating the Sociopathic Client.* (Georgetown, TX, Armadillo Press).

Delano, C. (1873) 'United States Indian Policy: A letter from Honorable Columbus Delano, Secretary of the Interior'. *Yankton Press,* 30 April.

Delgado, R. (2000) 'Goodbye to Hammurabi: analyzing the atavistic appeal of restorative justice'. *Stanford Law Review* 52(4), 75.

DeMalle, R.J. (ed.) (1984) *The Sixth Grandfather: Black Elk's Teachings Given to John G. Neihardt.* (Lincoln, University of Nebraska Press).

Gibbons, A. (1998a) 'Solving the Brain's Energy Crisis'. *Science* 280, 1345–7.

—— (1998b) 'In Mice, Mom's Genes Favor Brains Over Brawn'. *Science* 280, 1346.

Haberfeld, S. and Townsend, J. (1993) 'Power and Dispute Resolution in Indian Country'. *Mediation Quarterly* 10, 405–22.

Hammond, E. and Chayen, E. (1963) *Persistent Criminals* (London, HMSO).

Herman, J. (1992) *Trauma and Recovery* (New York, Basic Books, Harper & Collins).

Hora, P.F., Schma, W.G. and Rosenthal, J. (1999) 'Therapeutic Jurisprudence and the Drug Treatment Court Movement: Revolutionizing the Criminal Justice System's Response to Drug Abuse and Crime in America'. *Notre Dame Law Review* 74, 439.

Jensen, E., Geber, J. and Mosher, C. (2004) 'Social Consequences of the War on Drugs: the Legacy of Failed Policy'. *Criminal Justice Policy Review* 15(1), 100–21.

Justice Center (2001) 'Emmonak Juveniles and the Elders' Group'. *University of Alaska Anchorage, Alaska Justice Forum* 18(2), Spring.

Koetting, M.G. and Schiraldi, V. (1997) 'Singapore West: The Incarceration of 200,000 Californians'. *Social Justice* 24(1), 40.

LeResche, D. (1993) 'Editor's Notes'. *Mediation Quarterly* 10(4), 321.

Lipton, B.H. (1998) 'Nature, Nurture and the Power of Love'. *Journal of Prenatal and Perinatal Psychology and Health* 13, 3–10.

—— (2001) 'Insight into Cellular "Consciousness"'. *Bridges* 12(1), 5.

Mails, T.E. (1991) *Fools Crow: Wisdom and Power.* (Tulsa, OK, Council Oaks Books).

McCold, P. and Wachtel, B. (1997) 'Community Is Not A Place: A New Look at Community Justice Initiatives'. *International Conference on Justice without Violence: Views from Peacemaking, Criminology and Restorative Justice* (Albany, NY, Real Justice).

Melton, A. (1999) 'The concept of indigenous justice'. *Alternatives to Incarceration* Jul/Aug. (Hicksville, NY, Criminal Justice Media, Inc).

Meyer, J.F. (2002) 'It is a gift from the Creator to keep us in harmony: Original (vs. Alternative) Dispute Resolution on the Navajo Nation'. *International Journal of Public Administration* 25, 11.

Meyer, J.F. and Zion, J.W. (2000) 'Navajo Nation, Post-Traditional State'. In G. Barak (ed.), *Crime and Crime Control: A Global View.* (Westport, CT, Greenwood Press).

Moore, D.B. (1997) 'Pride, Shame and Empathy in Peer Relations: New Theory and Practice in Education and Juvenile Justice'. In K. Rigby and P. Slee (eds.), *Children's Peer Relations.* (London, Routledge).

Neihardt, J.G. (1932) *Black Elk Speaks.* (Lincoln, University of Nebraska Press, Bison Books).

Peroff, N. and Wildcat, D. (2002) 'Who is an American Indian?' *Social Science Journal* 39, 349–61.

Prescott, J.W. (1979) 'Deprivation of physical affection as a primary process in the development of physical violence'. In D.G. Gil (ed.), *Child Abuse and Violence* (pp. 66–137) (New York, AMS Press).

—— (1980) 'Somatosensory affectional deprivation (SAD) theory of drug and alcohol use'. In D.J. Letieri, M. Sayers and H. Pearson (eds.),

Theories On Drug Abuse: Selected Contemporary Perspectives. NIDA Research Monograph 30 (March), pp. 286–96 (Rockville, MD, National Institute on Drug Abuse, Department of Health and Human Services).

Presser, L. and Gaarder, E. (2000) 'Can Restorative Justice Reduce Battering? Some Preliminary Considerations'. *Social Justice* 27, 175.

Ridley, M. (2003) 'What Makes You Who You Are'. *Time Magazine*, 8 June, 55–63.

Ross, A.C. (1989) *Mitakuye Oyasin: We are all related.* (Denver, CO, Wicóni Wasté).

Ross, R. (1992) *Dancing with a Ghost: Exploring Indian Reality.* (Markham, Ontario, Octopus Publishing).

—— (1996) *Returning to the Teachings: Exploring Aboriginal Justice.* (Toronto, Penguin Books).

Rubin, T. (2001) 'Peacemaking: From Conflict to Harmony in the Navaho (sic) Tradition'. *Juvenile Justice Update* 7(1), 1–16.

Schma, W. (2000) 'Judging for the New Millennium'. *Court Review* 37, 4.

Siegel, D.J. (1999) *The Developing Mind.* (New York, The Guilford Press).

Siegel, D.J. and Hartzell, M. (2003) *Parenting from the Inside Out.* (New York, Penguin Putnam).

Thaler, D.S. (1994) 'The Evolution of Genetic Intelligence'. *Science* 264, 224–5.

Umbreit, M. and Bradshaw, W. (1997) 'Victim Experience of Meeting Adult vs. Juvenile Offenders: A Cross-National Comparison'. *Federal Probation* 61(4), 33–40.

Vicenti, C. (1995) 'The reemergence of tribal society and traditional justice systems: In their efforts to establish tribal culture, Indian tribes are relying on the restoration of traditional forms of adjudication'. *Judicature* 79(3).

Voss, R.W., Douville, V., Little Soldier, A. and Twiss, G. (1999) 'Tribal and Shamanic-based social work practice: a Lakota perspective'. *Social Work* 44(3), 228.

Waldram, J.B. (1994) 'Aboriginal Spirituality in Corrections: a Canadian Case Study in Religion and Therapy'. *American Indian Quarterly* 18(2), 197–214.

Whitney, D. and Trosten-Bloom, A. (2003) *The Power of Appreciative Inquiry: A Practical Guide to Positive Change.* (San Francisco, Berrett-Koehler).

Winck, B.J. and Wexler, D.B. (1996) 'Law in a Therapeutic Key: Developments in Therapeutic Jurisprudence'. Reviewed in Thomas T. Merrigan, 'Law in a Therapeutic Key: A Resource for Judges'. *Court Review* 37, 8.

Yazzie, R. (2003) 'Indian Law and Assimilation'. Presented at the University of Oregon Law School, February.

372 Barbara Mendenhall and James Dumesnil

Zion, J.W. (2002a) 'Indian Restorative Healing'. Session presented at Dreaming of a New Reality, Third International Conference on Circles and other Restorative Practices, August, Minneapolis, MN.
—— (2002b) 'The Varieties of Therapeutic Experience; Excerpts from The Second International Conference on Therapeutic Jurisprudence'. *Touro Law Review* 18 (Spring).
—— (undated) 'Punishment versus Healing: How Does Traditional Indian Law Work?' www.usask.ca/nativelaw/publicatons/jah/zion.html. (Native Law Centre of Canada).

16

The Juvenile Justice Forums of Malawi: A Case Study of the Lilongwe Juvenile Justice Forum

DESMOND KAUNDA

INTRODUCTION

THIS PAPER SEEKS to share the experiences of a new juvenile justice program in Malawi—the Juvenile Justice Forums of Malawi. The Lilongwe Juvenile Justice Forum (a regional/district forum) will be treated as a case study. This is a relatively new initiative intending to provide various interventions leading to the improvement of the juvenile justice delivery system in Malawi by adopting an 'integrated approach' to juvenile[1] justice issues.

THE MALAWI NATIONAL JUVENILE JUSTICE FORUM (NJJF)

One of the biggest constraints for the Malawi juvenile justice system has been the lack of a policy developing body and no development of procedural rules, guidelines and tools. Based upon a successful model tested in Namibia, Malawi established its own National Juvenile Justice Forum (NJJF) in 2000. The task of addressing the gaps in juvenile justice has been the responsibility of this forum. The NJJF is part and parcel of the judiciary, and is chaired by a High Court judge who works in consultation with the relevant authorities and stakeholders in the juvenile justice sector. The establishment of the working committee within the NJJF will result in a major improvement in the development of policy on juvenile justice. The NJJF has made progress in achieving its goals, some of which are highlighted below.

---

[1] The term 'juvenile' is here applied to young suspects aged 12–18. The minimum age of criminal responsibility in Malawi is currently 12.

Office setup and regional/district forums

The Malawi Judiciary donated office space at the High Court in Zomba. The offices have been refurbished and furnished by British funds through the DFID-Malawi Safety, Security, and Access to Justice (MaSSAJ) program and UNICEF, who are also funding the operations of the National Office. The office has recruited staff.

Three new Regional/District Forums (Blantyre, Lilongwe and Mzuzu) have been formed. Blantyre and Lilongwe have been launched and are now fully functional. The Regional/District Forums are headed by the Judiciary (a Magistrate) but co-ordinated by NGO partners. The Forums were formed and funded by UNICEF and they also receive support from the Danish Institute for Human Rights (DIHR).

All the Forums have held training sessions and awareness campaigns. They are also spreading to communities and establishing community committees. They have now been recognized, and children with problems are referred to them by the communities. The communities are slowly accepting that 'problem' children are not always police material.

Activities undertaken by the NJJF

Firstly, the NJJF, with the assistance of the American Bar Association (ABA), has produced draft Rules of Juvenile Procedure to create uniformity of approach and ensure that the constitutional rights of the child are protected. In addition to this, the NJJF has secured the authority of the Judiciary to have courts specializing in Juvenile Justice in the four Regional centers of Malawi. Twelve Magistrates will initially be trained to run these courts. This will reduce or hopefully remove the errors in procedure so far experienced. Further, the Malawi Police Service is compiling statistics on the arrest of children district by district. It is the intention of the NJJF to target districts with high arrest rates for specialization of courts.

With the collaboration of the Para-Legal Advisory Services (PAC), the NJJF has compiled comprehensive statistics on juveniles in custody, and juveniles convicted and sentenced to imprisonment contrary to the Children and Young Persons Act (CYPA). Also, in collaboration with the Board of Visitors established under the Children and Young Persons Act, funding has been secured from the British DFID-MaSSAJ Program to refurbish and furnish two dormitories at Mpemba Reformatory Centre to receive, assess and counsel juveniles who have been wrongfully convicted and sentenced to imprisonment. In collaboration with the Malawi National Council on Community Services (MNCCS), the NJJF is working to establish comprehensive rules and procedure for community service and diversion of juveniles. Diversion will be at pre-trial level; both at community and court level, and post-trial. In this regard, the NJJF has drafted Screening Guidelines for juveniles with a view to emphasizing diversion. The establishment of community committees is instrumental to the success of pre-trial diversion at community level.

In conjunction with the Ministry of Gender and Community Services, the NJJF is establishing a working committee that will develop further policy on juvenile justice under the direction of the National Council for Safety and Security, which is headed by the Vice President of Malawi. And finally, with the agreement of the Judiciary and donors, the NJJF has secured separate chambers from adults for trials of juveniles charged with homicide.

Although the National Forum will be launched after a trial period of two years, it has satisfactorily networked with other institutions and NGOs. A directory of institutions and NGOs dealing with juveniles will also be compiled and published.

OVERVIEW OF THE LILONGWE JUVENILE JUSTICE FORUM

The Lilongwe Juvenile Justice Forum (LJJF) was established as a result of recommendations made following a pilot project on juvenile justice that was implemented in the Zomba District, one of the urban centers of Malawi. The Zomba pilot project commenced in 2000 and ended in 2001. This part of the paper will focus on progress made since the establishment of the Lilongwe Juvenile Justice Forum.

Establishment of the LJJF

The forum was launched in Lilongwe in March 2002 with all the key stakeholders in support of the program. This was in line with the Government of Malawi's intention to support the establishment of Juvenile Justice Forums in all the cities of the country where the crime rate (largely due to urbanization) was generally high, including that of juvenile delinquency. Members of the LJJF are drawn from the stakeholders in the juvenile justice sector and include persons from such wide-ranging institutions as the police, social welfare programs, judiciary branch, prisons, NGOs, traditional leaders, religious leaders, the Malawi Human Rights Commission, the National Youth Council, and the Ministry of Education.

Objectives of the LJJF

The four main objectives of the LJJF are: (1) to attempt to provide a platform for exchange of information among the stakeholders regarding juvenile law and practice, (2) to contribute to improvements in the delivery of juvenile justice in Malawi, (3) to contribute to the realization of the standard minimum rules on juvenile justice, and (4) to improve the working relationship among the stakeholders.

Through such objectives, the forum will ensure adherence to Article 37(b) of the Convention on the Rights of the Child, which states that:

> No child shall be deprived of his/her liberty unlawfully or arbitrarily. The arrest, detention or imprisonment of a child shall be in conformity with the law and shall be used only as a measure of the last resort and for the shortest possible period of time.

The overall objective of the Forum is to contribute, through the establishment of a fair and humane juvenile justice system, to the protection of the rights of children in conflict with the law and to promote a culture of human rights in Malawi.

Structure

The LJJF is chaired by a judicial officer (Magistrate) and is co-ordinated by a Non-Governmental Organization (NGO) dealing with issues of children. Supporting the chair and co-ordinator is a core group of members who are responsible for planning, guiding and monitoring the implementation plan of forum activities. Table 16.1 illustrates the structure of the LJJF.

Table 16.1: Structure of the LJJF

Structure of the LJJF

Chairperson
(Judiciary)
Chief Resident Magistrate

Coordinator
(NGO)
CEYCA

Core Group
(Representatives from Institutions)
Judiciary, Police, Social Welfare, Prisons

| Members | Members | Members | Members | Members | Members |

Activities

During its launch, the LJJF developed an action plan which spelled out activities to be undertaken, and identified the institutions that would be responsible for undertaking these activities. The activities included the following:

Capacity building

This activity took the form of a workshop. It was intended to provide forum members with skills and knowledge about juvenile justice procedures so that they could return to their institutions and share those skills and knowledge.

Community sensitization, mobilization and formation of juvenile justice community monitoring committees

Members of the forum agreed to focus not only on children that have committed offences but also on the preventive aspects of crime. Members therefore decided that part of their program would be to mobilize the communities at both the local and city levels, the goal being to sensitize them and to form community monitoring committees on juvenile justice. These community committees were also meant to provide alternative, traditional means of dispute resolution for minor offences. The committees were there to provide civic education on crime prevention and generally to act as watchdogs in the communities. The committees would act as links between the forum and the community.

Forum meetings

Forum meetings were intended to provide a platform for discussion where the members would periodically come together and update each other on progress. The meetings were also meant to contribute towards enhancement of their working relationship. Problems to be faced by respective institutions were to be tabled at such forum meetings with a view to finding possible solutions. The meetings also provide the core group members with an opportunity to give progress reports.

Monitoring and prison visits

The purpose of the visits to prisons and other institutions was to enable forum members to periodically assess the cases and welfare of the young offenders in order to ensure proper intervention. It was noted that paralegal reports alone would not be sufficient.

Progress on the activities

So far, the forum has been able to sit for meetings and attended to some of the issues raised in the meetings. These issues have been in reference to the day-to-day experiences of respective institutions. A case in point is that police officers are continuing to handcuff young offenders on arrest and during trial at the court. The forum has been concerned with this practice and has tried to find out the reasons for its continuation contrary to legal requirements. Mostly, the police have been at pains to defend themselves, stating that children are 'slippery' to the extent of running away from the police officers, especially when not in handcuffs and as they go to court. It must be noted that police officers and the accused usually walk to court due to a shortage of transport.

With the training complete, there are now fewer allegations among various institutions that others are in the wrong, that they caused the delay of a juvenile's case or that they mishandled a case. The forum meetings have strengthened the relationships between the different institutions: they assist in identifying where the problems in the system are located and encourage the institutions to work together to attempt to rectify those problems.

Support structures, such as community monitoring committees relating to the preventive aspects of young offenders committing crimes, are still in the early stages of development. The committees have been able to provide the Forum Co-ordinator with reports regarding their community outreach initiatives. These have included the sensitization of village chiefs through meetings, the gathering of students and out-of-school youth, and several community sessions targeting various groups.

In terms of policy, the Chief Justice has recently directed the judiciary that juveniles be considered for placement in community service, depending on the nature of the offences committed. The system will work in a similar way to community service for adult offenders, the difference being the number of hours and type of work that may be given to young offenders. This direction came about upon recommendations being sent to the Judicial Service Commission for consideration following research in the area.

Key issues as identified by the LJJF

The LJJF has identified some vital issues as being in need of immediate attention, including the need for a change of 'Institutional Mindset' within the juvenile justice delivery institutions. This lends itself to lack of mental transformation of the Justice Officers. The 'Presumption of Guilt' of juveniles in conflict with the law is also a serious problem. Poor facilities, which lead to lack of separation of juveniles from adult inmates, present a danger to juvenile offenders. Finally, there are concerns about lengthy stays of juveniles in detention on remand awaiting trial, and poor qualifications of Juvenile Justice Officers.

Immediate challenges

Some immediate challenges facing the LJJF are as follows:

- **Resource constraints and inadequacies:** These threaten to kill the current juvenile justice initiative as the institutions are likely to become frustrated the longer this problem persists.
- **High staff turnover:** Those officers trained by the LJJF are frequently transferred to other districts, thereby necessitating continuous training for replacement officers.
- **Consolidation of the forum:** The forum is an effective platform for the sustenance of the project; however, it is not fully established in terms of strategic thinking for long-term impact.

A CASE STUDY OF THE LILONGWE JUVENILE JUSTICE FORUM

Background

With financial support from the DIHR(Danish Institute for Human Rights), the LJJF embarked on a project: *Advocating for the improvement of criminal justice system for juveniles in conflict with the law*. The project has three main focus areas: (1) capacity development of the juvenile justice institutions through training, (2) continuous research/monitoring and data collection on juvenile issues through monitoring, and (3) advocacy and lobbying for the improvement of juvenile justice. The project, which began in August 2002, is being implemented by two leading NGOs—the Centre for Youth and Children Affairs (CEYCA), and the Centre for Legal Assistance (CELA), with co-ordination and technical support from the Malawi Human Rights Resource Centre (MHRRC).

This particular case study will focus on the research and data collection component of the project (the monitoring exercise). The monitoring exercise began in September 2002 with the following objectives. First, to identify key stakeholders in the juvenile justice system; next, to measure knowledge and practice among the stakeholders; also to find out how different institutions handle and view juvenile offenders; to find out what actions are viewed as appropriate when different institutions discharge juvenile justice; and finally, to establish whether the Children and Young

Persons Act (CYPA) and the Convention on the Rights of the Child (CRC) are recognized and applied when discharging juvenile justice.

By early September, the monitoring exercise had made strides in fulfilling the first objective, having identified the following institutions as key stakeholders in the LJJF: police, prisons, courts, social welfare, the community, and civil society. The monitoring exercise was largely facilitated by a set of guiding tools (questionnaires) which were specifically designed to gather various information concerning juvenile offenders as well as the knowledge, practice and attitudes of various identified stakeholders. Apart from administering the questionnaires, the information was also gathered through continuous observation as well as perusal of official files and records. The information sought included the following: characteristics of juvenile offenders, roles of the various stakeholders, handling of juvenile cases, and relationships among the stakeholders as well as their limitations. A sample questionnaire targeting social welfare appears in the Appendix to this chapter.

Although the Lilongwe Forum has registered some positive developments, the case study below reveals a picture which demonstrates that the various stakeholders do not fully appreciate their role in juvenile justice; that there are persistent problems in the handling of juvenile cases; that there is a lack of communication between stakeholders; that the responsibilities are unclear among the stakeholders; and that the various stakeholders face limitations (particularly resource constraints) and lack adequate knowledge and training on their legal obligations and duties relating to juveniles. All of this prevents the stakeholders from carrying out their duties and delivering effective and efficient juvenile justice. Further, other stakeholders/duty bearers (such as traditional authorities, families, businesses, churches and NGOs) do not fully understand that they too have a role to play in the delivery of juvenile justice.

Childhood and characteristics of young offenders

A review of the Monitoring and Advocacy Reports of the LJJF for September and October 2002 suggests that the majority of young offenders are male and live in urban and peri-urban areas. Approximately 80% of them come from high-density areas, Kawale being a good example. Approximately 50% of these young offenders are street children coming from broken and low-income households. While some have both parents, there is a growing trend of children from single or female-headed households and indeed others who are orphans. There is also ample evidence to suggest that poverty and HIV/AIDS are the major contributing factors causing children from such homes to come into conflict with the law or commit crimes.

Most of the juveniles in the Kawale study are within the age range of 12–18 years, and the average age of young offenders is 15.

Statistics available from Kawale Police Station, a local police station, indicate that the most frequently committed offences by young offenders within Lilongwe are assaults, thefts and robbery, in order of decreasing frequency. However, statistics emanating from Lilongwe Police Station (a receiving and holding station for juveniles from all districts in the Central Region of Malawi) point to the fact that at the Central Region level, the most frequently committed offences are theft, burglary and robbery, in that order.

Pre-trial

While the law states that juveniles should not be handcuffed, throughout the monitoring period police officers were observed handcuffing juveniles. When asked why they were doing this, the frequent response was 'to prevent them from escaping'. While it may be the case that some of the officers were not aware of the international and domestic rule against handcuffing juveniles, it was also evident to the monitors that such attitudes and practices were a major problem for other officers, especially those who took part in recent training on juvenile justice provided by Centre for Youth and Children Affairs (CEYCA). However, issues of capacity also contribute to the problem. With the current police to population ratio of 1:1667[2] and officer/prisoner ratio of 1:14,[3] law enforcement officials find themselves—and were observed—escorting large numbers of prisoners (adults as well as juveniles) and are therefore compelled by such circumstances to handcuff all of them (Malawi Government 2002, 75). This is compounded by a lack of transportation, which means that officers often have to walk with prisoners to and from the court/prison/police station. As the penalty for 'allowing a prisoner to escape' is heavy, most officers would rather contravene the international and domestic rule against handcuffing juveniles than face the harsh sanctions for facilitating their escape.

While police officers try their best to separate juveniles from adults, they are often faced with the reality that there are no separate cells for juveniles. Consequently, some juveniles are kept at the OB Counter. Once juveniles are remanded to prison, both Maula and Kachere Prisons have separate cells for juveniles. The observed practice, however, is that juveniles are only

---

[2] The current Police to population ratio of 1:1667 is against an SADC regional standard of 1:500.

[3] The Warder to Prisoner ratio of 1:14 is against an international standard of 1:5.

separated from adults during the night when they are locked up; during the day, they are largely allowed to move freely within the prison.

Although police officers did often state that once a juvenile is arrested, they immediately inform probation/social welfare officers, probation officers often complained that they are not informed early enough for them to be able to play their role in the process. Prison officers confirmed this as they also complained that police officers rarely follow up on juveniles once they are committed to prison. At the same time, prison warders do not consider that they have a special mandate towards juveniles. Consequently, prison officers do not compile or keep separate information or submit returns to police, court or social welfare officials. The observation of the monitors was that since there were no specialized officers within the police, at the courts, or within social welfare and prisons to deal with juvenile matters, juveniles may often be 'lost' in the system. Further, it was quite apparent to the monitors that some law enforcement officials found cases of juveniles very involving and intimidating due to the strange and special regime of rules governing juvenile justice. It therefore does not come as a surprise that none of the police officers mentioned special handling and treatment of juveniles from the moment of arrest as part of their role as law enforcement officials.[4]

The monitors observed that juveniles are not provided with any food in police cells. The only food available has to be brought in by relatives and those with no relatives may end up with empty bellies unless they are given a share by their fellow inmates. For those who end up on prison remand, they have to make do with the monotonous diet of *Nsima* (maize meal) and beans which is taken once a day. Sanitation and ventilation in both police and prison cells were observed to fall well below minimum international standards.

The constitutional requirement for juveniles to be remanded for the shortest possible period is one that is often flouted. Statistics obtained from both Maula and Kachere Prisons indicated that most juveniles are often left on remand for too long, the majority staying for more than six months. During September 2002, there were approximately 54 juveniles at Maula Prison. Of these, 33 were being held on remand for homicide cases. Most had been held for so long that they were no longer children. One had been on remand for more than six years. Table 16.2 provides a picture of the numbers of juveniles held in Maula and Kachere Prisons during the six months between July and December 2002.

---

[4] Police officers mentioned their traditional roles of arresting offenders, investigating crime and temporarily detaining criminals.

Table 16.2: Number of juveniles in Maula and Kachere Prisons,
July to December 2002

	MAULA	KACHERE
JULY		
Juvenile Remand	31	15
Juvenile Remand Murder	37	0
Juvenile Convicted	82	0
AUGUST		
Juvenile Remand	30	11
Juvenile Remand Murder	37	0
Juvenile Convicted	86	0
SEPTEMBER		
Juvenile Remand	31	17
Juvenile Remand Murder	37	0
Juvenile Convicted	83	0
OCTOBER		
Juvenile Remand	27	12
Juvenile Remand Murder	37	0
Juvenile Convicted	88	0
NOVEMBER		
Juvenile Remand	21	14
Juvenile Remand Murder	37	0
Juvenile Convicted	85	0
DECEMBER		
Juvenile Remand	21	16
Juvenile Remand Murder	39	0
Juvenile Convicted	84	0

Trial

There are no specialized courts for juveniles at the Lilongwe Magistrates
Court. The reason advanced for this is that 'there are only very few juvenile
cases which are handled by Magistrates Courts'. When asked about delays
in handling juvenile cases, magistrates responded by saying that it is court
clerks and social welfare officers who are supposed to follow up on such
cases. However, court clerks attributed the blame to police officers and
magistrates, whom they said often renew remand warrants without the
involvement of court clerks, who are supposed to keep court records on them.

It would appear that there has been a gradual breakdown of co-ordination between court clerks and magistrates as a result of police officers dealing directly with magistrates, especially on renewal of remand warrants. While police officers pointed their fingers at social welfare officers for their delays in preparation and submission of court social reports to courts, social welfare officers blamed both the police and magistrates for taking centre stage in handling juvenile justice issues and only involving social welfare officers at a later stage in the process.

Despite the lack of specialized courts for juveniles, juvenile cases are handled *in camera* in the presence of the police, social welfare officers and parents or guardians. Only those juveniles jointly charged with adult offenders have their cases handled in open court.

Despite the law specifically prohibiting imprisonment unless it is a measure of last resort and then only for the shortest period possible, magistrates continue to pass fixed prison sentences on juveniles. Some of the sentences well exceed the set maximum periods for imprisonment, as evidenced by the prison files and records of some of the juveniles at Maula Prison. It would appear that the problem relates to the lack of training and specialization of non-professional magistrates in this field. The reluctance of prison authorities to check on such excesses and the demand that certain minimum standards be followed by all stakeholders also compounds the problem.

Although the Chief Justice has promulgated a special directive allowing magistrates to assign juveniles to community service, there are very few juveniles, if any at all, who benefit from such a provision within the Lilongwe area.

Post-trial

The researchers observed that convicted and remand juveniles at Maula and Kachere Prisons are not kept in separate cells, and they are only separated from adult prisoners during lock-up hours. Juvenile cells lack sufficient mats, which are used as mattresses. There is also insufficient bedding and the few blankets that are available are torn.

Both convicted and remand juveniles are given the same food as all other prisoners: maize meal with beans, which they take once a day. There is no special diet for juveniles requiring special meals.

There is very poor sanitation in the juvenile blocks at both Maula and Kachere Prisons due to a lack of disinfectants and cleaning materials. With the overcrowding situation, the prisons become fertile ground for diseases such as scabies.

It was observed that the only recreation activity available at either prison is football, and even this is only played once in a while when footballs are available. There is no formal education and training or rehabilitation program in place at either of the two prisons. The conditions observed by the monitors at both Maula and Kachere Prisons can hardly be described as 'taking into account [the juvenile's] age and the desirability of promoting his or her reintegration into society to assume a constructive role', as the Constitution requires (Malawi Constitution 1995, section 42(2)(g)(v)).

Relationship among stakeholders

Relationship between police, prisons, courts and social welfare

Although most of the respondents from the various institutions and stakeholders stated that their relationship with others in the juvenile justice arena was good or satisfactory, our observation is that this response is either (a) in line with a Malawian culture which avoids negative comments, or (b) due to low levels of knowledge or awareness of child rights/juvenile justice and their corresponding duties as duty bearers. The actual situation is that, on the one hand, the police complain that social welfare personnel are responsible for delays in juvenile processing due to delays in preparation and submission of court social reports and, on the other hand, that social welfare personnel perceive the police and courts to be the centre of juvenile justice and that social welfare plays a peripheral role. This indicates that much of the relationship is self-centred and therefore one-sided. There is generally a lack of communication among the juvenile justice stakeholders.

Although some of the institutions have taken certain initiatives to improve their relationship with other institutions, there is much left to be done. The Prisons Department is a case in point: after several visits by the Monitoring Team, staff at Kachere Prison have begun compiling statistics and returns on juveniles and providing the same to police, courts and social welfare. Our observation is that much as this may be the case, it is being done more by way of personal initiative and the commitment of individual prison staff rather than as an approach which follows any professional juvenile justice standards. This observation may be supported by the fact that the prison staff have not undergone any juvenile justice training.

Relationship between courts, police, prisons, social welfare and community/NGOs

Court, police, prison and social welfare officials described their relationship with NGOs and other civil society organizations as 'good', 'satisfactory', or 'just starting'. Certainly, such relationships are improving, especially with the presence of the LJJF as a meeting and discussion forum. However, it may be observed that the expectations of the communities in their demand for juvenile justice/child rights may not be properly conceived unless they are well informed and sensitized regarding the rights of the child. Attitudes of community members and some traditional authorities may offer some illustrations, such as the fact that juveniles are reported or handed over to the police with the expectation that the police will perform the role of parents or guardians (e.g. provide counselling sessions), or punish the juveniles. On the other hand, the police, courts, prisons and social welfare officials may not effectively deliver and discharge their roles as 'duty bearers' unless they too have the requisite knowledge and training in juvenile justice issues followed by a deliberate change in attitudes and practices regarding the manner in which juveniles are handled.

Limitations

All the juvenile justice institutions cited a number of limitations that impeded their effective delivery of juvenile justice. These limitations revolved around 'resources' and may be summed up as follows:

- Lack of stationery to record information properly;
- Poor and manual (as opposed to computerized) system of keeping juvenile records;
- Lack of transport to conduct visits to juvenile institutions, transfer juveniles from one institution to another, take juveniles to court, etc.;
- Lack of proper facilities to hold and properly care for juveniles;
- Lack of specially trained and specialized staff in juvenile justice matters.

However, the research team also observed that in addition to the limitations outlined above, there are generally low levels of morale and poor commitment to work on the part of most officials in all the key juvenile justice institutions (police, courts, prisons and social welfare). The Malawi Poverty Reduction Strategy Paper (MPRSP) has recognized this problem and formulated strategies to change and improve on what it calls 'political will' and 'mindsets' (Malawi Government 2002, 72–3). This may be attributed to poor salaries, lack of resources, and lack of training and knowledge. The research team would, however, wish to register its observation of the shared interest and willingness to learn in order to improve the delivery of juvenile justice among the stakeholders in the LJJF.

REFERENCES

Constitution of the Republic of Malawi (1995)
Laws of Malawi, *Children and Young Persons Act* (1969)

Lilongwe Juvenile Justice Forum (2002a) *Research Report on the Juvenile Justice Situation in Malawi: a Case Study of the Lilongwe Juvenile Justice Forum* (unpublished)

Lilongwe Juvenile Justice Forum (2002b) *Monitoring Reports* for the months of September, October, November and December (unpublished)

Malawi Government (2002) *Malawi Poverty Reduction Strategy Paper*

United Nations Convention on the Rights of the Child (1989)

APPENDIX

Sample Questionnaire Used by the Lilongwe Juvenile Justice Forum as a Checklist for Monitoring
(Note: there are other sets of questionnaires adapted for monitoring other institutions and stakeholders such as police, courts, prisons, NGOs, community, etc.)

SOCIAL WELFARE

1.0 **BIODATA OF THE INTERVIEWEE**
 1. Name:
 2. Positions: ....
 3. Stations: ....

2.0 **ROLES OF SOCIAL WELFARE.**
 1. What is the role of social welfare in-terms of juvenile justice delivery systems?
 ....
 ....
 ....

3.0 **HANDLING OF CASES**
 1. Do you receive juvenile offenders at your office?
 ....

 2. How many cases of juveniles per: week... month... year... do you receive?

 3. What is the common age range: 7–10 yrs.......... 11–14 yrs.......... 15–18 yrs..........

 4. Sex: Male.................................Female...........................

 5. Nature of cases: theft.........assault.........murder...........others.........
 6. What cases do you regard as the most common offences?
 ....
 ....
 ....

 7. What steps do you take when you receive a juvenile offender in your office?
 ....
 ....
 ....

8. What factors do you consider when determining the type of action/ recommendation which you may come up with when dealing with a juvenile offender?..
....
....
....
....

9. Do you have follow up programs on juveniles committed to a particular recommendation?
....
....
....
....

10. What do you know about the CYP Act and CRC? How do you apply them to your actions?
CYP Act...
CRC...
Application...
....

4.0 FAMILY

1. What is the common life history of the young offenders?
....
....

2. Do you contact their parents or guardians?
....

5.0 RELATIONSHIPS WITH OTHER STAKEHOLDERS:

3. What relationships exist between you and the:

4. Prisons..

5. Police...

6. Court..

7. NGOs..
8. Community...
9. Placement Institutions...
10. Families...

6.0 What factors may hinder your operations in delivering juvenile justice?
....
....

17

Combining Juvenile Justice with Family Law Reform in Serbia

IVANA STEVANOVIC

INTRODUCTION

EVEN THOUGH THE status of children in Serbia is directly contingent upon political, economic and societal circumstances, it also depends on attitudes toward children, and the understanding of what their rights should be. The patriarchal extended family still plays an exceptionally important role in Serbia and Montenegro—as the main provider of support and influence. These patriarchal characteristics are more visible and dominant in the south of the country. Attitudes toward women, therefore, and toward female children as well, are predominantly discriminatory, and, again, more so in the south of the country than in the north. One of the most prominent characteristics of the traditional approach toward children is the tendency to overprotect them, at least declaratively, undermining their right to participation, as well as their right to privacy and expression of thought and opinions.

Similar attitudes and practices are visible in the education, health and social care and protection systems, as well as in judicial bodies. Traditional attitudes are clearly held by the majority of those who are major political decision-makers and policy-creators. Of course, it would be unrealistic to expect different attitudes and treatment toward children in a country where even the most basic human rights are not yet accepted and adopted in society. The family situation—crucial for the proper development of every child—is very bleak. Most families in Serbia face a growing threat of poverty and an inability to maintain basic household standards. At the same time, the state cannot provide adequate help, not only because a growing number of families need help, but also because the state itself is extremely poor, and must use its limited budget for the basics—social security allocations, replenishing dilapidated pension funds—but also to support a gigantic administration, army and police.

Furthermore, children are not yet accepted in Serbia as holders of rights. Key principles regarding 'best interests', and a child's right to be listened to and to participate in decisions are not yet understood in society. Although the situation of children in Serbia is directly affected by political, economic and social circumstances, it is also conditioned by local attitudes to children themselves and their rights. One of the basic characteristics of the attitude towards children is over-protectiveness, at least in its verbal expression as the typical family structure in Serbia is patriarchal with the extended family playing an important role in provision of support and advice. Going from the north of the country southwards, the features of patriarchy are increasingly expressed and prevalent. This family structure with the extremely dominant *pater familias* directly influences attitudes to children and their rights to participation, privacy and expression of opinions. Attitudes to women and girls are often discriminatory, which is again more evident in the south of the country.

The consensus seems to be that many laws relating to children and their rights are ineffective, anachronous, and need modernizing in line with international legal documents and guidelines such as the Beijing Rules. Our politicians have a sinewy tendency to change parts of certain laws every time a switch in power occurs, while rarely creating new laws corresponding to international standards. For example, since the Law on Social Security of Citizens and Financial Protection of Families was adopted fourteen years ago, there have been nine laws amending and adding to its original text, which means that this particular law changed, on average, every seventeen months. Conversely, some laws remain unchanged for decades, in spite of being totally out of step with international conventions and treaties ratified by Serbia.

THE RIGHT OF THE CHILD IN THE JUVENILE JUSTICE SYSTEM IN SERBIA

As an extremely complex theme, juvenile justice encompasses the system and organization of the protection of rights for the most vulnerable groups of children: those exposed to abuse and neglect, those whose development is at risk due to family malfunction, and those in conflict with the law. With regard to new knowledge about the consequences of child abuse and etiological factors of delinquency, it is often possible to equate these groups of children.

The Convention on the Rights of the Child, along with other international documents, contains standards and norms indicating the obligations of the state and governmental bodies concerning the preservation of the family, legal protection of the child in family relations, and protection of the child from specific forms of violence in a wider social environment.

Complementary provisions of the Convention refer to the protection of rights of those children who breach certain norms of behavior.

Based on current knowledge regarding the legislation and experience in practice, it is possible to attempt a basic assessment of the level of compliance of Serbian family law and criminal law in this area with the principles and content of international documents as well as with the real needs and interests of children.

Legislation concerning child abuse and neglect is divided into three systems: social legislation, family law, and criminal law, which prescribe various legal measures for prevention and the protection of children from abuse. The situation of children who are in conflict with the law is generally based on principles contained in the above-mentioned international documents. However, implementation of this model has many shortcomings and contradictions.

According to the Statistics Institute of the Republic of Serbia, juvenile delinquency rates stagnated in 2004, as evidenced by the number of motions filed for criminal prosecution of juveniles. For various reasons, however, these statistics must be taken with a pinch of salt. Data indicate that crimes against life and bodily harm increased. Juveniles are most frequently sentenced to probationary/socialization measures, while incarceration remains rare. However, there are no set follow-up methods for youth sentenced to increased supervision or other probationary measures, resulting in their ineffectiveness.

According to current criminal legislation in Serbia, juvenile delinquents can be sentenced to: educational measures, juvenile prison (1 to 10 years) and safety measures. Criminal legislation differentiates two categories of juvenile delinquents: younger minors (14 to 16 years of age) and older minors (16 to 18 years of age). Persons under the age of 14 are not considered criminally liable and cannot be subject to criminal proceedings or criminal sanctions.

Educational measures, as a type of criminal sanction, are established as basic criminal sanctions that can be inflicted on these persons. The penalty of juvenile prison, which can be inflicted under certain conditions on juveniles aged between 16 and 18, is a criminal sanction that is imposed only in exceptional cases, when the legal conditions have been cumulatively fulfilled. Even then, it is imposed only if the court finds that it is the only possible way of reacting to the concrete criminal act perpetrated by an older minor.

Educational measures are grouped into three basic categories according to severity: disciplinary educational measures, educational measures of strong supervision, and institutional educational measures. Juvenile delinquents can be sentenced to all the same safety measures as adults, except those concerning prohibition from performing a profession, duty or work. In addition, safety measures of mandatory treatment of alcoholism and drug addiction may be imposed on them only in special circumstances. This system of criminal sanctions dates from 1959 and requires substantial revisions. Professionals in practice regard the system of criminal sanctions as inefficient, inadequate and obsolete. A reform of criminal proceedings against juveniles is also necessary in the sense of improving institutional and organizational solutions. In this area, so far, only partial specialization has been achieved. On the other hand, the model of social protection in criminal juvenile justice is criticized by the contemporary concept of child rights. Bearing this in mind, in 2001, the Belgrade Child Rights Centre, with the support of the Danish Institute for Human Rights, set up the project *Legal Reform in the Area of Juvenile Justice in Serbia*. The Ministry of Justice realized the need for legislative reform in the system of juvenile justice. A proposal for a new Law on Juvenile Justice was made in 2004. This proposal comprehensively defines the responsibility and status of minors who commit a criminal act, legal proceedings, and the sanctions that can be applied. It also contains articles pertaining to the protection of children who are victims of crimes, or witnesses in criminal proceedings. Juveniles are separated from the adult criminal justice system and all matters relating to minors in conflict with the law are addressed by one comprehensive law. The Serbian Assembly adopted the new Juvenile Justice Law in September 2005. The New Law being implemented the 1st of January 2006.

THE PROCESS OF PROJECT IMPLEMENTATION

Implementation of the project *Legal Reform in the Area of Juvenile Justice in the Republic of Serbia* began on 1 June 2001. In the first month—the preparatory phase of the project—the following activities were completed: organization of two groups of experts, establishment of contacts with the relevant ministries—the Federal Ministry of Justice, the Ministry of Justice of the Republic of Serbia and the Ministry of Social Affairs of the Republic of Serbia—who were informed on the project, and preparations concerning the acquisition of relevant foreign laws and publications in this field, to be used at a later stage of the project—the comparative analysis.

The research phase started with an analysis of the relevant legislation in Serbia, both family and criminal law (substantive and procedural law), from the viewpoint of international standards on child rights. Also analyzed were models of juvenile justice in comparative legal systems (national legislations of Croatia, Slovenia, Republika Srpska, Federation of Bosnia and Herzegovina, Macedonia, as well as Norway, Denmark, England, Wales, Germany, Belgium, Hungary, Scotland and the practice of the European Court in Strasbourg). Two study visits were undertaken—to Norway and to

Croatia—with the aim of studying best practices in this field. These countries were selected as representatives of Western Europe and as the regions with juvenile justice systems serving as good examples.

Within the research part of the project, one of the planned activities was a survey of the viewpoints of professionals and of their views on possible future directions for legal reform. Bearing in mind the experiences from practice, which indicate deficiencies and inadequacies in some legal solutions that diminish the efficacy of the protection of rights, we reached the conclusion that it was necessary to obtain the viewpoints of professionals, and insights into practice and problems in the implementation of the current regulations, as well as to obtain proposals for possible amendments.

Therefore, the aim of the research was to discover the views of professionals working on the implementation of regulations in the domain of family and criminal law and related to juveniles more specifically on current practice, on some contemporary concepts and legal solutions in comparative law, and on the possible and necessary changes to be made in this field in order to comply with the conditions and capacities of our country.

Two working groups—dealing with criminal law and family law respectively—began their activities on 1 October 2001. In October and November they worked on defining legal models of protection in line with international standards and basic characteristics of our legal tradition, as well as on defining the basic theses of the legal projects. The result of their work was the Policy Proposal, a document submitted to the relevant ministries in the Republic of Serbia at the beginning of November 2001.

In the following five months, the working groups focused on defining the final version of legal models for the protection of child rights in the legal system, in compliance with international standards and contemporary scientific knowledge, as well as the needs and specifics of practice.

With regard to assessment of priorities, the work focused on the following areas:

(1)   *Criminal legislation in relation to the criminal-legal treatment of juvenile offenders:* criminal responsibility, proceedings enabling diversion from the classic criminal-legal procedure, the system of criminal sanctions, the criminal process, organization of the judiciary.

(2)   *Protection of abused children in criminal law:* criminal liability of adults with regard to acts of violence against children, rules of criminal proceedings and organization of the legal system.

(3)   *Protection of child rights in family relations:* child rights and forms of violation of their rights, ways of ensuring the 'best interests of the child', the child's participation in the exercise of his/her rights, organization of the judiciary and specialization of the procedure, proceedings for the protection of rights.

By working on these issues in the domain of criminal law, the working group defined the model pertaining to (1) the rights of juveniles in conflict with the law, and (2) the right of the child to protection from abuse and neglect.

The criminal-legal working group of the Belgrade Child Rights Centre created the Draft Law on Juvenile Justice, basing its work on contemporary concepts of the system of juvenile justice, on international documents on human rights and child rights, on the latest solutions in comparative law, and on practical experience and local legal tradition.

Although the project proposal planned the lobbying phase for the adoption of the new model in May 2002 (the end of the project), bearing in mind that lobbying is a long process, the members of the Child Rights Centre team started the activities from the very beginning, i.e. when the project was accepted by the DCHR.

From our very first contact with the relevant ministries and the beginning of project implementation, to the Policy Proposal, which was submitted at the beginning of November 2001, up to the final submission of the Draft and its explanation, we were in direct contact with the governmental bodies responsible for the field that was the subject of our activities. It is important to emphasize that the Ministry of Justice of the Republic of Serbia and the Ministry of Social Affairs of the Republic of Serbia, through their representatives, participated directly in both working groups.

In the course of our work on the project, the Government of the Republic of Serbia established the Council for Child Rights (*Savet za prava deteta Vlade Republike Srbije*), an advisory governmental body for these issues. We presented the results of our year-long work to this Council in order to gain their support for our mission.

The draft model law on justice for the young brought together the provisions of criminal legislation, both substantive and procedural. The novelty of the proposed model lies in the fact that it requires juvenile judges to be specialized, a requirement also set for the state prosecutor, attorneys and the police. The model requires all of these to acquire special expertise in the field of child rights and juvenile delinquency. The reason for this is the fact that all normative interventions, even if the best laws and regulations are created, cannot have even a modest effect, let alone full effect, unless this is accompanied by the development of high-quality professionals. This has prompted us to refer to the well-known saying: 'All laws are worth as much as the people called upon to apply them.' In this regard, and in order to ensure the acquisition of professional expertise in the field of child rights and juvenile delinquency, the transitional provisions that should form part of this piece of legislation (in case it is adopted) should stipulate the obligation on the part of the Ministry of Justice of the Republic of Serbia and the Supreme Court of the Republic of Serbia to oversee the advanced training of personnel working in this field by arranging scientific and professional consultations, seminars and other forms of additional professional training.

In regulating the legislative response of society to crime among minors, the draft law on justice for the young proceeds from the principle of the subsidiary nature of sanctions—preferring out-of-court forms of intervention. The model expands the possibility of applying diversion procedures and non-custodial measures. In this manner, it provides for diversion from the conventional criminal procedure and for defining the rights of minors relative to their entry into the diversion procedure. In selecting a sanction, the model gives maximum emphasis to the principle of education rather than punishment. It points out that the purpose of criminal sanctions against minors is to influence their development, through supervision, by giving protection and assistance as well as by providing general and vocational education and training, to make them feel more personally responsible and to positively affect their education and the proper development of their personality.

The educational measures stipulated by the model are the following: warning measures (court reprimand and special obligations); reinforced supervision measures (reinforced supervision by the parent, adoptive parent or guardian); reinforced supervision in another family; reinforced supervision by the guardianship authority; reinforced supervision with day care at an appropriate institution for education of minors; and institutionalized educational measures (referral to a correctional institution, referral to a reformatory, and referral to a special institution for treatment or training).

The most important novelty in the field of substantive law envisaged by the model is the possibility of a special obligation being imposed as an autonomous educational measure. However, this educational measure may be pronounced together with the educational measures of reinforced supervision.

These types of sanctions are often, in the professional literature, called alternative sanctions because their main aim is either to demand that the minor—by appealing to him to show personal responsibility and actively co-operate—fulfils a certain obligation or to impose a certain prohibition against him. The model enumerates ten special obligations item by item, giving the court the authority to pronounce one or several such obligations dovetailed to suit the minor's personality and his living conditions. In order for these special obligations to be able to serve their purpose, they must be strictly individualized but, on the other hand, they may entail the full individualization also of criminal sanctions against juvenile delinquents. Likewise, it is very important to bear in mind that they should never be imposed as an additional disciplinary measure whose purpose it is to additionally burden the minor with particular duties, orders or prohibitions.

In addition to the special obligation, as a novel educational measure, the model introduces into the register of educational measures another such measure: reinforced supervision with daily care at an appropriate institution for the education of minors. The introduction of this measure is in line with modern trends, by introducing new semi-institutionalised forms of education for minors with larger or smaller behavioural disorders, to avoid their total removal from their living environment.

As for the procedural substance, the model proceeds from the redefined social-protective model which has been predominant in this field so far. Its aim is to better protect the basic human rights of the minor in the proceedings that concern him, namely: urgency of proceedings with specifically defined terms; redefinition of the provisions on detention in order to more fully define this measure as the ultimate and extraordinary tool; proportionality between the offence and the sanction (Obretković 1996, 136–63; Freeman 1983, 86–92).

Criminal proceedings against minors are instituted only at the request of the State Prosecutor for Minors. The model proposes that in the event that the State Prosecutor for Minors fails to make a request for proceedings against the minor to be initiated, he shall be obliged to inform the aggrieved party accordingly within eight days. The aggrieved party may not institute a criminal prosecution but has the right to demand, within eight days of the date of receipt of notification from the State Prosecutor for Minors, and if he has not been informed then within three months as of the date of rejection of the criminal complaint, that the issue of initiation of proceedings be decided upon by the juvenile chamber of a higher court. If the juvenile chamber of a higher court decides that the proceedings should be initiated or continued, the State Prosecutor for Minors must participate in these proceedings and has all the powers that belong to him under the draft.

The model highlights the role played by the Guardianship Authority in these proceedings.[1] Indeed, the State Prosecutor for Minors has to notify the Guardianship Authority of any initiated proceedings against a minor and if he fails to do so, this will be done by the juvenile judge while the failure will be brought to the attention of the Higher State Prosecutor for Minors.

In the creation of this legal model, the members of the working group were guided particularly by the need to make the national legislation comply with the Convention on the Rights of the Child—in particular with its Articles 37 and 40—in the sense of creating the legislation, procedures, bodies and institutions that specifically deal with children alleged as, accused of, or recognized as having infringed the criminal law (Art. 40, para. 3 of the Convention on the Rights of the Child). In relation to that, we were guided by recommendations of the United Nations and the European

[1] In the proceedings against a minor, the centre for social work as a guardianship authority has the right to be acquainted with the course of the proceedings as well as to make proposals in their course and point to the facts and evidence of relevance to the adoption of a correct decision.

Council contained in: the UN Standard Minimum Rules for the Administration of Juvenile Justice 1985 (Beijing Rules), UN Guidelines for the Prevention of Juvenile Delinquency 1990 (Riyadh Guidelines), UN Rules for the Protection of Juveniles Deprived of their Liberty 1990 (Havana Rules), UN Standard Minimum Rules for Alternative Penal Measures 1990 (Tokyo Rules), and European Rules on Social Sanctions and Measures 1992 (CER(92)16); for more detail see Vučković Šahović 2000, 145–9, 254–9; Krech 1997.

Also considered in the creation of the model were contemporary European laws. In that sense, we consulted the following legislation: English, German, Belgian, French, Austrian, Norwegian, as well as the current solutions in this domain in the former Yugoslav countries. We also consulted professional literature (Mehlbye and Walgrave 1998; Jensen 1996) as well as research results (among others, the survey carried out for the purpose of the project on the professionals' views in this domain).

After the year-long work on the project, the Draft Law on Juvenile Justice was completed. In order to stress the importance of the criminal-legal position of juveniles and younger adults, it contains both substantive and procedural criminal-legal provisions in one act. Such a solution we considered logical and justified, and functionally connected with the need for the special protection of juveniles, whether they are offenders or victims.

Of course, this included a proposal for amendments and supplements to the existing substantive criminal legislation. In that sense, the legislative bodies were presented with the new and redefined specific incriminations contained in substantive criminal law, with the clear definition of crimes.

The model for the protection of child rights in family relations required the construction of some new solutions in the domain of substantive and procedural law, which would make the position of the child as a subject of family relations comply with international standards and which would produce more comprehensive and efficient protection of his/her rights in the legal system. Although the project focused on the protection of children from abuse and neglect, this part, concerned with family law, was necessarily supplemented by material concerning the definition of child rights in family relations and the ability of the juvenile to exercise his/her rights, parental responsibility and ways of exercising parental responsibilities and rights, as well as the grounds and criteria for the intervention of the state in these relations. Therefore, the draft of normative solutions included some elements of substantive family law in parent-child relations, procedural stipulations with regard to the organization and composition of a specialized family judiciary, and specific court proceedings for the protection of child rights. It should be emphasized that the model is limited to the protection of personal rights of the child to health and development, endangered or violated by parents. In that sense, we did not include the status rights of the child in family relations, or the right to be maintained. This was due to the primary focus of the project on the protection of the child from family violence. Supplements were imposed by the need to place this protection in a broader framework, which defines the legal status of the child and the parent.

The model is primarily based on the concept of child rights contained in the Convention on the Rights of the Child and the European Convention on the Exercise of Child Rights, as well as other international human rights documents. In its creation, we consulted the solutions from comparative legal systems, particularly of the countries that had adopted modern standards of legal protection of child rights and family relations. Thus, we considered the legislations of Norway, the U.K., Germany, Denmark and Hungary, as well as Croatia and Slovenia, with which we share legal traditions.

The working groups (criminal-legal and family-legal) organized professional discussions in which they presented the results of the survey, the Draft Law on Juvenile Justice, the proposed amendments and supplements to the substantive criminal law (in the part concerning incrimination in which the child is the victim) and the Draft Family Law (in parts concerning parent-child relations, with corresponding procedural regulations). This constituted the first phase of the project.

The second phase began upon completion of the first, in August 2002. It ended in February 2003. In phase two the CRC working group undertook two important activities:

(1)   Writing up a business plan for the administration of juvenile justice, which would serve as a guideline for mainstreaming juvenile justice into the justice sector reform program.

(2)   Linking up with relevant working groups to provide advice on how to incorporate the area of the administration of juvenile justice into the justice sector in question.

The second group of activities in this phase focused on the CRC working group liaising with other relevant working groups addressing reform of the justice system, as well as on including the issue of the establishment of the juvenile justice system in the justice system of the Republic of Serbia. This involved liaising with the working group for the system of courts organised as part of the Danish Centre for Human Rights project in Belgrade. In meetings with experts of this group it was agreed that the proposed solutions of the Child Rights Centre would be included in their activities, in the sense of the competence and composition of courts in the proposed establishment of the juvenile justice system in the Republic of Serbia.

It is important to emphasise that throughout the second phase of the project, presentation of the Model to the relevant subjects (seminars, conferences and in the media) as well as lobbying for its adoption was continuous. In November 2002, we had the opportunity to present the Model at the annual gathering of the Supreme Court of Serbia to all judges for juveniles in Serbia. At the round table organised during this event, we had the opportunity once again to emphasize the necessity and urgency of the proposed legal changes in this domain. The family law draft was also presented at the same event and a discussion followed on the problems that the justice system is facing in this domain, particularly in relation to the issue of specialization.

Another important issue should be emphasized here—the problems that were encountered in the realisation of this phase. After the final versions were submitted to the Ministry of Justice of the Republic of Serbia, which was directly involved in the implementation of the first phase of the project through its representatives in working groups, the Ministry provided neither a positive nor a negative response to the initiative of the Child Rights Centre. Consequently, all our lobbying activities were redirected to the Council for the Rights of the Child of the Republic of Serbia, some members of the Government of the Republic of Serbia and the Prime Minister.

In December 2002 our efforts were rewarded—we were invited to present and explain the Model to the Council for the Rights of the Child. As a result, the Council supported the Model and sent out a request to all competent ministries of the Republic of Serbia for active involvement, with special emphasis on the High Council for the Reform of the Justice System of the Republic of Serbia (the Model is presented on the official website of the Republic of Serbia).

It is also important to stress that the UNICEF Belgrade Office participated very actively in all these activities and that they strongly support the Model.[2]

THE MODEL OF THE CHILD RIGHTS PROTECTION IN FAMILY RELATIONS

A model for the protection of child rights in family relations implies the design of some new arrangements in the field of substantial and procedural law, whereby the child's legal position, as a subject in family relations, is harmonized with the international legal standards, which produces a more comprehensive and efficient protection of his/her rights within the judicial system.

Basic approach

The novelties of the proposed model are based on modern theoretical concepts of family-legal relations, on international human rights and child

---

[2] We need to emphasize, though, that during the organization of round tables and public debates of this Model Law the following was pointed out: the need to modify certain things and the need to introduce into the text of this legal act a section on execution of criminal sanctions on children in conflict with the law. UNICEF Belgrade Office supports these activities.

rights instruments, and on practical experience. The key concepts used in drafting this model were the concept of child rights and the concept of parental responsibility. In that regard the structure of the model and the order of its provisions were changed. The basic premises for defining this model were the following:

(1)　The rights of the child have been formulated as special rights, separate from the parents' rights, with corresponding legal requirements regarding parents and state institutions.

(2)　Parental responsibility towards children should be joint and it implies active exercise of parental rights and duties.

(3)　The child's right to family life is essentially conditioned by the family's integrity and is secured through appropriate social support to parents.

(4)　The family's autonomy presupposes strictly limited intervention on the part of the state based on detailed legal requirements and conditioned by the principle of the child's 'best interests' or well-being.

The procedural operationalization of the new model of family-legal relations calls for changes to be made in the sphere of organizational and functional procedural family law. The basic premises of the proposed arrangements derive from the need to ensure lawful, effective and economical legal protection, to adapt the procedure as much as possible to suit the characteristics of the legal matter at hand, and to enable the child, as well as other family members, to have full procedural competence in all proceedings in which their rights are being decided.

Proceeding from the fact that 'law suits' in the field of parent-child relations are among the most complex legal matters and that there is an evident need for the courts to become specialized, the Draft proposes that a specialized chamber should conduct proceedings in these legal matters. Such a chamber would be set up in both first- and second-instance courts. Specialization would be achieved by appointing professionals, specifically educated in family relations, as judges in trial chambers. As for lay judges, they would have expertise and experience in family problems.

General procedural rules also envisage a much more concrete principle of urgency of proceedings, which is essential in all matters pertaining to the protection of the child's rights and ensuring his/her well-being. Since proclamation of the principle of urgency alone does not ensure the required practical expediency of proceedings, as evidenced by previous practice, it has been proposed to give this procedural principle a more concrete form. This could be achieved by prescribing a short term for scheduling the first hearing in the first-instance proceedings and a term for reaching a decision in second-instance proceedings.

One of the basic novelties of this Draft is a totally new concept of the child's procedural position and the legal representation of his/her rights in court proceedings. Bearing in mind the fact that the child's rights in matters of parent-child relations are directly affected in each of the special court proceedings, the child has been granted the status of a party to the proceedings. Proceeding from the fact that the child's interests cannot be automatically identified with the interests of his/her parents, or his/her legal representatives, or, for that matter, the interests of the state, whose representative is the guardianship authority, it has been proposed to prescribe a possibility for the court to appoint, *ex officio*, a special counsel for the child as the independent legal representative of the child's rights.

General provisions envisage the special representative's authority, created after the example of modern arrangements contained in comparative law and international instruments (the Convention on the Rights of the Child and the European Convention on the Exercise of Children's Rights). For the purpose of protecting the child and implementing his/her rights, the child's special representative shall have a duty, in addition to taking actions during the proceedings, to provide the child with all relevant information and explanations regarding the legal matter at hand and to explain to the child the meaning, objective and consequences of procedural actions before taking them, in a way suitable for his/her age and development level, except when it is contrary to the child's well-being. The special representative will also be obliged to assist the child in expressing his/her views and opinions, to explain to him/her the consequences that could arise in case his/her opinion is accepted, and to inform the court of the child's opinion.

In order to make the modern concept of the child's rights operational and ensure full procedural competence in proceedings for the child whose rights are being decided upon, the Draft proposes that a provision be made for the court to have the duty to enable the child, in accordance with his/her age and development level, to receive all relevant information on the proceedings and legal matter at hand; to be consulted and to express his/her opinion; to be informed of the consequences that could arise from the acceptance of his/her opinion; as well as the possible consequences of the court's ruling. In line with this aim, the court should be able to appoint a special service or person that will supply the child with relevant information, consult him/her, find out his/her opinion, assist the child to express his/her views and report to the court thereon. This would create real conditions for the child, as a party to the proceedings, to implement his/her right to be informed and to express his/her own opinion in the course of proceedings. It should also be necessary to envisage the court's duty to conduct an interview with the child, without the presence of third persons, in a place and way suitable for the child's age and evolving capacities.

Specific approach

In the new Juvenile Justice Model, in the area of family law reform the position of the child who is under the age of criminal responsibility (under 14 years), according to the proposed Draft Family Law, underwent a change.

According to the proposed Draft law, fairly detailed criteria have been set for the implementation of the child's compulsory referral to an appropriate institution or another family.[3] This measure is to be implemented if the child demonstrates a certain level of social deviation, which necessitates special education and the child's removal from its immediate living environment. Since this measure is of a repressive character and entails the child's separation from his/her parents, it is proposed that the existing competence of the guardianship authority be replaced by that of a court in non-contentious proceedings. The duration of the measure is limited, but the measure may be extended or the selected measure may be replaced with another protective one. The court may institute proceedings either in the line of duty (*ex officio*) or at the request of the Guardianship Authority, a parent or the person entrusted with the child's care. Just as with respect to the decision to temporarily suspend the parent's right to actual custody of the child, in this case, too, the guardianship authority will make the decision on the child's referral on the basis of the court's ruling.

The new Family Law was passed in 2004—this delineates many procedural solutions that respect and recognize the various needs of the child, provide for more adequate addressing of those needs, and ensure the child's active participation in accordance with his/her developmental levels and abilities. The State should develop the mechanisms for its enforcement, implementation, monitoring and evaluation.

---

[3]Article 43: 'The court may decide in non-contentious proceedings to place the child in a social care or educational institution or with another family under the following conditions:

1. when the child demonstrates social deviations;
2. when the level of that deviation necessitates special educational forms; and
3. when the child needs to be removed from his/her immediate living environment.

No decision on referral to an institution or another family may be imposed in respect of a child who has turned 16 years of age.

The court may institute the decision-making procedure from paragraph 1 hereof, ex officio or at the proposal of the guardianship authority, a parent, a guardian or a person entrusted with the child's care.

By its decision from paragraph 1 hereof, the court shall specify the duration of this measure which may be imposed for one year at maximum. Prior to the expiry of the period specified by the decision, the court may either ex officio or at the proposal of the guardianship authority, the child or a parent prolong the duration of this measure or pronounce another measure for the protection of the child's right.

On the basis of the court's decision as set out in paragraph 1 hereof, the guardianship authority shall bring a decision on the child's referral to an adequate institution or his/her placement with another family.

The Ministry of Labour, Employment and Social Policy project *Integrated Reform of the Social Protection System* produced documents outlining specific, concrete steps to be taken in reforming the social protection system, specifically: creation of new standards of work in centres for social work, transformation of residential institutions, integrated social protection on the local level, development of foster care systems and improvement of the system of adoption, and the protection of children against abuse and neglect.

CONCLUDING REMARKS

Reform of the legislation in the above-stated areas represents only the first step in improving the legal protection of child rights. An integral approach in the realization of these rights requires a systematic development of the legal, institutional and methodological bases of the matter, both in justice and social care, police and other services participating in the process of protection. In that sense it is necessary to comply and complement the regulations on social care, practice of law, execution of criminal sanctions, internal affairs service, etc. However, a reform of the legal system can only achieve the expected results if relevant standards of professional work are developed simultaneously and if staff working on its implementation are continuously educated.

REFERENCES

Freeman, M.D.A. (1983) *The Rights and Wrongs of Children.* (London, Frances Pinter).

Jensen, M.F. (1996) *Alternative Approaches to Juvenile Delinquency.* (Copenhagen, Association of Danish Lawyers and Economists).

Krech, R. (1997) 'Implementation of UN Juvenile Justice Instruments'. In Verhellen, E. (ed.), *Understanding Children's Rights.* (Belgium, University of Ghent).

Mehlbye, J. and Walgrave, L. (eds.) (1998) *Confronting Youth in Europe: Juvenile Crime and Juvenile Justice.* (Copenhagen, AKF Forlaget).

Obretković, M. (1996) 'The Rights of Equal Treatment in the Legal System'. In Janjić Komar, M, Obretković, M., *Prava deteta prava čoveka.* (Beograd, Dosije).

Vučković Šahović, N. (2000) *Rights of the Child and International Law.* (Beograd, Centar za prava deteta).

18

The Inherent Tension of Social Welfare and Criminal Social Control: Policy Lessons from the American Juvenile Court Experience

BARRY C. FELD

E VERY SOCIETY CONFRONTS similar problems when childhood and criminality intersect. How should we respond when a child is a criminal and a criminal is a child? How should we balance youth policy and crime policy? In American juvenile courts, a tension has always existed between social welfare and social control—between rehabilitating the young offender and punishing her for the offence, between safeguarding children and protecting society (Feld 1999a; McCord 2001). Resolving these tensions entails a choice between policies of paternalism and protectionism or liberation and autonomy. How should the legal system treat the criminal conduct of adolescents compared with that of adults? In part, the answers reflect broader social structural processes, political economic arrangements, media depictions and public perceptions of youth, the politics of crime, and other legal policies that affect the conditions under which young people develop and attain adulthood.

American juvenile courts focus primarily on youths' criminal behaviour and replicate many characteristics of the adult criminal justice system. The juvenile court's criminal law foundations and its relationship to the adult criminal justice system implicate issues of both youth policy and crime policy and raise questions about its basic purposes (Zimring 1998). Is the juvenile court's primary purpose to function as a rehabilitative social welfare system and to intervene and change young peoples' lives? In the alternative, is its main function simply to divert youth from and to serve as a barrier against the life-harming sanctions of the criminal justice system (Zimring 2000a)? Should the juvenile court function as a modified criminal justice system, but one which recognizes young offenders' reduced competency and diminished responsibility, and which provides additional procedural safeguards and mitigates the harshness of penalties?

During the past three decades in the United States, the public and politicians have perceived a frightening increase in youth crime and violence. Many people question juvenile courts' ability to rehabilitate violent young offenders and, simultaneously, to protect public safety. Sensational media depictions of young criminals as a different breed of 'super-predators' further heightened public anxiety and fanned a 'moral panic' (Feld 2003). A politically popular desire to 'get tough' has provided the impetus to transfer more youths to criminal courts for prosecution as adults and to increase the severity of sentences juvenile courts impose on delinquents. Such a shift has repudiated traditional assumptions of childhood blamelessness, disregarded adolescent immaturity, and punished youths as the moral equals of adults (Scott and Steinberg 2003).

Since 1967, judicial decisions, legislative amendments, and administrative changes have transformed the juvenile court from a nominally rehabilitative social welfare agency into a scaled-down, second-class criminal court that provides young offenders with neither therapy nor justice (Feld 1993a; 1999a). This transformation occurred because of the migration of African-Americans from the rural South to the urban North that began three-quarters of a century ago, the macro-structural transformation of American cities and the economy over the past quarter of a century, and the current linkages in the media, popular and political culture between race and serious youth crime (Feld 1999b; 2003).

Two competing cultural and legal conceptions of young people have facilitated this transformation. On the one hand, law and culture view young people as innocent, vulnerable, fragile, and dependent *children* whom their parents and the state should protect and nurture. On the other hand, law and culture perceive young people as vigorous, autonomous and responsible almost *adult-like* people from whose criminal behavior the public needs protection. Policy makers selectively manipulate these competing social constructs of *innocence* and *responsibility* to maximize the social control of young people (Scott 2000). Most states' juvenile justice systems provide neither special procedures to protect juveniles from their own immaturity nor the full panoply of adult procedural rights. Instead, they treat delinquents like adult criminal defendants when formal equality redounds to their disadvantage and use less-adequate juvenile procedures when those deficient practices provide a comparative advantage to the state.

For the past three decades, states' juvenile law reforms have used the competing imagery of *immaturity* and *responsibility* to engage in a process of 'criminological triage'. At the 'soft end' of juvenile courts' jurisdiction, reforms have shifted non-criminal status offenders out of the juvenile justice system into a 'hidden system' of social control in the private-sector mental health and chemical dependency industries. At the 'hard end', states transfer larger numbers of youths into the criminal justice system for prosecution as adults with no formal recognition of youthfulness as a mitigating factor. In the 'middle', juvenile courts increasingly punish those delinquents who remain within a more criminalized juvenile system.

The first part of this chapter describes the transformation of the juvenile court from a social welfare agency into a deficient criminal court over the past three decades. It analyzes broader macro-structural, legal and political forces that have abetted the transition to a more punitive juvenile system. Although juvenile courts attempt to combine social welfare and penal social control in one agency, these goals embody inherent contradictions. Juvenile courts do both badly and subordinate the former to the latter because their primary mission is crime control. By the late twentieth century, the American juvenile court failed to provide child welfare, failed to protect society, discredited the idea of rehabilitation, and undermined the image of the child-offender as innocent and blameless (Scott 2000). If crime control, rather than social welfare, is the main reason that juvenile courts intervene in young offenders' lives, then we need a different justification for a separate juvenile justice system. Although recent research in adolescent developmental psychology provides a strong foundation for constructing an age-appropriate justice system, policy makers have not sufficiently availed themselves of this information.

The next part analyzes developmental psychological research on adolescent competence and culpability. It extracts from those insights a rationale for an age-appropriate justice system for younger offenders. A justice system for young offenders must take cognizance of developmental differences in youths' competence and criminal responsibility. Research on adolescent competence suggests that youths should receive greater procedural protections than they currently receive in either the juvenile or criminal justice systems. Culpability entails a normative judgment about the degree of deserved punishment for making blameworthy choices (Feld 2004). Psychological research, criminal jurisprudence, and sentencing policy provide a rationale formally to recognize youthfulness as a mitigating factor when judges sentence young offenders in either a juvenile or criminal justice system. And, as a political matter, only a separate justice system can fully recognize differences in youths' competence and culpability, provide more youth-sensitive procedural rights and more humane sanctions, and insulate adolescents from the harshness of the criminal justice system.

THE JUVENILE COURT

The juvenile court is the by-product of changes in two cultural ideas that accompanied modernization and industrialization a century ago: *childhood* and *social control*. The shift from an agricultural to an urban industrial society and the separation of work from the home produced a new social construction of children as innocent, dependent and vulnerable

(Ainsworth 1991). Progressive 'child-savers' used the new imagery of childhood to advance a number of reform agendas—compulsory school attendance, child labor, and child welfare laws. A more modern, scientific conception of social control embraced positivist criminology and adopted medical analogies to treat offenders rather than to punish them for their offenses. Positivism sought to identify the antecedent forces that caused criminality and challenged the classic formulation of crime as the product of blameworthy, free-will choices (Allen 1964; 1981). By attributing criminal behavior to external and deterministic forces, Progressive reformers reduced actors' responsibility for crime and focused on efforts to reform rather than punish them. Juvenile courts combined the new conception of childhood with a new model of social control to produce a judicial-welfare alternative to criminal justice, to remove children from the adult process, to enforce the newer conception of children's dependency, and to substitute the state as *parens patriae*. The juvenile court's 'Rehabilitative Ideal' assumed the malleability of children and the availability of effective strategies to intervene in their 'best interests'.

Procedure and substance intertwine in the juvenile court. Because juvenile courts assumed that almost all delinquents lacked criminal responsibility, they avoided questions of juveniles' legal competence and reduced culpability (Bonnie and Grisso 2000). Procedurally, juvenile courts used informal processes, conducted closed, confidential hearings, and employed a euphemistic vocabulary to obscure the reality of coercive social control. Substantively, juvenile courts used indeterminate, non-proportional dispositions, emphasized rehabilitative treatment and supervision rather than punishment, and focused on offenders' future welfare rather than past offenses. Despite benevolent rhetoric, however, the Progressive 'child-savers' who created the juvenile court deliberately designed it to discriminate, to 'Americanize' immigrants and the poor, and to provide a coercive legal tool to distinguish between 'our children' and 'other people's children' (Feld 1999a).

Conceptually, punishment and treatment—crime control and social welfare—are mutually exclusive penal goals and make markedly different assumptions about the sources of delinquency and the nature of interventions. Punishment assumes that responsible people make blameworthy choices and deserve the sanctions assigned to their acts. The past offense provides the basis for scaling proportional punishment. Rehabilitative treatment or social welfare assumes a degree of determinism—antecedent factors caused the undesirable behavior. Intervention seeks to alleviate the sources of deviance in order to improve the offender's future welfare. Because circumstances differ, welfare dispositions are indeterminate and non-proportional and reflect a diagnosis and prediction about the effects of intervention on future behavior (Feld 1988).

In their pursuit of the 'Rehabilitative Ideal', Progressives situated the juvenile court on several cultural, legal and criminological fault lines. They juxtaposed binary conceptions for the juvenile and criminal justice systems: either child or adult; either determinism or free-will; either immature or responsible; either treatment or punishment; either social welfare or just deserts; either procedural informality or formality; either discretion or the rule of law. During the last third of the twentieth century, juvenile justice policies witnessed a marked shift from the former to the latter of each of these pairs in response to the structural and racial transformation of cities, the rise in youth crime, and the erosion of confidence in rehabilitation (Garland 2001).

The transformation of the juvenile court

During the 1960s, the Warren Court's civil rights decisions, criminal due process rulings, and 'constitutional domestication' of the juvenile court responded to broader structural and demographic changes taking place in America, particularly those associated with race and youth crime (Feld 1999a; 2003). In the decades prior to and after World War II, black migration from the rural South to the urban North increased minority concentrations in urban ghettos, made race a national rather than a regional issue, and provided the impetus for the Civil Rights movement (Lemann 1992). The 1960s also witnessed 'baby boom' increases in youth crime that continued until the late 1970s. During the 1960s, the rise in youth crime and urban racial disorder provoked cries for 'law and order' and provided the initial political impetus to 'get tough'. Republican politicians seized crime control as a wedge issue with which to distinguish themselves from Democrats and crime policies for the first time became a central issue in partisan politics (Beckett 1997; Feld 2003).

The Supreme Court's due process decisions responded to macro-structural and racial demographic changes, and attempted to guarantee civil rights, to protect minority citizens, and to limit the authority of the state (Feld 2003). *In re Gault* (1967) began to transform the juvenile court into a very different institution from that contemplated by the Progressives. The Court identified two crucial disjunctions between juvenile justice rhetoric and reality: the theory versus the practice of rehabilitation, and the differences between the procedural safeguards afforded adult criminal defendants and those available to delinquents. Rather than uncritically accepting the Progressives' rehabilitative rhetoric, *Gault* examined the punitive realities of juvenile justice—high rates of recidivism, the stigma of a delinquency label, harsh conditions of confinement, and the arbitrariness of the process. The Court mandated some basic procedural safeguards for delinquents charged with crimes and facing confinement: advance notice of charges; a fair and impartial hearing; a right to counsel; a right to confront and cross-examine witnesses; and the privilege against self-incrimination (Feld 1984).

In subsequent decisions, the Court further noted the criminal nature of delinquency proceedings. In *In re Winship* (1970), it held that the state must prove delinquency by the criminal standard of 'beyond a reasonable doubt' rather than by lower civil standards of proof. It required the highest standard of proof to protect against unwarranted convictions, to guard against abuses of government power, and to ensure public confidence in justice administration. In *Breed v Jones* (1975), the Court held that the constitutional prohibition against 'double jeopardy' precluded prosecuting a youth as an adult after a delinquency adjudication for the same offense. The Court posited a functional equivalence between delinquency and criminal trials.

In *McKeiver v Pennsylvania* (1971), the Court declined to extend to juveniles all the procedural safeguards of adult criminal prosecutions. *McKeiver* held that the Constitution does not require a right to a jury trial in delinquency proceedings because 'due process' entailed only 'accurate fact finding', which a judge could provide as well as a jury. *McKeiver* relied on the differences between juvenile courts' *treatment* and criminal courts' *punishment* to justify the procedural distinctions between the two systems, although the Court did not analyze what the differences in purposes actually entailed. Unlike *Gault*, which relied on procedural safeguards to ensure both accurate fact finding *and* protection against governmental oppression, *McKeiver* denied that delinquents needed protection from the state, invoked the mythology of the paternalistic judge, and rejected concerns that closed juvenile hearings actually could prejudice the accuracy of fact finding (Feld 1999a).

Gault and its progeny precipitated a procedural revolution that eventually transformed the juvenile court from its original Progressive conception of a social welfare agency into a more legalistic, and ultimately criminal, one. Progressive reformers based intervention on a child's 'real needs'—social circumstances, environment, need for treatment—and regarded proof of a crime as secondary. Despite *McKeiver*'s denial of a jury trial, *Gault* and *Winship* imposed an adversarial model—defense attorneys, privilege against self-incrimination, criminal standard of proof—and required proof of legal guilt as a prerequisite to state intervention. Even though juveniles enjoy fewer procedural rights than adults, the Court's emphasis on some degree of criminal procedural regularity altered juvenile courts' focus from 'real needs' to 'criminal deeds' and shifted delinquency proceedings' focus from a social welfare inquiry into a quasi-criminal prosecution. Formalizing the connection between criminal behavior and delinquency sentences highlighted juvenile courts' criminal law foundations. Providing delinquents with some criminal procedural safeguards legitimated the imposition of more punitive sentences. Once states granted youths even a semblance of procedural justice, juvenile courts more readily departed from a rehabilitative model. Although the Court provided procedural rights as part of its civil rights agenda to protect minorities' liberty interests, those safeguards

permitted punitive sanctions to escalate and ultimately to fall disproportionately heavily on minority offenders.

Juvenile Courts' procedural deficiencies

Unfortunately, *Gault* constituted an incomplete procedural revolution and
a substantial gulf still remains between the 'law on the books' and the 'law
in action'. States manipulate the fluid concepts of children and adults, or
treatment and punishment in order to maximize the social control of young
people. On the one hand, states treat juveniles just like adults when formal
equality results in practical inequality. For example, states use the adult
legal standard—'knowing, intelligent, and voluntary under the totality of
the circumstances'—to gauge the validity of juveniles' waivers of rights
(*Fare v Michael C.* (1979); Feld 1984), even though juveniles lack the competence of adults. Compared with adults, adolescents differ in cognitive
capacity, maturity of judgment, risk perception, susceptibility to peer influence, and future orientation, all of which cause them to make characteristically poorer legal decisions (Grisso *et al* 2003). Adolescents younger than
sixteen years of age are as seriously impaired as those mentally ill adults
whom clinicians deem incompetent to stand trial (Grisso *et al* 2003). The
research on youths' lack of competence is consistent with research on juveniles' waivers of *Miranda* rights (Grisso 1980) and waivers of their right to
counsel which also provide compelling evidence of the procedural deficiencies of the juvenile court (Feld 1989; 1993b).

Procedural justice hinges on access to and the assistance of counsel. In the
decades since *Gault*, the promise of legal representation remains unrealized
(Feld 1993b). In many states, half or fewer of all juveniles receive the assistance of counsel to which the law entitles them (ABA 1995; GAO 1995;
Feld 1993b). Most juveniles appear without lawyers because juvenile court
judges allow and even encourage them to waive their right to counsel.
However, for youths fifteen years of age and younger, research strongly
questions their ability to make a 'knowing, intelligent, and voluntary'
waiver of legal rights without consulting with an attorney (Grisso 1997).
However, a lawyer's presence seems to aggravate the severity of sentences
that juveniles receive and calls into question the quality of representation
and the fairness of delinquency trials (Feld 1993b).

Even as juvenile courts have become more punitive, most states continue
to deny delinquents access to jury trials and other basic criminal procedural
rights guaranteed to adults (Feld 1988; 1995). As a result, juvenile courts
provide a procedural regime in which few adults charged with crimes would
consent to be tried. They provide neither procedural parity with adults nor
additional safeguards that fully recognize the developmental limitations and
limited competence of youth.

Criminological triage

Despite their procedural inadequacies, the increased formality of juvenile courts provided the impetus to adopt substantive 'criminological triage' policies. This process entails diverting non-criminal status offenders out of the juvenile system at the 'soft' end, waiving serious offenders for adult criminal prosecution at the 'hard' end, and punishing more severely the residual, 'middle'-range of ordinary delinquent offenders (Feld 1993a).

Status offenders

At the 'soft' end, policy makers' disillusionment with juvenile courts' responses to non-criminal youths led to diversion, deinstitutionalization and decriminalization reforms (Feld 1999a). Deinstitutionalization reduced access to secure facilities for non-criminal offenders, and provided the catalyst to transfer many white, female and middle-class youths whom juvenile courts formerly handled as status offenders into private sector mental health and chemical dependency treatment facilities (Schwartz 1989). Most states' civil commitment laws do not provide juveniles with the same procedural safeguards as they do adults. Instead, states' laws invoke the imagery of immaturity and dependency to allow parents 'voluntarily' to commit their children to secure treatment facilities based solely on a physician's determination that such confinement is medically appropriate (Feld 1999a).

Serious and violent offenders

At the 'hard end' of juvenile courts' jurisdiction, judges, prosecutors and legislators transfer increasing numbers of younger offenders to criminal courts for prosecution as adults (Snyder and Sickmund 1999). In the late 1980s and early 1990s, virtually every state enacted 'tougher' laws either to simplify transfer of young offenders, or to require juvenile court judges to impose determinate or mandatory minimum sentences on those youths who remained within an increasingly punitive juvenile justice system (Torbett *et al* 1996; Feld 1998). Both transfer and sentencing strategies de-emphasize rehabilitation and the needs of offenders, stress personal and justice system accountability and punishment, and base sentences on the seriousness of the present offense and prior record. Cumulatively, these changes reflect an inversion of juvenile jurisprudence and sentencing policies—from rehabilitation to retribution, from an emphasis on the offender to the nature of the offense, and from concern with 'amenability to treatment' and a child's 'best interests' to public safety and punishment.

Sources of punitiveness

The sources of these changes in penal policies lay in broader social structural changes, media coverage of crime, and the politics of race (Feld 2003;

Garland 2001). Macro-structural changes in cities during the 1970s and 1980s led to the emergence of a racially isolated and impoverished black underclass. These economic and racial demographic changes contributed to the escalation of black youth homicide rates in the late 1980s, facilitated the politics of crime, and produced more punitive juvenile justice policies in the 1990s (Feld 1999a). One factor contributing to 'get tough' politics was the epidemic of 'crack' cocaine and the gun violence and youth homicides that accompanied the de-industrialization of the urban core and the emergence of the black underclass (Blumstein 1995). A second factor was media coverage that disproportionately put a black face on young criminals and reinforced the white public's fear of and racial animus toward Blacks (Feld 2003). The immediate source of the 'crackdown' was conservative politicians who used crime as a 'code word' to make racial appeals for electoral advantage (Mendelberg 2001).

Rise of the urban underclass

Between World War II and the early 1970s, semi-skilled high school graduates could get well paid jobs in the automobile, steel and construction industries. Beginning in the 1970s, the transition from an industrial to an information and service economy reduced employment opportunities in the manufacturing sectors and produced a bifurcation of economic opportunities based on skills and education. In less than twenty years, the gap between what high school and college graduates earned almost doubled both because the former made less and the latter received much more (Wilson 1996). However, only 13.1% of Blacks aged 25 to 34 had college degrees compared with 24.5% of Whites, and the proportion of Blacks aged 18 to 24 enrolled in college declined during this period while that of Whites increased (Edsall and Edsall 1991).

During the post-World War II period, government highway, housing and mortgage policies encouraged suburbs to expand around urban centers (Massey and Denton 1993). The migration of whites to the suburbs, the growth of information and service jobs in the suburbs, the bifurcation of the economy based on education, and the de-industrialization of the urban core increased racial segregation and the concentration of poverty among blacks in the major cities and altered the political balance. The emergence of the suburban population as a virtual electoral majority enables the predominantly white voters to satisfy most of their public service needs—schools, parks, police and roads—through local and county tax expenditures, weakens their ties to increasingly black cities, and reduces Whites' self-interest in state or federal programs which primarily benefit Blacks and the poor (Hacker 1995; Edsall and Edsall 1991).

In the mid-1980s, the emergence of a structural underclass, the introduction of crack cocaine into inner cities, and the proliferation of guns among youth produced a sharp escalation in black youth homicide rates (Blumstein 1995). The increase in youth homicide provided the immediate political impetus to 'get tough' on youth crime generally. States changed their juvenile waiver and delinquency sentencing laws in the late 1980s and early 1990s in response to two specific changes in patterns of youth crime and violence—race and guns. Lethal violence and victimization are highly concentrated in interstices of social disadvantage and since the mid-1960s, police have arrested black juveniles for violent crimes—rape, robbery and aggravated assault—at a rate about five times greater than that of white youths, and for homicide at a rate about seven times greater than that of whites (Zimring 1998; Feld 1999a). Beginning in 1986, youth homicide rates escalated sharply and the arrest rates of black and white juveniles diverged abruptly (Cook and Laub 1998). Between 1986 and 1993, arrests of white juveniles for homicide increased about 40% while those of black youths jumped by 278% (Snyder and Sickmund 1999). Juveniles' use of guns accounted for most of the escalation in youth homicide, as arrests of adolescents for homicide nearly tripled *and* firearms use by juveniles accounted for almost the *entire* increase (Feld 1999a). Analysts attribute the dramatic increase in black youth homicides to the violent drug industry that 'crack' cocaine spawned in large cities during the mid to late 1980s (Blumstein 1995). The mass media depict and the public perceive crime and juvenile courts' clientele primarily as poor, urban black males. Politicians exploited these racially-tinged perceptions with demagogic pledges to crack down on youth crime, which has become a 'code word' for black males (Beckett 1997).

Youth crime in the media

As a result of social and urban demographic changes since World War II, most black and white Americans live more residentially segregated lives now than they did a century ago (Massey and Denton 1993). Most Whites' knowledge about Blacks comes from news reports about welfare, crime and unemployment which tend to reinforce racial prejudice and stereotypes (Edsall and Edsall 1991; Dorfman and Schiraldi 2001). Whites' stereotypes of Blacks function as a perceptual 'screen' that admits supporting negative evidence and blocks contradictory positive data (Entman and Rojecki 2000).

Crime is socially constructed and 'frames' represent alternative ways of understanding it and carry different policy implications (Beckett and Sasson 2000). The policy choice to 'get tough' on youth crime reflects the ascendance of certain ways of interpreting and framing crime in the political and media cultures and a decision to emphasize punishment and imprisonment policies over other, more humane alternatives. In recent decades, the nature and content of media coverage have reinforced conservative interpretations of crime, put a Black face on it, and intensified public support for punitive policies. News media coverage systematically distorts reality by over-reporting violent crime and over-emphasizing the role of minority youths committing violent crimes (Dorfman and Schiraldi 2001). The emphasis on violence and race primes Whites' stereotypes and prejudice, and amplifies, rather than challenges, politicians' claims about the need for harsher policies toward criminals.

The social construction of news is a complex process that reflects journalistic values and routine practices, the entertainment value of the content, and the socio-political context of its creation. To increase audience shares and advertising revenues, local news programs favor an 'action news' format which focuses on frightening and sensational violence because these stories are concrete, visual, and emotionally powerful. A local crime news standard script typically contain two elements (Gilliam *et al* 1996; Gilliam and Iyengar 2000). The first element is that crime is violent—murder, rape, robbery, or gang behavior. The second element features the 'usual suspects'—minority perpetrators. Combining images of violence and race exerts a pervasive and cumulative effect on public opinion, because viewers exposed to violent and racial imagery then tend to support more punitive policies (Peffley *et al* 1996; Gilliam *et al* 1996).

Media depictions of crime do not accurately reflect real rates of crime, the proportion of crime that is violent, or the proportion of crime that minority youths commit (Dorfman and Schiraldi 2001). Local and network television news and news magazines devote more coverage to violent crime than they do to any other subject and disproportionately over-report the rarest types of crime, such as murder—'if it bleeds, it leads' (Entman and Rojecki 2000). Moreover, the media typically depict violent crimes involving strangers even though acquaintances or intimates commit most violent crimes and such coverage tends to reinforce a perception of criminals as outsiders and predators.

Crime news coverage tends to be episodic rather than contextual, to focus on individual stories rather than the broader social context, and rarely to analyze neighborhood conditions or individual or community risk factors that contribute to crime (Entman and Rojecki 2000). The lack of reporting about context leaves a misleading impression that violence is attributable exclusively to individual offenders' bad choices rather than to structural factors and thereby reinforces conservative interpretations of crime. News coverage fails to provide the information the public needs to make reasoned judgments or to evaluate politicians' claims about crime and justice policies (Dorfman and Schiraldi 2001).

The bias toward over-reporting violent crime reinforces the connection between race and crime. While Blacks commit violent crimes at higher rates than Whites, crime news features Blacks even more disproportionately than their actual rates (Gilliam *et al* 1996; Hurwitz and Peffley 1997). Media reports portray black defendants arrested for violent crimes negatively—anonymously, spread-eagled or in police custody, and poorly dressed—more often than they do white offenders (Entmann and Rojecki 2000; Peffley *et al* 1996). Conversely, crime news depicts victims disproportionately as female, white and affluent, even though they are victimized less often than other demographic groups, such as Blacks. Crime stories' 'newsworthiness' increases with white victims, decreases with black victims, and is strongest when crime is inter-racial (Dorfman and Schiraldi 2001). Such distorted coverage promotes pejorative stereotypes, reinforces Whites' perceptions of Blacks as dangerous and bolsters conservative interpretations of crime and punishment (Gilliam and Iynegar 2000; Mendelberg 2001).

Politics of race and crime

The adoption of laws to punish youth crime in the early 1990s culminated the politicization of criminal and juvenile justice policies that began several decades earlier. Social problems, such as crime, emerge in a process of social construction with conflicting interpretations and different policy prescriptions. Claims-makers, such as politicians, compete for public acceptance of the interpretations or frames they advocate and the policies they prescribe (Entman and Rojecki 2000). Over the past three decades, conservative politicians have successfully influenced public perceptions about the threat of crime, attributed the causes of crime to individuals' bad choices rather than to social structural forces, assigned responsibility for unacceptably high crime rates to lenient justice system policies, and promoted campaigns to 'crack down' on crime as part of a broader electoral strategy.

Divisions within the Democratic Party between racial and social policy liberals and conservatives, and northerners and southerners first emerged in 1948. By the 1960s, the Civil Rights movement heightened the visibility of Blacks in the south and forced the national Democratic Party to choose between its white southern and black northern constituencies. Although most Americans agreed in theory with norms of racial equality, many disagreed with the specific means that the courts and regulatory agencies developed to remedy inequality and the harbored continuing racial resentments (Mendelberg 2001). Many of the remedies the Warren Court instituted to end discrimination and racial segregation and to grant legal and procedural rights to unpopular groups such as criminal defendants became associated in the public mind with the liberal agenda of the Democratic Party. The 'rights revolution' and the associated social and cultural changes disturbed and angered many members of the white ethnic working- and lower-middle classes who bore the brunt of change—civil rights for minorities, employment and reproductive rights for women, protection for criminal defendants, affirmative action and racial preferences in hiring (Edsall and Edsall 1992).

During the turbulent 1960s, the sharp rise in youth crime and urban racial disorder evoked fears of 'crime in the streets' and provoked cries for 'law and order'. Republican politicians blamed escalating crime, campus disorder, urban riots, and social upheavals on the Warren Court and liberal Democratic policies. Crime and welfare policies became issues of partisan politics and acquired a racial quality as conservatives cast Blacks and their Democratic allies as the villains (Gilens 1999; Mendelberg 2001). The polarization between Democrats and Republicans on issues of race became explicit during the 1964 presidential contest between Lyndon Johnson, whose leadership led to the passage of the 1964 Civil Rights Act, and Barry Goldwater, a staunch conservative who opposed the law (Edsall and Edsall 1992). Democrats' support for black civil rights alienated white southern voters and presaged a racial realignment in American politics as voters began to identify clear differences between the two parties on a host of race-related public policy issues. Although the civil rights movement initially focused on achieving basic citizenship rights for Blacks, such as the right to vote and equal access to public accommodations, the post-1964 agenda addressed broader goals of implementing rights and assuring equality of outcomes for Blacks, often through the use of racial preferences.

Conservatives strongly opposed governmental actions to redistribute public and private goods—jobs, education and housing—to achieve greater racial equality. Negative media coverage of crime and welfare reinforced public perceptions and political depictions of Blacks as criminals and undeserving (Edsall and Edsall 1992; Gilens 1999). The civil rights movement changed perceptions of the Democratic and Republican parties and conservative politicians used crime and welfare as racially-tinged 'wedge issues' with which to distinguish themselves from Democrats in order to woo southern white and ethnic voters (Edsall and Edsall 1992).

In 1968, Richard Nixon's presidential campaign attributed urban riots and rising crime rates to liberal 'permissiveness' and criticized the Warren Court for 'coddling criminals' and 'handcuffing the forces of law and order'. Nixon's strategy effectively straddled the conflict between public support for the abstract principle of racial equality and resistance to government-prescribed remedies to end inequality. Nixon articulated the views of many white Americans who believed that it was wrong to deny Blacks basic citizenship rights, but who also opposed government-imposed residential, employment and educational integration (Mendelberg 2001).

Republican political strategists found a responsive audience among white southerners, suburbanites, socially-conservative ethnic Catholics and blue-collar workers to foster a political realignment around racial issues. Pursuing Kevin Phillips' 'southern strategy', Republicans courted these constituencies with racially-charged 'code words', such as 'law and order,' that indirectly evoked racial themes without explicitly challenging egalitarian ideals (Phillips 1969; Omi and Winant 1994). The Republicans' 'southern strategy' ruptured the Democrats' New Deal economic coalition of the 'have-nots' and produced a party realignment around issues of race rather than socio-economic class. As more progressive forces dominated the Democratic Party, Republicans depicted them as liberal elitists bent on imposing an alien racial and cultural agenda (Edsall and Edsall 1992). Because of the perceived association between race, on the one hand, and violence, disorder, crime, illegitimacy and welfare dependency, on the other, liberals failed convincingly to address the increasingly conservative public attitudes spurred by rising crime and welfare rates. The inability of liberals effectively to debate issues associated with race enabled conservative Republicans to propose simplistic, politically popular policies on many contentious issues and to push the debate in a conservative direction (Mendelberg 2001). Only in the 1990s under Bill Clinton, for example, could national Democrats respond to Republicans' exploitation of the crime issue by embracing an equally tough rhetoric and fostering a bi-partisan policy consensus for 'law and order' (Garland 2001; Beckett and Sasson 2000).

'Code words' to appeal to anti-Black sentiments

It is 'politically incorrect' to express overtly racist sentiments and research on 'modern racism' attempts to identify closely related, indirect indicators of racial hostility such as anti-black emotional affect, resistance to Blacks' political demands, and a denial that racial discrimination or racism persists (Entman and Rojecki 2000). 'Code words'—phrases that indirectly conjure racial themes, but do not directly challenge egalitarian ideals—enable politicians to appeal implicitly to racial resentment without providing clear evidence of racism or an intent to discriminate (Omi and Winant 1994). In the 1970s, conservative politicians recognized that words like 'law and order' and 'individual rights' evoked racial understandings and, by the 1980s, words like 'welfare' 'fairness' and 'groups' had acquired racial meanings as a backlash against liberal policies (Edsall and Edsall 1992). Crime and welfare serve as 'coded' issues that enable politicians implicitly to activate some white Americans' negative views about Blacks without explicitly playing the 'race card' (Gilens 1999; Mendelberg 2001).

For the past thirty years, 'sound-bite' politics, symbols and rhetoric have shaped penal policies as politicians fear being labeled 'soft-on-crime' and avoid thoughtful discussions of complex issues (Beckett 1997). In this unreflective environment, politicians exploit racially-tinged words and perceptions for political advantage with promises to 'get tough' and 'crack down' on 'youth crime' which the public understands as 'code words' for young black males. The use of 'code phrases' enables politicians to convey a well-known but implicit meaning—such as an appeal to whites' racial hostilities—while being able to deny any racist interpretation (Mendelberg 2001).

In this time, conservative politicians and the mass media have pushed crime to the top of the political agenda by focusing on sensational and violent crime to promote more punitive policies for political purposes. Politicians generate crime-news stories in order to shape public attitudes and promote crime policies that they believe will provide them with a political advantage. The 1988 Bush presidential campaign's focus on Willie Horton—a convicted black murderer released on furlough who burglarized and stabbed a white middle class man and raped a woman—tapped voter anger over criminal defendants' and prisoners' rights through the threatening archetype of the black male rapist of a white woman (Mendelberg 2001). By the early 1990s, 'youth crime' had acquired a coded meaning and juveniles had become a symbolic 'Willie Horton' (Beckett 1997; Beckett and Sasson 2000).

Punitiveness in juvenile transfer and sentencing policy

The politicization of crime policies and the media and public connections between race and youth crime provided a powerful incentive to transform juvenile justice jurisprudence (Zimring 1998). Questions about the effectiveness and legitimacy of the 'Rehabilitative Ideal' that emerged in the 1960s increasingly eroded the treatment rationale of the juvenile justice system and evoked a sense of failure among both practitioners and the public (Zimring 2000a; Garland 2001). Political opportunism and an erroneous perception that 'nothing works' fostered a greater legislative emphasis on punishment. The overarching jurisprudential themes of these legal changes include a shift from rehabilitation to retribution, from sentences based on the offender's needs to the seriousness of the offense, from 'amenability to treatment' to public safety and accountability, and a transfer of sentencing discretion from judges to prosecutors (Feld 1998; 1999a).

Within the past two decades, and particularly in reaction to the increase in black youth homicides in the late 1980s and early 1990s, virtually every state revised its transfer laws to facilitate the prosecution of more juveniles in criminal court (Torbet 1996; Feld 1995; 1998). Juvenile justice policies became especially punitive toward youths charged with violent and drug crimes, the offense categories to which black youths contribute disproportionately. Statutory changes use offense criteria in waiver laws either as dispositional guidelines to structure and limit judicial discretion, to guide prosecutorial charging decisions, or automatically to exclude certain offenses from juvenile court jurisdiction (Torbet *et al* 1996; Feld 1998; McCord 2001). The changes in waiver laws reflect a cultural and legal reconfiguration of youth from innocent and dependent children to responsible and autonomous adult-like offenders. Politicians' sound bites—'adult crime, adult time' or 'old enough to do the crime, old enough to do the time'—exemplify the reformulation of adolescence and represent crime policies that provide no formal recognition of youthfulness as a mitigating factor in sentencing (Feld 1997). After controlling for the seriousness of the offense, juvenile court judges are more likely to transfer minority youths than white youths to criminal court and the disparities are greatest for youths charged with violent and drug offenses (Poe-Yamagata and Jones 1999). Once states try youths as adults, criminal court judges sentence them as if they are adults, impose the same sentences, and send them to the same prisons (Feld 1998). On 1 March 2005, the U.S. Supreme Court, in a controversial 5-4 decision, barred states from executing offenders for crimes they committed while under the age of 18 (*Roper v Simmons*, 125 S.Ct. 1183 (2005)). The dissent in *Simmons* strongly criticized the majority for relying on international law as authority for its decision and for citing Article 37 of the United Nations Convention on the Rights of the Child, which the United States has not ratified.

Sentencing delinquents

The jurisprudential shift from treatment to punishment that inspired changes in waiver policies increasingly affects the sentences that juvenile court judges impose on delinquent offenders as well. Progressive reformers envisioned a social welfare system for youths that minimized procedural safeguards and maximized discretion to focus on youths' 'real needs'. The recent impetus to 'get tough' also impels juvenile judges to punish delinquents more severely and these harsher sanctions disproportionately affect minority youths (Feld 1999a; Poe-Yamagata and Jones 1999).

Legislative preambles and court opinions explicitly endorse punishment as an appropriate delinquency sanction. States' juvenile codes increasingly employ the rhetoric of accountability, individual responsibility, punishment, and public safety rather than a child's welfare or 'best interests' (Feld 1988; 1998). Half the states' juvenile sentencing laws use some type of offense-based criteria—determinate or mandatory minimum sentences—based on the seriousness of the offense to structure sentencing discretion (Torbet *et al* 1996; Feld 1998; Sheffer 1995). Some use sentencing guidelines to impose presumptive, determinate sentences based on age, offense, and prior record (Feld 1998; Sheffer 1995). Others impose mandatory sentences that define minimum terms of confinement or level of security placement based on age and offense (Torbet *et al* 1996; Sheffer 1995). States' departments of corrections administratively have adopted security classification and release guidelines that use offense criteria to specify proportional or mandatory minimum terms of confinement (Feld 1998). All of these sentencing provisions—determinate and mandatory minimum laws, and correctional and parole release guidelines—base the length of time delinquents will serve on the seriousness of the crime they committed rather than their 'real needs' or future welfare (McCord *et al* 2001). Offense criteria achieve proportionality in sentencing, increase the penal bite of sanctions, and allow legislators symbolically to demonstrate how 'tough' they are.

In addition to formal changes in sentencing laws, two general findings emerge clearly from empirical research evaluating juvenile court judges' dispositional practices. First, the present offense and prior record account for most of the variance in juvenile court sentences that can be explained. Studies of sentencing practices report that judges focus mainly on seriousness of the present offense and prior record when they sentence delinquents (Feld 1998). Secondly, after controlling for legal variables, the individualized justice of juvenile courts produces racial disparities in the sentencing of minority offenders (Bishop and Frazier 1996). According to juvenile courts' treatment ideology, judges' discretionary decisions *should* disproportionately affect minority youths, because the Progressives intended judges to focus on youths' social circumstances rather than simply their offenses and designed them to discriminate between 'our' children and 'other people's children'.

Examining juvenile correctional facilities and evaluating their effectiveness provides another indicator of the increased punitiveness of juvenile justice. Evaluations of juvenile correctional facilities in the decades following *Gault* reveal a continuing gap between the rhetoric of rehabilitation and the punitive reality (Feld 1977; 1981). Criminological research, judicial opinions, and investigative studies of delinquency institutions and training schools report staff beatings of inmates, use of drugs for social control purposes, extensive reliance on solitary confinement, and a virtual absence of meaningful rehabilitative programs (Feld 1998; Parent *et al* 1994). Despite 'rehabilitative rhetoric' and a euphemistic vocabulary, juvenile court judges increasingly consign disproportionately minority offenders to overcrowded custodial warehouses that constitute little more than youth prisons.

Evaluations of juvenile treatment programs provide little evidence that training schools, the most common form of institutional treatment for the largest numbers of serious and chronic delinquents, effectively rehabilitate youths or reduce their recidivism rates (Feld 1998). Unlike training schools, meta-analyses of other types of interventions report that some treatment programs produce positive effects on selected clients under certain conditions. A recent, comprehensive meta-analysis of 200 studies of treatment programs for serious juvenile offenders reported significant and positive effects that reduced recidivism by about 6%, from 50% to 44% (Lipsey and Wilson 1998). Positive outcomes most often occur in small programs that provide intensive and integrated responses to the multiple problems that delinquent youths present. Favorable results occur primarily under optimal conditions, for example, when mental health or other non-juvenile correctional personnel provide services with high treatment integrity in well-run programs. Even though some programs produce positive changes, most states do not provide these services to delinquents generally and instead confine them in euphemistically-sanitized youth prisons.

The inherent contradictions of the juvenile court

Today, American juvenile courts punish rather than treat young offenders and use procedures under which no adult charged with a crime would consent to be tried. The fundamental shortcoming of the juvenile court reflects a failure of conception and not simply a century-long failure of implementation. The juvenile court's creators envisaged a social service agency in a judicial setting, and attempted to fuse its welfare mission with the power of state coercion. Combining social welfare and penal social control functions in one agency ensures that juvenile courts do both badly. Providing for child welfare is a societal responsibility rather than a judicial one. Juvenile courts lack control over the resources necessary to meet children's welfare needs because of the social class and racial characteristics of their clients and because the public fears 'other people's children'. In practice, juvenile courts almost inevitably subordinate welfare concerns to crime control considerations.

If we created a child welfare system *ab initio,* would we choose a court as the best agency to deliver services and would we use criminality as the criterion to define eligibility for benefits? If we would not initially choose a court to deliver social services, then does the fact of a youth's criminality confer upon it any special competence as a welfare agency? Many young people who do not commit crimes need social services and many youths who commit crimes do not require or will not respond to social intervention. In short, criminality is an indiscriminate criterion upon which to allocate social services. Because we fail to meet the welfare needs of all young people, juvenile courts' treatment ideology serves primarily to legitimate judicial coercion of some youths because of their criminality.

The attempt to combine social welfare and criminal social control in one agency constitutes the inherent flaw of the juvenile court. The juvenile court subordinates social welfare concerns to criminal social control functions because of its penal focus. Legislatures do not define juvenile courts' jurisdiction on the basis of characteristics of children for which they are not responsible and for which effective intervention could improve their lives. For example, juvenile court law does not define eligibility for welfare services or create an enforceable right or entitlement based on young people's lack of access to quality education, lack of adequate housing or nutrition, unmet health needs, or impoverished families—none of which is their fault and all of which are risk factors for subsequent criminality (McCord *et al* 2001). In all these instances, children bear the burden of their parents' circumstances literally as innocent bystanders. Instead, states define juvenile court jurisdiction based on a youth's criminality, a prerequisite that detracts from a compassionate response. Unlike adverse social conditions for which youth are not responsible, criminal behavior represents the one characteristic for which young offenders do deserve at least some blame. In short, juvenile courts define eligibility for services on the basis of the feature least likely to elicit sympathy and compassion and ignore social structural conditions and personal circumstances more likely to evoke a desire to help. Juvenile courts' defining characteristic strengthens public antipathy to 'other people's children' by emphasizing primarily that they are criminals. Recent policies that stress punishment, accountability and personal responsibility further reinforce juvenile courts' penal foundations and reduce the legitimacy of youths' claims to humanitarian welfare assistance.

COMPETENCE AND CULPABILITY: FOUNDATIONS FOR YOUTH AND CRIME POLICY

For more than a decade, the John D. and Catherine T. MacArthur Foundation has sponsored research on Adolescent Development and Juvenile Justice. Despite American politicians' embrace of punitive policies, recent psychological and neuroscience research on how adolescents think differently from adults, how they exercise rights less effectively than adults, and the underlying neurobiological bases of these differences provide a strong foundation for the creation of a developmentally appropriate youth justice system (e.g. Grisso and Schwartz 2000).

States recognize that adolescents have different legal competencies and greater potential for change than adults. Paternalistic and protective legal policies that restrict youths' rights to vote, drink, smoke, drive, enter a binding contract, donate blood, and the like, reflect these insights. If states de-couple social welfare from crime control and acknowledge that juvenile courts function primarily as youth-based criminal justice systems, then they need to make similar modifications to accommodate the youthfulness of defendants.

The fundamental premise of a criminal justice system for youth is that adolescents differ from adults in their legal competence and criminal responsibility, and these developmental differences require substantive and procedural modifications of the justice system to accommodate them. Young offenders deserve less severe consequences for their misdeeds than more mature offenders simply because they are young and have less capacity for self-control (Feld 2004). A paternalistic youth and crime policy would protect them from the age-linked developmental characteristics that lead them to make poorer judgments (Scott and Steinberg 2003). Substantive justice requires states formally to acknowledge youths' diminished responsibility, to sentence them more leniently than older defendants, and to provide them with greater opportunities for change (Feld 2004). Procedural justice requires full procedural parity with adults and additional safeguards to account for youths' lesser adjudicative competence.

Competence

As juvenile justice becomes more punitive and states transfer more youths to criminal courts, difficult questions about immature youths' ability to understand the trial process and to make critical legal decisions have emerged (Redding and Frost 2001; Bonnie and Grisso 2000). The welfare-oriented juvenile court assumed an informal and co-operative process. But as juvenile courts have become more adversarial and legalistic, they confront issues of youths' competence. Waiver reforms to lower the age of criminal responsibility to 14 years or younger present criminal courts with larger numbers of youths whose developmental immaturity, rather than mental illness, presents significant issues of competence (Grisso 1997b; Feld 2000).

Competence refers to a person's ability to understand the nature and consequences of legal proceedings and to make decisions, to participate, and to assist counsel (Grisso 1997b; Grisso and Schwartz 2000). More commonly, mental illness or disability provide the primary reasons to question defendants' competence to stand trial and to doubt their ability to understand proceedings and assist counsel—'sufficient present ability to consult with his lawyer with a reasonable degree of rational understanding' and a 'rational as well as factual understanding of proceedings against him' (*Dusky v United States* (1960)). However, developmental immaturity also may render juveniles incompetent to stand trial. States adopt protective policies toward minors in most activities because they assume that adolescents' legal competencies—reasoning, understanding, appreciation, decision-making, maturity of judgment—are not equal to those of adults (Scott *et al* 1995; Grisso *et al* 2003). Juveniles' diminished understanding of rights, confusion about trial processes, limited language skills, and inadequately developed decision-making abilities undermine their ability effectively to participate or to assist counsel. Most youths younger than 13 or 14 years of age lack the basic competence to understand or meaningfully participate in their defense (Redding and Frost 2001). Many youths younger than 16 years of age lack adjudicative competence either to stand trial as adults or to make legal decisions in juvenile court without the assistance of counsel (Steinberg and Cauffman 1999). Juveniles' lesser competence does not derive from mental illness, as is the case for adult defendants, but rather from generic developmental limitations—immaturity, lack of knowledge, attitude toward risk, emphasis on short-term rather than long-term consequences, susceptibility to peer and parental influences—which affect their ability to communicate, to reason and understand, and to exercise judgment and make sound decisions (Grisso 2000). Thus, states must provide greater procedural safeguards in order to offset the inherent limitations of youth.

Culpability and diminished responsibility

Despite a state's desire or ability to treat miscreant youth, juvenile courts function primarily as agencies of criminal social control. Youths experience delinquency sanctions as punishment regardless of states' benevolent motives or the quality of treatment. Punishing young offenders rests on the premise that adolescents possess sufficient moral reasoning, cognitive capacity and volitional control to hold them partially responsible for their behavior, although not to the same degree as adults. Developmental psychological research, jurisprudence and criminal sentencing policy provide reasons to punish younger offenders less severely for their misdeeds than older offenders (Feld 2004). Sentencing policies must recognize youthfulness as a mitigating factor in both the juvenile and adult criminal justice system (Scott and Steinberg 2003).

Deserved punishment entails condemnation and consequences for making blameworthy choices and imposes sanctions proportional to the seriousness of a crime (von Hirsch 1976; 1993). Penal proportionality limits the state by restricting the exercise of power to deserved punishment commensurate with blameworthiness and the seriousness of the offense. Two elements—harm and culpability—define the seriousness of a crime. A perpetrator's age has relatively little bearing on assessments of harm—the nature of the injury inflicted, risk created, or value taken (Scott and Steinberg 2003). But, evaluations of seriousness also involve the quality of the actor's choice to engage in the criminal conduct that produced the harm. Youthfulness and immaturity bear quite directly on the quality of choices and the culpability of the actor. Criminal responsibility hinges on cognitive and volitional competence. Youths differ socially, physically, and psychologically from adults: they have not yet fully internalized moral norms, developed sufficient empathic identification with others, acquired adequate moral comprehension, or had sufficient opportunity to learn to restrain their actions. They possess neither the rationality—cognitive capacity—nor the self-control—volitional capacity—to equate their decisions and criminal responsibility fully with that of adults. Adolescence is a period of rapid growth and transition, and youths are 'works in progress' who have not quite become the people they will be as adults. As a result, their bad decisions reveal less about their character and blameworthiness than do the criminal choices of adults. Adolescents differ from adults in their psychosocial immaturity and greater responsiveness to external pressures that can lead to criminal conduct (Scott and Steinberg 2003; Feld 2004). While penal proportionality suggests shorter sentences for youth because of diminished responsibility, a protective youth policy also must avoid life-destructive consequences and provide 'room to reform' (Zimring 1982; 2000b). A youth policy should enable young offenders to survive the mistakes of adolescence with their life chances intact.

Adolescence as a generic form of diminished culpability

Certain developmental differences distinguish the quality of decisions that young people make from those of adults and justify a more protective stance when states sentence younger offenders (Feld 2004). Psycho-social 'maturity of judgment' and 'temperance' provide frameworks through which to examine adolescents' competency and culpability (Cauffman and Steinberg 1995; Scott 1992; Scott and Grisso 1997). Maturity of judgment can be assessed across a variety of domains—responsibility, temperance and perspective—that bear on blameworthiness, culpability and sentencing policy (Steinberg and Cauffman 1996; 1999). Youths' immature judgment contributes to a tendency to make poor choices that ultimately may harm themselves and others. Differences in judgment, self-control and criminal responsibility are attributable to youths' developmental differences from adults—breadth of experience, short-term versus long-term time perspectives, attitudes toward risk, impulsiveness, and the importance they attach to peer influences (Feld 1997).

Young people are more impulsive, exercise less self-control, fail adequately to calculate long-term consequences and engage in more risky behaviors than do adults. Adolescents are less risk-averse than adults in a wide range of activities affecting health and safety—speeding, unprotected sex, the use of drugs and alcohol, and criminal conduct. Adolescents may estimate the magnitude or probability of risks differently from adults, use a shorter timeframe, or reckon opportunities for gains rather than possibilities of losses differently than adults (Furby and Beyth-Marom 1992). Young people may discount negative future consequences because they have more difficulty than adults integrating a future consequence into their more limited experiential baseline (Gardner and Herman 1991). Disadvantaged youths, in particular, feel a sense of 'futurelessness', fatalism and despair which inclines them to discount future consequences even more than do other teenagers when they make cost and benefit calculations (Grisso 1996). Adolescents' disposition toward sensation-seeking encourages them to seek exciting and novel activities, and causes them to take greater risks than adults. Impulsiveness may stem from hormonal and physiological changes or mood volatility and may compromise decision making (Cauffman and Steinberg 1996).

Adolescents respond to peer group influences more readily than adults because of the crucial role that peer relationships play in identity formation (Scott 1992; Zimring 1998). Most adolescents commit crimes in a group context, and group-offending places normally law-abiding youth at greater risk of involvement and reduces their ability publicly to withdraw. Because of the social context of adolescent crime, young people require time, experience and opportunities to develop the capacity for independence and autonomous judgments and to resist peer influence.

Developmental processes affect youths' judgment and self-control, reduce their degree of criminal responsibility and deserved punishment, and justify a different youth sentencing policy. While young offenders possess sufficient understanding and culpability to hold them accountable for their acts, their crimes are less blameworthy than adults' crimes because of diminished responsibility and limited appreciation of consequences *and* because their life-circumstances understandably limited their opportunities to learn to make more responsible choices.

When youths offend, the families, schools and communities that nurture them bear some responsibility for the failures of those socializing institutions. Children depend on adults to care for them and to help them to develop the moral capacity for constructive behavior. The ability to exercise self-control is not simply a matter of luck, but a socially constructed developmental process. Community structures affect the conditions and contexts within which adolescents grow and interact with peers. Many characteristics of delinquents—lower intellectual ability, poverty, social disadvantage, cultural isolation—hamper cognitive and moral development (Grisso 1996). Moreover, unlike presumptively mobile adults, juveniles' dependency limits their ability to escape from criminogenic environments (Scott and Steinberg 2003).

Adolescence is a period of 'semi-autonomy' and youths require a 'learner's permit' that gives them opportunities to learn to make responsible choices but without suffering fully the long-term consequences of their mistakes (Zimring 1982). The ability to make responsible choices is learned behavior and the dependent status of youth systematically deprives them of chances to learn to be responsible. A youth and crime policy must manage the risks that youths pose to themselves and others while reducing the harmful consequences the justice system inflicts on them as they negotiate the transition to adulthood. Youths' socially constructed life situation limits their capacity to develop self-control, restricts opportunities to learn and exercise responsibility, and supports a partial reduction of criminal sanctions (Zimring 1998).

Like other risky behavior, most adolescent criminality is normal and transitional, and does not indicate the onset of a criminal career. Adolescence is a time of experimentation and exploration, and youths' character remains somewhat unformed and malleable. Penal policy must recognize the rapidity of adolescence development and avoid consequences that destroy a youth's life-chances. Because of immaturity and diminished culpability, a youth sentencing policy would entail shorter sentence durations than for older offenders. Because incarceration disrupts normal development, a sentencing policy also requires a higher seriousness threshold before states confine youths.

Policy and prescription

A justice system for youths must recognize adolescents' limited competence and diminished culpability, and avoid imposing life-destructive sanctions.

States confront several policy choices when they devise such a justice system. Should they create a separate juvenile justice system or adopt special procedures and sentencing provisions within criminal courts? How should they organize such courts? How should they balance welfare and crime control goals? If they create a separate juvenile court, should it exercise jurisdiction over non-criminal misconduct? What procedural safeguards are necessary to compensate for youths' limited competence? How should they incorporate principles of penal proportionality into the justice system? What is the appropriate age for criminal responsibility? How should criminal or juvenile courts respond to the youngest offenders, those below the ages of twelve or ten? Who should decide which youths to try in criminal courts? Although the United States' experience provides primarily cautionary answers to these difficult questions, developmental psychological research provides the basis for better-informed decisions.

Separate juvenile court?

Should a state have a legally separate juvenile justice system or simply a youth-adjunct of its criminal justice system? Scandinavian countries, for example, eschew juvenile courts, deal with younger offenders exclusively within the child welfare system, and try youths 15 years of age and older in their criminal justice system with special procedures, sentencing provisions and welfare dispositional options in lieu of criminal sanctions (Mehlbye and Sommer 1998; Feld 1994; Tonry and Doob 2004). On the other hand, most other western democracies create separate juvenile justice systems to institutionalize the diminished culpability of most young offenders and to insulate the juvenile system against the political pressures to punish endemic in the criminal justice system (Mehlbye and Walgrave 1998; Tonry and Doob 2004). A separate juvenile court may develop expertise in youth development and create special institutions to respond to youths' needs (Zimring 2000b; Allen 1964). More importantly, a separate juvenile court may protect youths from destructive penalties imposed in criminal courts. While the public unknowingly may tolerate modest sanctions administered to young offenders in low visibility delinquency proceedings, politicians may baulk at acknowledging openly a policy of moderation and resist formally recognizing youthfulness as a mitigating factor at sentencing (Scott 2000). Many elected officials prefer to demagogue about crime and posture politically about 'cracking down' on youth crime rather than responsibly educating the public about the realistic limits of the juvenile justice system to control it.

With the erosion of juvenile courts' historic rehabilitative and interventionist rationales, the strongest argument for the juvenile court remains a diversionary one—it is not a criminal court and it is not as susceptible to political pressures for repression and disfiguring punishments (Zimring 2000a). The primary argument for diversion is one of doing less harm than criminal punishment of the young. Because criminal courts presume the competence and culpability of defendants, a separate juvenile court may be a better venue in which to institutionalize the idea of reduced competence and diminished responsibility (Steinberg and Cauffman 1999). The ultimate policy question is one of 'compared to what?'—in which venue are youth consistently more likely to receive a less punitive and more humane outcome?

Jurisdiction—age

Both minimum and maximum ages define a juvenile court's jurisdiction. In terms of minimum age jurisdiction, older children and younger adolescents may lack the cognitive capacity to know the nature and consequences of their acts or to conform to the norms of the criminal law. The infancy defense of Anglo-American common law constituted an absolute defense and excused from criminal liability younger offenders who failed to appreciate the wrongfulness of their acts (Feld 1999a). Once states recognize the punitive nature of the delinquency docket, then there must be some age below which youths lack requisite criminal capacity. States should be able to deal with children younger than 10 or 12 years of age in a non-criminal social welfare setting and exclude them from the juvenile court.

In terms of maximum age of jurisdiction, a focus on diminished culpability encompasses more than simply cognitive capacity. The developmental psychology reviewed above indicates that by about 16 years of age most youths cognitively understand the prohibitions of the criminal law. However, it may take them several more years to develop sufficient maturity of judgment, ability to resist peer influences, and capacity for self-control to be fully criminally responsible (Feld 1999a; Zimring 1998). Thus, the maximum age of juvenile court jurisdiction should extend until at least 17 or 18 years of age.

Jurisdiction—dispositional age

The dispositional authority of a criminal justice system for youth should continue for several years beyond the maximum age of jurisdiction, for example until 19 or 21 years of age. Juveniles' time remaining within the dispositional jurisdiction of juvenile courts often provides impetus to transfer them to the criminal court. Most youths whom juvenile courts currently transfer are 16 or 17 years of age and nearing the maximum age of jurisdiction (Feld 1995). The availability of a delinquency disposition that extends several years beyond the jurisdictional age would reduce the pressure to transfer all but the most serious and criminally responsible older juveniles.

Jurisdiction—subject matter

Violations of the criminal law should be the exclusive jurisdictional basis of a criminal justice system for youths (ABA-IJA 1980). Of course, criminal violations may be found in statutes other than the penal code, for example, major traffic offenses, municipal ordinances, and the like. However, juvenile court jurisdiction should encompass only conduct that would be a crime if committed by an adult. It should not include so-called 'status offenses'—incorrigibility, indecent or immoral conduct, running away from home, being beyond the control of parents, truancy, curfew, and the like. The appropriate social and legal response to minor, nuisance and non-criminal misconduct goes to the heart of the juvenile court's mission and the normative concept of childhood on which it is based. The debate pits advocates of authority and control of youth against those who view intervention as discriminatory, a denial of rights, and ultimately ineffective (Feld 1993a). While helping troubled children in conflict with families and schools is inherently attractive, little evidence supports the effectiveness of coercive intervention to resolve these difficulties (Feld 1999a). States most appropriately address these issues directly through the child welfare, social service and educational systems rather than via the justice system and delinquency institutions.

Procedural safeguards

Because a justice system for youth is first and foremost a criminal justice system, youths should receive all of the procedural safeguards that adult defendants charged with comparable crimes receive. Many states provide summary procedures for simpler cases and more elaborate procedural safeguards for more serious offenses. If states create a youth-adjunct to the criminal justice system, it would be easier initially to institutionalize procedural parity with adults. If they create a separate juvenile system, then the presumption should be for procedural parity and additional protections to compensate for youths' lack of adjudicative competence. This also includes consideration of whether proceedings should be open to the public and records sealed and confidential.

Procedural justice hinges on the delivery of effective legal services (Feld 1993b; ABA 1995). The first issue is simply to assure the delivery of legal services to youths. In many states in the United States, for example, simply providing defense representation remains highly problematic (ABA 1995; GAO 1995). Many states fail to provide adequate funding for defense services and others allow delinquents to waive their right using the adult waiver standard even though youths lack adjudicative competence (Feld 1993b; ABA 1995).

Once attorneys represent youths, defining their proper role poses a separate question. Because of the punitive and adversarial nature of delinquency proceedings, most professional organizations assume that a defense attorney's proper role is to advocate zealously on behalf of her client (e.g. ABA 1995). However, delinquents experience considerable difficulty understanding either that they have legal rights or the role of counsel on their behalf. The issues of adjudicative competence—understanding, verbal communication, decision-making and participation—require lawyers to modify their adult-representation strategy when they serve younger clients and to provide support and explanations to enhance their clients' competence.

Sentencing as delinquents

Even as juvenile courts punish youths, they still must provide delinquents with 'room to reform', impose sanctions that provide delinquents with opportunities to change, and protect their long-term life chances (Zimring 1998; 2000b). While restrictions and unpleasant consequences are elements of any sanction, punishment must not permanently disfigure or stigmatize (Zimring 2000b). Delinquency sanctions that deter, incapacitate or punish can still provide an offender with the opportunity to change. 'Room to reform' has both prescriptive and proscriptive qualities. Affirmatively, states must prepare a young person for adulthood and this includes education, vocational training, and appropriate social services. Proscriptively, delinquency sanctions cannot be so severe as to destroy any possibility of a successful transition to adulthood.

The sanctions imposed in a criminal justice system for youth should be proportional to the gravity of harm and the culpability of the actor. Unlike a welfare-oriented disposition which is 'future-oriented', indeterminate and non-proportional, penal proportionality imposes limits on the state and provides for equality among similarly-situated young offenders. Within the limits defined by proportionality, states should provide youths with opportunities to change. If a state fails to provide opportunities for growth and further debilitates already disadvantaged youths, it guarantees that it will incur greater long-term human, criminal and correctional costs. A sentencing and correctional policy that offers young offenders 'room to reform' does not covertly reinstate a treatment ideology but facilitates young offenders' constructive use of their time and the resources available. Although the state bears an obligation to provide the means and incentives for personal change, the length of a youth's sentence should not depend on perceived treatment needs or responsiveness. Uncoupling social welfare from criminal social control and divorcing treatment from punishment means providing opportunities to change voluntarily.

Transfer to criminal court

Contrary to the recent American policy of transferring more and younger offenders to criminal court based primarily on the seriousness of their offense, judges, rather than prosecutors or legislators, have the greatest institutional competence to make this difficult sentencing decision (Feld 2000). A judicial hearing conducted in juvenile court—guided by substantive offense criteria, considerations of the offender's amenability to a noncriminal sentence, and subject to rigorous appellate review—constitutes the 'least bad' solution to the sentencing problems posed by serious offenders (Feld 2000; Zimring 2000b). Evaluation of a youth's maturity and culpability would also include an assessment of adjudicative competence (Grisso 1997). Because the premise of a youth justice system is criminal social control, states should only consider waiver for those few youths whose present offence, prior record, culpability and criminal participation deserve sentences substantially longer than those available in juvenile court. In most cases, this would involve only older youths charged with homicide (Zimring 2000b). An adversarial hearing at which both the state and defense can present relevant evidence to a judge is more likely to produce accurate and fair decisions than prosecutors make in their offices without access to critical information and subject to political considerations (Feld 2000; Zimring 1998). Juvenile court judges bring greater competence and youth perspective to these sentencing decisions than any other institutional actors.

At what minimum age should a youth be considered eligible for prosecution as an adult? The developmental psychological research reviewed above consistently reports that youths younger than 16 years of age are qualitatively different from older adolescents and young adults in competence and culpability (Scott and Steinberg 2003). Because of the unevenness of psycho-social development, even as to these older youths, a transfer hearing should include an assessment of adjudicative competence.

Sentencing as adult criminals

Following transfer to criminal court, both youth protection and diminished responsibility sentencing policies should still shield young people from the full penal consequences of their poor decisions and preserve their life chances and ability to make more mature and responsible choices in the future

(Zimring 1982; 2000b). Such a policy holds young offenders accountable for their acts and yet mitigates the severity of sanctions because of their reduced responsibility. Sentencing policy that integrates youthfulness, reduced culpability and restricted opportunities to learn self-control with penal principles of proportionality would provide younger offenders with substantial fractional reductions of adult sentences. If youths as a class characteristically make poorer choices than adults, then sentencing policies should protect them from the full penal consequences of their bad decisions. To punish less responsible youths like adults would be disproportional and impose a harsher penalty than the amount of culpability deserves (Steinberg and Cauffman 1999).

Because youthfulness constitutes a universal form of reduced culpability, states should treat it categorically as a mitigating factor, without regard to nuances of individual developmental differences or to the nature of the offense for which the youth was transferred. Youth development is a highly variable process and chronological age is a crude measure of criminal maturity and the opportunity to develop the capacity for self-control. Despite the variability of adolescents, however, a categorical 'youth discount' that uses age as a conclusive proxy for reduced culpability and shorter sentences is preferable to an individualized inquiry into the criminal responsibility of each young offender (Feld 2004). There are no clinical indicators of moral development or self-control that equate readily with criminal responsibility and accountability. Once we recognize that young criminal actors are only partially responsible, clinical testimony aimed precisely at tailoring sanctions to culpability is not worth the burden or diversion of resources that the effort would entail. Because diminished criminal responsibility is a legal concept, there is no forensic analog to which clinical testimony would correspond. Rather, a youth discount categorically recognizes that criminal choices by young people are qualitatively different from those of adults and constitute a form of diminished responsibility per se. Because reduced culpability provides the rationale for mitigation, younger adolescents are less responsible and deserve proportionally shorter sentences than older youths (Feld 1997; 2004). With the passage of time, age and opportunities to develop self-control, social tolerance of criminal deviance and claims for youthful mitigation decline. Discounted sentences that preserve younger offenders' life chances require that the maximum sentences they receive remain substantially lower than those imposed on adults. Capital penalties and mandatory minimum terms, for example, life without parole, have no place when states sentence presumptively less-blameworthy adolescents. Because of the rapidity of adolescent development and the disruptive consequences of incarceration, the rationale for a 'youth discount' also supports requiring a higher in/out threshold of offense seriousness and culpability as a prerequisite for imprisonment.

Age-segregated youth prisons

Where states should confine youths and what services they should provide are separate questions from those of criminal liability and accountability. States should maintain separate age-segregated correctional facilities to protect both younger offenders and older inmates. Even though youths are somewhat responsible for their criminal conduct, they are not the physical or psychological equals of adults in prison. While some youths may be vulnerable to victimization or exploitation by adults, other youths' lack of self-control may pose a threat to older inmates.

Because all young offenders will eventually return to society, the state must provide them with resources for self-improvement on a voluntary basis because of its basic responsibility to its citizens and in its own self-interest. A correctional policy that offers youths 'room to reform' opportunities and resources does not reinstate a welfare or treatment ideology, but facilities youths' constructive use of their time. With maturity, most young offenders develop a capacity for self-control. Youths require education, social and clinical services, and economic and vocational training for their personal growth and future life chances, regardless of the impact on recidivism rates.

CONCLUSION

A century ago, the transition from an agricultural to an industrial society changed our cultural ideas about childhood and strategies of social control, and led to the creation of the juvenile court. More recent structural changes have eroded support for the 'rehabilitative ideal' and modified the social construction of childhood (Feld 1999a; Garland 2001). The shift from an industrial to an information and service economy, the migration of rural southern blacks to cities and whites to suburbs, the deindustrialization of the urban core, and the concentration of poverty among urban blacks have changed the patterns and public perceptions of youth crime and the justice system's responses to it. States' juvenile justice systems now emphasize personal accountability and punish young offenders rather than treat them. To support more punitive policy, public officials invoke images of young offenders as responsible and autonomous people, rather than as dependent and vulnerable children. The depiction of delinquents as responsible offenders has eroded the Progressives' social construction of childhood innocence and vulnerability. As a result, neither the 'treatment' nor 'childhood' foundation remains and very little distinguishes America's juvenile and criminal justice systems' ideologies and practices. Most of the remaining differences put young people at a disadvantage because states provide an inferior justice system to maximize their social control and because policy makers do not regard youths as 'real' people entitled to the same legal protections or rights as other citizens.

States bring youths to the justice system because they committed crimes, not because they need social services. Accordingly, states should uncouple social welfare from social control. This would enable them to pursue child welfare directly, unencumbered by penal considerations. A society that cares for the welfare of its children does so by supporting families, communities, schools and social institutions that nurture all young people, and not by cynically incarcerating its most disadvantaged children and pretending that it is 'for their own good'. Separating social welfare and social control would also honestly acknowledge that the real business of juvenile courts is crime control. Once we recognize that the child is a criminal and the criminal is a child, we must make substantive and procedural modifications to accommodate the youthfulness of some defendants. Only by doing so can a state achieve justice and fairness for its children.

REFERENCES

Ainsworth, J.E. (1991) Re-imagining Childhood and Re-constructing the Legal Order: The Case for Abolishing the Juvenile Court. *North Carolina Law Review* 69, 1083–133.

Allen, F.A. (1964) Legal Values and the Rehabilitative Ideal. In *The Borderland of the Criminal Law: Essays in Law and Criminology*. (Chicago, University of Chicago Press).

—— (1981) *Decline of the Rehabilitative Ideal*. (New Haven, CT, Yale University Press).

American Bar Association (1995) *A Call For Justice: An Assessment of Access to Counsel and Quality of Representation in Delinquency Proceedings*. (Chicago, American Bar Association).

American Bar Association and Institute of Judicial Administration (1980) *Juvenile Justice Standards Relating to Juvenile Delinquency and Sanctions*. (Cambridge, MA, Ballinger Publishing).

Beckett, K. (1997) *Making Crime Pay: Law and Order in Contemporary American Politics*. (New York, Oxford University Press).

Beckett, K. and T. Sasson (2000) *The Politics of Injustice: Crime and Punishment in America*. (Thousand Oaks, CA, Pine Forge Press).

Bishop, D. and C. Frazier (1996) Race Effects in Juvenile Justice Decision-Making: Findings of a Statewide Analysis. *Journal of Criminal Law and Criminology* 86, 392–413.

Blumstein, A. (1995) Youth Violence, Guns, and the Illicit-Drug Industry. *Journal of Criminal Law and Criminology* 86, 10 B 36.

Bonnie, R.J. and T. Grisso (2000) Adjudicative Competence and Youthful Offenders. In T. Grisso and R. Schwartz (eds.), *Youth on Trial: A Developmental Perspective on Juvenile Justice*. (Chicago, University of Chicago Press).

Cauffman, E. and L. Steinberg (1995) The Cognitive and Affective Influences on Adolescent Decision-Making. *Temple Law Review* 68, 1763–89.

Cook, P.J. and J.H. Laub (1998) The Role of Youth in Violent Crime and Victimization. *Crime and Justice: A Review of Research* 24, 27–64.

Dorfman, L. and V. Schiraldi (2001) *Off Balance: Youth, Race & Crime in the News*. (Washington, D.C., Youth Law Center, Building Blocks for Youth).

Edsall, T.B. with M.D. Edsall (1992) *Chain Reaction: The Impact of Race, Rights and Taxes on American Politics*. (New York, W.W. Norton & Co).

Entman, R.M. and A. Rojecki (2000) *The Black Image in the White Mind: Media and Race in America*. (Chicago, University of Chicago Press).

Feld, B.C. (1977) *Neutralizing Inmate Violence: Juvenile Offenders in Institutions*. (Cambridge, MA, Ballinger).

—— (1984) Criminalizing Juvenile Justice: Rules of Procedure for Juvenile Court. *Minnesota Law Review* 69, 141 B 276.

—— (1988) Juvenile Court Meets the Principle of Offense: Punishment, Treatment, and the Difference it Makes. *Boston University Law Review* 68, 821 B 915.

—— (1989) The Right to Counsel in Juvenile Court: An Empirical Study of When Lawyers Appear and the Difference They Make. *Journal of Criminal Law and Criminology* 79, 1185 B 1346.

—— (1993a) Criminalizing the American Juvenile Court. In M. Tonry (ed.), *Crime and Justice: A Review of Research*, vol. 17. (Chicago, University of Chicago Press).

—— (1993b) *Justice for Children: The Right to Counsel and the Juvenile Court*. (Boston: Northeastern University Press).

—— (1994) Juvenile Justice Swedish Style: A Rose By Another Name? *Justice Quarterly* 11, 625–50.

—— (1995) Violent Youth and Public Policy: A Case Study of Juvenile Justice Law Reform. *Minnesota Law Review* 79, 965 B 1128.

—— (1997) Abolish the Juvenile Court: Youthfulness, Criminal Responsibility, and Sentencing Policy. *Journal of Criminal Law & Criminology* 88, 68–136.

—— (1998) Juvenile and Criminal Justice System's Responses to Youth Violence. *Crime & Justice: An Annual Review* 24, 189–261.

—— (1999a) *Bad Kids: Race and The Transformation of the Juvenile Court*. (New York, Oxford University Press).

—— (1999b) The Transformation of the Juvenile Court—Part II: Race and the 'Crack Down' on Youth Crime. *Minnesota Law Review* 84, 327–95.

—— (2000) Legislative Exclusion of Offenses from Juvenile Court Jurisdiction: A History and Critique. In J. Fagan and F. Zimring (eds.),

The Changing Border of Juvenile Justice: Transfer of Adolescents to the Criminal Court. (Chicago, University of Chicago Press).

—— (2003) Race, Politics, and Juvenile Justice: The Warren Court and the Conservative 'Backlash'. *Minnesota Law Review* 89, 1445–575.

—— (2004) Competence, Culpability, and Punishment: Implications of *Atkins* for Executing and Sentencing Adolescents. *Hofstra Law Review* 32, 463–553.

Fordham Law Review (1996) Special Issue on Ethical Issues in Legal Representation of Children. *Fordham Law Review* 44 .

Furby, Lita and Ruth Beyth-Marom (1992) Risk Taking in Adolescence: A Decision-Making Perspective. *Developmental Review* 12, 1–44.

Gardner, William and Janna Herman (1990) Adolescents' AIDS Risk Taking: A Rational Choice Perspective. In W. Gardner *et al* (eds.), *Adolescents and the AIDS Epidemic.* (San Fransisco, CA, Jossey Bass).

Garland, David (2001) *The Culture of Control: Crime and Social Order in Contemporary Society.* (Chicago, University of Chicago Press).

General Accounting Office (1995) *Juvenile Justice: Representation Rates Varied as Did Counsel's Impact on Court Outcomes.* (Washington, D.C., U.S. General Accounting Office).

Gilens, Martin (1999) *Why Americans Hate Welfare: Race, Media, and the Politics of Anti-poverty Policy.* (Chicago, University of Chicago Press).

Gilliam, Franklin D., Jr., Shanto Iyengar, Adam Simon and Oliver Wright (1996) Crime in Black and White. The Violent, Scary World of Local News. *Harvard International Journal of Press/Politics* 1(3), 6–23.

Gilliam, Franklin D., Jr. and Shanto Iyengar (2000) Prime Suspects: The Influence of Local Television News on the Viewing Public. *American Journal of Political Science* 44, 560–73.

Grisso, Thomas (1980) Juveniles' Capacities to Waive *Miranda* Rights: An Empirical Analysis. *California Law Review* 68, 1134–66.

—— (1996) Society's Retributive Response to Juvenile Violence: A Developmental Perspective. *Law and Human Behavior* 20, 229–47.

—— (1997a) The Competence of Adolescents as Trial Defendants. *Psychology, Public Policy & Law* 3, 3–19.

—— (1997b) Juveniles' Competence to Stand Trial: New Questions for an Era of Punitive Juvenile Justice Reform. In Patricia Puritz, Alycia Capozello and Wendy Shang (eds.), *More Than Meets The Eye: Rethinking Assessment, Competency and Sentencing for a Harsher Era of Juvenile Justice.* (Washington, D.C., American Bar Association Juvenile Justice Center).

—— (2000) What We Know About Youth's Capacities as Trial Defendants. In Thomas Grisso and Robert G. Schwartz, *Youth on Trial: A Developmental Perspective on Juvenile Justice.* (Chicago, University of Chicago Press).

Grisso, Thomas and R.G. Schwartz (2000) *Youth on Trial: A Developmental Perspective on Juvenile Justice.* (Chicago, University of Chicago Press).

Grisso, Thomas, L. Steinberg, J. Woolard, E. Cauffman, E. Scott, S. Graham, F. Lexcen, N.D. Reppucci and R. Schwartz (2003) Juveniles' Competence to Stand Trial: A Comparsion of Adolescents' and Adults' Capacities as Trial Defendants. *Law and Human Behavior* 27, 333–62.

Hacker, A. (1995) *Two Nations: Black and White, Separate, Hostile and Unequal.* (New York, Macmillan).

Hurwitz, J. and M. Peffley (1997) Public Perceptions of Race and Crime: The Role of Racial Stereotypes. *American Journal of Political Science* 41, 375–401.

Lemann, N. (1992) *The Promised Land: The Great Black Migration and How It Changed America.* (New York, Vintage Books).

Lipsey, M.W. and D.B. Wilson (1998) Effective Intervention for Serious Juvenile Offenders. In Rolf Loeber and David P. Farrington (eds.), *Serious and Violent Juvenile Offenders: Risk Factors and Successful Interventions.* (Thousand Oaks, CA, Sage Publications).

Massey, D. and N. Denton (1993) *American Apartheid: Segregation and the Making of the Underclass.* (Cambridge, MA, Harvard University Press).

McCord, J., C.S. Widom and N.A. Crowell (2001) *Juvenile Crime, Juvenile Justice.* (Washington, D.C., National Academy Press).

Mehlbye, J. and B. Sommer (1998) Denmark. In J. Mehlbye and L. Walgrave (eds.),*Confronting Youth in Europe: Juvenile Crime and Juvenile Justice.* (Copenhagen, AKF Forlaget).

Mehlbye, J. and L. Walgrave (eds.) (1998) *Confronting Youth in Europe: Juvenile Crime and Juvenile Justice.* (Copenhagen, AKF Forlaget).

Medelberg, T. (2001) *The Race Card: Campaign Strategy, Implicit Messages, and the Norm of Equality.* (Princeton, Princeton University Press).

Parent, D.G., V. Lieter, S. Kennedy, L. Livens, D. Wentworth, and S. Wilcox (1994) *Conditions of Confinement: Juvenile Detention and Corrections Facilities.* (Washington, D.C., Office of Juvenile Justice and Delinquency Prevention).

Poe-Yamagata, E. and M.A. Jones (1999) *And Justice For Some.* (Washington, D.C., Building Blocks For Youth).

Omi, M. and H. Winant (1994) *Racial Formation in the United States: From the 1960s to the 1980s.* (New York, Routledge).

Peffley, M., T. Shields and B. Williams (1996) The Intersection of Race and Crime in Television News Stories: An Experimental Study. *Political Communications* 13, 309–27.

Peffley, M., J. Hurwitz and P.M. Sniderman (1997) Racial Stereotypes and Whites' Political Views of Blacks in the Context of Welfare and Crime. *American Journal of Political Science* 41, 30–60.

Phillips, K. (1969) *The Emerging Republican Majority.* (New Rochelle, NY, Arlington House).

Redding, R.E. and L.E. Frost (2001) Adjudicative Competence in the Modern Juvenile Court. *Virginia Journal of Social Policy & the Law* 9, 353–409.

Schwartz, I.M. (1989) *(In)Justice for Juveniles: Rethinking the Best Interests of the Child* (Lexington, MA, Lexington Books).

Sheffer, J.P. (1995) Serious and Habitual Juvenile Offender Statutes: Reconciling Punishment and Rehabilitation within the Juvenile Justice System. *Vanderbilt Law Review* 48, 479–512.

Scott, E.S. (1992) Judgment and Reasoning in Adolescent Decisionmaking. *Villanova Law Review* 37, 1607–69.

—— (2000) The Legal Construction of Adolescence. *Hofstra Law Review* 29, 547–98.

Scott, E.S., N.D. Reppucci and J.L. Woolard (1995) Evaluating Adolescent Decision Making in Legal Context. *Law and Human Behavior* 19, 221–44.

Scott, E.S. and T. Grisso (1998) The Evolution of Adolescence: A Developmental Perspective on Juvenile Justice Reform. *Journal of Criminal Law and Criminology* 88, 137–89.

Scott, E.S. and L. Steinberg (2003) Blaming Youth. *Texas Law Review* 81, 799–840.

Snyder, H. and M. Sickmund (1999) *Juvenile Offenders and Victims: A National Report.* (Washington, D.C., Office of Juvenile Justice and Delinquency Prevention, National Center for Juvenile Justice).

Steinberg, L. and E. Cauffman (1996) Maturity of Judgment in Adolescence: Psychosocial Factors in Adolescent Decision Making. *Law and Human Behavior* 20, 249–72.

—— (1999) The Elephant in the Courtroom: A Developmental Perspective on the Adjudication of Youthful Offenders. *Virginia Journal of Social Policy & the Law* 6, 389–417.

Tonry, M. and A.N. Doob (2004) *Youth Crime and Youth Justice: Comparative and Cross-National Perspectives. Crime and Justice: A Review of Research* vol. 31 (Chicago, University of Chicago Press).

Torbet, P., R. Gable, H. Hurst IV, I. Montgomery, L. Szymanski, and D. Thomas (1996) *State Responses to Serious and Violent Juvenile Crime: Research Report.* (Washington, D.C., Office of Juvenile Justice and Delinquency Prevention, National Center for Juvenile Justice).

von Hirsch, A. (1976) *Doing Justice.* (New York, Hill & Wang).

—— (1993) *Censure and Sanctions.* (New York, Oxford University Press).

Wilson, W.J. (1987) *The Truly Disadvantaged.* (Chicago, University of Chicago Press).

—— (1996) *When Work Disappears: The World of the New Urban Poor.* (New York, Alfred A. Knopf).

Zimring, F. (1982) *The Changing Legal World of Adolescence*. (New York, Free Press).
—— (1998) *American Youth Violence*. (New York, Oxford University Press).
—— (2000a) The Common Thread: Diversion in Juvenile Justice. *California Law Review* 88, 2477–95.
—— (2000b) The Punitive Necessity of Waiver. In J. Fagan and F. Zimring (eds.), *The Changing Borders of Juvenile Justice: Transfer of Adolescents to the Criminal Court*. (Chicago, University of Chicago Press).

Cases Cited

Breed v Jones, 421 U.S. 519 (1975).
Dusky v United States, 362 U.S. 402 (1960).
Fare v Michael C., 442 U.S. 707 (1979).
In re Gault, 387 U.S. 1 (1967).
In re Winship, 397 U.S. 358 (1970).
McKeiver v Pennsylvania, 403 U.S. 528 (1971).
Roper v Simmons, 125 S. Ct. 1111 (2005).

19

Conclusions: Themes, Trends, and Challenges

ERIC L. JENSEN AND JØRGEN JEPSEN

SOCIAL CONSTRUCTIONS OF YOUTH AND JUVENILE JUSTICE POLICY

SEVERAL COMMON THEMES and related international trends become obvious from the chapters in this book. First, the notion of a separate justice system for juveniles is now and was at its origins grounded in the social construction of childhood (see deMause 1974; Platt 1977). That is, children or juveniles are perceived of as less cognitively and socially developed than adults, and cannot be held to a standard of adult culpability, or *mens rea*. Based on this conception of childhood, youth are in need of nurturing and guidance to grow into responsible adults, and deserve a chance to rectify their law violating actions short of feeling the iron hand of criminal punishment with the possible exception of those committing extremely violent crimes. This was the underlying philosophy of the original American juvenile court until the insertion of a crime control model in the early 1980s.

Variations on the original social welfare model were also subsequently adopted by many European countries from the early 1900s through the 1930s (see Dünkel in this volume; Edelbacher and Fenz 2002; Walgrave 2002; Gelsthorpe and Kemp 2002; McAra 2002). These actions were inspired in part by the international Criminalist Conferences and the coming into power of the social democrats.

Setting the stage: changing constructions of youth in the U.S.A.

In reality, the traditional cultural construction of childhood has been somewhat mixed in the U.S. with children often suffering harsh treatment throughout history (see Empey, Stafford and Hay 1999 for an overview). A more modern conception of children arrived thanks to the efforts of the

Progressive Movement in the late 1800s. Cultural conceptions of children and their treatment in practice seemed to improve with the social activism, changes in law, and changes in social and educational policy that emanated from the Progressives.

Growing out of these cultural conceptions of childhood were policies that sought to minimize the stigma and resulting negative consequences for youth who were involved in the juvenile justice system. While these policies were the basis of the original juvenile court model, some had effectively been laid aside in practice in the U.S.A. by the late 1960s. This dereliction of least intrusive policies was brought to the national attention of juvenile justice professionals and scholars with the *Gault* case of 1967. In that case Gerald Gault was given an indeterminate sentence of up to six years in a correctional facility for juveniles because he was alleged to have participated in telephone call to a woman in which undesirable language was used. The actions in this case caused many to re-think the reality of the notions of minimal intrusion by the juvenile justice system and proportionality under law for juveniles (see Jensen's chapter in this volume).

A movement in the late 1960s and 1970s in the U.S. initiated an attempt to return the juvenile justice system to its roots (see the chapter by Jensen in this volume). These renewed efforts were aimed at avoiding the stigma associated with processing in the justice system. They included an active campaign of utilizing the authority and funding resources of the federal government to enforce least restrictive alternative policies including diversion from formal juvenile justice system processing for minor violations of law and status offenses, and the avoidance of incarceration whenever possible. Thus, the policy direction of this era was an attempt to humanize the system of juvenile justice which had changed over nearly eighty years and return it to its philosophical origins.

Societal contexts, cultural values and norms change over time, however. The efforts of these reform movements were based on the notions of the modern cultural constructions of childhood. The construction of childhood has been changed by powerful political forces in the U.S.A. since the early 1970s, however. The political agenda of the administration of President Richard Nixon was to create a political strategy in American society which would take the traditional voting blocks of the white working class in the Northern states and whites in the Southern states away from the Democrat party (i.e. the Southern strategy). In their efforts to enhance their personal political power and the long-term power of the Republican party, the Nixon administration painted a picture of young people—particularly young African Americans—as leftist political radicals who were opposed to the war in Vietnam, users of illegal drugs, and violent criminals.

Thus, the youth movements of the time, emerging minority self-empowerment movements, drugs, and crime became one-in-the-same in the minds of many Americans. This was a clear example of scapegoating the problems of society on various 'dangerous classes' of people ... in order to gain political support. For example, Baum (1996: 13—emphasis added) quotes an entry made by H.R. Haldeman, Nixon's White House Chief of Staff, in his personal diary: '[President Nixon] emphasized that you have to face the fact that the whole problem is really the blacks. The key is to devise a system that recognizes this *while not appearing to.*' (Jensen and Gerber 1998, 13).

Beckett and Sasson (2004, 54) have noted how this political strategy was translated into popular discourse:

> New sets of Republican constituencies were thus courted through the use of racially charged code words—phrases and symbols that 'refer indirectly to racial themes but do not directly challenge popular democratic or egalitarian ideals' (Omni and Winant 1986, 120). The discourse of 'law and order' is an excellent example of such coded language, and allowed for the indirect expression of racially charged fears and antagonisms.

These political claims-making activities instituted a change in the very cultural conceptions of youth, and later, by extension, those of children. The most important legacy of these claims-making activities of the Nixon administration is that this rhetoric has persisted in the minds of Americans for nearly three decades, largely due to the crusading efforts of the neo-conservatives and the uncritical distribution of these images by the mass media—not only in news productions but also on 'talk radio' and 'reality' crime television programming (Jensen and Gerber 1998, 13; Beckett and Sasson 2004 chapters 5 and 6; Cavender 1998).

The seeds were planted by the Nixon administration but this altered social construction of young people re-emerged with the presidency of Ronald Reagan, beginning in 1980. As shown in Jensen's chapter in this volume, the Reagan administration shifted public attention and federal juvenile justice policy to a focus on youth violence—which was not supported by statistics on crime, unbeknownst to the market-driven media and the misinformed public. The neo-conservative image of youth was, and continues to be, of adult-like persons who make rational decisions to commit a disproportionate number of serious crimes. The modern social construction of the cognitively developing child in need of nurturing and assistance was under attack by this intense political claims-making. The public appears to have been increasingly susceptible to this myth of youth dangerousness, due in part to the economic crises of the late 1970s and early 1980s (see Wilson 1987). The acceptance of this view of youth has also been reinforced by the substantial growth of the religious right in the U.S.A. and their patriarchal, punitive worldview (see Grasmick and McGill 1994; Jacobs, Carmichael and Kent 2005).

Several years after the Reagan claims about youthful violence, an epi-demic of violence swept the nation, especially in low-income neighborhoods of large cities. The rapid increase in murders coupled with the images of dangerous youth spread by the Nixon and Reagan administrations and rei-fied by the media resulted in a new social construction of teenagers and changed ideas about appropriate legal punishments for them in the minds of many Americans. When self-proclaimed experts on youth crime created the image and label of 'superpredator' it was widely covered in the media and firmly implanted in the minds of the public (see Bennett, Dilulio and Walters 1996). This rapid increase in violence by youth coupled with a changed cultural view of adolescents and the political dominance of the neo-conservatives at the time, combined to lead to the enactment of harsh penalties for serious youthful offenders and an explosion in the incarcera-tion of juveniles for many forms of law violation—not only violence (see Feld's chapter in this volume).

Moral panics as social construction of youth crime: variations by nation

While it appears that these negative constructions of youth and concomi-tant shifts toward harsher justice policies directed at young people began in the U.S.A. some thirty years ago, these constructions have now spread to other nations. As Estrada (2001, 639) has noted in the introduction to his constructionist analysis of perceptions of youth violence, 'As we enter the new millennium, academics, the media, politicians and the public seem for once to be in agreement, that the number of youths committing violent offenses is increasing rapidly in Europe' Estrada then goes on to demon-strate that this perception is not supported by empirical reality in most European countries.

Perhaps the first infusion of this ideology in Europe was under Margaret Thatcher in the United Kingdom.

> The *Criminal Justice Act* of 1982, which was passed by Mrs. Thatcher's Conservative party government, moved away from some elements of welfare and treatment to more punitive elements as it severely attacked the principles of wel-fare for juvenile delinquents that previous legislation had introduced [in 1963] ... The dramatic politically motivated shift embodies many of the elements of a crime control model. (Antonopoulos and Winterdyk 2003, 388)

Mrs. Thatcher's punitive ideology regarding young law violators paralleled the neo-conservative philosophy and policies in the U.S.A.

Why are some nations susceptible to the moral panic of youth crime and violence and others not? This is a complex question and our under-standing must be sought in the sociocultural, economic and political con-ditions in these nations. Common themes that emerge are scapegoating minority/immigrant/racial groups, and the insecurities caused by rapid social change and economic decline.

One common theme that emerges in those nations covered in this book that have experienced a moral panic regarding youth crime is a connection to minority populations or immigrants. Indeed, the origins of the American juvenile court have been closely linked with attempts to control immigrant youth (Platt 1977). Feld (1999 and in the present volume) has shown a strong connection between race and the recent use of crime control policies in juvenile justice in the U.S.A.

After reviewing the situations in eight Western European nations and the United States, Marshall (1997, 224–5) noted:

> political and public debate on the link between criminality and minorities/migrants ... is often highly politicized and volatile, sensitive, and emotionally charged. More often than not, the 'minority-crime' connection is enthusiastically embraced by political extremists in Europe. Likewise, in the United States, public and political discourse on native ethnic and racial minorities, 'new immigrants', undocumented aliens, and foreigners (and crime) tends to be highly controversial and emotional ...

Often a kernel of truth exists in these claims that may lead to moral panics (see Reinarman 2003). In general, street crime, interpersonal violence and victimization occur at higher rates among marginalized populations, and in nations with weak social welfare systems among the lowest income strata. The research shows that the socio-economic living environments of the marginalized are an important influence on the prevalence of law violation, especially serious offenses (Jarjoura, Triplett and Brinker 2002; Elliott and Huizinga 1983; Sampson 1995; Sampson and Groves 1989; Anderson 1999).

Marginalized populations are more likely to be immigrants or people of color in the U.S.A. and Western Europe. As Feld (1999, 290) has pointed out, a tendency exists to perceive the children of these marginalized groups as different and more deserving of harsh punishments when they violate the law. In addition, there is a tendency for politicians to make scapegoats of these less powerful groups. Politicians often deflect attention from inequalities in society and the resulting harmful consequences of these structural problems to the life problems of less powerful groups in the society (see Baum 1996; Jensen and Gerber 1998; Beckett and Sasson 2004).

In the U.S.A., Denmark, South Africa and the former West Germany, the social construction of dangerous youth is firmly connected to images of young people in non-white, marginalized populations. On the one hand, this connection has been made rather covertly by politicians and the media in the U.S. On the other hand, in Denmark the immigrant-crime connection has been made quite openly and frankly by major national political figures. In South Africa the image of the poorest, marginalized black street children as the major source of youth crime appears to be thoroughly embedded in the minds of the white minority.

We also observe a clear 'sense of popular punitiveness' in both the U.S.A. and South Africa. The origins of this punitiveness are found in the individualistic ethos of the dominant cultures within these societies, and the racial and social class tensions therein (see Austin and Irwin 2001; Beckett and Sasson 2004). This situation has been exacerbated in American society by thirty years of divisive claims-making activities by neo-conservative politicians and the rise of the religious right.

Denmark has also experienced claims-making activities regarding youth crime and violence which have resulted in some movement towards 'get tough' legislation. As Jepsen points out in his chapter, from the late 1990s through 2002 three factors were involved in the move toward more serious sanctions: (1) a relatively minor increase in violent crime among youth 10–17 years of age up to 2002, and since then a clearer rise in serious violent youth crime; (2) the 'Great Danish Rocker War'; and (3) xenophobic reactions to increased immigration combined with several highly publicized crimes of violence perpetrated by immigrant youth or second generation immigrant youth. While a kernel of truth regarding increases in youth violence existed in Denmark, the media and politicians have greatly exaggerated the problem. These claims-making activities by the media and politicians were further solidified into criminal policy under the Social Democratic government in the late 1990s and 2000–1 in the form of two consecutive and comprehensive 'violence packages'. With the election of a right-wing government in late 2001 a campaign was launched for anti-immigrant and even anti-asylum policies (in particular influenced by the Danish People's Party). Since taking power, the new government has zealously pursued a 'get tough on crime' program with an emphasis on law violations by young immigrants and particularly young second generation immigrants. Public concern regarding violence and crime actually decreased from 1993 through late 2003, however, until the highly publicized murders of two little girls and group rapes committed by second generation immigrant youth in mid-2003 stimulated increased concerns. Thus, public opinion was not originally the driving force underlying these policy changes. Political claims-making was the initial primary influence (see Jensen and Gerber 1998).

Feelings of insecurity are also a major theme in the changing social contexts of several of the nations represented in this book. In this context, Scheingold (1984, 87) has noted: 'The politics of law and order thrive only together with a more extended sense of social malaise, which drives the public toward the consolations provided by the myth of crime and punishment.' Further, 'punishment, as Durkheim has pointed out, provides an unequivocal reassurance that the society's norms and values are still intact—fully supported by the powers that be' (Scheingold 1984, 86).

South Africa is perhaps the most obvious case here with a sense of underlying fear following the move to democracy. Given the wide racial divisions in South Africa and the insecurities of many elements of society with the change to democracy, Skelton points to a regressive shift from a modern developmental view of children to a 'popular punitiveness'. She writes, 'The fears of the white minority about the myriad of societal changes they were experiencing tended to be most effectively articulated in terms of fear about crime' (this volume). As in the U.S.A., political and media constructions of youth—especially non-white youth—as dangerous and violent have been influential in South Africa recently.

This growing fear of crime and violence among the public has led to 'law and order' changes in the proposed South African juvenile justice legislation. What was initially a progressive, restorative justice and child rights-based proposal has been partially transformed due to this fear and the sense of 'popular punitiveness'.

In the U.S.A., the economic position of the average family has steadily deteriorated since the mid-1970s. People sense their increasing insecurity but are often not aware of the structural, and indeed global, sources of their frustrations. Thus they are more susceptible to the politics of fear. In Denmark, one of the most comprehensive social welfare systems in the world has been slowly weakened over time. While these changes are at least in part due to the baby boom generation approaching retirement and the anticipated increased demands that will be made on the social welfare system in the near future, the situation was exacerbated by claims-making in the tabloid media and political campaigns of the right-wing focused on alleged abuses of the social welfare system by immigrants. The Danish case reminds observers of the code words and symbolic politics used so often by neo-conservatives in the U.S.A.

American society was suffering massive structural economic dislocations in the 1980s when the neo-conservatives came into power. The unemployment rate was high, especially in the 'rust belt' Northeast, poverty rates soared in large cities of the Northeast, and well-paid unionized, industrial jobs were being moved to other nations or Southern non-union states by major corporations. The neo-conservative politicians would rather make issues of the myth of youth violent crime—at that time—and illicit drugs than face the serious economic problems which the nation was facing. At the same time, the public was hoping for a promise of stability and economic well-being. As Scheingold (1984) has noted, these conditions are fertile ground for 'get tough' crime policies.

Although Sweden was subject to claims-making activities about youth violence from the mid-1980s through the mid-1990s, this nation resisted the path taken by so many other countries (see the chapter by Sarnecki in this volume). At least during the mid-1990s, Sweden was going through a period of concern about immigrants and an economic downturn. More recently, Sweden has returned to a position of economic strength in Europe.

The nature of reporting violent crime in the media has influenced public opinion in Sweden to believe that youthful violence is on the rise, despite research to the contrary. Despite the shift in public concern about youth violence, the cultural values and the societal institutions of Sweden have resisted massive movements toward demonizing youth and a related crime control model—the basic welfare approach to delinquency has not been altered. However, a special new sanction of 'secure (closed) youth care' has been developed for the 'hard end' of the spectrum of Swedish juvenile crime. At the same time, mediation and other community-based non-punitive types of reactions have also been developed.

Poland has also experienced a moral panic regarding youth crime and violence since the early 1990s (see Krajewski's chapter in this volume). 'Due to growing problems with juvenile delinquency and foremost juvenile violence, *or rather public perception that such processes take place*, the public, media, and politicians increasingly support a more punitive approach to the problems of juvenile delinquency' (emphasis added). Today Poland has the highest unemployment rate among the major nations of Western and Eastern Europe. When combined with reductions in benefits to pensioners since the regime change and low wages for the employed, economic insecurities and social malaise in Poland are rife.

Conservative political pressures have also been exerted in Germany to move toward a crime control model. As elsewhere, feelings of insecurity associated with a major transition in society (i.e. reunification) have been exploited by most German political parties (except the Green party), with law and order being hot topics. To date, however, these repressive efforts have failed. Apparently somewhat unique to Germany, an organization of juvenile justice practitioners has been quite influential in resisting the conservative push for 'get tough' policies.[1]

Socio-cultural constructions of youth and juvenile justice policy: variations by nation

The factor that appears to differentiate the nations represented in this volume more than moral panics regarding youth crime are their respective socio-cultural constructions of youth. This point became clear to the authors when we heard reports of conditions in Malawi at the Oñati conference, read the chapter on Nepal, and read drafts of chapters for the Durban volume from Uganda and Tanzania (see Sørensen and Jepsen 2005). These papers confirmed Jepsen's observations while participating in pre-appraisal missions to Africa as part of the DIHR juvenile justice program.

---

[1] This situation is in sharp contrast to Denmark, where the new conservative government has publicly criticized academic experts on criminal justice issues.

The manner in which children and youth are treated under the rubric of the legal system in these nations reflects cultures that have not adopted the modern social constructions of childhood and adolescence that were the philosophical underpinnings of child welfare-based juvenile justice systems and the Convention on the Rights of the Child. This situation is clearly understandable since the modern constructions of childhood and adolescence were reified with the movement from agricultural to urban, industrial economies in Western societies (see Feld 1999). The developing nations are presently moving towards a contemporary version of this structural socio-economic transition experienced earlier by Western societies.

Sweden, Poland, the reunified Germany, Catalonia, and to some degree Serbia, continue to hold to cultural traditions of treating youthful law violators as victims of their life circumstances and in need of support and assistance due to their developmental stage of life. These sentiments are clearly stated by Krajewski:

> It [the social welfare approach] is based on the assumption that persons below a certain age, because of their mental development, shall not and cannot be held responsible for their wrongful acts in the same way as adults. This excludes ... retributive purposes of punishment ... Moreover, it is assumed that possibilities of changing youthful law violators, or rehabilitating them, are, because of their young age, much better than in the case of ... adults. (this volume)

Achieving the tenets set out in the Convention on the Rights of the Child requires cultural and by extension legal systems that recognize the special needs of children (see Grisso and Schwartz 2000). On the other hand, powerful conservative political forces in many Western nations adhere to a model of children and youth as simply little adults who are rational decision makers. Speaking on crime, then President Reagan (1984, 886) said, 'Choosing a career in crime is not the result of poverty or of an unhappy child or a misunderstood adolescence; it is the result of a conscious, willful choice made by some who consider themselves above the law, who seek to exploit the hard work and, sometimes, the very lives of their fellow citizens'. When applied to children and adolescents, this philosophy is a regression toward cultural values that had been replaced hundreds of years ago in Western cultures by a modern social construction of childhood. This backward step has also occurred, at least in juvenile justice policy, in South Africa, the United Kingdom (see Antonopoulous and Winterdyk 2003), and recently in Denmark.

THE RESTORATIVE JUSTICE MOVEMENT

Another theme that runs through several of the chapters in this book is the movement toward restorative justice concepts and alternatives to the traditional juvenile justice system. Restorative justice is an ancient practice.

452 *Eric L Jensen and Jørgen Jepsen*

> Restorative justice has been the dominant model of criminal justice throughout most of human history for perhaps all of the world's peoples. ... Beyond the parts of the globe ruled by European kings (among the Indigenous peoples of the Americas, Africa, Asia, and the Pacific), restorative traditions persisted into modern times ... remaining today as a resource of cultural diversity that can be drawn upon by European peoples whose justice traditions have been more homogenized and impoverished by central state power. (Braithwaite 2002, 5)

Although the renewed attention to restorative justice principles and programming in the West began in Canada with an experimental victim-offender reconciliation program in the mid-1970s, some indigenous peoples have continued to use this alternative to traditional justice practices to the present time (Braithwaite 2002). Thus, the West has learned from the indigenous practices of non-western cultures. The most well-known of these practices is family group conferencing in New Zealand. This program grew out of the traditional Maori practices for handling dispute resolution. The re-birth of traditional native justice practices in Canada and the U.S.A. have also brought attention to the restorative justice movement. Thus, one of the founding questions behind the Oñati conference was: what can the West learn from restorative justice practices in developing nations?

As noted in the chapter by Mendenhall and Dumesnil, native communities in the U.S.A. and Canada are increasingly moving toward restorative practices with juvenile law violators. Although the research on the effectiveness of these programs is still in its initial stages, these practices appear to be well-received by many stakeholders and residents of these communities where they are established.

The South African Law Reform Commission has also worked intensively to develop legislation and realistic policy objectives for a restorative-based juvenile justice system. The process has been going on for several years, but as noted in the chapter by Skelton, public fears and a moral panic reminiscent of those in the West have created obstacles to the passage of this progressive juvenile justice proposal. The original restorative-oriented work in South Africa may inspire similar developments in other African nations such as Malawi, and in other developing countries such as Nepal—a partner in the DIHR juvenile justice program.

Today restorative justice is also a well-established movement in the West. One of the first systems was set up in Norway, in part as a result of Nils Christie's work on 'Conflicts as Property' (Christie 1977; see also Miers 2001). Mediation boards became part of national legislation in Norway in 1991. Restorative justice policies were included in the 1990 German reform law. These programs were implemented rather rapidly in the former East Germany (Dünkel, this volume). As of the mid-1990s, there were at least 300 restorative justice programs in North America—with the majority in Canada—and over 500 in Europe (Braithwaite 2002, 8). The U.S. federal government has advocated the adoption of restorative justice models and practices (see U.S. Office of Juvenile Justice and Delinquency Prevention 1998; Bazemore and Umbreit 2001; Umbreit 2000). These practices have been comprehensively adopted in only a few jurisdictions in the U.S.A., however. Recent legislation in the United Kingdom, Canada, Poland and Austria has also attempted to establish restorative justice practices for juveniles (see Antonopoulos and Winterdyk 2003; Löschnig-Gspandl 2001; Krajewski, this volume).

Braithwaite (2002) reports support from both sides of the ideological continuum for restorative justice alternatives:

> In New Zealand, the country with the most developed programmatic commitment to restorative justice, the mainstream conservative and social democratic parties have been joined by Christian pro-family parties of the Right in their support for restorative justice. In New Zealand ... and Australia ..., the evidence is surprising on how supportive of restorative justice can be the police, that traditional ally of law-and-order politicians. (Braithwaite 2002, 10)

Of course, the process of instituting new policies often faces obstacles during implementation. The 1998 restorative juvenile justice model in the U.K, for example, has experienced forms of punitiveness that would not be expected from a truly restorative system. For example, restorative conferencing has become dominated by the police officer. In practice, the offender and the victim play minor roles in the process. In addition, if the offenders are not willing to comply with a reparation order, 'the reparation order automatically becomes punishment. In other words, "the offender may be coerced into reparation"' (Antonopoulos and Winterdyk 2003, 394).

Based on observational research on youth justice conferences in Australia and New Zealand, Daly (2002, 72) stated, 'there appears to be limits on "repairing the harm" for offenders and victims'. On the one hand, juveniles often lack the empathetic orientation toward others which is necessary for a restorative process—often a developmental issue. On the other hand, the victims are limited by 'the capacity to be generous to lawbreakers and to see lawbreakers as capable of change' (Daly 2002, 72).

The state of Idaho in the U.S.A. formally adopted the Balanced and Restorative Justice Model as the theoretical basis for its new juvenile justice system in 1995 (see U.S. Office of Juvenile Justice and Delinquency Prevention 1998), yet long-term incarcerations of juveniles increased substantially following the implementation of this legislation absent a clear indication of a rise in serious youth crime (see Chinn Planning, Inc. 1998; Office of Juvenile Justice and Delinquency Prevention 2004). An increase in long-term incarceration in this case directly opposes Braithwaite's (2002) view of restoration.[2]

---

[2] These increases in the incarceration of juveniles following the adoption of a model intended to be restorative parallel those of the 'widening of the net' phenomena experienced with some programs in the American experiences with diversion.

Based on these observations in three societies, it becomes obvious that attempts to implement restorative justice practices will face serious obstacles in societies and communities with widespread sentiments of popular punitiveness.

Outlining the basics of the restorative justice model, Strang (2002, 44) states:

> Restorative justice takes many forms, but usually refers to the restoration of victims, offenders, and community. ... Bazemore (1997) observed that restorative justice encourages a shift towards less formal responses to crime that emphasize the role of citizens, community groups, and other institutions of civil society. Bazemore and Umbreit (1995) believe that in fact a core value in restorative justice is to balance offender needs, victim needs, and the needs of the community.

The Scandinavian welfare board includes several of the elements of the restorative justice model outlined in this quotation: a less formal response to crime than in the traditional juvenile court; a response that includes citizens and specialists in the membership of the board; concern with offender needs; and concern with the needs of the community (i.e. to reintegrate the offender).

In Norway, the 'conflict councils' involve victim-offender mediation and have been operating in all Norwegian communes for more than a decade as a way of diverting minor cases from the criminal justice system. A similar system was attempted in Denmark but only on a limited experimental basis. On the other hand, Denmark has for several years elaborated a structure for co-operation between the social welfare sector, schools and the police (the 'SSP-system'). Denmark has also recently begun to introduce family conferencing as inspired by the New Zealand model.

Thus, only an emphasis on the needs of the victim remains to be integrated into the Scandinavian model to make it a comprehensive restorative justice practice. In fact, the Scandinavian municipal social welfare board model is remarkably similar to community reparative boards, one of the four restorative conferencing models discussed by Bazemore and Umbreit (2001).

Such a synthesis of these models could represent a path for developing, transitional and developed countries to pursue in designing, revising and implementing juvenile justice systems: a Scandinavian-style community social welfare board model with an added focus on meeting the needs of the victim and taking care of the concern for the community through structures similar to the Danish model for co-operation among schools, social services and the police. This new model could result in balancing the needs of offenders, victims and the community. In developing nations, traditional culture-specific modes of restorative practices could be added to this new model. Due process protections for the accused must also be included in this model as per the Convention on the Rights of the Child by introducing an element of judicial control. Such a model may overcome many of the recurring disappointments experienced with both the social welfare models and the crime control model, and assist in bringing reparation to victims.

IMPLEMENTING JUVENILE JUSTICE SYSTEMS

A major objective of both the conference at the International Institute for the Sociology of Law in Oñati, Spain and this book is to assist practitioners, jurists, NGOs, etc. in developing and implementing humane, effective juvenile justice systems within the principles set out in the Convention on the Rights of the Child and other international instruments. It is obvious from the cumulative empirical and practical knowledge represented in this book that all nations can learn from the experiences of others. Developed nations are learning from the traditional restorative practices being used in developing nations and native communities of North America. Developing nations and nations in transition are learning from the years of experience and research on juvenile justice programming in developed nations. The experiences of nations in transition and those of developed nations that have recently undergone major changes in their juvenile justice systems may provide guidance for developing nations in the legal, political and 'how to' (and 'how not to') realities of implementing new systems (e.g., by organizing and supporting regional co-operation—see Stapleton's chapter in the present volume).

In addition, responsible juvenile justice practitioners, researchers and activists must be aware of the deleterious consequences of the widespread moral panics about young people, youthful law violators and violence that plague many Western nations and often become the ideological underpinnings of repressive practices. We can then work together to create strategies to overcome this false information and the public fears associated with these claims-making activities (see Herring and Ebner 2005 for a related policy example).

Models of juvenile justice systems and specific programs can only be effective in achieving the objectives set out for them if they are correctly implemented (see Sherman *et al* 1997). As part of effective implementation, it is critical that all stakeholders are represented in the processes leading up to the creation and implementation of new or revised juvenile justice systems. This may indeed be one of the most important contributions that a community-based restorative justice model can make to this implementation process (see the chapters by Flindt-Pedersen and Stapleton in this volume; Mashamba 2005; DeGabriele 2005). Effectively implemented restorative justice models not only include the various stakeholders in the community, but once operating also appear to receive the support of nearly all stakeholder groups (see Braithwaite 2002). This unique appeal of restorative justice principles and practices to interests at both the 'soft' and the 'hard' ends of the spectrum can be a crucial element in the development of new human rights-based juvenile justice systems. The chapter on Malawi in the present volume illustrates this process in practice.

As Jepsen (2005, 13–14) stated in the Durban volume:

> It is worth noting that the push for reforms come not only from donors and foreign advocates of juvenile justice reform but also from national and regional sources. It is important that juvenile justice reform is not pushed upon the less developed countries by foreign donors. Programs of development are sustainable only to the extent they build upon local partnerships in the participating countries. These partners include persons and institutions with actual and potential standing and influence in the individual countries. It is therefore paramount to include all major stakeholders in the reform process, both in relation to goals and deciding on appropriate mechanisms. ... The use of advocacy—for human rights in general and for juvenile justice in particular—is an important element in these efforts. Raising awareness about problems and solutions is a first and indispensable element in the process of reform.

Successful implementation of juvenile justice practices also depends upon basing policy and practice decisions on the extant empirical research. A wealth of research on 'what works' or 'best practices' in juvenile justice programming has accumulated during the past fifty years (see Sherman *et al* 1997; www.mstservices.com; http://depts.washington.edu/sdrg/index.html; http://www.strengtheningfamilies.org/html; Armstrong's chapter in this volume; Jensen and Eilers 2005). Although policy decisions are often made by political officials based on their personal philosophies, advocates of humane, human rights-based, effective juvenile justice policies must be intimately familiar with the most methodologically rigorous research—or engage consultants with this knowledge—and continually work for the best programs possible.

We will conclude this statement of themes and future challenges with a quotation from Barry Krisberg, president of the National Council on Crime and Delinquency:

> ... it is patently clear that most of us would seek a justice system that is founded on core principles of charity and redemption if it were our own children who were in trouble. This, of course, is the key issue. If we recognize the truth that all children are our children, the search for the juvenile justice ideal [of the original juvenile court] is our only choice. (2005, 196)

Treating young law violators humanely and fairly is part of the effort to secure the future of society and lies at the heart of the Convention on the Rights of the Child. This instrument envisions delinquent youth as part of society now and in the future as they mature, not as objects for punishment and marginalization.

REFERENCES

Anderson, E. (1999) *Code of the Street: Decency, Violence, and the Moral Life of the Inner City.* (New York, W.W. Norton).

Antonopoulos, G.A. and Winterdyk, J.A. (2003) The British 1998 Crime and Disorder Act: A 'Restorative' Response to Youth Offending? *European Journal of Crime, Criminal Law and Criminal Justice* 11, 386–97.

Austin, J. and Irwin, J. (2001) *It's About Time: America's Imprisonment Binge.* 3rd edn (Belmont, CA, Wadsworth/Thomson Learning).

Baum, D. (1996) *Smoke and Mirrors: The War on Drugs and the Politics of Failure.* (Boston, MA, Little, Brown).

Bazemore, G. and Umbreit, M.S. (2001) *A Comparison of Four Restorative Conferencing Models.* (Washington, D.C., Office of Juvenile Justice and Delinquency Prevention, February).

Beckett, K. and Sasson, T. (2000) *The Politics of Injustice: Crime and Punishment in America.* (Thousand Oaks, CA, Pine Forge Press).

—— (2004) *The Politics of Injustice: Crime and Punishment in America.* 2nd edn. (Thousand Oaks, CA, Sage Publications).

Bennett, W.J., Dilulio, J.J. and Walters, J.P. (1996) *Body Count: Moral Poverty and How to Win America's War against Crime and Drugs.* (New York, Simon and Schuster).

Braithwaite, J. (2002) *Restorative Justice and Responsive Regulation.* (Oxford, Oxford University Press).

Cavender, G. (1998) In The 'Shadows of Shadows': Television Reality Crime Programming. In M. Fishman and G. Cavender (eds.), *Entertaining Crime: Television Reality Programming.* (Hawthorne, NY, Aldine de Gruyter).

Chinn Planning, Inc. (1998) *Statewide Needs Assessment Study. Final Report.* (Columbia, South Carolina, September).

Christie, N. (1977) Conflicts as Property. *British Journal of Criminology* 17, 1–19.

Daly, K. (2002) Restorative Justice: The Real Story. *Punishment and Society* 4, 55–79.

DeGabriele, D.A. (2005) Juvenile Justice in Malawi: Progress Since the 1999 Regional Conference. In Johnny Juhl Sørensen and Jørgen Jepsen (eds.), *Juvenile Justice in Transition: Bringing the Convention on the Rights of the Child to Work in Africa and Nepal* (Copenhagen, The Danish Institute for Human Rights).

deMause, L. (1974) The Evolution of Childhood. In Lloyd deMuase (ed.), *The History of Childhood.* (New York, Harper).

Edelbacher, M. and Fenz, C. (2002) Juvenile Justice System: An Austrian Perspective. In John A. Winterdyk (ed.), *Juvenile Justice Systems: International Perspectives.* 2nd edn (Toronto, Ontario, Canadian Scholars' Press Inc).

Elliott, D.S. and Huizinga, D. (1983) Social Class and Delinquent Behavior in a National Youth Panel: 1976–1980. *Criminology* 21, 149–77.

Empey, L.T., Stafford, M.C. and Hay, C.H. (1999) *American Delinquency: Its Meaning and Constructions.* (Belmont, CA; Wadsworth Publishing).

Estrada, F. (2001) Juvenile Violence as a Social Problem: Trends, Media Attention and Societal Response. *British Journal of Criminology* 41, 639–55.

Feld, B.C. (1999) *Bad Kids: Race and the Transformation of the Juvenile Court.* (New York, Oxford University Press).

Gelsthorpe, L. and Kemp, V. (2002) Comparative Juvenile Justice: England and Wales. In John A. Winterdyk (ed.), *Juvenile Justice Systems: International Perspectives.* 2nd edn (Toronto, Ontario, Canadian Scholars' Press Inc).

Grasmick, H.G. and McGill, A. (1994) Religion, Attribution Style, and Punitiveness toward Juvenile Offenders. *Criminology* 32, 23–46.

Grisso, T. and Schwartz, R.G. (eds) (2000) *Youth on Trial: A Developmental Perspective on Juvenile Justice.* (Chicago, University of Chicago Press).

Herring, L. and Ebner, J. (2005) Sociologists Impact Interpretation of Federal Welfare Legislation. *Footnotes* 33, 5.

Jacobs, D., Carmichael, J.T. and Kent, S.L. (2005) Vigilantism, Current Racial Threat, and Death Sentences. *American Sociological Review* 70, 656–77.

Jarjoura, G.R., Triplett, R.A. and Brinker, G.P. (2002) Growing Up Poor: Examining the Link between Persistent Poverty and Delinquency. *Journal of Quantitative Criminology* 18, 159–87.

Jensen, E.L. and Eilers, S. (2005) An Annotated Bibliography on Diversion, Restorative Justice, and Least Restrictive Alternatives. In Johnny Juhl Sørensen and Jørgen Jepsen (eds.), *Juvenile Justice in Transition: Bringing the Convention on the Rights of the Child to Work in Africa and Nepal.* (Copenhagen, The Danish Institute for Human Rights).

Jensen, E.L. and Gerber, J. (1998) The Social Construction of Drug Problems: An Historical Overview. In Eric L. Jensen and Jurg Gerber (eds.), *The New War on Drugs: Symbolic Politics and Criminal Justice Policy.* (Cincinnati, OH, Anderson Publishing Co. and the Academy of Criminal Justice Sciences).

Jepsen, J. (2005) The DIHR Support Programme and International Trends. In Johnny Juhl Sørensen and Jørgen Jepsen (eds.), *Juvenile Justice in Transition: Bringing the Convention on the Rights of the Child to Work in Africa and Nepal.* (Copenhagen, The Danish Institute for Human Rights).

Krisberg, B. (2005) *Juvenile Justice: Redeeming Our Children.* (Thousand Oaks, CA, Sage).

Kyvsgaard, B. (2003) Bekymring for Vold og Kriminalitet 2003 (Worries about Crime and Violence). *Justitsministeriets Forskningsenhed*, 10 December.

Löschnig-Gspandl, M. (2001) Diversion in Austria: Legal Aspects. *European Journal of Crime, Criminal Law and Criminal Justice 9*, 281–90.

McAra, L. (2002) The Scottish Juvenile Justice System: Policy and Practice. In John A. Winterdyk (ed.), *Juvenile Justice Systems: International Perspectives*. 2nd edn (Toronto, Ontario, Canadian Scholars' Press Inc).

Marshall, I.H. (1997) Minorities and Crime in Europe and the United States: More Similar than Different! In Ineke Haen Marshall (ed.), *Minorities, Migrants, and Crime: Diversity and Similarity Across Europe and the Untied States*. (Thousand Oaks, CA, Sage).

Mashamba, J. (2005) Emerging Issues in Diverting Juvenile Offenders from the Criminal Justice System: The Socio-cultural Realities, Economics, and Politics of Administration of Juvenile Justice in Tanzania. In Johnny Juhl Sørensen and Jørgen Jepsen (eds.), *Juvenile Justice in Transition: Bringing the Convention on the Rights of the Child to Work in Africa and Nepal*. (Copenhagen, The Danish Institute for Human Rights).

Miers, D. (2001) *An International Review of Restorative Justice*. (London, Home Office. Crime Reduction Research Series Paper 10).

Office of Juvenile Justice and Delinquency Prevention (2004) *Juveniles in Corrections*. (Washington, D.C., Office of Justice Programs).

Omi, M. and Winont, H.(1986) Racial Formation in the United States. (New York, Routledge and Kegan Paul).

Platt, A. (1977) *The Child Savers: The Invention of Delinquency*. 2nd edn (Chicago, University of Chicago Press).

Reagan, R. (1984) Remarks at the Annual Convention of the Texas State Bar Association in San Antonio. In *Public Papers of the Presidents 1984* vol 2. (Washington, D.C., U.S. Government Printing Office) (as cited in Beckett and Sasson 2000, 61).

Reinarman, C. (2003) The Social Construction of Drug Scares. In Patricia A. Adler and Peter Adler (eds.), *Constructions of Deviance: Social Power, Context, and Interaction*. 4th edn (Belmont, CA, Wadsworth).

Sampson, R.J. (1995) Unemployment and imbalanced sex ratios: Race-specific consequences for family structure and crime. In M.B. Tucker and C. Mitchell Kernan (eds.), *The Decline in Marriage Among African Americans*. (New York, Russell Sage).

Sampson, R.J. and Groves, W.B. (1989) Community Structure and Crime: Testing Disruption. *American Journal of Sociology 94*, 774–802.

Scheingold, S.A. (1984) *The Politics of Law and Order: Street Crime and Public Policy*. (New York, Longman Inc).

Sherman, L.W., Gottfredson, D., MacKenzie, D.L., Eck, J., Reuter, P. and Bushway, S. (1997) *Preventing Crime: What Works, What Doesn't, and What's Promising*. (Washington, D.C., National Institute of Justice).

Sørensen, J.J. and Jepsen, J. (eds.) (2005) *Juvenile Justice in Transition: Bringing the Convention on the Rights of the Child to Work in Africa and Nepal*. (Copenhagen, The Danish Institute for Human Rights).

Strang, H. (2002) *Repair or Revenge: Victims and Restorative Justice*. (Oxford, Oxford University Press).

Umbreit, M.S. (2000) *Family Group Conferencing: Implications for Crime Victims*. (Washington, D.C., U.S. Department of Justice, Office for Victims of Crime, April).

U.S. Office of Juvenile Justice and Delinquency Prevention (1998) *Guide for Implementing the Balanced and Restorative Justice Model*. (Washington, D.C., Office of Juvenile Justice and Delinquency Prevention Report Series).

Walgrave, L. (2002) Juvenile Justice in Belgium. In John A.Winterdyk (ed.), *Juvenile Justice Systems: International Perspectives*. 2nd edn (Toronto, Ontario, Canadian Scholars' Press Inc).

Wilson, W.J. (1987) *The Truly Disadvantaged*. (Chicago, University of Chicago Press).

Index